GUGLIELMO FERRERO

THE LIFE OF CÆSAR

Translated by

A. E. ZIMMERN

Montague Burton Professor
of International Relations, Oxford University

The Norton Library
W · W · NORTON & COMPANY · INC ·
NEW YORK

FIRST PUBLISHED IN THE NORTON LIBRARY 1962

Printed in the United States of America

CONTENTS

CHAPTER I

ROME AND ITALY A CENTURY BEFORE CHRIST

A CENTURY before Christ, Rome was already the first Mediterranean power. Although she was only a small republic, governed by not more than a hundred noble families, she had already conquered and latinized almost the whole of Italy; she was mistress of the coasts of Gaul, Spain, Greece, and had firmly established herself on the African and the Asiatic coasts. But at the same time she was suffering from a terrible internal crisis which affected her political, economic, moral and intellectual life. A close acquaintance with the history of this crisis is necessary if we are to understand the stormy history of the famous man with whom this book is concerned. What was its cause?

For more than a century, Rome and Italy had been achieving remarkable progress in very many directions. The diffusion of Greek philosophy, the progress of education and the increase of wealth had made men more sensible of the severity of the old legal code, and the stupid and barbarous superstitions which it embodied. The last vestiges of human sacrifice disappeared within a few years of this date. The decrees of the Prætors marked a continuous development of the principles of equity: Roman law, as we know it, began gradually to take shape It was about this time, for instance, that the *lex Aebutia* swept away the cumbrous and pedantic machinery of the so-called *legis actiones*, replacing it by a more flexible and rational procedure better suited to a business age. Both in literature and art there was evidence of considerable activity. Nobles and merchants began to build handsome palaces in the metropolis, using marbles from Hymettus, and other exotic materials in place of the familiar Italian travertine. Literary dilettantism became a prevailing fashion; distinguished Senators dabbled in history and philo sophy,and scribbled verses both in Latin and in Greek. There were orators to be heard in the Forum, such as Antonius and Licinius Crassus, who had elaborated their style with care upon Greek models. The arts of Greece and Asia found an ever widening circle of admirers, and Greek sculptors and painters, among them even a woman, Iaia of Cyzicus, were employed in increasing numbers by wealthy patrons in the capital.

Yet in whichever direction we look, whether at political or social conditions or at the sphere of individual morality, we see signs of encroaching disorder and decay. The rise in the standard of living was forcing the old aristocracy into strange shifts for a livelihood: some kept afloat by peculation or extortion or the simpler expedient of debt; others by acquaintance or marriage connection, wholly regardless of appearances, with wealthy tax-farmers or financiers. Many of the country proprietors studied agriculture in the writings of the Greeks, or in the Carthaginian treatise of Mago, which had been translated by order of the Senate. They borrowed a little capital, planted olives and vineyards, and tried to improve their methods of cultivation. But want of experience, together with difficulties of transport, imperfect organization, and the high rate of interest, generally ended by bringing failure both upon the experiments and those that made them. Moreover, the law of Spurius Thorius, by converting so large a part of the public land into private property, had encouraged landlords to be extravagant, and thus, after a burst of short-lived prosperity, ended by leaving them worse off than before.

These tendencies were only accentuated by the spread of education. In the metropolis and in the Latin and allied towns new schools of rhetoric were opening their doors to train young Italians in a common language and a national oratory; and Latin gained ground daily, both as a spoken and a written language, upon the Sabellian and Oscan dialects of the countryside. But this new and coveted culture was as yet out of touch with the life of the community. Many of the young advocates turned out by the schools found neither patrons to befriend them, nor clients to plead for; and emigration into the provinces became a tempting and often a necessary expedient. Many Italians made fortunes in the slave-trade, which was now largely in the hands of the pirates; for the few slaves captured in war and trade with the barbarians no longer sufficed for the increasing demand. Delos became a huge slave market for the whole of the Mediterranean basin; and many a young Italian fresh from school sold his manuscripts of Homer and Plato to make a living as a buccaneer. Others found their way into Egypt, or oftener still to the new province of Asia, where, thanks to the arrangements of Caius Gracchus, the exploitation of the old kingdom of Pergamus had proved immensely profitable. The tax-farmers, all of them either Romans or Italians, enjoyed the open patronage of the governors in their systematic pillage of the province.

But there were far more, of course, who went under, and the glaring contrast between the ill-gotten gains of the few and the penury of the many did much to accentuate the general unrest. A new line of cleavage appeared in Italian society. On the one side was the great host of men who had lost all they had to lose in the world, the bankrupt traders and ruined landowners who were to be found in every corner of Italy; on the other, a small and grasping clique of parvenu millionaires. The moderate incomes, which might have bridged the gulf between the two, were gradually disappearing. It was a narrow and exclusive ring of capitalists, composed of a few surviving nobles, of some of the ancient Italian aristocracy and of knights, plebeians, and freedmen, which was thus accumulating land in Italy, wringing fortunes out of the unhappy natives of Asia, and paying for them with the universal detestation of their countrymen.

Meanwhile the Treasury was empty, the army disorganized, and the fleet which had conquered Carthage was left rotting in the harbours of Italy; Rome had hardly strength enough to quell the slave revolts which were continually breaking out in Sicily and Campania. Yet she would soon need all the forces at her command. Mithridates, always on the alert, had profited by the Cimbric war to break his alliance with the King of Bithynia and to seize Cappadocia, while in Italy the rivalry between the knights and the Senate, between the rich financiers and the nobility, grew daily more acute. After the Senators, the knights were the most eminent class in the social order, forming between the plebs and the hundred families who represented the senatorial nobility, a kind of secondary aristocracy, through which one had to pass to become a member of the Senate and the senatorial nobility. For many centuries the knights had respected and served the senatorial nobility with deference; but during the last twenty-five years they had become unruly. Caius Gracchus had enriched them by allowing them to exploit the old kingdom of Pergamus, a province of Asia; and by approving a judiciary reform by which the Tribunals, which until then had been composed of Senators, were to be composed only of knights, thus unduly increasing their political power.. They now formed a class of rich capitalists and financiers, independent of the senatorial nobility which consisted of big landowners.

Their wealth, their newly acquired rights in the law-courts all justified self-assertion. Although they generally left politics to the aristocrats, and stuck to business and money-making, they felt themselves the equals or even the superiors of the old bankrupt nobility. All this was not unnaturally resented by the aristocrats. Disgusted with the universal disorder, for which the intrusion of the plutocracy seemed the most obvious cause, embittered by the sting of unaccustomed poverty and by the insolence of their newly discovered rivals, they looked longingly back upon the days of their undisputed supremacy, and clamoured for rigorous legislation against the abuses of capitalism. They could not forgive a member of their own class like Caius Julius Cæsar, who bound himself by friendship and marriage with an obscure equestrian family, or defied the ostracism of society by embarking upon a business career.

But if the nobility as a body was opposed to the knights, the nobility itself as a united body was no longer what it was a century before. For thirty years, since Tiberius and Caius Gracchus had founded a Democratic or popular party, the hundred families which represented the Republic, had also been divided. The majority still formed a party which might be termed Conservative, and which represented the traditions of a time when the aristocracy had governed the Republic as a united and unanimous body. A small minority supported by the common people and the middle classes, carried on the struggle which the Gracchi had initiated and attempted to reform and rejuvenate the Republic, but with vague and changing programmes. Their aim was to modify the rigorous oligarchical rule of the old nobility, to improve the standard of living of the common people, the small landowners, and the middle class; but by what means they did not know precisely. Every few years, new schemes were launched for the people's approval—only to be rejected as revolutionary by the Conservative nobility.

This incessant rivalry and unrest in the upper ranks of society was a fresh incitement to the Democrats, who had for the last decade been resuming a vigorous agitation both in the Assembly and the Law-courts. But the old popular party too had fallen on evil days. It had declined from the pinnacle to which the Gracchi and their enthusiasts had raised it. Two wild and insolent politicians, Saturninus and Glaucia, were the leading popular agitators of the day. Though its leaders went on repeating the old invectives against the nobles, and bringing forward fresh Corn Laws just to flavour their abuse, no serious attempt at constructive legislation had been made.

The respectable members of both parties, excluded from a political career, found a cheap consolation in lamenting the evils of their times. Justice had become simply one more instrument of oppression in the hands of the wealthy. Fraud and violence, extortion and bribery, were the familiar incidents of public life. At Rome, as at Carthage in the days of her decline, money was fast becoming the sole goal of ambition and the supreme measure of worth. Yet there were hundreds foolish enough to give up an assured, if modest, position in the country in order to risk their fortunes in some business venture: and many more who reduced themselves well-nigh to bankruptcy to give a superior education to their children. The younger generation, flushed with the rhetoric of their school training, thought that a year or two's chattering in the Forum would talk them into wealth and power. They produced a not unnatural reaction among the upper classes, where the opinion was commonly held that the spread of education was in itself an evil: that all it achieved was the manufacture of a superfluous intellectual proletariat of upstarts, agitators and criminals. "To learn Greek is to learn knavery," was a proverb common on men's lips.

That there was some truth in the taunt is proved by the corresponding increase of crime, which was connived at and fomented by the authorities. Murder, poisoning, theft, assassination, even family tragedies, became alarmingly frequent. The Roman household no longer fufilled the disciplinary and judicial functions that had been given it by the old constitution, and the domestic tribunal was regarded as a mere relic of a bygone age. There was a large category of crimes committed by women and young persons which went entirely un-punished, being still outside the cognizance of the law, and no longer dealt with by the family. Moreover, even recognized offences, when committed by Roman citizens, often evaded a penalty. The rough and primitive provisions of the ancient penal code knew no other punishments to the person beyond flogging or death. Imprisonment was not recognized as a penalty, prisons serving merely for the detention of the accused before being brought up for trial. Flogging and the death penalty having been abolished for Roman citizens, there was no alternative but exile; and exile still meant what it had meant in the old days when Rome was an isolated town among a number of hostile rivals—a convenient retirement to Palestrina or Naples. And even this not very formidable prospect was easily averted by a little skilful expenditure. Roman citizens, in fact, were practically immune from every sort of penal jurisdiction.

Hence the increasing desire among the Italians to obtain the privileges of citizenship. For the agitation was now spreading far and wide through the peninsula to the consternation of the Conservative party. The intellectual and economic unification of Italy was gradually breaking down all distinctions between Romans, Latins and allies, and the old political organization of the separate districts had by now lost all reality and meaning. Middle-class Italians, often heavily in debt and deprived of the patronage of the old local nobility, were now united in their demand for emancipation, and in their hostility to the clique that held the reins of power at Rome. The franchise seemed the remedy for all their grievances.

This wild and disordered conflict of material interests could not fail to find reflection in the world of ideas. But here the confusion was intensified by the innumerable and contradictory doctrines of Greek philosophy. It was the fashion for men to consult the philosophers to find out their political bearings; and every educated man had his own particular standpoint from which he looked down upon the distress of the time. The theories thus evolved marked the final extinction of any ancient and definite doctrines which still survived into the new era. There were interminable discussions on the diseases from which Rome was suffering. No one tried the remedy of action. Men frittered away their energies in a morbid inertia, pouring vain encomiums upon a golden past, and childishly appealing for the intervention of some heaven-sent deliverer. Intellectuals singled out the unfortunate Caius Gracchus (it was characteristic that they should choose just the greatest of their statesmen for their scapegoat) as the originator of all the various mischiefs of the time. It was Gracchus who by his corn laws had emptied the Treasury; it was Gracchus who by his judicial arrangements had made the plutocracy all-powerful; it was Gracchus who had let loose the demagogues, disorganized the army and abandoned the provinces to capitalist rapacity. All Italy cried aloud for a saviour.

In the year 100 B.C. a man named Caius Marius believed himself to be the desired saviour. A knight by origin, he embarked, like almost all of them, on a business career, but failed. He then devoted himself to politics and warfare, in which he was more successful. Thanks to the support of the Democratic party, he became Consul in 107, in spite of the old nobility, who resented this office being filled by a knight. He defeated Jugurtha and afterwards repelled the Cimbri and the Teutones with great slaughter in the valley of the Po. His action in checking the invasion of the Cimbri led to his being elected Consul five times in succession with the support of the Democratic party, although this was contrary to the laws.

Intoxicated by his successes on the battlefield, he regarded them as preludes to new triumphs in the Forum. At the particular moment which we have reached, his efforts were centred upon the attainment of a sixth spell of consular office. But he would have to step down for once into the party arena. Hitherto the proud and masterful soldier had disdained to take sides with either party; nor had it been necessary for him to do so. During the continuance of the Cimbric war he had accepted the suffrages of the Democrats without even having to ask for their support. But now that the invaders were finally repelled he had to face a very different situation. The spontaneous enthusiasm in his favour, generated by the Cimbri, had evaporated at their disappearance, and he could now only become Consul as the representative of one of the two parties in the State. The choice was not so difficult. The Conservatives could never forgive him for having been for four years the champion of the democratic party. The moderate party, as usual in a crisis, was a wholly negligible factor. There remained the Democrats. Marius entered into a compact with Saturninus and Glaucia, securing the Consulship for himself, the Tribuneship for

Saturninus, and the Prætorship for Glaucia. Together they formed the Popular government of the year 100, a government in which the conqueror of the Cimbri practically became the instrument of the two demagogues. His colleagues soon set to work. Saturninus produced a Land Bill, which appears to have assigned the land devastated by the Cimbri in Transpadane Gaul to the Romans and the poor Italians, a Corn Bill reducing the price of the State-sold corn, and a Colonial Bill in which, reviving the idea of Caius Gracchus, he created settlements in Greece, Macedonia, Sicily and Africa for the veterans of Marius.

These schemes were all of them well enough in the abstract, but in the disturbed state of public opinion no serious discussion of them was possible. In the excitement of controversy the two parties soon came to blows. The turbulent demagogues summoned bands of armed peasants to Rome, and by this means secured the passing of their proposals in the Comitia. Worse was to follow. At the consular elections for 99, Saturninus gave the signal for open insurrection by putting to death Caius Memmius, one of the most capable and respected members of the opposite party. This was the turning-point in the struggle. The rich capitalists, who had so far lent powerful support to the popular party, were frightened into the camp of law and order. The Senate decreed a state of siege, and all respectable citizens armed themselves in self-defence. It was a difficult situation for Marius; an old man's ambition and a soldier's instinct fought hard in him for supremacy. Discipline won in the end; but it was a doubtful victory. He put himself at the head of the Senators and Knights to suppress the rising of his colleagues; but his action displayed so much weakness and vacillation that the Conservatives believed him to be an accomplice of the rebels, while the advanced Democrats of course regarded him as a traitor. Finally, however, he succeeded in quelling the revolt, and Saturninus and Glaucia were put to death by a band of incensed nobles and capitalists under his command.

It was in this troubled year of Marius's Consulship that his sister Aurelia bore her husband, C. Julius Cæsar, a son, who was given his father's name.

The cry of revolution or spoliation never fails to bring Conservatives to heel. The rich financiers had been scared out of their Democratic allegiance, and the general public, disgusted at the turn matters had taken, veered round with equal rapidity. Marius soon felt his position undermined. Suspected by all parties within a year of his triumph over the Cimbri, he discreetly set out on a long journey to the East. The Conservatives thus returned both to office and to power. The more enlightened members of the party timidly urged the claims of social reform. But their feeble protests passed unheeded, and the government preferred to stake its credit upon a spirited foreign policy. It succeeded indeed in inducing the Senate to refuse the legacy of the Cyrenaica, which had been left to the Roman people by Ptolemy Apion on his death in 96, being reluctant at a time of military and financial embarrassment to assume fresh responsibilities in a disturbed and semi-barbarous country. But it was all the more anxious definitely to re-establish Rome's waning prestige in the East. There was no lack of opportunity for interference. In 95 Nicomedes of Bithynia was commanded to restore the territory he had taken, and given to understand that disobedience would be disastrous. Galatia was then given back to the Tetrarchs, Paphlagonia declared a free country, and Cappadocia put under the charge of a Parthian noble called Ariobarzanes, who was given the title of King. When two years later Mithridates concluded an alliance with Tigranes, King of Armenia, invaded Cappadocia and drove out Ariobarzanes, the aristocratic party proved equal to the emergency, and the Proprætor Lucius Cornelius Sulla was at once despatched with a small army to re-establish Ariobarzanes on his throne.

But these foreign successes were wholly insufficient to ensure peace in Italy. Distress was growing on every side. The Italians were haunted by their ambition for the franchise and a jealous hostility to the small oligarchy at Rome; and the Democrats were moving heaven and earth to recover their predominance. Marius had now returned from the East and could not resign himself in his own lifetime to the rôle of a mere historical personage. The financiers, driven temporarily by Saturninus into an unnatural allegiance, were rekindling their old fires against senatorial rivals. In 93 a comparatively unimportant incident, the trial of Publius Rutilius Rufus, provoked the long expected crisis.

Rufus was a Conservative and an aristocrat, a man of unblemished record and unquestioned courage, hostile both to the demagogues and the capitalists, and an outspoken admirer of the old *régime*. During his government of Asia as *Legatus Pro prætore*, he had had the misfortune to offend the capitalist interest by vigorous action against the rapacity of the Italian financiers. His enemies vowed vengeance. On his return to Rome they concocted against him a charge of extortion, and secured his condemnation by a tribunal of their friends. Rufus went off quietly into exile; but his martyrdom was not suffered in vain. It awakened all that was best in the old aristocracy to what was going on all round them, to the decay and disappearance of the old order and the ugly and unscrupulous injustice of the new. They saw that it would soon be too late to resist, that they must fight, and fight at once; and fortune provided them with a leader.

Livius Drusus, an ambitious and passionate young aristocrat, was the man of their choice. Elected Tribune of the people in 91, Drusus endeavoured to adopt against the financiers the policy which Caius Gracchus had found so useful against the big landlords. His idea was to isolate the moneyed interest by means of an alliance between the aristocracy and the popular party. He brought forward a number of laws designed to secure him the favour of the democracy; amongst them a Bill depriving the knights of their powers in the law-courts, and a measure making the tardy concession of citizen rights to the Italians. The idea of Italian emancipation had been slowly making way among the Roman electorate; but it had still to encounter very obstinate resistance. Not a few of the aristocrats had been converted to its support, though they could not help being conscious of the danger it involved to their class and party. But a great number were blinded by a prejudice so traditional as to be almost a second nature, and they confirmed it by the argument that any increase in the number of poor and ignorant electors would aggravate rather than allay the disorders in the capital. The financiers and the rich Italians were bitterly and outspokenly hostile. They were convinced that political reform would only be the prelude to a huge social upheaval, and that the Italians, most of whom were poor and indebted, would promptly make use of the franchise to introduce those bogies so familiar to students of ancient history, a revolutionary Land Law and the wholesale abolition of debt. A terrible agitation now broke out, dividing the aristocracy into two angry camps, and stirring all the old embers of controversy into flame. One morning Livius was found assassinated in his house. Profiting by the disturbances which followed his disappearance, the knights hastily passed through a bill creating an extraordinary tribunal to try all who were suspected of sympathy with the Italians, thus ridding themselves by prosecution and exile of all the chief of their opponents among the aristocracy and the Democrats.

But this paltry retaliation was soon rudely interrupted. The death of Livius had sent an earthquake shock through the Peninsula, and Rome soon felt the ground trembling beneath her feet. The whole country south of Liris raised the standard of revolt. Men rushed to arms in the cause of a united Italy, against Rome, the allied cities, and the Latin colonies of the centre and north of the Peninsula, most of which remained faithful to their allegiance. Rome was taken utterly by surprise. For once all party quarrels were hushed. The legions scattered broadcast throughout the Empire were hastily recalled to Italy; naval contingents were brought up from Heraclea, Clazomenæ and Miletus, and arms distributed among all classes both free and slave. Even Marius, mindful of his reputation, begged for a command. Then ensued a war whose horrors can be but dimly descried behind the scanty records that have come down to us. Roman generals marched ruthlessly up and down Italy, burning farms, sacking towns, and carrying off men, women and children, to sell them in the open market, or work them in gangs on their own estates.

It was in these campaigns that a studious young man named Marcus Tullius Cicero, born in the year 106, and belonging to a well-to-do family at Arpinum, first saw active service.

It was the very barbarism of such a warfare in the very heart of their own country which brought about its cessation. Romans were forced to realize that magnanimity was a safer policy than conquest, and the party among the nobles which was opposed to the financiers and sympathetic to the Italians came once more into power. In the year 90 the Consul Lucius Julius Cæsar was able to pass a law providing that citizen rights should be extended to the States which had remained faithful to Rome. Not long afterwards, at the end of the same year or at the beginning of the next, two Tribunes proposed the *lex Plautia Papiria,* according to which any citizen of an allied town domiciled in Italy could acquire the rights of Roman citizenship on making a declaration within sixty days to the Prætor at Rome. Other measures soon followed. In 89 a *lex Plautia* took away the law-courts from the knights, and enacted that judges should be chosen by the tribes from among every class in the State. It was perhaps in the same year that the Consul Cneius Pompeius Strabo proposed to extend the rights of the Latin colonies to the towns of Cisalpine Gaul, in order to relieve them from the obligation of military service and as a compensation for the losses they had suffered by serving in the Allies' Revolt. These concessions were far more effective than military operations in bringing the war to a close, and it was not long before only the Samnites and Lucanians remained in the field.

Italy had hardly begun to recover from the horrors of civil war when she was darkened by the shadow of a far worse calamity in the East. Mithridates had been surprised by the Social War just at the moment when he was preparing to embark on a great campaign to drive Rome out of Asia. As, however, at the moment of the outbreak of the Allies' Revolt his preparations were not yet concluded, he had assisted a younger brother of Nicomedes of Bithynia to seize that kingdom, and had joined hands with Tigranes, regardless of possible Roman intervention, in reconquering Cappadocia and putting his son on the throne. This was a direct challenge to the Romans, and it had been unexpectedly taken up. The aristocratic party, eager to win its spurs in foreign policy, sent out Manius Aquilius in the year 90 with a special mission to re-establish the two kings in their States, with the help of the small force of the Proconsul Lucius Cassius. Aquilius and Cassius had no difficulty in accomplishing their mission. But Aquilius had not come to the East to be bought off by the promises of Nicomedes. Thirsting for operations on a large scale against Mithridates, he tried to induce Nicomedes and Ariobarzanes to make filibustering expeditions over the frontier of Pontus. The unfortunate King showed a very reasonable hesitation. But Nicomedes was in the debt of the Roman bankers at Ephesus for large sums of money borrowed at Rome and in Asia during his exile to facilitate his restoration. Aquilius demanded payment. Nicomedes had no alternative but to raise the money out of the spoils of a raid into Pontus. Anxious to gain time and anxious also to put his adversary in the wrong, Mithridates sent in to Aquilius a modest and reasonable claim for damages, which was of course refused. At the end of the year 89 his preparations were complete. Sending his son to invade Cappadocia, he continued to bombard Aquilius with vigorous requests for reparation. Aquilius replied by a demand for unconditional submission. The result was a declaration of war.

When operations commenced in the spring of 88, Mithridates had at his command a fleet of four hundred ships, and one of those enormous armies, comparable to the conscript levies of modern Europe, which Oriental strategy, reckoning solely by quantity, has always insisted on regarding as formidable. It is said that he had a horde of 300,000 men, composed of Greek mercenaries, Armenian cavalry, and an infantry force of Cappadocians, Paphlagonians, Galatians, Scythians, Sarmatians, Thracians, Bastarni and Celts. Aquilius on the other hand had only been able during the winter to collect a small fleet from Bithynia and Asia, and a small army, including the raw Asiatic recruits of the King of Bithynia, which had been incorporated among the scanty Roman contingents. The result was as might have been foreseen. The four corps into which the Roman army was divided were defeated or dispersed within a few weeks; the Roman fleet surrendered to the superior force of the enemy; the King of Bithynia fled into Italy; the Roman generals were taken prisoners, and Mithridates proceeded at leisure to the invasion of Asia.

Great was the consternation when this news reached Italy. The Allies' Revolt had already been sufficiently disastrous. It had ruined many of the small and moderate proprietors by the destruction of their farms and cattle, and had interfered with the rents drawn by many of the rich aristocrats from their South Italian estates. The invasion of Asia now snatched away at one blow all profits on the vast capital expended by Roman financiers throughout the province. A serious financial crisis ensued. The tax-farmers refused payment, while owing to the prevailing conditions of trade the other imposts brought in but little. The Treasury was empty. Capitalists were too

frightened to invest, and made strenuous efforts to recover all outstanding liabilities. There was a general scarcity of money, and much
of what was in circulation was counterfeit. A Prætor who set his
face against the brutality of creditors was assassinated one morning
at sacrifice by a band of financiers. Rome was filled with riot,
assassination and robbery. The old and the new citizens seized the
occasion to vent their grievances in street-fighting. The Italians
complained that the Senate had refused to inscribe them within the
thirty-five tribes, and was trying to gain time by proposing all manner
of schemes to nullify their new rights; one proposal, for instance, was
to inscribe them in ten new tribes; another to include them in only
eight of the old thirty-five. But worse news from the seat of war in
the East broke into these petty bickerings.

What faced Rome in Asia was not, as she had first thought, a mere
struggle between an Eastern and a Western Power, but an organized and widespread revolution against plutocracy. Mithridates was
posing, not simply as the hero of Hellenism, but as the avenger of
the artisans and the peasants, the middle-class traders and landlords
of Asia, who were suffering under the extortions of Roman bankers
and of Levantine, Jewish and Egyptian usurers. He had sent orders
to the governors of all the conquered provinces warning them to
prepare for a general massacre of the Italians on the 30th day after
the date of his letter, and had skilfully inflamed the passions of the
common people, already hotly excited by the condemnation of their
protector, Rutilius Rufus. He promised liberty to all slaves, and a
50 per cent. remission to all debtors who killed their creditors. On
the day fixed, 100,000 Italians, men, women and children, were
attacked and cut down in the streets, or drowned, or burnt alive, by
the furious populace in all the greater and smaller towns of Asia.
Their slaves were set free, and their goods divided between the towns
and the Royal Treasury. The same treatment was accorded to the
possessions of non-Italian capitalists such as the Jewish bankers of
the Island of Cos. The spirit of rebellion soon spread to Greece. At
Athens the people rose in insurrection, philosophers and University
professors helping to fan the flame. Mithridates, having laid the
train, was well prepared for the explosion. His general, Archelaus,
was immediately despatched with a fleet and an army to reduce the

towns which had not yet revolted against the Romans and to conquer and devastate the rich trading centre of Delos. It was a great and far-reaching struggle for mastery in the Greek world. On the one side was an Asiatic monarchy reinforced by a revolutionary proletariat, on the other the Italian plutocracy reinforced by a decadent aristocracy and a democracy still unconscious of its strength. The intellectual classes, the men of letters and philosophers so numerous in the East, were ranged, as in all great social conflicts, some on one side and some on the other, according to individual sympathies, interests and attachments.

The Senate rose at once to the emergency. It entrusted Sulla, who was Consul in 88, with the direction of the war, and, finding the Treasury empty, it took the decisive step of selling all the goods which were under mortmain, including the whole of the treasures in the temples at Rome. Yet there was treachery almost in their own camp. Nothing is more significant of the bitterness which possessed all parties in Italy at this time than that they should have seized this moment of national danger to pursue their internecine conflicts. The Samnites and Lucanians, who were still under arms, sent ambassadors to Mithridates with proposals for an alliance. A large number of ruined Italians incited by hatred of the Conservatives, who were trying to evade their concession of citizen rights, and by the necessity of somehow making a livelihood, fled to Asia and joined the army of Mithridates. At Rome a party among the knights, who resented the loss of their judicial power, were preparing to recover it by revolutionary means, with the sinister assistance of Marius. The old veteran, who had long been fuming at the loss of his old popularity, was now indulging in wild and fantastic dreams of glory; to deprive Sulla of his command against Mithridates, win the fabled treasures of Pontus, and live over again before his death the great days of his Cimbric triumphs. The coalition found a ready instrument in Publius Sulpicius Rufus, an aristocrat who had been driven by his debts and also, it appears, by personal animosities to become an ardent member of the Democratic party. Rufus was at this time Tribune of the people. On the pretext of giving a tardy satisfaction to the new citizens, he proposed a law according to which the Italians should be partitioned out among the thirty-five tribes, and had it passed by hiring bands of cut-throats to terrify the electors and do violence to the Consuls. Both Consuls were forced to leave Rome. Sulla went off to join the army which was being assembled at Nola. Thereupon Marius, who was now in company with Rufus supreme master of Rome, had a law passed conferring the Eastern command upon himself, and sent orders to Sulla to give up his troops.

CHAPTER II

THE SULLAN REACTION

IF the wealthy classes so often come off second best in a struggle with the democracy, the cause is generally to be found in their disinclination to submit to leadership. The prospect which faced the Roman Conservatives at this moment, when the Revolution, in the person of Marius, had made itself complete master of the State, was indeed dark enough to close up the party ranks. Yet it was only by accident that they discovered in Sulla a fit champion for their cause. Sulla had up to this time been one of those superior but solitary figures who are sometimes to be found in an aristocracy when its old governing *régime* is on the eve of dissolution. Too intelligent and cultured to cherish the old prejudices of his class or to ignore the symptoms of its inevitable decadence; too conscious and contemptuous of the true value of success to court power by the meannesses on which fame in a democracy nearly always depends; energetic, fond of money, and impatient of inaction, yet with a marked inclination to scepticism and self-indulgence, he seemed to most of his contemporaries so indifferent to all distinctions between right and wrong, and so desirous for mere sensual and intellectual enjoyment, as never to be willing to sacrifice his own interest or pleasure to any ideal cause of principle. Hitherto his career had been rather military than political. He had preferred campaigning against Cimbri and revolted Italians to joining hands with one or other of the two parties at Rome. Although his origin and connections attached him rather to the Conservative than to the popular party, he had taken as small a share in party struggles as was compatible with the attainment of political and military promotion. His advance had thus been very slow, and he was over fifty when, in this year, he finally reached the Consulship. It is likely enough that, in his impartial contempt for both parties, he would have allowed Conservatives and Democrats to go on massacring one another indefinitely, if the revolutionaries had not suddenly marked him out for attack by attempting to deprive him of his Eastern command.

His reply to the summons of Marius was the first revelation of his characteristic daring and rapidity of decision. Having first made sure of the fidelity of his troops, he marched straight up from Nola upon Rome and occupied the city. Marius, utterly dumbfounded by the suddenness of the attack, had no alternative but flight; and Sulla thus became at one blow sole master of the situation. But since his object had merely been to preserve his command and not to make a counter-revolution in the Conservative interest, he used his victory with moderation. He prosecuted only twelve of the insurrectionary leaders, annulled the unconstitutional laws of Sulpicius, and allowed the elections for the following year to take place undisturbed. A Conservative, Cneius Octavius, was elected to the Consulship, with Lucius Cornelius Cinna, a man who passed for a Democrat, as his colleague. Sulla did no more than make them take an oath to respect the laws.

At the end of the year he left for Brindisi, where he embarked for Greece. He had with him five legions, a few incomplete cohorts, and a small force of cavalry, in all about 30,000 men. Never perhaps did so small an army set forth to accomplish so huge a task. Mithridates was preparing to defend his conquests with his wonted vigour and to make full use of his great numerical superiority. Archelaus and Aristion, who were already in Greece at the head of considerable armies, were to withdraw their troops to Athens and the Piræus, and allow themselves to be besieged, while a new army was to be assembled in Asia, and to be sent to Greece in due course when the Romans had become exhausted by the siege of Athens. As a plan of campaign, this left nothing to be desired. It compelled Sulla, as soon as he had disembarked in Epirus, to march South with his 30,000 men on the heels of the retreating enemy, and eventually to tire out his totally inadequate forces in a long and difficult siege. Meanwhile the Pontic fleet endeavoured to intercept communications with Italy, and to hamper the provision of Sulla's supplies.

Sulla's situation was thus already sufficiently precarious. But it became ten times more so when the Democrats recaptured the reins of government in Italy. No sooner had Sulla departed than the Consul Cinna again raised the question of the new citizens and their enrol-ment in the thirty-five tribes. His colleagues of course opposed the project. Both sides proceeded to arm their respective partisans and a pitched battle was fought in the streets of Rome. Ultimately Cinna was deposed and proscribed. He immediately retired to raise the standard of revolt in the country, collecting troops and money through the whole of Italy, and encouraging the Samnites, who were still under arms, to prolong their resistance. In the midst of this confusion Marius reappeared upon the scene from Africa, where he had been in hiding, accompanied by a small troop of Numidians, and began to enlist an army of freedmen and slaves in Etruria. The Senate attempted to prevent the outbreak of a second Social War by granting citizen rights to all the Italians who had not benefited by the *lex Julia* and the *lex Plautia Papiria*; only the Samnites and the Lucanians, as being still in revolt, were to be excepted. Unfortunately there was no second Sulla in their hour of need, and Marius had no difficulty in seizing Rome. The embittered old soldier wreaked a cruel vengeance on the proud nobles who had always refused him their admiration. A large number of aristocrats were executed, and their heads carried to the house of Marius, or fixed as an adornment to the Rostra. Sulla was declared the enemy of his country and deposed from his command; his house at Rome was razed to the ground, his villas pillaged, and his goods confiscated.

Meanwhile the little army before Athens which was to reconquer the East was being abandoned by the home government just at the moment when the hardships of a long siege were beginning to tell upon its strength. Disease and skirmishing were daily thinning its ranks, and the stock of supplies was running dangerously low. If the relieving army from Asia arrived in time to avert capitulation, the besiegers would be cut off without hope of retreat. In this supreme crisis of his career, Sulla showed the stuff of which he was made. The contemptuous sceptic, the man who seemed to have taken part in all the fighting of his age simply to secure for himself the riches indispensable for self-indulgence, stands forth at last in his true character, strong-willed, merciless, and absolutely self-centred. Entrenched before Athens, he was like a Titan at bay. To save himself and his army he swept off every obstacle from his path. He cut down the thickets of the Lyceum and the plane-trees of Plato's Academy to accommodate his siege works; he established a mint in the Peloponnese, to provide sufficient pay for his troops; he made ruthless requisitions throughout Greece, pillaging temples, regardless of the sacrilege, converting tripods, and vases, and jewels, all the artistic treasures dedicated by countless generations of worshippers, into silver and gold to meet his needs. He sent one of his younger officers, Lucius Lucullus, with six ships to break through the cordon of the Pontic fleet and bring up vessels from all parts of the Mediterranean, and to restore the Roman sea-power in the Ægean. He did all that was possible, and far more than was conventional, to encourage his men; he shared every hardship and joined in every skirmish, appearing in person to lead them to the attack, and distributing prize-money among all ranks. Marius had been the first in the war against Jugurtha to see that under the changed conditions of the age Rome must be content to recruit her legions from amongst the lowest stratum of the Italian populace; that the conquests on which she had entered with a national militia of yeomen could only be continued by a standing army of paid soldiers. But it was Sulla who first realized that this new breed of soldiers could be treated in all ways like regular mercenary levies and submitted to every severity of discipline, hardship, and danger, provided only that they were skilfully commanded and generously paid.

During the whole of 87 Athens continued to offer a desperate resistance against all assaults. Archelaus was an excellent general, and if the fortunes of the war had depended entirely upon him, Sulla would perhaps have succumbed. But the reinforcing army, which was due to arrive from Asia in the autumn of 87, did not make its appearance. Hampered by its own unwieldy size, and delayed by a disorganized commissariat and indifferent leadership, its advance was slow and fitful. The governor of Macedonia, Caius Sentius Saturninus, set himself across its path with the few troops at his disposal, and succeeded in intercepting it in Macedonia at a difficult season of the year. It was obliged to go into winter quarters in that not very hospitable country, and Sulla was thus set free to make the most of his time till the spring.

But hardly was this danger removed when another storm-cloud beat up from the west. At the beginning of 86 death put an end to the troubled career of Marius. But his disappearance did nothing to settle the dangerous dispute over the Eastern command, a dispute which had already lasted two years, and had almost added the horrors of a second Civil War to the vexations of a party conflict at Rome. There were many reasons why the Democrats could not leave the command in the hands of a man like Sulla, who, though by no means a whole-hearted Conservative, was yet thoroughly out of sympathy with the popular party. The most pressing were no doubt provided by the numerous aspirants in its own ranks, who were ambitious of high military command. But private interest could be speciously reinforced by the fancied necessities of policy. The party which inherited the traditions of the Gracchi and Marius needed to restore its prestige by some striking military success. By the repulse of the Cimbri and Teutones it had saved Italy; by the discomfiture of Mithridates it would reconquer Asia. Nor did it shrink from accepting the legacy of personal bitterness bequeathed by its dead leader, and from treating Sulla frankly as an implacable enemy. Lucius Valerius Flaccus, the Consul who was elected in the place of Marius, was ordered to go to Greece with an army of 12,000 men to relieve Sulla of his command. The new Consul was an ardent Democrat who had just passed a law releasing all debtors from 75 per cent. of their debts; if he arrived before Athens capitulated, Sulla would be caught in a vice between the legions from Rome and the armies of Mithridates.

But Flaccus' preparations took time. He was still in Italy when on March 1, 86, Sulla succeeded, after a desperate assault, in capturing both Athens and the Piræus. These successes infused new life into his soldiers; but they were not decisive for the issue of the campaign. Without the command of the sea Sulla was not yet in a position to inflict a crushing blow upon the enemy. Archelaus retired into the peninsula of Munychia, where he embarked his whole force in good order, and sailed to Thermopylæ to join the invading army. Thus after the capture of Athens, Sulla had still, as before, three armies to face, the forces of Archelaus, his Asiatic reinforcements, and the legions of Flaccus, who had by now disembarked in Epirus. Sulla realized that he must rout the Pontic armies before the arrival of the new Consul. Although the enemy were in considerable numerical superiority, he marched with all his forces to meet Archelaus, and defeated him in the great battle of Chæronea, in Bœotia.

This victory, the first won by Roman troops over Mithridates, produced an immense sensation all through the Empire. Its con-

sequences were far more momentous than those of the capture of
Athens, and it led to a situation which was favourable both to Sulla
and to Roman interests in general. For some months past the
respectable classes in Asia, aghast at the massacres of 88 and at the
revolutionary methods of Mithridates, had begun to intrigue with
Rome against the Pontic domination. They found it easy to make use
of the discontent of the common people at the continual levies of the
new government. Already by the end of 87 Ephesus had revolted in
favour of Rome. The battle of Chæronea, following close upon this
revolt, encouraged the Roman party throughout Asia, broke down
the wavering fidelity of the towns, and forced Mithridates to new
shifts to recover his prestige. He now adopted the most interesting,
and the most ominous, of the Protean disguises of his career, proclaiming himself throughout Asia as the champion of the Social
Revolution, abolishing all debts and promising liberty to all States
which remained faithful to his cause. He then prepared to send a new
army, under the orders of Dorilas, for the invasion of Bœotia and
the reconquest of Greece.

But the most important consequence of the victory of Chæronea
was to facilitate what had hitherto seemed as unlikely as it was
indispensable—peace between Sulla and the Democratic party.
Flaccus, who seems to have been less unreasonable than his kind, had
no sooner landed in Epirus than he realized the full nature of his
mission: that he was expected to reopen the Civil War at the very
moment when the common enemy was about to throw new forces
into the province he had conquered. He saw that to dispute the honour
of holding the chief command against Mithridates, when the united
forces of the two rival generals were hardly in a position to defeat
him, would be criminal folly. Sulla, for his part, was not the man to
be blinded either by success in battle or by the bitterness of party; he
was fully alive to the dangers of a simultaneous campaign against the
King of Pontus and the forces of the Democrats. Unfortunately,
Flaccus was prevented by Sulla's proscription from throwing the two
armies into one, and Sulla had to be content with a secret arrangement,
according to which the two forces were to act in agreement without
their co-operation being generally known. Flaccus was to use his
authority as Consul to induce the people of Byzantium to fit out a

fleet, thus carrying the war into Asia. Sulla was to remain in Greece to await Dorilas, who was now advancing, after taking on board off Eubœa Archelaus and 10,000 survivors of the battle of Chæronea. This sensible arrangement produced excellent effects. By the close of 86 both armies had won considerable successes. Sulla attacked and annihilated the army of Dorilas at Orchomenos, sent him flying into Eubœa, where he was unable to follow him, and then retired into Thessaly for winter quarters. Flaccus invaded Macedonia, drove the last remnants of the Pontic army before him into Asia, and crossed the Bosphorus with the help of the Byzantine fleet. Thus all Mithridates' schemes had been checkmated. When the year ended, so far from having recovered the ground lost at Chæronea, he had definitively lost all his European conquests.

The armies of the proscribed Proconsul and the legitimate Consul had co-operated in this happy result, though Sulla's achievements outweighed those of Flaccus. If the Italian Democrats had been inclined to follow the wise example of Flaccus, if they had revoked Sulla's proscription, and accepted his services on reasonable conditions, the crisis which had almost entailed the loss of the Empire would have been over within a few more months. But the course of politics in Italy rendered this easy solution impossible. The Conservative party had been almost entirely exterminated by the Revolution. A large number of the aristocracy and the wealthier citizens had been killed, others had escaped to Sulla or into distant provinces, those who remained in Rome were paralysed with fear. The equestrian order had fared little better. The financiers and merchants who composed it felt themselves threatened on both sides. They hardly knew which to shun as the greater evil: a Conservative reaction that would take away all their privileges, or a social revolution that would follow the precedent of the reduction of debts which had just been decreed. The Democratic party, strong in the support of the middle class, felt too sure of its own power to make any agreement with Sulla.

Flaccus' conduct found so little favour with the Democrats that during the winter of 86–85 Fimbria, one of his lieutenants and a member of the popular party, suspecting the secret agreement between Flaccus and Sulla, succeeded in rousing the soldiers to mutiny; Flaccus was put to death by his troops, and Fimbria proclaimed Commander-in-Chief. This petty military revolution made all hopes of conciliation futile. Sulla now found himself once more in a very critical situation. He could not afford to let Fimbria conclude the conquest of Asia; for the Democrats, already sufficiently his enemy, would only use their success to turn their arms against himself and his army. On the other hand, it was very dangerous for him to attack Fimbria, for Mithridates, in spite of his loss of prestige since the defeats at Chæronea and Orchomenos, would be certain, on the outbreak of Civil War, to recover everything that he had lost.

Such was the situation which forced Sulla to take a step which was destined to be decisive for his whole future career, and to exercise a baneful influence upon Rome for the next twenty years of her history. Unable to fight a double war against Fimbria and Mithridates, and equally unable to come to terms with Fimbria, he decided to negotiate with Mithridates for the conclusion of peace upon reasonable terms. The moment seemed auspicious. The length of the operations and the defeats of the last year had exhausted the military and financial resources of the King of Pontus. Greece was entirely lost, and almost the whole of Asia in revolt. By the offer of land and money and other tempting promises, Sulla gained the ear of Archelaus, persuaded him to surrender his fleet, and to approach his master with definite proposals. The *status quo* of 88 was to be restored; Mithridates was to keep the whole of his old kingdom of Pontus, to receive the title of friend and ally of the Roman people, and to pay over to Sulla 2,000 talents and a fixed number of warships. Sulla even promised to facilitate his retreat and to draw a veil over his failure by granting an amnesty to the rebel States of Asia.

Regarded from the standpoint of the military and political traditions of Rome such a treaty was almost an act of high treason. The King who had massacred 100,000 Italians and devastated the fairest provinces of the Empire was to keep his kingdom, to receive the title of friend and ally, and to pay a comparatively trifling indemnity. But the condition of Italy after half a century of political and social conflict was so disastrous that Sulla was practically forced into buying safety for himself and his soldiers by a formal alliance with the butcher of the Italians. Yielding to the solicitations of Sulla, Archelaus visited Mithridates, and used all his influence to persuade him. The wily

Oriental, who well understood why Sulla's terms were so favourable, at first attempted to improve them by the threat of an alliance with Fimbria. But Fimbria did not give him the chance. Burning to achieve something that would justify his anomalous position, he took the field in the spring of 85, marched into Asia and won several signal successes over the armies of Mithridates, culminating in the capture of Pergamus. Meanwhile Lucullus, who had at length succeeded in collecting a fleet, appeared on the Asiatic coast to incite the cities to revolt. Mithridates, seeing his army disorganized and his power in Asia slipping from his grasp, was finally persuaded that it would be simpler to make an agreement with Sulla than with Fimbria. He sought an interview with the Proconsul at Dardanus, accepted his terms, and embarked the survivors of his army for Pontus.

Thus rid of Mithridates, Sulla advanced to meet Fimbria in Lydia. The murderer of Flaccus had proved himself a violent and exacting commander, and had quickly forfeited the sympathies of his army. At Sulla's approach his men broke up to join forces with the victor of Chæronea and Orchomenos, and Fimbria himself found refuge in suicide. Sulla thus remained sole master of Asia at the head of a large fleet and a considerable army, together with the resources secured by the indemnity from Mithridates.

This success was indeed no more than his due. It was Sulla who had really destroyed the power of Mithridates, and restored to the Empire the provinces he had overrun. Had it not been for Chæronea and Orchomenos, Fimbria could never have entered Asia, still less have captured Pergamus. Yet there was one grave blot on his record. The Treaty of Dardanus had granted what was virtually a free pardon to the Hannibal of the East. This was a concession in which neither party, however greatly it desired peace, would have dared to acquiesce, unless Sulla had been absolute master of the situation. Sulla, of course, was very well aware of this, and did his best to meet the difficulty. During the years 85 and 84 he worked hard, not only to strengthen his personal position with the legions, but to make his peace with the Democrats at home. He was anxious to conclude some satisfactory arrangement which would allow him to return quietly to Italy for the enjoyment of the immense wealth which he had amassed during the war. If his opponents had only guaranteed to maintain his Eastern settlement, and engaged not to go back upon the Treaty of Dardanus, he would have been quite ready to abandon the Roman Conservatives, who had not raised a finger to help him in his moment of danger. But the spirit of universal distrust which is so deep-rooted at all times of revolution, and so complicates the conflicts of political parties, made any such agreement impossible. A good many nobles had taken refuge in the camp of Sulla, and were continually urging him to overthrow the Democratic government. All over the Empire the survivors of the Conservative party had been persuaded by the news of Sulla's victories into the belief that they had at last lighted upon a true champion who would be prepared to repeat against the existing *régime* his bold stroke against the revolution of Sulpicius in 88. Intrigues and conspiracies were already in the air, and an active agitation now broke out amongst the youth of the wealthier classes. Sulla was far too clever a man to become the blind instrument of a party which was itself to blame for its disasters; yet the turn which events were taking could not help proving injurious to his attempts at conciliation. The Democratic government, always suspicious of his past, scented treason at once. The middle class were afraid that he would attempt to deprive the Italians of their citizen rights. The popular party was, of course, burning to have its revenge on the Conservatives. The disavowal of the Treaty of Dardanus, which would deprive their opponents of all credit for the conquest of Asia, was a tempting battle-cry for party warfare. They would refuse to recognize a treaty containing provisions so humiliating to the Republic: the so-called victory of a Conservative general over Mithridates were better-named a national humiliation.

If the moral and political situation of Italy made an agreement unlikely between Sulla and the Democrats, the conflict of economic interests soon rendered it impossible. The knights, many of whom had invested money in the province of Asia, had now become as powerful with the Democratic government as they had been under every preceding *régime;* for the wave of feeling which had stirred the whole State and thrown together men of all parties against the exactions of the financiers had passed away as suddenly as it had come. It was inevitable that the plutocrats in the equestrian order should take sides against Sulla. It was true that he had reconquered Asia; but events had forced him to injure many of their interests in the process. He had restored their value in law to contracts concluded between individuals, and had re-established the old local obligations between debtor and creditor; but he had also abolished the farming of the land-tithe upon land decreed by Caius Gracchus, and decided that all taxes should be levied by the province itself. It is not surprising, therefore, that the long negotiations between Sulla and the Democrats led to no result. Sulla had done his best. He held his hand during the whole of the year 84. At last at the beginning of 83, when the ports of Italy were being closed against him, he left the two legions of Fimbria behind him in Asia, and set out on his homeward journey, to declare war on the Democratic government. He brought with him to the West not only the gold of Mithridates and the spoils of the temples of Greece, but a more precious possession in the books of Aristotle, which he had seized in the library of Apellicon at Athens.

It is unnecessary to deal in detail with the history of the Civil War that followed; it must suffice merely to emphasize its one most important result. Sulla, hitherto the representative of neither party in the State, ended by becoming the leader of the extreme reactionaries. On his arrival in Italy, the survivors of the Conservative party flocked from all sides to his standard, and hailed him as the deliverer they had so long expected. Attempts were at once made to use him as the instrument of their partisan interest, and before long some of the younger men of the party found courage to take action. One of the number, Cneius Pompeius, son of the Consul of the year 89, and a member of a noble but wealthy family, recruited a small force in Picenum. Another young noble, Marcus Licinius Crassus, who had lost a brother in the Revolution, followed his example; so did Metellus Pius, son of the general who had fought against Jugurtha. Sulla, however, was not yet willing to become the tool of a party clique. He reassured the Italians by declaring that he would not go back upon the great measure of Italian emancipation, and consented further to treat with the popular party through the mediation of the Senate. But it was all in vain. The chiefs of the popular party, who do not seem, with the exception of Sertorius, to have been men of any mark, were too distrustful of his intentions. With the whole of Italy at their back, they were not disposed to be frightened by the few legions of

Sulla, and met all his advances with polite but determined evasion. Thus Sulla was at last driven to accept the offers of the Conservatives. He entrusted important commands to Pompey, Crassus and Metellus, and took up arms as the champion of the counter-revolution. His operations were marked by his customary rapidity and decision. Before long, by a skilful admixture of force and conciliation, he had restored some semblance of order to a society in which a long period of unrest and revolution had broken down all the ordinary restraints of morality. By the adroit use of his money he detached from the Democratic party a large number of its civil and military supporters, and those who resisted his temptations were discouraged by his decisive victories over all the leaders of the Democratic forces. One after the other they fell before his sword; Sertorius alone succeeded in escaping to Spain. Within a few months Sulla had overturned the revolutionary government and become supreme master of Italy, with an armed force at his back, while the popular party lay crushed beneath his heel, and the Senate sat by, an interested but impotent spectator.

From this time forward Sulla seems a changed man. The proud, lofty and cynical aristocrat had always kept concealed in his nature a strain of sensual brutality, which at last burst out in full force. His imperious disdain for his fellow-men and the resentment inspired by his perils in the Civil War now turned him, whether by instinct or calculation, into a butcher. He was not to be deceived by the flattery men paid him after his victory. He realized that those very Conservatives to whom his victories had been so useful, and for whom he entertained as sincere a contempt as for their opponents, would be the first to bring against him all the old party reproaches, the Treaty of Dardanus, the death of Fimbria, the Civil War, and the first to abandon him to the tender mercies of the Democrats unless order were re-established upon so secure a basis that his arrangements remained unassailable either in Italy or in the East. For the restoration of order he needed no party allegiance. He resolved to do his work thoroughly, and to do it alone.

His first step was to claim from the Senate the office of Dictator, which brought with it the right of life and death over every citizen for an indefinite period, and plenary powers for the reform of the Constitution. The Senate was not in a position to resist, and the

Lex Valeria granting him the office was passed without opposition. Armed with these powers, he put to death an enormous number— according to one account 5,000—of those who had in the present or previous generation, supported the Democratic movement; he persecuted their families, reduced them to poverty by confiscations, annulled all their marriages with aristocratic houses, and decreed that the sons of the proscribed should be excluded for ever from every office in the State. Whole cities were punished by the infliction of fines, the demolition of fortifications, and the confiscation of public and private lands. He distributed these wholesale amongst his veterans, whom he settled upon the country, like colonists in a conquered province. Two thousand seven hundred knights and about 100 Senators were put to death, and anyone who had sinned in the least against the interests or the prejudices of the Conservative party went in danger of his life.

Unfortunately in a country already suffering from the effects of a whole generation of social disorder, a political reaction soon degenerated into an organized pillage. Sulla could hardly avoid collecting round him a heterogeneous crowd of adventurers—slaves and freedmen, plebeians and patricians, bankrupt nobles like Lucius Domitius Ahenobarbus and aristocratic financiers like Marcus Crassus. These men succeeded in piling up enormous riches by the simple process of buying up cheap the goods of the proscribed. Sulla could do nothing to interfere: perhaps he would not have wished to had he been able. Cold and merciless in the hour of victory as in the hour of danger, he was untouched by that desire for adulation so characteristic of usurping greatness; he seems to have felt an exquisite satisfaction in showing his comprehensive contempt at once for Conservatives and Democrats, rich and poor, Romans and Italians, nobles, financiers and plebeians. All equally trembled in his presence, as he sat enthroned and indifferent, in his palatial home, to receive the homage of all the greatest personages in Rome, when with hatred in their hearts they came to pay their humble respects to the supreme arbiter of life and death. He derived a cynical enjoyment from the spectacle of all that was noble or illustrious or aristocratic in Roman society, the young and old representatives of historic families and the fashionable ladies of the nobility, squabbling and elbowing for admission to the sumptuous dinners at which he sat, surrounded by his favourite singers, thinking only of his meat and drink, and not taking even the trouble to ask the names of his innumerable and illustrious guests. With the same sublime indifference he allowed his relatives and the friends of his youth to wrangle with the crowd of ambitious and greedy parasites in his vestibule and to trifle with his complaisance to secure the lands, the houses or the slaves of the proscribed; to extract a pardon for some less conspicuous victim or the condemnation of some innocent citizen whose wealth or character had exposed him to the hatred of his accusers. The number of persons ruined in this way was very considerable. A great many took refuge with the barbarians in Spain and Mauretania, or at the Court of Mithridates. All who failed to secure the protection of some friend at Court spent their days in continual apprehension of arrest. The young son of that Caius Julius Cæsar, whose sister Marius had married, and who had died at Pisa of apoplexy a few years before, was one of those whose life was in especial danger; for he was not only the nephew of Marius, but had committed the additional offence of marrying Cornelia, the daughter of Cinna. The Dictator commanded him to divorce her; but Cæsar, who was very fond of his young wife, in whose favour he had refused a rich heiress, Cossutia, refused to obey. He preferred to see the confiscation of his own patrimony and of the dowry of his wife, and to leave the city at the imminent risk of proscription. Soon afterwards, however, Sulla was induced by the intervention of some of his relatives to extend him a free pardon.

The popular party was crushed for the moment; but it was necessary to provide against its possible revival. It was with this object that Sulla, who had now developed into a true representative of the Conservative cause, attempted to effect a great reform of the constitution on the lines foreshadowed by Rutilius Rufus and his small group of aristocratic followers, who now suddenly saw almost the whole of their programme put into execution. Sulla abolished the Censorship and the public distributions of corn; he increased the number of the Prætors to eight, and of the Quæstors to twenty; he took away from the Assembly the power of discussing laws without authorization from the Senate; he transferred to the Assembly of the Centuries the powers which had belonged to the Assembly of the

Tribes; he deprived the Tribunes of the people of the right of proposing laws, and of standing for the higher magistracies, leaving them only the right of hearing appeals. He decreed that no one should be elected to an office except in the normal order of promotion, and that re-election should only be possible after the lapse of ten years; he attempted to check the increase of crime by sharpening the penalties for offences of violence and fraud. He freed no less than 10,000 slaves and gave them full citizen rights, selecting the youngest and bravest of those who had belonged to the proscribed, added 300 equestrian members to the Senate, and restored to that body its old judicial prerogatives.

His main object, in short, was to break down the influence of the two new powers in the State, the middle class and the equestrian order, by a re-establishment, with slight modifications, of the old aristocratic constitution which had existed at the time of the first Punic War, when Italian society, then predominantly agricultural, aristocratic and military, had been composed of a perfectly rigid stratification of classes. By the time when Sulla attempted to restore this old order, all these separate layers had become folded and broken and inextricably confused, at first by the gradual weakening of the aristocracy, then by the steady pressure of the middle class from below, and finally by the violent earthquake of the Revolution. He selected for the change the very moment when slaves had been incited to betray their proscribed masters, and when his own parasites were banding together in associations in which slave and freedman, aristocrat and bourgeois joined hands to do violence to law and custom, and to involve the whole of Italy in bloodshed and devastation. His settlement can hardly be classed as an aristocratic restoration. Rather it was a wild and sanguinary carnival, in Italy and Asia and throughout the Roman dominions, of a small oligarchy of slaves and assassins, of needy aristocrats and unscrupulous adventurers, remorseless usurers and professional *condottieri*, triumphing over a vast Empire of oppressed millions who in one passionate and impotent access of fury had risen against their oppressors. Impassive amidst the carousals of the actors, singers and dancers who nightly flocked to his halls, Sulla looked complacently on at a victory which he had not sought, but for which, nevertheless, he was alone responsible. The moment he felt secure of his life as a private individual in the Empire which he governed as Dictator, he abdicated his office to devote himself more completely to a life of pleasure. It did not spare him long. At the beginning of 78 he died.

It would be unjust to credit Sulla with the worst sort of ambition; he was a sincere Republican who hastened to give up his power the moment it was possible for him to do so without danger to his own life and that of his friends. But the force of circumstances and the peculiar limitations of his own nature caused him to play a less conspicuous part in history than might have been expected from a man of his activity and intelligence. He was far from being a model of the true Republican; to compare him with a man like Washington, for instance, would be ludicrous. Remarkable as he was for the clearness with which he conceived his ideas, and the infinite energy and resource which he displayed in their execution, he was incapable of any great depth of passion or of any really creative intellectual conception; he lacked just that spark of divine madness, that almost mystical power of inspiration which is reserved for the greatest spirits and seems somehow to embody, in confused and unconscious form, the vital instinct of our race as it presses onwards towards the future. Thinking only of self-indulgence, and indifferent to all that was outside this narrow range, nothing seized his attention in the life of his time but the confusion introduced into the structure of its society— a confusion due apparently to the perverseness and folly of mankind, and needing only, he thought, to be set right with the sword. Thus he succeeded in creating, not a Constitution or an Empire, but simply a gigantic system of police—conceived with unerring clearness, and executed with superhuman energy. These police measures were perhaps necessary at that moment to save the Empire and the whole of ancient civilization from the destruction with which they were threatened by the desperate revolt of the oppressed thousands in Italy and Asia. But its value in history does not exceed that of all similar systems. Order, even in the best organized State, is only a smooth and specious fiction in the place of justice and wisdom. An ordered society is like a field which has periodically to be touched and torn by the plough before the soil receives the virtue to renew its creative power. The terrible upheaval in Italian society may perhaps be compared to a ploughshare penetrating into the very depths of the old order, turning and returning the soil of which it was composed, bringing to light much that had been hidden, breaking up into powder much that for many months had been hardened in the sun, opening new pores for the showers of heaven, waking into activity all the living seeds within as a preparation for a new and abundant harvest. Marius had contributed his part to this great revival, in spite of the criminal ambitions of his later years, by tracing the large outlines of the new military organization of Rome, and by helping to solve the question of Italian emancipation. Sulla contributed nothing at all. His work was even more self-contradictory than that of the Gracchi. He climbed into power by wielding the chief weapon of the new plutocracy, by the lavish use of money among friends and opponents. He used it to restore the political institutions of the age of agriculture. No wonder that his work and his influence were short-lived. The imposing edifice of his constitution was like a cabin of reeds put together on the sea-shore, that is carried away with one burst of rough sea wind. Nothing survived of his work but the fear inspired by a type of statesman new to the history of Rome.

Thus ended the stormy generation which had opened with the assassination of the Gracchi. In the midst of all this confusion, one great historic process had been quietly completed. The old Italy, the Italy of Oscans, Sabellians, Umbrians, Latins, Etruscans, Greeks and Gauls had disappeared into the past. In place of a number of small federal republics, there was now a single Italian nation, with an agriculture, a commerce, an army, a civilization and a culture of its own, welded together into a solid and compact middle class out of a medley of human units from all parts of the peninsula who had been thrown together, in close and intimate relations, by the tie of a common ambition, by fellowship in study, in commerce, or in arms.

CHAPTER III

CÆSAR'S DÉBUT IN POLITICS

AFTER his narrow escape from Sulla, Caius Julius Cæsar decided to go away from Rome on an extensive journey. He left Italy in the suite of the Proprætor Marcus Minutius Thermus for the siege of Mitylene, the last of the rebel cities in Asia to hold out against the Romans. From Mitylene he went on to Bithynia, sent by Thermus on a mission to the old king to demand ships to assist in the siege. His stay in the palace of Nicomedes, far from Rome and his family, afterwards became a by-word with his enemies, who were fond of relating how the young Cæsar plunged deep in all the vices of an Oriental Court. What is certain is that he made repeated visits to the Court of Nicomedes between this time and 78, when Publius Servilius, Proconsul of Cilicia, undertook a campaign against the pirates of Lycia and Pamphylia. Cæsar then joined Servilius, and held a subordinate command in the operations; but shortly afterwards, on the news of Sulla's death, he returned to the capital.

He found Rome, with the great Dictator removed, far from happy under the rule of the oligarchs. Sulla's successors were neither united amongst themselves nor confident in their powers. In spite of the gigantic effort made by Sulla, the aristocratic constitution he had established was by no means well founded; it offended a great number of individual interests without responding in any way to the needs of the age. Nor could it be expected to work smoothly and successfully in the absence of the old Roman nobility, for whose use or in whose memory it had been devised. It is true that the survivors of the hereditary aristocracy, in particular the representatives of its most respected houses, such as Quintus Lutatius Catulus, rallied vigorously to the support of a constitution which had realized all the reactionary ideas of their class. They imagined that the tide of democratic advance, which had been encroaching so perilously during the last two generations, had been swept back for ever; that the old aristocratic constitution, the sole foundation of Roman greatness, had been firmly and finally secured against attack. But a small group of noble families does not make up a nobility, and these respectable aristocrats formed in reality but a minority of the ruling caste. Side by side with them, and bound by the same party allegiance, there were the associates and the hangmen of Sulla, enriched by the confiscation of the goods of the proscribed; there were stragglers and deserters from the party of Marius; there were the old moderate Conservatives, now transformed by the Revolution into reactionaries of the deepest dye; there was the whole familiar class of trimmers and turncoats whose gaze is always turned towards the rising sun. So far from being representative of one section or order in the State, the Conservative party was little better than a band of political adventurers, of a predominantly low-class character, manifestly unworthy of that respectful obedience which is the very essence of aristocratic government.

The ruling faction may have been fully conscious of their lack of moral authority: but they might still hope to hold Italy together in a common detestation for the party of their opponents. It was a congenial policy, and they adopted it with alacrity. They set consistently to work to brand the revolutionaries as pariahs. They excluded from the Senate, the magistracies and the provincial governorships all who would not bow the knee to Sulla and the Conservative chiefs as the sole great men of the preceding generation, or refused to heap contumely upon the Democr tic party and its representatives, and upon the ideas and causes for which Marius in particular had fought. Yet the pretence was too unreal to impose on men for long. If the men now in power affected to class Marius with the corsairs and criminals, and took an unworthy delight in overturning his trophies, it remained none the less true that it was Marius who had repulsed the Cimbri and Teutones, and Sulla who had signed the Treaty of Dardanus. It was impossible therefore for the Conservative clique to parade their hatred of the democrats and their chiefs without wounding the national susceptibilities of Italy. And indeed the Italians regarded them with anything but favour. With no moral or sentimental prestige to protect them, Sulla's successors were encamped in the centre of the country like a small army of occupation in a conquered land, surrounded and harassed on all sides by bands of watchful and implacable enemies. The reaction had meant insult, humiliation, and ruin to a large circle of individuals: Sulla had sown a crop of bitter and painful memories in every corner of Italy. The sons of the proscribed who had lost parents, possessions and political rights, the cities which had been robbed of territory and Roman citizenship, the knights who had forfeited their power in the law-courts and almost all their old political influence, the great Italian middle class which was afraid of losing the privileges it had so painfully won, all these formed an angry and restless multitude of opponents in face of which the strongest government might well have felt dismay. Several of these factions were indeed temporarily disorganized and dispersed by the terror of persecution. But what would happen on the day that they were reunited under a single leader?

There was one way indeed in which the oligarchs might hope to gain strength and prestige—the adoption of a bold foreign policy, and the achievement of some striking military and diplomatic success. The Government might, for instance, have won pardon for many of its failings by wiping out the stain of the Treaty of Dardanus. But a small political cabal hastily made up, in the midst of a great political upheaval, out of a number of discordant and vacillating elements, and paralysed by the very horror of the experiences through which it had passed, had no energy left for a vigorous initiative. Its most powerful instrument, the Senate, remained entirely inactive, attempting to avoid every occasion of war in the fear of the possible consequences of defeat, and refusing to risk on distant expeditions any considerable part of the forces whose presence seemed indispensable to maintain order at home. This was curiously exemplified in the year 81, when Alexander II, King of Egypt, followed the example of the King of Pergamus and bequeathed his country to the Senate. Egypt was the richest kingdom of the ancient world: yet the Senate rejected it outright, merely taking over the money treasure of the deceased king which had been deposited at Tyre. It is true that when Mithridates demanded the recognition of the Treaty of Dardanus the Senate refused to comply. But, however unwilling it might still show itself to share Sulla's responsibilities, it did not seem to be aware that its refusal made a second war inevitable, and made no preparations whatever for meeting it.

It is not surprising therefore that on the death of Sulla the surviving members of the Democratic party began to show signs of activity.

A serious incident, which happened while Cæsar was in the East, soon demonstrated to all the world the inherent weakness of Sulla's government without a Sulla to direct it. On the first outbreak of the new popular agitation the Democrats actually secured for their chief a certain Marcus Æmilius Lepidus, one of the Consuls for the year 78. Lepidus was rich and of noble family, and the owner of the grandest palace in Rome. He had hitherto been a Conservative, and in Sulla's circle, and had even enriched himself by buying up the goods of the proscribed. But he was ambitious, volatile and headstrong, and had taken offence because Sulla had tried to prevent his election in the Consulship. After Sulla's death, he secured the leadership of the popular party by proposing to re-establish the distributions of corn, to recall the exiles, and to restore their electoral rights and their lands to the towns which had been robbed of them. His agitation proved unexpectedly successful.

The weakness of the government was manifest from the very first. Although Lepidus stood almost alone in his propaganda, the Senate, which had no trustworthy troops at its disposal in the capital, was intimidated into partial submission. It yielded on the question of the distributions of corn and the return of the exiles, but offered vigorous opposition to the other proposals, particularly that of the restitution of lands. But the agitation of Lepidus had roused a spirit of revolt all over Italy. In the neighbourhood of Fiesole, in Etruria, many of the landlords who had been despoiled by Sulla took up arms to drive out the occupants of their old domains. At Rome the extreme Conservatives, headed by the other Consul, Quintus Lutatius Catulus, accused Lepidus of fomenting rebellion, and proposed energetic measures of suppression, which the Senate had not the courage to adopt. It was thought simpler to remove Lepidus from Rome by finding various pretexts for hastening the departure of the two Consuls for their provinces before the election of their successors had taken place. It appears that their provinces had already been assigned to them, Narbonese Gaul to Lepidus, Italy to Catulus; they were now given large sums of money for their administration, and compelled to take an oath not to turn their arms against one another.

Returning to Rome in the midst of these commotions, Cæsar naturally met with anything but a cordial reception from the ruling clique, who had by no means forgotten his parentage and his past. His sudden arrival, timed apparently just on the eve of a new popular rising, must have seemed to them very suspicious. The Marian party were, in fact, already planning an insurrection. Lepidus had taken the Senate's money and left for his province; but he interrupted his journey in Etruria, and began openly calling the poorer classes in that district and other parts of Italy to his standard. Meanwhile Marcus Junius Brutus, another noble who had been compromised by the revolution, and owed his pardon by Sulla simply to family connections, was recruiting an army amongst the dregs of the population in the Po valley, almost certainly in connivance with Lepidus. At Rome there were many who were in the secret of the conspiracy and prepared to follow the two revolutionary chiefs. Cæsar's brother-in-law, Cinna, tried to persuade him to join; but Cæsar refused.

On the outbreak of the war the Senate needed two safe generals to take command against Lepidus and Brutus. One was very naturally the Consul Catulus; the other should have been a magistrate in high position. But among the conspicuous members of Sulla's party it was impossible to overlook the young Cneius Pompeius. Pompey was born in 106, of a rich and noble family. We have seen that, while still a youth, he had distinguished himself at the head of an army during the civil wars carried on by Sulla after his return to Italy; since then he had married a niece of the Dictator, and was now the most promising of the younger members of the party. His ambition prompted him at this juncture to ask the Senate for the chief command of the war, in spite of the fact that he was a private citizen occupying no official position. That such a demand should be presented by a friend and follower of Sulla, who had imposed so strict an observance of the old rules for the succession of offices, was indeed incongruous: it only serves to show once more that even the intimates of the Dictator only took his constitution seriously where it happened to coincide with their own personal interests. The Senate, with its usual timidity, did not venture to rebuff a young man with Pompey's record. Heedless of the stipulations of the constitution it was professing to defend, it entrusted him with an army for the campaign against Brutus.

Fighting began soon afterwards. Lepidus made a bold attempt to seize Rome, but was successfully held at bay by the Consul Catulus and by Appius Claudius, whom the Senate had been prevailed upon to nominate *interrex* with plenary powers. In the North Brutus was defeated by Pompey and shut up in Modena. He eventually surrendered on condition that his life should be spared, but was treacherously put to death by his conqueror, leaving behind him at Rome a young widow named Servilia, and a son, a little more than a year old, who bore his father's name. Owing to the defeat of Brutus, and possibly also to the losses which he had suffered in his attacks on Rome, Lepidus retired again towards the North. He was, however, defeated once more at Cosa in Etruria, and embarked with the rest of his army for Sardinia, where he fought several unsuccessful actions against the Governor Caius Valerius Triarius; he died not long afterwards, a victim to the hardships of campaigning, and also, it is said, to chagrin at the infidelity of his wife. The surviving members of his army were taken to Spain by an officer named Perpenna, to join forces with Sertorius.

Cæsar had been both prudent and fortunate in steering clear of these complications: but he was now longing to make his mark. He was a member of an ancient family which had for the last six generations obtained no higher office than Prætorship and had forfeited its position by forming connections with parvenus like Marius, and with members of the capitalist bourgeoisie, thus escaping financial disaster, but without successfully attaining to wealth. If Cæsar was able to play a prominent part and to live on a lavish scale, he owed it to the wisdom of his mother, Aurelia, who was an admirable specimen of the old-fashioned Roman matron. The time had come for him to make his *début*. Feeling better fitted for experiments in the field of eloquence than in that of revolutionary action, he began in 77 by prosecuting two powerful personages in Sulla's clique, Cornelius Dolabella, a friend of the Dictator and ex-Governor of Macedonia, and Caius Antonius Hybrida, another of Sulla's generals. He accused them, of course, with a purely political object, of crimes committed in Greece during the late war.

There could be no doubt that the Conservative government had grossly abused its powers. In spite of all Sulla's efforts, his reaction had only tended to increase the corruption and debasement of Roman politics. It had reduced to silence the tribunes of the people, whose unquestioned rights in the Roman democracy were analogous to those enjoyed by the Press in the Western world of to-day: it had crushed the Democratic party, and terrorized the middle class and the knights who had been the backbone of its strength. The result was that, in the absence of free speech, the pushing and unscrupulous members of the party had easily driven all their more respectable competitors into the background. The financial administration was in the hands of the Quæstors, light-headed young aristocrats with no taste for the complicated mathematics of their department, who allowed the officials of the Treasury to abuse their confidence by drawing up false balance sheets, neglecting to force payment from the State debtors, and playing havoc in a hundred ways with the public revenues. Violent, avaricious and unscrupulous politicians, including many who had won a disagreeable notoriety during Sulla's proscriptions, such as Caius Verres, Cnæus Dolabella and Publius Cethegus, had no difficulty in securing election to high office and exercised a dominant influence amongst the languid and fashionable crowd which filled the Senate house. Their hand was even heavier on the provinces than on Italy. In Narbonese Gaul, for instance, the financiers were continually bringing pressure to bear upon dishonest governors to filch the lands of the free tribes on the frontiers, and lease them out at low rates to Roman capitalists. All through the provinces governors committed acts of cruelty and spoliation which practically always went unpunished. At Rome itself there was no guarantee for justice; the senatorial tribunals reconstituted by Sulla were even more inefficient than those of the knights; no rich and powerful man had any difficulty in securing an acquittal provided he employed the necessary intrigues and disposed of the necessary wealth. There was scope enough and to spare, as Cæsar knew, for the prosecution of a provincial governor, and he might reasonably expect to find public opinion on his side.

Yet for all this Cæsar had selected a most unpropitious moment. No sooner was the scare from Lepidus dispelled than a new danger appeared from two opposite quarters of the horizon. The first sign of trouble came from Spain, where Sertorius, originally a small peasant proprietor from Norcia, who had been sent by his mother to study law, and who had turned instead to soldiering, had unfurled the drooping standard of the revolutionary cause. He had overrun almost the entire peninsula, built himself an arsenal, organized an army, and founded a school to give a Latin education to the sons of the Spanish nobility. He had, moreover, welcomed the fugitives of the party of Marius, chosen a Senate from amongst their number, and inflicted numerous defeats upon the Sullan commander, Metellus Pius. But he was not the champion of a mere local movement. At the other end of the world Mithridates, stung by the refusal of the Senate to put its signature to the Treaty of Dardanus, was exercising all his energy to prepare for a new war, laying up huge supplies of money, stores and arms, and entering into secret agreements with the pirates, who had profited by the anarchy of the Revolution to renew their exploits in all parts of the Mediterranean. Persuaded by his previous experience that a small but efficient body of troops was far more serviceable in the field than the huge and cumbrous array of the ordinary Oriental army, he was trying to organize a force on the Roman model with the help of numerous Italians who had entered his service. There was grave anxiety at Rome amongst those who remembered the stormy days of 89. Once again they seemed face to face with the three-fold danger of a Civil War in Italy, Mithridates in the Eastern provinces, and the obstinate and daring resistance of the pirates. Nor did they fail to suspect some mysterious agreement between Mithridates and Sertorius.

In such a crisis as this, accusations brought, however justly, against persons in high position were too reminiscent of the futile tribunician scandals of old to disturb the political equilibrium. Unprincipled politicians denounced them as subversive and revolutionary, and the moderates, too nervous, despite the honesty of their intentions, to back up the accusers, disguised any satisfaction they may have felt at this bold attack on the ruling faction. Thus, in spite of the daring eloquence of their assailant, the two accused were safely acquitted, and Cæsar found himself more deeply compromised than ever in the eyes of a Government which already suspected him as the nephew of Marius. All the luck fell to the young men of the opposite party. Pompey had returned from his war against Rufus more vain and self-confident than ever. Not satisfied with the laurels he had already won, he kept his troops under arms in the neighbourhood of Rome, and began intriguing to be sent to Spain to reinforce Metellus against Sertorius. Although Pompey had not yet been elected to a single magistracy, the Senate was too apprehensive of a second military revolt to refuse its sanction to the arrangement.

On Pompey's appointment Cæsar decided to renew his Eastern travels. He set out at once for Rhodes, at that time the favourite resort of rich young Romans who wanted to perfect their oratorical style. But an unpleasant adventure befell him on his way out: he was captured by a crew of pirates, who kept him prisoner on board ship for some fifty days, and only released him on the return of the trusty messengers, his slave Epicrates amongst others, whom he had sent on to Asia for a ransom. It was an annoying mishap, which could not fail to cause amusement at his expense in Roman society. But he consoled himself on the recovery of his liberty by sending home a delightful romance about his captivity, telling how he had lived for forty days with the pirates like a prince among his slaves, joining in their sports, reading them his poems, and threatening to have them all hanged if ever they restored him to liberty. The end of it was, of course, that as soon as he recovered his freedom he had actually manned a vessel, tracked his captors, and had several of them crucified. Whatever the truth underlying the tale, Cæsar settled down quietly and seriously to study at Rhodes, while round about him, unsuspected by him as by all his contemporaries, a new society was slowly being formed and perfected, as the straggling survivors of the great age of Revolution passed away to make room for a fresh generation, born about the year 100.

For indeed the pessimists had once more been refuted. The ordeals of recent years had not hurt Italy beyond healing. Once the terrors of the Revolution and the Reaction were removed, she began slowly to adapt herself to the changed conditions they had created, and to find in them new instruments for social well-being. That, after all, is a constant law of national life; and there were many influences at work which permitted Italy to obey it. Massacres like those which culminated in the Civil War and the Mithridatic campaigns would no doubt have been sufficient to overwhelm a small subject or tributary nation, poor in capital and slaves and living on the produce of its own labour, which must have failed to repair the loss of so much capacity from its fields, its workshops and its army. But this was far from being the case with Italy. Here, where thousands were struggling to make profit out of Rome's political supremacy over the Mediterranean peoples and to live upon the labour of slaves and subject nations, these wars and massacres entailed advantages of their own: they reduced the competitors and improved the conditions in the race for riches and renown. In not a few families decimated by the Revolution, the surviving members found themselves on the return of peace, notwithstanding all the losses they had sustained, more comfortably off than they had been before. Moreover, the revolutionary government had in 86 decreed the reduction of all debts by 75 per cent., thus relieving many a patrimony of its heaviest burdens and compensating a large number of individuals, at the expense of quite a few, for the injuries inflicted by the civil wars.

Italy emerged from the crisis with her finances repaired and her army reorganized. If she had only been able to save her Empire by acquiescence in a humiliating treaty, she was still strong enough after her victory to force Greece and Asia to pay a part of the costs of her revolution. Sulla alone had captured in Asia and sold to Italians vast quantities of slaves; he had confiscated throughout Greece many lands belonging to towns and temples, and leased them to Italian capitalists; and had paid into the Treasury all that remained of his Asiatic spoils, 15,000 pounds of gold and 115,000 pounds of silver, equivalent to-day to about £800,000, and worth a great deal more than this according to the ancient standard of prices. If we add to this the sums given by him to his troops in Asia and brought by them to Italy, those spent in Italy to win over the men of the Democratic army, and those which he kept for himself or gave away to his friends, we shall probably arrive at a total four or five times as great as this.

Another still more important effect of his victories must not be overlooked. They revived, on something very like its old scale, the old system of exploiting the provinces. This was especially the case in Asia, where Sulla had vainly attempted to introduce better methods by his abolition of tax farming. Though the land taxes were no longer leased out to Italian knights, the cities of Asia had still to pay Sulla a contribution of 20,000 talents and five years' arrears of taxation, a crushing exaction, which, falling upon a country already crippled by revolution and war, drove towns and private individuals to borrow largely from the only great capitalists of the time, the Italian financiers. The condition of Greece, by nature a poorer province, was still more unfortunate. Called back to the country by towns and private individuals in need of funds, the Roman capitalists, who had been hunted down with so much fury but ten years before, made their way back one by one to snatch all that remained over after the great upheaval. We find them at Delos, which had suffered so cruelly from Mithridates, at Patras and Argos, in Elis and Laconia, at Tenos, Mitylene, Assos and Lampsacus, even in the still independent State of Bithynia. Wherever they appeared they lent money to towns and private persons, secured part of the local commerce and export trade, and took the place of the native merchants ruined by the war. Amongst their number was a young man named Titus Pomponius Atticus, a knight who had inherited a big fortune from his uncle, one of the richest tax-farmers in Rome. Atticus had gone to Athens after Sulla's victory, to study at the University and so escape the dangers of the Revolution; but finding in the fallen greatness of Hellas a fruitful field for the investment of his capital, he had been able to combine business with learning and so to increase both in wealth and wisdom. Greece and Asia were indeed no longer so rich a prey as at the time of their original annexation. Yet there was still, especially in Asia, much treasure to be won by Western enterprise; there were works of art, precious metals and splendid buildings, artisans skilled in every branch of labour, and peasants who could make wealth out of the inexhaustible resources of the soil. Capitalists were able to secure mortgages on future harvests, to seize statues, pictures and goldsmiths' work, houses, estates, public buildings, and finally the native inhabitants themselves, reducing to slavery all peasants who were unable to pay their debts or accepting in lieu of payment the sons and daughters of their debtors. Many financiers now also turned their attention to Narbonese Gaul, where the taxes raised for the army which was fighting in Spain against Sertorius drove many private individuals and cities into debt. Finally, in Italy itself, if the Revolution had destroyed a large amount of wealth, it had put into circulation a great deal more which had lain idle for centuries, such as the Treasures dedicated in temples and the sacred property sold by the Senate.

All this serves to explain how, during the years when Cæsar was studying at Rhodes, almost on the morrow of a sanguinary internecine struggle, there was yet a marked increase in the general luxury and comfort. Amongst the slaves captured in Asia by Sulla during the Mithridatic War and sold to Italian merchants, and amongst those whom the financiers afterwards bought in Asia or who were kidnapped by pirates, there were skilful field labourers, gardeners, dyers, weavers, perfumers, cooks, sculptors, painters, smiths, metal workers, musicians, engineers, architects, writers, grammarians, all of them men and women of fine and active intelligence quick to pick up any new accomplishment, licit or illicit, at the bidding of their masters. Hundreds of Italian families had been prepared by the slow infiltration of Græco-Oriental influences to welcome the great inrush from the East when it came; they were receptive of new manners and ideas and ready to enjoy what they had saved or gained during the Revolution. These slaves were just the teachers they needed; under their supple tuition the masters of the world no longer dispersed the wealth of their conquests in barbaric profusion to satisfy the grosser appetites; they learnt to improve their agriculture, to refine their manners, to study and enjoy the fine arts, and to make vice itself compatible with elegance and distinction.

Thus, while Cæsar was quietly studying at Rhodes, life and fashions at Rome were being completely transformed. The new influences from the East had created a new social atmosphere. Old distinctions were being broken down, old prejudices overcome, and the most different tastes and occupations found common interests and enthusiasms in a common world. Among those admitted within the charmed circle of Society were cultivated financiers, like Titus Pomponius Atticus, who took no part in public life, millionaires like Pompey and Crassus, whose ambitions were centred upon politics, scions of old aristocratic houses who had recovered their fortunes during the Revolution, such as Lucius Domitius Ahenobarbus, and young men of rich or well-to-do municipal families, who after having received a careful education at home, had come to Rome to lead a life of fashion or acquire fame in the law-courts or in a political or military career. Amongst these were Cicero, Varro and Caius Octavius, son of a rich money-lender from Velletri: well-known advocates like Hortensius, who made large fortunes by defending provincial governors against charges of extortion; students like Valerius Cato and Cornelius Nepos; courtesans from the East whose beauty had won them universal notoriety; savants from Greece and Asia who had found a welcome in all the great houses; and Roman ladies of advanced opinions who took a serious interest in politics or dabbled in Greek and philosophy. The different members of this diverse and cosmopolitan society stimulated one another with their particular enthusiasms; the student inspired the financier and the politician with a taste for culture; the *gourmet* infected the writer and the business man with the delights of self-indulgence; the financier interested the dilettante, the soldier and the statesman in the excitements, if not perhaps in all the detailed and doubtful operations, of investment and speculation.

As all these various passions took fire from mutual contact, fashionable life gradually increased in profusion and complexity; everyone hastened to fit up a villa in the country and in the watering-places, like Baiæ, which were now coming into favour; to keep up a large staff of slaves, each of whom had his particular duties, valets, litter-carriers, and men to look after the lamps during the night, besides musicians, secretaries, librarians, copyists, and even doctors; to have all that he needed in daily life prepared in the house by his slaves, except in the case of rare and costly objects which could only be procured from distant countries; to exhibit a good assortment of Greek works of art, tables from Delphi, vases from Corinth, cups, candelabra, statues, paintings, bronzes, and even a sculptured basin for the pond in his park. Many of the rich financiers and Senators now gave up the primitive and inconvenient houses in which they had grown up, and built themselves palaces rivalling that of Lepidus in size and magnificence, full of adaptations from Græco-Asiatic designs, with reception- and drawing-rooms, a library, a palæstra, and even a bathroom with stucco ornamentation and wall paintings. The habit of corresponding by letter began to be widespread; through the desire for intercourse between friend and friend, and the impatience to find out what was happening in Rome or in the provinces, confidential slaves were frequently despatched into the most distant parts of the Empire. Invitations to dinner or to stay in the country became a usual form of entertainment, and a generous standard of hospitality came to be regarded as obligatory. Men no longer travelled with a small suite, but attended by a huge retinue of slaves. Funerals became increasingly costly, and it became fashionable to erect huge family monuments upon the main roads of Italy, to attract the attention of the passing public. With the changes in the prevailing style of jewellery and in the variety and the cost of the fashionable stuffs, dress, too, became more distinctive and costly. The wealthy class in Rome and all over Italy began to conform to that conventional code of propriety by which the rich seem always destined, in the progress of civilization, to become more and more enslaved, till finally they lost all feeling for what is serious and genuine in life. The new generation followed their example with alacrity, and preached the new conventions with a passionate vehemence which must have been highly exasperating to those of their seniors who were still attached to the simplicity of primitive manners. Amongst those who protested against this development there was, however, one prominent figure of the younger age, Marcus Porcius Cato, a man of rich and noble family and a descendant of Cato the Censor. His puritan spirit revolted against the tyranny of fashion to which the golden youth of Rome wished to make him conform; he would walk in the streets without shoes or tunic, to accustom himself, as he said, only to blush at things which were shameful in themselves, and not merely by convention.

Side by side with this new standard of luxury, the needs of the intellect began to claim closer attention. Amongst the upper classes of Italy we find widespread evidence of that burning thirst for knowledge which is characteristic of all the really great epochs of history. A young man of distinguished family like Cæsar could not complete his education without a stay of some years in Greece or in the East to attend a course of rhetoric, or the class of some well-known philosopher. Everyone learned to make speeches and to write in verse and prose, and there was a general desire for a wide and many-sided culture. Books were read upon all conceivable subjects, rhetoric, æsthetics, history, geography, agriculture, strategy, tactics, siege operations, philosophy, medicine; the encyclopædia of Aristotle, which Sulla had brought to Italy, suddenly came into an immense vogue It had been but little appreciated by the specialists of the last two centuries who had studied particular sciences like astronomy, mathematics and literary history in the restful solitudes of the big museums maintained by the Hellenistic sovereigns of the East; but it found a large and ready public of admirers now that the educated classes in Italy were conscious of the responsibilities of a world-wide Empire. There was a large class of men whose occupations can only be described as encyclopædic, who had been successively soldiers, statesmen, orators, judges, financiers, organizers of festivals or public works, admirals, landlords or ambassadors, and who needed to have at their command, not this or that special science, but a vast fund of general information which would enable them to pick up with rapidity any subject they desired. Aristotle, the philosopher of imperial expansion, the master first of Alexander and later of the Arabs, presented the Empire-builders of Italy with a vast and well-arranged handbook of information, written in a plain and unadorned style, and stored not only with facts, but with a sufficient supply of those general ideas which, however imperfect in themselves, are yet indispensable to all who venture as pioneers into unknown regions, reminding them of the general direction in which they are moving and preventing them from changing their line of march at the first serious obstacle or rebuff.

All this increase in luxury and expenditure among the upper classes was in itself an encouragement to the prevalent spirit of speculation. Sulla had indeed been able to re-establish the old Roman institutions; but the sentiment of aristocracy soon succumbed to the temptations of the new era, and even members of the old historic nobility were ready to forget their old repugnance for business undertakings. Financiers and landlords, blue-blooded aristocrats and parvenu millionaires, began to break down the old barriers of caste and rank, and to merge into a single class of enterprising traders and financiers, under conditions in which the old political antagonism between the knights and the Senate, the capitalist bourgeoisie and the ruling military aristocracy could not help becoming gradually effaced.

At the same time a profound change was coming over the whole social economy of Italy. During the preceding half-century Italian capital had by preference been sent abroad, more especially to Asia, where it had helped to exploit the recently conquered provinces; comparatively little had been invested in Italy upon agricultural purposes. Generally speaking, while the moderate landlords had in some cases endeavoured to effect improvements in cultivation, the large proprietors, who had taken over the lands of the impoverished small farmers, were too preoccupied with increasing the acreage of their holdings to spend time and trouble over modernizing their methods. They contented themselves with forming huge estates (*latifundia*) rudely cultivated by slaves, or with transforming the old yeomen into small farmers (*coloni*) who were contented to work on by the old superannuated processes. But now that the provinces, and particularly Asia, had been over-exploited by Italian financiers and ruined by a devastating war, they ceased to be so profitable a field for new investment, and capital began once more to flow back to the land.

Thus it was that the wasted Italian countryside began to blossom once more into its old prosperity. The first signs of fresh vigour had been manifest half a century ago; and another three or four generations were to pass before the whole miraculous transformation could be finally perfected. But it was during these few years, when a new life was pulsating through the cities of Italy, that the spirit of enterprise and improvement burst the close confines of their walls and gave the decisive impulse to the rural revival. It was the slave immigrants who were the chief agents in the reanimation of Italy. The great and moderate landlords continued to buy their field workers from abroad, but, with more capital at their disposal, displayed a care in their selection which would have been inexplicable to their fathers. Besides the ordinary human chattels purchased for hard manual labour and shut up at night in the fetid shelters or *Ergastula*, they took pains to acquire a certain number of highly skilled cultivators, who were less harshly treated and expected to amend the methods and increase the profits of cultivation.

It was upon the vine and the olive that their efforts were most naturally expended. The world market for wine at this time was Rhodes, while Greece, the Ægean Islands and Asia Minor were the great wine-growing countries, the Burgundy and Champagne of the ancient world, which exported the drink of the gods to regions where the grape did not grow, or where the wealthier classes had no taste for the rough wine of the country. But their supremacy was no longer to remain unchallenged. Amongst the hordes of Oriental prisoners whom Sulla sold into Italy, or whom the pirates and Italian tax-farmers and merchants kidnapped and bought in Asia and packed off westwards for home employers, there were many peasants who understood the cultivation of the vine and the olive and all the processes in the making of wine and oil. Financiers, who had grown rich on tax-farming or army contracts or provincial money-lending, landlords and aristocrats who had a little capital to dispose of, were quick to realize that they might wrest their old monopoly from Greece and Asia and meet the increasing consumption of the Italian market. They proceeded to invest largely in Oriental slaves and employ them as planters of vines and olives wherever the district was favourable, choosing situations near the sea or the roads, such as many parts of Sicily and the neighbourhood of Faenza in the plain of Romagna. Greater care, too, was expended upon the construction of farms, so that slaves could live and work there under healthier conditions.

Another new development in Italian country life was scientific cattle-breeding. The Roman nobles of the previous generation had preferred to stake their money on nomadic prairie pasturage—a form of speculation dating back to the good old days of the Common Land, when the aristocracy paid little attention to business enterprise. But now that the price of land, and with it the cost of living, was steadily rising all over Italy, they were learning perforce to perfect their methods of rearing, to choose for their chief shepherds slaves of a certain measure of intelligence and knowledge, to study the breed of their animals, their intercrossing, their feeding, and their general health. Many landlords devoted themselves to raising stock outside Italy, in thinly populated and barbarous districts: Atticus, for instance, possessed enormous lands and huge herds in Epirus. Experiments were also made in Italy in the direction of the selective breeding of the horse and the donkey. Governors and officials made use of journeys undertaken for military and administrative purposes to observe plants, animals and herds, and the particular treatment each required, asking questions of the natives, and bringing home much useful information.

A large number of Italians, too, even among the aristocracy, devoted themselves to financial speculation, endeavouring by means of couriers and agents to lend money at high rates, especially in Asia, depositing capital for interest with bankers at Rome and Ephesus, and buying the debentures or shares (*partes* or *particulæ*) of the syndicates of "publicans," who leased the public lands, the taxes and the military and civil contracts of the Empire. Others exploited workings of clay to manufacture bricks, and built houses in the capital which they let to the middle class or to the ever-growing swarms of the proletariat. Many speculations were made in Oriental slaves, who were skilful in those higher arts of production for which there was a steadily increasing demand. Others invested their money in grammarians, doctors, architects, master-masons or stucco workers, letting them out to anyone who had need of them, or setting them free on condition that they reserved for their old patrons a part of their professional earnings.

The result of these many-sided activities may be stated very shortly. Rome like a great spider was sucking blood from the provinces. The Italian upper classes were engaged in weaving a vast web of financial interests to secure the treasure that they needed for their own growing demands. The middle class in the less important cities of Italy, less powerful but quite as greedy, hastened to ape their superiors. So did the class beneath them, the small farmers, the day labourers, the artisan immigrants from the East, the freedmen from all parts of the world, and all those who had been ruined by the Civil War. At Rome the rich were gradually infecting the whole community with their passion for amusement and good feeding, increasing the magnificence of the festivals which candidates and magistrates gave to the people, and the sumptuousness of the public banquets, at which poor men learnt to appreciate the taste of good wine, as of thrushes, chickens, geese, and even peacocks. In the small towns and in the country districts of Italy, the soldiers of Sulla had become living exponents of the vices and luxury of the East, of drunkenness and debauchery and the ostentation of riches. Their example awoke slumbering instincts of adventure and commercial enterprise among the younger generation in the families of the smaller landlords and farmers. The poorer among them enlisted in the army, hoping to make a fortune in distant expeditions; others who had a little money set themselves up in business; whilst others again who had inherited a tiny farm or allotment tried to imitate their wealthier neighbours by the purchase of a slave or two, reckoning they would only have to sow the seed necessary to feed themselves and their dependents, and to plant vines, olives and fruit trees and a few flowers for the bees, in order to sell a fine store of produce and live a life of ease and comfort. The increase of general expenditure among all classes gave a stimulus to the speculations of the rich capitalists and nobles, several of whom even embarked upon retail dealing, opening a shop in their palaces (like some of the Florentine nobles a generation ago) and there selling the produce of their estates through an assistant, who was generally a slave or a freedman.

Thus the survivors of the Civil War had wooed back the old prosperity of Italy. The mercantile spirit was even more widespread and infectious than in the previous generation. There was a general rise in wages and prices, and in the value of land. Italy was passing through one of those happy periods of affluence when opportunities of profit arise one out of another and seem to multiply on all sides with progressive rapidity. Out of the depression and anarchy of the Revolution had emerged an era of plenty in which the competition of all the various elements in the community to acquire wealth, power and pleasure became even more breathless and exciting than in the preceding generation. The new Italian bourgeoisie composed of landlords and merchants, cultivated gentlemen and ambitious politicians, which had been slowly consolidating its power for the last half-century, was becoming daily better fitted by wealth, capacity and education to contend with the hereditary republican aristocracy for the power and responsibilities of Empire. Meanwhile Cæsar was living quietly at Rhodes, deep in the study of orators and philosophers.

CHAPTER IV

THE CONQUEST OF BITHYNIA

THIS great and rapid transformation of social life and conditions entailed corresponding adjustments in the sphere of politics. It was inevitable from the first that Sulla's settlement should be merely temporary and provisional. As the old generation passed away from the scene, the classes and parties which had contended so violently but a few years before, laid aside their animosities and drew together almost unconsciously in a common mood of conciliation. The Italian middle class learnt to abate the revolutionary and anti-Roman enthusiasm which had involved their country in the miseries of the Social War and driven hundreds of their countrymen to join the army of Mithridates. The healing process of time and the general increase and diffusion of prosperity slowly appeased the agitation of a class which had long been devoted to Roman interests and was imbued with Italian patriotism and Italian good sense. As they planted their vines and olives, built farms and cottages, bought slaves out of their savings, or enlisted in the legions, the small landlords and labourers, the merchants and contractors all over Italy became the supporters, sometimes even the devoted partisans, of order and the established authority. They forgot the great services which the Revolution had rendered to their cause; they branded as traitors the many enthusiasts of the preceding generation whom distress and persecution had driven to the banners of Mithridates; they abandoned Sertorius, the last surviving champion of the Marian party and the revolutionary movement. A few trifling successes over Sertorius were enough to win Pompey a lasting popularity in all parts of the peninsula.

Meanwhile the rich classes and even the aristocracy itself were gradually losing much of their reactionary fervour. The Social War, the reduction of debts, even Sulla's proscriptions were becoming dim and distant memories. Men began to be convinced that the talk of a coming revolution was mere idle chatter. They saw that the emancipation of Italy, a reform which was for some fifty years the bugbear of the Conservatives, had been carried through without any of the calamities predicted. Although the number of electors had been increased and was now almost 900,000, the small oligarchy of resident voters at Rome, whose opposition to an extended franchise had precipitated the whole crisis, found that it still remained, as before, the controlling force in the government of the Empire. As the elections could only be held at Rome, voters who lived in other parts of Italy were unable to undertake the long journey to the capital several times during the year; until some reform was passed to abolish the present centralized system, they were practically debarred from using their privileges. But all agitation in this direction had been severely kept under during Sulla's reign of terror, and other interests very soon intervened to make the majority of the new voters quite indifferent to the exercise of the rights for which they had fought. A generation ago, the extension of the franchise had seemed a panacea for every evil, and all parties in turn had found in it a battle-cry for rousing the public to political enthusiasm. But now that opportunities of money-making had become so much more frequent, the middle class preferred to emigrate to the provinces, or, if they stayed in Italy, to stick to their own proper business of growing rich. It seemed foolish to waste time over political conflicts in which the ordinary voter found it difficult to remain constant to any definite aim, when it was within the reach of any member of the community, by attending to his private affairs, to rise high on the social ladder. Of all the privileges that Roman citizenship brought with it, the right to vote at elections was that by which most men set least store. They were content to leave the political offices in the gift or the sale of the small oligarchy of residents; in other words, in the control of the Roman upper classes.

For in the capital the middle class, so predominant in the Italian country towns, was practically non-existent. The vast majority of the Roman electorate was composed of an indigent class, either free or freedmen, which made a precarious livelihood as a parasite upon the upper ranks of society, its members finding employment in the State services or contracts, or working as masons, weavers, waggoners, stone-cutters or gardeners, or living as clients or dependents of the wealthy houses. It was thus perfectly simple for the moneyed classes, provided only they remained united and homogeneous, to keep a firm hold over the needy proletariat of electors, and to secure the success of their own favoured candidates. A man of rich or noble family, who had connections with the aristocracy or with the world of finance, could thus almost make sure of being elected to office: the only opposition he need fear would be from rivals in his own class. So the extension of the franchise had only strengthened its old opponents. The old Roman oligarchy of Senators and knights, bound together by ties of friendship and very often of marriage, was left, in the growing indifference of the Italian middle class, practically undisputed master of the great executive offices, and of the government of Italy and the Empire.

The rulers soon discovered the new basis of their power, which Sulla had been unable to descry. Its detection led to a very curious result. It made the whole elaborate buttress work of Sulla's constitutional structure seem artificial and even precarious as a safeguard of aristocracy. The younger members of the caste were quick to draw the inference. They argued that his settlement was neither secure nor efficient, and utterly unsuited to the needs of the age. Some of the older men, of course, saw matters very differently. In many of the great houses Sulla's reaction had provoked an outburst of exaggerated Conservative feeling; there was a section of the nobility which again tried to keep to itself, to avoid, so far as possible, all contact with their inferiors, and to behave and speak as if all the Italians were still in the position of humble dependents. But circumstances were too strong for these childish eccentricities. As the proscriptions were slowly forgotten, clear-sighted observers were forced to admit that the wealth of the knights was indispensable to the supremacy of the aristocracy. But the knights, whose powers had been curtailed and dignity wounded by Sulla and his partisans, could not be expected to remain loyal to the existing *régime*. Yet they could sway the electorate, and some concession to their demands could not long be delayed. It was the same, in a lesser degree, as regards the Italian middle class. It might make small use of the franchise; but it had earned in the Social War its good right to consideration. It was impossible to behave as though the Revolution had never been. The public opinion of Italy was a force to be reckoned with; it represented the homes from which the government drew almost all its common soldiers, its centurions and its subalterns.

The effect of these tendencies became increasingly apparent during the time when Cæsar was studying at Rhodes. The ruling cabal was becoming detested throughout the whole length of Italy. Even among its own nominal supporters disaffection was widespread. The abominable behaviour of the provincial governors, the corruption of the senatorial tribunals, the odious intrigues for *legationes liberæ*[1] excited general disgust. Moreover there had been a wearisome succession of blunders and panics, intrigues and scandals, to exasperate an already restless public. The most vital interests were shamefully neglected; Mithridates was allowed time quietly to mature his revenge; the pirates continued to capture Roman citizens on the high seas. In Spain Sertorius advanced from triumph to triumph. The Senators who had not been able to prevent Pompey from taking command, indignant at the promotion of so young a rival, did their best to make his enterprise a failure by refusing to vote the necessary funds, and Pompey had himself to advance the sums necessary for his soldiers and equipment. It was now some years since Rome had displayed any signs of real energy on her frontiers. There had been a petty expedition under Appius Claudius, Proconsul of Macedonia, into Thrace, and another small campaign against the Dardani under Caius Scribonius Curio, who had advanced as far north as the Danube. There had also been a small war in Dalmatia which had ended in the capture of Salona. But this exhausted the record of senatorial achievements. Amid the inertia of his successors the exploits of Sulla were forgotten and even the nobility harked back to the memories of his rival. Marius no doubt had tampered with revolution, but at least he had given Rome a new Army and led a loyal democracy to victory over the invader. Men more and more looked back with longing on the free speech of former days; they forgave the blunders of the old popular champions, and remembered only how they had caused evildoers in office to tremble at their invective. Year after year some violent tribune, Lucius Licinius in 76, Quintus Opimius in 75, each bolder than the last, incited the people against the Sullan Constitution and the aristocratic tribunals. At last, in 75, the Consul, Caius Aurelius

[1] The name given to a privilege sometimes granted by the Senate to one of its members allowing him to travel *gratis,* even upon private affairs, and obtain free lodgings and means of transport in the provinces for himself and his suite.

Cotta, uncle of Cæsar, won the first success in the new struggle by abolishing Sulla's provision that a Tribune of the people should be ineligible for any other office.

The results of this movement were to be most strikingly exhibited in the field of foreign policy; the decisive change took place during the years when Cæsar was still at Rhodes. Towards the end of the year 75 or the beginning of the next, King Nicomedes of Bithynia died bequeathing his kingdom and all that was in it to the Roman State. This was the second bequest within quite a short time which had fallen to the Senate; but Bithynia was less easily dealt with than Egypt, for its acceptance was certain to involve war with Mithridates. The King of Pontus could not permit a Roman occupation of Bithynia without endangering his prestige among the Eastern nations. After the timidity and indifference it had recently displayed regarding Egypt, the Senate was at a loss how to act. Its first inclination apparently was to refuse the legacy; but public opinion soon interfered to forbid it. Already in the reign of the late king, Roman financiers had begun to find their way into Bithynia and knew something of its resources. Nicomedes had owned a vast domain of Crown lands with mines and fisheries of very considerable value which annexation would put at the disposal of Italian capitalists, while considerable profits might also be expected from the taxes of the rich Greek cities on the coast. With this tempting bait within reach Rome's destiny of conquest seemed too manifest to be evaded. An agitation of the familiar sort was set on foot. War with Mithridates was in any case only a question of years and no good Roman could be in two minds about avenging Dardanus. The Senate was finally compelled to annex Bithynia and to declare the son of Nicomedes illegitimate. A syndicate was immediately formed at Rome to administer the possessions of the Bithynian Crown, and disputes arose over the command of a war which seemed likely to be rich in profit and glory.

One of the Consuls for the year happened to be Lucius Lucinius Lucullus, member of a family which could lay claim both to fame and notoriety. His father was suspected of foul play during the Sicilian slave revolt of 102 and his mother, the sister of Metellus Numidicus, had been accused of infidelity. His grandfather had been mixed up during his Consulship in a robbery of statues, while his great-grandfather had been indicted when Ædile for concocting a false accusation. The record is so sinister that its veracity may be questioned. It is certain, at any rate, that the family, despite its nobility, was poor, and that Lucius, like his younger brother Marcus, though he received a very careful literary education, grew up in modest surroundings and with simple habits, imbued from boyhood with all the pride of his caste and with the principles of the old Roman nobility. During his youth he had taken some part in the terrible class conflicts which preceded the Revolution; though in matters of the intellect a passionate Hellenist, he took his stand in politics, with all the better elements of the poorer nobility, on the side of Rutilius Rufus and the party opposed to all the new social forces, whether democratic or capitalist. He had married a wife who brought him no dowry, though a member of a very aristocratic family: Clodia, daughter of Appius Claudius, Consul in 79, Prætor after the Civil War in 77, who in 76 had obtained the government of Africa, coming home with a reputation for upright administration. Able, resolute and energetic, he had been, as we have seen, one of the few members of the aristocracy who took part in the Civil War. He had distinguished himself as one of Sulla's lieutenants in his Eastern campaigns, fought recklessly against the revolutionaries, and yet, despite his poverty, took no part in the wholesale plundering of the vanquished. Lucullus, in short, was one of the few who represented with sincerity and conviction the one respectable element in Sulla's government, the primitive and genuine aristocratic tradition which had been brought back to power with such disappointing results. He had offered a vigorous opposition to all attempts made to overturn the Constitution of Sulla, yet at the same time without showing the least consideration or indulgence towards the baser elements of the ruling *régime*, the vicious and needy aristocracy and their parasites. He had had several violent altercations with Lucius Quintius, tribune of the people in 75, and with the notorious Publius Cethegus, one of the most prominent agents of the existing cabal, who had originally deserted from the party of Marius to enrich himself over the proscriptions, and was now like many another influential scoundrel under similar *régimes*, universally detested in secret, but treated by the aristocracy on all public occasions with a respect not unmingled with awe. By this old-fashioned and uncompromising attitude Lucullus had not unnaturally attracted to himself the impartial hostility of all parties in the community.

When the question of a war with Mithridates came up for discussion Lucullus considered that there was no one more entitled than himself to the command. He had already once conducted operations against Mithridates under Sulla, and was completely conversant with Eastern affairs. Unfortunately the consular provinces had already been distributed and the lot had designed him for Cisalpine Gaul. Moreover, there were numerous candidates for the command. Besides his own colleague Cotta, there was Marcus Antonius, son of the great orator, who had been Prætor in the preceding year; and possibly also Pompey, who was still in Spain but, indignant at the dilatory support of the Senate, was threatening to return to the capital with his legions. At this opportune moment news arrived of the death of Lucius Octavius, Governor of Cilicia. Lucullus at once conceived the idea of exchanging Gaul for Cilicia; for the Governor of Cilicia would certainly be entrusted with the duty of invading Pontus through Cappadocia, and nobody at Rome doubted that it would be easy to carry the war triumphantly into the enemy's country. But the re-distribution of the provinces was by no means easy to manage. Lucullus had far more enemies than friends in influential circles, and excitement was running high at Rome over the command. There was a general feeling that this campaign would mark the end of the old timid and negative policy, and there was a host of competitors ambitious for its laurels.

Lucullus realized that the moment was decisive for his future, perhaps also for that of his party, and resolved for once to let ambition take precedence over prejudice. To the amazement of fashionable circles he began to intrigue in his own interest with a keenness and subtlety for which no one would have given him credit. Throughout Italian society the women had been far more Conservative than the men in maintaining the customs and feelings of older generations. In many of the noble houses there were still Roman matrons, like the mother of Cæsar, who lived in a primitive and old-world simplicity, even preferring to keep up the old-fashioned pronunciation of Latin, which had long ago become clipped and vulgarized by the cosmopolitan chatter of the tavern and the market-place. But the all-pervading influences in Italian society were beginning to leave their mark even upon the women. The perversions which are introduced into the feminine world by a rich and mercantile civilization and the culture and pleasures which accompany it were no longer a novelty in Roman houses. They brought with them all the familiar corruptions—the shameless venality of fashionable ladies who rely for their expenditure upon the attentions of their admirers; the ascendancy of skilful and depraved intriguers over victims enervated by self-indulgence and sensitive to all the arts and witchery of seduction; the open rivalry between young competitors for dowries; the tyranny of rich wives over impecunious husbands; the tendency of women to live the same life as men, to study and to speculate, to ride and to play, and even to dabble with delight in the muddy waters of politics. Amongst the prominent representatives of the "new women" at Rome at this time was a certain Precia, a clever specimen of her class, who, thanks to a number of illustrious lovers and above all to the notorious Cethegus, was in a position to dispose of extensive influence. This was the woman whom Lucullus selected to be his instrument. He condescended to compete with Antonius and probably a good many others for her kindness, seconding his appeals with the substantial compliments of the day. He even made his peace with his old enemy Quintius and bought his favour at a considerable price. Precia deigned to be moved by these assiduous attentions from the proudest of Roman aristocrats, and undertook to promote a reconciliation between Cethegus and Lucullus. The rest was easy.

Fortune came to the assistance of the fair intriguer and her admirers. Mithridates had already for some time been preparing for a new attack upon Rome. He had accumulated huge supplies of money, and won the support of the barbarians of Thrace and the Greek cities to the north-west of the Black Sea, including Apollonia, Odessus and Tomi. Moreover, through the intervention of Lucius Fannius and Lucius Magius, two ex-officers of Fimbria, who had taken refuge at his Court after the murder of their general, he had actually concluded an alliance with Sertorius; the stipulations were that Asia was to remain Roman, while Bithynia, Paphlagonia and Cappadocia were to go to Mithridates, who was to furnish Sertorius with 4,000 talents and forty ships, in return for the services of a Roman general, Marcus

Marius. But the death and testament of Nicomedes forced the King's hand, and drove him to premature and precipitate action. In the spring of 74, while the metropolis was still quietly discussing who should take command in the far-away Eastern campaign, Mithridates surprised his enemies by taking the field.

He despatched part of his forces under Taxiles and Hermocrates to invade Bithynia, where they drove a swarm of Italian concession hunters and traders before them to take refuge in Chalcedon. At the head of the rest of his army he marched into the Roman province of Asia, no longer, as on the preceding occasion, as an Oriental conqueror, but as the ally of the Roman Sertorius. Every town on occupation was solemnly liberated by Marcus Marius, acting as Proconsul, in the name of Sertorius, and exempted from the payment of part of its taxes. Finally, in the hope of exciting a general revolt, he sent out small flying columns of cavalry under the orders of Eumachus, Fannius and Metrophanes, in different directions across great Phrygia into Cilicia and to the recently subjugated Isaurians of Mount Taurus. The significance of this strategy is unmistakable. Mithridates was returning to his old policy of raising up against Rome a great revolution. If his success was not so striking as on the former occasion it was still at first very considerable. In Asia several towns on the Sea of Marmora, including Parium, Lampsacus and Priapus, surrendered to Marcus Marius. In Bithynia all the towns declared for Mithridates, with the single exception of Chalcedon. The fear of a new revolution spread far and wide through Asia. It was an ominous situation. The only troops in the province were the two old legions of Fimbria under the orders of a simple Proprætor, while the two legions in Cilicia had been left without a leader by the death of their Proconsul. The towns which remained loyal hastily improvised defences, and Cæsar, his military ambitions rekindled by the outbreak of hostilities, interrupted his studies in oratory, hurried from Rhodes to the continent, and formed a small militia to check the rebellion in the towns of Caria. His behaviour was less important for what it achieved than for what it signified. It showed that he had definitely broken with Sertorius and the survivors of his uncle's party, and regarded himself as a true Constitutionalist—an adversary of the revolutionary and anti-Roman programme, and a partisan of the new policy the primary object of which was to increase the prestige of Rome.

This unexpected invasion caused all the more alarm because of the painful memories it reawakened in Italy. The government at once threw off all hesitation and prepared to act with promptitude and vigour. Everyone believed the danger to be as great now as it had been in 88; and it was at once felt that it was impossible to leave Asia at such a moment to a Proprætor with two legions, or to allow Cilicia to be without a Governor till the following year. Lucullus, who had won his spurs in the previous war, was universally considered the man for the post. Thus Precia was able to carry through her contemplated arrangements to the satisfaction of all parties. Pompey was given funds to continue his operations against Sertorius; Antonius was made admiral of the fleet with a command over the whole coast-line and the special duty of tracking the pirates to their Cretan stronghold; Cotta was ordered to defend Bithynia and the Sea of Marmora; whilst Lucullus was made Proconsul of Cilicia, and entrusted with the task of driving Mithridates out of Asia, with the two legions of Asia and a legion of conscripts recruited in Italy. This was a great success in the sphere of drawing-room diplomacy; but incidentally it involved a serious military blunder, dividing the operations of the campaign between three generals, without giving any one of them the supreme command.

The danger was pressing and the two Consuls hastened their departure; it was probably about the end of spring, or the beginning of summer, when they left Rome. Lucullus sailed to Asia with his legions of conscripts; Cotta first collected a fleet from among the allies and then proceeded to Chalcedon, which was still in the hands of the Romans, intending to use it as his base of operations for the reconquest of Bithynia. Lucullus found the situation in the province less critical than had been thought in Italy. In spite of the suddenness of its outbreak, the revolution had not spread so quickly as on the previous occasion. The wealthy classes were not entirely unprepared for it, while among the common people the revolution of 88, with its miserable *dénouement*, was still a lively warning against disorder. None of the great cities had joined the revolt, and the large sea-port towns, notably Cyzicus, were prepared to fight to the death against the patron of the social revolution and the ally of the pirates. Moreover, Mithridates had been detained in the interior by the slow progress of the rebellion, and he did not now venture to advance very far into the province. It was therefore easy for Lucullus to bring up the two legions from Cilicia, to re-establish discipline in the old army of Fimbria, and to do something to alleviate the economic depression in the towns of Asia, while he continued to make arrangements for his impending campaign.

He was engaged in these measures of preparation when a serious disaster occurred in the North. It seems that Mithridates, having ascertained the destination of Cotta's fleet, hastily left the army of Asia, joined that of Bithynia, and led it to the attack of Chalcedon. Chalcedon was situated on the Bosphorus, opposite Byzantium, and the Roman fleet had been stationed in its harbour to intercept the Pontic ships carrying corn for the troops from the Black Sea into the Sea of Marmora. It is easy to imagine the panic in Chalcedon when Mithridates took up his station outside the town. The rich financiers who had fled there for refuge and were impatient to return to their business, fell upon the unfortunate Cotta with entreaties to march out boldly against Mithridates and strike a signal blow for the liberation of Bithynia. Cotta reluctantly yielded to civilian advice. After a battle which ended in a grave land defeat and in the loss of his entire fleet, he was forced to shut himself up within the walls of the city.

So signal a reverse at the very commencement of the campaign had at least the merit of establishing unity in the chief command. Lucullus, who had by now advanced with 30,000 men and 2,500 cavalry as far as the Sangarius, assumed the chief command of the entire operations on the Asiatic Continent. Turning a deaf ear to those who counselled the immediate invasion of Pontus, he continued his march against the Pontic army operating in Asia, to which Mithridates had no doubt returned after his victory at Chalcedon. But he realized the decisive importance with which the impending battle was now invested, and acted with the prudence of a consummate general. When his army approached Mithridates he sought first of all to obtain exact information as to the forces of the enemy. Finding them in a considerable superiority he decided not to stake all upon a single fight. He therefore bought up all the available supplies, loaded them up on his baggage animals, and began to follow obstinately on the heels of Mithridates without ever accepting battle, retiring every evening into his camp, and using his cavalry to hamper the enemy in replenishing his supplies.

Mithridates had only been partially successful in organizing an army on the Roman model. In spite of the efforts of the numerous Italians whom he had taken into his service, he had been compelled once more to take the field with a large and unwieldy force, which it was difficult adequately to provision. His perplexities were increased at every step of his advance into Asia, as he drew further away from the Pontic harbours on the Black Sea to which his ships conveyed corn from the Crimea. The port of Lampsacus probably gave him but slight assistance, and the convoys which came by land moved so slowly and arrived so irregularly that the army often remained without bread for three or four days at a time. Lucullus was soon enabled so to harass the enemy by attacks upon his already precarious communications, that Mithridates was faced with the necessity of retreating towards his base of supplies in the Pontic coast towns on the Black Sea. But to abandon the Roman province and all hope of a general rising, and to confine himself to defensive action in his own country, would be a disastrous confession of failure. Unwilling to acquiesce without a struggle, the proud monarch threw himself once more upon fortune, and attempted a manœuvre of characteristic daring. His plan involved nothing less than the seizure of Cyzicus, the most important harbour on the Sea of Marmora, the revival of the revolutionary movement in Asia, and the vigorous resumption of military operations in that province against Lucullus, with Cyzicus as a base for the landing of supplies from Pontus. One evening he suddenly broke up his camp, moved off in silence, undetected by the army of Lucullus, and arrived at dawn, after a forced march, within sight of Cyzicus.

He at once attempted a surprise attack. On its repulse he laid siege to the town by land and by sea. Lucullus had, of course, followed close on his heels, and Mithridates might have seized his long-sought opportunity of giving battle to the Romans. But he did not dare to use against them the troops he needed to press the blockade, and was thus compelled to let himself be surrounded in his turn within a vast line of siege works and trenches without ever engaging in a regular engagement. He still hoped that he would ultimately be able to capture the city, and reckoned that he could keep open his communications by sea even if the Romans were to close them by land. A long and obstinate double siege ensued, during which the fortunes of war depended on the resistance of the Cyzicenes. If the town had capitulated, Mithridates would have commanded an excellent base of operations and could easily have driven Lucullus out of Asia. If on the other hand it held out, Mithridates might eventually find himself in terrible straits, enclosed between the besieged and Lucullus. Lucullus succeeded in reviving the courage of the Cyzicenes by giving them news of his presence. The siege dragged slowly on through the year. Mithridates remained obstinately on the defensive and allowed himself to be surprised by the coming of winter. Month by month his situation grew more difficult. Storms interfered with his supplies, and bread and forage began to run low. The unburied corpses of men and animals poisoned the air, and a horrible epidemic broke out in the trenches. At last Mithridates decided to attempt a retreat by misleading the enemy. Directing the cavalry and baggage animals to move eastwards towards Bithynia, he himself took the coast road, and led his army westwards towards Lampsacus, where he hoped to form a junction with the fleet. It was a well-devised stratagem. Lucullus was enticed to march his army across the snow-covered plains in pursuit of the Pontic cavalry, which retired slowly before him. He caught up the baggage train at the passage of the Rindacus and cut it in pieces with enormous slaughter. Then suddenly discovering that the greater part of the army must have fled in another direction, he turned as rapidly back. Fortune came to his aid. Heavy rains had brought the army of Mithridates to a halt at the banks of the Edepus. Here it was overtaken and cut to pieces by Lucullus. Only a few stragglers succeeded in following their king to Lampsacus, where they were hastily embarked for home. Thus Bithynia was reduced and Chalcedon relieved in the early months of 73: and the first round of the struggle ended in a brilliant victory for the small but active and well-disciplined army of Rome over the numerous and unwieldy forces which Mithridates had in vain attempted to train on the Roman model.

CHAPTER V

THE INVASION OF PONTUS AND THE
PRÆTORSHIP OF CRASSUS

MEANWHILE, in the course of the year 73, Cæsar had returned to Rome. We do not know the upshot of his small expedition against Mithridates, but it is likely enough that when his fears of a general revolution proved groundless, he disbanded his small force soon after the arrival of Lucullus in Asia. He returned to Rome shortly afterwards on the news that he had been elected Pontifex in the place of his uncle Caius Aurelius Cotta, who had lately died in Gaul.

Cæsar must have found the situation at home very different from what it had been on his return from his earlier journey. Much had happened in Italy during his absence; but the alteration he probably noticed most of all was in the character of his fellow-countrymen. Here the change had indeed been both rapid and far-reaching. The action and interaction of a number of causes—the increase of prosperity, the diffusion of culture, the rise in the standard of comfort and luxury, the intermingling of the races in different parts of the peninsula—in a word, the general progress of what we call civilization had now finally completed a transformation in the Italian character which had been preparing for at least a century. In the old days, Italy had been a nation of peasants with few needs and as few ideas: the typical Italian qualities had been patience, doggedness, and a certain impenetrable toughness of fibre. But of late years the Italian had become nervous, excitable and unbalanced. He seemed continually to be oscillating between the opposite poles of character—between an egoism brutalized by sensuality and a moral sensibility sharpened by education and refinement, between wild and spasmodic outbursts of pride and cruelty, and the lingering influences of patriotism, piety and justice, to which he was acutely and morbidly responsive whenever personal pleasures and ambitions remained unaffected. It was a condition with which the modern world is painfully familiar.

The change, which was felt throughout the peninsula, was of course more particularly noticeable in the metropolis, where it stirred up new bitterness against senatorial inefficiency. The people of Rome had one especial reason for discontent in the increasing frequency of famines; that of the year 75 had been particularly severe. The problem of supplying the metropolis became more difficult every year. The complaints brought against the negligence of the government were so loud and numerous that the two Consuls of that year, Caius Cassius Longinus and Marcus Terentius Licinianus Varro, the younger brother of Lucullus and adopted son of Marcus Terentius Varro, though Conservatives in politics, proposed a law to increase the tribute of corn supplied by the Sicilians.

But far more serious anxieties were in store for the government A band of slaves, runaways from a school of gladiators at Capua, had developed, under the leadership of a Thracian called Spartacus, into a small but formidable army, which had attacked and defeated several legions hastily despatched to disperse it. As an exceedingly large number of slaves had recently been imported into the country, all the bolder and more violent spirits began to escape from their masters and join the standard of Spartacus. For a moment Italy seemed face to face with the prospect of a huge slave rising.

There were other losses too to set off against the triumphs of Lucullus. Marcus Antonius had utterly failed in his projected enterprise against Crete, and had finally, after some desultory ravaging in Sicily, suffered a complete defeat at the hands of the pirates. Great, therefore, was the consternation when a short time afterwards news reached Rome that Mithridates, defeated by land, was vigorously reopening operations by sea with the help of his old friends and allies among the States and tribes of Thrace. While Lucullus' two subordinates, Caius Valerius Triarius and Barba, were marching against the towns in Bithynia which were still holding out against Rome, Mithridates had devastated the coasts of the Sea of Marmora, besieged Perinthus, threatened Byzantium and sent a part of his fleet into the Ægean under the orders of Marius, to join hands with the pirates of Crete and Spain.

This was very serious news. The Ægean fleet might very well be directed against Italy, and the coastline, it was recollected, was entirely undefended. Furious reproaches were brought against the Senate and the magistrates for their criminal neglect of the public interest. The Senate took hurried steps to meet the situation. It decided that the Consul Marcus Lucullus should be sent to Thrace next year as Proconsul with a large army to crush the allies of Mithridates in those districts. It allowed his brother Lucius 3,000 talents for the construction of a fleet—as if a fleet could be turned out in a night and a day—prolonging his command by a year, and perhaps also entrusting him with the government of Bithynia with Cotta for his subordinate. Circumstances had now, in fact, compelled it to do what its own common sense should have suggested at the beginning of the operations—to put the military and naval commands into one hand.

All these events intensified the discontent against the existing *régime*, which had now become widespread among all classes of the community. Their reaction was soon felt in the world of politics. They helped to complete the reconstitution of the old Democratic party, which now re-emerged into prominence upon a new basis and in a changed form. It was no longer a motley assemblage of bankrupts and desperadoes agitating for a social revolution, but a sober and orderly body composed of men from the upper and middle classes, claiming before all to be efficient in its methods and constitutional in its aims. What it demanded was simply a more upright and energetic administration : to be saved from the barefaced exactions of extortionate officials and the perilous intimidation of revolting slaves. Many of the best houses soon became something very like Opposition clubs, where young men made passionate speeches in favour of restoring the democratic Constitution and revived the old battle-cries of Gracchan reform. One of their favourite meeting-places was the house of Servilia, the young, witty and intellectual widow of the Marcus Brutus who had been killed by Pompey in the revolution of 78. She had contracted a second marriage with Decimus Junius Silanus, an aristocrat of advanced ideas, who kept open house for all the ardent spirits in the upper ranks of society, conspicuous amongst whom was, of course, Cæsar. Cæsar was indeed beginning to find his way into houses which had been very unwilling to welcome him on his first return from the East. About this time he was elected by the people a *tribunus militum*, an appointment carrying with it the command of a thousand men in time of war. It was now all in his favour to be the nephew of Marius.

He began to look round for the chance of some stroke of popularity which would launch him successfully upon a political career.

This was no easy task even for a nephew of Marius. The Roman electorate numbered at this time some 910,000 voters. Only a part of this total, however, was resident at Rome, and the remainder, who were scattered up and down the country, could not be relied upon to come up for the annual elections. This alone introduced a great element of uncertainty into the voting, which was intensified by the nature of the resident electorate itself. The larger part of it consisted of small shopkeepers and workmen, clients and dependents of men in high station, petty officials occupying posts in the administration reserved for free citizens, and the familiar derelict assemblage of unemployed and unemployable loafers and beggars. Few of these would scruple to sell their vote for a consideration. Skilful wire-pullers had thus gradually been enabled to elevate dealing in votes to the level of a regular trade. They formed the dregs of the electorate into organized clubs or "colleges," and made sure of their men by a careful system of free dinners and petty largess. They then sold their votes by contract to the several candidates, with complicated precautions to ensure the faithful execution of promises. The remainder of the electorate, on the other hand, consisting of the well-to-do bourgeoisie in Rome and Italy, the contractors and tax-farmers, merchants and landowners, wealthy freedmen and men of leisure and culture, voted, when they voted at all, for some candidate they happened to like or to respect, on the inspiration of some momentary enthusiasm or animosity, or of some item of intelligence, whether true or false, which chanced to be circulated at the time of the elections. The treacherous breeze of popular favour might thus veer round from one hour to the next. The merest trifle, a well-placed rumour or a fortunate phrase, would sometimes alter all the probabilities of the situation between night and morning, leading perhaps, by some sudden freak of popular feeling, to a result which was equally surprising to all parties concerned.

To acquire influence over so fluid and heterogeneous a body of electors, unassisted by the ruling caste, was no easy matter. Cæsar began by serving a sedulous apprenticeship in that forced labour of adulation to which all Roman politicians of that day were condemned.

He rose from his bed at dawn to receive every busybody or nonentity in Rome or from the country who cared to come either simply to pay his respects to a man of influence and reputation, or with the more practical object of demanding his assistance in a law-suit or asking for pecuniary help, or for the farming of some tax, or for exemption from military service, or for a letter of introduction to the Governor of some distant province. He then went down still early into the Forum to plead causes, or to have a word with a magistrate or Senator or banker in the interests of some unfortunate client. The rest of his day was spent in the same laborious tedium. He allowed himself to be stopped in the street by any worthy citizen who chose to claim his acquaintance, racked his over-laden memory to recollect who he might be, or employed the indispensable services of the slave or *nomenclator*, whose special business it was to remember the names of the greatest possible number of electors and to prompt his master so skilfully as to give the elector the illusion of being known by sight. He kept a pleasantry or a compliment or a promise ready on his lips for all-comers, invited necessary acquaintances to dinner every evening, put in an appearance at the marriages, funerals, and family festivals of all classes of citizens, worked in support of some particular candidate in every election that took place, and gave hospitality in his house or provided regular assistance for a certain number of dependents from amongst the poorer classes in Rome, who served as his spies amongst the people, as his agents during elections, as a claque during his speeches in the Forum, or as his cut-throats in any personal quarrel.

But Cæsar's hour was as yet far distant. For the moment other men loomed large in the public eye. Pompey in Spain was slowly, but steadily, gaining ground upon Sertorius. Lucullus, elated by his success at Cyzicus, had hastily collected a fleet from the allies and pursued the Pontic squadron into the Ægean, where he attacked and destroyed its several detachments in detail and put relentlessly to death all the Italian deserters whom he captured, including their commander, Marcus Marius. His subordinates were engaged meanwhile in besieging the refractory cities of Bithynia and amassing great wealth in slaves and loot. Thus by about the middle of the year 73 Lucullus had succeeded in reducing the whole of Bithynia with the exception of Heraclea, and had forced Mithridates to return by sea into his own kingdom with the remains of the army with which he had invaded Bithynia in the previous year. It was at this moment of the campaign, some time during the summer, that Lucullus summoned a council of war at Nicomedia.

Almost all his generals were in favour of allowing the troops to rest till the following spring; but the Commander-in-Chief did not endorse the advice of his subordinates. Whilst they regarded the situation from a strictly military standpoint Lucullus was passing through a decisive crisis in his career—a crisis that was to be of far-reaching significance, not only for his own personal character, but for the whole moral and political development of the age, of which he may be regarded as a typical representative. It was, indeed, more than a mere matter of strategy which he had summoned his generals to decide. At once impatient and far-sighted, he had made up his mind for a course which would at last resolve the contradictions from which Roman policy had so long been suffering.

Lucullus, who had now nearly turned fifty, had up to this moment been an almost perfect specimen of that old Roman aristocracy which might, by the exercise of its traditional qualities, have made the Constitution of Sulla a genuine and durable settlement. Austere and primitive in his habits, he was a sworn foe to all ostentation and luxury and, with the sole exception of Greek culture, to every kind of influence from abroad; he gloried in his own poverty and had a true noble's disdain for popularity and all vulgar and petty ambitions. Unfortunately an aristocrat of this nature was a sort of archæological rarity at Rome, one of the last representatives of a race of men that had long since vanished from the world. While he continued thus to profess the old inherited Roman virtues, Lucullus had watched the temptations of the new age growing up all round him. He had seen friends of his own, who had enriched themselves in the proscriptions, honoured with more consideration than a poor man like himself. He had watched Pompey, who had risked so little in the Civil War, rise fast and high by the mere power of popularity. A man of his activity, intelligence and ambition must long since have asked himself whether, if he went on playing this obscure and old-fashioned part, he would not end by sacrificing his influence to men who shared his ambitions without partaking of his scruples. He had reluctantly acknowledged that the timid and hesitating policy of his party was justly exciting the reproaches of Italy, and that the government of Sulla was certain to be overturned if it did not show itself capable of any service to Rome. The intrigues to which he had descended in order to obtain his command had been the first visible sign of a change in his character. His success as a general precipitated the crisis. His victories at Cyzicus and in the Ægean had completed his conversion to the political methods of Pompey, whose fortune had been made by his cool disregard of the requirements of the constitution. He decided not to await the orders of the Senate, but to set out immediately and on his own initiative upon the invasion of Pontus.

He knew the home government too well to doubt that, if he had stayed to wait for instructions, he would eventually, after a wearisome delay, have received orders to remain inactive or to return to Italy. If, on the other hand, he set forth on a distant expedition, during the course of which it would have been highly imprudent to recall him, he would easily secure a prolongation of his powers. The avenging of the Treaty of Dardanus and the chastisement of Mithridates were surely well worth this concession to the perverted political morality of the age. At the council of war at Nicomedia he therefore declared his determination, in face of the opposition of almost all his generals, to attempt the immediate invasion of the kingdom of Mithridates. While Cotta undertook the siege of Heraclea, and Triarius remained with seventy ships in the Hellespont to intercept the Pontic vessels on their way from Spain and Crete, the Commander-in-Chief was to march with all his army upon the two ports of Amisus and Themiscyra, to secure a base of supplies for a long campaign in the mountainous districts of Pontus. Mithridates had meanwhile retired into the recesses of his kingdom, into the triangle formed by Cabira, Amasia and Eupatoria, to prepare for a fresh campaign and await the arrival of the reinforcements he had requested from his son-in-law Tigranes, King of Armenia, his son Macares, Viceroy of the Crimea, and from the Scythians.

Lucullus wasted little time over his preparations. Within a few weeks he had led his army across Bithynia and Galatia into the defenceless kingdom of Pontus and abandoned a rich, populous and peaceful country to his Italian soldiers, to rob cattle and stores, precious metals and curios, and make enormous and indiscriminate captures of slaves, men and women, rich and poor, peasants and burghers. All who could produce a sufficient sum to buy their freedom were set at liberty: the rest were sold to the merchants who followed the army. The price of a slave in the Roman camp soon sank to 4 drachmæ. Yet the troops were still unsatisfied. They complained that their impetuous general allowed them no time to carry off their loot at leisure, that he often even accepted the surrender of towns and villages on the condition that private property should be respected. Their murmurings passed unheeded by Lucullus, always the strictest of disciplinarians. He marched his legions rapidly through the country up to the walls of Amisus and Themiscyra, where an obstinate resistance obliged the Roman army to spend the winter of 73–72 in the trenches. The foe who had so often threatened the Romans in offensive campaigns was at last brought to bay. But the campaign involved far more than the ordinary military operations, even of a war of the first magnitude. By his invasion of Pontus, Lucullus was not only precipitating the decision of a long and serious conflict; he was making a revolution in the international relations of his country. He was introducing a new conception into Roman policy—the idea of aggressive Imperialism. The invasion of Pontus was the first symptom of that policy of the personal initiative of provincial generals which was destined, in the course of a single decade, to replace the feeble and inconsistent control of the Senate and become the strongest force in Roman government. By being the first to make trial at his own risk of the policy to which Pompey and Cæsar were later to owe their glory, Lucullus revealed to Italy the new prospect which lay before her. He showed her how far stronger she was than the great neighbouring States which had always seemed so formidable, and stirred all her new passions in the temptation to despoil them.

In the spring of 72 operations were vigorously resumed against Mithridates and his allies in Pontus, Thrace, and Spain. Lucullus, hearing that the new army of Mithridates was nearly ready and not wishing to be attacked under the walls of Amisus and Themiscyra, marched out to meet it with part of his army, while the remainder continued to siege under the command of Lucius Licinius Murena. Difficulties of commissariat made the expedition both trying and dangerous, but Lucullus was assisted by the treachery of several of the Pontic generals. He was thus able to inflict a decisive defeat on Mithridates, who had lost the best of his troops in the invasion of Asia and Bithynia in the preceding year, and had received none of the reinforcements which he had demanded. Lucullus seized the camp and the treasures of Mithridates. The king himself once more escaped him; in the disorder of the retreat he succeeded in slipping away, after leaving orders that all the women in his harem should be put to death. Meanwhile Marcus, brother of Lucullus, who had been sent as Proconsul into Macedonia and was engaged on the conquest of Thrace, had crossed the Balkans and even reached the Danube. He cut off the hands of whole tribes to strike terror into their neighbours, and not only pillaged the settlements of the Barbarians, but even the renowned Greek cities on the coast, which maintained friendly relations with Mithridates.

At the other end of the world, in Spain, Pompey was at length able to bring his campaign to a close, thanks chiefly to the treachery of Perpenna, who had brought the strange career of Sertorius to an end by assassination. He was now beginning a war of plunder and extermination against the towns which had sided with Sertorius or welcomed his partisans.

In Italy on the other hand, Spartacus after defeating the two Consuls of the year, was engaged in a triumphal progress from one end of the Peninsula to the other, followed by a crowd of traders, who shamelessly provided the slave-leader with all the materials that he needed for the manufacture of arms. In the nervous and impressionable state of national feeling, courage and cowardice, like everything else, had become contagious. The soldiers sent to fight against Spartacus, like the officers who commanded and the politicians who enrolled them, were now completely demoralized. At the elections in 71 there were actually not sufficient candidates for the vacancies, so terrible was the prospect of having to command an army against the invincible slave-leader.

The Senate realized that this scandal would fill the measure of popular indignation to the brim, that it was imperative at all costs to find some capable and energetic commander to put in command of the war. It found him in the person of one of the Prætors for that year. Marcus Licinius Crassus was the descendant of a noble family which we have already seen distinguishing itself during the Sullan reaction. A spoilt child of Fortune, he had received from her every possible gift—illustrious birth, a rich patrimony, quick and easy opportunities for prominence, and an excellent education. He was alert, cultivated and inquisitive: and had shown gifts both of patience and initiative. He had already won a considerable military reputation by bringing help at a critical moment, during the battle of the Colline Gate, one of the most important of Sulla's victories, which was at one moment nearly turned into a defeat. Moreover, although he was born rich, he had increased his fortune by buying the goods of the proscribed, and his wealth, together with the part he had played in the repressive measures of Sulla, made him an important personage in Roman society. He had since been elected without difficulty and in the regular order to all the offices up to the Prætorship, had devoted himself successfully to business and become one of the most powerful capitalists in Rome. Nor was he averse to the new movement in education. Distinguished teachers from Greece and Rome found a ready welcome in his house, and he himself had studied philosophy and cultivated a natural gift for literature and eloquence. Crassus was rich and intelligent; he enjoyed an assured position and a large measure of power. Yet he was tormented by jealousy of the reputation of Pompey, who was almost his own age and had been his fellow in arms in the war against the Revolution. Unfortunately Crassus was by nature rather a careful and hard-headed man of business, than a prodigal and high-spirited politician capable of dominating and inspiring a city crowd. He was a man of moderate needs, of unblemished private character, greatly attached to his family life and accustomed, in all departments of life and in every enterprise to which he put his hand, to exercise the minutest and most painstaking supervision. He made it his business to take advantage with infinite prudence and perseverance of every favourable opportunity, whether great or small; he advanced money to a large and influential circle of dependents; he defended every case that was offered him, even pleading for men so vile and abject that Cæsar refused to take up their case; he was lavish in paying respects and compliments to persons of all kinds. Yet, in spite of all, he was far less admired and popular than Pompey. He had no qualities that caught the imagination of the people. His minute attention to business and his aptitude for figures, hindered rather than helped his political advance. There was nobody whom he hated to the death, but there was nobody that he would follow to the death. He was not cruel for the pleasure of being cruel; yet he was utterly without the scruples either of native honesty or of the caste to which he belonged. A *grand seigneur* by deliberate policy rather than by native instinct, he alternated displays of the most lavish munificence with small exhibitions of pettiness; he was inexorable, for instance, in demanding the restitution of sums lent originally out of complaisance, if, when the time came, he thought he had no more need of his debtor. Thus all his elaborate and painstaking generosity left him no more popular than before.

The widespread influence and the military reputation of Crassus marked him out as a natural commander in the war against Spartacus. Excited by the fame that Pompey had won by his Spanish victories, and conscious that still greater distinction awaited the conqueror of the slaves, Crassus set himself to his task with characteristic energy. He broke down the infectious cowardice of his soldiers by reviving a penal measure which had been obsolete for many years, punishing the first cohorts who fled before the enemy with decimation. But although he succeeded in inflicting several defeats upon the slaves he was unable either to crush them completely or to capture their chief. At length the Senate took the step of recalling Pompey from Spain to entrust him with the task of bringing Spartacus to bay.

Crassus was not the man to surrender the fame which had seemed almost within his grasp, and was goaded to redouble all his previous exertions. Spartacus was a military genius and had worked miracles: but his heterogeneous army could not hold out indefinitely. Discord and desertion came to Crassus' aid, and he was finally able to win a victory, in the course of which Spartacus was killed. When Pompey returned from Spain he found no more of the enemy than a small band of refugees whom he met in the Alps. Six thousand slaves who were taken prisoners were crucified along the Appian Way, as a warning example to their companions in captivity.

Meanwhile Lucullus, who had spent the winter of 72–71 at Cabira in the palace of the fugitive king, was training his small army for the final conquest of Pontus, treating it rather as an inanimate instrument than as a body of living and feeling men. In a nature so violent and passionate as his, the change which had begun after the victories in 74 and 73 had run its course very rapidly. It would have been difficult to recognize the proud and penurious young aristocrat, once the chosen lieutenant of Sulla, in the greedy, ambitious and intriguing commander who had secured for himself the government of Asia, brought the whole of the East within his power, and kept the chiefs of the popular party at his beck and call in the capital by sending home after every victory in the field, or surrender of a city, long trains of mules bearing gifts of gold and silver and works of art. Contact with the wealth and luxury of the Eastern world had awakened all the latent cupidity of a nature which had resisted even the facile temptations of the proscriptions. But with a strange but very human inconsistency he still remained, as a general, the stern unbending aristocrat of the old days, barely admitting that his legions had any other rights but to obey. Lucullus was not exactly a cruel man, but, like all haughty and passionate natures, he was little tolerant of opposition whenever his mind was filled with one idea or one aim. His absolute power as a general, the intoxication of his successes, the vastness of the schemes which he was maturing, together with the temptations of ambition and avarice, which were all the more insidious because so recently awakened, had swollen his natural arrogance and brutality to unmeasured dimensions. The soldiers complained that he no longer came among them like a comrade, passing from tent to tent with a kindly word of praise or encouragement, but passed by impatiently on horseback with an escort, and only when military reasons demanded it: that he had become taciturn and preoccupied, never recognizing or addressing them except to point out or to punish shortcomings, or to demand the fulfilment of one difficult and perilous duty after another; and that, if he did occasionally allow them some share in the loot, he did so with a miserly reluctance, and as though he were afraid of spoiling them by indulgence. The officers, who were members of the best families in Rome, were indignant at his continual reprimands for slackness and incapacity: they chafed at his complete indifference to name or rank, at his burdening them with order after order and service after service; and they declared that, work as hard as they liked, they could never succeed in winning his approbation. And yet Lucullus was attached to his men, and had a sincere respect for many of his officers; but he was too absorbed and harassed by his own multifarious projects to reflect on the immense value which would have been attached to an occasional word of commendation or kindness. He had no eyes for the incongruity of a situation which permitted him to send off to his representatives in Italy vast stores of money and works of art, while he went on labouring to repress the rapacity of his soldiers, and seemed to expect them to toil only for the advancement of his own personal renown.

The soldiers had naturally expected that Lucullus would attack the mountain strongholds where all the treasures of the Court were deposited, and thus reward them for their long hardships with the treasure chests and the furniture of the Pontic king. But Lucullus, unblinded by the prospect of loot, intended first to make himself complete master of Pontus by taking the large Greek cities, Amasia, Amisus and Sinope; and he followed his usual custom, and the example of the old Roman generals, in paying no attention to the wishes of his soldiers. After securing the surrender of a few fortresses by treachery, he led his grumbling legions against these last relics of the civilizing power of Greece upon the Black Sea. Ever since Rome's maladministration of the Pergamene bequest, her power had become hated and feared by all the Greeks in Asia; and the cities had thus prepared to make a long and obstinate resistance. By the end of 71 only Amisus had as yet surrendered. It had been a terrible night for Lucullus when his soldiers, after seizing the town in a surprise assault, had rushed through the streets by torch-light, rioting, sacking and butchering, and setting many of the houses on fire. Lucullus was a typical Roman general, but he had been brought up under the influences of Greek culture, and he reverenced the memory of Hellenism. When he saw Amisus, the Athens of Pontus, a prey to the flames, he threw himself among his troops, seeking to bring them back to reason and discipline, and beseeching their help to save the city from extinction. But he was asking too much. The patience of the long-suffering legionary had broken down. Now that he was at last finding compensation for long months of hardship, and finding it after his own brutal and terrible fashion, it was in vain for his general to interfere with the old catch-words of moderation. Lucullus only narrowly escaped being torn to pieces; and he had reluctantly to allow his unruly condottieri to do their will on the daughter city of Athens. They were symbolic of the age in which they lived, an age in which the highest powers of the human spirit were becoming refined in their desires, and in the enjoyment of the noblest things the world has to offer, while at the same moment all the bestial instincts were let loose in the struggle of man against man for the acquirement of wealth and power. The old military severity personified by Lucullus was forced to give way before a mob of mutinous soldiers. Their general could do no more than set at liberty all who survived from the carnage, and rebuild the fallen city.

CHAPTER VI

THE NEW POPULAR PARTY

WHILE Lucullus was fighting in Asia, the Conservative party continued to lose ground in Italy. The successes of its general in the East caused no improvement in its own position at home, for everyone realized that they were due solely to the personal initiative of Lucullus and not to the policy of the Senate. Even aristocrats began to turn towards ideas of democratic reform; and one of the most active and prominent young men of the party was even now preparing to secede from its ranks. In the second half of the year 71, when he returned to Rome from the Spanish War, Pompey was no longer what he had been at his departure, a young *protégé* of Sulla, for whom everyone predicted a brilliant career. By his victory over Sertorius, he had become, at the age of thirty-six, one of the great personages of the Republic, a man who, although he had never held any public office, and was not even a Senator, could take equal rank beside the most influential and respected of his contemporaries. No member of the younger generation, not even Crassus, had had greater chances offered him than Pompey. But the rapidity of his rise, as he could not help being aware, had excited much jealousy among the ruling caste. On his return from Spain he felt his anomalous situation was becoming precarious; and he resolved to secure himself once and for all by standing in the ordinary course as a candidate for public office. Unfortunately, it is sometimes just as difficult to find the way out of a privileged position as to find the way in. After commanding armies as a Proconsul and receiving the title of Imperator, Pompey could not very well begin his career over again, as the laws demanded, with the Quæstorship and the Ædileship. He decided, therefore, to concentrate his efforts on the highest office of all, and to appear as a candidate for the Consulship in the year 70, thus returning into the ordinary groove through an irregularity greater than all that had preceded: for he had neither the age nor any of the other qualifications requisite for becoming Consul.

The moment seemed propitious; but there were the old difficulties in his way, and the means which had hitherto proved successful in overcoming them would no longer suffice. It was certain that the Conservatives, many of whom were jealous of his promotion and had hampered his Spanish campaign by the refusal of supplies, would use every effort to oppose his candidature. On the other hand, the relative positions of Pompey and his party had altered considerably during the years of his absence in Spain. While the Conservatives had been declining in popular estimation, Pompey had been steadily gaining ground, till he was now, in company with Crassus, the man of the hour, and the most popular general in the State. Like most of his generation, he held but lightly by principle; his successes had filled him with self-confidence, and roused his indignation against a party from whom he had received nothing and expected nothing. It was a tempting prospect to woo himself into favour with the Democrats, and come back to power at the head of his new party to exact retribution from the treacherous allies who had played him false during the war. He began by making advances to the tribunes of the people, promising, if he obtained the Consulship by their support, to re-establish the old prerogatives of the Tribunician power. These proposals were received with enthusiasm by the popular party, who were lacking in influential leaders. It was felt that a man so distinguished by his ancestry and achievements, his social position and assured popularity, was well worth the sacrifice of a few terrible memories. Within a few days, the friend of Sulla, the man who had murdered Junius Brutus and quenched in bloodshed the revolt of Lepidus, had become the admired leader of the popular party and its candidate for the Consulship.

Yet it is likely enough that for all this Pompey's candidature would not have succeeded if chance had not come once more to his assistance. Crassus, whose old chagrin had been reawakened by the intervention of Pompey in his campaign against the slaves, was himself casting an eye on the chief magistracy when he learnt of his rival's intention. Now the candidature of Crassus, who was still in command of an army, although less irregular than that of Pompey, was also unconstitutional. The two generals decided to forget, if not to forgive, their differences and to join forces for mutual advantage. Crassus needed the popularity of Pompey to recommend him to the suffrages of the people. Pompey needed the mediation of Crassus to overcome the opposition of Crassus' debtors in the Senate. Their calculations proved correct. Under the pretext of waiting for a triumph both generals kept their troops under arms outside Rome, and the Senate was soon intimidated into admitting the legality of both candidatures. Crassus and Pompey were thereupon elected without opposition to the Consulship for the year 70, and Pompey begged his friend Marcus Terentius Varro to write him a memorandum on the duties of a Consul, of which, as he said, he was completely ignorant.

Pompey's promises to the democrats and his popularity with the middle class gave hopes of a memorable Consulship. But during the months that elapsed between the election and the end of the year (the Consuls entered upon their duties on January 1st), the prospect was clouded by the renewal of hostility between the two allies. Crassus declined to follow Pompey in his conversion to democracy or to lend him assistance in his schemes of reform. In carrying through a programme of this nature the very foundations of Sulla's work, its moral authority no less than its legal guarantees, seemed likely to be affected; and Crassus, of course, had not only been one of the most useful of Sulla's agents; he had also bought up, for enormous sums, the goods of the proscribed. The Consuls were thus unable to come to any agreement. Neither of them dismissed their legions. Even after entering Rome and celebrating an ovation, Crassus declared that he would keep his army under orders so long as Pompey did the same. Pompey on his side only increased the emphasis of his Democratic professions. When, between the end of November and the beginning of December, the Tribune of the people, Marcus Lollius Palicanus, conducted a huge crowd outside the walls to his camp to hear a statement of his consular programme, he made them an exceedingly violent speech. Too long, he said, had they watched votes being sold by auction to the highest bidder in the tribunals; too long had they groaned under the intolerable iniquities of official plunderers in the provinces. He declared openly that he would set his hand to the redress of these abuses, and gave them also to understand that he would re-establish in their entirety the prerogatives of the Tribunes. His oration was immensely successful. Yet Crassus was still undecided:

and the unhappy disagreement between the Consuls might make havoc of all Pompey's excellent designs.

Their friends attempted to interpose. Great popular demonstrations were organized to coax the two into a reconciliation. At last, when, on January 1st, Pompey entered upon his office, Crassus was so far overcome by public opinion as to declare himself ready to support the policy of his colleague. The reconciliation took place in public, apparently in the first days of their Consulship, and their troops were forthwith dismissed. Soon afterwards, assisted by the huge distributions of corn made by Crassus and the sumptuous festivals arranged by Pompey, the latter opened his attack upon the Constitution of Sulla, demanding that the Tribunes should be given back the powers taken from them by Sulla, particularly the power of proposing laws without authorization from the Senate. As this last proposal required to be approved by the Senate, a huge agitation was set on foot to intimidate the majority. Cæsar, always on the look-out for opportunities of self-advertisement, dashed into the fray and made intemperate speeches at public meetings, while Crassus made quiet but effective use of his subterranean channels of influence in the Senate.

Encouraged by Pompey's proposals and by the manifest weakness of the Conservatives, the animosities which had long been smouldering against the Sullan clique now broke out on all sides. Public feeling was soon excited to fever heat. Whilst their leaders were satisfied with attacking the system, the people cried out for a victim in flesh and blood. Fortune delivered one into their hands in the person of Caius Verres, an ex-officer in the revolutionary army, who, like Cethegus, had known exactly when to leap from the sinking ship; passing thence into the service of the Conservative party, he had been elected Prætor for the year 74, and then sent as Proprætor to Sicily where, thanks to the influence of his friends at Rome, he had succeeded in remaining three years instead of one. Whether his ravages and exactions in the island were really so shameless as his accusers declared, or whether the story of his crimes is not, in part at any rate, a legend skilfully set in circulation by the enemies of his party, must remain one of the secrets of history. It is difficult to judge a man's conduct fairly when we only possess the articles of his prosecution. It is certain, at any rate, that people in Rome had been saying for a long time past that Verres was guilty of countless offences, not only against Sicilians, but even against Roman citizens; and his scandalous misrule was thought to be ruining the greatest and most indispensable of the Roman granaries. So loud was the outcry that his successor, a Conservative named Lucius Metellus, had gone to Sicily with the sincere intention of repairing his maladministration, and the Sicilian cities had been so far encouraged as to send a deputation to accuse him at Rome.

At a quieter moment this prosecution would have had no better chance of succeeding than the many others attempted by provincials during the Sullan *régime*. It was almost impossible that they should find a sympathetic hearing. The unhappy complainants invariably failed to find an influential patron among the Conservatives, and were generally forced back upon the feeble resources of the Democrats for some defender devoid of influence or reputation, thus entering upon their struggle against the formidable conspiracy of class interests armed only with the weapon of the justice of their cause. But for once the Sicilian deputies had arrived at Rome in the nick of time. The agitation for reform was just being inaugurated, and public opinion at once declared vehemently in their favour. Pompey and the chiefs of the Democratic party snatched at the opportunity. Perceiving that a great case against extortion would be an excellent means of fomenting their agitation, they took the affair directly under their patronage and resolved not to let it drop. The Sicilians did not even now find an influential advocate to defend them; but they chose better than they knew when they secured Marcus Tullius Cicero, a young man of thirty-six, of great ability, and unusual eloquence, who was free from all connections with the Conservative party, and yet ambitious of achieving a great position in the State.

Cicero was born at Arpinum of an equestrian family of small means. He belonged to what we should call the provincial bourgeoisie, and was being brought up in the old-time simplicity of an Italian country town. He had received a very careful literary education, and had gone on to Greece to attend courses of philosophy and eloquence. With his time fully occupied in study he had spent his youth, like the Romans of the older generation, undistracted by the amusements and temptations on which so many of the young men of his day wasted time and money. Yet it was not political ambition or the hope of playing a leading part in the Republic which had given him strength to serve so thoroughly in the hard apprenticeship of eloquence. When, on the death of his father, he had inherited his modest fortune, an estate at Arpinum and a house at Rome, and had come to establish himself in the metropolis, he found Sulla all-powerful and the younger members of the equestrian families excluded from politics. Endowed with all the qualities that go to make up the artistic temperament, with imagination, sensibility and a feeling for beauty, but ambitious at the same time for recognition and renown, Cicero had perhaps not found it difficult to renounce all dreams of political greatness for the more congenial ideal of becoming a prince of the Forum, a worthy rival of Hortensius and the great masters of Roman law and oratory.

He had made a striking *début*. Spurred on by the ambition of youth, and by a genuine detestation of violence, he had accepted the defence of several unhappy men, Roscius amongst others, persecuted, under different pretexts, by the creatures of the Dictator. His generous hardihood, aided by truly exceptional powers of eloquence, had soon brought his name into celebrity and enabled him, about the year 77, to contract a successful marriage with Terentia, a lady belonging to a rich and distinguished family, who brought him in a dowry of 120,000 drachmæ and owned several houses at Rome and an estate near Tusculum. This marriage had made Cicero, who lived in a simple style, extremely comfortable, if not exactly rich. He continued to plead in the law-courts, keeping himself honourably independent of the Conservative party and acting up to the ideal of the older lawyers, who refused to admit the giving of legal assistance to be a regular profession, preferring to regard it as a social duty performed gratuitously by the wealthy. While Hortensius and other celebrated advocates of the Conservative party gladly undertook the defence of provincial governors for a reasonable share in the spoils, Cicero was pre-eminent among his contemporaries for his strict observance of the *lex Cincia*, which debarred advocates from the acceptance of a honorarium from their clients. His impeccable honesty, the simplicity of his life, and his courageous independence of the Conservative clique, together with his great intellectual and oratorical gifts, had attracted to him general esteem and sympathy, not only among active Demo-

cratic partisans, but among all ranks of society. His political career
had borne witness to his popularity. Although he had little money to
spend on elections and cherished few political ambitions, he had
already been elected to the Quæstorship without even the expense of
a contest.

Cicero accepted with enthusiasm the defence of the Sicilians. It
appears that he succeeded already in January in inducing the Prætor,
Manius Acilius Glabrio, to refuse to entertain an accusation directed
against Verres by Quintus Cæcilius, his old Quæstor; possibly with
the connivance of Verres himself. Then, having secured a delay of
one hundred and ten days for the collection of evidence, he left for
Sicily.

Meanwhile the Conservatives had been unable to repel the attacks
of Pompey. When the Bill dealing with the powers of the Tribunes
was discussed in the Senate, only a small number of members ventured
to oppose it, amongst them Marcus Lepidus, Marcus Lucullus and
Catulus. Even Catulus, however, went so far as to acknowledge that
Pompey's measure might seem to be justified by the corruption of
the senatorial tribunals. The large majority of Senators approved of
the Bill.

Here surely we have decisive proof that, after ten years of scandal
and conflict, opposition to the aristocratic *régime* was widespread in
all classes and even extended to the nobility. Curiously enough, it
seems to have been most felt amongst the two extreme wings of the
aristocracy, comprising its best and its worse elements: amongst the
able and vigorous young men who were its most stalwart and promising
upholders, and among the ambitious and unprincipled products of the
changed conditions of the time.

The old land-holding aristocracy had by now become transformed
into a society of financiers and plutocrats. Of the historic nobility of
Rome but a small circle of families remained, almost all of them in
straitened circumstances. The upper class was no longer composed
solely of the nobility, but included many wealthy knights and some
men of humbler origin but distinguished gifts like Cicero; it found
room, in fact, for all the boldest and most skilful competitors in the
universal struggle for wealth, education and power. There were still,
it is true, a certain number of old families which preserved the

characteristic ideas which all aristocracies seem to have the power of crystallizing long after their political decay, ideas which had at Rome been reawakened and intensified by the reaction of Sulla. There were still men who felt the old hostility against the upstart classes, the old contempt for the present generation as vulgar and corrupt, the old prejudice for the principle of authority, and a horror of all political change. Such men could not conceive how the son of a peasant at Velletri or Arpinum, who happened, through fortunate speculations, to have become a millionaire, could venture to rival them in the display of riches and share in the distribution of political offices. They could not bear to see a crowd of obscure lawyers and Tribunes, who had fought their way up from the lower ranks of society, hurling accusations against the patricians who had once been the demi-gods of the people. They hated to see the cobblers and artisans, the shop-keepers and freedmen of Rome hissing their superiors when they appeared in the Forum, and refusing them their votes when they were canvassed at elections: and they turned away more in sorrow than in indignation from an age which seemed to have lost all respect for birth or breeding or inherited wealth or intelligence.

Yet there were nobles who perceived that the rising power of the middle class and the knights could no longer be treated in the spirit of two centuries ago; that the times were changed, and new aspirations must perforce be satisfied; and who were prepared, whether through philosophic conviction or personal ambition, to adapt their opinions to a new society, in which intelligence and wealth were bound to take precedence over the claims of manners and ancestry. Such men realized that the surest way of preserving the social power of the nobility was through a conscious adaptation to the new Democratic régime. Nor need they despair of fully holding their own. The centralization of the political offices at Rome, the claims of business, the absence of a political tradition or of easy means of advancement, the terrible memories of the Civil Wars and the reaction, all tended to divert from the political arena almost the whole of the equestrian order and the new middle class. Had it not been for the surviving aristocratic families, there would actually not have been a sufficiency of magistrates of all sorts to provide for the government of the Empire. If only, therefore, the aristocracy consented to abandon absurd and superannuated pretensions, it could still continue to divide among its members almost all the offices of the State.

After this initial success with the Tribunician Bill in the Senate, Sulla's work was attacked on all sides. Plautius, one of the Tribunes, who was seconded by Cæsar, secured the passing of an amnesty for the survivors of the Civil Wars, including all who had fought for Lepidus and Sertorius. The Censorship, which had been suspended seventeen years before, was re-established, and, in April or May, the new Censors, Lucius Gellius and Cneius Lentulus, cleared the Senate of many of the friends of Sulla, driving out amongst others Caius Antonius Hybrida, whom Cæsar had unsuccessfully attacked in 77.

This was only the prelude to a more determined onslaught. Lucius Aurelius Cotta, a noble of Democratic opinions, now proposed to restore to the knights their old power in the law-courts, on the ground that, as they were almost all of them rich, there would be no object in attempting to corrupt them. But here the issue was no longer so simple; and the reform of the law-courts met with a far more strenuous opposition than any of the preceding proposals. Brought forward at a moment when the public was taking so lively an interest in the case of Verres, it caused consternation in the Conservative camp. The Tribunes had now recovered their old prerogatives, and it was enough to prosecute anyone of any wealth or distinction for his condemnation to be assured without prospect of appeal. It was an ominous moment to select for allowing the knights to sit in judgment over their senatorial enemies. Henceforward every provincial Governor would be, like Verres, at the mercy of his subjects. Year by year deputations would stream in from the provinces clamouring for justice against the oppressor, and, backed by a sentimental public, the knights would be relentless in exacting it! The excellent intentions of a class or a party normally last just so long as they maintain it in power. This case was no exception to the rule. Many Conservatives had long ago admitted that it was necessary to improve the conditions of justice and to repress abuses; yet, in their apprehension lest that justice might be exercised upon themselves, they were not content with opposing Cotta's proposed legislation; they even undertook the rescue of Verres, whose attack and condemnation seemed likely to involve the whole party in disaster. It was decided to run Conservative candidates for all the more important offices and to employ every means for securing their success. Quintus Hortensius, the celebrated lawyer, and Quintus Metellus, were to stand for the Consulship, and Marcus Metellus, brother of Quintus and of Lucius, the Governor of Sicily, for the Prætorship. These candidates and other leading members of the nobility, including Caius Scribonius Curio, soon came to terms with Verres. Verres engaged to use all his influence on their behalf during the election, while Hortensius promised to undertake his defence. Quintus and Marcus Metellus wrote to their brother Lucius in Sicily asking him to hush up the evidence of Verres' misdeeds. If they were elected, and the law of Cotta thrown out, they would try to postpone the case till the following year; it would then come before a tribunal of Senators presided over, most probably, by Marcus Metellus, and Verres would have a Consul for his defender.

Meanwhile, despite the intrigues of Metellus, Cicero had been diligently pursuing his inquiries, and when he returned at the date fixed, about the end of April, he brought with him a pile of documentary evidence. But his case did not at once come on for hearing. He had to wait till the end of another suit brought against the Governor of Macedonia, put up or, at the least, prolonged, to cause the postponement of his own. To Cicero himself this delay was by no means inconvenient; for it left him free to devote himself to his approaching candidature for the Ædileship. Now that the case against Verres had been put off, and Cotta's Bill blocked by Conservative opposition, the forces of both parties should have been concentrated upon the elections, which were to take place, as usual, about the middle of the year. Unfortunately, when Cicero returned from Sicily, the Democratic party was distracted, within a few months of its first successes, by unhappy divisions within its own ranks. The quarrel between the two Consuls had broken out afresh.

The ancient historians give us little information as to the motives and details of a difference which was to be momentous in its effects. It is probable that it was brought about by the ambitions of Pompey. Pompey was a perfect specimen of the man of talent, who, though himself devoid of any real originality or creative power, is quick to pick up and to profit by new ideas brought within his reach by men of genius. If he had been sent to the East in the place of Lucullus, he would never have ventured to stake all upon the invasion of Pontus, but would have preferred to proceed with the leisurely prudence traditional among Roman generals. But now, after the amazing successes of Lucullus, his imagination suddenly awoke to all that these conquests had to teach him. He saw that the timid Eastern policy of the Senate was unnecessary and incongruous, that the great Asiatic monarchies, so imposing to the outside observer, were helpless and invertebrate organisms, which could easily be mastered by energetic aggression; and that the adoption of such a policy would lay open a new and wealthy field to the administrators and financiers of Italy, and provide soldiers and politicians with new sources of wealth, influence and renown. He had therefore conceived the idea of pro-curing an appointment in the East as Proconsul, in the place of Lucullus, to take his share of gleaning in the field where Lucullus had been working for the last four years. In this way he would ensure for his party the direction and exploitation of the new Eastern policy devised by Lucullus, to the importance of which the Conservatives still seemed so strangely blind.

Unfortunately Crassus, always jealous of his colleague, once more took delight in barring his advance. So vigorously did he defend the foreign policy of Lucullus that the two Consuls were soon at variance on all matters of policy. A quarrel of this nature could not but be disastrous for the popular party, which was only just recovering its strength after a long period of persecution. It was, in fact, so greatly demoralized by the dissensions of its leaders that all political operations came to a standstill. Towards the middle of the year Cotta was left to defend his law by himself, and in the elections for 69 the Con-servative candidates were allowed to secure the Consulship and Marcus Metellus the Prætorship. These were happy auguries of acquittal for Verres. With the connivance of his patrons, he now attempted to use Hortensius and Metellus to intimidate the Sicilian ambassadors and induce them to withdraw from their accusation, at the same time using all the money at his command to procure the defeat of Cicero's candidature for the Ædileship. Cicero's failure would have been a final blow to the Sicilians, who were already disquieted by the result of the Consular elections; and the whole trial would probably have been over after a hearing of a few days.

The disastrous impression caused by the elections roused Pompey and the Democratic chiefs out of their torpor, and Cicero, energetically supported by the party, was elected to the Ædileship. Thanks to hard work and to a few skilful concessions, the law of Cotta, too, was finally approved; in the form in which it became law the judges were to be chosen not from amongst the knights only, but from amongst the Senators, the knights and the richer plebeians. The Sicilians were thus encouraged to hold firm, and the arrangements for the prosecution of Verres, the first hearing of which was fixed for August 5th, were vigorously pushed forward. Soon nothing else was talked of in Rome and all over Italy but the approaching trial. Men thought of it as they might have thought of a gladiatorial spectacle, where under the eyes of a public eager for sensations, a young and rising lawyer was to fight over the body of a Proprætor with the prince of Roman orators. Gossip and prophecy flowed fast and full. Some knew that attempts would be made to tamper with the judges designated by lot. Others spoke of overpowering evidence collected in Sicily which would be held in reserve till the crowning moment. More sceptical observers declared that, like so many other foxes previously caught in the same trap, Verres too would escape without even leaving his tail behind him. All the amateurs of oratorical warfare were impatient to be present at the battle of eloquence between Cicero and Hortensius. Cicero, said those who pretended to experience in these matters, was a young man of great erudition and brilliant gifts, but he would sorely miss the experience of his distinguished opponent.

Meanwhile both sides completed their preparations for the great conflict. Cicero felt instinctively that this was to be a decisive moment in his career. He gave up the idea of fighting opponents of such skill and influence with the customary weapons of his profession, realizing that, with the public already prepossessed in his favour, the bludgeon would serve him better than the rapier. It would be best, he saw, to abandon dialectics and dexterities for a bold and slashing onslaught, and to endeavour to take the feelings of the public by storm through some amazing and unexpected sensation. He took pains therefore to arrange his material in the manner most calculated to make an impression upon the crowd, preparing, together with each group of evidence, a brief but clear and trenchant address. Verres and his friends, on the other hand, elated by their success at the elections, attempted to circumvent and cajole the witnesses, arranging, for instance, to have panegyrics of the accused sent up from all the towns of Sicily. They also devised ingenious tactics against the fury and impatience of the prosecution, by endeavouring to make the proceedings drag on until August 16th, the date when all hearings would be suspended for a fortnight to celebrate the games promised by Pompey ever since the war against Sertorius. They would then continue the same manœuvre until the case was postponed into the following year. There was considerable prospect of their success, for there were several legal holidays during the remaining months of the year—from September 4th to 19th for the Roman Games, from October 26th to November 4th for the Games of Victory, and from November 4th to 17th for the Plebeian Games.

On the morning of August 4th, when the hearing began, a huge crowd was collected in the Forum, round the seats set apart for the judges, the witnesses, and the parties to the action. Verres appeared upon the scene with Hortensius, attended by many of the greatest personages in Rome. Unfortunately for him, his case was not simply an ordinary suit for extortion; it was closely bound up with the struggle of political parties, and Cicero had formed a better estimate than Hortensius of the state of general opinion. When the documents and evidence skilfully drawn up by the prosecution were laid bare before the public, when the long tale of sufferings endured by the people of Sicily was recited and exaggerated in the Forum by a succession of passionate and eloquent witnesses, the tide of indignation that had been slowly gathering for a decade in all classes of the community against Sulla, the reaction and the Conservative cabal, suddenly burst the flood-gates. Some of the more pathetic incidents in the evidence even moved the public to tears; others provoked murmurs of disgust; others drove them to cries of inarticulate rage. At the end of each hearing the revelations made during the day were circulated broadcast through the city, and thus, with changes and accretions as they passed from mouth to mouth, they roused the entire population to sympathetic interest. The next day a still greater crowd would press round the Forum, hoping to catch something of the tale of horrors, and crying out in wild indignation, without understanding a word, when it perceived the growing excitement of those who stood nearer to the Tribunal. One day when a witness told how Verres had crucified a Roman citizen who had in vain made the appeal: *Civis Romanus Sum*, the audience was stirred to such ungovernable fury that, if the Prætor had not immediately adjourned the hearing, Verres would have been lynched in the open Forum. It was indeed no single individual who was on his trial; it was a party, a system of government, a whole epoch, come to judgment. The public conscience, so long bound down to a hateful silence, sought relief at last by pouring out all its long-stored wrath on the miserable Proprætor whom accident had delivered to its hatred, and made him expiate in his single person, not only his own private sins but all the crimes of Sulla and his detested accomplices. So overwhelming was the fury of the people that Verres and his friends, taken utterly by surprise, felt their case to be hopeless and lost heart. For thirteen days they attempted to stem the violence of the current: day by day they watched it rising higher. The moment came when they realized that no judges could dare to acquit the accused. On the fourteenth day the sitting was suspended. Verres, to save a part at least of his fortune, abandoned the conflict and went into voluntary exile. He disappeared for ever from the presence and the memory of his countrymen; while Cicero, now become one of the chief men in Rome, went fast and far on the path of renown. Neither of the two men suspected, as they parted to pursue these different destinies, that the roads they took would bring them together once again, twenty-seven years later, on the brink of the same abyss.

While these events were taking place in Italy, Lucullus had gone to spend the winter of the year 71 in the province of Asia, of which he had been made Governor. He found it ruined by the exactions that the Italian financiers, in their wanton impatience for quick profits, had inflicted upon the population. If Lucullus had become in many respects a changed man, he still preserved the old aversion of an hereditary aristocrat for the whole breed of financiers, and he now displayed his usual impetuosity in a courageous attempt to renew the policy of Rutilius Rufus. He proceeded to take measures to check the cupidity of the tax-farmers, without in the least reflecting, in the self-confidence of temporary omnipotence, what powerful enemies his magnanimity would provoke. Moreover, he was now revolving a still grander and more ambitious design—nothing less than the invasion and conquest of the whole monarchy of Tigranes, King of Armenia and son-in-law and protector of Mithridates. Thanks to the weakness of Roman policy during the last half-century, and latterly also to the distractions of the Bithynian War and the conquest of Pontus, Tigranes had been able, during the last fifteen years, to enlarge his Empire in all directions by the methods of conquest and alliance. His power now extended as far North as the Caucasus, where his rule was acknowledged by the semi-barbarous populations of the Albanians and Iberians; while on the South, East and West he had conquered almost the whole Empire of the Seleucids, in Cilicia, Syria and Phœnicia, and robbed the Parthians of several of their provinces by the submission of the Satraps of Great Media, Media Atropatene and Gordiene.

It was against this unwieldy and ill-assorted Empire that Lucullus now intended to direct his newly discovered imperialism. But before invading Armenia, he wished first to secure himself against the enemy in his rear by completing the conquest of Pontus. Sending his brother-in-law, Appius Claudius, to demand from Tigranes the surrender of Mithridates, he had left in the spring of 70 to continue the siege of Sinope and Amasia. He was certain that Tigranes would refuse his demand and thus provide him with a pretext for a declaration of war. Sinope and Amasia surrendered in the autumn with a large number of prisoners, and Lucullus was for once able to put some check upon the brutality of his soldiers. A worse fate had befallen Heraclea in the previous spring. Cotta had besieged it by land, while Triarius besieged it by sea. When the town finally capitulated, they pillaged houses and temples without mercy, ransacking all their store of treasure; massacred or reduced to slavery the entire population and even took away the far-famed statue of Heracles, with its arrows of solid gold. They had then set fire to the town and, while the smoke mounted to the sky, the Roman ships sailed out of port so crammed with booty that several foundered on the voyage.

Meanwhile a defiant answer had arrived from Tigranes. Influenced, it appears, by a party among his councillors who feared a possible rival in Mithridates, the King of Armenia had been unwilling at first to receive him, and had consigned him to honorary banishment in a distant fortress; but he had no intention of yielding to the wishes of a Roman general or of descending to the position of a subject monarch. There was now a pretext for invasion. In the spring of 69 the campaign was to begin.

CHAPTER VII

THE CONQUEST OF ARMENIA AND THE FINANCIAL CRISIS IN ITALY

MEANWHILE at Rome the year 70 had ended unfavourably for the popular party. Pompey had been so much disconcerted and exasperated by the intrigues of Crassus that he had given up the idea of replacing Lucullus and declared that at the end of his Consulship he would retire into private life without accepting a province. Crassus, delighted to have interfered with Pompey's calculations, had also preferred to stay at Rome. The Conservatives were somewhat reassured by Pompey's discomfiture, more particularly as nearly all the offices were in the hands of their nominees. For the rest, since the defeat of Mithridates, there was peace within the Empire. The only war on hand for the moment was that against the Cretan pirates who, after the defeat of Marcus Antonius, had in vain sent ambassadors to Rome to sue for peace.

Lucullus alone allowed himself no rest. In the spring of 69 he set out without authorization from home on the hazardous adventure of the conquest of Armenia, with two legions and some bodies of Asiatic auxiliaries, mostly Galatians and Thracians, scarcely 20,000 men in all, and with only the vaguest information about the geography of the country. Mithridates and Tigranes, who had patched up their quarrel when they realized the intentions of Lucullus, had prepared a strong army to meet him. If, in the conquest of Pontus, Lucullus had given a rather liberal interpretation to the orders of the Senate, his invasion of Armenia marks the definite inauguration, at his own risk, of a policy of personal initiative. Halting only by night and allowing his army no breathing-space, he followed the great caravan route across Melitene, descended to the Euphrates, crossed the river and marched upon Tigranocerta. Here he inflicted so signal a defeat upon the army of the Armenian general Mitrobarzanes that Tigranes retired hastily to the north of Armenia, leaving behind him at Tigranocerta a general in charge of his treasure and his harem. Lucullus now laid siege to Tigranocerta. Tigranes soon recovered from his alarm, changed his tactics, and advanced, as Lucullus had expected, with an army, to relieve the city, without even awaiting Mithridates, who was on his way to join him with a large force of cavalry. Lucullus at once adopted the right manœuvre for a besieging general against a relieving force; he left 6,000 soldiers in the trenches under the command of Murena, and marched to meet the second army with about 14,000 men, horse and foot. When the two forces came in sight of one another on opposite sides of the Tigris, Tigranes and his staff, with the exception of a few old campaigners who knew the Roman temper, expected that in accordance with the routine of their profession the enemy would retire before an army five times their number. But Lucullus was not the man to falter. One morning he forded the Tigris, threw his small army upon the Armenians like a pack of mastiffs upon a huge flock of sheep, and broke them up into such hopeless confusion that the king himself was glad to escape with an escort of about a hundred and fifty horse. Having thus rid himself of Tigranes, Lucullus returned to the siege of Tigranocerta, which surrendered soon afterwards.

In the elation of this signal success, Lucullus gave a sudden revelation of the generous instincts of his nature, which had been eclipsed and almost extinguished by his ambition, and the tension at which he had lived during the last few years. He seems to have desired to show, by some act of striking magnanimity, his respectful admiration for Hellenic culture. The vassals of Tigranes who surrendered to Lucullus were treated with clemency; Antiochus Asiaticus was recognized as King of Syria; the wives and property of all the Greeks in Tigranocerta were scrupulously respected; and the many Greeks and barbarian settlers whom Tigranes had forcibly deported to people his capital were sent back to their native countries. At the same time he recognized that for once his legions had a right to a part of the 8,000 talents which he found in the royal treasury and of the other 2,700 talents which he made by the sale of loot, while, in addition, as an agreeable surprise after the hardships of the campaign, each soldier received a personal present of 800 drachmæ. The army was then sent into winter quarters in Gordiene. In this delightful country Lucullus, now master of the Armenian provinces south of the Tigris, spent the winter months dreaming of still grander exploits for the following year, when he would revive the adventures of Alexander the Great, invade Persia and conquer the Parthians, to whom he had already sent an embassy to dissuade them from an alliance with Tigranes.

The headstrong Senator who, amid the petty intrigues of a frivolous aristocracy at Rome, had painfully secured for himself the command of a small mountain province, and who had disembarked in Asia at the head of an insignificant and hastily trained army—the last expiring effort, as many thought, of a decaying Empire—had now, within six years, and with no addition to his forces, become a worthy rival or successor to Alexander himself. Bold, untiring, and unwaveringly self-confident, never an instant in hesitation, acting always on his own responsibility and as if there were no home government to be considered, he seemed to know no obstacle that could block his triumphal advance. Always on the march, whether over the plains of Syria and Cilicia or through the snowy defiles of Taurus, he would face armies five times as numerous as his own, and set out on the morrow of victory upon some new and still more hazardous enterprise as though he needed no repose and had no vision of the last limit of his ambition. After ransacking store upon store of Oriental treasure, he yet enjoyed playing the part of the great patron of Hellenism, and playing it in his own characteristic fashion by a capricious extravagance of generosity unparalleled in the military history of Rome.

Now that the superstitious populace of the East revered him almost as a god, Italy might surely have been expected to admire him as the creator of the new imperialism. But the mysterious demon of adventure and unrest, which was to grant Lucullus and the other great spirits of his generation no peace till they had left an enduring mark in the records of humanity, racked thousands of their humbler fellow-countrymen also. Italy was indeed just entering upon a grave economic crisis, pregnant with great issues for her future development. At this moment, indeed, there was a great abundance of money throughout the country. In addition to the stores accumulated by preceding generals, there were new masses of treasure, won in the war or as interest on the booty previously acquired; there was the capital that Marcus Lucullus had brought back from the pillage of Thracian villages or Greek towns on the Black Sea; that sent home by his brother Lucius; the interest on capital let out at usury or invested in land and buildings in different parts of the Empire; loot that private soldiers and officers had brought home on their return from active service, and finally the tribute paid into the State Treasury. The Republic had at that time an annual budget of 50 million drachmæ. Calculating a ratio of 15 to 1 between silver and gold (which is that which subsisted in Europe previous to the last fall in silver), this would mean a total of over £1,500,000, the greater part of which came from the provinces.

But the demand for money was increasing even more rapidly than the supply. It was needed, and in ever-increasing quantities, to buy from all parts of the Empire the corn necessary to feed the metropolis. It was needed for military preparations, and to maintain the armies of Spain, Macedonia and Narbonese Gaul. It was needed for loans to private individuals, to cities, and to foreign sovereigns, for the satisfaction of the growing taste for luxury among all classes, and, above all, and in enormous sums, for speculation, which was now beginning to infect the public with the gambling spirit in every part of Italy. Within the last few years the commercial movement which originated in the re-establishment of order after the Revolution had continued on its course with ever-increasing velocity. Men and women, nobles and plebeians, rich capitalists and country landowners, small merchants, artisans and freedmen, were engaged in a wild scramble for the sale and purchase of the soil of Italy. Others bought slaves capable of being trained into good cultivators, and planted vines, olives and fruit trees to compete with the produce of the East. But as the great majority of speculators were not in possession of sufficient capital to gamble with, they hastened to employ and, of course, to abuse, the expedient of the mortgage, which had recently been introduced from Greece, and greatly facilitated the giving of credit. One man who had bought a piece of land mortgaged it to buy slaves and plant vines. Another, who possessed a site in a town, mortgaged it to raise money to build on it. Others mortgaged their lands to invest sums in the provinces, either in Asia or in Africa, to private individuals, or cities, or sovereigns, hoping that the venture would be profitable in the long run. No one felt any disquietude at the rapid rise which was simultaneously taking place in the price of money. After having lightly contracted one debt to improve conditions of cultivation, to build a house, and live in great style, a man would as lightly incur a second to pay off the excessive interest on the first, thus sinking deeper and deeper into debt, always in the hope of eventually repaying in full, and risking, of course, the loss of everything that he had. There was a surprising number of Italians who found themselves in this predicament. On the other hand, anyone who was in possession of capital and knew how to lay it out with skill was, of course, in a position to amass fabulous wealth.

No one used his opportunities more successfully than Crassus, who devoted all his energy to this one object. He did not, like so many of his less cautious contemporaries, buy up land at absurdly high prices in the expectation that it would rise still further in value. His favourite speculation was to assist speculators who had embarked on an enterprise without the necessary capital. For instance, he bought up a large number of slaves in the East, choosing with care those who understood the art of building, such as engineers, architects, and master masons. He then established in his house a regular school to teach the art of masonry to young slaves, and hired these out to small builders who were too poor to buy them out of their own pocket. Another new source of income which he tapped proved exceedingly lucrative. Since the houses at Rome were mostly built of wood and the Ædiles had so far neglected to organize efficient measures of prevention, fires were at this time exceedingly frequent. This suggested to him a very ingenious idea. He organized a regular fire brigade from amongst his slaves, and established watch stations in every part of Rome. As soon as a fire broke out, the watch ran to give notice to the brigade. The firemen turned out, but accompanied by a representative of Crassus, who bought up, practically for nothing, the house which was on fire, and sometimes all the neighbouring houses which happened to be threatened as well. The bargain once concluded, he had the fire put out and the house rebuilt. In this way he secured possession of a large number of houses at a trifling cost, and became one of the largest landlords at Rome both in houses and land, which he was then able, of course, to exchange, to sell and to buy up again almost as he chose. Having become in this way one of the richest, if not the richest, man in Rome, his power steadily increasing with every rise in the price of money, Crassus soon became a dominating figure in the Senate and the electorate, and indeed among all classes of the community. Behind him he had a whole troop or army of assistants, administrators and secretaries, and amongst the innumerable names that figured in his ledgers were tax-farmers and merchants, builders to whom he had lent slaves, numberless persons who were tenants of his houses, and even Senators to whom he had made private advances.

This growing embarrassment gradually brought on a financial depression, which reacted in its turn upon politics. The popular movement became more violent and assumed a social rather than a political form—no uncommon development in a democracy where there are glaring inequalities in the distribution of wealth. There was no more enthusiasm for the continuance of the constitutional reforms which had been so hopefully undertaken in 70. The question which had stirred the passions of Italy for an entire decade now scarcely excited a spark of interest. The Democratic party seemed to have relapsed into its old weakness and disorder.

It lacked both programme and leaders. Crassus, who was now completely out of touch with Pompey, had re-entered the ranks of the Conservatives, with whom he now habitually acted. Pompey scarcely showed himself in public, seldom came down to the Forum to plead and admitted only a small number of intimates to the privilege of his friendship. Cæsar, for his part, having nothing better to do in this period of political truce, was profiting by the relations of his family with the high capitalist bourgeoisie to run into debt, and attempting to court popularity with the people by his prodigal expenditure, his winning manners, his persuasive eloquence, and any ingenious and daring stroke which was calculated to impress the popular fancy. This was hardly perhaps a very exalted form of activity, but for the moment there seemed nothing better to do.

But the lull was more apparent than real. If Pompey was affecting to be tired of politics, his silence and reserve were only adopted to make the people feel his loss. He was determined to have his revenge upon Crassus and the Conservatives, and to be sent, he cared not how, to replace Lucullus in the East. As he had nothing more to hope from the Senate, where Crassus was supreme, he was secretly maturing a far-reaching scheme which would force the government to recall

Lucullus and put him in his place. The movement was inaugurated in 69 by a skilful agitation among all classes of the community. Pompey's share in the campaign cannot be fixed with certainty. It is probable that he used his influence to back the widespread complaints against Lucullus' provincial reforms, trying to win over the financiers by pledging himself to their abolition. Of his activity in other directions we can speak with more assurance. There is no doubt that it was Pompey who was the soul of the agitation set on foot at this time by the Tribunes of the people, who employed against his rival every artifice of popular insinuation and invective. It is never difficult to play upon the passions of the mob at a period of commercial depression. The Tribunes harped steadily on the same telling refrain. At a moment when thousands in Italy were on the verge of starvation or bankruptcy, a small knot of millionaires was quietly appropriating enormous masses of booty which belonged by rights to the State, that is to all the citizens. They directed their most venomous shafts against Lucullus, who was just now conducting the most lucrative campaign of all. The public listened gladly to their onslaughts. If a few rich and eminent citizens testified to their admiration according to a growing custom, particularly among bachelors, by leaving him substantial bequests at their death, the poor and ignorant populace gave credence to every rumour circulated by his enemies about the treasures which he was sending home from the East. Men even went so far as to expend pity on the Kings of Armenia and the Orient whom he preferred to rob, so it was said, in order to fill his own purse rather than carry on regular warfare and execute the orders of the Senate. Thus it came to be thought that his Eastern command had already lasted too long. After the battle of Tigranocerta he was even accused by common report of having omitted to pursue Tigranes simply in order to prolong the war and keep open opportunities for plunder. Some almost went so far as to reproach the Senate for not checking him midway in his career of victory.

Far away in the interior of Asia, Lucullus gave little heed to an agitation, which, had it been what it seemed, he might safely have ignored. But behind the trumpets of the Tribunes and the shouting of the populace Pompey and the financiers lay securely entrenched. It was a powerful coalition; and, with public opinion to back it up, it became irresistible. In the course of the year 69, although Lucullus was strongly supported in the Senate by Crassus and the Conservatives, the Senate was compelled by an angry public and the intrigues of the financiers to take some action. Desirous to do the least possible injury to Lucullus whilst removing the most obvious of the capitalist grievances, it deprived Lucullus of the government of the province of Asia for the year 68, entrusting it instead to a Proprætor. This was the recompense of a grateful country for his victories of the preceding year.

But Pompey was still unsatisfied. It was not long before he found supporters on whom he had scarcely reckoned in the soldiers of Lucullus themselves. Lucullus was now ready for his great expedition into Persia. But when in the spring of 68 his subordinate Sornatius received orders to join his general for the march upon Ctesiphon the legions, which had been wintering in Pontus, refused to obey The old-fashioned martinet had succeeded in exhausting the patience of his soldiers, who were tired of being treated like the legionaries of a Cincinnatus or a Scipio. Their example was infectious. Even the forces that Lucullus had with him in Gordiene showed a disinclination to be marched into Persia. The unbending disciplinarian was for once obliged to yield. Abandoning his proposed plan of campaign he decided instead to invade Armenia. Little did he suspect that he and his army were being slowly enmeshed in the invisible network of intrigue which was being woven at Rome in the house of Pompey. From the moment when Pompey realized the prevalence of discontent in the legions of his rival, he set himself to devise a terrible vengeance—to compel the recall and degradation of Lucullus by provoking a general mutiny among his soldiers.

CHAPTER VIII

THE FALL OF LUCULLUS

It was in this same year that Quintus Metellus went out as Proconsul to Crete, and Cæsar set foot upon the lowest rung of the political ladder, the Quæstorship, as one of the most brilliant among the younger members of the Democratic party. His ability no less than his illustrious birth and distinguished bearing attracted sympathy in all classes, even amongst the less fanatical Conservatives. Our evidence does not enable us to judge what were the articles of his political creed at this time, but it is fair to infer from his rank, as from his character and actions, that they were not such as to alienate him from men of moderate and serious opinions in all parties.

It is indeed impossible to understand Cæsar's extraordinary career and the singular place which he occupies in the history of Rome without keeping continually in view the variety of the influences which enriched his strange and many-sided individuality. Cæsar had not the reckless and impulsive temperament, or the unbridled imagination, which so often distinguish the leaders of great movements. He was still simply an elegant young political aspirant, of winning manners and prodigal habits, but hampered by delicate health, keen, alert, ambitious, and excellently endowed for every kind of intellectual activity. He had been able to make himself one of the best speakers of his age. He had devoted himself passionately to the study of astronomy, a science which had been virtually discovered about a century before this time by Hipparchus, and had since made great progress in Asia and Egypt. But the studies in which he was most deeply interested were of a more purely æsthetic character; for he was refining and cultivating his taste in the hope of applying it to the organization of popular festivals and the designing and building of public works. In short, he was a man of fine, lively and supple intelligence, who, despite his highstrung nature, could by no means be called headstrong or unbalanced. At heart he was an artist and a student; yet so manifold were his gifts and so great his skill and energy in applying them that he might be sure of success, if he desired it, in the arena of politics or war.

Such a man on his entry into politics would naturally feel an affinity for the moderate school of thought. It is not impossible, therefore, to form a more or less probable notion of the opinions which a young man of his class would be likely to hold. His teachers were, of course, not Romans but Greeks, and the ideas with which they inspired him were not of native Italian growth. We shall most easily detect them by glancing for a moment at the great contemporary Renaissance—at the peculiar influence exercised by the civilization of Greece upon the educated classes of Cæsar's day.

When the Italians first began to be the pupils of the Greeks, they looked back over two great ages of Hellenism which had followed one upon the other and passed away. There was the classical Greece of Sophocles and Phidias, Pericles and Plato, Demosthenes and Aristotle, with its countless small independent city communities, its glorious and turbulent democracies, its local schools of art, each characteristic of a separate people, its dialect-literature, its private schools of metaphysical philosophy. There was also the cosmopolitan Greece of the great bureaucratic kingdoms founded by Alexander in Asia and Africa, with their splendid capitals, their common language, their Court literature, their accumulations of knowledge, their royal institutions for the encouragement of learning, their taste for special sciences and for the new philosophies of conduct, like those of the Stoics and Epicureans. In the Rome of Cæsar's day, all that was most living and expressive in this long filiation of ideas found a ready and welcome acceptance. The various currents of thought and feeling in the two great ages of Hellenism met to foam and clash in the whirlpool of an imperial metropolis. Here the student of philosophy found disciples of Plato disputing against the followers of Zeno and Epicurus, and the young poet could choose between the decadent romanticism of the Alexandrians or the strict classical tradition of the great tragedians and lyrists. In the field of eloquence, the flowers and mannerisms of the Asiatic orators vied with the pure and delicate graces of the Attic stylists; in art, those who found no pleasure in the dexterous refinement of the Hellenistic masterpieces of Asia and Egypt could reserve a fastidious admiration for the archaic sobriety of the age of Phidias. There were scholars who spent their lives upon minute researches in some special science that had been painfully nurtured amid the solitudes of a royal museum, while others, with a more catholic, if less conscientious, application, wandered gaily over the vast range of encyclopædic study opened up by the private teachers of the classical period. Within the space of one short generation, Rome was living, with a feverish intensity, through the successive phases of a civilization which it had taken five centuries to bring to perfection.

But in the midst of all these contending and contradictory influences, it was the elder Greece which men recalled with the sincerest enthusiasm. Demosthenes became the model of perfection imitated by every orator; Cicero loved to associate the florid magnificence of Asiatic eloquence with the old classical sobriety of form. The pure artistic tradition of Phidias and Polyclitus, of Scopas, Praxiteles and Lysippus, established a lasting supremacy over the Rhodian and other Asiatic schools. The greatest sculptor of that age, Pasiteles, who was a Greek of South Italy and thus a Roman citizen, was the head of a school of Neo-attic sculptors who made copies of old classical master-pieces; he also produced original work distinguished by an elegance of form and a simplicity of execution which were the fruit of his study of nature and the great archaic models.

It was the same ruling tendency in another field of operation that drove the political thinkers of Rome to the study of Aristotle. What appealed to them most of all in the master of Alexander was his theory of a government which should harmonize the principles of monarchy, aristocracy and democracy. According to this conception, which is one of the fundamental political ideas of Aristotle, the people should possess sufficient authority to repress the tyranny of government, while the chief power should be in the hands of the rich and noble families, who are to exercise it for the public good and provide an example of civic virtue. A magistrate may, in case of need, be placed in a position of supreme control and invested with the powers of a President of the Republic; but such a President must himself be one of the best citizens in the State; he must govern in strict accordance with the laws, and must, above all, live in scrupulous observance of them himself. The law must, in fact, be regarded as the true, if impersonal, sovereign of the Republic. Without this necessary balance of opposing principles, democracy must inevitably degenerate into mob rule, aristocracy into the tyranny of a caste, and monarchy into that worst of all possible governments, an autocracy of the familiar Asiatic type, good enough perhaps for the emasculated nations of the East, but ill-suited to the superior peoples of Greece. These Aristotelean theories, which had been taken up again by Polybius in his study of Roman society in the age of Scipio Æmilianus, were just now coming to be widely held. Their popularity is easily explained. They harmonized the anti-monarchical and aristocratic traditions of Roman history with the new and encroaching tendencies of democracy, and brought with them the hope of some happy and lasting solution of the political difficulties under which the Republic had been suffering for the last half-century.

It is very probable that Cæsar shared the ideas of his class; that, like most of the nobles who at that time owed allegiance to the popular party, he was inclined to some policy of conciliation between aristocracy and democracy on the lines of the ideas of Aristotle and Polybius: that he dreamed of a free and conquering Republic, with an art and a culture like those of Athens, but of wider extent and greater powers, a State which would be governed by a hereditary aristocracy, vigorous in administration but emancipated from class prejudice and unfettered by tradition, and which would make Italy the metropolis of the world for power and riches, for art and science, for eloquence and liberty.

But even if he had himself been untouched by these tendencies, interest alone would have inclined him to the moderate school. His personal fortune was by no means equal to the expenses entailed by a political career, and he had for some time past been compelled to borrow. As his family had many connections with the knights, it was not difficult for him to raise the money. Many of the rich tax-farmers were ready to lend to the young nephew of Marius, for whom every one predicted a great future, even if they felt by no means sure of recovering their money. Wealthy capitalists had indeed come to regard these loans to politicians as a means of indirect corruption, which ingeniously fortified their influence over the government whilst they themselves remained aloof from political conflicts. But Cæsar could only rely upon the powerful financial support of the knights so long as he took care to retain their confidence; and this he would very soon have forfeited if he had allowed himself to be involved in the revolutionary propaganda of the new tribe of demagogues.

As a matter of fact his Quæstorship, so long as he remained at Rome, was entirely uneventful. He was content with paying exaggerated homage to the ghost of his proscribed uncle, behaviour which might perhaps technically have been classed as revolutionary, though in the existing state of opinion it was agreeable to all classes. It was generally recognized that the hero of the Raudine Fields deserved to be set among the number of great historical personages, in the place of honour from which party hatred had expelled him; and Cæsar, who had in the course of this year lost both his wife and his aunt, the widow of Marius, was not afraid to carry the statue of the great popular general in the funeral procession. Soon afterwards he set out for Spain as Quæstor to the Prætor Antistius Vetus, while Pompey remained at Rome to plan the fall of Lucullus.

In the spring of this year Lucullus with his usual hardihood had thrown himself into Armenia dragging after him a small, weary and grumbling army, largely officered by men who were working for Pompey. Amongst those who were sedulously kindling the spirit of mutiny was a brother-in-law of Lucullus himself, a young aristocrat named Publius Clodius, who was suffering from penury and, like so many of his neighbours, hoped to redress this disability in the career of politics. Yet not even the suspicion of traitors amongst his own family could deter the intrepid Lucullus from endeavouring, with the same small force at his disposal, to eclipse even the daring of his earlier conquests. What induced him to attempt so incredible a feat? It is possible that in the flush of unprecedented success he was blind to the intrigues and disaffection all round him. Yet since the records of this last campaign are too scanty to elucidate his conduct, it is justifiable to offer an alternative suggestion. It may be that, suspecting the treachery of his officers, and not daring to repress it by overt measures, Lucullus, always inclined for the bolder course, resolved to meet the danger half-way, and to stifle the discontent of his army by a new success as striking as the conquest of Armenia.

But if his intentions are conjectural, there is no doubt as to his movements. He advanced in a series of great marches as far as the plateau of Lake Van, where he came upon the united armies of Mithridates and Tigranes. The two allies had decided to wait in an entrenched camp on a hill-top, on the Roman model, until the early Armenian winter compelled the Roman army to a disastrous retreat. Lucullus, after vainly endeavouring to force on an engagement, attempted to draw the enemy from his camp by an advance upon Artaxata, the Armenian capital. Tigranes, fearing for his harem and his treasure, broke up his camp, followed the Romans and endeavoured to dispute the passage of the Arsaniades. A battle took place on the banks of the river and the Armenian king suffered another defeat. After this victory any other general would have arrested his advance on the approach of autumn. But Lucullus, like a passionate gambler who risks all that he has won by doubling the stakes, decided to drive home his success by dealing a sudden blow at the very heart of the Empire of Tigranes and marched at once upon Artaxata.

This daring strategy may partly have been prompted by the news from Italy. His position at Rome was now indeed extremely precarious. The popular agitation, which had been almost extinct since the year 70, was once more in full flame. The financial depression had excited all the worst passions of the mob. Italy was beginning to pass through a period of violent ferment in which every act or proposal against the rich and powerful was certain to win the popular approval. It was easy for Pompey to stir up feeling against an aristocrat of old lineage like Lucullus, in spite of all that he had achieved for the Roman name. There had been a close and exciting struggle over Eastern policy. After much painful intriguing, the friends of the Proconsul had secured that the commission entrusted with the organization of the government of Pontus should be composed of his own partisans. They had even succeeded in making his brother Marcus one of the number. But on another very important point they had been forced to give way before Pompey and the public. Lucullus had been deprived of the Governorship of Cilicia for the following year. It is true that, as some small compensation, they had given Cilicia to his brother-in-law, Quintus Marcius Rex, who was Consul for that year, in the hope that the conqueror of Pontus would continue to govern the province through his relative. But the contest was becoming more and more unequal, and in spite of all the efforts of Crassus,

Pompey and the democrats gained ground daily. Only the capture of Artaxata and the final conquest of Armenia by Lucullus could have revived the fortunes of his partisans at Rome.

Although the autumn was now approaching, Lucullus ordered his troops to advance upon Artaxata. Once more, by a supreme application of discipline, he broke down the resistance of the legions. The march was begun; but it did not continue. When the Armenian autumn began to give warning of the early approach of winter, the soldiers revolted and refused to go further. As almost all the officers supported the mutiny and many had even helped to excite it, Lucullus was forced to yield. By the end of October he was back with his army in Mesopotamia.

This inglorious retreat was the first great success of Pompey's cabal. Unfortunately for Lucullus, it soon entailed others of a far more serious character. Once back in Mesopotamia, Clodius, resolved to strike home at once, profited by a temporary absence of Lucullus to provoke a general revolt among the legions, depicting to them in glowing colours the easy conditions of service enjoyed by the troops of Pompey. Lucullus hastily returned and Clodius was forced to fly. But this series of petty mutinies had infused new spirit into the enemy on whose discouragement they had too confidently reckoned. At the end of the year 68, Mithridates suddenly reappeared in Pontus with a small army of 8,000 soldiers, appealed to the loyalty of his old subjects, and succeeded in shutting up in Cabira the officer whom Lucullus had left in charge. Lucullus was anxious to relieve him, but the troops refused to march before the spring of 67. It was left to his admiral Triarius to bring reinforcements to Pontus by sea and extricate the garrison of Cabira. Unfortunately Triarius was not able to drive Mithridates out of the country, and was forced to go into winter quarters within view of the hostile army, at Gaziura in the very heart of Pontus. Meanwhile the soldiers of Lucullus were engaged in trading and other delights of relaxation, as though Asia were in a state of complete tranquillity, and no Roman legionary in the slightest danger.

This news appears to have reached Rome towards the end of the year 68. It only intensified the excitement that was already raging. The situation was a very curious one. The various parties and cliques were in desperate conflict; yet none had so far succeeded in gaining any definite success. The consequence was that all State business was indefinitely delayed; no administrative questions were being decided, and everyone was in a state of nervous exasperation. The Conservatives were grumbling at the turn matters had taken in the East, while Pompey and his clique were in no way satisfied with the successes they had so far gained. For all their efforts, Crassus still remained more powerful than Pompey in the Senate, and Pompey did not seem to have improved his chances of obtaining for himself the powers wrested from Lucullus. It was becoming clear every day that his right policy was to appeal directly to the tribes and demand from the people what was refused him by the Senate. This would involve gaining his position by one of those skilful election manœuvres which the political parties of a generation ago had been in the habit of adopting whenever they felt sufficient confidence in their powers. But Pompey was probably aware that he could not safely reckon upon the success of such an attempt. The great mass of the lower classes was certainly on his side; but it was totally without organization, whereas the Senators and the knights had a great influence over the voting. He could not therefore be sure that his popularity alone would suffice to win him the elections; and although he used every means to increase his influence he did not feel justified in taking the risk. It was probably with his connivance and on his advice that one of his old Quæstors, Caius Cornelius, a man of integrity but of very mediocre ability, who had been elected Tribune of the people for the year 67, proposed two exceedingly popular Bills, one a law forbidding Roman citizens to lend money in the provinces, which was intended to allay the financial crisis in Italy by stopping the export of capital; another a law taking away from the Senators and bestowing upon the people the right of giving dispensations from the observance of a law. But all these manœuvres would probably have been of little use if an unexpected incident had not upset all calculations and given a different direction to the conflicts of parties, the intrigues of Pompey and the agitation of the public. The change was caused by the outbreak of a terrible famine during the winter.

Men are always inclined to impute their misfortunes to the misdeeds of others. On this occasion the people threw the blame for the famine upon the pirates who intercepted the corn-ships on the high seas, upon the Senate and the magistrates who had for years been unable to repress them, and finally upon Lucullus, whose general Triarius had been sent with a fleet into the Ægean, where he had shown his helplessness by allowing the pirate Athenodorus to sack Delos under his very eyes. The widespread feeling against the Senate and its slackness, which had contributed so greatly to the Democratic victories of the year 70, now showed itself afresh. In the midst of this ferment the two laws proposed by Caius Cornelius provoked what was almost a miniature civil war. There was fighting and bloodshed between armed bands in the Forum. It seemed almost like a return to the old days before the Social War and the Revolution of Marius.

Pompey was quick to realize that all questions of home and foreign policy must be subordinated to the exigencies of the food supply, and that he had only to appeal to the electors on this question to obtain from them any answer he wished. Renouncing for the moment all schemes of Eastern conquest, he put up one of his supporters, Aulus Gabinius, a man of low origin and moderate fortune, who was then Tribune of the people, to propose in the Assembly a Bill empowering the people to choose, from amongst the Senators of consular rank, a Dictator of the seas to conduct the campaign against the pirates. The holder of this new post was to have a fleet of 200 ships, a large army, 6,000 talents, 15 lieutenants and absolute proconsular authority for three years over the whole Mediterranean and its coasts up to fifty miles inland, with additional powers of recruiting troops and collecting money in all the provinces. His plan was exceedingly ingenious. The Conservatives attempted to oppose the project in the fear that Pompey's novel Dictatorship would eventually affect the commands of Lucullus and Metellus. But the fear of starvation had stirred Rome to the depths. There were noisy demonstrations in the streets, with threats of a revolution if the law was not approved. In the end Pompey was entrusted with powers even wider than those which Gabinius had originally proposed. He was authorized to enrol an army of 120,000 men with 5,000 horse, to form a fleet of 500 ships and to nominate 24 subordinate commanders.

Cæsar, who had lately returned from Spain, was among those who backed up the proposal of Gabinius. The law was indeed far too popular for him to venture to oppose it. But if he was anxious to avoid displeasing the people, he was still more anxious to make the greatest possible number of friends in rich and powerful circles. It was with this object that, some time in the last three years, he had married the wealthy and influential Pompeia, daughter of Quintus Pompeius Rufus, an aristocrat and ardent reactionary who had been killed in 88 by the partisans of Marius, and of Cornelia, daughter of Sulla. For the nephew of Marius to marry a grand-daughter of Sulla and the daughter of a victim of the popular revolution is a proof of the shortness of political memories at Rome; but it also throws an interesting light on the ambitions which Cæsar was entertaining at this time. Aristocratic marriages were now only regarded as means to maintain or to increase political influence. Cæsar would probably not have married Pompeia if he had not been anxious to ally himself with the great Conservative nobility. A wealthy marriage of this sort at once raised his credit amongst the knights, connected him with many influential Senators, and helped the party of Sulla to draw a veil over his origin and the democratic incidents of his early career. Thus, if the agreement made in 70 between the advanced aristocrats and the popular party proved to be lasting, Cæsar might one day be the nominee both of the people and of the better elements among the Conservative classes. His marriage shows that Cæsar was at this moment in no way preoccupied by the fresh outbreak of hostilities between the Conservatives and the popular party, and did not regard it as sufficiently important to impede the gradual process of conciliation between all classes and parties which had been going on since the death of Sulla.

Meanwhile, at the beginning of the spring of 67, military operations were again resumed. Lucullus moved to the help of Triarius, and Pompey set out to recruit his forces. He could only beat up a small army in the place of the 120,000 soldiers allowed him, while, in the neglected condition of the Roman Navy, the harbours of the allies yielded him no more than 270 of the 500 ships which he was assigned. He distributed them among his numerous subordinates, who were chosen from amongst prominent members of the upper classes and the Conservative party, amongst them Marcus Terentius Varro, entrusting each of them with the task of clearing a given portion of the Mediterranean. Meanwhile Lucullus had ascertained in the course of his march that Triarius, either through defective information or in the desire of winning a campaign by himself, had given battle to Mithridates at Gaziura and been defeated with great loss. Lucullus asked his brother-in-law Marcius for reinforcements from Cilicia and marched rapidly to his assistance. But when he had come up with Mithridates, he was unable to force a general engagement, or to efface the impression produced by the defeat of his subordinate.

Pompey, on the other hand, was surprisingly successful in what was generally considered a very formidable task. In an impressionable society like that of Rome, and at a time of universal excitement, it had been possible to regard the pirates as a dangerous adversary. In reality their apparent strength was due entirely to the negligence of Rome. The only country over which they exercised any effective control was Crete, where they had established a sort of military government which Quintus Metellus had been engaged for a year past in attacking. Their forces were not numerous and had, since the fall of their powerful patron Mithridates, fallen into complete disorganization. The news that a Dictator of the seas had been appointed at Rome and was collecting a large force against them soon spread round the Mediterranean coasts to add to the discouragement already caused by the annexation of Pontus. This impression was only increased by the fate of the first captures made by the Dictator. Pompey, who was working for a rapid success rather than for a permanent settlement, made a clever use of the momentary confusion of the enemy. After treating the first batches of prisoners with excessive severity, he suddenly modified his methods, offered a free pardon to all who submitted, and sent them to repeople deserted and devastated towns. This policy laid him open to grave criticism, for, in accordance with Roman law and tradition, it was shameful and almost criminal to treat pirates with such clemency. The Conservatives, of course, attempted to make capital out of his behaviour. But Pompey, strong in the popular support, was only anxious for an immediate victory. The pirates were reassured by a policy which was tantamount to amnesty. Before long they appeared spontaneously from all sides to surrender their ships and their arms to the Roman generals. For some time afterwards the sea remained comparatively unmolested, and Pompey was greeted at Rome as the wonderful hero who had cleared the seas in a few weeks. In reality he had accomplished very little. As soon as the panic inspired by his Dictatorship had passed off, the pirates rearmed their ships and began once more to sweep the seas as of old.

Meanwhile Lucullus, who had really given the death-blow to a mighty monarchy, was on the point of being robbed of all the fruits of his labour. As soon as the news of Triarius' defeat reached Rome, the noisy troop of Pompey's partisans set to work once more. Gabinius proposed a second Bill depriving Lucullus of the command of the war against Mithridates and the provinces of Pontus and Cilicia, and bestowing them on the Consul Manius Acilius Glabrio; at the same time the legions of Fimbria were recalled and all who disobeyed were threatened with the confiscation of their property. In the face of strong popular demonstrations the Senate had for once to let the Bill pass.

Lucullus was now in a terrible dilemma. Marcius, unwilling to compromise himself in the cause of his brother-in-law, refused to grant him the reinforcements he asked, on the pretext that his soldiers were unwilling to march. Meanwhile a rumour spread that Tigranes was moving up with a large army to join forces with Mithridates, and almost simultaneously the new Proconsul of Asia made public the edict of his recall. But Lucullus was as yet in no mood to submit. Calmly ignoring the senatorial decree, he proceeded to march upon Tigranes, in the hope of surprising him on his way, hindering his junction with Mithridates and inflicting upon him a defeat that would give a new turn to events. But this desperate effort was his last. In the course of the march his weary troops broke out into open mutiny, and, relying upon the decree of recall, refused to follow a man who could no longer claim to be their general. Lucullus suddenly awoke to the mistaken severity of his *régime*, and with characteristic impetuosity attempted to redeem it. He visited his old campaigners in their tents, spoke to them with the genuine affection that his ambitions and anxieties had too long obscured, and made familiar and personal appeals to the leaders of the revolt. It was all in vain. The soldiers declared that they were ready to wait until the end of the year; if by that time the enemy had not shown his face, they would severally disperse, those of them who had been dismissed, to their own homes, the others to join the standard of Glabrio. Lucullus had no alternative but to yield. While Mithridates was reconquering his old kingdom and Triarius pillaging Cappadocia, the man who two years before had dominated Asia like a second Alexander became in his own camp the butt and the laughing-stock of his soldiers.

Thus strangely and suddenly ended the political and military career of Lucullus. During the six years which he spent in the East he had made a revolution in Roman politics which it would be impossible to over-emphasize. He found the foreign policy of the Roman Republic embarrassed by traditions of slackness, paralysed by an indecision which took alarm at shadows and gave way at once before any determined opposition, and accustomed to regard intrigue and procrastination as satisfactory substitutes for rapid and resolute action. It felt an almost sacred respect for the established order, and an extreme terror of laying a finger upon its familiar workings. It habitually preferred diplomacy to war, and never understood how to make the most of a success or drive home any vigorous effort, generally accepting some compromise which settled the question for the moment along the line of least resistance at the risk of raising new and inevitable complications in the immediate future. This policy was not indeed without a certain sagacity of its own, but it had become stultified by the very exaggeration of its own virtues. Lucullus substituted war for negotiation as the usual method of solving the difficulties of Eastern policy. He replaced the interminable machinations of Senatorial intrigue by the sharp and vivid impression of his swift campaigns, with their bewildering attacks and their complete and amazing victories. By the adoption of a strong and sustained policy of aggression he succeeded in becoming the arbiter of the entire East, reducing one State after another to helplessness in a series of almost foolhardy campaigns. A policy capable, if not carried to exaggeration, of doing Rome such service as this was certain to find converts and imitators. Pompey and Cæsar were to be the two great pupils of Lucullus and to reap in the field where he had sown. For Lucullus was reserved the part, pathetic but not inglorious, of the pioneer who encounters all the risks and enjoys but the scanty first-fruits of success. His fall was not simply the result of the intrigues of Pompey. Those intrigues would have been powerless if they had not revealed to his enemies the one weak point in his armour. It is indeed the cause of Lucullus' downfall which is perhaps the most significant lesson of his career. By an effort of genius the aristocrat of ancient lineage, who had learnt in the school of Rutilius Rufus and was the devoted and disinterested friend of Sulla, had been able to liberate himself from the deadening fetters of caste and become the creator of the new imperialism. But there was one sphere in which he had still remained the inflexible aristocrat of the olden time. He had never outgrown the old-fashioned conception of the duty of a general towards his soldiers. In this strange inconsistency lay the seeds of his disgrace. The new imperialism required generals of a different type from the men who had held command during the first two Punic Wars. For the troops had been changing with their generals. The discipline and obedience of traditional soldiering had passed away beyond recall with the opening of the East. When it was too late, Lucullus awoke to his mistake. Not all his signal qualities availed to save him from one of the cruellest humiliations a Roman general ever suffered. His fall marks the final failure of the aristocratic restoration attempted by Sulla. It was because he remained faithful to the old ideals and customs, in one of their noblest and greatest applications, that the noblest and greatest of the friends of Sulla had to pass on to others the gain and the glory of the new policy which he had been the first to conceive and to execute.

CHAPTER IX

CICERO AND THE MANILIAN LAW

WHILE Pompey was conquering the pirates by kindness, Quintus Metellus was spreading fire and bloodshed throughout Crete, massacring his prisoners and growing rich on their loot. Metellus belonged to the small circle of the old nobility who would have liked to govern the Empire on the system of Scipio Æmilianus, and his severity was a deliberate protest against the clemency of the demagogue Pompey who was not ashamed to court the favour of the people by making terms with the evil-doers. In their desperation the pirates appealed to Pompey with offers of submission, and Pompey, only too glad to humiliate Metellus, eagerly accepted them. On the pretext that the Gabinian Law put Crete under his orders, he despatched Lucius Octavius to replace Metellus; but Metellus retorted with a declaration that Crete was outside Pompey's jurisdiction and inflicted condign punishment upon the cities which, in reliance upon Pompey's decree, had refused him obedience. Lucius Octavius was very nearly forced into maintaining the rights of his chief by defending the pirates against a Roman Proconsul. Happily more serious incidents intervened to distract Pompey from this awkward quarrel.

Towards the end of the year 67, grave news reached Rome from the East. Financiers received letter upon letter from their correspondents in Asia giving alarming reports about the state of the province. Lucullus was no longer in command of the army, and Glabrio and Marcius were men of little capacity. Mithridates had again become master of Pontus. Tigranes had broken into Cappadocia and flying columns had burnt the frontier villages and made their appearance in the heart of Bithynia. These reports caused a regular panic in the capital. Men thought of Mithridates as already at Pergamus, of a general massacre of Italians and confiscation of property on the model of 88. Before long everyone was agreed that the ordinary magistrates were insufficient to deal with so serious a situation —a view not infrequently taken by the Democrats, but shared for once on this occasion by many of the Conservatives and financiers.

The friends of Pompey were not slow to turn all this to their advantage. At the beginning of 66 the Tribune Manilius proposed that Pompey should be entrusted, in addition to the powers which he already held, with the government of Asia, Bithynia, Cilicia, the chief command in the operations against Mithridates and Tigranes, and the right of declaring war and concluding alliances as he thought good, in the name of the Roman people. This was nothing less than a legal authorization in Pompey's favour of the policy of personal initiative which Lucullus had been the first to apply. Crassus was disgusted to see his rival carrying off the palm in their four years' duel of intrigue. The Conservative party was unwilling to pass a second law in his favour, thus openly recognizing a policy which it had tolerated or ignored in the case of Lucullus. Some of its more eminent members, such as Catulus and Hortensius, even endeavoured to oppose the project by appealing to Republican sentiment and demonstrating that a Dictatorship of this sort would be monarchical in character.

But Pompey's success over the pirates was for the moment more influential than the coalition of Crassus, the Conservatives, and tradition. A new power had appeared in Italian politics, intermittent in its working, but invincible whenever its influence was exerted— the force of public opinion. It had already once made trial of its power; for in 70 it was the violent outbreak of a long-stored resentment against the Conservative government which stirred many Conservatives to transfer their support to the opposite party. But the enthusiasm had cooled down as quickly as it had been roused: and it was in vain that Cæsar, Pompey and the Tribunes had attempted to reawaken it. Now, however, quite suddenly there was a fresh outburst of excitement. In the enthusiasm of Pompey's success against the pirates, all Italy acclaimed him as the greatest general of the age, the man who alone had proved himself worthy of their confidence and capable of dealing a death-blow to the indomitable Mithridates.

It was indeed not merely the irresponsible enthusiasm of the man in the street which clamoured for Pompey to be Dictator of the East. The wealthy classes, the numerous Senators and knights who had invested capital in Asia, joined with young aspirants like Cæsar in the general outcry. Pompey obtained support, too, from what was perhaps a still more significant quarter. Since his sensational prosecution of Verres, Cicero had quietly continued his training, reading and studying very widely, refining his oratorical style, and exercising his facility for composition so successfully as to become one of the quickest and most concentrated workers of the day. In a society that hungered for intellectual gratification, he had succeeded, notwithstanding the obscurity of his origin and the smallness of his means, in winning sufficient influence and popularity to be elected to the Ædileship and the Prætorship. He now counted as one of the most conspicuous figures in Roman life. His influence was of a peculiar and unprecedented kind. Like all typical men of letters, he was better able to sway the imagination and emotions of masses of men than to dominate the will of single individuals. When he stood up to speak before a large popular audience, the power which he seemed to wield was extraordinary. The marvellous hold which he had thus obtained over the minds of his hearers in an age where no one was untouched by the flame of personal ambition, had kindled in him a vague passion to become the Demosthenes of Rome. Like many another soldier and man of letters before and since, he began to delude himself with the notion that he was destined to be a great administrator. Yet all the time, for each of the separate individuals out of whom the huge crowds which he held spellbound with his eloquence were composed, Cicero was little more than a weak little figure in the rough arena of politics; not all his fine moral qualities or professions of independence could shield him against the arts of intrigue and intimidation. He was neither cruel, nor rapacious, nor insincere; his morals were pure, and his affections strong and deeply rooted. But there were qualities in his nature which forbade him to be powerful. He was of a morbidly nervous and susceptible disposition, tormented by the pinpricks of an almost feminine vanity and by a sensibility that was alive to every petty annoyance. Above all, he was never able to free himself from a certain attitude of snobbishness towards the upper classes. If he was very greedy of notoriety and proud of being known to everyone, he was much more afraid lest a word should be breathed against him in the greatest houses of Rome, and longed ardently, and for a long time hopelessly, for an *entrée* into the house of any aristocrat of authentic lineage and untarnished record. He was also radiant with satisfaction at the many friendships which his oratorical renown had brought him among the rich capitalists, particularly if they were men of culture like Atticus. In a word, even after he had become a great figure in history, Cicero remained in many respects what he had been from the beginning—a small bourgeois from a country town, whose vanity fell an easy prey to the compliments of the plutocracy and the nobility. All this serves to explain why, at this critical juncture in his career, he followed Cæsar's example, and courted admiration simultaneously from the Democrats and the Conservatives: although unlike Cæsar, and just because he was a bourgeois born, he inclined rather towards the nobility. It explains also why he had prosecuted Verres and assailed the corrupt Conservative administration in the year of the Democratic revival, and why he had afterwards refused to be a candidate for the Tribuneship in order not to compromise his reputation in the eyes of the aristocrats.

The Bill of Manilius now offered an extraordinarily favourable opportunity for pleasing several parties at once—not only the rich capitalists and a large part of the aristocracy, but also the whole of the proletariat. Cicero, who was at that time Prætor, came forward in support of the bill in a speech of great eloquence, delivered in his best manner. He knew his public. He assured the rich merchants and Senators, who were trembling for their investments, the well-to-do tax-farmers, the shopkeepers and the artisans, that the old kingdom of Pergamus was the richest province of the Empire, that not only did it supply the Treasury with a large part of its revenues, but that most of the invested capital of the tax-farmers, merchants and other private individuals was laid out there, and that it was therefore the duty of all classes to unite in defending it to the death. Cæsar, who intended to stand for the Ædileship in 65 and was using every effort to gain popularity, also appeared in support of the Bill, which was thus eventually passed, much to the indignation of Crassus. Pompey received the good news in Cilicia where he had gone into winter quarters, and immediately set about making preparations for his campaign.

We have now reached the spring of 66. Still, as ever, the favourite of fortune, Pompey had been entrusted with the despatch of a man already wounded to the death. Mithridates had quarrelled with

Tigranes, who suspected him with sowing disaffection among his sons in the hope of raising to the throne of Armenia a man more devoted to his cause. Abandoned by Tigranes, without a fleet, and with no more than about 30,000 infantry and a few thousand cavalry, he had only one more chance, and that but a weak one. There was just a hope that Phraates, who had succeeded Arsaces on the throne of Parthia, would come to his aid. But Pompey hastened to send an embassy to Phraates to persuade him to turn his arms against Tigranes, and recover the lost provinces of his kingdom. He was anxious to be done with intriguing and to strike a rapid blow against Rome's old enemy.

But before his hands were free to act there was one delicate duty to perform. He had come out to relieve Lucullus of his command; but Lucullus was still obstinately encamped in the midst of his mutinous legions. Leaving behind him in Cilicia the three legions of Marcius, Pompey advanced with a large force which was to serve both for the campaign against Mithridates and to persuade Lucullus of the necessity of submission. The young favourite of fortune advanced in the flush of success to encounter the sour and war-worn veteran. There were many in both camps who awaited the meeting with unconcealed anxiety. It was impossible to predict the effect of an interview. Mutual friends did their best to secure that all might go off with dignity and without scandal. The two generals were induced to meet at Danala in Galatia. The interview opened auspiciously with mutual compliments, but Lucullus who had never been a skilful diplomatist, endeavoured to maintain an impossible position. He declared that nothing remained for Pompey but to return to Rome, since he himself had already brought the war to a conclusion. Hot words ensued, and the generals parted after an unpleasantly violent scene. Lucullus even went so far as to publish decrees and distribute the lands he had conquered in Galatia, trying in his way to make others believe, or perhaps rather to make himself believe, that he had no intention of giving way. But Pompey had no difficulty in drawing off all his soldiers to his own standard, with the exception of 1,600 whom he left to accompany their general to Italy.

With an army of scarcely 30,000 men, Pompey now crossed the frontier of Pontus. Following the precedent set him by Lucullus in the campaign of 74, Mithridates first tried by skirmishing to hamper the commissariat of the enemy. But when he had lost part of his cavalry in an ambush and Pompey had succeeded in opening a quicker and surer means of communication by Acelisene, he abandoned offensive tactics and retired to a strong position at Dasteira. Pompey then sent for reinforcements from Cilicia. Mithridates now realized that he would soon be surrounded by overwhelmingly superior forces. One night he eluded the vigilance of the Roman sentinels, and slipped out in the hope of crossing the Euphrates and continuing the war in Armenia. But Pompey went in pursuit, overtook him after three days, and inflicted upon him a severe defeat, during which Mithridates only just succeeded in escaping. With the remnant of his army he made his way to Sinoria, on the borders of Armenia, the strongest of his fortresses. There he took possession of a huge sum of money, gave his soldiers a year's pay, distributed amongst them a great part of his other riches, and sent to ask the hospitality of Tigranes, on whose frontier he was. Then, not daring to await a reply within such easy reach of the Romans, he started off once more with a small escort, recruiting troops as he went, marched up the right bank of the Euphrates to its source and down again into Colchis, which, amid the disorder of the last few years, had practically recovered its independence, and finally succeeded in reaching Dioscurias, the last of the great Greek cities on the coast, at the foot of the Caucasus.

Pompey, whose strategy had been seen at its best in the campaign, was now temporarily helpless. He was not in a position to lead his whole army across the mountains in pursuit of this band of fugitives. Nor was there anything to be lost by postponing the invasion of Colchis till the following year. Mithridates was surrounded and practically taken in a trap. He could not return to Armenia; he could not elude the Roman squadrons by sea; nor could he fly to the Crimea, where his son Machares was now on the throne, for Machares had become an ally of the Romans; moreover he was cut off from the Crimea by the barbarous tribes of the Caucasus, whom even at the time of his greatest power he had always been unable to reduce. Pompey therefore preferred to turn aside to Armenia, which he overran without difficulty. While Pompey had been fighting against Mithridates, Tigranes had been attacked by Phraates and his own rebellious son. But Phraates had soon retired and his son, alarmed at his isolation, had sent to Pompey for help. Tigranes attempted to resist, but when he ascertained that Pompey was preparing to attack him, he put the envoys of Mithridates in chains, set a price upon his head, and came alone and on foot as a suppliant to the Roman camp. Pompey received him kindly, reassured him by the restoration of all the hereditary domains of his family, and reconciled him to his son, who was rewarded with the grant of Sophene. Tigranes received the title of friend and ally of the Roman people and was forced to pay 6,000 talents to Pompey personally, 50 drachmæ to each of the soldiers, 1,000 to each of the centurions and 10,000 to each of the military Tribunes. Pompey then led his troops northwards to winter quarters on the banks of the Kur on the extreme northern frontier of Armenia and prepared for his invasion of Colchis by entering into relations with the Albanians, who inhabit Cirvan and Daghestan, and with the Iberians of Georgia. But if he thought that he had at last cornered Mithridates, he was mistaken. The indomitable veteran had himself been making overtures to the Iberians and Albanians and had persuaded them to help him in a last effort against Rome. In December the legions in winter quarters on the banks of the Kur were suddenly surprised by the Albanians. The attack was repulsed; and Pompey thus received a useful warning to be thoroughly on his guard against these treacherous barbarians.

CHAPTER X

THE EGYPTIAN PROJECT

THE surprise attack of the Albanians was the last moment of real danger in the campaign. In the spring of 65 Pompey set out on what turned out to be a triumphal progress through Western Asia, slowly wending his way, gathering spoils as he went, through the great monarchies, the free cities, the maritime republics, the petty theocracies, and the numerous brigand or private communities which had sprung up out of the chaos of the Empire of Alexander. He passed by the legendary scenes of the poetry and mythology of Greece; he visited lands and cities and battlefields whose names had long been familiar to the Western imagination; he contemplated the infinite variety of barbarous nations scattered through Asia between the Caucasus and Arabia, with every diversity of language, custom and religion; he became acquainted with the wonders and the depravity of that ancient industrial and Hellenized Orient which lived by exploiting the barbarians in its service and differed so profoundly from the younger and more buoyant civilization of Italy: its weird and impressive cults compounded of layer upon layer of superstition, its intensive and laborious agriculture, where the soil allowed it, the arts and industries of the famous cities which manufactured the luxuries of the whole of the Mediterranean world: above all, the men and women who lived in these great industrial centres—their labouring population, sober, hard-working and thrifty, yet quick and intelligent and strangely sensitive to the influence of religion: their class of professional intellectuals, philosophers and scientists, still so rare a phenomenon in Italy: and the royal Courts with their vice and luxury, their untold treasures, and the elaborate and striking ceremonial which excited so much curiosity amongst the simple-minded democracy of Italy.

At the beginning of the spring Pompey invaded and overran the country of the Iberians, beneath the snow-peaks of the mountains where Prometheus had once been chained. He passed on into the valley of the Rion, the ancient Phasis, and descended into the plain of Colchis. Here, in the country of Medea and the Argonauts, he had thought at last to lay hands on Mithridates. He was too late. The undaunted veteran had once more performed an exploit that seemed outside the range of possibility. Forcing a passage with his small army through the tribes of the Caucasus, he had penetrated successfully along the four hundred miles of hostile and difficult coast which separated him from the Crimea. Once in the Crimea, he fell upon his rebellious son, forced him to fly for his life, and thus conquered himself a new kingdom. Pompey was too cautious a general to attempt to invade the Crimea by sea. Having arranged for a blockade during his absence, he set out along the valley of the Kur, upon an expedition against the Albanians, whom he seems to have surprised by the aid of treachery. Thence he returned into Lesser Armenia bringing back to the adventurous Italian merchants exact and welcome information about the mysterious overland trade route to India. This route started from the port of Phasis, ascended that river to its source, crossing thence into the valley of the Kur, and over the country of the Iberians and Albanians to the Caspian; once across the Caspian, it made for the valley of the Amu Daria (the ancient Oxus), which did not flow, as to-day, into the Sea of Aral, but into the Caspian.

In the course of these expeditions the troops had naturally amassed large stores of precious metals and slaves. When he reached Lesser Armenia, Pompey spent the rest of the year in reducing the last resisting fortresses and taking possession of the immense treasures of Mithridates. The greater part of it he found in the citadel of Talaura, which contained 2,000 coffers of onyx encrusted with gold and so huge a store of phials, vases, couches, beds, bridles and breastplates, covered with gold and precious stones, that it took a month to make their inventory. In another citadel he came upon the correspondence and secret memoirs of Mithridates, the recipes for his poisons, and an interesting correspondence between the King of Pontus and his favourite Monima. The whole of the treasure of the last great Hellenizing monarch of Asia had now passed into the possession of the Italian democracy.

But the democracy was in no mood to enjoy its victories. All through 66 the Italian situation had grown steadily worse. After the passionate interest taken in the debates on the Manilian law and in the course of affairs in Asia, the public had relapsed into its normal condition of sulky torpor. The financial crisis was becoming acute. All classes in the State were suffering from the pressure of debt; all felt the irritation that waits on disappointed expectations. Now that order had been re-established in the East, there was in fact only one great problem which really interested the mass of the nation, the problem of debt; and this neither of the two parties dared to bring to the front. In default of more serious questions the two small cliques of politicians who represented the Conservative and popular parties, were reduced to a war of intrigue and slander, carried on principally in the law-courts, which seemed to increase in violence as it diminished in interest.

A situation difficult enough in itself was still further complicated by a manœuvre on the part of Crassus. The millionaire, who ever since his Consulship had given his support to the Conservatives in their struggle against Pompey, had now passed over to the popular party, and, in the place and during the absence of Pompey, undertaken to be its leader. His object is not difficult to divine. After the two rebuffs he had suffered by the Gabinian and Manilian laws he was longing for a revenge, and he proposed to obtain it by an imitation of the intrigues of his successful rival. The democracy wanted conquests and victories and the sack of cities; Pompey had gained his great popularity because his success against the pirates was thought to have checked the famine in the metropolis. Crassus was a man of business. He was prepared to accept the public in their present mood and to supply them with just what they desired. He would come forward as their general in a new enterprise which would for ever assure to Rome the blessing of cheap food. Here was a second disciple for the unhappy Lucullus. Whilst Pompey continued to apply his policy in Asia, Crassus was dreaming of carrying it into an altogether new quarter of the world, into the great and wealthy kingdom of Egypt.

It must be confessed that Crassus had shown perspicacity in the selection of his victim. Egypt was not only the richest country in the world; it was also one of the few countries so fertile that the annual harvest largely exceeded the needs of the people and was available, with the royal permission, for export to less fortunate regions. If Egypt were annexed to Rome the surplus of its annual harvest could be exported in its entirety to the metropolis. The conquest of Egypt therefore meant for the Romans what the abolition of corn duties means for us; it meant cheap bread. No doubt some pretext was needed for the Roman intervention; but this was easily found in the will of Alexander II, who at his death in 81, had bequeathed Egypt to the Romans. There were many now who regretted that the Senate had at that time been so timid as to refuse his bequest. There would, however, be no difficulty in going back upon its decision, for with its habitual want of logic the Senate had at the same time refused to recognize the new King Ptolemy Auletes, whose royal descent was somewhat dubious and who had for years been vainly intriguing to secure recognition.

Crassus, who knew his fellow-Senators, was well aware that some sharp external pressure would be needed if this traditional policy was to be reversed in favour of aggressive measures against a peaceful country which had done nothing to provoke hostility. He must therefore follow the precedent of Pompey in raising some excitement in the public mind. But this manœuvre was bound to fail unless he had first made his peace with the Democratic party and gained over to his side all the more active and skilful members of Pompey's clique. After several years of conflict such a reconciliation was by no means easily achieved. Crassus appears to have found the personal friends of his rival a serious obstacle in his path, since in the agitation which follows we find none of the men who had helped Pompey taking a prominent part. One only among the more prominent popular politicians was found favourable to Crassus, but he was the ablest and most adroit of them all—Cæsar.

Cæsar was now approaching a critical moment in his career. He had hitherto given a general support to the popular party but without forming any close personal relations or joining in any intrigues of the kind which his friend Clodius had undertaken in the army of Lucullus. Thanks to this policy, he had remained, more than any other of the rising members of the Democratic party, in the confidence of his Conservative opponents. Yet for all this he was as yet only on the threshold of a political career. He had gone no farther than the

Ædileship, to which he had been elected for the following year. What exercised a still greater influence over his actions was that he was in serious pecuniary straits. At a time when popular enthusiasm was at a low ebb it was more than ever necessary for him to have plenty of money; there was every prospect that his expenditure would rise steadily, and no prospect of meeting it till he eventually reached the Prætorship and recouped himself out of the spoils of his provincial administration. In this situation the ambition and jealousy of Crassus were a very gold-mine for an impecunious aspirant. Under the imperative necessity of making some money, Cæsar braved the hostility of his party colleagues and, for the first time in his life, allowed himself to become the instrument of the millionaire. But he still hoped that it would involve no breach with Pompey. The latter surely could not complain if Cæsar, after doing his best to obtain him his command in the East, now performed a similar service, in respect of Egypt, for his distinguished fellow-citizen. It was easy for him to argue down his scruples in the ingenuous irresponsibility of youth. He would be useful to Crassus, and Crassus would be exceedingly useful to him; at the same time he would be maintaining his friendly relationship with Pompey, and doing nothing to compromise the position he had already acquired. In short it was a master-stroke, which would leave him on good terms with everyone.

Not long after he had concluded this coalition with Crassus in 66, we find Cæsar involved in a very unpleasant intrigue. At the Consular elections for 65 the Senate was most anxious to secure the return of Lucius Aurelius Cotta and Cneius Manlius Torquatus; it had therefore erased from the list of candidates the name of Lucius Sergius Catiline, an old partisan of Sulla who had just returned from a Proprætorship in Africa, on the double pretext that his nomination had not been received in time and that he was under prosecution for extortion. When, in spite of this intrigue, two other candidates, Publius Autronius and Publius Sulla, nephew of the Dictator, had been elected, the son of Torquatus had accused the two Consuls designate of extortion and he intrigued so successfully that they were both condemned and a new election proclaimed. This time the Senatorial candidates were duly elected. The popular party, which had taken up the cause of Autronius and Sulla as a convenient weapon against the Conservatives, had succeeded in rousing a good deal of public feeling on the subject, and some disorders had actually broken out during the hearing of the trial. This encouraged them to still bolder measures after their condemnation, and they entered into a conspiracy to bring about a third election by assassinating the new Consuls on the first day of the year.

The conspiracy was joined by Catiline and a few other needy young aristocrats, such as Cnæus Piso; and, what is more serious, it appears to have been approved in secret by Cæsar and Crassus, though, for fear of compromising their reputation, they refused any active support. This was an act of very great imprudence on their part, and politicians of their skill and adroitness would never have committed it if they had not practically been forced into dangerous measures by the difficulties attending their Egyptian project. In spite of his personal solicitations, the supporters of Pompey obstinately refused to lend Crassus any assistance, and Cæsar and the millionaire still remained alone in the field. It was not easy for them by their own unaided efforts to stir up the people and override the opposition of the Senate and the magistrates. In this situation it would have been exceedingly useful to have two Consuls favourable to their scheme, and it was this that induced them to countenance the projected *coup d'état* of Sulla and Antonius. Unfortunately the conspiracy was discovered, and public opinion was much disturbed at the strange light it threw on the morals of the upper classes. All parties united in demanding an exemplary penalty. But when the Senate met to discuss it, Crassus intervened so vigorously in the debate as not only to save the conspirators from punishment but even to secure them compensation for their defeat. Perhaps he thought that a bold attitude would most effectually silence the unpleasant rumours that were abroad about his complicity in the plot; or it may have pleased him to give a display of his influence over the Senate. At any rate that body yielded to his appeal, and no prosecutions were undertaken. Piso was sent on an extraordinary mission to Spain, while Torquatus himself prepared to defend Catiline in his case for extortion. In this way the matter was soon hushed up.

Meanwhile Lucullus had returned to Italy with his miserable escort of 1,600 soldiers and huge stores of gold and silver in bullion and ingots. He brought with him to the West a more precious possession than these in the cherry-tree, which began from this time onwards to be generally cultivated in Italy. It is strange to reflect that in the snowy plumage of a cherry-tree in a spring orchard we have a trophy, that has survived the convulsions of twenty centuries of history, of the great Eastern conquests of Lucullus. But if posterity forgets the men to whom its thanks are due, their contemporaries too often ignore them. Despite all his victories and his spoils, and despite the unknown treasure he carried in his train, Lucullus found the gates of Rome sternly closed against his modest triumphal procession. Feeling was running high between the two political groups, and the most trivial incident was used by one party or the other as a pretext for attacking their rivals. Suddenly re-entering the world of politics after years of absence, Lucullus found himself being assailed by the popular party as though he were a criminal or a brigand. In the hope of exciting the passions of the mob against the upper classes, demagogues threw into his teeth, as the friend of Sulla, all that they had been ready to tolerate and even praise in Pompey, his indiscriminate looting, his unauthorized campaigns, and the blunders and brutalities of his generals. Every time the Senate met to discuss the triumphs of Lucullus, the Tribunes interposed their veto.

Nor did they reserve their criticisms for Lucullus; they soon turned their attention to his officers and subordinates, in particular to Cotta, the captor of Heraclea. On Cotta's return the Senate had decreed him unusual honours and allowed him the title of Ponticus. But when he began to make display of the wealth he had acquired during the war the Tribunes took up his case, threatened to bring a prosecution against him, and demanded the release of the prisoners of Heraclea. Perceiving the storm-clouds gathering on the horizon, Cotta prudently decided to cast out ballast. But though he disgorged large sums out of his booty to the public Treasury, the Democratic party continued its attacks. Cotta's contributions, they declared, were an insult and an absurdity; he had kept the greater part for himself. When the law by which his prisoners were to be released was brought before the Assembly, the popular leaders arranged a pathetic scene for the occasion. They hunted up from the highways and hedges, from private houses and the barracks of the slave-merchants, all the

Heracleote captives that they could find, dressed them in mourning, presented them with wreaths of olive, and sent them thus attired into the assembly. Then a certain Thrasimedes of Heraclea rose to speak. He recalled the old friendship between Heraclea and Rome, he described the long-drawn agonies of the siege, the horrors of the sack, the carnage and the fire, to the accompaniment of a pitiful chorus of sobs from the slaves. The public was so impressed that Cotta was hardly allowed to open his mouth, and thought himself exceedingly lucky to escape a sentence of exile.

The Conservatives replied to all this by accusing their opponents of working for a revolution. When Pompey returned from the East, they declared, at the head of his victorious legions, he would have himself proclaimed sole ruler and overturn the government of the Republic. Yet these alarms did not prevent them from picking a quarrel with Crassus and Cæsar. After the failure of their conspiracy the two allies had reverted to their original project of provoking a great popular agitation for the conquest of Egypt, and they were now attempting by various ingenious expedients to gain the favour of the people. Crassus, who was Censor, proposed to inscribe in the registers of the citizens the inhabitants of Transpadane Gaul—a thoroughly democratic idea which might be regarded as the natural sequel and conclusion of the great popular movement for the emancipation of Italy. Meanwhile Cæsar, who was Ædile, was trying to take men's breath away by prodigies of extravagance, of course at Crassus' expense. He had the Capitol, the Forum, and the basilicas decorated with pictures and statues, celebrated the Megalesian and Roman games with unprecedented magnificence and gave a splendid gladiatorial show in memory of his father, in which the fighters for the first time used spears and arrows of gold and silver. He further organized, in booths temporarily constructed on the Forum and in the basilicas, an exhibition of all the objects used in the games and in the decoration of public buildings.

But if the Senate had been intimidated by Crassus to close its eyes to the conspiracy, this barefaced bribery now stirred the more reactionary Conservatives to indignation. They showed particular hostility towards Cæsar, who was less powerful than the millionaire; their old distrust against the nephew of Marius, a strange compound of genuine alarm and aristocratic contempt, was once more awakened. Catulus, the most respected figure among the old Conservatives, at length found courage to show open resistance. In his capacity of Censor he opposed the project of Crassus for granting citizenship to the Transpadanes, and acted with so much vigour that Crassus was forced to give up the idea. But suddenly one morning a strange rumour ran through the city. The trophies of Marius, which had been removed by Sulla, had been re-established on the Capitol during the night. It was Cæsar who had prepared this surprise, which was immensely successful. During the next few days there was a general rush to the Capitol to see the trophies of the wars against Jugurtha and the Cimbri and gaze on the venerated features of the hero whom the nobility had so implacably pursued. Many of Marius' veterans were seen to break into tears, as they recalled the incidents of their campaigns. The Senate felt its weakness in the face of this popular outburst, and did not venture to have the trophies removed. But Catulus openly attacked Cæsar in the Senate, and charged him with attempting to subvert the State, no longer by methods of subterranean conspiracy, but openly and in the eye of the public.

This attack by Catulus marks the commencement of the new struggle between Cæsar and the Conservatives, a struggle which was to last for the rest of his life and entail consequences of such far-reaching importance. The idea of conciliation between the two parties, of which Cæsar in his student days had been so confident, was now abandoned. Excited by these preliminary skirmishes, the Conservatives now redoubled their efforts and extended their attacks to Gabinius, whom they attempted to prevent from leaving for the East to take up his duties as Pompey's subordinate. In this they were unsuccessful; but when Cæsar, thinking his ground had been sufficiently prepared, at length brought forward with the help of the Tribunes the question of the conquest of Egypt, they opposed it with an energy which was no longer looked for from the Senate. As Cæsar appealed to the will of King Alexander, they naturally fought him by throwing doubts upon its authenticity; but they went further, and affirmed that, even granting it to be authentic, Rome had no business to cast longing eyes upon every country and pick a quarrel with every nation.

This opposition of the small Conservative clique to the projects of Cæsar and Crassus is significant not so much for its immediate as for its more distant consequences. So far the party had not adopted a clear attitude towards the new imperialism which had been created by one of its members. It had allowed Lucullus freedom of action, but it had opposed the ambitions of Pompey and declared them contrary to the spirit of the Republican constitution. Upon the policy in itself there had as yet been no pronouncement. But from this time onwards the Conservative party took a clear stand against aggression and expansion, and associated itself with the cause of peace, of which Italy must sooner or later feel the need.

The Conservatives could at first only congratulate themselves on their choice of policy. They succeeded without difficulty in checkmating the designs of Crassus and Cæsar. Ingenious as it was in itself, the scheme for the conquest of Egypt never succeeded in taking hold of the popular imagination. There were several reasons for its failure. A considerable number of the partisans of Pompey distrusted Crassus and refused to support him. Nor was Crassus helped by the chance occurrence of any striking incident, like the final attack of Mithridates upon Asia, which had been so useful to Pompey. The moment, too, was not well chosen. The rich classes, who had hitherto favoured and encouraged the Democrats, were beginning to fight shy of the violent propaganda of the popular movement and the legislation in which it resulted; they were gradually inclining once more to the Conservatives, whose leaders were cleverly holding out baits, such for instance as the restoration to the knights of the privilege abolished by Sulla of sitting on the senatorial seats in the theatre. As for the middle class, the late Democratic victories had brought it nothing except possibly a general discontent at the excessive debts which it had contracted. It was disillusioned, disgusted, and out of spirits. Cæsar saw that the agitation had no future and soon induced Crassus to abandon the whole project.

CHAPTER XI

HOW CÆSAR BECAME A DEMAGOGUE

THE conspiracy of 66, the agitation for the conquest of Egypt, his bribery and indebtedness, and the suspicions aroused by his coalition with Crassus had all reacted unfavourably on Cæsar's reputation. He had alienated the support of many who had previously admired him and were disappointed to see him giving way to the temptations of political intrigue. The ideal of his youthful ambition had now lost its appeal. It was but only too manifest that the Aristotelian harmony between aristocracy and democracy was an impracticable dream. The well-to-do classes, preoccupied with their financial embarrassment and disgusted by a succession of futile or dangerous political agitations, were becoming indifferent or even Conservative in their political views: while the popular party was seeking its supporters deeper down amongst the dregs of the Roman population—amongst the bankrupt landlords and merchants of Italy and disappointed and desperate outcasts from all classes of society. There began to be talk of Land Laws, of the abolition of debt, of confiscating the plunder of the generals, and other revolutionary measures for the relief of the poor. As a reaction against this development, the small clique to which the great Conservative party seemed now to be reduced, professed sentiments of the utmost fury and contempt against their opponents: though it had no more hopeful items in its own programme than the antiquated expedients of massacre, execution and *coups d'état*.

Cæsar must often, during this period, have cast envious eyes on Pompey, so happily removed from these troublesome agitations. Pompey was indeed being extraordinarily successful in the two schemes which had taken him to the East; he was increasing his power and he was amassing an immense fortune. By extracting huge sums from the Kings of the East, by large organized slave-raids, by the sale of the poorer prisoners, and the ransoms of the rich, he had already become as wealthy as Crassus. Part of his money he had immediately invested in the East, contracting loans at excessive rates of interest with small sovereigns who were in debt, such as Ariobarzanes the King of Cappadocia. By this time, after years of unimpeded success, he had become a sort of King of kings over the entire East with an authority such as no Roman had ever wielded before him. In the spring of 64 he gave a display of his power and magnificence at Amisus, where he had assembled a Court of kings to distribute pardons and favours in the name of Rome. He gave new kings to Paphlagonia and Colchis, increased the dominion of the Tetrarchs of Galatia, appointed Archelaus, son of the defender of Athens, to be high priest of Comana, and divided the territory of Pontus between eleven towns, where, under the supervision of the Roman Governor, he set up the Republican constitution of a pure Greek πόλις. Like all educated Italians of his day, Pompey regarded Republican institutions of the Græco-Italian type as the best of all possible governments, and eagerly re-established it among the Greek populations freed by Roman arms from the yoke of Oriental autocracy. Not content with having successfully concluded the task undertaken by Lucullus, he was about to seek fresh laurels in the kingdoms of Parthia or Syria. He had not yet made up his mind which of the two to invade, but, after the fall of Pontus, one or the other was a predestined victim. Having now completed his reorganization of the East, Pompey was naturally anxious to put the crown to an achievement in which no rival could share his glory. He had wealth, power, renown, everything in fact that his heart could desire.

Cæsar, on the other hand, needed to perform prodigies of ingenuity to avoid capsizing, as he navigated his small craft among the democratic rapids. In the early months of the year 64, Crassus had revived his old project of securing the election of two Consuls pledged to favour his designs; and, of course, it was once more Cæsar who was to play the most hazardous part in the enterprise. There were seven candidates for the Consulship of 63. They were Publius Sulpicius Galba and Caius Licinius Sacerdos, two honest but not particularly influential nobles; Caius Antonius Hybrida, who had held command under Sulla and been accused of extortion by Cæsar in 77, and who now came before the electors burdened with debt and with all his possessions mortgaged; Quintus Cornificius and Lucius Cassius Longinus, who were out of the running, and finally Cicero and Catiline. Catiline was a man of great ability, but exceedingly unscrupulous in his ambitions and violent in his methods, who had been attracted to the popular party by the intrigue of which he had been the victim in 65.

A contest between so miscellaneous a selection of candidates at so critical a moment was foredoomed to be intricate and full of surprises. Cicero at first lost heart on seeing that the Conservatives preferred the claims of the two nobles to those of an interloper like himself, who was compromised by relations with the popular party; and he had serious thoughts of joining forces with Catiline, with whom he was personally acquainted, although he was in no way his friend. But Crassus and Cæsar were too quick for him. Catiline, with his unsleeping energy and bitterness against the Conservatives, and Antonius, who was too unprincipled and too penurious to reject a golden opportunity, were exactly the instruments that they needed. They therefore made terms with these two and prepared to lend them vigorous support as the Democratic candidates for the Consulship. It looked as if Cicero, who had reached his other offices by the unanimous consent of all parties, would, for once, be unanimously rejected. But the Conservatives were so alarmed by the prospect of two Consuls pledged to Crassus' designs, that in order to have a serious candidate to set against Catiline, they offered their support to the parvenu. Abandoned by his own party, Cicero, who had for some time been growing disgusted with the excesses of the Democrats, readily consented to become the candidate of the Conservatives, without realizing the dangers which, in a system of party government, threaten an honest politician who suddenly changes his party allegiance.

Both parties now put forth all their strength. Catiline spent a great deal of his own and a great deal more of Crassus' money; Cæsar used his utmost efforts to help Catiline and the ex-general of Sulla whom he had accused thirteen years before; and Crassus mobilized his army of clients, freedmen and defaulting tenants. For once the public was thoroughly excited, and the elections passed off in the midst of a huge agitation. The result bore witness to the perplexity of the voters. Neither of the two parties was triumphant, but neither was entirely defeated. Catiline, the most dangerous of the popular candidates, was beaten, but Antonius was successful, with Cicero for his colleague. But in any case Crassus had once more been checkmated; for it was of no use to him to have only one of the Consuls on his side, particularly as that one was the less capable of his two nominees.

After this excitement a brief truce intervened, and public attention was again directed upon Pompey, who had at last made up his mind for the invasion of Syria. The majority of his staff had strongly urged him to carry out the old designs of Lucullus upon Parthia. Perhaps Pompey, who was less of a genius but a wiser man than Lucullus, had some inkling that the task of conquering the Parthian Empire was beyond his strength, and beyond the strength of Rome. If so, it is a remarkable proof of his penetration. But there are several small facts which indicate that he had not as yet, in 64, so clear a vision of the real conditions, and that he continued to hesitate between his dislike of leaving the glory of overrunning Parthia to another and his fear of risking his life in an over-hazardous adventure. This, at any rate, seems the best explanation of his curious military dispositions. He divided his army into two bodies, one of which was to enter Syria under his orders by the safe route through Cilicia, while the other, under the command of Lucius Afranius, was to occupy Gordiene and then to meet him in Syria, after passing through Mesopotamia, which was a province of the Parthian Empire. This violation of Parthian territory was a deliberate provocation, and it was no doubt intended as a concession to the party which demanded war with Parthia. Unwilling to declare war openly, Pompey contented himself with making a military demonstration to show the peoples of the East that he had no fear of Parthia and would not shrink in case of need from undertaking a campaign. These were still the aggressive tactics of Lucullus; but they had degenerated by passing into feeble hands. Pompey no longer struck quick and boldly like his master; he preferred a more cautious game of fence and parry.

Despite its ingenuity, this strategy proved unsuccessful. Afranius was very nearly lost with the whole of his army in Mesopotamia, which he rashly invaded without trustworthy guides or accurate knowledge or adequate preparation. But Pompey, who had been clever enough to reserve the easier part of the enterprise for himself, accomplished his task without risk or hardship. The old kingdom of the Seleucids, once a great and conquering power, was now broken up into a large number of rival principalities, no single one of which had the courage or the forces to resist the Roman invader. Pompey had only to show his face to be recognized as master. He sent troops into Phœnicia and Cœlesyria to occupy Damascus, under the command of Aulus Gabinius and Marcus Æmilius Scaurus, son of that Marcus Æmilius Scaurus who, himself son of a coal-merchant, had become *Princeps Senatus*. Then he proceeded to make a distribution of kingdoms and territories. He gave Commagene to Antiochus, whom Lucullus had already made King of Syria, declared Seleucia a free city, and promised protection to Antioch in return for a large sum which it had paid him. He showed generosity towards the King of Osroene and the Chief of the Ituræan Arabs. Finally, under the pretext that the national dynasty was extinct, he declared Syria a Roman province with the obligation of paying a tribute of one-twentieth of its revenues. Pompey had thus, like Lucullus, added immense new provinces to the Roman Empire.

Meanwhile new troubles had broken out in his rear. Provoked by the march of Afranius, yet not daring to attack Pompey himself, King Phraates had declared war upon the King of Armenia. Tigranes sent to Pompey for aid. Many of his officers again urged Pompey to invade Parthia and incorporate it in the Empire. But if the march of Afranius had caused alarm to Phraates, his narrow escape had made a very lively impression upon Pompey. Rejecting the foolhardy counsels of his officers he decided to adopt a more reasonable attitude towards the King of Parthia and to curb his own ambitions. He contented himself with despatching three commissioners to decide the questions which had risen between the two kings. Meanwhile Scaurus and Gabinius had found a perfect gold-mine in Judæa, where a Civil War was raging between two members of the royal family of the Asmonæans, Aristobulus and Hyrcanus. Both had sent appeals to the Roman generals to ask for their assistance. It was granted to Aristobulus on payment of nearly two millions to Scaurus and nearly a million and a half to Gabinius.

While conquest thus succeeded conquest in some of the richest regions of the world, no one suspected that at three score and ten and in the depths of the Crimea, Mithridates still dreamt of renewing the enterprise of Hannibal. He had spent the whole of the year 64 in recruiting a small army. His plan of campaign showed all or more than all his old audacity. He intended to march along the north coast of the Black Sea, attracting the Sarmatians and Bastarnæ to his standard as he passed, thence up the valley of the Danube, where the Celts would join him; then, crossing Pannonia, he would hurl himself at the head of a powerful army into the plain of Italy. What induced him to adopt this extraordinary plan? It is just possible that he may have kept himself informed from the Crimea of the situation in Italy or that he hoped to rekindle the social war by inflaming the passions of the two parties at Rome. We shall probably be safer in attributing his scheme to the ambition or monomania of a veteran campaigner who refused to submit to his destiny. We are not in a position to decide. But this much is certain. If Mithridates had been in constant communication with Italy, he could only have been inspired with a fresh energy for his project.

Meanwhile the Italians were as unconscious as Pompey and his Syrian army of this storm cloud in the North. All eyes were now turned upon the wild and confused social conflict which was being fought out under the shadow of the Capitol. The truce which followed the elections did not last for long. It was probably during November that a report began to circulate through Rome which produced lively excitement in all classes. The Tribunes of the people were said to be preparing a Land Bill. The rumour was significant. Since Sulla's Dictatorship, no one at Rome had even ventured to mention the name of a Land Bill. The popular party must be very confident of its strength to be rekindling a brand that had already so often been snatched from its grasp. Soon afterwards men saw the Tribunes, and more especially the projected proposer of the Bill, a certain Publius Rullus, adopting strange disguises, appearing in public with dishevelled hair and unshorn beard, and dressed in rags. This masquerading was a still more ominous symptom. The measure must be revolutionary indeed if the Tribunes began courting the worst section of the electorate by adopting its dress. But great as was the excitement among the Conservatives, it was nothing to that felt by Cicero.

Cicero was an artist of the first rank, an incomparable writer, a man of delicate sensibility, lively imagination and strong and subtle intellect, whose supreme ambition was not to amass wealth or to exercise authority over his equals, but to win admiration. Apart from these great intellectual qualities and this characteristic ambition, he reproduced the distinctive traits which centuries of submission had imprinted on the Italian middle class from which he sprung. He had the same frugal and cautious habits, the same almost morbid disdain for luxury, combined with great strictness in private life, strong family affections, and a somewhat exaggerated respect for aristocracy and wealth. The public life of his time, with its violence and its unrealities, its bitterness and its treachery, with the cynical opportunism and frivolous ostentation of its leading men, and the avowed self-interest and unscrupulousness of its parties, offended against all his deeper instincts. So well, indeed, had he realized this himself that he had hitherto been quite satisfied to remain the greatest orator and lawyer in Rome, and had only sought public office because he had obtained it unopposed.

Thus Cicero had calculated upon his Consulship as a pleasant continuation of this tranquil career and as a graceful recognition of his eminent services to literature. If he had accepted the support of the Conservatives, he had not in the least desired to compromise his popularity with the people. He wished to preserve, even as Consul, his privileged place in public life as a statesman above party. Unfortunately the impending Land Bill involved a policy of this sort in a serious dilemma. However conciliatory his attitude, it would scarcely be possible to please all parties. Confident in his prestige, Cicero was at least prepared to try. He visited the Tribunes and told them that he too was desirous of doing something useful for the people and that they might very well work in common. To his unfeigned surprise, his advances were by no means welcomed. The Tribunes, not without a certain pointed irony, refused to give him any information about the projected Bill and declared that they had no need of his services. After this rebuff, Cicero was forced to wait for the details of the Bill until, towards the end of December, Rullus read it out to the people. The law was more complicated and revolutionary than its predecessors upon similar lines, and contained many clauses whose obscure terminology was very alarming. It instituted a sort of economic Dictatorship of ten commissioners chosen by the seventeen tribes for five years with full powers, and exempt from the Tribunician Veto.

These commissioners had power to sell, both in and outside Italy, all property that had fallen in to the State in and after the year 88, together with all property whose sale had been discussed in the Senate since the year 81. They had also power to make an inventory of the booty of all generals with the exception of Pompey, to force them to give back what they had taken, and with the money accruing from these sales and from the spoils of the generals, to buy land in Italy to distribute among the poor.

Cicero guessed at once, and rightly, that Rullus was acting in the interests of Crassus and Cæsar. It is quite impossible that at a time when Crassus and Cæsar were controlling the policy of the popular party, an obscure Tribune should have been bold enough to propose so revolutionary a law without the secret support of his chiefs. Moreover it is difficult to see what aim the Tribune could have had in proposing such a law upon his own initiative. It is probable that Crassus and Cæsar were pursuing a double end. They were endeavouring at once to rob Cicero of his popularity and to raise anew, under a different form, the great question of Egypt. Once elected commissioners, Cæsar and Crassus would be able to declare that amongst the property that had fallen into the State since the year 88 were the possessions of the Ptolemies, which had been bequeathed with the kingdom of Egypt by Alexander II in 81; by making use of the enormous powers of corruption that the Land Law placed in their hands they could then make war upon Egypt to recover them. They might expect the people at last to conjure up some enthusiasm for the annexation of Egypt, when it knew that the profits to be derived from it would be used for buying up land.

Once this is explained, it is easy to understand why Crassus and Cæsar had the Bill proposed by a Tribune instead of openly coming forward as its promoters. A Bill so revolutionary in its scope wounded too many susceptibilities and alarmed too many interests. The Conservatives saw in the new commissioners a sort of disguised Dictatorship of the Democratic chiefs. It was resented by the generals who amassed large fortunes in the recent wars, by the tax-farmers who had had leased public lands in Bithynia and Pontus, the sale of which would come under discussion, by all those, in short, who had profited most from the conquests of Lucullus and Pompey, and who were now to be despoiled for the benefit of the distressed proletariat. The result of the conflict which was inevitable before such a law could be approved must have appeared so dubious that neither Crassus nor Cæsar was willing to set his reputation and prospects at stake. Indeed the Conservatives and the wealthy classes took up the struggle with enthusiasm. They began by exaggerating the revolutionary aspect of the law. They declared that it would entail a general liquidation of the State property, because the commissioners would include in it the public estates in Greece and Asia, on the pretext that these provinces had been reconquered by Sulla after 88. Attempts were made to frighten all who had bought the goods of persons proscribed by Sulla by persuading them that the law would be enforced against their property. Some colour was lent to this assertion by a proposal of Rullus to annul the civic penalties pronounced by Sulla against the sons of the proscribed. In spite of his desire to stand well with all parties, Cicero was thus forced to defend the interests of his friends the knights and the cause of Conservatism.

This was the first great encounter of his Consulship, and he emerged with flying colours. Cæsar and Crassus were profoundly mistaken in thinking that a Bill of so serious and revolutionary a character had any chance of being proposed with success by an obscure and incapable Tribune—a man of straw who had neither the prestige nor the ability to counteract such a combination of interests. Nobles, knights and generals, all prospective victims of the law, joined vigorously in the campaign, and the Tribunes were unable either to baffle their intrigues or to stir the unruffled composure of the people. By their reluctance to throw themselves openly into the struggle Cæsar and Crassus had done no more than provide the Consul with a magnificent opening for his gifts. Cicero secured the rejection of the Bill at the Assembly by the delivery of two orations, pitched in his most democratic key, in which he declared that his ambition was to be a great popular Consul, and gave himself out as a sincere admirer of the Gracchi and the old Land Laws, which had been truly designed for the good of the people. He declared that he opposed the measure of Rullus because it was contrary to the popular interest and injured rather than assisted the prosperity of the poorer classes.

Cæsar and Crassus thus had once more received a check. But they were far from being ready to acknowledge defeat; there were other questions to be raised which might yet serve to inflame the passions of the people and cause Cicero greater embarrassment to dismiss. One after the other the Tribunes of the people introduced revolutionary proposals. One Tribune demanded nothing less than the abolition of all debts; another desired that the penalties pronounced against Publius Autronius and Publius Sulla, the conspirators of 66, should be revoked. Yet all these attempts seemed somehow to miss fire. No one was prepared to take this sort of proposal seriously, and the appeals of the Tribunes fell upon deaf ears.

Yet Cæsar and Crassus had not entirely misjudged the situation. These feints and manœuvres, if they effected nothing else, increased the exasperation of the Conservatives and the general feeling of insecurity among all classes in the community. Money, scarce enough at ordinary times, became dearer and dearer. Many debtors found themselves in the gravest embarrassment. According to the severe regulations which were then in use regarding mortgage, if the debtor was unable punctually to meet his obligations, the creditor was entitled to take possession of the property mortgaged, even if it were two or three times the value of the amount lent. Many people who were unable to raise the money necessary to pay off their interest or reimburse the capital they had borrowed, were forced to part at ridiculous prices with their lands, their houses, their jewels, or their works of art. There was a rapid fall in prices throughout the market from which all classes suffered in varying degrees. Among those who felt it most were the rich Senators who were no longer able to raise the large sums necessary for the complicated administration of their huge hereditary estates.

All this led to the outbreak of a lively agitation, not only among the politicians of the Conservative party, but among the whole of the wealthy class. The responsibility for the depression was thought to rest with the Tribunes and their masters; but, if Crassus was shielded by his wealth, no such consideration was felt for the unhappy Cæsar. Cæsar was poor, he was unpopular, and he was deeply in debt. Moreover he had no powerful relatives to stand by him. It is probable that the aristocratic connections that he had made by his marriage were by now gradually falling away from his side. As to the members of his own family, they continued to ally their fortunes with parvenus in hopes of recovering some of the money wasted by Cæsar's extravagance. It was probably with this object that one of his nieces had lately married a certain Caius Octavius, the wealthy son of a usurer at Velletri, who was using his father's fortune to make friends in Roman society and to pave the way for a political career. It was therefore simple enough to spare Crassus and reserve all the stripes for Cæsar. This convenient and satisfactory operation was so frequently performed as to give rise to the very natural question: was not Cæsar actually paid by Crassus to bare his back for a double share of the whippings?

It is probably this year that marks the invention of the first Cæsar legend, the story in which, by no very exaggerated process of distortion, Cæsar appears as the representative of all that most shocked the old Latin conscience in the "new manners." No doubt he was in debt: but Conservative gossip made his liabilities mount up to fabulous figures: men talked of millions. Again, Cæsar had, of course, realized what enormous power was dispensed by the women of his day in the family circle, and he had certainly tried to make friends with the wives of Crassus, Pompey, Gabinius, and the other popular chiefs; he was a frequent guest, for instance, at the house of Servilia, the widow of the Marcus Junius Brutus who perished in the revolution of 78, and sister of Cato, a clever and influential woman who had found a second husband in Decimus Julius Silanus. None of these women, with the exception of Pompey's wife, Mucia, appear to have been his mistress. Yet, in Conservative gossip, the legend of Cæsar's amours soon took its place beside the legend of his debts, and he was accused of carrying on intrigues simultaneously with Servilia and with the wives of Pompey, Crassus, and Gabinius, in short with the wives of all the leaders of the popular party. His relations with Mucia were the subject of particularly biting sarcasms. It was now clear as daylight why Cæsar had been so enthusiastic in his support of the Gabinian and Manilian laws. All that he wanted was to despatch on a distant mission the husband of the fair but fickle Mucia. Cæsar had in fact become for the Conservatives the incarnation of all the new abominations of the time: the young libertine who gains his ends through women, the unscrupulous bankrupt, whose debts drive him into crime, the adventurer who to satisfy his greed and ambition is prepared to go the length of overturning the commonwealth. Yet legend may sometimes assume the importance of history; and the absurd exaggerations of his enemies were gradually to drive Cæsar to transform some of these imaginary vices into the real revolutionary forces of his age.

These attacks put Cæsar on his mettle. He was indeed in a position of real danger. If the agitation were to provoke the outbreak of disorders and the Senate were prevailed upon to decree a state of siege, he might easily perish like the Gracchi and Saturninus. The contemplation of the fate that had befallen his forerunners in the party could not help causing their natural successor, both in policy and popularity, the liveliest disquiet. Cæsar with his energy, his quickness of apprehension and his extraordinary lucidity of judgment, at once saw the line of safety. His best defence was to startle his opponents by some stroke of propagandist daring. But to do this successfully he must shift his ground. He must abandon the field of economic reform and Land legislation for a more purely political issue. This would not only be less dangerous in itself, but it would give far greater scope for a genuine popular agitation; it was never difficult to stir the jealous and ignorant proletariat against the aristocrats.

He succeeded in trumping up a political question of a very curious kind. In an obscure corner of Rome there lived an old Senator named Caius Rabirius, who was said to have killed with his own hand a Tribune of the people, thirty-seven years before, at the time of the riots of Saturninus. Of course there was no one who still remembered the details. Cæsar hunted him out and suddenly had him accused of *perduellio* by a certain Titus Atius Labienus, a newcomer in politics, who was one of his adherents and was at that time Tribune of the people. He then secured that the Prætor, also an accomplice, should send the case before two judges, of whom he himself would be one. Rabirius was of course declared guilty; and the penalty for *perduellio* was death. The Conservatives were stirred to action, quite as much by Cæsar's unheard-of audacity as by anxiety for the fate of the unfortunate old Senator. Rabirius appealed to the people, and Cicero readily undertook his defence. In tones of impassioned eloquence he told the people that the object aimed at in the agitation was not the head of the unhappy Rabirius, but the weakening of all ties that held together the established order, so as to pave the way more easily for a complete overthrow of the State. But the people, who had remained cold over the Land Law, were now thoroughly in earnest; the memories of the great revolution had stirred their blood, and Rabirius would certainly have been condemned if a Prætor had not hit upon an ingenious excuse for dissolving the assembly. Cæsar, who was not thirsting for the life-blood of Rabirius, let the old man go in peace. His object had been fully attained. He had cooled the enthusiasm that the Conservatives had been displaying for a state of siege and "short work with the demagogues," and he had shown them how easy it was, even after a lapse of thirty-seven years, to excite the anger of the people against the mere suggestion of Sullan methods.

About this time the post of Pontifex Maximus became vacant through the death of Metellus Pius. It was a lifelong office, the holder of which had the supreme direction of the official religion and the privilege of living in a public residence. The right of electing the Pontifex had been taken away from the people by Sulla and restored to the College of Pontiffs. Cæsar conceived the idea of reintroducing, by a law which Labienus was to propose, the popular election of the Pontifex Maximus and of coming forward himself as candidate. If he succeeded in becoming the head of the established religion, a Consul would scarcely dare to make away with him in a massacre on the proclamation of a state of siege. There were several distinguished personages, amongst others Catulus and Publius Servilius Isauricus, standing for the office. These eminent persons thought it an excellent jest when they heard that a man under forty, a bankrupt atheist, mixed up with all the demagogues in Rome, and a devotee of the astronomy of Hipparchus, was a candidate with them for so blamelessly Conservative a post. Catulus even ventured to insult Cæsar by offering him money for the abandonment of his candidature. The suggestion that he was no more than a common hireling touched Cæsar to the quick. He threw himself into the conflict with the impetuosity of a man who feels that his whole career is at stake, and assisted by the substantial advances of Crassus and by his skill fought his campaign so successfully, that the mode of election was changed, and he was finally elected Pontifex Maximus.

CHAPTER XII

CATILINE

THE Conservatives found some slight consolation in a small success. They at length succeeded in passing a decree for the triumph of Lucullus. The Proconsul was allowed to enter Rome at the head of his soldiers. But in spite of the hundred thousand barrels of wine which he distributed among the people to celebrate the occasion, it was a frigid and cheerless ceremony. One would have thought that it was only some obscure commander returning from a paltry expedition against barbarians and not the teacher of the new imperialism now so much in vogue, and the originator of the conquests and the glories of Pompey. But Lucullus cared little for the noise of notoriety. After ten years in the East he re-entered his father's house disgusted with mankind, deaf to the plaudits of the masses, and prepared to find a congenial reward for his achievements in the enjoyment of his riches and the respectful admiration of his peers.

In the spring of this same year a petty revolution rid the fortunate Pompey of Mithridates. His son Pharnaces, his own soldiers and the people of the Crimea, alarmed by his project for the invasion of Italy, turned against the heroic old monarch and forced him to commit suicide.

Thus ended a man who to the ability, the energy and the daring of a self-made adventurer united the unmeasured pride and the unchallenged egoism of an Eastern potentate. Like Hannibal before him, he had risked his life on a single-handed struggle against Rome and Italy. But once again the single fighter, powerful though he was, and in spite of the encouragement of opening successes, retired broken before the forces of a system. As Hannibal had failed to beat down the Roman aristocracy strengthened by centuries of national life, so Mithridates had failed to beat down the young and vigorous Italian people. In vain had he conceived the audacious project of destroying his enemy by kindling all round her, throughout the Mediterranean and in Italy itself, the most extensive and devastating outburst of revolution that the ancient world had ever seen. The son of the man who had dreamed of being the Emperor of the East was content to accept, as a gift from the conqueror, the petty principality of the Crimea. Genius had once more to succumb before organization, before the concerted action of those manifold political and military forces in which, despite the shock and havoc of crisis after crisis, Italy was still so powerful.

The news of Mithridates' death was received at Rome with clamorous rejoicings. It formed a new title of glory for Pompey, to whom the popular party gave credit for every success in those regions. Cæsar hastened to urge the people to decree the most solemn honours in his favour. Then the reports from the East again began to grow monotonous. Pompey was traversing Phœnicia and Cœlesyria, taking ransom from the petty chieftains. He had met with no resistance except from a small town called Jerusalem amongst a petty nation with whom the Romans had since the year 139 been on amicable terms. But the difficulty which faced Pompey here was a mere trifle. The two monarchs of the Jews, who were engaged in fighting one another and from whom Scaurus and Gabinius had already extracted their pile of treasures, had now had recourse to Pompey. After some hesitation, and on the promise of a substantial sum, Pompey had decided to come to the assistance of Aristobulus; but when Gabinius came to Jerusalem to fetch the money, a popular outbreak compelled him to fly, and Pompey had been forced to lay siege to the city.

The public had no time to pay attention to this little war, for the political struggle in Italy was now growing greatly in violence. The year 63 was to be a year of Conservative panics. Already in the spring they witnessed the arrival in Rome of a prospective candidate for the Tribuneship in Quintus Metellus Nepos, brother-in-law of Pompey, and one of his generals. This Metellus was son of the Consul of 98, nephew of the conqueror of the Balearic Islands, and great-nephew of Metellus Macedonicus. He thus belonged to one of the greatest families in Rome, but like many other members of the aristocracy he had followed Pompey, in the hope of hastening his promotion and filling his coffers. The numerous escort of slaves and baggage animals which came home with him showed that his second object at least had been successfully achieved.

The arrival of Metellus produced a great sensation among the

Conservatives. It was generally thought that he was pursuing his candidature in concert with Pompey, and that Pompey must therefore have some special object in view. Men anxiously enquired what this object might be. So great was the disquietude that it was decided to put forward a Conservative candidate for the Tribuneship, a thing which had not been done for years. But what Conservative was ready to face the risks of an almost desperate contest? Among the Conservatives as among the Democrats, there was no great store of earnest and honourable partisans. In default of a better candidate it was decided to fall back on a man for whom the Conservatives entertained a distrust not unmixed with ridicule—on Cato, that isolated and whimsical figure whom we have already seen protesting against the fashionable elegance of his contemporaries. He was a man of narrow views but unswerving consistency, upright, virtuous, inflexible, without fear and without reproach, an enemy of compromise on any question and with any person. It was only his supreme contempt for his opponents that could have induced this most obscurantist of Conservatives to attempt the incongruous enterprise of standing just now for so popular an office as the Tribuneship. But the danger from Metellus was pressing, and Cæsar too had just announced his candidature for the Prætorship. Here were two great reasons for alarm; and a third soon came to reinforce them.

Catiline was once more standing as candidate for the Consulship, and garnishing his *menu* to meet the public taste. He promised, if elected, to propose a measure dispensing all debtors from paying their creditors. It cannot be denied that this savoured somewhat of revolution: yet it is mistaken to regard it as a deliberate preparation for what afterwards developed into the famous conspiracy. Catiline was still simply trying to court popularity by a proposal which, detestable though it appeared to creditors, was far from displeasing to the majority of citizens, a proposal which, however violent and categorical in form, was not very different from that of a Socialist member to-day who should promise his electors to reduce the interest on the national debt to 2 per cent. The reduction and abolition of debt had been frequent incidents in the history of Greece, which was being so closely studied at Rome at this time. Nor was it unknown even in the Roman annals, from the very earliest times down to the last attempt in 86. Moreover it is an expedient to which all nations tend periodically to recur when they find themselves staggering beneath the weight of their obligations. Catiline was in fact merely following up the Democratic propaganda of Crassus and Cæsar by the selection of a project no more revolutionary, but simpler and more definite, than the Land Bill of Rullus. This time there would be no misunderstanding among the electorate. The plain offer to relieve them from their debts could not fail to rouse them.

It is highly probable, though there is no evidence for the supposition, that Catiline first endeavoured to act in concert with Cæsar and Crassus, but failed to arrive at a satisfactory agreement. No reasons are preserved to us for his ill-success. It may be that Crassus and Cæsar, disillusioned by the fate of the Land Bill, despaired of attaining their objects by so dangerous a means. It must never be forgotten that Crassus was one of the greatest creditors in Rome. It is likely enough that, placed in the dilemma of risking either the loss of his money or the failure of his pet project, he made up his mind to postpone Egypt once more.

Catiline was forced to proceed by himself. He threw himself into the battle with the energy of despair, resolved, if necessary, to expend the whole of his fortune. The experiment of launching his revolutionary propaganda into a society already seething with discontent was instantaneously successful. His proposal so exactly harmonized with the secret desires of a large section of the population that their author leapt at once into unexpected popularity. He found ardent and enthusiastic supporters in the most diverse quarters—amongst the dissipated youth and the decadent aristocracy of Rome, among the poor in all parts of Italy, and even among the middle class of well-to-do proprietors, whom the passion for speculation had driven deep into debt. Where Rullus had only ruffled the surface, Catiline moved society to the depths. It was not long before he had gathered round him a band of devoted partisans at Rome and in many of the towns of Italy; old soldiers and settlers of Sulla's army, like Caius Manlius from Fiesole, inglorious prodigals from the middle classes, well-to-do landlords from small country towns, needy nobles like Publius Lentulus Sura, Caius Cethegus, Publius Sulla, Marcus Portius Læca and Sempronia, an extravagant and fashionable lady in the best society, the wife of Decimus Brutus, the Consul of 77—in short a whole company of light-headed adventurers, who set themselves to the task of expropriating the rich as though it were the easiest thing in the world, to be carried through in peace and comfort by the constitutional method of legislation, approved by the majority of the electors.

This pleasant illusion was soon to be dispelled. The danger of an abolition of debt seemed so stupendous that it grouped together in a coalition two bodies of men who had for the last half-century regarded one another with distrust and contempt. It provoked an alliance between the knights and the respectable aristocrats, who still clung to the wealth and the traditions of older days. The capitalists had at first regarded the whole movement with contempt. But when they saw how it gained ground with the people, they began to feel uncomfortable. Before long discomfort had developed into anxiety, anxiety into dismay and even into panic. The whole political situation thus underwent a complete transformation. Goaded on by their fears, the knights threw off their habitual indifference to politics, and declared themselves ready to give help by all means in their power to the party which stood for the defence of law and property. The group of respectable aristocrats, though scarcely threatened by the law of Catiline, readily joined hands with the wealthy knights, partly out of a vague feeling for order and security, partly through their detestation of a propaganda which aimed at uprooting all established institutions. A coalition was thus speedily formed which had for its object, not merely the defeat of Catiline at the elections, but also, as it was said, the re-establishment of the reign of authority, tranquillity and order in a State infested by the upholders of robbery, sedition, and crime.

Catiline and his supporters had thus to face a far greater resistance than they had ever expected. Yet, unfortunately for the coalition, the very excess of their precautions had tended rather to intensify the perils that they apprehended. In the midst of all this excitement trade and enterprise were at a standstill; money grew alarmingly dear and the failure of debtors became increasingly frequent. But this only provided fresh material for the propaganda of Catiline and gave debtors a more lively sense of the necessity of a revolution. The capital and the country were soon reduced to a state of absolute chaos, during which Crassus took fright and disappeared from Rome and Cæsar discreetly kept aloof from affairs.

Cicero would have been glad enough to behave likewise; but his position as Consul allowed him no choice. Once more he found himself in an exceedingly embarrassing situation. No doubt the coalition of all the respectable classes was a great encouragement to stand firm against Catiline and his agitation. But he could not help knowing that Catiline enjoyed considerable support among the mass of the people, whose admiration he was very reluctant to sacrifice. He made up his mind that if he opposed Catiline—as he must—he would do so rather by indirect means than by an open declaration of war. He therefore began by purchasing the neutrality of his colleague by surrendering to him his own province of Macedonia; and then proceeded to draw up a Bill increasing the severity of the penalties for corruption and modifying the methods of voting in a manner that would be disadvantageous to Catiline. A well-known lawyer, Servius Sulpicius, was entrusted with the drafting of this measure.

Such was the situation when, towards the beginning of July, amid general uncertainty, the electoral campaign was set on foot. The Conservatives were angry, the middle class doubtful and wavering, the popular party openly divided against itself. Besides Catiline there were three other candidates for the Consulship: Servius Sulpicius, who had drawn up the Electoral Bill, Lucius Licinius Murena, an ex-general of Lucullus, and Decimus Junius Silanus, the husband of Servilia. Crassus seems to have given his support to Murena, while Cæsar entered the lists for Silanus, and Cato for Sulpicius. Disquieting rumours soon began to circulate. It was said that Catiline was summoning Sulla's veterans from Etruria for the elections: that, if they came, they would shrink from nothing, not even from the assassination of Cicero. The truth was simply that Catiline had brought up bands of peasants from the neighbourhood of Arezzo and Fiesole to swell the ranks of his supporters. It can easily be imagined what popular report, among Italians, and at a time of unusual excitement, contrived to build up out of this simple circumstance. Everyone in Rome had his own version of the tale, and everyone was anxious to outdo his neighbour in divulging it. Men exaggerated what they had been told, declared they had seen what they had only heard, and added a wealth of picturesque detail, till, after passing through some thousands of mouths, what had originally been hazarded as a flimsy conjecture reappeared as a substantial and detailed narrative. Rome was full of people who had heard, or had seen, or knew for certain, and could not contain themselves from telling all they knew. In an unwonted epidemic of civic zeal many ran off to give full information to the magistrates, in the vague desire of emphasizing their own share in the general commotion and of posing not as simple spectators but as important actors in the drama of the hour.

In political circles these rumours were much discussed and very varying estimates formed as to their meaning. The Conservatives not only accepted the entire story, but insisted on denouncing as accomplices all who ventured to question its credibility. In the popular party, on the other hand, there was a general inclination, even among the Senators, to dismiss the whole tale as a wild fiction. Meanwhile the elections were at hand and popular excitement was still steadily rising. Money had been lavishly distributed by Cæsar, by Metellus, by Catiline, and by Murena, who had come back wealthy from the East. Bands of peasants and labourers brought up by Catiline were entering the city daily, whilst the Conservatives and the capitalists were straining every nerve against his candidature. Day by day the reports grew more alarming. It was said that soldiers were being enrolled in Etruria at Catiline's cost, that a general insurrection in imitation of Lepidus was being prepared, and that Catiline was bent on a wholesale massacre of the Senate.

The forecasts became more and more uncertain. The ominous rumours of civil war, the violence of the Conservative campaign and the acute financial depression had done much to frighten the middle-class proprietors. But Catiline was meeting with considerable success in his appeal to the desperate and discontented classes at Rome; and he was calling the whole proletariat population of Italy to the metropolis. The Conservatives grew daily more insecure. They continued to repeat their story that the Republic was being threatened by a widespread conspiracy, in which not only Catiline but also Cæsar and the whole of the Democratic party were concerned. Angry spirits amongst them began to cry out for stern measures. Cicero did his best to give his new-found allies proof of his anxiety for the maintenance of order. He listened to every report and followed up every clue. There was hardly an hour in the day when he was not giving audience to professional spies, or to informers not yet initiated into that odious brotherhood. He made it his business to credit all the rumours unfavourable to Catiline, and there was scarcely a sitting of the Senate in which, reinforced by Cato, he did not attack Catiline for corruption and threaten him with a prosecution. But he steadily refused to move a single step further. He was not so blind as to be unaware that the matter was still in the region of suspicion and presumption, and that no such substantial evidence had as yet come into his hands as would justify him in the adoption of drastic measures.

An unforeseen incident now intervened still further to complicate an already perplexing situation. Servius, the lawyer who had drafted the Electoral Bill, had put himself forward for the Consulship, but, keeping strictly within the terms of his own Bill, was refusing to expend any money on his candidature. Unfortunately, amongst a number of candidates who were lavish with their funds, nobody was disposed to pay serious attention to a politician who behaved as if his precious law were really intended to be observed. Servius was so disgusted at this treatment that, in the very midst of the electoral campaign, he announced his intention of withdrawing his candidature and prosecuting Murena for bribery. He set to work on the collection of evidence for his charge with the assistance of Cato, who was indignant that the best of the Conservative candidates should be excluded from the contest.

A scandal of this sort on the very eve of the voting disheartened the Conservatives and was a great encouragement to Catiline. In the confidence of impending victory he delivered a great speech a few days before the election telling the voters that it was now futile for the poor to rely upon the rich for the improvement of their lot. Cicero, bent upon wrecking the candidature of Catiline, but without exposing himself to unpopularity and with the semblance of having popular interests at heart, was soon forced to take the field against his enemy with some more serious accusation than an absurd charge of corruption. It is possible that the peasants brought up by Catiline to vote, many of whom were accompanied by Sullan veterans, may have let fall some imprudent remarks, as they sat chattering in the taverns at Catiline's expense. It is likely enough that the old Sullan Manlius waxed sarcastic against a timid and vainglorious breed of talkers who harboured new-fangled constitutional scruples and relied on legislative action for the abolition of debt. The survivor of a generation of revolutions could tell them that the only way to free debtors was the short way with the sword. All this was skilfully exaggerated by the Conservatives, and Cicero made use of it to disguise his hostility to Catiline under the all-embracing pretext of national defence. He pretended that it was not the man of the people whom he was fighting, but the felon from whom even Cæsar and Crassus had held openly aloof, the enemy of the public peace who had vowed to make the metropolis a scene of fire and carnage. But would the electors attach sufficient credence to these reports? Would the tide of indignation rise high enough for Catiline to be submerged?

Yielding most probably to pressure from the Conservative chiefs, Cicero prepared a master-stroke which was to give the death-blow to Catiline's candidature. On the day before the date fixed for the elections he suddenly convened the Senate and, with a great parade of solemnity, demanded that the voting should be postponed for several days in order that an inquiry might be held next day on the dangers which threatened the life of the State. On the following day he gave an elaborate and emphatic recital of all the reports which were current as to Catiline's intentions and practically challenged Catiline to clear himself, in the hope of extracting some compromising confession. Catiline replied, with laconic insolence, that his intention was to become the head of the sole vigorous organ which still existed in the State—the people.

Cicero's manœuvre had failed, and it was now necessary to proceed with the elections, which took place in the last days of July or the first days of August. On the morning of the voting the result was still so uncertain that both sides made unprecedented exertions to bring up supporters. Cicero took his place as President of the Assembly surrounded by a bodyguard of friends; he was wearing a cuirass which gleamed as he opened his toga. All this was contrived to make an impression upon the public, and particularly upon timid and undecided electors who might possibly be persuaded to vote for Catiline. The neighbouring temples were guarded by soldiers; practically the whole of the equestrian order was mobilized; nobles and knights who had never appeared in the Campus Martius in their lives came with set and anxious faces to the voting booths, followed by a procession of friends and clients. The voting was very close; but once more money had overborne numbers. In spite of the support of the proletariat, Catiline was not elected. Cæsar, however, secured the Prætorship, and Metellus the Tribuneship, but with Cato for a colleague.

There was still one chance open to Catiline. If Murena were condemned in the suit which Sulpicius was bringing against him, the election would have to be fought over again. But Cicero took up Murena's case in an eloquent speech which has come down to us, and Murena was acquitted.

After this third defeat Catiline had no other alternative but to renounce all hopes of the Consulship and retire into private life. Cicero could congratulate himself on having emerged skilfully and honourably from the painful position in which Catiline's candidature had placed him, without sacrifice of his popularity. But Catiline was too proud and violent a nature to acquiesce in defeat. Furious at his discomfiture and dreading reprisals, he took a daring and decisive step. He entrusted Manlius, who was returning to Etruria, with a sum of money, charging him to recruit a small army among the distressed; and he persuaded the most desperate of his partisans, relying on the support of the troops of Manlius, to attempt a *coup d'état* by the assassination of Cicero and the forcible seizure of the Consulship. August and September went by in the preparations for this attempt.

But it was impossible to preserve secrecy during the whole of this time. Before long the comparative tranquillity which had followed on the elections, was ruffled anew with rumours of revolution, and Cicero was again assailed with the familiar outcries and exhortations to take measures in self-defence. What was he to do? Once more he displayed the greatest assiduity in collecting information, but carefully avoided bringing matters to a climax or adopting any measures of severity which might have seemed odious to the people. But the Conservatives were not to be placated. They cried out for the proclamation of a state of siege; and as the rumours of the conspiracy became increasingly definite, they put greater and greater pressure upon the unfortunate

Consul. Cicero, who had long been wavering, was at last moved to action, not only by the agitation among the upper classes, but also by the danger to which he was personally exposed. With everyone round him calling out for drastic repression, he made up his mind to convene the Senate for October 21st, and to give an account of the most serious reports which were then in circulation, declaring them to be substantially true and confirmed by information which he, in his capacity of Consul, had succeeded in procuring. In this way the Senate would be induced to proclaim a state of siege, and the Conservatives would be satisfied. In the sitting of October 21st, at which Catiline boldly put in an appearance, he declared that he "knew all," that he had the most certain proof of the gravest charges that were made against Catiline—which was certainly not the case at that time. Amongst other things he declared that on October 27th, Caius Manlius was to take up arms in Etruria at the head of an army, and that Catiline had fixed the 28th for a massacre of the Senate. Catiline was invited to clear himself, and gave an insolent reply. But the Senate, convinced by the explicit declarations of Cicero (for no one thought it possible that he could make such serious statements without certain proof), no longer ventured to hesitate and a state of siege was proclaimed.

Great was the sensation at Rome when this news became known. Men always tend to judge the present by their memories of the past; and there was a general expectation that, as the time of the Gracchi and of Saturninus, the Consul would be seen calling Senators and knights to arms and making a massacre of the leaders of the popular party. Cæsar must have passed several hours of terrible suspense. But nothing of the sort took place. In spite of the impression caused by the speech of Cicero and the precautions adopted in consequence, the Senators returned quietly to their homes. Nothing more was done except to place garrisons in different parts of the city. The times had changed; and the impetuous passions of a more primitive era no longer held sway. Some of the Senators still boldly affirmed that Cicero was lying Others declared that, the panic once over, the popular party would not leave the murder of its chiefs unavenged. Others had consented to decree the state of siege, but were not really persuaded that the danger was sufficient. Others again were restrained by moral, legal or constitutional scruples. Cicero, who should have given the order putting the decree into execution, was afraid of doing anything which might draw down upon himself the traditional hatred felt for a Nasica or an Opimius, or of posing in any way as a latter-day Sulla. Moreover, the mere threat of coercion now produced upon a sensitive public an effect quite as great as coercion itself in a less civilized epoch. The Conservative party was therefore easily satisfied with the vague threat of martial law, and with a prosecution for assault brought against Catiline by the young Lucius Æmilius Lepidus, another son of the revolutionary chief of 78, who was, however, a member of the aristocratic party.

Yet somehow the agitation in the city did not abate, and the stream of rumours flowed on unchecked. Persons in high position were constantly receiving anonymous letters purporting to contain extraordinary disclosures. Cicero must have felt himself particularly insecure. Conscious that part at least of the revelations he had made before the Senate was untrue, he must have feared that he might have to pay dearer than any of his partisans. He began to be slightly reassured when one day Crassus brought him in a bundle of miscellaneous letters and denunciations which he had received. It was some satisfaction to know that the powerful banker thoroughly believed in the reality of the danger. It was now Catiline's turn to play at bluff. Somewhat discouraged by the universal hostility and suspicion with which he saw himself regarded, he adopted an ingenious stratagem in order to shelter himself and watch for an opportunity of recovering his ground. He paid a visit to Marcus Lepidus and asked him for permission to live in his house. This would show the public that he was so confident in his own innocence that he was not afraid to live under the daily observance of an aristocrat in high position. When Lepidus refused to become his honorary gaoler, Catiline, with still greater hardihood, turned to Cicero for an asylum. When Cicero in his turn rejected him, he appealed to a certain Marcus Marcellus, who took him in.

Impartial members of the public were now completely at sea. Whom were they to believe—Cicero or Catiline? Cicero was certainly a man of distinguished position and recognized integrity. But it was truly singular that after solemnly proclaiming the imminence of a revolution, he took no measures against the man whom he had declared to be its chief. Catiline was no doubt a man of great daring, but was it credible that, if he were maturing a revolution, he would have the effrontery to visit the Consul who accused him and ask him to be so good as to put him up in his house? From time to time there was a lull in the great storm of rumours, and then the suspicion would gain ground that Cicero had invented the whole story. Fortunately for Cicero, official news arrived within a few days that Manlius had shown himself openly in Etruria at the head of a small army; and a short time afterwards letters came in from Manlius himself to Quintus Marcius in which he declared that he and his supporters had taken up arms because they could no longer endure the debts with which they were burdened.

This news caused a tremendous sensation. So Catiline was the knave, and Cicero the model citizen! If the public was excited, the Conservatives went almost wild. There was no time to be lost. This was a genuine Civil War, and "thorough" must be the word. The Senators were thrown completely off their balance. After hesitating for so long, they decided in a fit of nervous hurry to adopt the most extreme measures of precaution. If the whole of Italy had been in revolt they could not have done more. Rewards were promised to all who would give information about the plot. Quintus Metellus, who was still awaiting his Cretan triumph, was sent into Apulia, Quintus Marcius into Etruria, Quintus Pompeius Rufus to Campania, Quintus Metellus Celer to the Marches. Cicero, to his huge surprise and delight, became, within a day and a night, the object of universal admiration. He was thought to have brought to the defence of the Republic an energy and a clear-sightedness that were little short of miraculous.

Yet for all this he did not yet see his way to taking action against Catiline. But Catiline played into his hands. Feeling the sympathies of his few remaining allies slipping from him and watching the violence of his enemies growing daily in intensity, he decided at last to throw off the mask. He seems to have entertained for a moment the plan of making an attack, on November 1st, upon the fortress of Palestrina. When, owing to the vigilance of Cicero, this project had to be abandoned, he escaped the watch of his host and on the night of November 6th, in the house of Læca, assembled a meeting of those of his friends who were most deeply compromised in his schemes. He demonstrated to them the necessity for a universal insurrection throughout Italy to reinforce the movement of Manlius, and gave an outline of his plan, which was to begin with the assassination of Cicero, whom he regarded, like his opponents, as his most formidable enemy. Two knights who were present agreed to visit Cicero next morning and despatch him; but Fulvia, the mistress of Catiline, immediately informed the Consul, who convoked an extraordinary meeting of the Senate on the following day, November 7th. Catiline, unabashed to the last, duly attended the meeting; but at his entry into the room he was shunned by all his colleagues. Alone upon his seat he listened to the violent invective directed against him by Cicero, amidst the applause of the entire Senate. Catiline realized that he had nothing more to hope from the Senators. He rose, uttered a few ominous words, and went out. He left the same evening for Etruria, completely at liberty and with a numerous following. Cicero was so anxious to avoid responsibility for violence that he did not dare to hinder his departure. Rather he rejoiced at his escape, even though it might lead to a Civil War. If Catiline took up arms he would shake off his last defenders and Cicero would once more have extricated himself from all complications amid universal applause.

It is true that Cicero's triumph was not wholly uncontested. A few furious Conservatives boldly maintained that the Consul should have laid hands on Catiline and put him to death, while there was a small number who declared that Catiline had been maligned. But these criticisms hardly touched Cicero, who had now suddenly eclipsed both Cæsar and Crassus and become second only to Pompey, the most popular man in Rome. Unfortunately the struggle was not yet over. Those among Catiline's partisans who were most deeply concerned in his plot, Lentulus, Cethegus, Statilius, Ceparius, lost their nerve after Catiline, the only man of ability in the movement, had left them. They had now been abandoned by the great majority of their supporters, who had expected to secure the abolition of debt by easy and constitutional means, and were in no mood for war and bloodshed. Realizing the danger of their position, they hurriedly pieced together a ridiculous conspiracy on the lines of the plan sketched out by their leader. Their idea was to raise a movement among the proletariat and the slaves, to set light to the city in several quarters at once, and so increase the general disorder at the moment when Catiline was approaching with his army. It was the foolish concoction of men half frightened out of their wits by their danger. The next step was feebler still. They approached certain ambassadors of the Allobroges who had come to Rome to lay some grievances before the Senate, and asked whether their people would consent to come to their assistance with pikemen and cavalry.

This was their supreme mistake. Of course the Allobroges denounced them, and Cicero at last procured written prooofs of their treachery. Acting for once with great rapidity, he had the chief conspirators arrested on the morning of December 3rd, and brought them before the Senate. There he showed them the letters given to the ambassadors for the chieftains of the Allobroges and confronted them with the ambassadors themselves. In their confusion they were all surprised into a confession.

The report of their detection was at once dispersed and distorted in every corner of the city. Rumour declared that there had been a vast conspiracy to burn down Rome and bring the Gauls into Italy. The impressionable metropolis was horror-struck at the suggestion. The public which Cæsar and Crassus had tried in vain to awaken was at length touched to the quick. It had been touched in the year 70: but how changed was the situation seven years later. It was now to the Conservatives that it appealed for help, and appealed so emphatically that even the chiefs of the popular party, even the proletariat itself, always faithful to its demagogues, was carried away in the swirl of the tide. From all sides a great and anxious crowd made its way to the Senate-house to hear the news; and when, at the end of the cross-examination, Cicero made his appearance outside he received a great ovation. That night hardly anyone slept at Rome Men went to visit one another in their houses to ask counsel and comfort, and to nerve themselves for the unknown dangers of the morrow. The Conservatives, at once angry and exultant, were chafing to have done with all weakness towards the Democrats. They desired to strike not only at the accomplices of Catiline but at all the popular leaders and especially at Cæsar. The capitalists and the middle classes, in the full flush of their patriotic fervour, prepared to appear in arms the following day to keep the revolutionaries in order. So loud was the outcry for making an example that certain citizens whose sons were compromised in the agitation bethought them that according to ancient law they had the right to sit in judgment on their own children and had them put to death by their slaves.

Next day the Senate met to continue the inquiry and hear further witnesses. But it was almost impossible to maintain a judicial atmosphere. The chiefs of the Conservative party, Catulus in particular, began to put captious questions to the conspirators, to induce them to confess that Cæsar had been privy to the plot. An informer, no doubt in the hope of helping the conspirators, declared that Crassus was involved, but the outcries of the Senators stopped him midway in his statement. At one moment report spread through the House that the populace was rising to deliver the prisoners. The confusion was indescribable. All had lost their presence of mind, except Cicero and Cæsar. The extraordinary outburst of popular excitement had rudely awakened Cicero out of the delirious dream in which he had been living for the last month and recalled him to something like his natural caution. Even in the thick of the excitement he described the dangers which would be entailed by the adoption of too revolutionary measures. But what was to be done? The public was angry and was appealing to him as the pillar of the Republic. It was impossible for him now to draw back; or he at least had not the courage to do so. He fell back, in the difficulty, on an old and tried expedient. He resolved to precipitate the crisis, and to make the following day decide the fate of the conspirators. As for Cæsar, he too saw the dilemma in which he was placed. If he kept silent he would be charged with meanness or cowardice. On the other hand, in the excited state of public opinion, if he defended the accused, he would be almost encouraging his enemies to employ violence against him.

On the 5th the Senate met again; a huge and excited crowd blocked up the Forum, the temples and all the streets in the neighbourhood of the Senate-house. Silanus, the first Senator to be asked his opinion, voted for death. All the others who were asked after him voted the same way, until it came to the turn of Cæsar. Cæsar, after some severe reflections upon the crime of the accused, pointed out that the death penalty would be both illegal and dangerous, and proposed in its place compulsory detention in a municipality and the confiscation of their property. His skilful and vigorous appeal shook the resolution of many of the Senators, and opinion seemed more or less evenly divided. Cicero spoke in ambiguous terms, but gave it to be understood that he inclined to Cæsar's view. But Cato rose to speak definitely against Cæsar's suggestion and he pleaded so vehemently, he was so emphatic in his demand that respect for law and order should be enforced by the pronouncement of a death penalty, that the Senate was converted to his view and capital punishment decreed.

To Cicero was left the duty of carrying this order into execution. His task would be to collect the conspirators from the different houses where they were guarded and conduct them to the Mamertine prison, where they would be strangled by the soldiers who acted as public executioners. But the extreme Conservatives proposed to escort the Consul on his funereal mission through the city and to the prison and make an impressive demonstration of law and order before the noisy and riotous populace of the metropolis, which was itself, as they declared, morally implicated in the treason. Most of the Senators joined in the escort; there were a few exceptions, one of whom was Cæsar, whom a group of knights had threatened with swords as he left the Senate-house. So the streets of Rome witnessed the passing of this strange and solemn hangman's procession, composed of the whole senatorial aristocracy, the rich financiers and the well-to-do merchants, who had paused in their wrangling for the moment, with the chief executive officer of the Republic at its head. When the ceremony was over, Cicero was escorted back by the crowd to his house amidst enthusiastic demonstrations of confidence. Justice had had her victims. A few weeks later Catiline, who had only been able to arm a few thousand men, was easily defeated and killed at Pistoja in Etruria.

Cicero fondly imagined that with these drastic measures he had quenched the flame of revolution which had been spreading through Italy. In the complacency of success he forgot his own doubts and hesitations. In reality, if a wild and dangerous conflagration had been quickly and triumphantly stamped out, it was merely because Italy had never been inflammable. Italians had indeed been very ready to respond to Catiline's original proposal for the abolition of debt, when it appeared for a moment both compatible with security and easy of attainment. But when what had claimed to be an ordinary political agitation became the nucleus of an oligarchical and revolutionary conspiracy, shaped rather by the inevitable pressure of events than in accordance with any clear and persistent policy, the country had condemned and even opposed the enterprise. The old revolutionary generation of the Social and Civil Wars, the contemporaries of Saturninus and Marius, of Sulla, Carbo and Sertorius, had disappeared from the scene. The increase of wealth and comfort, of enjoyments and education, among the masses, the manifold refinements of urban life, the general diffusion of a more lavish and commodious style of living, had combined to make Italians more timid and irresolute, more easily susceptible to panic, and more convinced of the desirability of law and order. The new bourgeoisie which had grown up in the various cities of Italy was a prosperous and pleasure-loving society, entirely unfamiliar with military life, owning property in land and houses and slaves, and chiefly preoccupied with commerce and industry, speculation and contracts, and the other manifold varieties of money-making. Such people asked for nothing better than to be dispensed from paying their debts if a mere legislation could relieve them from the disagreeable obligation. But they did not intend to pursue this pleasing illusion by staking their present possessions and future expectations upon the perilous hazard of a revolution. The landed proprietors, especially, dreaded the prospect of civil war, owing to the increasing cultivation of the vine and olive, which only bear fruit after many years of growth and thus entail far more serious losses through war and devastation than crops which are sown, gathered and consumed from one year to the next.

CHAPTER XIII

THE RETURN OF POMPEY AND THE TRIAL OF CLODIUS

POMPEY meanwhile was still detained before Jerusalem. With the help of Hyrcanus the city itself had been easily captured; but a part of the inhabitants had taken refuge in the Temple, which they defended with the stubborn desperation of their race. The Temple was built on a hill dominating the city, and was surrounded by a fortress with walls of enormous height. Pompey had sent to Tyre for siege engines, which he erected against the rock; but the defenders retorted so furiously with arrows and stones that the operations had been protracted into a long and difficult siege.

The surrender came about at last in a curious manner. Once every seven days Pompey noticed that the besieged seemed to be stupefied into inactivity and allowed the Romans to work unmolested at their engines. He inquired of Hyrcanus, who told him that every seventh day was the Sabbath, the day on which the law obliged the faithful to abstain from all labour, which, as interpreted by the devout, included even self-defence. Pompey ordered his soldiers to work only on the Sabbath; he was thus enabled, within three months, to raise his towers up to the height of the walls and to move to the attack. Faustus, son of Sulla, was the first over the ramparts; but there was horrible carnage before the capture was completed. Curious to inspect the sanctuary which had cost him so much pains, Pompey made his way into the inmost shrine of the Temple, where none but the high priest was allowed to enter. But he looked in vain for a statue or a picture of the Godhead. He admired the strange seven-branched candlestick, which the Jews seemed specially to venerate, the table of gold, the huge store of incense for worship, and, hidden away in the cellars, the store of treasure which should have served to recompense the Roman legionary for his labours. But the God of the Bible then gave not the least striking proof of that power whose fear was soon to be spread so far throughout the world Alone of all the gods of the Orient his gold was respected by a Roman adventurer. Pompey was so overcome by the weird fanaticism of his Jewish surroundings that he dared not lay hands on the treasure.

Pompey was still in Palestine when he was met by an embassy from the King of Egypt, which had come to do him homage, to make him a large present of money and to deliver him a strange invitation. He was to go with his legions into Egypt to assist the King to quell a revolt which had lately broken out. Disquieted by the schemes of Crassus and Cæsar and despairing of recognition as King by the Senate, Ptolemy Auletes was now endeavouring to gain a new ally in his defence. If Pompey accepted the invitation and re-established order in Egypt, he could hardly help pleading his cause in the Senate on his return and securing him the coveted title of Friend and Ally of the Roman people. The scheme was characteristically crafty; but it was not without a dangerous side. It might help Ptolemy to win his country; but it might also help him to lose it. What was he to do if the Roman defender, after quelling the disaffection, refused to evacuate his country and annexed it to Rome? With a Lucullus this would have been a very serious risk. But Ptolemy had to do with a general who was too cautious rather than too daring for his purpose. Pompey reflected that an Egyptian adventure would most probably expose him to a double attack; it would offend the party that refused to recognize Ptolemy and was opposed altogether to Egyptian intervention; still more would it offend the noisy clique which was just now crying out for intervention, under the influence of Crassus and Cæsar. He was therefore soon finished with the embassy; he pocketed the money, but refused the invitation. He then declared Palestine and Cœlesyria a Roman province, laid Jerusalem under a tribute, gave the high priesthood to Hyrcanus, and, taking Aristobulus away with him as a prisoner, returned to Pontus.

Meanwhile Italy was slowly recovering from the Catilinarian terror; but it had left an indelible mark on her public life. In times of quick excitement and unstable balance, a trivial incident, if it chances to coincide with the close of a long and unconscious development, may be charged with far-reaching significance. The conspiracy of Catiline had not been formidable in itself, but it had burst in with a storm of fresh air upon the sultry atmosphere of Roman politics; it had touched every class and party and individual in the State; it had loosened long-standing agreements and snapped many ancient attachments; and when it passed away as quickly as it had come it left the whole field of policy transformed.

Its most immediate effect was the break-up of the post-Revolutionary Liberalism, with its temperate and patronizing projects of reform, which had grown up around Pompey in the year 70. This party had drawn its strength from the middle class and a part of the aristocracy, from a union of landlords, merchants and financiers with the progressive nobility and men of means and leisure; but it had been gradually enfeebled, partly by the growth of political indifference, partly because it had falsified the expectations and wearied the short-lived patience of its promoters; and partly because its members had been frightened or excited into the two extreme camps by the emergence of the question of debt. The respectable and educated classes conceived an incurable distrust for the politicians and pro-grammes of the Democrats, without a recovery of confidence in their Conservative opponents; and with a comprehensive contempt for all political squabbling, left the two parties to fight it out as best they could. The results of this sudden paralysis of public opinion can hardly be exaggerated. It transformed the Conservative party into a knot of furious reactionaries. All the wildest and most fanatical spirits in its ranks, encouraged by their easy success against Catiline, and confident that the sudden divorce between democracy and respectability would prove to be lasting, domineered over the moderate section in the Senate and entered, under the leadership of Catulus and Cato, into a life-and-death struggle against the popular party. Their plan of campaign was to use the prosecutions of the accomplices of Catiline as an opportunity for a far-reaching and systematic persecution of their opponents.

The moment seemed propitious. Pompey was still at a distance; Metellus Nepos, his Roman representative, could safely be ignored. Crassus had been frightened by the conspiracy out of his popular sympathies. Cæsar alone remained: and Cæsar was discredited and detested. Upon his devoted head the storm that had only just been lulled threatened to descend once more in all its fury. We may wonder what would have become of him at this moment had he been of a more sensitive and delicate temperament, or disposed to allow aristocratic prejudice or ethical scruples to dictate his action. But it was his conduct at this difficult crisis which first showed how marvellously Cæsar was adapted for the conflicts of his turbulent age.

The knights and all the wealthy had deserted the party and were not to be wooed back; Democracy was more than unpopular: it had become disreputable. Cæsar's remedy was to make it more disreputable still—to transform it avowedly into what it had begun to be during the last four or five years, a party of social discontent. Concealed in the holes and corners of Rome, in the enormous lodging-houses of the speculative builders of the day, there seethed an innumerable population of freedmen, artisans, pedlars, small shopkeepers, adventurers, beggars and malefactors, swept in from all parts of Italy and the Empire. These men made a living by any occupation, licit or illicit, which the slaves left open to them. They were employed on the public works; they plied their trades as masons, stone-cutters and waggoners, potters and weavers, cooks, florists and flute-players; they put themselves at the service of cabals and individual politicians as cut-throats or spies or go-betweens; they crept on to the register and sold their votes; they stole, they swindled, and they took their part, and more than their part, in the political banquets. Many of them had organized themselves into "Colleges" or associations of working men, which the Senate was now attempting to dissolve as illegal. Indolent, thriftless, discontented and incapable, perpetually clamouring for employment, yet perpetually cast adrift, this underground population had responded readily to the battle-cry of Catiline and had rallied enthusiastically to promote his campaign. It was still prepared, if it found a leader, to do yeoman service in the cause of anarchy. These were the men who were elected by the Pontifex Maximus, with his henchman the great-nephew of Metellus Macedonicus, to repulse the attacks of the fanatical Conservatives, the chosen allies with whom they were now prepared to attack them, no longer on the dangerous battle-ground of economic reform, but in the easier and more accessible arena of ordinary politics.

No sooner had Cæsar entered upon his Prætorship than he opened the attack upon Catulus in person. The Conservative leader was accused of having misadministered the funds for repairing the Capitol from the damage inflicted in the Civil War, and it was proposed to transfer this duty to Pompey. The proposal was defeated by the vigorous opposition of the Conservatives. But soon afterwards Metellus, with the assistance of Cæsar, came forward with a still more daring demand—nothing less than that Pompey should be recalled to Italy with his army in order to prevent any further illegal executions of citizens. This frankly raised the question whether the condemnations pronounced by the Senate against the accomplices of Catiline were legal, and was an open threat to those who were using the memories of the Terror to reap an aftermath of vindictive denunciation. The Conservatives were furious at what they considered a flagrant breach of patriotism. Not content with accusing men who had risked their lives in the cause of order, the party of revolution now wished officially to entrust Pompey with the duty of making the *coup d'état*! On the morning of the day when the Bill was to be discussed at the Assembly, Cato, who was still Tribune, went unattended to oppose his veto: but Cæsar and Metellus had him chased away with stones by bands of ruffians. Their example was contagious. The Conservatives ran off in their turn to fetch help and appeared in time to drive off Cæsar and Metellus before the Bill was passed.

The question was thus settled for the moment; but the scandal had been too great for things to remain as they were. It was only intensified when Metellus left Rome, with threats of vengeance, to return to Pompey's camp. In spite of the awakening protests of the moderates, the Senate was unable to resist the pressure of the reactionaries and took the grave step of deposing Metellus and Cæsar from their offices. But Cæsar was no stranger to the arts of injured innocence. At the cry of injustice the noisy rabble of his supporters rose in wrath against the decision, and the Senate, still more frightened of disorder than it was of the reactionaries, was obliged to reinstate him in his office. The Conservative leaders were mad with rage. They attempted to turn the tables by implicating him in the prosecutions against the accomplices of Catiline; but this only increased the dangerous ferment among the populace. Finally, as a sop to the many-headed Cerberus, the uncompromising Cato had perforce to increase the distributions of corn to the people to a sum of about seven millions, with a proportionate increase in the number of beneficiaries.

If within the last twelve months the whole political situation had been entirely transformed, the attitude of individuals needed corresponding readjustment. For two persons in particular, for Pompey and for Cicero, the change was of vital consequence. It was known that Pompey was preparing to return home, and everyone was asking what part he would play under the altered rules of the game. The Conservatives were very uneasy. They declared that he would use his army to make himself Dictator and abolish the Republic. And yet, but for the difficulty which even the ablest men seem to experience in analysing character amid the heats of a political conflict, nobody could possibly have imagined Pompey assuming the rôle of a second Sulla. He himself was indeed at that very moment earnestly considering how he could become reconciled to the Conservatives. During his long absence in the East, Pompey had at last found his true bearings. He was indeed a typical example of the hereditary aristocrat as he is sometimes developed under the influence of an advancing civilization. A graceful and not unsuccessful dilettante in art, literature and science, in politics and war, the very variety and facility of his accomplishments unfitted him for any intense and concentrated endeavour. Skilful and even crafty within his own range, he was yet easily deceived by an active intriguer or unbalanced by the shock of an unexpected rebuff. Though he served ambition and was gratified by power, like the rest of his grasping age, neither violence, nor greed, nor any active self-seeking lay truly at the bottom of his nature; but beneath that kindly and amiable, yet dignified demeanour, as so often in an aristocratic nature, lay cold and unstirred depths of complacency and selfishness.

Such a man was by nature allied rather to a moderate Conservatism than to the doctrines of revolution. In his youth he had rushed to arms in the cause of Sulla. But his early successes had stirred ambitions which linked his fortunes with the popular party. These ambitions he had been enabled to gratify; the East had given him, what it gives to few, the whole of his heart's desire. He returned to Rome at once the most renowned, the most powerful and one of the wealthiest of her citizens. He had added new provinces to the Empire, he held kings in the East at his mercy, and he had amassed and safely invested as much money as even a Roman could need. The claims of ambition once finally quieted, his aristocratic and Conservative temperament reasserted its sway. He began to feel a repugnance against the vulgar and turbulent propaganda of his party, and his disgust was increased when he learnt the intrigues of Crassus, the rumoured adultery of his wife Mucia, and the notorious position of Cæsar as the chief of all the rabble of Rome. Whilst the political wiseacres were shaking their heads over his supposed ambitions, he was simply concerned how to secure a successful triumph with the least possible friction and annoyance. In his letters to the Senate he never mentioned the Catilinarian imbroglio. He had thoughts of divorcing Mucia and contracting some new marriage which would pave the way for his reconciliation with the Conservatives; and he proposed, on his way home, to make a sort of royal tour through the Greek world, partly in order to gain time, but partly also to make a final and magnificent display of his greatness and dignity. He crossed first to Mitylene in Lesbos, which he made a free city to please his favourite Theophanes, who was a native of the place; he admired its fine theatre and conceived the project of building one similar, but on a larger scale, at Rome. From Lesbos he went to Rhodes, where he interviewed Posidonius, the philosophic historian so much in vogue among wealthy Romans, and distributed money to the professors. Then he moved on to Ephesus, where his army and fleet were collected.

If the Conservatives might have found an ally where they suspected the deadliest enmity, they had but a lukewarm supporter in Cicero, whom they might justly by now count as one of their own leaders. The conspiracy of Catiline marks a turning-point in the life and character of the great writer. Hitherto he had posed as a thrifty and retiring citizen, untouched by the temptations of power and luxury, whose ambitions were reserved for the Republic of letters and who had rather accepted than courted high office in the State. But his encounter with Catiline had turned his head. The emphatic laudation of the knights and the nobility, ordinarily so reserved towards any middle-class achievement, the unprecedented privileges decreed in his honour, including the sounding title of "Father of his Country," all the thousand exaggerations which fear or folly will always circulate on the morrow of even the most trivial disturbance, had combined to take his vain and sensitive nature by storm. He ended by being convinced that he had really saved the Republic from a horrible cataclysm, that he was in fact a capable and far-seeing statesman. Ideas of greatness began to float before his mind. He was no longer contented either with the unsubstantial glories of literature or with the modest life which he had hitherto been leading. Just in this very year, during the growing intensity of the party struggle, he committed one of the greatest indiscretions of his career by buying from Crassus, at the huge sum of $3\frac{1}{2}$ million sesterces, an enormous house on the Palatine. Anxious to possess a residence more worthy of his new position than the modest and old-fashioned home of his fathers, and unable to provide the necessary means, he was forced to depart from his strict observance of the Cincian law, and to ask the clients whom he defended to advance him large sums, of course without interest—to borrow money in fact from a wide circle of friends. One of his clients alone, Publius Sulla, lent him 2 million sesterces. It is true that he reckoned on his colleague Antonius, then in Macedonia, to pay his debts; for when he had surrendered him his province, it had been agreed between them that Antonius should give him a part of the booty he would make in his wars. For all that he was contracting enormous debts with very uncertain prospects of payment, and committing the same mistake as Cæsar in fettering his personal liberty with a chain which he would not easily succeed in snapping.

Moreover, if his ambitions were growing, his vigour and industry were far from keeping pace. While he was busily contracting debts in order to live up to his new position, he was unconsciously changing his personal habits. He had of late become strangely indolent, leaving it to others to defend his actions and not daring to range himself resolutely on the Conservative side. In their attacks against the Conservatives the Democrats still showed a certain respect for his name, and perhaps he hoped by a judicious withdrawal to preserve, if not his old popularity, at any rate a certain prestige among the popular ranks. Whilst parties were coming to blows in the Forum, he therefore remained in the background and confined himself to constant and vainglorious repetitions of the achievements of his Consulship, even making arrangements, it appears, to write a history of the year in Greek.

Pompey was now, towards the middle of 62, just about to leave for home. Before embarking, he made the customary distribution of prize money to his companions in arms. Each private soldier received 6,000 sesterces (about £60) and Centurions and Tribunes large sums up to a total which would amount to about £3,000,000. His generals alone had 100,000,000 sesterces, so that if we suppose there were twenty-five of them, each would have a sum equivalent to about £40,000, a substantial recompense for campaigns involving a minimum of danger, and which had not lasted in all more than a short four years. Finally, he embarked his army and set sail for Greece. He went first of all to Athens, where he stayed some time hearing philosophical lectures, and offered 50 talents to restore the finest of the ancient buildings. From Athens he sent his wife Mucia a letter announcing her impending divorce. Then he embarked for Italy, and landed towards the end of the year at Brindisi, while the Conservatives were trembling in expectation of a Democratic Sulla and Crassus was making hasty arrangements to leave Rome with his family.

Meanwhile at Rome, the hush of suspense which preceded Pompey's arrival had been rudely interrupted in the first days of December by an exciting scandal. Pompeia, the wife of Cæsar, had an intrigue with Clodius, the man who had suborned the legions of Lucullus. Clodius was one of those degenerates who are sometimes found in noble families in the last stages of their decadence, with weak and almost girlish features and the movements and tastes of a woman (to go about in female costume was one of his greatest delights). Since it fell to Pompeia, as Prætor's wife, to preside over the ceremony of the Bona Dea at which only women could be present, he conceived the fantastic idea of making an assignation with her during the ceremony.

Unfortunately he was found out. But a society so frankly sceptical and incredulous as that of Rome at this time might have been expected to pass off the scandal with a laugh, more especially as serious subjects were not lacking to claim the attention of the public. It is true that the alarm caused by Pompey's arrival was rapidly passing off. On his disembarkation at Brindisi, to the great delight and astonishment of the Conservatives, he had disbanded his army, and was making his way towards Rome with a small suite to demand a triumph. But disquieting news was coming in from Gaul. The Allobroges had risen in revolt and had devastated part of the Narbonese province, which the Senate, always weak and hesitating in its foreign policy, had for some time past left to itself. Moreover the Helvetii, who had taken part in the invasion of the Cimbri and Teutones and who had since settled down round the Lake of Geneva, were being pressed on the north-east by the Suevi and were anxious to cross the Roman province on their way to emigrate to the western seaboard.

But the Conservative party had no ears for all this. It could think of nothing but Clodius, whose adventure was regarded in the most tragic light. So horrible a sacrilege must not be left unpunished. Clearly Catiline's fate had proved an unsufficient warning. Here was the younger generation threatening to become even more seditious and dissolute than that which had preceded it. It was time to make a summary and deterrent example. The Senate consulted the College of Pontiffs to know if the act of Clodius constituted a sacrilege. When the College replied in the affirmative, it ordered the Consuls for the year 61, Marcus Pupius Piso and Marcus Valerius Messala, to propose a law fixing the procedure to be adopted and establishing a special tribunal to judge the case. To propose an extraordinary tribunal at a moment when the popular party was protesting daily against the illegal condemnation of the accomplices of Catiline was a deliberate provocation; and the Democrats immediately took Clodius under their protection. A violent agitation broke out against the Bill, largely fomented by a Tribune of obscure antecedents, named Quintus Fufius Calenus, who was anxious to obtain notoriety. The Conservatives remained firm in their demand for the condemnation of the sacrilege. Thus by the beginning of 61 the foolish adventure of Clodius had caused the outbreak of a regular political tempest, from which the most eminent men found it impossible to find shelter.

Cæsar, who was just about to go as Proprætor to Spain, was forced to delay his departure, and took prompt advantage of the scandal to divorce Pompeia, whose aristocratic connections were rather embarrassing than useful now that he was in open war with the aristocratic party. Pompey was of course appealed to by both parties; after resisting as long as he could, he was finally forced into a declaration which in its ambiguity seemed more favourable to the Conservatives than to the Democrats.

Even Cicero could not keep aloof. He was indeed carried far further than he wished by a curious intrigue undertaken by Clodius.

Anxious to make sure of his support, Clodius attempted to entangle him through the second of his sisters, the wife of Quintus Metellus Celer, a woman of the most evil reputation. But Cicero's wife, Terentia, was on the look-out; and the "Father of his Country" only recovered his customary portion of household peace by pledging himself to work for the passing of the judicial Bill directed against Clodius. Clodius was furious at his failure; he broke out in violent invectives against Cicero for his conduct with regard to Catiline, and, with a malicious allusion to the declarations made by Cicero in the Senate, fixed upon him the nickname of the "all-knowing" Consul.

These attacks came at an awkward moment; for Cicero had just now other reasons for anxiety and chagrin. Antonius was sending him no money; worse still, since he had failed in an expedition against the Dardani, public opinion at Rome was clamouring for his recall, and Cicero was forced to intervene to keep him in command. But rumours had got abroad of Cicero's agreement with his colleague, and the popular party began to make him their target. It was said that the knights had paid him to have the accomplices of Catiline condemned. He was already smarting under these stings when the attacks of Clodius came to increase his discomfort, and worried him at last, in a longing for retaliation, to plunge imprudently into the midst of the fray. The Bill was thus approved with modifications favourable to Clodius, proposed by Calenus. The next step was the trial itself. Crassus, now more easy in his mind, was ready to re-enter the world of intrigue and consented, at the instigation of Cæsar, to disburse enough money to corrupt the judges; while the Conservatives on their side were preparing the most damning evidence against Clodius. When the trial took place Clodius impudently denied that he had been present at the festival of the Bona Dea at all. The man who had been surprised there must have been someone else, for he had not even been at Rome that day. Cæsar was examined as a witness and declared that he knew nothing. Lucullus came forward to testify to the incestuous union of Clodia, his wife, with her brother. But it was Cicero who gave the crowning evidence by declaring that Clodius had been at Rome on that very day and had come to see him three hours before the sacrilege. Everyone believed his condemnation to be inevitable, but the gold of Crassus was more decisive than any evidence, and to the jubilation of the Democrats and the confusion of the Conservatives, Clodius was actually acquitted.

The Conservatives now sought to turn the tables upon Cæsar, who was making his arrangements to leave for Spain. Several of his creditors, suborned by his political enemies, produced a bundle of old unpaid *syngraphæ*, or bills of exchange, and threatened in default of payment to confiscate the pile of baggage which Cæsar, like most governors, was taking out with him to his province. These threats must certainly have been due to some political intrigue, for his creditors would scarcely have been so foolish as to keep Cæsar at Rome at the very moment when he was going into the province to enrich himself. Cæsar again addressed himself to Crassus, who offered a guarantee which the creditors did not venture to dispute. Thus released from his obligations Cæsar set out for Spain.

He left behind him at Rome Pompey, busy in the preparations for his triumph, Lucullus, now living quietly in retirement, and Cicero, since his defeat in the trial of Clodius, a prey to gathering anxieties. Stimulated by Clodius the Democrats were once more taking up the whole Catilinarian affair, throwing doubts upon Cicero's good faith and declaring that on the famous December 5th, Roman citizens had not so much been judged as assassinated. If only he had been compensated for this ingratitude by some sufficient admiration from the other side, he would not have been so grieved. But many of the people who had admired and applauded him during the crisis had now fallen under the spell of the agitators, and were beginning to ask if Cicero had not exaggerated the danger. He was at a loss where to turn. Too honest and, to speak truth, too vain to turn his back upon his own achievements in order to satisfy his critics, he yet lacked both the courage and the energy necessary to attach himself whole-heartedly to the extreme Conservatives.

For the moment, however, all was quiet; nor was the quiet even disturbed by an embassy which reached Rome from Gaul just about this time. The peoples of Gaul had now for some years been convulsed by an endless series of internal dissensions and disastrous wars. During the course of one of these wars, a short time before, one of the most powerful of the Gallic tribes, the Sequani, had called to their aid from beyond the Rhine a German chieftain, Ariovistus, who with his Suevian tribesmen had helped to conquer the Ædui. The Ædui, who had been in alliance with Rome since the conquest of the Narbonese Province, sent the Druid Divitiacus to Rome to appeal for assistance. Cicero now entertained him in his house; but despite the hospitality of the ex-Consul Divitiacus did not succeed in arousing Rome out of the complacent indifference with which she had treated the affairs of Gaul for the last sixty years. The Senate escaped from the difficulty by decreeing that the Governor of the Province, who as a matter of fact had very small forces at his disposal, was to protect the Ædui against any attempt of their enemies. Thus the Gallic question soon passed once more out of the public mind.

There was now a slight lull in the storm of politics. Generals and statesmen may make way for a moment for a greater representative of the spirit of their age—no soldier, nor demagogue in the public eye, but an obscure man of letters, a friend of Cicero, who, unknown and unregarded in a sequestered corner of Rome, was labouring at the most daring and characteristic monument of her imperial literature. His name was Titus Lucretius Carus. He was a man most probably of independent means who lived in a small house in the metropolis on the income derived from his landed property, in the midst of his books, with a few friends among the upper classes, but without ambition or desire for wealth. All his pleasure lay in the contemplation of the infinite world which Epicurus had opened to his gaze, a world flooded through and through with a rain of atoms, alight with countless stars and peopled with countless worlds, maintaining its equipoise by a gigantic effort of vitality in which Rome and her Empire were but one tiny eddy, lost in the immense and moving ocean of eternity.

But Lucretius was no idle dilettante who had fled from the violence and passions of mankind to distract an overladen brain with the selfish pastimes of the intellect. He was an ardent worker, an untiring craftsman of the imagination, who in the solitude of his study showed an ambition as insatiable as Lucullus himself in the thickest of the fight. He was conceiving a great poem upon Nature, bidding his contemporaries depose from their heavenly thrones the false gods whom they had too long worshipped, and attempting single-handed to win, not a new province with an army of soldiers, but rather, with a Titanic aspiration of the intellect, the lordship and comprehension of the natural world.

In the travail of self-expression the master of thought became a master of language; for he was the first to mould Latin to the uses of poetry. At the time when Lucretius began to write, the speech of the peasants of Latium was still primitive and confused, ill-fitted for abstract thinking, and its versification rude and imperfect; but, as Lucullus, with but 30,000 ignorant Italians, had set forth to trample down the Empires of the East, so Lucretius dared to do violence to those massive accents which men had thought destined for uses no more noble or enduring than the enactments of legislators, the reckonings of merchants, and the disputes of politicians. Lucretius took the language of his fathers, softened and purified it in the fire of his enthusiasm, hammered it long and patiently on the anvil of his thought, till it had lost all the dullness and opacity of its origin; he took the rough metres of the older poets, shaped and re-shaped them with vigorous workmanship till they rang clear and true in the stirring rhythm of his sonorous hexameter lines; and this instrument of language thus laboriously formed he applied to express, no metrical and meaningless analysis of an abstract doctrine, but his own deep-felt and romantic philosophy of the universe. He gave vivid utterance to the intensest exaltation, the most voluptuous abandonment, that the mind of man has ever felt before the everlasting and everchanging spectacle of the life of the Universe. He projected upon the infinite background of Nature the light and the shadows, the joy and the despair which came and went in his own spirit. He depicted in the colour and radiance of reality all the tender and terrible incidents of existence, the smiles that wreathe green meadows in the spring-time after rain, the gambolings of animals at pasture, the rushings of mighty tempests over field and forest, the great floods and rushings of rivers, the calms and storms on the high seas, the puny efforts of man still in the animal stage to preserve and to beautify his precarious existence, the horrors of plague and war, the folly of the fear of death, the burning thirst for love among all living creatures, the eternity and identity of the life which pulsates through the universe in all the myriad and mutable forces of animal being. The exposition of the philosophy of Epicurus binds together the detached and broken masses of his thought into the living unity of a single great poem, a solemn and indeed almost a religious book, not the most perfect but the most powerful achievement in the literature of Rome, in which posterity should recognize, not the caprice or the miracle of a solitary thinker lost in the wilderness of an imperial metropolis, but one of those manifold efforts to win power and knowledge and the heights of human greatness essayed by the men of that giant generation in the world of action and the world of thought. He stands for the heroic upward struggle of a reason which, in the sacred cause of truth, crushes indignantly beneath its feet the paltry superstitions of authority and religion. There are few greater gifts which Rome has bestowed upon mankind than the *De Natura* of Lucretius, which, little regarded among the men amongst whom it was written, has found its way across the ages, while the trophies, the monuments and the glory of so many of Rome's generals have perished in the gulf of time.

CHAPTER XIV

THE THREE-HEADED MONSTER

AFTER the narrow escape from his creditors on the eve of departure, Cæsar was doubly sensible of the necessity of repairing the family fortunes. No sooner had he arrived in Spain than he devoted himself systematically to the amassing of money. After recruiting ten new cohorts and adding them to the twenty already in the province, he undertook expeditions against the Callæci and the Lusitanians, and was merciless in sacking their villages even when they were ready to offer him allegiance. As the province was burdened with debts contracted with Italian capitalists during the war with Sertorius, he applied the Catilinarian remedy of a diminution of interest, and was paid huge sums by the cities in compensation.

At Rome Pompey had succeeded in securing his general Lucius Afranius as Consul for the year 60 with Quintus Metellus Celer, brother-in-law of Clodius, for a colleague. He was still putting off his triumph to await the arrival of his Asiatic spoils. At the end of September all was ready, and on the 29th the procession set forth on the Appian Way. It was preceded by two great placards giving a full account of Pompey's achievements and proclaiming that by the tribute from the new provinces he had raised the revenue of the Republic from fifty to eighty million drachmæ. Behind these placards came an interminable procession of waggons filled with armour and helmets and the prows of pirate ships. Then came mules bearing the money treasure, some sixty million drachmæ, which the conqueror was paying into the treasury of the State. Then followed a marvellous collection of jewels belonging to Mithridates, carefully exhibited for the public gaze. Then, each on a special vehicle, all the most valuable objects he had brought home—a playing-table composed entirely of two enormous precious stones, three magnificent beds, a couch of massive gold given by the King of the Iberians, thirty-five bands of pearls, three colossal gold statues of Minerva, Mars and Apollo, a miniature temple of the Muses covered with gems and surmounted by a timepiece, a bed in which Darius, son of Hystaspes, had once slept, the throne and sceptre of Mithridates, his statue in silver, a bust of Pompey in pearls by a skilful Oriental artist, and a collection of strange tropical plants, amongst others the ebony. For hours and hours the treasures of the last Hellenistic monarch of Asia wound through the narrow streets of Rome, before the eyes of a huge and excited crowd which cheerfully faced the sun, the dust, the noise and the long waits of the huge procession, seemed never to grow tired of staring at the show, and kept up a running fire of applause or criticism at each strange and wonderful object as it passed, while the eyes of the women brightened at the magnificent jewellery which they saw set out.

But this was only a first instalment. On the following day, which happened to be Pompey's birthday, came the turn of the living. First walked large groups of prisoners from all countries, from the pirates to the Arabs and Jews, all at liberty and unchained—a picturesque ethnographical display of the immense variety of nations over which Rome had extended her Empire. Then followed a crowd of princes and hostages, two celebrated pirate chiefs, the son of Tigranes, who had quarrelled with Pompey and had been deprived of his principality of Sophene, seven sons of Mithridates, Aristobulus with a son and two daughters, and numerous Iberian and Albanian chieftains. Then came huge pictures depicting important episodes in the campaign, such as the flight of Tigranes and the death of Mithridates; then strange idols worshipped by the barbarians. Last of all came the lord of the triumph himself, on a chariot decorated with pearls. He was clothed in a tunic said to have been worn by Alexander the Great, and followed by a glittering escort of commanders and tribunes on foot and on horse-back. But the strangest sight of the day, and that which gave the Italians the most lively sense of being in truth the first among the nations, was when, at the end of the long progress through the streets, the hero of the triumph, who claimed to have extended the limits of Empire to the further end of the world, put off the garb of Alexander and modestly retired, a simple citizen, to the house of his fathers.

Not long after the festival, towards the end of the year 61, and in the early months of 60, discord broke out anew. Pompey was still desirous of a reconciliation with the Conservatives, and with this object he had asked Cato, according to one account for his two nieces, according to another for his two daughters, to marry the one and give the other to his eldest son. Cæsar's fortunes had never been in greater danger. But Cato, the uncompromising reactionary, gave a curt refusal. He did not care to see politics brought into family life, nor did he trust the conversion of a man who had already once deserted the Conservative side. None of the extreme reactionaries were in the mood to forgive Pompey, and now that he had disarmed himself by dismissing his troops, their thoughts were only of vengeance. They replied to all Pompey's advances by insulting attacks. When he asked the Senate to ratify the arrangements he had made in the East, he found numerous Senators against him. Crassus and Lucullus opposed him out of spite, Cato and the Conservatives in order to destroy the credit he had gained with the Eastern monarchs, and also perhaps to endanger his chances of recovering the huge sums he had lent them.

Another serious subject of dispute arose with regard to the disposal of the new provincial revenues. Pompey made the very reasonable proposal of distributing part of them among his soldiers by buying land for them in Italy and spending the rest on Italy as a whole by abolishing all import duties. The disbandment of troops which Pompey had just made was, next to Sulla's, the largest that had ever taken place since soldiering had become a profession for the poor. Since many of the troops, in spite of their twenty or twenty-five years in the East, had not succeeded in saving up enough money for their old age, it was necessary to provide them with pensions by the assignment of land on which to build themselves a cottage out of their savings, buy a few slaves and attempt to make a living by agriculture. The abolition of import duties was generally desired by the whole of Italy, for the consumption of wine, perfumery, furniture, dyes, stuffs and artistic work of all sorts from the East was steadily growing, even in towns of secondary importance, many of which were increasing greatly in prosperity. If the frontiers of Italy were thrown open, not only would Eastern imports be cheaper, but there would be an end of the interminable disputes with the financiers who farmed the taxes.

Pompey at once took steps to carry out these projects. It was at his instigation that the Tribune Lucius Flavius now proposed a Land Bill, and Metellus Nepos a Bill abolishing import duties in Italy upon imported products. Unfortunately the sudden increase of revenue had, as usual, whetted too many appetites. The Conservatives were anxious that the new funds should remain at the disposition of the Senate to increase the sums assigned to the provincial Governorships and other branches of the public service in which Senators found a living. The powerful company which had contracted for the taxes of Asia seized the opportunity to petition the Senate, with the assistance of Crassus, who was probably a shareholder, for the reduction of their contract prices, urging that it had offered too high a figure and stood to lose upon the transaction. The result was a long-drawn series of political squabbles which finally succeeded in driving Pompey off his balance and shattering the already weakened nerves of Cicero.

Pompey, who had come to Rome sated with success and with the sole intention of basking in the sunshine of renown and riches, now found himself entangled in a miserable network of intrigues, which were all the more aggravating because, in spite of his affectation of contempt for his enemies, he was quite unsuccessful in defeating them. Cicero, disgusted at the Conservatives, disquieted by the growing violence of the demagogues, and distressed above measure at his own rapid loss of prestige, endeavoured to disarm the hostility of the tax-farmers by undertaking their defence in the Senate. He confided, however, to Atticus in a private letter that he thought their cupidity outrageous. He was anxious too to draw near to Pompey, though he had not the courage to take the necessary steps. He told Atticus in self-defence that he had hopes of converting the chief of the popular party. He had at length completed and published the Greek history of his Consulate, but not without a serious mishap. In order to prove that he was not lightly influenced by vague reports, and to shield himself, though without saying so, from the accusations of Clodius, he mentioned in the book that Crassus had one evening brought him a bundle of informers' letters against Catiline. Crassus, who had recovered from his alarm and was once more angling for popularity, was furious at a revelation which placed him among the number of the persecutors of Catiline. So Cicero had succeeded in making another enemy.

Meanwhile, apart from the question of the abolition of the import duties, the numerous discussions which had taken place in the Forum and the Senate had led to no result of importance. Neither Pompey's general administration in the East nor the Land Bill, nor the reduction of the Asiatic contract, had yet been ratified. To crown all, there now suddenly arrived very alarming news from Gaul. The spectre of a new German invasion suddenly loomed up again on the horizon. It was reported that the Helvetii, one of the most warlike peoples in Gaul, who had taken part in the invasion of the Cimbri and Teutones, were preparing to leave their mountains and to invade and subdue Gaul; they were said to be aiming at the establishment of a great Celtic Empire beneath their military hegemony, and to be looking about for allies to support them in their enterprise. It was generally agreed that if the Helvetii succeeded in conquering Gaul, they would at once hurl their forces upon Italy. This alarming intelligence finally dispelled the easy confidence which it had been customary to preserve on Gallic affairs. All other questions were ruled out of court and the Senate decided that the two Consuls should draw lots for the two Gallic provinces, the Cisalpine and the Narbonese, that a levy should immediately be made, that all exceptions from military service should be suspended, and finally that three ambassadors should be sent to Gaul to study the situation on the spot. One group of politicians, headed by the Consul Metellus, went still further. They proposed to declare war at once upon the Helvetii to crush them before they left for their own country. The imperialist spirit which had been so lively at Rome since the conquests of Lucullus and Pompey snatched at every opportunity that arose; and all over Italy there were ruined nobles and ambitious adventurers only thirsting for an opportunity to win glory and plunder. Since the interminable discussions on Pompey's administration closed the East just now to Roman enterprise, the opportunity afforded by a war in Gaul was not lightly to be dismissed.

Meanwhile, towards the middle of the year 60, Cæsar hurriedly returned from Spain to contest the Consulship for 59. There were this year three candidates for the Consulship: Cæsar, a dilettante historian called Lucius Lucceius, who had lived long in Egypt and was exceedingly wealthy, and Marcus Bibulus, a reactionary Conservative, who had already been Cæsar's colleague both as Ædile and Prætor. Lucceius, who belonged to neither party and was merely anxious to be elected for the honour of the position, was appealed to by both candidates in the hope that he would defray their election expenses. But the popular demagogue was more persuasive than the nominee of the reactionaries, and Bibulus was obliged to have recourse to his own friends, who raised a subscription for his expenses. Even Cato consented for once to subscribe, in his apprehension as to what the Consulship of a Cæsar might bring forth. Cæsar and Bibulus were elected, and the unfortunate millionaire who had paid the expenses was left in the lurch. As a set-off against this election, the Conservatives induced the Senate to decide that the Proconsular duty of the two Consuls for 59 should consist in the overseeing of roads and forests, an administrative position of quite secondary importance. By this ludicrous stratagem the Senate thought to guard itself beforehand against the design which was commonly attributed to Cæsar of applying in some new corner of the world the political methods of Lucullus and Pompey.

As to what Cæsar's schemes at this moment precisely were we have no information. Three great enterprises still lay open at this time to Roman policy—the annexation of Egypt, the invasion of Parthia, and the extension of the Roman dominion in Europe towards the Danube and the Rhine. In spite of the imminence of a Gallic war at this moment, Cæsar could hardly be thinking of any enterprise in that country: for Cisalpine Gaul had fallen to Metellus Celer, who was just arranging to leave Rome for his army.

Nor can Cæsar be credited with harbouring any designs upon Egypt. The Democratic party had abandoned the schemes it had entertained in 65 and was now showing a greater zeal even than the Senate for the preservation of Egyptian independence. It was Ptolemy Auletes who had brought about this miraculous conversion. No longer hoping for any assistance from Pompey, he had conceived the daring design of wringing out of the very politicians who a few years before had tried to rob him of his kingdom that recognition of his authority which the Senate still hesitated to grant him. He was engaged in negotiations with Crassus, Pompey and Cæsar and had promised them an enormous sum—6,000 talents—if they secured his recognition by Rome as a legitimate sovereign.

It is the most likely solution, therefore, though it is a conjecture unsupported by evidence, that Cæsar was already at this time dreaming of the conquest of Parthia, which Lucullus had designed but been

forced to abandon. Since then it had fallen to Pompey to undertake it;
and though both Pompey and Lucullus had turned back upon the
frontier, the idea that it was Rome's destiny to conquer the great
Parthian Empire was already widespread. A confirmation of this
conjecture may be found in the emphasis with which, four years
afterwards, Cæsar urged Crassus to this very undertaking.

But these were dreams in the far distance; and just now present
troubles were sufficiently pressing. The petty manœuvre of the Senate
was a warning to the Consul designate to entertain no illusions on the
attitude of his opponents. Cæsar at once made preparations for the
struggle; but he acted in the style which his enemies least expected.
While the Conservatives were on the look-out for a year of turbulence,
Cæsar was gradually returning to those moderate ideas which were
more in harmony with his character, his social position and his interests.
His scheme for fighting the Conservative party was a very simple one.
He intended to reorganize the moderate and reforming Democratic
party of the year 70, which had enlisted the support both of the upper
and middle classes. Enfeebled by events and by the blunders of its
leaders, this party had been finally dispersed by the conspiracy of
Catiline. But it could easily be brought together again if only
its more powerful chiefs could be induced to join hands: if only,
that is, a coalition could be formed between Crassus, Pompey
and Cicero.

It was a difficult undertaking, but it was far from impossible.
Pompey needed the ratification of his administration in the East;
Crassus, discredited among the Conservatives by his Egyptian project
and among the Democrats by his ambiguous attitude during the
conspiracy, was anxious to recover his old popularity. As for Cicero,
all he wished was to efface the impression of the condemnation of
Catilinarians. During the months which he spent at Rome as Consul
designate, Cæsar manœuvred so adroitly that he succeeded in breaking
down the old hostility between Pompey and Crassus. The reconciliation was of course still kept secret; neither of the three wished it to
become publicly known, lest their enemies, who were still powerful,
should be frightened into fresh energy. At the same time, Publius
Cornelius Balbus, a Spaniard from Cadiz, whom Pompey had made
a Roman citizen, and who was a friend of several important personages

at Rome, was entrusted with the task of negotiating with Cicero and suggesting an alliance with Crassus and Pompey.

The scheme for the coalition thus gradually took shape. By taking up a conciliatory attitude and securing the support of Cicero, Crassus and Pompey, Cæsar hoped to bring over to his side those moderate Senators, actually a majority in that body, who had ever since the conspiracy of Catiline voted in blind terror for the small group of extreme Conservatives. He hoped to bring matters back to the good old days of the year 70 and to have public affairs again transacted by a coalition of four. Had not the great battles of those days against the Conservative cabal been won in the Senate, the Assembly and the Forum by the joint action of Pompey, Crassus, Cicero and himself? Cicero was exceedingly flattered by the offer: but he had fallen into a morbid and vacillating state and could not be persuaded into answering either yes or no. Disappointing as this was, it did not interfere with the project as a whole. Even without Cicero the coalition of Crassus and Pompey would be sufficient to reconstitute the party, and it was Cæsar himself who would gain all the advantages of the arrangement. Not only would he secure an important Proconsular command but he would use his office to gain himself a fortune. It was as impossible then, as it is nowadays, to play a prominent political part without considerable expenditure. On his return from Spain, Cæsar had given nothing to his creditors, or at least to those among them who did not make his life a burden; he continued to owe a large sum to Atticus and also to be in the debt of Pompey. He now therefore accepted the extremely favourable advances of Ptolemy Auletes and further promised during his Consulship to effect a diminution of the contract of the company which farmed the taxes of Asia. The directors were pledged, in exchange, to give him a large number of shares in the company.

While Cæsar was making these preparations for his Consulship, there was a curious development in the Gallic situation. If the sensation caused by the first news about the Helvetii had slightly worn off, Metellus was continuing his preparations with undiminished activity. But in the midst of his arrangements he had been surprised and embarrassed by a very singular proposal. Profiting by the anxiety felt at Rome about the Helvetii, Ariovistus, King of the Suevi, proposed himself to Rome as an ally; he offered, that is, if occasion arose, to fight on the side of the Romans against the new Cimbri and Teutones. Ariovistus was the enemy of the Ædui, the old allies of Rome, in whose favour the Senate had passed an important decree only the year before. If Rome accepted the alliance of Ariovistus, she would be cancelling this Æduan decree, which had been specially directed against the King of the Suevi, and would be declaring herself the Friend and Ally of two peoples hostile to one another, a situation which might some day give rise to serious complications. Nevertheless the offer of Ariovistus was very tempting. The help of the Suevi, the most warlike people in Gaul, might prove exceedingly useful in a war against the Helvetii. There was therefore a party in Rome favourable to the alliance with the Suevi and anxious to sacrifice the Ædui and the original object of the alliance with them to the necessity of preventing a possible coalition between Ariovistus and the Helvetii. Moreover Ariovistus for his part seemed very anxious for the Roman alliance and made large presents to Metellus, who seems to have been doubtful about entertaining the offer.

In the midst of these preparations and vicissitudes the year 60 expired and Cæsar became Consul. He had at length attained the supreme ambition of the political career of every Roman. No sooner had he entered upon his office than he made a speech in the Senate protesting his anxiety to act on every occasion in agreement with Bibulus, and he took several opportunities of testifying to his respect for his colleague.

He also made an administrative reform which must have pleased the middle class and for which Cæsar deserves a small place in the history of journalism. With the increase of wealth and education curiosity had very naturally kept pace, and there were people in Rome who sought to gain a living by doing something analagous to the modern journalist. They collected what they considered to be the most important and interesting public and private information of the day, and at regular intervals every few days they collected it into a small handbook and had it copied several times by a slave, distributing the copies to subscribers. Naturally this was a luxury which only the rich could afford. Cæsar seems to have passed a decree that one of the magistrates should be entrusted with the duty of causing a *résumé* of all the most important news to be inscribed on whitewashed walls in different parts of the city, with the arrangement that when the news was stale, the wall should be whitewashed again for other news to take its place. In this way even the poorest of the people could be kept informed about all that went on. Cæsar also arranged that reports of sittings of the Senate should be made in a more regular manner and put at the disposition of the public.

Thinking that he had paved the way for more extended action, Cæsar now put forward a Land Bill. It enacted that twenty commissioners should be entrusted with the duty of distributing to the veterans and the poor all that remained of the public land with the exception of Campania, with the addition of other land to be bought on reasonable terms with the money brought in by Pompey. This was both a wise and a moderate proposal, and on presenting it to the Senate Cæsar declared that he was ready to listen to any objections that might be offered. But he was very soon deceived in his hopes of a return to the Democratic victories of the year 70. Times and tempers had changed too much in the interval. The ominous conjunction of the words Cæsar and Land Bill was too much for the reactionaries; and the landlords, who were strongly represented in the Senate, particularly those who were in possession of land bought during the proscriptions of Sulla, were much dismayed at a Bill which put into the hands of twenty commissioners a power which it would be easy to abuse. The Conservatives thus easily succeeded, under one pretext and another, in postponing the discussion of the Bill in the weak and irresolute Senate.

Cæsar was patient for some time, while Calenus, who was Prætor, and Publius Vatinius, an obscure political adventurer who was Tribune, proposed reforms in the law regulating the courts. At length, seeing that neither Crassus nor himself would be successful in securing that the Bill should be discussed by the Senate, Cæsar declared that he would simply have it proposed to the electors. This caused a great sensation. With the assistance of Cato and the Conservatives, Bibulus entered into a violent campaign of obstruction on religious grounds to prevent the meeting of the people. Cæsar's patience broke down, and he began to work upon the feelings of his supporters. Finally, after doing all he could to win Bibulus to his side, he played his trump card. He appealed openly to Crassus and Pompey for their help. Crassus and Pompey came down to the Forum and declared that the factious obstruction of the Conservatives must be broken down by force if persuasion proved insufficient. On this the Bill was approved amidst a scene of tumultuous excitement. A clause added at the last moment forced the Senators to swear that they would faithfully observe it.

But this success was as nothing in comparison with the effect produced upon the public when it became known that the three powerful personages whom everyone had thought to be enemies had all the while been acting in concert. It was the struggle between Crassus and Pompey which, in spite of rebuff after rebuff and scandal after scandal, had made it possible for the reactionaries to remain in power so long; and the quarrel between the two men was so bitter and of such long standing that the world had come to regard it as permanent. Now, suddenly, and almost by miracle, the two enemies were seen to be sworn allies: and both came forward in the cause of Cæsar, the redoubtable leader of all the rabble in Rome. The discovery caused an immense sensation. It was evident that if Pompey, Crassus and Cæsar united their forces, they could do what they liked with the electors, and that henceforward without their consent it would be well-nigh impossible to obtain either an office or a command or a mission or a loan. The majority of the Senators thought only of office, money and influence. As usual, therefore, they took sides with the big battalions and hastily trooped away from the small faction of reactionary Conservatives, who had rallied, since the death of Catulus, round the standard of Cato.

When the body has prepared itself for an effort far out of proportion to the obstacle to be encountered, it is apt to lose its equilibrium; and the same law holds good of the action of character. This was curiously exemplified by Cæsar's behaviour at this juncture. If Cæsar's was a nature naturally prone to moderation, he was yet quick to catch fire from the influence of the moment, and he could hardly escape being inflamed by the political society around him—a society from which all the reasonable spirits were being gradually withdrawn, and where, from Cato to Clodius, from Gabinius to Bibulus, sound and fury were the powerful and predominating elements. He had begun by being cautious and respectful; but emboldened by the success of the Land Bill and by the unexpected display of his recent increase of power, and furious at the factious opposition of the Conservatives, he changed his tactics with a swiftness and agility of which only he was capable, and swung round to the idea of an unadulterated democracy. His notion was now to found at Rome a democracy similar to the democracies of Greece, which dispensed with a Senate and governed their Empires single-handed through the deliberative assembly of the people. Such a democracy, with three men distinguished for eloquence, riches and renown at its head, would be capable, as it had already shown by its settlement of the Land Bill, of dealing satisfactorily with all those questions of foreign policy and finance of which the Senate had hitherto had the supreme control.

An unexpected event brought Cæsar's resolve to a head. Towards the middle of February, Quintus Metellus Celer died on the eve of his departure for Cisalpine Gaul. He was still so young, and his death was so unexpected, that his wife Clodia was suspected of having poisoned him. The government of Gaul, which meant the command in the imminent war against the Helvetii, became vacant through his death. It was at this moment undoubtedly that Cæsar first entertained the idea of securing an extraordinary command in Gaul. Though he knew very little about Gallic affairs, the idea of conducting a campaign against the nation whom Italy regarded as a new German invader could not fail to attract him. By a campaign against the Helvetii he would be following in the great tradition of his uncle and his party, and would show Italy once more that only the Democrats could defend her against the northern barbarians.

But the Senate could not be expected to sanction such an arrangement. He must appeal, as Pompey had appealed in similar case, direct to the Assembly of the people. Cæsar did not lose an instant. He gave up any other ideas of conquest which he may hitherto have entertained, and tried to spread the belief that a serious war in Gaul was perilously imminent. Profiting by the impression created by his alliance with Crassus and Pompey, he made Vatinius propose to the people a Bill entrusting him for five years with the government of Cisalpine Gaul and Illyria with three legions, dating from the date of the promulgation of the Bill. In case war broke out before the end of the year, he would thus be enabled to take command at once, following the example of Lucullus. Thanks largely to the stupefaction which reigned in political circles, as well as to his own activity and the help of Crassus and Pompey, the Bill was passed without difficulty and promulgated on March 1st.

When this stroke had gone safely home, Cæsar went on to three further projects. He persuaded the people to acknowledge Ptolemy Auletes as a friend of the Roman people, sharing with his friends the reward which he received for his success. He persuaded them also to reduce the contract which the tax-farmers had demanded from the Senate, and to approve the Asiatic administration of Pompey. The shares in the tax-farming company of Asia immediately rose in value.

Cæsar thus moved from success to success. Nor did he rest content even here. Hoping to ensure the permanence of the coalition, he persuaded Pompey in April to marry his daughter Julia, who was betrothed to Servilius Cæpio. Cæpio was to be consoled with a daughter of Pompey instead. Then, towards the end of April, Cæsar proposed a second Land Bill according to which the land in Campania from which the State drew a considerable revenue, was also to be distributed among poor citizens with families. The principal object of the measure was to impoverish the Treasury and thus to injure the Conservatives, who had repeatedly used their power in the Senate to spend public money in defence of their own interests. Its principal effect was to complete the Agrarian revolution begun by Spurius Thorius in 118 and to destroy the last vestiges of the Common Land system in Italy.

Never before had the Senate been so boldly assailed in its most ancient and revered prerogatives. In comparison with these attacks, how futile seemed the projects for which Caius Gracchus had met his death! For Cæsar now went so far as not to convene the Senate at all. He acted, and showed that he acted, as the master of the situation, without anyone daring to offer him a serious resistance. Futile recriminations, elaborate witticisms, a few vain and sporadic outbursts of temper—this was all that the Conservative party could set against a revolutionary Consul. Bibulus, still obstinate in his ritualistic sophistries, had declared the last meetings of the people to be null and void, and continued to emit a stream of violent decrees against Cæsar, Pompey and Crassus.

Varro had christened the alliance of Cæsar, Pompey and Crassus the Three-Headed Monster, and the jest had been successfully repeated in the aristocratic *salons*, where from morning to night the names of the three chiefs of the victorious democracy were taken in vain. Crassus was a disgusting usurer, who sold his vote in the open Senate and received criminals in his house for a consideration. Pompey was a farcical hero in a campaign without battles, who had married the daughter of the man who had had relations with his first wife. Cæsar was the accomplice of Catiline and the favourite of Nicomedes. Among the middle and upper classes, in the wealthy and cultured circles which took no part in politics but criticized all that went on in the spirit of detached and impartial spectators, the overwhelming power of the Caucus attracted to Cæsar, Crassus and Pompey a great part of the aversion which at Rome, as in all democracies, is always reserved for any party or group of men, whatever their character, who succeeded in securing the sweets of power. At the street corners where the furious edicts of Bibulus were exposed, the crowd was so great that it was almost impossible to pass by. Bibulus was in fact becoming almost popular, while Cæsar, Pompey and Crassus were sometimes given a chilling reception at festivals and public ceremonies. The younger generation in the upper classes, more vain and precocious even that that which had preceded it, affected an exalted contempt for the vulgar demagogy which Cæsar seemed definitely to have established at Rome.

Cicero was particularly grieved about the "Dynasts." He wrote to Atticus that Pompey was certainly aspiring to the tyranny, and that the indifference of the great and the impudence of a few ambitious upstarts was transforming the Republic into a Monarchy. Nor could he easily resign himself to playing the rôle of a secondary personage. He had good reasons for anxiety, not only because of his sincere repugnance against the tyranny of demagogues, but also owing to the growing audacity of Clodius, who was under the open protection of Pompey and Cæsar and desired to renounce his patrician rank to become Tribune of the people. The legal difficulties involved in this step were considerable, but Cæsar came to his help and succeeded by a *Lex Curiata de Arrogatione* in making him a plebeian. He was certain to be elected Tribune in the following year.

But these outbursts of hostility and fury seemed to exercise not the slightest influence. It is true that Pompey, who had expected to become, as in 70, the chief of a new Democratic party, composed of distinguished and constitutional politicians, had been a little surprised to find himself ranked beside Cæsar and Crassus as the chief of a mob-government repugnant to his aristocratic temper. He was also somewhat disturbed by Cæsar's domination and attempted by skilful sophistries to divest himself of his share of responsibility for his behaviour. But Crassus was free from all such qualms; at once less burdened with prejudices and more frankly egoistical, he thoroughly enjoyed his new post of power.

Meanwhile Cæsar, who seemed to grow bolder daily, was the open and undisputed lord of Rome. Neither he nor Crassus was much concerned by the animosity of the upper classes. Open opposition against them there was none. No one ventured to repeat in public what everyone was saying in the privacy of his own house. The rare sessions of the Senate were thinly attended, and the Conservative party meetings at the house of Bibulus were emptier still. Cicero in his letters to Atticus spoke bitterly of the cowardice of the Senators; but he followed the discreet example of the rest of the citizens.

Meanwhile even if the Democratic party was not, as Cato maintained, composed solely of drunkards, Cæsar, Pompey and Crassus were in reality nothing more than the chiefs of a political following which was detested by those classes of the State which were in possession of wealth and culture. How could a rabble of this sort continue to be supreme in a free Republic with elective institutions? What mysterious agency had suddenly destroyed the whole strength of the upper classes and of that august assembly which had for centuries governed first the small province of Latium, then the Italian peninsula, and lately a world-wide Empire?

In the old agricultural society with its organized military aristocracy, the Senate derived its energy and authority from the fact that it represented a single governing class, a class consisting of a landed nobility, which had been fitted by a special training for war and government, which had been subjected to a stern discipline at home and in society, and which was in essential agreement on the few vital questions that political life in a simple state of civilization brought forward for settlement. But with the growth of imperialism, with the progress of the commercial spirit, with the temptations of culture and luxury, in a word with the progress of all that we are accustomed to call civilization, the old traditions had become extinct. The development of the selfish passions, of cupidity, ambition and self-indulgence, had driven many members of the upper classes from political life. There was no longer at Rome, as of old, a disciplined and homogeneous body of citizens ready to undertake the responsibilities of government. Instead there was an infinite variety of individuals each of whom was greedy for special pleasures and attracted to special occupations or special vices. All were too much engaged at home, too selfish, too unsympathetic to one another, to be able to work harmoniously in an interest common to them all.

It was just at this time that Rome brought forth her first and greatest lyric poet, whose wild and passionate notes, with their touch of personal anguish, are symbolic of a tempestuous change of climate in Roman society. Born in the year 84 of a rich family at Verona, Caius Valerius Catullus received an excellent literary education and at twenty years of age had made his way to the capital. Introduced into high society by Cornelius Nepos, he soon made the acquaintance of all the well-known politicians, the rich merchants, and the distinguished ladies of the city. While he continued to buy books and to study, he had given himself up with almost barbaric impetuosity to a life of pleasure, running recklessly into debt, quarrelling with an over-thrifty father, and paying court to fine ladies. He had fallen passionately in love with the beautiful but notorious Clodia, wife of Metellus Celer. It had not been difficult to break down the hesitation of an easy-hearted woman who must have been pleased for a moment with the half-mad outbursts of a country youth, as a new solace and distraction after the light lovers of the day. Catullus answered the evasive caprices of Clodia with a jealous passion for his Lesbia, whom he claimed entirely as his own and for whom he wore himself out during these years in a succession of quarrels and reconciliations, appeals and invectives, despair and appeasements, which in no way disturbed their object in the even tenor of a life of pleasure.

It was to console himself amid the torments of his passion that Catullus took refuge in his extraordinary poetic genius. In verses of an almost brutal sincerity, of a marvellous power and variety of rhythm, subject and expression, he put into music all the most trivial and sorrowful moments of his life, the sudden and violent onset of sensual appetite, the tender confidences of friendship, the melancholy of departure on a distant voyage, the mourning for a brother who died young in Asia, the breezes and bluster of fugitive anger, and the tender and fleeting play of fancy when, amid the noise and frivolity of Rome, his thoughts won back to his native Lake of Garda in its lonely peace, to the little house at Sirmio which waited for him as an old nurse awaits a wandering child, who is astray in a wide and hungry world. Above all he is the poet of love—love in the fierceness and jealousy of its longing, with all its tortures and all its poignancy, and the insoluble contradiction that seems to gnaw at its heart.

> Odi et amo. Quare id faciam fortasse requiris.
> Nescio, sed fieri sentio, et excrucior.

The lyric poetry of Catullus would be sufficient by itself to explain the success of the political revolution made by Cæsar during his Consulship. Poetry so personal and passionate in its expression could surely only proceed from an age in which the upper and cultivated classes had dispersed upon an individual search for the diverse enjoyments of life, from wealth up to love, from play to philosophy, abandoning the affairs of government to a class of professional politicians, the majority of whom was at the beck and call of any clique or party which for the moment seemed to be in power.

Now that Cæsar had boldly usurped the powers of the Senate, the majority of the Senators were afraid to be on bad terms with the three chiefs of the all-powerful democracy. Cato and Bibulus tried in vain to organize an opposition; the upper classes, dissatisfied but resigned, tamely submitted to the tyranny of the caucus. Lucullus alone attempted for a moment to oppose the triumvirs; but when Cæsar threatened him with a prosecution about the booty he had made in his Eastern wars he relapsed once more into silence.

But Cæsar's habitual prudence had not entirely deserted him. He never allowed himself to forget that a power so rapidly acquired might as rapidly be lost. True, he had succeeded in passing a striking series of revolutionary laws; but he knew well that the moment he left Rome the Conservatives would attempt to annul them. He therefore spent the whole of the rest of his Consulship in a characteristically vigorous attempt to consolidate the power of the Triumvirate. It was necessary before all things to secure for the Consulship in the following year men devoted to his own and his friends' interests. The candidates he selected were Aulus Gabinius, a faithful adherent of Pompey, and Lucius Calpurnius Piso, a member of an old noble family which had, however, deserted the traditions of its past. Piso's father had lost his patrimony and had then devoted himself to business. After making a considerable fortune in military contracts at the time of the Social War, he had married a rich plebeian, the daughter of a merchant at Piacenza. So far as we can judge, Piso was a man of some intelligence, but prepared in his own interests to take service under any banner. In order to make quite sure of him, Cæsar became engaged to his daughter Calpurnia.

But above all it was necessary to make certain of a permanent majority in the Electoral Assembly. This was the only way of securing that the Conservative party should not take advantage of Cæsar's absence to persuade the people to annul his laws. Granted the selfishness and hostility of the upper and middle classes, it was only amongst the poor and the dregs of the population, amongst the artisans, the freedmen and the beggars, that a mass mob of reliable electors could be found who would be ready to vote at the orders of a leader. But the events of the last few years had shown the danger of trusting blindly in a populace that was as loose and uncompacted as the sand on the seashore. Cæsar therefore determined to organize at least a part of this mob into a regular electoral corps. Looking out for a man for his purpose, he skilfully fixed upon Clodius. Cæsar proposed to assist him to the Tribuneship on condition that he became his chief electoral agent. Clodius accepted. He was only too ready to enjoy a year of power in order to take his vengeance on Cicero, against whom he had nursed a wild hatred ever since his denunciation in the matter of the sacrilege.

But Bibulus had the elections postponed from July to October. Meanwhile Cicero, who about the beginning of July had returned from Campania, noticed that, amid the general agitation, his prestige was again beginning to rise. Pompey missed no occasion of saying him a gracious word, while Cæsar proposed to take him to Gaul under his command. Both were clearly anxious not to have him as an adversary. The malcontents, the Conservatives, and the younger generation, all the forces of the opposition, besieged his house as in the great days of the Conspiracy and seemed to regard him as the only man capable of restoring the Constitution. Only Clodius was his enemy, and filled Rome with invectives and menaces against him. But Cicero was weary and doubts preyed upon his mind. The flatteries of Cæsar and Pompey had little hold on him, for his aversion for the coalition was deep and sincere. But he had no longer the courage to undertake an energetic opposition. He was perpetually changing his mind, sometimes eager for the fray, sometimes discouraged by the slackness of the Conservatives. In their private meetings, they all roundly abused Cæsar; but in public there was nothing that they would say or do. Only one of the candidates for 58 had refused to swear to his laws.

Moreover the threats of Clodius were beginning to be so disquieting to Cicero that he gradually forgot all public disorders. He had spoken of them to Pompey and had been reassured by a declaration that Clodius had promised the Triumvirs to do nothing against him. This kept him quiet for some time, but when he saw Clodius continuing his campaign of invective, his anxieties broke out afresh. He wrote to Atticus to come hastily to Rome to discover the intentions of Clodius through Clodia, with whom Atticus seems to have had intimate relations. As a matter of fact Clodius was purposely deceiving Pompey. He was really anxious to have Cicero condemned to exile on the accusation of having illegally executed the accomplices of Catiline. But he was clever enough to conceal his purpose from the world; he was well aware how difficult it was to secure the banishment of so distinguished an orator, and was hoping for some opportunity of taking him by surprise.

In the meantime Cæsar had proposed an admirable Bill, definitely worded, though no doubt difficult to apply, placing a check on the conduct of provincial governors. He further induced Vatinius, who was well paid for his trouble with shares in the company of tax-farmers, to propose a second Bill authorizing him to settle 5,000 colonists with Latin rights at Como. And he also took another and

a far more momentous step. He made up his mind in favour of alliance
with the Suevi, and induced the Senate to give Ariovistus the title of
Friend and Ally. He was anxious to secure beforehand every chance
of success in the war against the Helvetii, which he reckoned on
conducting in the following year. He intended to attack them in their
own country before they had time to make a move; and his object in
conciliating Ariovistus was to set his mind easy on the score of the
Suevi and to ensure the isolation of the Helvetii.

But Pompey still hesitated and seemed even to regret that he had
become involved in the coalition. Cæsar, in his perplexity, adopted an
ingenious manœuvre to break down his colleague's irresolution. He
induced him to believe that the Roman aristocracy had entered into
a plot against his life. Vatinius persuaded a police agent called Vettius
to induce some frivolous young members of the aristocracy to concoct
and then confess a conspiracy against Pompey. Vettius spoke of it to
a son of Scribonius Curio. Curio, too clever to swallow the bait, at
once told his father, who revealed it to Pompey. Vettius was arrested
and put into prison, where he laid information against several young
aristocrats, amongst others Brutus, son of Servilia. It is not impossible
that Vettius may actually have spoken to Brutus on the matter and
that Brutus was imprudent enough to listen, which would indicate
that Vettius had an ominous insight into character; in any case Servilia
hastened to Cæsar, who went to visit Vettius in prison. Cæsar then
assembled the people and confronted them with Vettius, who told a
long story of a plot in which Brutus no longer figured, but in which
vague accusations were brought against powerful personages in the
Conservative party, against Lucullus, Domitius, Ahenobarbus and
Cicero himself. After that the matter was hushed up. It was even
asserted that Cæsar had Vettius secretly put to death in prison.

In October the elections at last took place. Piso and Gabinius were
elected Consuls and Clodius Tribune of the people. The Prætors
were all Conservatives; and amongst them was Lucius Domitius
Ahenobarbus. Soon afterwards the Senate, in which the Conservative
party had lost a great part of its influence, on the proposal of Crassus
and Pompey, added the government of Narbonese Gaul with one
legion to the province already given to Cæsar. Cæsar, now sure of
his Proconsular command, was occupied in definitely consolidating

his position amongst the electors by the organization of what we may not unfairly describe as the Tammany Hall of antiquity. Clodius had hardly entered upon his office when, on December 10th, he announced a series of Bills, each outbidding the other in popularity, which had certainly been approved beforehand by Cæsar. First came a Corn Bill, according to which poor citizens could be provided with corn by the State, no longer at a low figure but gratis; next a Bill permitting the people to meet and pass laws on all feast days; finally a Bill granting complete freedom of association to the working classes at Rome. Some of the Conservatives, including Cicero, wished to meet these proposals with a vigorous opposition, but Clodius adroitly quieted them by giving them to understand that if they consented to approve them, he would cease to attack Cicero. Thus it came about that in the first days of 58 they were all of them approved without opposition. Clodius thereupon proposed a new law entrusting one of his clients, Sextus Clodius, a man of poor and obscure family, with the task of drawing up the list of those who should be admitted to the free distribution of corn.

This led to a curious and unexpected development. A large number of shopkeepers, pedlars and artisans who possessed slaves and had difficulty in supporting them on account of the high price of corn gave them their freedom in order that they might be fed at the public expense. The saving in food was calculated to compensate their masters for the loss of service entailed by their enfranchisement. This caused a rapid increase in the number of those entitled to the distribution: for Sextus was not scrupulous as to what names were inserted on the list. The law was thus of very considerable benefit to the poor, and the popularity of Cæsar, Pompey, Crassus and Clodius was correspondingly increased. With the aid of Sextus and the Consuls, Clodius now found it easy to establish associations among the working classes in every quarter of the city, which were to serve at once as labour and electoral guilds. He further organized into troops or *decuries* a large number of freedmen and even of slaves, under the command of corporals who were to lead them to the vote on the receipt of orders from headquarters. This electoral army, recruited from amongst the poor cosmopolitan electorate of Rome, was entirely at the service of the three leaders; yet thanks to the new Corn Law, its maintenance was actually paid for by the government. In order to facilitate his distribution of corn, Clodius passed through the Assembly a Bill decreeing the annexation of Cyprus and the confiscation of the treasures of its King, on the pretext that he continued to give assistance to the pirates.

Clodius had served his leaders with both zeal and ability; he was now ready for his reward. He clamoured for the condemnation of Cicero. Cæsar, Crassus and Pompey would gladly have withdrawn Cicero from Rome, but in some less ignominious fashion. Cæsar, who had already left Rome and was on the point of setting out for Gaul, went so far as to renew his offer to take him as legate; but the wily Clodius, who had repeatedly assured the Triumvirs that he desired no more than to make Cicero uncomfortable, held his hand until he had organized his electoral associations. When his preparations were complete he darted upon his prey. He suddenly came forward with a law threatening with exile all who had condemned or should in future condemn to death a Roman citizen without giving him the chance of appealing to the people. This is exactly what had happened in the case of the Catilinarians. At the same time, to secure that the Consuls should give him free action in the persecution of Cicero, Clodius proposed a Provincial Bill according to which, notwithstanding the recent arrangements of Cæsar, Macedonia was to be given for five years to Piso, and Syria to Gabinius with the right of making war outside the province and of administering justice among the free nations. The proposal was strengthened by the grant of a large sum of money.

Cicero and his friends attempted to resist and a deputation of Senators and capitalists visited the Consuls. Cicero begged Piso, Pompey and Crassus to intervene, and his friends attempted to summon public meetings to protest against the law of Clodius. It was all in vain. The Triumvirs complained bitterly of Clodius' adroitness in making them partly responsible for the scandal of banishing a man so illustrious as Cicero; but they did not dare to enter the lists against the all-powerful demagogue. Crassus contented himself with letting his son Publius, a young man of great ability and high aspirations, act in his place. But, intimidated by Clodius and discouraged by the silence of his three chiefs, the public refused to stir in Cicero's defence. Overcome by the suddenness of the attack, his friends felt obliged to

urge submission for the moment, and advised him to go into exile
with the hope of a speedy and honourable return. Cicero wrung his
hands and vowed he would refuse to go. But the situation left him
no choice; and he finally took the only wise course which remained
to him, and left Rome in the first days of March 58. As soon as he
was gone Clodius had his exile confirmed by law and destroyed his
houses and villas.

A short time afterwards Cæsar left Italy on the receipt of disquieting news from Gaul, and Cato left for Cyprus as the nominee
of Clodius, to carry out the provisions of his law of annexation. Cæsar
took with him to Gaul a large band of friends who were to serve
under his orders in the army. Amongst them were Labienus, who had
been Tribune in 63, Mamurra, a knight from Formia who had
probably up to this time been a tax-farmer, but was now to be his
chief engineer, and Publius, the son of Crassus. As for Cato, he had
long hesitated to accept the extraordinary mission to Cyprus. He
realized that Clodius had merely selected him in order to make sure
of his withdrawal and to leave the path clear for the Triumvirs and
himself. But he reflected that Clodius might bring an action against
him for disobeying an order of the people. Moreover there was nothing
to be done at Rome, while in Cyprus he would at least be ensuring
that the riches of the king passed into the Treasury of the Republic.
He therefore decided to go, taking with him his nephew Marcus
Brutus, who needed a change of air after his entanglement with
Vettius. Brutus was a young man who was passionately devoted to
books and who had already won a great reputation at Rome not only
for his studious tastes but also for his still rarer qualities of personal
character.

CHAPTER XV

EMPIRE-BUILDING

MEANWHILE all over Italy the rapid progress of luxury went on unchecked. On his return from the East Lucullus had almost, if not absolutely, withdrawn from politics, and as though he felt that he had carried one great historic task to conclusion, set out to work with all his powers upon another. After having excited in his countrymen the passion and the daring for the indefinite extension of Empire, he was now teaching them, the unconscious possessors of the greatest treasure-house in the world, how to employ the riches which he had placed in their hands. With an energy which seemed to grow rather than diminish with his years, the man who had lived till fifty in conditions of old-fashioned frugality, and had then, late in middle life, overrun the kingdoms and despoiled the treasures of two great Oriental monarchs, was now dazzling Italy with his display of Asiatic magnificence as he had formerly dazzled her with the risks and the romance of his campaigns.

Out of the spoils of Mithridates and Tigranes he constructed on that part of the Pincian now called La Trinita dei Monti, between the Via Sistina, the Via Due Macelli and the Via Capo le Case, a magnificent palace with halls, loggias, gardens and libraries and embellished throughout with the finest works of art. He purchased the Island of Nisida and spent huge sums in turning it into a delightful summer resort. He built a villa at Baiæ, and bought vast estates at Frascati where he employed a large number of Greek architects, in the construction, not of ordinary farm-houses, but of splendid mansions on each of the properties, with luxurious banqueting-halls and every artistic embellishment. Here he invited all the learned and artistic Greeks of the day, together with troops of his personal friends, to sumptuous feasts prepared by the best cooks in Rome to satisfy the gluttony which was the one sensual indulgence that appealed to the veteran who had come to his enjoyments so late in life. Aphrodite herself never deigned to cross the threshold so impatiently thrown open to the ministrations of pleasure. As he sat installed at these magnificent repasts, the thought can surely never have crossed his mind that, while the glory of the policy which he had conceived and initiated was to fall almost entirely to a younger disciple, his own name would survive upon the lips of men associated only with the memories of luxurious entertainment; that posterity would forget that he had given Italy the cherry-tree, and misconstrue the historic importance of his conquests, to linger and moralize in half-envious disgust over the prodigious Sybaritic hospitality of his dinners. And yet this strange mania for building and banqueting was itself but the sequel to the work which Lucullus had inaugurated in Pontus, when he ransacked its treasures and took captive its inhabitants. All that he had achieved in the East was one long protest against the simpler traditions of Italian life; and it was by a true if unconscious instinct that at the close of his life, on his return and retirement, he became the apostle of the civilization of the Hellenized Orient, with all its refinement and all its depravity.

Nor indeed was his teaching neglected by his countrymen. Society was being transformed with almost dizzy rapidity. The assimilation of Orientals into the Italian population, the special characteristic of the great imperialist era, was already far advanced. Never before had Italy been so crowded with slaves. The conquests of the two Luculli and of Pompey, the continual warfare and raiding on the frontiers, and the familiar traffic in men sold by their creditors or kidnapped by the pirates, had already brought, and were still bringing, to Italy a vast multitude of men and women. They formed a strange and motley assortment. There were architects, engineers, doctors, painters, goldsmiths, weavers and metalworkers from Asia, singers and dancers from Syria, hucksters and fortune-tellers from Palestine, sellers of medicinal and poisonous herbs, shepherds from Gaul, Germany, Scythia and Spain, all equally and indiscriminately dispersed among the houses of the upper and middle classes in Rome and Italy. Every one of these immigrants had been robbed of home and fortune by the stress of the struggle between man and man and had been obliged, whether young or old, to begin his life over again.

Gradually, as time went on, a division of labour was formed in their ranks. Some refused to submit and were done away with by their masters. Some escaped from their captors and turned to brigandage and piracy, or were lost in the metropolis or on the roads of Italy, or met their death in a brawl or a rising or some natural accident. Others succumbed to disease or exhaustion, or were unable to survive the degradation of their state and the loss of all that was dear to them. In every great migration of the human family from one part of the earth to another, whether freely or forcibly undertaken, there are thousands of stragglers who fall thus by the way.

But these, after all, were a minority. There still remained a large body of immigrants, including most of those drawn from the civilized lands of the East, who were skilful workers in the arts and slowly became acclimatized to the inhabitants and the conditions of their new country. As the memory of their home died out of their souls, they consented to acquire the language of their conquerors and taught them in their turn what they had to teach. Sometimes they were allowed to exercise their profession in a shop opened by their patron, partly for their own profit and partly for his. Sometimes they even obtained complete liberty on condition that they paid over to their patron a part of their earnings. They began to be regarded as the natural free workers of the community, who surrendered a portion of their profits to their superiors to maintain upper- and middle-class Italians in a luxurious idleness. Their ranks were being continually swollen by recruits from below: for with the improvement in the relations between slaves and their masters it became customary before long to grant liberty to faithful and skilled slaves after six years of servitude. Thus was formed the nucleus of a new freedman class, with definite rights in the Roman courts; for the laws regarding the moral and economic position of freedmen were gradually modified, as definite decisions were given upon particular cases which arose.

The slave immigrants found a ready outlet for their abilities in the engrossing speculations of their adopted countrymen. Many Italians bought skilled slaves with the object of using them to instruct their fellows; and there were upper- and middle-class households in Rome and throughout Italy which had become regular schools of arts and crafts. To take but one instance, a perfumer of Mithridates who had been the slave and then the freedman of a certain Lutatius opened a shop at Rome, where he prepared his perfumes, no longer for the harem of an Eastern Sultan, but for the fashionable ladies of Rome.

All over Italy in the houses of the rich and well-to-do there were slaves and freedmen acting as blacksmiths, carpenters, weavers, tapestry workers, master masons, painters and upholsterers, who were employed for their owners and for an outside public whose necessities increased as the years went on. Out on the countryside the same process might be witnessed. Men who had started life as peasants in the Cyclades and Syria were busy perfecting the cultivation of the vine and the olive, teaching improvements in the preparation of oil and wine and in the scientific raising and feeding of stock.

Thus among all classes of the Italian community there was an increasing variety and refinement of demand and a progressive specialization in the employments of skilled labourers and brain workers. The spread of education through the whole of the middle class provided openings for hundreds of rhetoricians and grammarians; the humble but hard-working profession of teaching was rapidly crowded with quick-witted freedmen. But this by no means exhausted the intellectual occupations. There was a large class of slaves living upon the ignorance and the weaknesses of masters who had failed, or refused, to outgrow the old-fashioned Italian simplicity. The men among them became accountants, land-agents, major-domos, confidants, librarians, copyists, translators, secretaries or intermediaries, while the women found open still easier pathways to becoming at once the servants and the rulers of their masters. The houses of politicians like Pompey, Crassus and Cæsar were miniature government offices where numberless freedmen and slaves from the East were engaged on their master's work, organizing their festivals, answering their correspondence, and keeping up to date the ledgers, the lists of dependents and the family archives.

Side by side with this influx of immigrants from the provinces into Italy, there was a very large emigration of Italians into the newly annexed parts of the Empire. Countless Italians had by now become established all over the Mediterranean basin, not only in Greece and in the province of Asia, but on the recently conquered coastline of the Adriatic, as at Salona and Alessio, in Narbonese Gaul, in Spanish towns such as Cordova and Seville, at Utica, Hadrumetum and Thapsus in Africa, at Antioch and other towns in Syria, whither numerous adventures and traders from Italy had followed in the wake of Pompey's army. These Italians engaged in the most manifold employments. They were contractors to the army, farmers of the taxes, dealers in slaves or the other produce of the country, managers, sub-managers or employees in big financial companies, agents of rich Italians who had lands or money invested in the provinces, landowners or occupiers of public land, and finally and most frequently, professional usurers. Leaving home, as a rule, utterly planless and penniless, whatever the corner of the Empire to which fortune had led them, these Italian settlers soon became living and integral portions of that single and spreading organism which was slowly drawing its tentacles over the whole coastline of the Mediterranean. They organized themselves into clubs or associations regulated by statute, called *Conventus Civium Romanorum*; and they were the natural escort and Council of governors, who, despatched at short notice to an unknown country, always ended by becoming either their tools or their accomplices. Thus they came to regard themselves as a select and limited aristocracy among the indigenous population, protected and privileged by their wealth, their rights as Roman citizens, and the patronage of the governors. Thus the two great migrations of conquered and conquerors met and crossed face to face on the high roads of Empire, each moving foredoomed to a historic destiny; the one with its gaze toward the West, seeking service for a quick hand and a ready brain with the arts and the education, the wisdom and the depravity of the Orient: the other hastening Eastward to use and abuse all the powers of Empire, with arms and authority and riches, and the blind pride of a master who little knows what a future lies ambushed in the docility of his slaves.

But both, in their new homes, looked to the same metropolis; and Rome, the mother of conquerors, had changed with her children. The imperial metropolis still preserved a few landmarks of the old capital of Latium: venerable and unsightly temples of worm-eaten timber, patrician houses in the old Latin style, basilicas and monuments decorated with rude Etruscan terra-cottas. But the old order was passing, both in spirit and appearance. The modest provincial city, with its restricted working-class quarter and wide strips of field and grove pleasantly diversified by the little detached houses of the patricians, each with its small garden, was now everywhere outgrowing the old circuit of her walls. The disorder of the slums now encumbered and encroached upon the rich. The immense and towering lodging-houses, which formed the principal dwelling of the poor, were packed together in great numbers one against the other, fastened on to the slopes or raised upon the summits of the seven hills. The careful and almost monastic combination of instruction and example, of mutual supervision and discipline, which had taught the old Roman nobility to conquer the world by apprenticeship in the school of self-control and responsibility, had now long since become obsolete. Ambition and avarice and all the minions of Lust, Aphrodite and Dionysus, the nine Muses and the Philosophy of Greece, had burst in upon the city like a troop of Bacchantes; and from Rome they had won their way through the Peninsula, filling men's hearts, wherever they passed by, with an unsatisfied longing for wealth and power and pleasure and knowledge. The proud and mighty Empire disdained to recall the obscurity of its origin, as the conqueror of Pontus, amid the splendid opulence which distracted his last years in his villa on the Pincian, just dimly remembered, as from some former existence, the austere young aristocrat who had gone to his first battle by the side of the great Sulla.

Yet reflection such as this would have availed but little. Contemporaries who had been at once spectators and actors in the great transformation spoke of it as a "corruption of ancient manners," as a disease inevitable from the frailty of mankind, whose amazing and ominous progress no foresight of statesmen could stay. But we, who have a longer and riper experience of human nature and history, can form a clearer and less clouded vision; across the gulf of intervening centuries the lamentation and invective of the ancients fall strangely familiar on our ears; and by listening faithfully to their echoes, and meditating on their meaning, we may penetrate at last to the very heart of their complaint. Only so shall we comprehend the true nature of Roman Imperialism.

When they spoke of "corruption," Roman writers were thinking of the upheaval occasioned in the aristocratic, agricultural and military society of ancient Italy by the progress of Imperial expansion. The transformation which was thus brought about is analogous to that effected by the progress of industry in England and France during the nineteenth century, in North Italy and Germany since 1848, and in America between the days of Washington and Franklin and the time of the War of Secession. Almost identically the same effects which have been produced in these countries by the increase of wealth and the progress of industry were produced in ancient society by the extension of the Roman power over the whole of the Mediterranean basin.

The symptoms are almost too familiar to need recapitulation. An increasing percentage of the nation abandoned labour in the fields for commerce, money-lending and speculation. Agriculture itself became an industry requiring capital and constantly demanding speedier and more skilful methods. The expense of living, and the standard of comfort and luxury, went up in all classes of the community, and rose from generation to generation with progressive rapidity. There was an increase of the artisan population in all the cities and an increasing variety of professions in which it was employed. The old territorial nobility fell into decay, while the rich merchants and capitalists gradually developed into a powerful, numerous and exclusive caste. The middle class grew steadily in wealth and independence. Education, once the luxury and prerogative of a small aristocracy, was eagerly sought after by its rivals from below, as an instrument for the acquisition of power and riches, and for the revival and adaptation to the needs of a new age of the ancient traditions in all departments of life, whether public or private, from law, education and medicine, to agriculture, politics and war. Money and brains became synonymous with power. Rome grew rapidly; and the widespread inclination for urban life was causing even the smaller towns to increase in size and improve in appearance.

Thus Italy was no longer a nation of thrifty and hard-working peasants, but the conqueror and usurer of the Mediterranean world. She was now a united and homogeneous community in which, with the exception of a few outcasts, all ranks in the State, nobility, financiers and merchants, had been drawn together into a single class, living in ease and comfort on its invested capital: on the quick profits derived from Imperial expansion, and on the labour and services of multitudinous slaves, who worked in their fields, or looked after their houses, filled the intellectual professions or engaged in commerce, administration and politics. The suspense and depression which had provoked the disorders of the Catilinarian agitation had been removed by the vast treasure which Pompey and his men had brought back to the West, and by the taxes and exploitating of the newly conquered provinces. Once more precious metals were cheap and abundant; and trade and speculation were proportionately brisk.

And Italy, of course, bore marks of the change. All over the country the virgin forest was disappearing before the axe, and the primitive farm buildings with which even the larger landowners had once been content were being rapidly demolished. The hideous slave-shelters or compounds, with their gangs of forced labourers, vanished from the scene, together with the huge desolate tracts of pasture where they had spent their days, to be replaced by vineyards, olive-groves and orchards, now planted in all parts of the Peninsula. All round the great cities there was a gay belt of villas and gardens, surrounded by larger estates on which the new slave immigrants contentedly cultivated the vine or the olive, or bred animals for the stable or transport, under the direction of a Greek or Oriental bailiff; while the countryside was dotted with the pleasant cottages of land-lords, who farmed their own holdings with the help of a few slaves. The ancient townships of Italy, still engirdled with walls of Cyclopean masonry from the old days of incessant and ubiquitous warfare, hastening to don the adornments of a new era of peace, planned temples and squares, handsome basilicas and sumptuous palaces, to the designs and direction of Eastern architects. To match the changeless beauty of her sky and sea, Italy eagerly cast off her old barbaric trappings of corn and woodland for a more smiling vesture of vine and olive, fine cities and bright gardens, the gifts or the plunder of the bounteous East.

Italy was thus passing through the same period of rejuvenation as Europe and the United States at the present day. She was being transformed from a caste aristocracy of nobles and peasants into a homogeneous democracy of merchants and bourgeois. We might expect her then to encounter some of our characteristic modern problems by the way. And indeed we discover that she was faced with the same three torturing contradictions which baffle the wisdom of twentieth-century statesmanship. There is the contradiction between the sentiment of democracy and the unequal distribution of wealth; between elective institutions and the political indifference of the upper and middle classes; and lastly between the weakening of the military spirit and the heightening of the national pride, between ambitious dreams of war and conquest and the distaste among all classes for active fighting.

The decadence of the ancient nobility and the loosening of its control over the lower ranks of society: the growing pride and independence and authority of the middle class and the diffusion of education and political discussion: and the formation in the capital of a numerous intractable and irresponsible proletariat, meant the close of the old era of efficient if narrow-minded aristocratic administration, when the nobles monopolized the offices, sat together in the Senate House, and imposed their own harmonious will and policy upon a submissive Italy. The idea that government should be by the people and for the people, that politics were subject to the criticism of public opinion, that the State officials were not the masters but the servants and Ministers of the nation, had become as prevalent in Italy then as in twentieth-century Europe. And yet, as in Europe and the United States at the present time, the great bulk of the upper and middle classes took but a languid interest in public affairs; they preferred to spend their time upon commerce or agriculture, study or pleasure.

Yet these political anchorites and abstainers lived no idle or careless lives. It was they who painfully imported and planted the trees of the East on their native hills, who laboured to increase and improve the vines, the olives and the cattle of Italy, who studied and wrote on the philosophy of Greece, who acclimatized the arts and the industries of Asia, who reformed the architecture of temples, houses and cities, and learnt to apply works of art in their decoration—who were the first, in short, to change an uncouth and agricultural country into what Italy has been for mankind ever since, a joy and admiration to generations of beholders. It is now sixteen centuries since the disappearance of the Roman Empire, and though in the pages of too many modern historians the mighty host of the workers lies concealed and contemned behind the dominant personality of a few soldiers and politicians, their work has lived after them. On the plains and hillsides of Italy to-day vineyards, orchards and olive groves shake out to the wind the last surviving trophies of the world-conquest of Rome.

Yet these were the men who gave the death-blow to the ancient spirit of Roman citizenship, and allowed the elective institutions of the State to sink into the hands of the ambitious dilettanti and grasping adventurers who disputed for the suffrages, and controlled the organizations, of the Roman proletariat. For the proletariat was the only part of the population which was still passionately interested in its rulers; it found in politics a pleasant and gratuitous entertainment, as absorbing as the more expensive diversions of the rich; and eking out as it did a precarious livelihood on the margin of subsistence, it had the largest stake and interest in the policy of the State. To have no politics would for the Roman poor have meant to have no bread. It was their politics that supplied them with deep draughts of good wine and feasts of pork and thrushes on the big State holidays, with the easy and well-paid labour on public works or the excitements of the gladiatorial show, or the petty cash to gamble at dice or recoup them for an evening's pleasure.

Does not all this correspond, in however rudimentary a form, to the growing power enjoyed to-day in all States which have elective institutions by the Socialist party, drawing its recruits amongst the urban labourers, who stand in especial need of the protection of government? And is there not a suggestive parallel between the well-to-do public of Italy and our modern bourgeoisie, which, dispensing more easily with direct help from the State, distracted by its own private interests and occupations, enervated by the succession and variety of its pleasures, satisfied with the influential privileges of education and riches and the helpless, if well-directed, criticisms of a congenial irritation, seems everywhere to be making a dignified withdrawal from the arena of politics? The political revolution of Cæsar's Consulship was only the last phase in a transformation which had long been taking place. In this department of his activity Cæsar may perhaps fitly be compared with a modern Socialist leader, or rather with a Tammany Boss in New York. Roman politics had become debased into an open and world-wide market for laws and appointments, kingdoms and provinces, exemptions and sinecures and the deals of financiers: a frenzied cockpit of intrigue and swindling, assassination and blackmail: the resort not only of the vilest and most violent of the men of the time, but of the corruptest and most insidious of the women: where, if any honest Roman strayed in by accident, he was either speedily extinguished or as speedily became soiled with the contagion of his company.

But the new bourgeoisie was losing more than a mere interest in home intrigues and elections; it was forfeiting its old aptitude for a military life. The conquests of Lucullus and Pompey had afforded vast gratification to the Imperialist susceptibilities of the middle class; they had disseminated a sentiment bordering on adoration for Alexander the Great, together with the most fantastic dreams of world-wide domination. But the great majority of the arm-chair strategists who were ready to overrun the world in the footsteps of the great Macedonian could not have endured a single day of genuine soldiering. The old law according to which all men from seventeen to forty-six were liable to military service was indeed still nominally in force; but merchants, landlords and professional men refused to suffer the interruption of their business or their pleasure by the inconsiderate obligations of military service; and the magistrates who were responsible for the levies now only enrolled volunteers. Those who enlisted were generally men who had failed in every other town or country occupation, and gladly entered a profession in which they received the pay of 224 denarri a year, and were not only fed and clothed, but had the chance of winning prize-money from their general or attaining the coveted position of centurion. It was only when there was a dearth of volunteers that the State used its authority of compulsion, and even then it drew its recruits exclusively from amongst the unemployed in the towns or from the free peasants and the smaller proprietors in the mountains, where some relics still survived of the old Roman fighting-stock. Yet, even with these resources to draw upon, the ranks were not replenished. Although the numbers in the armies were comparatively small, it was soon found impossible to maintain them at full strength with Italian recruits. Thus the military organization was gradually extended. It became necessary to keep the soldiers a great many years under arms, and to admit recruits from amongst the more primitive Latins of Cisalpine Gaul, where the original Celtic population had mixed with immigrants from Italy to form a class of moderate proprietors, who still preserved the large families, the simple manners and morals, and the adventurous temperament, which had beaten back Hannibal six generations before. Indeed, within the very next decade, we shall find the recruiting sergeants of the Republic withdrawing in despair from Southern and Central Italy and trusting to the Po Valley to fill the gaps in their ranks.

Yet from time to time black storm clouds of anger would beat up suddenly from the horizon to lash the stagnant waters of civic indifference; and the unsuspected passion of an apathetic electorate would surprise and overwhelm the proud coalitions and their chiefs. The unkingly usurpers, who feared neither the gods in heaven nor any lord on earth, sat trembling on their thrones before the invisible authority of general opinion, before the pent and gathering indignation of the educated public. The sleeping giant could be master when he willed. No party in the State could do systematic violence to a class who by wealth, numbers and knowledge was supreme in the community. Their influence can be felt through the whole field of policy. Why else was Pompey, despite his riches and renown, so scrupulous not to offend the Republican sentiment of Italy? Why was the all-powerful Crassus so impatient to obliterate the more discreditable incidents of a doubtful career? Cæsar himself was as greatly under their dominance. When he departed for Gaul the chief idea in his mind was to regain, by a brilliant succession of victories, the respect he had forfeited among a sensitive public by the extravagance and corruption of a disordered youth, the indecent propaganda of his years under Crassus, and the radical and revolutionary policy of his Consulship. It is singular indeed how results clash with motives when the actors are moving in a changing scene.

Yet it would be foolish and misleading to exaggerate the parallel. If our modern civilization is struggling under the burden of very similar problems, we are far less acutely conscious of their incidence. To ancient Italy they were a matter of life and death. The political apathy of the civilized nations and their growing unfitness for a military life do not seem, for the present at any rate, to menace the very existence of white civilization. The mercantile democracies of our own epoch depend, like all communities, upon sustained effort;

but they depend upon an effort in which the struggle of man against nature exerts a more powerful leverage than the struggle of man against man. They depend, that is, upon industry: and the object of industry is to make the forces of Nature subservient to human use. But in the effort which brought a mercantile democracy into being in ancient Italy, the struggle of man against man was far more powerful than the struggle of man against nature. In the face and in defiance of all tempting analogies there remains this great and essential difference between ancient and modern life. It arises from the fact that the world of antiquity was poorer and less populous than the world of to-day, and its knowledge of nature and powers of production thus proportionately curtailed. A mercantile bourgeoisie of the type which circumstances enabled to be developed in ancient Italy can take root almost anywhere in the twentieth-century world—in a small and defenceless territory like Belgium, or a great and conquering sea-power like England, amongst a huge democracy in a comparatively empty continent like the United States, or in an industrialized country like Germany, established upon some of the most unfertile soil in Europe. All that is required for a country is that a small number of able and active men should form an industrial aristocracy, accumulate a certain amount of capital, lay it out with skill and offer abundant opportunities for labour. If labour is scarce in the country itself, it will soon come in from abroad. Workers will cross the ocean unasked in the search of employment, and accept it however painful and degrading its conditions; they will descend into the bowels of the earth; they will pass their life on a cockle-shell tumbling on the waves; they will spend their day from sunrise to sunset in Cyclopean caverns before furnaces of molten steel, in obedience to the iron laws of industrial discipline and subordination.

In the workshops of the United States there are busy hordes of cosmopolitan labourers who have voluntarily emigrated from all parts of the world. They find a parallel in ancient society in the multitude of slaves and freedmen from Greece and Asia, Gaul and Germany, Spain and Scythia, who were employed at Rome and throughout Italy in the possession and for the profit of the bourgeoisie. But these ancient immigrants did not come in freely; all, or almost all, were shipped to Italy as cargoes of human goods. Now we shall see in the sequel that the Roman slave-trade effected no permanent depopulation or damage in the slave-supplying countries of the East. It is clear therefore that there must have been an excess of population in those regions, as there is to-day in those parts of Europe whence the American emigrants chiefly flow. This suggests an interesting question. Why did not the skilled labourers and brain workers of the East emigrate voluntarily to the West in sufficient numbers to satisfy the Italian demand?

The answer is simple. Because ancient life was still too simple to draw them from their homes. In the modern civilized world the conditions of life in the different strata of society pass from wealth at the top to poverty at the base through an infinite gradation of intermediate stages of comfort. Thus in every section of the community from the highest to the lowest, but especially among the labouring population, there are minute differences between the standard of man and man and profession and profession, which are quite as important, in their peculiar function, as the larger differences between class and class. For this delicate and complicated gradation of differences is the never-failing instrument by which the capitalist bourgeoisie succeeds in attracting men to its service even across distances of thousands of miles. In a world so populous, and so eager for enjoyment, as our own, it is impossible that capital should ever fail, provided only that it offers a reasonable wage, to find men who, to attain some slightly greater measure of comfort and luxury, will consent to learn and to perform the most repellent or dangerous or exhausting labour.

But in the ancient world this instrument of persuasion was not available; there were practically no gradations between the demands of the workers. From an absolutely unmeasured luxury, which was only possible to the very richest, life passed down, at one step, to a primitive level, where food was of the very simplest and pleasure meant a rare evening of dissipation or inebriety, or a free festival provided by the priests or the plutocrats or the government. Since his needs were so much fewer, the free labourer in the East was less active and enterprising than the workman of to-day. Even if population increased and life became more difficult, he remained in his own country. Having neither the means nor the desire to improve his position, why should he face the pains and perils of an unknown journey to seek a distant master who would always remain a stranger? Adventurers and vagabonds flocked freely to Rome from every corner of her Empire; but the ordinary labourer remained in the provinces. He required to be brought.

Here at last we have the key to the great problem of ancient slavery. Rome was a Slave-State because slavery was essential to her production and development; because she could only obtain workers by the slave-trade and by conquest. Her slavery and her agression are inextricably intertwined; for prisoners, to-day a mere incubus of warfare, were then a substantial indemnity for the expenses of a campaign. Every increase in the demand for labour in Italy spurred the ambition and the audacity of the Roman generals; and the glamour of the feats of a Lucullus and a Pompey was enhanced by the workers they carried back to the West.

The same essential difference between ancient and modern life can be observed in another field. Whenever a capitalist and industrial bourgeoisie enjoys a period of prosperity, the population increases so fast that the surrounding territory is insufficient to supply its needs. This is happening, of course, all round us in the Europe of to-day; and it was happening in the same way in the Rome of Cæsar's time. Nowadays such a contingency causes no anxiety; for the need is at once met by the private enterprise of merchants. Means of transport are easy and inexpensive; and there are young and fertile countries where men of the same civilization and the same needs as ourselves grow far more corn than they consume, and are glad to sell it for our industrial products. These communities are thus in a position to supply us in such abundance that many industrial countries reject a part of what is offered them by putting an import duty on corn. If one of the ancients were to come to life again nothing would be more incomprehensible to him than our modern corn duties. In those days there was hardly a country which had not difficulty in producing the corn necessary for its own maintenance, and even countries like Sicily, Egypt or the Crimea, which ordinarily enjoyed plenteous harvests, preferred if possible to keep their corn for themselves. The result is obvious. Countries where capital was abundant, so far from putting any check on the import of corn, did all they could to promote it, and they were naturally tempted or even compelled to extend their power over corn-growing regions in order to be able to control the export. Thus, from the moment when Rome became the capital of the world, the question of her food supply became one of the most pressing in her politics. Here again we have a potent and never-failing stimulus toward aggression in the civilized societies of the ancient world.

Let us draw the argument together. The progress of a mercantile democracy was decided in antiquity, as it is decided to-day, by the progressive increase in demand from generation to generation, and by the number and character of the persons who are able or anxious to live up to a high standard of comfort. We have watched this progress from generation to generation, for a period of one hundred and fifty years, from the generation which was growing up at the end of the Second Punic War to the generation contemporary with Cæsar. We have only to look round to observe the same phenomena in the civilization of to-day. But the instruments of production at our disposal are so powerful, and the wealth already accumulated so great, that, so long as there is no slackening in the energy of our captains of industry, it is easy to satisfy the increasing demand of new generations by employing part of the wealth already produced, not to satisfy the needs of the present, but to contribute to the production of new wealth for the future. Our industries have at their command, not only the precious metals, increasingly employed as exchange becomes more frequent, but also vastly improved means of communication and transport and a growing store of raw material and foodstuffs. Precious metals in particular are so abundant and so easily borrowed that anyone who undertakes to pay a small interest and promises repayment never fails to secure them.

In the ancient world, on the other hand, where production was slower and less abundant, appetites increased far faster than the means of their satisfaction; and mercantile democracies suffered from acute temporary crises owing to their periodical inability to increase production and satisfy consumers. Above all they suffered from the scarcity of precious metals. Between 70 and 60 B.C., for instance, Italy was driven almost to distraction owing to the failure of the supply of gold and silver. There were constant complaints about the high rate of interest, accompanied by attempts to prevent the export of bullion, and by a serious agitation for the remission of debt. The demand for money, in fact, grew more rapidly than the supply, so rapidly that it is impossible to say what would have happened if it had not been relieved by the palliative of war, with its expedients of indiscriminate pillage from the treasures of temples, the palaces of kings and the houses of the wealthy, both among civilized and barbarous populations. Thus war performed a peculiar and valuable function in ancient society by quickening the circulation of capital, which was often too sluggish. Since the modern world has discovered other ways of promoting this object, the economic significance of war has now been entirely reversed.

Thus we see that poverty, scarcity of population, and the comparative want of productive power in the ancient world made it impossible that a capitalist bourgeoisie should be formed without warfare—without struggle that is, not between man and nature, but between man and man. Yet the carnage and destruction which war must always entail tended themselves to impede the growth of population, the progress of industry and the increase of wealth; though the cheapness of ancient armaments made war far less ruinous than to-day. Thus we reach the curious and tragic conclusion that an ancient community could only become wealthy and civilized by preying upon its neighbours. This was a fundamental contradiction in ancient life which Cæsar and his contemporaries in vain attempted to solve.

But there were lesser difficulties than this which they equally failed to meet. The army, the government and indeed all the public services, from the lowest to the most essential, were at Rome in a state of indescribable confusion. Owing to the fact that every single magistracy was elective, the government lacked what forms the stable foundation of all modern States, a permanent Civil Service, which, amid the struggles of party, can continue almost mechanically to fulfil the most necessary and elementary functions of national life. At Rome houses would catch fire or tumble to pieces while the Ædiles were busy with the organization of games. The supply of water was totally insufficient. The first aqueduct had been constructed in 312, a second in 272, a third in 144, a fourth in 125, but since that year the State had neglected the needs of an ever-growing population. The ships which brought corn for the metropolis were forced to cast anchor in the natural roadstead of Ostia, which was small and insecure and had never been improved, or else to sail up the Tiber, and discharge their merchandise at the docks or *emporium*, which had been constructed in 192 and 174 under the Aventine, on the site of the Lungo Tevere dei Pierleoni and the Lungo Tevere Testaccio. The streets of Rome were as unsafe as a forest full of brigands; besides the cut-throats and the pickpockets who infested them, the passer-by went in terror of his life from crowding waggons and tumbling walls, sudden fires and ill-built houses.

The disorder of the metropolis was equalled by the anarchy of government. Ever since Italian society had begun to display the variety of tastes and occupations with which we are so familiar in modern life, the Senate had degenerated into a fashionable club for aristocrats and dilettanti, financiers and barristers, men of letters and wire-pullers. It included large landed proprietors like Domitius Ahenobarbus, financial magnates like Crassus, illustrious generals like the two Luculli and Pompey, men of letters like Cicero, lawyers like Hortensius, scholars like Varro, students of astronomy and agriculture like Nigidius Fibulus and Tramellius Scrofa, and solicitors like Sulpicius Rufus—each one of them bent firstly upon his own private aims and ambitions, and next upon those of his class or his party, or his clients and dependents.

Thus the Senate lost its predominant position and degenerated into an instrument of which the complex social forces in the outside world attempted from time to time to make use. It was these powerful outside forces which were struggling together for supremacy, and it is with them that the true interest of the history lies. With the exception of the Civil Service and the great manufacturing interests, these forces were very much the same then as they are to-day. There were the financiers, the large landowners, the moderate proprietors, the surviving representatives of the aristocracy, the middle class with its social and pecuniary ambitions, the influences of militarism, and the demagogues. All were unsparing in the effort to use for their own purposes the powers which the Senate had inherited from the days when it was the organ of a single ruling class.

The history of the Roman coinage affords a good instance of its weakness. While Italy had become the financial metropolis of the Mediterranean, the Senate continued to coin nothing but silver money, and the innumerable loans arranged at Rome had to be paid out in a foreign currency or in ingots. The only Roman gold coins which were struck were due to the generals, who had the right to mint money to pay their soldiers, and used the privilege to put their own titles and effigies on the coins. The State finances were thus in a state of chaos. No further action was taken against the pirates whose activity had, it is true, been somewhat curtailed since the fall of Mithridates and the conquest of Crete and Syria; and there was hardly a district in the Empire which was not infested by brigands.

What was stranger still in an Empire that rested on force, the army was completely disorganized. Now that the ancient national militia had been transformed into a mercenary soldiery, it was imperative to establish a regular course of military training for recruits. Yet nobody thought of doing so. The legions which were left upon distant frontiers were often reduced to scarcely half their fighting strength and changed their generals from year to year. It is almost farcical to apply the name of general to politicians who hurried off from the Forum to take command of an army, surrounded by a staff of friends none of whom had the very faintest idea of what they were required to teach their soldiers. Moreover they were far more interested in the discovery of good investments for their capital than in studying the complex problems of tactics or strategy, and were always in a hurry to return to Italy. Cæsar himself went out to take over the command of four legions with no experience of war beyond the siege of Mitylene and the small punitive expeditions which he had directed in Spain in 61 The only men at all skilled in the profession of arms were the centurions, who were chosen from the common militia. Stranger still was the circumstance that the army now consisted entirely of infantry. In the old days the younger members of rich families formed corps of cavalry, but the youth of the new generation preferred to lend money at 40 per cent. in the provinces or to stay at Rome in the enjoyment of inherited fortunes. Moreover even if they had all been born soldiers, they could not have supplied the Empire with a sufficient force of cavalry. Roman generals were therefore obliged to levy horsemen from among barbarians in Thrace, Gaul, Germany, Spain and Numidia, and were actually reduced to giving orders through interpreters. Surprising indeed are the vagaries of history. Rome achieved her greatest conquests with an utterly disorganized army; and it was these very conquests which completed the military decadence of her people.

It would not be easy to discover in the whole course of history a State which effected conquests so extensive with resources so slender and ill-directed as Rome. Her political institutions matched the weakness of her army. The Senate, the constitutional instrument of foreign policy, had no regular means for securing information, and no servants acquainted with the principles and history of the numerous and difficult questions which came up for settlement. Its habitual expedient was to continue deliberation and postpone decision so long as was decently possible. Indeed for more than a century Rome had only increased her Empire with evident reluctance and in cases where there was no other possible alternative. Though Lucullus and Pompey had clearly demonstrated that this inherited policy no longer corresponded either with the changed conditions of the outside world or with the changed requirements of Rome herself, she still continually allowed herself, as in the case of Gaul, to be surprised and stupefied by the march of events. The numerous tributary or allied States were left to themselves; and no one was charged to watch them or to maintain constant relations with their chiefs. The policy pursued towards allied or independent neighbours varied from one year to the next according to the caprice of the governors sent out to the frontier provinces; and it sometimes happened that at a critical moment the most serious questions were simply left to chance.

This almost incredible want of organization in the sphere of foreign policy explains much of the success of the Democratic party. The attempt made by the Conservatives after the conspiracy of Catiline to restore the failing authority of the Senate had been overcome by the coalition of Pompey, Crassus and Cæsar, in the face of an almost incredulous aristocracy. The Consulship of Cæsar seemed to mark the definite conclusion, in favour of the Democratic party, of the battle which had been raging since the year 70. For the government was now no longer administered in the Senate House, but in the palaces of Pompey and Crassus and in the tent or litter of Cæsar, as he moved up and down his Gallic province. Cæsar, Pompey and Crassus together concerted measures for the administration of the Empire at home and abroad, for the distribution of offices and the outlay of public money; and their acts were ratified by meetings packed with the tame voters of Clodius and by the few complacent Senators who kept up, in an almost empty house, the sorry pretence of a deliberative assembly. For their correspondence and accounts, their information and intrigues, they fell back on the aid of the most able and skilful of their multitudinous slaves, who became in this way the irresponsible agents of a lawless and irresponsible Government of Three. Thus in spite of their blunders, the Democrats had triumphed in the long party duel; they won because they were quicker than their rivals to seize the importance of Lucullus' work in the East; because they promised to inspire, and had already succeeded in inspiring, Roman foreign policy with the energy in which it had long been lacking.

But could the huge mechanism of Empire continue to be set in motion by the weak leverage of the Workmen's Associations at Rome and the retainers of three far from unanimous politicians? Were the Three so immensely superior to their fellow-citizens as to divide between them with impunity the heritage of many generations of Empire?

The law of life was the same then as it has been in all ages. The great men of that day were just as ignorant as their fellows of the historic work of which they were at once to be the instruments and the victims. Like all other human beings, they were the plaything of what in history we can name Destiny, though it is nothing more than the unforeseen coincidence of events, the emergence into action of hidden forces which, in a complex and disordered society such as that of Rome or of our own day, no contemporary can be expected to discern. These men had risen to their high position, not through any superhuman powers of will or intellect on their own part, but through the singular conditions of the days in which they lived—because birth and reputation, riches, ambition and ability, and above all chance, had placed in their hands a power that grew resistlessly greater as the old State institutions crumbled steadily to decay. But the day was at hand when their coveted greatness would become revealed in a tragic and inextricable embarrassment: when it compelled them to assume labours and responsibilities which as far exceeded their strength as the honours they were now enjoying exceeded their deserts. Dark indeed was the issue which Destiny was reserving for each one of the three. Meanwhile, solitary amidst all the disorder of his time, Lucullus, the strangest and most isolated figure in the whole history of Rome, from his vast and sumptuous gardens on the Pincian, on the height where the Belvedere of the Medici Villa had since been placed, philosophized with the doctors of Greece on the corruption of his countrymen, as he looked quietly down from his calm island refuge over the great city at his feet—a vast and moving ocean for ever swept by the tides and tempests of human society. Alone among all the rivals of his power he was to have a gentle passing: Euthanasia, the Greek goddess of a Happy Death, came herself to fetch him home. Not long was to elapse before his wild and soaring spirit, after enjoying for a brief space the late-found happiness of repose, reached the end of its earthly term, having achieved, in ignorance, like all its fellows, one of the mightiest tasks in history; and while the world tragedy of the new Imperialism which he had created was drawing slowly to its climax, Lucullus, alone of the great men of his day, fell peacefully asleep in the arms of the silent goddess.

CÆSAR'S FIRST YEAR IN GAUL

THE news that the Helvetian emigration was about to take place hastened Cæsar's departure from Rome. In the February of the preceding year the government of the two Gauls had fallen quite unexpectedly to his share. Since then he had had little chance of preparing for his new duties. During his Consulship he was so taken up with the struggles and intrigues of home politics that he had no time to inform himself about Gaul. He had neither read books of travel nor consulted the merchants and politicians who were in relations with the *hinterland* through the Narbonese province. Thus he went out to his duties without any definite ideas of policy and with the meagrest knowledge of the country and its inhabitants. No doubt he had a clear notion of his general line of conduct. He intended, so far as possible, to apply to Gaul the methods of Lucullus and Pompey in Asia, to let slip no real or imaginary pretext for military operations, to acquire the riches and reputation so easily picked up in the provinces, to demonstrate to his fellow-citizens that he was a skilful diplomatist and a brilliant general. But he had as yet no particular ideas as to the possibility of such a policy, nor of the risks and vicissitudes it might be likely to involve. He would make up his mind on the spot, when he was face to face with the situation. His attitude was characteristic of the debasement of Roman statesmanship both at home and abroad. Politics had now become little more than the art of framing happy improvisations. Cæsar in Gaul was but following the common law. He went out at his own risk; and he worked for his own ends. Lucullus had succeeded; Pompey had succeeded; why should not Cæsar succeed also?

The first of these improvisations was the war against the Helvetii. There is no doubt that, when he left Rome, Cæsar's views about the emigration of the Helvetii were those which had been circulated through the political world at Rome from 62 onwards by the Æduan emissary, Divitiacus. Divitiacus was the spokesman of a political party in Gaul which had its own reasons for opposing the Helvetian movement. Rome had been taught by him to believe that the Helvetii had designs of invading the country and placing themselves at the head of a great coalition of the Gallic peoples. If they were prepared to be satisfied for the moment with the invasion of the province, in order to enter the country by the shortest route, they intended some day to be the nucleus of a great Celtic Empire which would dominate Gaul and menace the independence of Italy. With his views on the Helvetian movement inspired by Divitiacus, Cæsar naturally left Rome in excitement the moment he heard that the Helvetii were actually on the march. The danger to Roman interest seemed very real: and there was clearly not a moment to be lost.

The invasion of the Helvetii had been for some time on the horizon. Yet Cæsar, in his inexperience, had allowed himself to be surprised, with one legion in Narbonese Gaul and the three others at Aquileia, at the farther end of the Cisalpine province. Sending hasty orders to the legions at Aquileia to rejoin him, and travelling day and night, he hurried out to Geneva where he probably expected to find hostilities already begun.

It was between the 5th and 8th of April when he reached Geneva. Here, to his great surprise, he found, not war but an embassy from the Helvetii. They explained that a part of their nation desired to trek into Gaul with their women and children, and asked his permission to pass through the Roman province. It was a reasonable request, neither provocative nor menacing. But Cæsar had been taught by his Æduan advisers to regard the Helvetii as a horde of savages impatient to swoop down on the fertile lands of Gaul. Not unnaturally he suspected treachery. He asked for a few days' consideration, giving the deputation to understand that he would eventually consent. No sooner had they departed than he began, with the legion he had brought with him and some recruits enlisted on the spot, to fortify all the fordable points on the Rhone between the Lake of Geneva and the Jura. The object of these precautions is clear enough. They show that Cæsar expected serious hostilities to ensue after the refusal he had decided to give to the Helvetian demands. But once more he had miscalculated. A negative answer was returned to the Helvetii on the 13th, and the apprehended attack did not take place. The Helvetii made no attempt to invade the province, but sent instead to the Sequani to ask permission to cross the mountains at the Pass of the Écluse, which was readily granted them. Then they set out in their full numbers, with men, women, and children, some 150,000 persons in all, with three months' supplies and the few valuables they possessed stored in their waggons, under the conduct of an old chief called Divico, taking the Jura route.

The scare about the invasion of the Province had passed away as suddenly as it came, and Cæsar had lost his first opportunity for a campaign. But a second scare still remained. There was still the danger that, as the Ædui had so constantly preached, the Helvetii contemplated the foundation of a great Gallic Empire.

Here was Cæsar's chance. It was urgently necessary that he should have some feat to his credit as soon as was conveniently possible. He decided therefore to declare war upon the future Gallic Empire by pursuing the fancied Empire-builders into the heart of the country. A pretext was easily found. He was already in relations with the Æduan government, which thought itself threatened by the Helvetian trek; and the Governor of the Narbonese province had the Senate's instructions to defend the Ædui. First of all, however, it was necessary to have sufficient forces for a campaign. Four legions by themselves were hardly enough. Leaving Labienus to defend the Rhone, Cæsar hastily returned into Cisalpine Gaul, and, while awaiting the three legions he had already recalled from winter quarters at Aquileia, recruited two more. When these five legions were ready, he crossed the Col de Genèvre, descended on Grenoble, and marched rapidly northward along the borders of the province. Somewhere in the neighbourhood of the modern Lyons he was joined by Labienus with the legion he had left at Geneva; and it was probably about the beginning of June when, with six legions and their auxiliaries, some 25,000 men in all, he crossed the frontier of the Roman province and moved into Gallic territory along the left bank of the Saône.

His arrival was well timed. During the last two months the Helvetii had slowly traversed the country of the Sequani and had then entered Æduan territory; they had proceeded as far as the Saône with the intention of crossing it, probably at Mâcon. But whether they had really been pillaging the country or whether the party hostile to the trekkers, inspired by Cæsar, had concocted an agitation throughout the country, no sooner had the Proconsul crossed the Roman frontier than numerous Gallic peoples began to send him deputations begging for help. Petitions came from the Allobroges, who lived on the farther side of the Rhone, the Ambarri, the Ædui, and even from the Sequani, who had actually given the Helvetii permission to pass through their territory. With a legitimate pretext thus ready to his hand, Cæsar used his senatorial decree in favour of the Ædui to demand 4,000 horse and the necessary supplies from that nation, and threw himself headlong into the war. His plan was to surprise the Helvetii, who were beginning to cross the Saône, while they were still engaged in that slow and difficult operation. In a series of forced marches he moved upon Mâcon. When he arrived in the neighbour-hood he made a last effort, sending three legions in advance at full marching speed. But he had overestimated the delays of the passage. When his three legions arrived, only a small rearguard still remained on the left bank. To cut this to pieces was simple enough; but the success was but of trifling importance for his object. Cæsar took one day to throw his whole army on to the opposite bank, and started in pursuit of the Helvetii, who had moved off to the north-west across the undulating country of the Charolais.

Cæsar imagined that he was marching northwards to suppress a widespread and dangerous movement, perhaps the beginnings of a new Cimbric invasion among the Celtic populations. In reality he was merely blundering into a trap which had been skilfully laid him by Ariovistus. The Helvetii had not the least intention of founding a great Gallic Empire. This was a ridiculous popular fairy-tale to which the Romans and Cæsar, in their ignorance of Gallic affairs, had innocently lent credence, and which Ariovistus had done his best to circulate. There were no political designs in their trek at all. The real centre of political interest lay in quite a different direction. At the moment of Cæsar's arrival what really endangered Gaul was not the Swiss peril, personified in the Helvetian trekkers, but the German peril, personified in Ariovistus.

Divided for centuries past into a large number of unequal and independent republics which were continually fighting one another for supremacy, and distracted too by desperate party conflicts which often led to warfare through outside intervention, Gaul had been going through a period of particularly acute disturbance during the two decades preceding Cæsar's arrival, owing to a struggle for supremacy between the Ædui and the Sequani. The contest centred round the possession of the valuable toll-rights over the Saône; but it involved interests that affected, not the two nations only, but the whole of the country. Some years before, in the course of the struggle, the Arverni and the Sequani, having been defeated by the Ædui, had appealed for aid to Ariovistus, King of the Suevi, bribing him with the promise of territory in Gaul. Ariovistus had crossed the Rhone at the head of his Germans, and had duly helped the Sequani and the Arverni to defeat the Ædui.

The consequences of inviting the Germans west of the Rhine had been far more serious than the two Gallic disputants had foreseen. Once settled in Gaul, Ariovistus had no intention of remaining satisfied with the territory assigned him. He summoned numbers of his fellow-countrymen from Germany, and, with a victorious army at his back, profited by the divisions which paralysed the Gallic states, to establish, within a few years, a German supremacy over the whole of Gaul. The native population chafed bitterly at the invader, and a coalition of the states had attempted to liberate the country. But Ariovistus had defeated it, and had gone on, in the flush of his success, to extract tribute from the Ædui, and even to oppress his old allies the Sequani, who were responsible for his original intrusion into Gaul.

Thus for the last fourteen years there had been growing danger of a German supremacy over Gaul with its centre on the Rhine. Nor was this the most alarming feature in the situation. What was more ominous still was that the imminence of this national peril had intensified rather than allayed the struggle between the two dominant Gallic parties, the Conservative or aristocratic, and the Popular or rather the plutocratic interest. For some generations past the old Gallic nobility, like their Roman compeers at the time of the Gracchi, had been sinking steadily into the slough of debt, while a small knot of aristocrats, more skilful and venturesome that their fellows, had made use of the pecuniary difficulties of the upper classes to gather a great part of the wealth and authority of the country into their own hands. Some accumulated their riches in lands and capital, others monopolized the tolls and taxes and were the creditors of half the community. Between them they had an innumerable train of debtors, dependants, and servants; they controlled the proletariat by the wholesale distribution of largesse, and were trying to turn the old aristocratic republics of Gaul into something very like an ordinary monarchy. All over Gaul in almost every state there were millionaire demagogues, the Gallic analogues of Pompey, Crassus, and Cæsar, who were bidding for the support of the proletariat to strengthen their personal influence, and fighting a winning battle against the Conservative nobility, which stood for the old institutions and their old prestige. So fierce was the struggle and so absorbed the combatants that, when the German invader suddenly appeared on the field, both sides thought only of how they might use him for their own petty purposes.

Both parties had been quick to realize that the glory of having driven back Ariovistus across the Rhine would be sufficient to ensure them a long spell of power. But as each side desired to win this prestige as a weapon against the other, they were necessarily debarred from pursuing any common policy against the common enemy. They were thus each thrown back upon allies from outside. The Conservative nobility, which was most strongly represented among the Ædui, turned naturally to the Romans, and it was with the object of securing Roman help against Ariovistus that the Æduan Conservatives had been intriguing for some time past, through Divitiacus and others, to force the Senate to intervene in the affairs of Gaul. The Popular or plutocratic party, on the other hand, drew its strength from the masses, and the masses would not tolerate foreign intervention against the foreigner. To call in the Romans against Ariovistus would be to exchange one master for another. Its rallying-cry therefore was the liberation of Gaul by the united effort of the Gallic peoples. But since the most civilized and influential states in Gaul were not in a position to head the national cause, they looked for allies of a more martial and primitive strain. It was natural that at this juncture their eyes should turn eastwards, to Switzerland. The Helvetii were just the instrument they needed. It was the chiefs of the Popular party then who were responsible for the Helvetian trek. The Helvetii, who were finding their own territory too small for them, were promised new lands, we do not know in what part of Gaul, and were to be used as allies in the national uprising against the Suevi, whom they had met and conquered of old in their mountain home.

This then was the situation at the moment of Cæsar's arrival. Both parties preferred a prolongation of the existing anarchy and suspense to the possibility of a victory for their opponents; and the power of Ariovistus was being slowly consolidated, while the two factions were disputing as to the best means of overthrowing him. The Roman party had made a great *coup* by securing the senatorial decree in favour of the Ædui; yet, though two years had elapsed, the decree had not yet been put into force. The National party had succeeded in its turn in inducing the Helvetii to take up arms against Ariovistus; but for three years past one difficulty after another, to which the Conservatives, no doubt, contributed their share, had prevented the trek from taking place. In short, neither party was strong enough to secure a dominant position and lead the patriots of Gaul against the national enemy. Deplorable disorder reigned in every part of the country, and the intensity of the conflict, dividing not only nation against nation, and class against class, but even family against family, is well illustrated by the fact that the head of the National party, the Æduan Dumnorix, was the brother of Divitiacus, the chief of the Roman party.

The simplest way of stifling this insensate party struggle for supremacy would have been the conclusion of an alliance between Rome and the Helvetii against Ariovistus. But the foolish panic which had broken out in Rome, the obstinacy of the Italians in regarding the Helvetii as a horde of new Cimbri and Teutones, the ignorance of even well-informed Romans regarding Gallic affairs, the intrigues of Ariovistus, and the foolhardy mood in which Cæsar entered on his duties, all combined to make any such understanding out of the question. Italian public opinion favoured an alliance with Ariovistus; and Cæsar had gone out to Gaul determined to play the part of a second Marius by crushing the Helvetii.

This led to an exceedingly complicated situation in Gaul. The party which had demanded Roman intervention could not venture to oppose the Proconsul's projects; yet Cæsar's war against the Helvetii was exceedingly unpopular in Gaul; and to support the ally of Ariovistus looked like treachery to the national cause. Still more painful was the dilemma of the Nationalists. They did not dare openly to resist Rome, yet neither could they abandon the Helvetii to their fate. The Nationalist leaders were of course furious with Cæsar, but they soon realized that the only policy was to conceal their embarrassment. They must lie low, employ every artifice to gain time, work upon the ignorance of the Proconsul and the power that their popularity placed in their hands in order to slip in between Cæsar and their opponents and find some indirect means of relieving the Helvetii. The result was that both parties protested their friendship to Rome. Dumnorix came in person to the Roman camp and offered to pay the expenses of the Æduan cavalry on condition that he himself should be placed in command, intending of course to use his position to help his friends on the other side. Cæsar's campaign against the Helvetii was so unpopular in Gaul that the Roman party did not dare to inform him who his strange cavalry commander really was.

Thus Cæsar had succeeded in entangling himself in a whole network of difficulties of whose existence he was blissfully unaware. He went off in pursuit of the Helvetii, plunging into the depths of a vast and unknown country, without the faintest suspicion that his first campaign would stultify his position in Gaul from the very start by wounding the hopes and susceptibilities of the great mass of the Gallic people, or that a part of his escort, with their Æduan commander, set out on the expedition with the deliberate intention of betraying him.

The campaign so rashly undertaken was as rashly and strangely pursued. The Helvetii were anxious to carry through their trek as speedily as possible and had no desire to provoke the hostility of Rome. As soon as they learnt that the Roman general had crossed the Saône they sent an embassy, with Divico in person at its head, to give a reassuring statement and make a reasonable offer. Divico declared that, despite the unwarranted attack that had been made upon them on the banks of the Saône, the Helvetii did not desire war and were prepared to trek to any territory which Cæsar might suggest. To Cæsar, still under the influence of the Æduan intriguers, these declarations sounded too favourable to be sincere. So far from appeasing him, they only increased his apprehensions. Such proposals from the would-be rulers of Gaul could only be intended to hoodwink a foreigner. In his reply to the embassy Cæsar reproached them with their previous wars against Rome, declared that he refused to trust their word, and demanded hostages as the price of his abstention from attack. Divico replied that the Helvetii were more accustomed to receive than to give hostages, and broke off the negotiations.

This was an official declaration of war between Rome and the Helvetii. Yet once more there was a lull before hostilities commenced. The Helvetii, still anxious to avoid fighting, continued their march, prepared to defend themselves but resolved not to attack. Cæsar, fully conscious of the danger involved in a defeat, set himself to follow the Helvetii at five or six miles' distance, waiting for a good opportunity for attack, which the Helvetii abstained from giving him. For fifteen days the two armies followed one another in this manner, with only a few light cavalry skirmishes in which the horsemen of Dumnorix allowed themselves to be easily beaten. The Helvetii were marching northward towards the Côte d'Or, and Cæsar in his pursuit had been forced to move away from the Saône, which had been his line of communications hitherto. Before long the provisions which had been brought up from Mâcon on beasts of burden began to run low, the supplies promised him by the Ædui failed to arrive, and the Æduan nobles found all their volubility required to explain its non-appearance.

At last suspicion began to dawn on Cæsar's mind. He grew impatient, and at last ordered an inquiry. Then, from a hint here and a confession there, his eyes began to be opened to the trap into which he had been inveigled. Slowly the whole complicated political situation of Gaul began to take shape in his mind. He discovered that, if the Æduan aristocrats with Divitiacus at their head were friendly to the Romans, a large part of the Æduan nation was bitterly opposed to them, and that the leader of this section, Dumnorix, had only consented to equip and command the Æduan cavalry in order to assist his real allies the Helvetii. Moreover it was Dumnorix who, through his wealth and popularity, controlled the policy of the Æduan Senate and was endangering the success of the campaign by cutting off the supplies.

Viewed in this light the situation was exceedingly alarming.

Cæsar dared not take steps against Dumnorix for fear of exasperating the Ædui, but he saw that to go on pursuing the Helvetii without bringing them to an engagement was to discourage his own troops and to play into the hands of the traitors. Nothing but a speedy and decisive victory could turn the scales in his favour. His luck did not desert him. On the very day on which he discovered the danger of his position the scouts came in with the news that the Helvetii were encamped about seven miles off, at the foot of a mountain which they had as yet failed to occupy and which could be ascended by a different road from that which they had taken. Here was the long-expected opportunity. Cæsar's scheme was to send Labienus in advance with two legions to occupy the mountain at night; he himself would set out a little later with the rest of the army on the same route as the Ædui, arriving about dawn at their encampment to attack them in their sleep, while Labienus plunged down upon them from above. The plan was ingenious and it was executed with care. Labienus left in good time; Cæsar first sent a detachment of scouts commanded by Publius Considius, one of his most trusted veterans; then at the hour fixed in the dead of the night, he started in person with the legions. It was an anxious and agitating moment for a general who was making his first essay in strategy, with his supplies almost exhausted, with a host of traitors in his camp, and with legions whose courage was none too sure. And indeed, as it turned out, one moment of hesitation was enough to spoil the whole elaborate scheme of attack. At dawn, after a difficult night march, Cæsar had just come within sight of the Helvetian camp when Considius arrived at a gallop to say that the mountain was occupied, not by Labienus, but by the Helvetii. What then had taken place during the night? It looked as if Labienus had been overwhelmed and cut to pieces. In his dismay at the news Cæsar hastily withdrew, and, finding a hill in a favourable position, set out his legions in order of battle expecting an attack. It was not till some hours afterwards, when the sun was already high in the heavens and all remained quiet around him, that he sent out scouts to reconnoitre. Soon he heard that Considius' information had been mistaken. Labienus had successfully occupied the mountain and in vain awaited Cæsar's attack. Meanwhile the Helvetii had quietly broken up camp and moved on.

The situation was becoming critical. The troops had by this time only supplies for two days. The two armies had now arrived near Bibracte, the wealthy capital of the Ædui which lay nearly twenty miles to the west of the line of march. Cæsar had no alternative but to fall back upon Bibracte for supplies. He was just about to make the necessary arrangements when suddenly, on the site of the modern village of Ivry, the Helvetii threw themselves upon his legions and offered battle. When he learnt that only accident had saved his followers from a disastrous surprise, Divico probably felt unwilling to have the Romans any longer at his heels, and decided to give battle as the lesser evil. It may be that he was also unable to control the spirit of his men. However this may be, Cæsar had only just time, by dint of using his cavalry against the advancing enemy, to form up his army in order of battle. He arranged his four legions of veterans in three lines half-way up a hill on the right of the road, with the two new legions and auxiliaries above them, with orders to guard the baggage and prepare an encampment. Before long the Helvetii were upon them in full force, assailing the legions front to front with the headstrong bravery of mountaineers. Divico seems to have been one of those skilful and astute tacticians who, growing up among a primitive people exposed to constant guerilla warfare, like the Boers, learn their art by the continual exercise of a natural gift rather than by theoretical study. He was more than a match (and he knew it) for his ingenious but inexperienced Roman opponent, with his academic ideas of tactics picked up in the Greek manuals he had studied as a young man. Cæsar, who was probably much excited about his first big battle, took the frontal attack for the serious part of the engagement; when the ranks of the Helvetii began slowly to give way, he ordered his men to advance down the hill and attack the enemy, who were retiring to an opposite height. But the frontal attack and the retreat were only a feint to draw the Romans down the hill. Scarcely were they well on the level, than Divico drove in an ambush of 15,000 Boii and Tulingii on their right flank, while the retiring columns wheeled round and returned to the attack. The Romans were attacked simultaneously in front and on the flank, and also threatened in the rear; and the change had taken place so rapidly that Cæsar was unable to send to the troops on the top of the hill for help. A desperate hand-to-hand conflict ensued. What exactly took place we do not know. It is impossible to make sense out of the confused and contradictory account left us by Cæsar. What is clear is that he has something to conceal; for it will hardly be admitted that a writer so clear and definite in his descriptions as Cæsar can have left us a confused account of his first great battle out of pure negligence.

It is probable that the two new legions were panic-stricken, and, having received no orders, watched the conflict from above without daring to come to Cæsar's help: that Cæsar succeeded after considerable losses in extricating his men from the defile and gaining some strong position where they were able to resist the attack, and that satisfied with this success the Helvetii eventually retired. If so, the confused account in the *Commentaries* is merely a device to mask what was really a defeat. In any case, Cæsar was obliged to allow the enemy to break up their camp during the night and slowly continue their march towards Langres, leaving not a single prisoner in his hands, while he himself, owing to the large number of dead and wounded, and the fatigue and probably also the discouragement of his soldiers, was forced to remain three days on the field of battle.

Thus the Helvetii had fully attained their object. But after this initial failure Cæsar could not let matters remain as they were. He was just preparing to pursue the enemy afresh and to avenge his rebuff, cost what it might, when, to his great good fortune, the Helvetii asked for peace. Tired out by their long march, and perhaps somewhat bewildered by what had taken place, they had suddenly conceived a fear lest Rome might make them pay dear for their victory. They determined to make peace with the Proconsul, and declared that they were ready to return to their old country. Delighted at a proposal which rescued him without risk or dishonour from a dangerous war, Cæsar was prepared to be as magnanimous as circumstances required. Not only did he force the Allobroges to make the Helvetii large grants of grain to tide them over the time till their first harvest, but when the Boii flatly refused to return to their homes he made the Ædui grant them land in their own territory. It was Roman magnanimity at the expense of the Gauls. In his report to the Senate the result of the campaign was of course set down as a victory. The Helvetii returned home, with the exception of a small band of hotheads who insisted on continuing the trek towards the Rhine, and were easily cut off by the natives before they reached their destination.

If the Helvetii had been less frightened, not of Cæsar but of Rome, if they had attacked the tired and dispirited Roman army on the morrow of the battle, they might have saved Gaul from the Roman supremacy for ever. For twenty-four hours Divico had the destinies of Europe in his hands; but satisfied with having checked Cæsar for a moment, the ignorant tribesman continued on his way. Cæsar had therefore emerged not discreditably from the difficulties into which he had been rash enough to plunge. Unfortunately a negative success of this kind was not sufficient for his purpose. He needed some striking victory to revive his prestige in Italy, where his partisans were finding it increasingly difficult to hold their own.

It was while Cæsar was campaigning against the Helvetii that the first-fruits of the Democratic revolution began to show above the surface. They were as different from the rosy prophecies of Cæsar as from the jeremiads of his opponents. Cæsar had been mistaken in thinking that during his absence from Rome Crassus and Pompey would be able to control the Republic: that they could impose an unquestioned supremacy, amid a submissive and lethargic public, over a leaderless Opposition, a paralysed Senate and a dragooned and disciplined electorate. The habitual indifference of the upper classes had been rudely broken at last, soon after his departure, by an injustice done to a single Roman citizen, by the exile of Cicero. It is a curious and significant fact. In that troubled epoch iniquities just as crying were committed daily, and excited neither commiseration nor even comment; indeed Clodius had relied upon the moral apathy of the public for the success of his campaign against the popular writer. But for once the old Roman conscience asserted its claims. The first shock of stupefaction gradually passed away; and the public broke out into open discontent, when they saw their favourite driven out of Italy, his house on the Palatine solemnly burnt, his villas pillaged, and his exile decreed without a trial in a *privilegium* by an electoral majority, which assumed the function of a judicial tribunal to persecute one of the greatest of their fellow-citizens, contrary to every principle of law, for a crime which he had never committed. It was more than even the Roman public was prepared to tolerate. Rome would be for ever dishonoured if she made no amends. A violent agitation broke out for Cicero's recall, especially among his admirers in the upper classes.

While Cicero was mournfully sailing into exile his name began to be held in ever-increasing veneration in his own country among the public of knights and Senators. The first manifestation of sympathy in his favour was all the more impressive because it took place in silence. When Clodius held an auction for his possessions not a soul appeared to bid for them. But this was only a beginning. It was followed by demonstrations of all sorts, during which every opportunity was taken to testify to the exile's popularity. Many of the rich citizens placed their fortunes at his disposal; for Cicero was now practically a ruined man and had been reduced to living on the dowry of Terentia.

Unfortunately while the star of Cicero was thus in the ascendant among the wealthy classes, the light of his persecutor Clodius still monopolized his quarter of the heavens. Against the leaderless Conservatives and the dispirited Senate the Tribune was in his element. Inviolable by the nature of his office, unassailably popular through his recent corn law, director through his creature Sextus of the free distributions of food, chief of the voters' associations which controlled every election, closely allied to the two Consuls, for whom he had secured a five years' Governorship, Clodius began systematically to imitate and even to exaggerate the methods of his master. His particular predilection was to exploit the field of foreign policy for pecuniary purposes. He commenced by a stroke of characteristic daring in conniving at the escape of the son of Tigranes whom Pompey had condemned to a sort of honorary imprisonment in the house of a Senator. The Armenian had paid him well for his assistance; but it was a grave insult to Pompey, and everyone was wondering what action he would take. Men were already beginning to hope for an open rupture between the Democratic leaders. But Pompey was in no mood for a fight, and decided to overlook the matter altogether. So the irrepressible Tribune continued uninterrupted on his way, selling kingdoms, privileges, and priesthoods in all parts of the Empire, and rapidly rising to be the real master of the capital.

The demonstrations of Cicero's admirers, with no practical lever-age behind them, were not likely to impress a man cast in this mould. Clodius was not the kind of politician to be intimidated by an agitation concerted between the wealthy and middle classes, nor by decrees (or rather, in the modern phraseology, resolutions) passed by the big syndicates of tax-farmers, or the college of scribes and free officials of the Republic, or the numerous colonies and municipalities all over Italy which were enthusiastic for Cicero's recall. He would fight long and fiercely before he released his prey. The friends of Cicero had no illusions about their antagonist, and they set themselves patiently to the task of exerting pressure upon the Senate, and upon Pompey, the most naturally Conservative and the most impressionable of the three Democratic chiefs. It was useless to count upon Crassus, who had been stubbornly hostile to Cicero ever since the Catilinarian revelations.

Thus it was that an act of injustice to a single individual had gradually stirred up a serious political crisis which was now convulsing the entire community. As no one ventured to buy the site of Cicero's house, Clodius had it purchased by a man of straw, and to make its future restitution more difficult was contemplating the erection of a loggia and a little Temple of Liberty. The friends of Cicero, on their side, had on the 1st of June brought forward a proposal for his recall in the Senate; when Clodius had induced a Tribune to veto it, they had their revenge by organizing a huge popular demonstration to his brother Quintus, on his return from Asia. They had further com-pelled the Senate to declare that no other public matter should take precedence over the question of Cicero; and they were making arrangements to use all their influence at the elections for the success of his partisans.

Meanwhile the unhappy object of all this excitement and enthu-siasm in Italy was pining away his soul at Thessalonica. Cicero was thoroughly miserable in exile. All his ordinary tastes seemed for the time to have deserted him. He could neither write nor read (at other times his unfailing resource), nor enjoy the relaxations of travel. He refused to receive the visit either of friends or relations, and spent all his time devising and picking to pieces endless projects for his return, overwhelming his friends with letters sometimes plaintive and reproachful, sometimes buoyant and hopeful, in a continual alternation of confidence and despair. The times were changed and the part of Rutilius Rufus ill suited his temperament. Meanwhile the Conservatives did their best to keep open the question of his recall, speaking of him as though he were indeed a second Rufus and the victim, not of a personal animosity in a flimsy political disguise, but of the violence and rancour of the entire popular party. If the elections could only be fought upon Cicero, there was some chance of avenging the defeats of the preceding year. The most tempting prospects were thus opened up. Varro and other friends of Cicero, not content with urging Pompey to secure his recall, used the widespread agitation as an argument for the divorce of Julia and Pompey's eventual return to the Conservative side. In short, the political situation in Italy towards the middle of 58 was such as to cause serious anxiety to the absent Triumvir. Unfortunately, soon after the close of the Helvetian campaign he found himself confronted with new troubles even closer at hand.

After the conclusion of peace Cæsar had believed for a moment that his brief campaign against the Helvetii would have far-reaching and favourable results. He had seen assembled around him under his presidency, yet without his own initiative, the *Concilium totius Galliæ* or general assembly of Gaul, almost all the states having spontaneously sent him deputations. Nor had they come merely to offer empty congratulations, but to beg for Roman help against the national enemy, Ariovistus. This was in itself significant. It was no longer, as in the war against the Helvetii, one political party from among a single nation, the Ædui, but the whole of Gaul, without distinction of parties and states, which now declared its willingness to accept the suzerainty of Rome by appealing for her aid in the most important of national questions. It was hardly possible to doubt what this general assembly seemed in itself to prove, that the Helvetian war had done more to increase Roman prestige in Gaul than a generation of negotiations and senatorial debates.

Yet Cæsar was not slow to perceive that the situation was not altogether so favourable as it seemed. It was a solemn and decisive moment in the history of Gaul and of the world when the great Gallic assembly met for the first time under the presidency of the representative of Rome. It was then, very probably, for the first time, that Cæsar had a clear view of the whole political situation of Gaul in its proper perspective, that he was able to see both the real object pursued by the Helvetii in their trek and the essential fact, whose importance had hitherto escaped him, that the true enemy of Roman influence in Gaul was not the old tribesman Divico, but Ariovistus. It was evident that the Roman Proconsul could not obtain the supremacy he desired in Gaul, could not win a position which would enable him on one pretext or another to extract large sums of money from the free Celtic Republics, unless he first disembarrassed the country of his German competitor, who had stepped prematurely into his own coveted place. But as he gradually grew better to understand the political situation of the country he realized the full extent of his blunder in attacking the Helvetii, the brave little nation which had itself been prepared to play its part against the German. This campaign had indeed been trebly unfortunate. It had robbed him of an ally who might have been very useful in the coming struggle and thus considerably strengthened his real rivals, the Germans; it had alienated the powerful Nationalist party and the patriotic sentiment of Gaul, which could not forgive either the Roman Proconsul or his Gallic allies; and it had compromised the prestige of Rome in Gaul and lessened his chances in the war against Ariovistus—a war which must inevitably be fought out, if the Celtic Republics were ever to be brought within the circle of Roman influence.

It was not out of admiration for Rome that the whole of Gaul sent ambassadors to Cæsar to ask his help against the German intruder. That imposing demonstration of Gallic unity was merely the last despairing effort of the Roman and Conservative party to draw what profit it could out of the situation created by Cæsar's first campaign. The failure of the Helvetian trek, which was the direct result of Æduan intrigue, had excited so much indignation in Gaul that the Conservatives now recognized that their one and only chance was to induce Cæsar to turn his arms without delay against Ariovistus. If Cæsar remained quiet after the conclusion of peace the people would perforce have believed the popular Nationalist agitators, who accused the Ædui and the whole aristocratic party of having betrayed the national cause by calling in the Romans against the Helvetii and thus leaving Gaul in the hands of the Germans. On the other hand, if Cæsar drove the Suevi across the Rhine, the Conservatives would be able to declare that they had done far better service than the so-called Nationalists to the national cause, while at the same time in the victorious Proconsul they would secure a solid support for their future power. The one thing necessary, therefore, was to force Cæsar into the war with all possible speed.

Cæsar was not slow to perceive that the pressing and respectful solicitations of the Gallic representatives were practically a summons to arms. Already by the Helvetian war he had alienated the powerful National party and the mass of the people, and now, unless he crushed Ariovistus, the Roman party too would turn against him and he and his small army would be isolated in the midst of a vast and hostile country, with no chance of support from either side. He would have no alternative but an inglorious evacuation. A campaign against Ariovistus was the only means of winning the prestige he had hoped to find in his Helvetian campaign. Unfortunately this indispensable enterprise was not one of those adventures which can be improvised within a few weeks without serious danger. It involved marching into a strange country with a small army of six legions, with no good base of operations, against an enemy elated by a succession of victories, whose forces were believed to be indefinitely numerous. Cæsar could not depend upon the loyalty of the Gauls, upon whom he relied entirely for supplies; and he would leave behind him a powerful party which was longing for his overthrow. His experience in the Helvetian campaign enlightened him as to the full nature of his difficulties. Finally, and this might be most serious of all, in the case of a reverse, there were technical reasons against the course he was taking. Only a year ago, Ariovistus had been declared Friend and Ally of the Roman people, and no reasonable pretext of war could be alleged against him.

Cæsar had perhaps never yet been in so awkward a dilemma. He had to stake all that he had gained by a long and painful conflict, and all that he hoped to gain in the future, upon the doubtful result of a very hazardous campaign. A single defeat would mean the end of his whole Gallic adventure, and his fate in Italy was bound up with his fate in Gaul. But, with the lucidity of judgment and quickness of decision that never failed him in an emergency, Cæsar made up his mind that the ordeal must be faced; and he resolved to meet it at once by improvising a campaign to the best of his ability.

The first business was to find a pretext. He began by inviting Ariovistus to meet him because he had certain matters to discuss. It was insolently phrased, and the chieftain naturally replied that, if Cæsar needed him, he had only to visit him himself to tell him what he wished. Cæsar refused the suggestion, and asked him to make various concessions in favour of the Ædui and Sequani. Ariovistus, now thoroughly out of temper, not unnaturally refused. Cæsar then declared that he had been authorized to make war on him by the well-known decree in favour of the Ædui. Warned, however, by his previous experience, Cæsar was determined to run no risks of starvation or treachery in the course of his march. He occupied Besançon, the largest and richest town of the Sequani, organized a commissariat to be supplied by the Ædui and Sequani, and replaced Dumnorix as cavalry commander by Publius Crassus, son of Marcus.

But once on the road a new difficulty confronted him. The courage of his soldiers, already sorely tried by the perils and carnage of the Helvetian campaign, had been broken down by accounts given them about Germany and the Germans through the inhabitants and merchants of Besançon; and at the last moment they refused to march. They were far too few, they declared, to attack so formidable a foe, and would assuredly go astray and starve in the huge forests and deserts of a trackless country. Fear had reminded them too of the obligations of conscience. A war against a king whom the Senate had declared a Friend and Ally was hardly justifiable, and the gods would surely deny it a favourable issue. This was just the sort of difficulty Cæsar knew how to face. He called a meeting of officers and men, met their undeniable arguments with appeals to their self-respect, and stirred all their pride as Roman soldiers by dramatically declaring that if all the others refused he would set out alone with his 10th legion, which he knew would not fail him at need.

On the following day the army set out for the valley of the Rhine. After a march of seven days it arrived in the valley of the Thur, and soon afterwards came in sight of the army of Ariovistus. Cæsar, who knew that Ariovistus was expecting reinforcements, at once offered battle; but Ariovistus declined it for several days, telling his men when they grew impatient that the prophetesses would not let him fight before the new moon. Meanwhile he contented himself with threatening Cæsar's communications with the Ædui and Sequani and occupying his soldiers in cavalry skirmishes and surprise attacks, without ever venturing upon a general engagement. One day, however, it seems that one of these raids was carried farther than usual, no doubt owing to a mistake on Cæsar's part, and very nearly resulted in the capture of one of the two camps between which, for greater convenience in provisioning, Cæsar had divided his army. What then ensued is left obscure in our accounts. Perhaps Ariovistus placed too much confidence in his troops, or he may have been unable any longer to restrain their impatience. What is certain is that next morning, when Cæsar brought his troops out of camp, Ariovistus accepted battle. The right wing of the Roman army broke through the enemy's front, but the left wing could not resist the onset, and was already beginning to give way before Cæsar, who was on the right, became aware of what was going on. Fortunately Publius Crassus, who was in reserve with his cavalry, realized the peril and ordered the third line of reserves to move up in support. The experience of the Helvetian campaign had proved useful and the Romans emerged victorious. Ariovistus retreated precipitately across the Rhine, renouncing his Gallic ambitions for good. The German rule over Gaul was a thing of the past.

It is this victory over Ariovistus, and not his campaign against the Helvetii, which must be counted as Cæsar's first great political and military success. It was an important success because it transferred to Rome, at least for a time, the Protectorate which Ariovistus had hitherto been exercising over the divided republics of Gaul. So far this Protectorate was in no way comparable to the great Asiatic conquests of Lucullus and Pompey; yet in Cæsar's hands it might become a very useful instrument both for filling his own coffers and for bringing pressure to bear upon Italian politics. But for the moment Cæsar had no time to attend to his new conquests or to drive home his victory. All he could do was to send his legions into winter quarters

under Labienus in the territory of the Sequani and immediately
return into Cisalpine Gaul. Bad news had come up from Rome.

No one in Italy suspected the importance of what was taking place
in Gaul, and no one therefore displayed the least interest in its details.
Attention was exclusively directed upon Cicero, whose cause excited
ever-growing enthusiasm as the struggle between his friends and
Clodius became increasingly violent. At the elections Cicero's party
had won a striking success. The two new Consuls, Publius Cornelius
Lentulus and Quintus Cæcilius Metellus, were both favourable to
Cicero, besides seven out of the eight Prætors, and eight out of the
ten Tribunes. The public was delighted, and hoped that this result
would hasten the exile's recall, particularly as Pompey had promised
to bring the question before the Senate after the elections. But Clodius
was not easily discouraged. Knowing how easy it was to intimidate
Pompey and his senatorial flatterers, he had begun by attacking him
in a series of violent speeches; he had then appeared at the head of
his supporters to break up the public meetings of Cicero's partisans;
and had ended by posting up on the door of the Senate House the
preamble of his law against Cicero, forbidding the Senate hereafter
to discuss the question. Pompey was seriously alarmed. Finding no
help from Crassus he had thoughts of appealing to Cæsar. But Clodius,
growing daily more violent, actually threatened to burn his house and
put him to death, while, encouraged by the apathy of the Consuls,
he terrorized the whole city at the head of his bands. The public could
protest as much as it liked against the exile of Cicero: the politicians
were at the mercy of the irrepressible Tribune. For the time at least
all further advance was barred. Pompey retired to his house and refused
to show himself in public. No one in the Senate dared whisper a
proposal. At last a personal friend of Cicero's ventured timidly to
raise his voice. To evade the difficulty resulting from the veto posted
up by Clodius on the doors of the Senate House, Sestius endeavoured
to include Cicero's cause in a general formula which did not mention
him by name; but nothing came of the suggestion. Clodius made use
of the temporary paralysis of his adversaries to inaugurate the little
Temple of Liberty on the site of Cicero's house, putting up as an
image of the goddess, at least so Cicero tells us, a statue of a courtesan
from Tanagra. To increase the popularity of his cause he then began

to bribe the public with wholesale donations of corn bought up in all parts of Italy, wasting on this purpose the money brought home by Pompey, which was to have served for the administration of Cæsar's Land Law.

But this was at last too much for Pompey. He decided to put down his foot, and show Rome who was the master of the Republic. With this object he resolved to send Sestius to Cæsar to ask his consent to the recall of Cicero. He detached the Consul Gabinius from Clodius' side and persuaded him to form a band of supporters to resist the hired ruffians of Clodius. He also induced eight Tribunes of the people to propose, on the 29th of October, a law of recall in favour of Cicero. In order not to offend Pompey, the Tribunes consented; but at the same time, to avoid quarrelling with their formidable colleague, they inserted into the law a clause which practically stultified the whole, to the effect that no part of their proposals should repeal or decide any matter with which it had previously been declared illegal to deal. So another of these strange legal expedients ended in failure.

Amidst all these disorders, no one at Rome found time to pay attention to Cæsar, and the end of the German protectorate fell absolutely flat. Cæsar realized that just at present the Italian public had no ear for victories, and that the recall of Cicero might be far more useful to his cause. He therefore assented to Pompey's request. But a complicated question was not so quickly settled. Determined to use extreme measures to avert what was now seen to be inevitable, Clodius adopted the most unexpected of all his many devices. He turned against his old master, and made advances to the Conservatives, promising to declare Cæsar's laws null and void on the frivolous pretexts already brought forward by Bibulus.

Clodius' Tribunate ran out at last on the 9th of December; but it had been long enough to send Rome into a condition bordering on frenzy. It left the Democratic party hopelessly divided. Pompey had lost all confidence in Crassus; Crassus detested Pompey; Clodius and Pompey were at open war; there was dissension between the Consuls, Piso remaining friendly to Clodius, while Gabinius had taken sides with Pompey Public affairs were in a state of absolute chaos. The Senate had ceased to transact business; Crassus held his peace and did nothing; Pompey displayed a feeble and spasmodic activity; Cæsar's

Land Law, for which so many battles had been fought a year ago, had not begun to be administered. Gabinius alone showed signs of energy; he had passed an anti-plutocratic measure forbidding Italians to invest money outside Italy, in the hope of forcing capital to remain in the country and of diminishing the rate of interest to the advantage of debtors.

Meanwhile Cicero was still in exile. At the sitting of the 1st of January 57, his recall was at last discussed. Some of the Senators were bold enough to declare that Clodius' law was illegal, and that it was, consequently, unnecessary to make a new law to annul it. The law being void in itself, it was sufficient to invite Cicero to return. But Pompey, who was more cautious, suggested that it would be better not to enter into a conflict with the electors on a technical point, but to have a new law passed. Since the whole matter was merely a formality, the new law would be approved without difficulty. But he had left Clodius out of his reckoning. When on the 25th of January 57, the law for Cicero's recall was brought before the electors to be discussed, Clodius, though now but an ordinary citizen, appeared at the head of his bands to prevent its approval, and in the riots that took place the Forum was bathed with blood, which it took sponges to wash off again next morning.

CHAPTER XVII

THE ANNEXATION OF GAUL

The situation at Rome was indeed becoming critical; for during the winter of 58–57 famine supervened to intensify the prevalent disorders. Its cause is probably to be found in the enormous purchases made by Clodius in the preceding year and his reckless profusion in their distribution, perhaps also in the general anarchy and uncertainty, which frightened the merchants and paralysed the magistrates. The first explanation was at any rate that which commended itself to the enemies of the ex-Tribune, who were anxious to deprive him of his post under the corn law, and held him personally responsible for the distress.

But in spite of this accumulation of difficulties Cæsar was unable this year to keep in touch with Italian affairs as he would have liked. Disquieting news from Labienus forced him to cross the Alps again almost immediately. The victory over Ariovistus had not been sufficient to wipe out the Helvetian campaign; the consequences of this fatal blunder dogged him at every step. The Nationalists, who detested the Roman intruder, distrusted the assurances he had so readily given that he would respect the liberties of Gaul, and were preparing for a new war. Their plan was the same as that which they had adopted against Ariovistus: to secure the alliance of some primitive and warlike people against the national enemy. This time it was to be the Belgæ, a name which includes all the mixed populations of Celts and Germans living between the Rhine, the Scheldt, the Seine and the Atlantic.

When Cæsar received the early information of the coming trouble from Labienus, the full scheme of the war had not yet been sketched out. Yet its imminence in the near future was bound to cause him anxiety. It showed him that, unless he consented to withdraw his legions into the Narbonese Province and abandon all thoughts of intervention in Gaul proper, he must make ready for some hard fighting. On the other hand, the poor impression he had made at Rome by his victory over Ariovistus forced him to move on to some more important and sensational enterprise. He had the winter in which to make up his mind. He decided to let Crassus, Pompey, Clodius and Cicero fight it out between them in Italy, while he went back to Gaul to prepare a thrilling adventure recalling the exploits of Lucullus in the East. He proposed to anticipate the attack of the Belgæ by bearding them in their own native strongholds before their arrangements were complete. Their country was a long way off and utterly unknown to the Romans; and the Belgæ were regarded as an exceedingly formidable enemy, not only because of their valour, which was well known in Southern Gaul, but because of their numbers, upon which information was scanty, but quite sufficiently alarming. In all probability, therefore, it was a question of a long and difficult campaign; but Cæsar was not to be deterred. He was far too eager for some success that would consolidate his influence in Italy to make nice calculations about the risks he was taking.

But once clear as to his policy he did not rush blindly at his goal. The campaign against Ariovistus had warned him of the necessity of cautious and well-considered preparation. Since he could not calculate the enemy's forces with any exactitude he began by increasing his own. He sent agents to Africa, Crete, and the Balearic Islands for archers and slingers, and raised two new legions in the Cisalpine Province, sending them into Gaul under the command of Quintus Pedius. Shortly afterwards he crossed the Alps in person, and rejoined his army in the Franche Comté. Thence, after making careful arrangements for supplies, he moved rapidly, in a fortnight, into the enemy's territory, and surprised the first nation he invaded, the Remi, into submission. This initial success might be of considerable importance; for the Remi were in a position to give him more exact information as to the enemy's forces. The answer to his inquiries was not reassuring; the Belgæ, it appeared, could put some 350,000 men into the field. Cæsar had no means of testing the truth of this statement, or of judging whether the Remi were sincere in their professions of friendship. In any case, whether the information was correct or not, it was a call for caution. He therefore extracted hostages from the Remi, and persuaded the Ædui to invade the country of the Bellovaci, the most powerful of the Belgian peoples, to detach them from the general coalition, while he himself made a strong bridgehead on the Aisne, where he placed six cohorts under Quintus Titurius Sabinus and established his camp on the right bank with its flank on the river. Here, behind strong entrenchments, he waited with his eight legions for the approach of the Belgæ. When at last they came up, he refused to give battle. He was anxious first to study his new enemy and their method of fighting, and to prepare an elaborate battlefield by digging and fortifying two huge trenches 400 feet long, between which his army could fight sheltered from flank attacks. This was a precaution he had learned from Divico; but on this occasion it proved singularly useless. The enemy were not so naïve as to choose the ground he had prepared for their frontal attack; and though day after day they marched out in battle formation, and ranged up on the farther side of a small marsh, they too, like the Romans, kept stubbornly on the defensive.

In this way some time passed without any decisive action. Suddenly one day Cæsar was informed by Titurius that the Belgæ were attempting to turn his position by fording the river a little below the camp, to cut Cæsar's communications with the south. Cæsar hastily moved out across the bridge with the cavalry, archers, and slingers, and, arriving at the moment when the enemy were just entering the ford, charged them headlong into the bed of the stream. The engagement was short and sharp, and, after a feeble resistance, the Belgæ retired. Taken aback by this precipitate retreat, which did not seem justified by the losses they had suffered, Cæsar suspected stratagem and had the banks of the river watched all day. But at evening, when all remained quiet and he was just beginning to feel reassured, still more surprising intelligence was brought in. The whole Belgian army was in retreat. It seemed hardly credible after one slight skirmish; and Cæsar dared not move his troops out of camp during the night. It was only next morning, when the news was confirmed, that he threw three legions under Labienus on the heels of the enemy, together with a force of cavalry under Quintus Pedius and Lucius Arunculeius Cotta. Before long he discovered the explanation of a retreat which put a sudden end, after a short advance-guard skirmish, to what had seemed likely to develop into a formidable war. Only a few days before, the Bellovaci had heard of the Æduan invasion into their territory; they were clamouring to return to the defence of their country, but had been induced to stop for the attack on the day before their departure. When this had failed and supplies threatened to run short, they had broken up camp, and the rest of the army had followed them. Thus, after a brief and unsatisfactory campaign, the great Belgian coalition dispersed to the four winds.

Cæsar at once realized that if he acted quickly he could now take each state singly and subdue one after another. He was not the man to miss his chance. Without a day's delay he marched into the country of the Suessiones, surprised their force as they were just disbanding, and quickly persuaded them to submit. He was equally successful with the Ambianes. Then he moved on, with the same promptitude but still greater daring, to deal with the Nervii. The Nervii were the most warlike and barbarous people among the Belgæ. They were still so primitive as to grant no admittance into their cheerless and sparsely populated country to the insidious merchants from Greece and Italy who tried to tempt them with the cajolments of imported wine And they were crafty as well as brave, as the invading army found out to its cost. Joining hands with their neighbours, the Atrebates and Viromandi, they succeeded in surprising the Roman troops in their forests at twilight, just while they were constructing their camp for the night. A terrible hand-to-hand conflict ensued, in which the general himself had to fight like a common soldier. If the Roman troops had not learnt by the experience of the last two years to fight on their own initiative without awaiting orders from their officers, they would very probably have been annihilated. As it was, a hard-won fight ended in the submission of the Nervii. The only people now still remaining in arms was the Aduatuci, who on the news of the defeat of the Nervii burned their villages and took refuge in a fortress on the site of the modern Namur. Cæsar marched up and besieged it, and when, after a few days, proposals for capitulation were offered him he accepted on the usual condition that all arms should be given up. All day long the besieged busily carried out their arms from the fortress or hid them in the trenches; but at nightfall they took them from their concealment and burst out upon the Romans. The attack was repulsed, the town recaptured, and all the besieged, according to Cæsar, no less than 53,000 in number, were sold as slaves to the merchants who accompanied the army.

By this series of victories over such a number of semi-civilized and warlike peoples Cæsar caused a great sensation in the whole of Gaul and forced even doubters who had jeered at his exploits against the Helvetii to recognize the reality of the Roman supremacy. Most important of all, he had made large captures of prisoners, whom he generally sold on the spot, and of booty. There can be no doubt that in the course of his devastations he must have unearthed great quantities of precious metals, which the Belgæ, like all primitive peoples, were in the habit of hoarding. But the essential question still remained to be answered. Would his victories produce as great an impression in Italy as they had produced in Gaul?

The news from Rome was indeed far from reassuring, and led Cæsar to anticipate the break-down of the Democratic *régime*. Cicero had at length returned from exile, welcomed throughout Italy by enthusiastic demonstrations. Yet Clodius' law of banishment had only been repealed by Pompey's discovery, among the Tribunes for 57, of a man capable of standing up against the uncontrollable demagogue. The new Conservative hero was a certain Titus Annius Milo, a penurious aristocrat who shared the foolhardy ambitions and the unscrupulous methods of his Democratic rival. Sheltered, like Clodius, by the inviolability of his office, and excited by the promise of the Consulship for his exertions, Milo had recruited a private band of gladiators and cut-throats. By this means Pompey had at last been able on the 4th of August, amid scenes of riot and bloodshed, to vote the law recalling Cicero and ordering full reparation to be made for his sufferings.

But peace had not yet returned to the Republic. The Conservatives and Pompey had joined hands to make the famine an excuse for depriving Clodius of his superintendence of the corn-supply. Cicero, now once more among his peers, had gone further still. He had persuaded the Senate to approve a law giving Pompey for five years supreme control and inspection of all ports and markets in the Empire and the power of nominating not more than fifteen subordinates to keep Rome supplied with corn. This measure once more provoked the tempest which had been lulled for a moment on Cicero's return. Clodius attempted a revenge by raising the people against Pompey, declaring that it was he who had made food dear in order to make

himself king of Rome. He had announced his candidature for the
Ædileship in the following year; he had attempted through his friends
among the Tribunes to prevent Cicero from being indemnified for
the demolition of his house; and finally, at the elections for 56, he
had placed his bands at the disposal of the Conservatives and had
succeeded in carrying into power all their candidates for the Consulship and the Prætorship.

Thus the alliance between the demagogue and the Conservatives
was now formally recognized; and it proved so alarming to Pompey
that he arranged with Milo to postpone the election of the Ædiles
for fear of a fresh success for the new coalition. But now a new cause
of difficulty appeared on the scene, as if to add to the confusion.
Ptolemy Auletes, who had been driven out of Egypt by a revolution
among his subjects, came to Rome to tell his creditors that if they
ever desired payment they must help him to recover his kingdom.
Pompey, who was anxious to make a success of his new duties, had
been relying on the friendship of Ptolemy to secure the granary of
the Mediterranean. He received him in his palace and did his best
for his cause; but neither the Senate nor the public took much
interest in the poor king's fate.

In short, despite the weakness and incoherence of the Conservatives, the popular party, for all its spasmodic displays of energy,
seemed likely before long to have exhausted its strength. With the
exception of a few men of note, its ranks were filled with hotheaded
and brainless adventurers. Sooner or later the Conservative party,
which was not only wealthier but counted far more men of distinction
among its supporters, would regain its old power, repeal the Julian
laws and pay off its long score of grudges against their author.

Cæsar saw all this clearly enough from his distant vantage-post
in Gaul. He realized that he must somehow avert the impending
disaster. The situation was critical, for the collapse of his party might
occur at any moment. Amidst the labyrinth of difficulties which
hedged him round on every side, Cæsar's far-seeing genius hit on one
clear line of escape. It was a way of which no one else but he would
have·thought, for to traditional Roman ideas it involved what was
little short of madness. But, when the danger demanded it, Cæsar
had the daring to execute what others in his position would hardly

have dared to conceive. What he proposed to do was simple enough on paper—to annex the whole of Gaul as far as the Rhine to the Roman Empire, as Lucullus had annexed Pontus, and Pompey Syria; but it was a far more audacious scheme than either of these, or indeed than anything of the kind that had as yet been done in Roman history. Gaul was a country twice the size of Italy. It contained a number of independent states, with powerful aristocracies, influential priesthoods, and a long and tenacious tradition of national life. It had a population amounting most probably to some four or five million inhabitants, not debased and vitiated like so many of the peoples of the East, but inured to the experience of organized warfare.

To bring a whole medley of nations, from one day to the next, under the authority of Rome, and to remodel the whole structure of their life and government, was a stupendous undertaking. Without sinking to the level of the nervous diplomats who had refused to be embarrassed with the responsibilities of Egypt, serious observers were justified in asking if Rome was not undertaking more than she could possibly reform. But Cæsar could not now draw back. The temptations to attach himself to the new Imperialist school of policy were too great to be resisted. He saw how through the Helvetian war he had so thoroughly earned the hatred of the Nationalists that so long as he remained in Gaul they would never willingly accept the Roman protectorate. Yet, after his recent victories, even the more moderate party in Rome regarded that protectorate as just and necessary; and in any case he himself could not now possibly renounce it. Under these circumstances the Nationalists would be certain to use the semi-independent status under which the Gallic nations were now living to stir up constant difficulties for the Roman overlord. The only methods by which Rome could be rid of the whole trouble were by evacuation or annexation. This after all is a crisis in the history of every protectorate, and sooner or later it had been bound to occur in Gaul, where national feeling was exceptionally strong. This being so, it was surely not unwise to precipitate an inevitable development by making use of the impression produced by his victory over the Belgæ.

From the point of view of Italian politics his motives were still more pressing. Cæsar knew that he could never rescue the failing fortunes of his party unless he achieved some amazing and sensational success. The Belgæ had served him just as little as Ariovistus. He needed to make some far more stirring announcement: to proclaim that the age-long and ever-formidable enemies of Rome were now, after two years' hard fighting, at last effectually subdued; that the conquest of the Celtic lands, the great work undertaken by the first great representative of the Roman democracy, Caius Flaminius, had been finished a century and a half later by Caius Julius Cæsar; that the Roman Empire had been enriched by a fertile and populous territory, as vast as the provinces won by Lucullus and Pompey in the East. It is true that this conquest was still in great part imaginary. Aquitania and the other independent districts of Southern Gaul had not as yet seen a single Roman soldier or official; many of the peoples of Central and Western Gaul had not made their submission, and others had only done so formally; several, including some of the richest and most powerful, the Sequani, the Ædui, and the Lingones, had given the Roman general a friendly reception, but merely in the character of a powerful ally and without displaying the least inclination to accept the Roman overlordship. But at Rome immediate success, whatever the risk of distant danger, was the supreme law of political life. Once involved in a struggle where contending parties played upon the public by alternate violence and bluff, Cæsar devised what is probably the most skilful recorded exhibition of political charlatanism.

To give a little colour to his announcement, he sent Publius Crassus with one legion into Western Gaul hastily to receive the formal submission of the small nations between the Seine and the Loire. He despatched Servius Sulpicius Galba with another legion into Valais in the direction of the Great St. Bernard Pass to subdue the mountain tribes, whose toll-dues he regarded as excessive, and thus throw open to Italian merchants the new market that he had won them. He left the other legions in winter quarters among the Carnutes, the Andes and the Turones, and returned into Cisalpine Gaul, bearing the great news with him. Italy learnt that the Proconsul had finished his part of the work; it remained for the Senate to nominate the ten commissioners required to organize the new conquest into a Roman province. His calculation was that, taken thus by surprise, Gaul would remain quiet at least till the spring, and that during the winter, while the whole of Italy was still ringing with the news of his amazing achievement, he would have time to reshape the fortunes of his party.

The annexation seemed, however, for the time being, to be limited to the southern and western parts of Gaul. The most powerful tribes of central Gaul, such as the Sequani and the Ædui, who already had treaties of alliance with Rome, seem not to have changed their political status for the moment; but they found themselves surrounded and almost stifled by Gallic territories which had become Roman provinces overnight.

Thus it was that the Roman conquest of Gaul was, in the first intention of its author, simply an electioneering manœuvre to impress the Senate and politicians, the electors and the general public of Italy, in the midst of a confused struggle of cliques and parties, the inevitable, if unpremeditated, outcome of the revolutionary policy which Cæsar had been forced to carry through in his Consulship. Yet in those critical days, while he was bent solely on checkmating his Conservative opponents at Rome, Cæsar was in truth the blind instrument of destiny, moulding the whole future course of European history. Little though he guessed it at the time, that fateful proclamation was to be the prelude to a long and sanguinary struggle which would end in the decline or extinction of the old Gallic aristocracy. On the disappearance of their native rulers, who still preserved the old Celtic traditions, the people would easily adopt the Græco-Latin civilization of their conquerors, which thus found its way, unsuspected and unsupported by Gaul's first Proconsul, into the heart of the European continent, to form the basis of our modern society.

But Cæsar's only idea at the moment was to regain the ground lost at Rome by the blunders of his supporters. In this he was entirely successful. Exactly as he had calculated, the conquest of Gaul caused an immense sensation all over Italy. The proletariat, the middle classes, the financiers, the men of letters, the whole of the bourgeoisie which ordinarily stood aloof from political conflicts, in short, the entire nation, felt a glow of patriotic pride at his achievement, and, believing that somehow it would bring forth fruits as abundant as the Eastern wars of the last decade, indulged in one of those short but violent epidemics of enthusiasm which from time to time stir the depths of a civilized community. A deputation of Senators was sent by the people of Rome to Cæsar in Cisalpine Gaul to bear him congratulations. Many politicians who a year ago had passed severe strictures on his policy now returned to his support and hastened to meet him in the province. The Senate bowed before a unanimous public and decreed a supplication of fifteen days, the longest that had ever been known. The unregulated excitement which was at that time regarded as an adequate substitute for common sense and judgment in large matters of policy threw the credulous people of Italy completely off their balance during the whole winter of 57–56. There were very few who suspected that Gaul was not really conquered.

Cæsar was quick to apply the short-lived enthusiasm to the ends for which he had evoked it. During his last two years in Gaul Cæsar had benefited greatly by being continually in the open air, by the constant exercise and the enforced continence of an active military life. He had discovered that his delicate constitution had a far greater reserve of strength than he had ever imagined and that the hardships of campaigning agreed with him far better than the luxury and relaxation of civilian life at Rome. At the same time Gaul had revealed to him the possession of another quality which is given to very few, even among superior spirits—that intense and unflagging delight of the mind in the work upon which it is engaged which seems to make the powers of soul and body, of intellect and imagination, ever brighter and more vigorous as fresh prospects of activity are opened out to their labours. Thus it was that after his hard campaign among the Belgæ he crossed over into Cisalpine Gaul, not for repose but to undertake newer and more burdensome responsibilities. He traversed the province, administering justice and presiding over meetings of notables, travelling night and day to do more in the time; he received deputations, inquired into grievances, determined appeals, accepted invitations to meet the nobility, received the reports of his generals in Gaul, gave orders to Italian merchants for arms, horses and equipment, found recruits for the gaps in his ranks, attended daily to a huge correspondence from the capital, read all the latest books and the accounts of public and private doings at Rome, and entertained the many friends and friends of friends who came to visit him from Rome. The exaltation that is natural to every man who is conscious of his own greatness, the glory he had won by his striking victory over the Belgæ, the success of his pretended annexation of Gaul, combined with the mere physical pleasure of being restored to good health, spurred him on to the exercise of all his powers.

In the midst of all these distractions Cæsar found time to attend to the main object of his journey—the reconstruction of the Triumvirate, which during the latter months of 57 and the early months of 56 seemed to be slowly crumbling to pieces. Perhaps the Egyptian scandal contributed more than anything else to its discredit. Ptolemy's old creditors, in particular the rich banker Caius Rabirius Postumus, had again supplied him with money, and had managed to arrange, by dint of much intriguing, that the Consul Lentulus should be charged with restoring him to his ungrateful subjects at the head of the army of Cilicia. But the Conservative party, which had always been opposed to Egyptian entanglements, now claimed to have found it laid down in the Sibylline books, no doubt after a considerable search, that if a king of Egypt asked for help, he must indeed be helped, but not with an army. As the majority of Senators did not dare openly to offend against the popular superstition about Sibylline Oracles, the decree charging Lentulus to restore Ptolemy had to be discussed over again. The constant alternations of this everlasting affair were fast degenerating into farce, when it was rudely lifted back again to the region of high tragedy. For some time past it had been understood that an embassy of 100 Alexandrian notables was on its way to Rome to impeach their renegade monarch and to enlighten the Senate as to the real facts of the Egyptian situation; but the weeks passed and no deputation arrived. Various reasons had at first been given to explain the delay; but before long an unpleasant story began to go the round of Rome. Men whispered that Ptolemy had had his troublesome subjects put to death one after the other on the highroads of Italy and that the assassins were receiving their pay in the house of Pompey. The Conservative party was up in arms immediately. Favonius demanded an inquiry and promised to bring up the chief of the embassy, a certain Dio, who had escaped the assassins and was staying in Rome in the house of Lucceius. But before he could do so Dio disappeared in his turn and people did not hesitate to say that he had shared the fate of his fellows

Meanwhile other troubles were besetting the popular party. The Treasury was empty; Cato was shortly expected home with the gold and the slaves of the King of Cyprus; and the old quarrel between Crassus and Pompey was breaking out afresh. Crassus, who was still anxious to be sent to Egypt, was working in secret against Pompey, while Pompey, utterly tired and disgusted with politics, no longer appeared in the Senate and accused Crassus of paying Clodius to procure his assassination. At length after long discussion the Senate decided, early in January 56, that Ptolemy should be restored by a Roman magistrate without an army. But this only provoked new jealousies. Crassus and Lentulus were both eager for the mission, while Pompey, though he said and did nothing openly, had all his friends working to secure it for himself.

So the struggle recommenced with unabated violence. By the 15th of January no conclusion had yet been reached and the sittings of the Senate were suspended for the election of the Ædiles, which had been postponed to this date. Clodius was one of the candidates, and with the support of the Conservatives he defeated Vatinius, his most serious competitor. He was scarcely installed in office before he boldly prosecuted Pompey's henchman Milo for assault. The lawsuit that ensued surpassed everything of the sort that had ever been seen even at Rome. Pompey had agreed to defend Milo, but when he rose to speak Clodius' supporters began hissing and shouting, and the whole of his speech was drowned in a flood of irrepressible vituperation. When Pompey at length sat down Clodius rose, but Pompey's supporters played him the same trick; for two hours they deluged him with a shower of elegant invective in verse and prose. The whole scene was one of indescribable disorder. Suddenly, during a lull in the tumult, Clodius stood up and began to cry out with his supporters, "Who is it that is starving you?" to which his band replied in chorus, "Pompey, Pompey." Clodius went on, "Who would like to go to Egypt?" Again they replied, "Pompey, Pompey." "And whom are we going to send?" "Crassus, Crassus." Finally the suit was suspended and Pompey returned home in a fury. Milo was ultimately acquitted, but Sextus Clodius, the creature of Clodius, whom Milo had accused of assault, was also acquitted in his turn a short time afterwards because all the Senators in the jury voted in his favour.

By this time the Conservatives all openly favoured Clodius against the Triumvirate. So bold had they become that when, a short time afterwards, there was a discussion in the Senate on the forty million sesterces to be voted to Pompey for the purchase of corn several Senators complained in violent terms ("You would have thought," wrote Cicero, "that you were in a public meeting") that Cæsar's Land Law threatened to deprive the State of the revenue of the Campanian land. Fortunately the law had not yet been put into execution, and they asked if it could not be annulled. Cicero in fact had actually proposed that the question should be discussed on the 15th of May. From Cæsar's point of view then there was no time to be lost. Crassus had gone up to meet Cæsar at Ravenna, while Pompey had gone to Sardinia and Africa on his new commission. Cæsar arranged to meet them both at Lucca. He had already thought out a new and daring policy to save the Democrats and the Triumvirate from imminent dissolution, and was anxious to submit it to the judgment of his colleagues

CHAPTER XVIII

DEMOCRATIC IMPERIALISM

THE annexation of Gaul produced so powerful an impression in Italy because it was proclaimed at a crucial moment of her history. Cæsar had indeed been fortunate in his opportunity. We have seen how in the development of ancient Italy Imperialism plays the part of the industrial movement in the modern world; and it was inevitable that the attitude adopted by the public towards the policy of expansion should vary with every vicissitude in the conflict between the old social order and the new. The annexation of Gaul happened to synchronize with the renewal of the great struggle between the old and honourable traditions of Italy and the æsthetic and intellectual but corrupt and pleasure-loving civilization of the East.

For the ancient Latin spirit was still by no means extinct. It was yet to be found in those numerous families of the wealthy and well-to-do classes who remained faithful to whatever was best and most healthy in the old simple order, and it continued to fight manfully against the encroaching tendencies of the new era. It found support not only in the sacred memories of older times but also in some of the philosophies of the East itself. There were many Italian students of Aristotle who were ready to follow their master in his denunciations of excessive luxury and mercantile cupidity as the evils most fatal to republican states. Varro wrote his learned treatise on civil and religious antiquities in order to reconstruct for his contemporaries all that was most venerable in the life of the past. It was during this generation too that a mystical sect of moralists, founded at the beginning of the century at Alexandria under the name of Neo-Pythagoreans, endeavoured to circulate amongst Italian society certain ethical treatises attributed to the original Pythagoras, preaching all the virtues which were just now disappearing from the life of the upper classes: piety towards the gods, respect for ancestors, gentleness, temperance, justice, and the scrupulous examination every evening of actions accomplished during the day.

But these isolated efforts were powerless against the tendencies of the age. The influence of the East, in all its corruption and all its splendour, came flooding through Italy like a spring torrent swollen by the melting of the snows. The conquests of Pompey, the increase of the State revenues, the abundance of capital, and the prosperity which, after the depressions of the years 66–63, had been the natural result of these conquests, had once more intoxicated the imperial democracy. Italy was no longer the Amazon or the Minerva of the world; she had become a Bacchante. Aphrodite and Dionysus with their train of Mænads had flocked into Rome, leading their wild and stirring processions through the streets day and night, and inviting men and women, patricians and freedmen, slaves and citizens, rich and poor, to join in their festive revels. The banquets of the Workmen's Associations and Electoral Societies were so numerous and magnificent as to be continually raising the price of food-stuffs in the metropolis; although the State bought up grain in all parts of the world, there was yet a continual scarcity. The market gardeners in the suburbs, the breeders of animals, the innumerable publicans and wine merchants in the city, began to amass incredible wealth. Eurysaces, the biggest baker in Rome, an obscure freedman who had an enormous bakehouse and a great number of slaves, was one of the most successful of these purveyors to the government and to the great political and popular banquets; he ended by piling up so huge a fortune that he was enabled to leave behind him, as a lasting record of his wealth, that strange tomb in the shape of a baker's oven which is still to be seen, almost in its original form, in the neighbourhood of the Porta Maggiore. All over Italy there was a rage to build palaces, country houses, and farms, to buy slaves, and to increase the expenses of public and private life. Second only to Gaul and the business profits and festivals which its annexation would provide, what the inquisitive public cared most about was the theatre of Pompey, the first great stone theatre Rome had ever seen, which was being constructed by Greek architects on the spot now occupied by the Campo dei Fiori and the adjacent streets. At length there had arisen a man bold enough to revolt against the ridiculous law, imposed centuries ago by the narrow puritanism of the old era, which made the construction of stone theatres at Rome illegal. The building of this theatre was thus in itself symptomatic of the new order. It is true that

Pompey had tried to spare the feelings of the old-fashioned party, and to keep himself within the four corners of the law, by constructing a small temple of Venus on the top of the tiers of seats, which could thus be looked upon as a sort of huge staircase leading up to the temple. But Pompey was a man who was always afraid of his own successes, and he had no suspicion that for the great majority of Romans the construction of this theatre meant far more than the conquest of Syria.

In the meantime, while the big stone theatre was being completed, ambitious politicians spent fabulous sums upon giving the populace shows, which sometimes went on for several weeks, in provisional wooden playhouses: in engaging gladiators, musicians, dancers, and actors, and sending to the ends of the earth for lions, panthers, tigers, elephants, monkeys, crocodiles, and rhinoceroses to be exhibited in public and to fight in the arena. Every Asiatic and African governor was obliged to become a dealer in wild animals on behalf of his friends at Rome. In the year 58, in a festival for his Ædileship, Scaurus spent almost the whole of the proceeds of his Eastern campaigns in purchasing some 3,000 statues, some wonderful pictures from Sicyon, and about 300 columns of beautiful marbles, to decorate a wooden theatre which was to hold 80,000 spectators and was only to remain in use for a month.

The largest section of the upper classes, both in the aristocracy and the plutocracy, had entered upon a mad career of debauchery and self-indulgence. The old aristocracy and the rich bourgeoisie of the equestrian order had at length joined forces, but merely in the pursuit of common sources of enjoyment. The Empire was no longer administered by a martial aristocracy and a powerful class of financial magnates; at its head there was now a small clique of depraved and cynical materialists who were prepared to enjoy all the pleasures of the senses, and many of the intellect, provided only that high thinking did not seriously interfere with the paramount business of high living.

It was the same with their wives. In this shallow and dissipated society a woman who was not armed with the strongest and most refined of moral instincts soon lost all sense of shame and serious feeling, and became frivolous, fickle and corrupt. Roman ladies ruined their husbands to satisfy, not lust but a passion for precious stuffs and dresses, for sumptuous litters or costly furniture, for a well-groomed retinue of foreign slaves, above all for pearls and precious stones, such as they had seen in the treasure of Mithridates, when it was carried in Pompey's triumph, and were still able to stare at it any day when Pompey had exhibited it, in the temple of Jupiter on the Capitol. Their husbands squabbled between them as to whose cellar was best furnished with the most exquisite and expensive Greek wines, whose larder best stocked with costly victuals, whose country house best decorated, whose library best provided with books, whose gallantries and adventures were most to be envied.

The younger generation was still worse. We may typify it as a whole by taking five examples from among the best-known of the promising young men of the time. These five are Marcus Antonius, son of the Prætor who had fought so unsuccessfully in 74 against the pirates; Caius Scribonius Curio, son of the well-known Conservative who had been Consul in 76 and afterwards commander in Thrace; Caius Sallustius Crispus, son of a rich landowner from Amiternum; Marcus Cælius, son of a well-known banker from Pozzuoli, and lastly Catullus. Antony and Curio were so constantly together that slander called them husband and wife; between them they had run up so many debts and become entangled in so many adventures that Curio's father had forced him to leave Antony, and Antony, pursued by his creditors, had taken refuge in Greece; there he made pretence of leading a sober and studious existence, but when he found this too dull (as he very soon did) he went on to Gabinius in Syria, who made him a cavalry officer. Sallust, who had ability and a real taste for letters, wasted the whole of a considerable fortune upon women, and was considerately given the name of "Fortunate" by his friends because of the great number of his gallantries. Cælius had been an ardent follower of Catiline, chiefly owing to the debts he had already contracted. When he escaped the fate of his accomplices he continued his dissipations; he had become the lover of Clodia, had then broken with her, and been accused by her of having taken part in the assassination of the ambassadors sent from Alexandria to indict Ptolemy Auletes before the Senate. Catullus, now out of favour with his family, who were sick of his extravagance, burdened with debt, and heart-broken at the betrayal of Clodia and the death of a brother, who had died somewhere in Asia, had gone in the suite of the Prætor Caius Memmius to Bithynia to forget his sorrows and to fill his purse. Hardly had he reached Asia than he felt home-sick for Italy, and he soon began to make congenial preparations for his return and to satisfy a fantastic and prodigal caprice. In one of the sea-coast cities of the Black Sea, perhaps at Amastris, he had bought a dainty little yacht in which he proposed to sail home across the Mediterranean. He set sail in his boat with its crew of purchased sailors and took it to a port in the Sea of Marmora, joined it again at Nicæa, after an excursion to Troy to visit the deserted tomb of his brother, and then, like a king in his own ship of state, he coasted slowly along the seaboard of Asia Minor, threaded his way through the islands of the Ægean, and along the coast of Greece, and so up the Adriatic to the mouth of the Po, thus eventually, after a strip of land journey, reaching his native Lake of Garda.

Catullus and his companions are only typical members of the thoughtless and thriftless society in which they lived. Elated by a prosperity which everyone regarded as permanent, Italy was losing all sense of the distinction between justice and injustice, truth and falsehood, wisdom and folly. Yet in sober fact her prosperity was more apparent than real. If expenses were increasing on every side, incomes were by no means increasing in proportion. One of the sources of revenue which had been most lucrative ever since the time of the Gracchi, the financial exploitation of the provinces, was almost exhausted, and Italy was forced back, for her provincial profits, upon the more barbaric methods of political and military bleeding. This is one of the essential factors in the ten years which follow upon Cæsar's Consulship; it supplies the key, not only to the popularity which Cæsar's Democratic Imperialism enjoyed at this moment, but also to the terrible crisis which it was one day to bring forth. During the last quarter of a century Asia and Greece, which had already after Sulla's conquests shown symptoms of becoming a less lucrative field for Italian financiers, had been almost worked out. It was now impossible to make a large fortune out of the East by a year or two in business. All the wealth which could be most profitably transported to Italy or exploited on the spot had already fallen into the hands of Italian capitalists, and the new conquests, such as Pontus and Syria, having already been exhausted by long years of war, were not a profitable sphere for Western enterprise.

All this did not pass unnoticed by the money-lending classes in Italy, and capital was gradually withdrawn from all these departments of speculation. The sons, nephews, and grandsons of the knights who had made their millions in the half-century posterior to the death of Caius Gracchus were now comfortably settled at home, like Atticus, enjoying the fortunes they had inherited, and devoting themselves to politics or business, study or pleasure. The last remains of the old wealth of Asia were being scrambled for by a crowd of small money-lenders working with very little capital; and the class of wealthy, educated and influential financiers, who had been the greatest political power in Roman government from the time of the Gracchi to the time of Sulla, had almost entirely disappeared. It had been weakened first of all by the massacres and confiscations of Marius and Sulla; it had become enervated in the succeeding quarter of a century by the lack of opportunity for great enterprises and by the desire, to which a second business generation is always prone, to enjoy its inherited money; and it had now finally become merged with the old political aristocracy, surrendering its own peculiar advantages to a herd of obscure and ignorant capitalists who were unable to exercise any authority in the State.

Thus the political influence of the capitalists, which had been a source of so much danger to the Republic in the time of Marius and Sulla, was now scarcely more than an historic memory. The repression of the conspiracy of Catiline had been a desperate and expiring effort. The Catilinarian spirit was by now entirely triumphant; and the victorious Democrats were busily infecting Roman society and government with the bitter anti-capitalist prejudices and animosities of the masses, not without certain assistance from the aristocracy which, then as always, had a lurking hatred for usurers. Although the three chiefs of the popular party were not themselves hostile to the capitalists, the executive showed itself more and more opposed to their interests. In Macedonia, for instance, Piso was easily induced for a consideration to lower the interest owed by many of the towns. In Syria, Gabinius always put Italian capitalists in the wrong, interfering with their enterprises in every possible way to persuade them that

their capital would be much better invested in Italy than in Syria.
At Rome, after a long period of neglect, the old laws forbidding
Senators to engage in business began once more to be put into force.
For instance, Marcus Brutus, son of Servilia, when he went to Cyprus
in the suite of Cato, had made the acquaintance of two of those
obscure Italian capitalists who infested the East at that time, and had
been induced by their mediation to lend money to King Ariobar-
zianes and to the town of Salamis in Cyprus, at the rate of 48 per
cent.; but since business of this sort was directly contrary to the law
of Gabinius he was secretly intriguing to have his investment authorized by a special vote of the Senate.

But if the field of speculation and great financial enterprises was
becoming exhausted, what other pecuniary resources remained open
to the upper classes, and, above all, to the small ruling oligarchy at
Rome? There was only one form of provincial enterprise which was
still as lucrative as ever. Italy was driven back inevitably upon war
—with its manifold profits in booty and tribute, gifts and ransom.
After the huge fortunes amassed by Lucullus and Pompey, and the
millions made by their generals, and even by persons in lower positions
who had followed their standards, every politician in Rome, and all
his friends and relations, looked forward to securing a similar windfall
in some part of the world to which the Roman arms had not yet
penetrated.

It is easy to imagine how these demands and expectations diffused
the passion for Imperialism throughout Roman society. Military
plundering had now become the most lucrative industry in Italy.
When an army amassed a store of loot there was hardly anyone in
Italy who did not benefit by it, and it was the peaceable class, the
people who risked nothing at all, who benefited the most. It was the
merchants, the contractors and the workmen to whom the State,
with its Treasury heaped with spoils, and the generals, officers and
soldiers, with their pockets full of money, provided employment
and remuneration. This civil population, devoted though it was to
commerce and agriculture, was just as enthusiastic for Imperialism
as the world of politics. Perhaps its ardour for the aggrandizement
of the Empire was all the greater, because, like all stay-at-home
classes of society, it was easily moved by the glamour and excitement

of military life. The curious platonic affection among civilians for war, a phenomenon common in many advanced societies, had by this time become very widespread in Italy, and was a force which partisan interests well knew how to employ in the propagation of their policy of Imperialist adventure. If our modern Imperialists look to the great Roman Empire-builders for a model, their heroes went back boldly to the archetype in Alexander. No personage in history was more popular at this time than the mighty Macedonian, and most men seem to have imagined that Rome was about to accomplish very similar exploits.

But meanwhile, before the Empire of Rome became co-extensive with Alexander's, the most immediate and decisive effect of the universal enthusiasm was to impel men to incur the most impossible obligations. Nearly everyone was at once both creditor and debtor; men lent one another any little money they possessed, and borrowed again whenever they were in difficulties. Italian society had become an inextricable labyrinth of debit and credit, through the system of *Syngraphæ* or Letters of Credit, which were renewed as soon as they fell due; they were negotiated in the same way as securities and bills of exchange to-day, because the scarcity of capital and the frequent oscillations in prices would have made it ruinous for them to be redeemed too frequently. Those who were in need of money attempted to sell to some financier the claims they had on other persons, and the financier would give cash payment, of course with a proportionate discount according to the prospects of the debt, the needs of the creditor and the condition of the money market.

The new policy which Cæsar proposed to his friends harmonized admirably with the condition of opinion in Italy, and tended at once to stimulate and to satisfy the ruling passions of a commercial and democratic age—its imperial and military pride, its eagerness for quick profits, its infectious mania for luxury, self-indulgence, and ostentation, both in public and private life. Expansion on the frontiers, prodigality at home, gold and the sword: these were the two main points in Cæsar's programme, and the two were inextricably associated. Expansion would furnish the money necessary for prodigality; the prosperity created by home expenses would generate new energy for expansion.

Already in this very winter Cæsar had spent all the money he had made in his Belgian campaign by lending or giving enormous sums to politicians who had come from Rome to pay him court. But he entertained still vaster designs for the succeeding years. Crassus was to make Pompey's peace with Clodius; and Crassus and Pompey were to be candidates for the Consulship of 55. Once elected they were to induce the people to give them a Proconsulship for five years: they were to prolong Cæsar's Gallic command, also for five years, and to vote the sums necessary to pay all the legions which he had recruited since the beginning of the war. Having thus become masters of the Republic for an indefinite time, they were to follow out on a more extended scale the aggressive Imperialism which Lucullus had originated, and to achieve new and romantic feats of conquest. With the money these conquests brought in they were to execute huge public works in Rome and Italy, make profits for contractors and merchants, workmen and soldiers, buy up the Senate and the politicians, and provide the people with amusements on a scale of unparalleled splendour. Among other projects, a big gladiatorial school was to be established at Capua. As regards the conquests to be made, they had decided upon an enterprise which must appeal to every admirer of Alexander—a scheme too upon which Cæsar had long been bent, the conquest of Parthia. The man and the party who annexed to the Roman East this huge, mysterious and fabulously wealthy empire would win unrivalled glory in the world of his contemporaries and of posterity. Cæsar had indeed to resign himself to the abandonment of this adventure to one of his friends; for he was himself too much occupied by affairs in Gaul, where his recent conquests still required his presence. As for Egypt, Crassus and Pompey must give up their designs and dissensions, but were to charge Gabinius to restore Ptolemy to his country, without authorization from the Senate, on condition that he paid each of them a large sum of money. It seems that the amount demanded by Cæsar was about seventeen and a half million sesterces, or more than £160,000. The man who had attempted as Consul to find a legislative nostrum for the chronic corruption of all civil societies was now himself preparing to corrupt the entire electorate of Italy.

We do not know what took place in the discussions at Lucca

between Cæsar, Pompey and Crassus; but it is probable that Crassus' assent was more easily given than Pompey's. Crassus had enjoyed both wealth and power, but the popularity of Lucullus, or Pompey, or Cæsar had been denied him, and he had spent a long public life in different efforts to acquire it. At this moment of universal elation his old passion flamed up once more. The Imperialist policy of Lucullus had brought glory to its author and to Pompey, and it was already bringing glory to Cæsar. Why should Crassus remain content with being the victor of Spartacus, when it was open to a Roman general to match the exploits of Alexander? His ambition to be the conqueror of Parthia was alone sufficient to win his approval of Cæsar's designs.

Pompey, on the other hand, who was the only one of the three with the least knowledge of Parthia, and had refused the chance of attacking it in 63, may have felt inclined to oppose this whole policy of expansion and corruption. He was already beginning to be disgusted, and also a little frightened, by the shape which the policy of his party was assuming. Like many wealthy men who have everything that they need, he was strongly in favour of a simple life and an austere and unassuming morality—for other people. But it was impossible for him to break away from Cæsar and Crassus; he was fond of his wife; he felt that his reputation was endangered; and he had numerous enemies in the Senate. Clodius, already quite sufficiently impertinent, would shrink from no violence or stratagem against him when he ceased to be shielded by Cæsar and Crassus. The only way to consolidate his tottering influence was to become Consul, and then, after successfully accomplishing his new special mission, to secure some novel and extraordinary command. But for all this he needed allies. So he could not refuse assent to his colleague's proposals.

CHAPTER XIX

THE SECOND CONSULSHIP OF CRASSUS AND POMPEY

A SHORT time after the Conference at Lucca Cæsar was obliged to give up his intention of making a long stay in Cisalpine Gaul and to hasten back across the Alps. Revolts were already breaking out in the province which he claimed to have "pacified." Galba had been attacked by mountain tribes and his army almost cut to pieces; several of the peoples in Armorica who had made their submission in the previous autumn were again in arms; the Veneti, who were heading the movement, had put in chains the Roman officers sent to requisition supplies. Moreover, the announcement of annexation had caused universal discontent among the Gallic people, particularly among the Belgæ and Treveri; and the tribes of Aquitania, who had not yet submitted, fearing that Cæsar intended to include them in the comprehensive terms of his proclamation, prepared to assist the Veneti.

At a moment when his friends at Rome were so loudly proclaiming the conquest of Gaul, Cæsar could not afford to create the impression that he dared not treat the country like a subject province. He therefore imposed upon Gaul an annual contribution of forty million sesterces, prepared ruthlessly to suppress the revolt of the Veneti, and decided to proceed without delay against the peoples which still remained independent. He sent Labienus into the country of the Treveri to impress them and their neighbours, the Remi and the Belgæ, with the Roman power; he sent Quintus Titurius Sabinus with about 10,000 men to ravage the territory of the Vinelli, the Curiosoliti and the Lessobii, who were allies of the Veneti; he ordered Publius Cæsar to march into Aquitania with a small force of cavalry, and about 4,000 infantry; and reserved for himself the task of reducing the Veneti. As the Veneti were provided with a numerous fleet he had ships constructed on the Loire and enrolled all the pilots and rowers he could find. He ordered the Pictones and Santones, who were holding aloof from the revolt but had not yet made their submission, to provide him with ships, thus declaring them tributaries of Rome. For the command of the fleet he selected the young Decimus Brutus, son of the Consul of 77 and the well-known Sempronia; and even before the ships were ready he led his land forces into the territory of the Veneti.

Titurius and Publius Crassus were soon successful in their respective operations. Cæsar, however, was not equally fortunate. The Veneti had taken refuge within forts constructed on tongues of land jutting out into the sea, in positions where the great ocean tides defended them far better than any devices of human ingenuity; ebbing and flowing twice daily with a rhythmic force strange to dwellers by the Mediterranean, the high tide repulsed the army which was attempting the siege by land, and the low tide stranded the fleet which was moving to the attack by sea. Cæsar thus spent a large part of the summer in assailing a line of impregnable fortresses which were secured against capture either by land or by sea.

Meanwhile Pompey, after duly making his peace with Clodius, had again become reconciled with Crassus, and together the two chiefs exercised an undisputed lordship over Rome, Italy and the Empire. The reconstruction of the Triumvirate had reduced the Conservative opposition to a small knot of vain and violent Senators, headed by Cato, Favonius and Domitius Ahenobarbus, who had no influence over the majority of their colleagues. Even Cicero had reluctantly submitted. Cæsar had promised his brother Quintus a command in Gaul, and Pompey who had gone straight from Lucca to Sardinia to requisition corn, had asked Quintus to tell him that his speech in the Senate on Cæsar's Land Law had given him much displeasure. Cicero had consented to go into the country on the 15th of May when he should have been present in the Senate to speak on a motion of his own about this very subject.

He soon yielded still further, and promised actually to speak in Cæsar's favour, when at the beginning of June a debate took place on the proposed despatch of ten commissioners to organize the administration of Gaul and to vote the funds necessary for the four legions recruited by Cæsar in 58 and 57. In spite of his triumphal return to Italy, the wound inflicted on him by Clodius had left a lasting mark upon his nervous and impressionable temperament. The vague dreams of glory which had turned his brain after the conspiracy of Catiline had by now passed away. Content with having escaped from the arena with his life, he wished to remain outside as an intelligent onlooker. He was returning to his early passion for literature, to which he had been unfaithful since he laid it by years ago to become one of the leading lawyers in Rome. He was now engaged upon an ambitious work, the dialogue called *De Oratore*, a book written in his very best narrative and philosophical style, full of vivid personal touches and delightful pieces of characterization. The quiet pleasure which he derived from the composition of his book seemed for the moment far more enviable than the delirious excitements of ambition and the mad intoxication of power. There were private preoccupations too, such as the unsatisfactory state of his finances, which distracted him from devoting too much attention to politics. He had already been in some embarrassment before his exile, through the debts incurred to pay for his new house. Despite the indemnity voted him by the Senate, which, as a matter of fact, was wholly insufficient, and the advances of his friend Atticus, he had serious difficulty in satisfying his creditors and rebuilding his house and country villas.

There was yet another reason which deterred him from opposing the Triumvirate. As a man of right feeling he felt that he owed a debt of gratitude towards Pompey for his recall from exile—a debt which was something of the nature of a political obligation. Why, he asked himself, should he offend Pompey to please a small clique of obstinate aristocrats who had abandoned him in his hour of danger and were really not a whit better than their opponents? As for Cæsar, there might be much to be said against him, yet had he not also a good deal to his credit? What was the use of making life a burden by running full tilt against every difficulty that arose? Would it not be wiser to follow the example set by a man like Varro, who, though an aristocrat of wealth and culture, had filled numerous offices, been legate in the war against the pirates and at the end brought home a good million of money for his pains?

Varro had indeed understood how to preserve entire liberty of action in the midst of all the party struggles and intrigues of his day. Quite recently, after passing some trenchant criticisms upon the policy of his friend Pompey, he had retired from politics to his villa in the country where he occupied himself with improving the cultivation of his estates and helping by his studies and writings to keep alive all that was best in the old Roman traditions, reshaped and revivified by the influence of Greece. He did so in the form most popular with a dilettante and bustling age, which made action a fetish and thought a pastime, by writing handbooks, compilations and manuals; his great work in nine books, entitled *Disciplinæ*, is in fact a sort of encyclopædia. He was also a patron of art, and Archelaus, one of the first sculptors in Rome, was employed in his service. Cicero was quite ready to follow in the footsteps of his friend Varro. There were now but two objects which he had at heart: to show his gratitude to Pompey, and to take vengeance upon Clodius.

The public soon learnt of his change of attitude. In spite of his disapproval of the conference of Lucca, he shortly afterwards delivered a striking speech in the Senate, introducing a panegyric, in the fashion of the day, on the conquest and pacification of Gaul, and telling the arm-chair critics, who inquired why funds and reinforcements were still needed for a conquest which was already completed, that, although the larger operations had been triumphantly concluded, there was still a sort of war to be carried on against guerillas. The Conservative opposition was easily outvoted. It was decided to send ten commissioners to organize the new territory, and in the spring of 56 Gaul was officially proclaimed a Roman province by the Senate. It was also resolved that Piso should be recalled at the close of the same year, and that Gabinius should leave Syria at the end of 55, to be replaced by one of the newly elected Consuls.

For July with the elections was now at hand. Lucius Domitius Ahenobarbus had already announced his candidature for the Consulship, and it was generally expected that Pompey and Crassus would follow his example. The days passed: but Pompey and Crassus gave no sign. Either the report which had been circulated about their candidature was erroneous, or they had changed their minds. Soon it was observed that every time it was proposed to fix the day of the election two Tribunes systematically made use of their veto. The electors soon awoke to the meaning of this manœuvre. As public opinion was not generally favourable to their candidature Crassus and Pompey were unwilling that the election should take place under the presidency of the Consuls Cneius Cornelius Lentulus and Lucius Marcius Philippus, both of whom were Conservatives. One of the two would have to preside at the electoral assembly, which meant that it would be his duty to present the list of candidates to the people, and that he would have the right of refusing to inscribe any name of which he did not approve. There was some chance that he might be led on by public opinion to erase the names of Crassus and Pompey. Fearing a rebuff of this sort Crassus and Pompey had decided to have the elections postponed by the Tribunes until the following year. From the 1st of January onwards it would be necessary for the Senate to elect an *interrex* for five days at a time and this *interrex* would preside over the elections in place of the Consul. Their plan was thus simply to wait until chance gave them a Senator devoted to their own cause.

The Conservative clique urged the public, who had no taste for these intrigues, to compel Pompey and Crassus to abandon their obstruction, or at least to acknowledge their responsibility for its continuance. Lentulus made several attempts to force a declaration from them in the Senate as to whether they intended to come forward as candidates; he even summoned a large popular meeting at which, in the presence of all the Conservative Senators in mourning costume, he accused Pompey of tyranny. But it was all in vain. The public grumbled at Crassus and Pompey, but remained on the whole completely indifferent. Among politicians, on the other hand, there was so widespread a fear of the Triumvirate that many were afraid even to enter the Senate House. The months passed. The elections were still being postponed, and Pompey and Crassus still pretended to be innocent of the obstruction. The Conservatives attempted to retaliate by bringing an action against Lucius Cornelius Balbus, the skilful agent of Cæsar and Pompey, for the wrongful use of the title of citizen; but Pompey begged Cicero to defend him. Cicero made a speech which is still extant and successfully secured his acquittal.

Meanwhile the revolt of the Veneti had at last been quelled by the tardy appearance of Decimus Brutus with his fleet. Whether the tribesmen made light of a navy indiscriminately collected from all parts of the coast, or whether, weary of the long siege, they hoped to finish the war at one blow, they had at once taken to their ships and given battle; and Decimus Brutus had achieved so signal a victory that they had immediately sent in their submission. Cæsar, anxious to give a fresh demonstration that Gaul was now a Roman province, condemned all their chief men to death.

Then he moved on farther afield. At the end of the summer he undertook an expedition against the Morini and the Menapii who had not yet submitted; but the campaign was unsuccessful. These warlike tribes did not offer a collected resistance against the march of the legions, but dispersed in small bands through the forests and marshes, taking their treasure with them, and carried on an obstinate guerilla warfare by surprising and cutting off small detachments of Romans. Winter was now approaching, and Cæsar saw that it would be foolish to advance farther into a wild and totally unknown country. He therefore made good his retreat after inflicting some damage on the country, and sent his army into winter quarters in the territory which had revolted in the course of the year.

Thus a third year of the war had ended, leaving the Romans with some striking successes and a considerable supply of loot. The suppression of the various risings had given Cæsar abundant pretexts for devastation and pillage, and had enabled him and his officers, notably Memmius and Labienus, and indeed the whole army, to reap a handsome compensation for the hardships they had endured.

But Cæsar had now to meet a far more serious difficulty than the stubborn resistance of a few angry tribes. He had to organize a constitution for the conquered province. It was, of course, entirely beyond his power to destroy at one blow the whole existing framework of Celtic society and to replace it by a brand-new form of government. On the other hand it was not at all easy to adapt the old working institutions to the changed situation: to mould to his own extraneous purposes a complicated system of forces and attachments and interests, which still retained much of its vitality under the Roman *régime*. He was particularly embarrassed by the condition of the two prevailing political parties, the one Nationalist and popular, the other Conservative and aristocratic. Though their activity had been considerably curtailed since the annexation, neither of these parties had been wholly broken up; each still continued to maintain its old position and nurse its old grievances, endeavouring to apply the new conditions to the furtherance of its own particular interests. As Cæsar grew to have a better acquaintance with Gaul he realized that the Nationalists, relying as they did on the support of the masses, were far more powerful than the Conservatives and aristocrats who had invited him into Gaul. He learnt that all through the country the Diets or Assemblies of Notables were feeble and decadent bodies which enjoyed only a nominal authority in face of the growing power of the personage always known in Cæsar's writings as the king. The king was the chief executive officer of the government, generally nominated for a fixed period by the Diet, and not infrequently selected from among the demagogues at the head of the Nationalist party. Now this party, though it had bowed for the moment beneath the yoke, continued to distrust Cæsar's intentions and to detest the foreigner. This meant, of course, that a large part of the nation refused to accept the new *régime* with sincerity and loyalty, and would do nothing to bring the old institutions of the country into harmony with Roman demands.

The difficulty was undoubtedly very serious. But Cæsar, with his fine diplomatic ability and unequalled presence of mind, was not easily daunted. He came to the conclusion that he must alter the whole direction of his Gallic policy by transferring the weight of his influence from the one party to the other: in other words, he made up his mind to abandon the Conservatives upon whose help he had so far relied and to depend upon the popular party, which had been hitherto steadily opposed to him. He began by making advances of all sorts to the rich men who were engaged in winning a monarchical position in the old Gallic republics. By the exertion of his own personal influence or by usurping the powers of the Diets, he arranged that some of them should be appointed kings in their own country, hoping thus to have the policy of several of the people directed by chiefs devoted to the Roman interest and prepared to bring the masses over to his side. Sacrificing the friends who had hitherto stood by him, he summoned the Diets and used all his power to precipitate the revolution which the oligarchy of plutocrats had long been maturing. Amongst the new friends whom he made in this manner were Vercingetorix, the young and powerful chief of the Arverni; Tasgetus, King of the Carnutes; Cavarinus, King of the Senones, and Commius, King of the Atrebates. It appears that he even intended to make Dumnorix King of the Ædui. He was also thinking of applying the principle of *divide et impera* to help the Ædui and Remi to the supremacy which had been forfeited by their rivals the Senones, the Sequani and the Arverni. This was the policy he had devised to consolidate the Roman power in Gaul.

But whatever the troubles still in store for him, all went well for the moment both in Gaul and in the metropolis. Crassus and Pompey had succeeded in postponing the elections to the year 55, and in securing the nomination of an *interrex* favourable to their cause. The obstinate Domitius had been induced by his leader Cato to persist in his candidature; and on the morning of the election he left his house at dawn, with an escort of slaves and clients, to make a round of the city soliciting for votes. At the corner of one of the roads he was suddenly assailed by an armed band; the slave who preceded him with a torch was killed, many of the escort wounded, and Domitius himself frightened into an undignified retreat. Cæsar had given furlough to many of his soldiers to go up to vote, under the escort of Publius Crassus, and Crassus and Pompey were thus eventually elected without difficulty.

They set to work without delay. Their first and most pressing care was to put into execution the scheme agreed upon at Lucca. One of the Tribunes of the people, Caius Trebonius, son of a rich business man and a recent convert to the party of Cæsar, succeeded, despite the violent opposition of the Conservatives, in passing a law which made Syria and the two Spains the provinces to be assigned to the Consuls of the year, each to be held for five years with powers of peace and war. When this was off their hands, the Consuls proceeded to renew the government of the three Gauls to Cæsar for another five years. This proposal too was passed without serious disorder, although Cicero, in several friendly interviews, endeavoured to dissuade Pompey from its adoption. After a short holiday in the country Pompey and Crassus, who returned to Rome in April, brought forward various measures to put a check to the social disorders of the time. Crassus proposed a Bill against corruption, and Pompey a Bill containing rigorous provisions against parricide and a measure to amend the method of selecting juries for the courts. Pompey was also anxious to pass a law against luxury, which suggests that he was already inclining towards ideas which were utterly opposed to the flaunting Imperialism of Cæsar; Hortensius however persuaded him to withdraw it by an eloquent panegyric in which he described luxury as the natural and fitting ornament of power.

But no small reform of this nature could have availed in a society where anarchy and corruption were encroaching day by day. About the beginning of spring a singular rumour began to circulate at Pozzuoli, amongst the numerous Egyptian merchants who used that port in the direct trade between Egypt and Italy. It was whispered that Ptolemy had been brought back to Alexandria by the help of a Roman army. Considering that the Senate had as yet come to no decision upon the matter, the news seemed hardly credible. But for all that it was true. Ptolemy, tired of sending money to Rome and receiving nothing in return, had at length appealed to Ephesus where, shortly after the conference at Lucca, he had been met by Rabirius; they had then gone on together with Pompey's despatches to interview Gabinius in Syria. Gabinius, in obedience to Pompey's orders, at last consented to restore Ptolemy to his kingdom without waiting for the authorization of the Senate. He was to receive a handsome compensation from Ptolemy, and Rabirius was to become Minister of Finance in the Egyptian kingdom, to watch over the interests of the Italian creditors in that country. Thus, towards the end of the year 56, Gabinius had invaded Egypt and re-established Ptolemy on his throne, with an army in which Antony was an officer. The howl of indignation from the Conservatives can be imagined.

The impression of this scandal had not yet died away when the public awoke to a still more startling piece of news. It suddenly became manifest that Crassus intended to attempt the conquest of Parthia. The evidence was indeed too plain to be gainsaid. He was now openly making preparations for the campaign, recruiting soldiers, selecting officers, putting his affairs in order and making a detailed inventory of his fortune. He was able to set down in his book, that having been left 300 talents by his father he was now in possession of some 7,000. Yet he was still dissatisfied. The megalomania which was so widespread an ailment at the time, coupled with the vanity of a headstrong and grasping nature, had turned the veteran politician, hitherto, despite all his defects, a serious and sagacious man of business, into a lighthearted swaggerer who was a prey to the strangest and most impossible delusions. He intended to beat the record of Lucullus who had passed away in the previous year in a state of childish senility, to follow on the track of Alexander into India, and go down as the greatest of all great conquerors. The excitement caused by this news and by the preparations with which it was accompanied proved infectious, and it was not long before enthusiasm was enlisted far and wide for the idea. Many of the younger men attempted to secure positions as officers, amongst them Caius Cassius Longinus, who had married a daughter of Servilia and thus become the brother-in-law of Brutus. But the small Conservative clique persisted in predicting disaster; the country, they declared, was distant and unknown and the Parthians redoubtable assailants in the field. They even ventured upon the paradox that the war must be unjust because the enemy had supplied no excuse for its declaration. It was long since anyone at Rome had paid serious heed to arguments of this description; and indeed neither party seems to have had any real conception of the difficulties of the enterprise.

Cæsar allowed himself even less breathing-space than Crassus and Pompey. In the spring of 55 he had crossed the Alps into Gaul with the intention of spending the summer on a small expedition into Britain, to see if the island offered facilities for the winning of fresh laurels. But his attention had been distracted by an invasion of two German tribes, the Usipetes and the Tencteri, who had perhaps been secretly induced by the Nationalist leaders to cross the Rhine against the Romans. Alarmed at the number of their forces, Cæsar had employed the dishonest stratagem of keeping them busy with negotiations and then attacking them by surprise. He decided to follow up this success by an expedition across the Rhine, to intimidate the Germans against future interference. He ascended the valley of the Rhine as far as Bonn, threw a bridge over the river within ten days and made a hasty raid into the territory of the Suevi and the Sugcambri. It was only after the conclusion of these operations that his hands were free for the British enterprise. He had only time to make a hasty disembarkation with two legions, reserving a larger expedition till the following year.

In spite of their comparative insignificance the news of these exploits caused great enthusiasm at Rome. Rumour said that Cæsar had conquered 300,000 Germans, and his descent upon Britain seemed little short of miraculous. If Cæsar's information about Britain was meagre, people at Rome were utterly in the dark as to conditions of the country, and could therefore say for certain that the wealth concealed in the recesses of that fabulous island would provide an unparalleled opening for profitable enterprise. But the Roman public had long ceased to employ its reason, and in its appetite for amusements, sensations and holidays it swallowed anything that was offered it with indiscriminate credulity. At the end of the summer the palings round the theatre of Pompey had at last been removed and Rome had been dazzled by its huge masses of glittering marble and by the superb square colonnade for shelter in rainy weather, which was built behind the stage and decorated with paintings by Polygnotos and statues representing the nations conquered by Pompey. According to one tradition place was found there for the magnificent statue by Apollonius, son of Nestor, part of which has come down to us under the name of the Belvedere Torso. One part of the colonnade was walled off to form a magnificent room called the Curia of Pompey, which was large enough to hold the entire Senate. A magnificent festival was held to inaugurate the first building truly worthy of the metropolis of Empire. Amongst other marvels there was a wild-beast hunt in the course of which the wounded elephants began to trumpet, emitting cries so distressing, we are told, as to move the hearts of the public—that same public which used the dagger so freely in its Forum scuffles, and drew an exquisite pleasure from the death-struggle of a gladiator.

These reports of uninterrupted military success, together with such displays of almost regal munificence and delirious popular enthusiasm, must have been profoundly discouraging to the Conservative party. Its ranks grew scantier daily, till they were gradually thinned down to a mere handful of politicians. But these at least made up for lack of numbers by violence; as they saw their forces diminishing, they joined more persistently in the combat. They had secured the election of Domitius Ahenobarbus to the Consulship for the year 54 in company with Appius Claudius, the elder brother of Clodius and a friend of Pompey, and had also been successful in winning the Prætorship for Cato and Publius Servilius, son of the conqueror of the Isaurians, as the colleagues of Caius Alfius Flavius and Servius Sulpicius Galba, the one a friend and the other an officer of Cæsar's. They now prepared a counterblast to the popular demonstrations in Cæsar's honour. Cato proposed that, in accordance with ancient Roman custom, he should be delivered up to the Usipetes and Tencteri for having violated the law of nations.

Nor did this satisfy their meddlesome weakness. Before long they resorted to a still more daring manœuvre. Crassus had been enrolling soldiers in Italy to make up, together with the legions of Gabinius, the army which he thought necessary for his Parthian expedition. Unable to raise a sufficient number of volunteers, he had fallen back at last on compulsory enlistment. This hurried resort to the press-gang wounded the susceptibilities of a public which had long lost all taste for military service. Profiting by the agitation thus provoked, the Conservative party attempted to veto the levy of Crassus by means of two Tribunes, Caius Ateius Capito and Publius Aquilius Gallus. But the stratagem only intensified the impatience of Crassus, who now arranged to leave Italy already in November. The Tribunes were thus robbed of their victim. But at least they could offer a dignified protest. When Crassus left Rome with his suite and his son Publius, whom Cæsar had sent to accompany him with a troop of Gallic horse, Ateius escorted him to the City boundary, assailing him as he went with evil prophecies and maledictions.

CHAPTER XX

THE "CONQUEST" OF BRITAIN

THE elderly banker who was thus buckling on sword and armour to slake an old thirst for popularity was at least expeditious in his methods. He set off on the conquest of Parthia in the most relentless and peremptory haste, taking the straightest possible line towards his objective, regardless of the impediments in his path. On his arrival at Brindisi he insisted on immediately putting out to sea in the stormy season, and thus lost a number of ships and men in the crossing. Disembarking at Durazzo, he set out without delay in the depth of winter, taking the Egnatian Road across Albania, Macedonia and Thrace towards the Bosphorus, and ignoring the effect that this disastrous and hurried advance produced upon the spirits of his recruits.

Meanwhile Cæsar had decided to spend the following year in an attempt on Britain. We have no information as to his object, but it is hardly likely that he expected to effect the conquest of the whole island. Perhaps he intended nothing more than a filibustering expedition on an unusually large scale, to bring home fresh stores of booty, and to give the Romans new material for celebrations and vainglory. He may also have wished to diminish the unrest prevalent throughout Gaul since the peace he had so unexpectedly imposed upon a country where war had for centuries been the normal condition of life. Sudden social changes of this kind never fail to produce a crop of unexpected disturbances; and no difficulty perhaps caused Cæsar more trouble in his settlement of Gaul than the unemployed soldiers. There were hundreds of men in the country who were solely dependent upon warfare for power and position. Suddenly cut off by the peace from what had been the whole source of their social importance, and indeed their livelihood, such adventurers inevitably drifted into discontent and sedition. Cæsar was so well aware of this that he attempted to occupy the soldier class by recruiting amongst them a large number of volunteers and to flatter the military vanity of the Gauls by forming a legion, the famous Lark, composed almost entirely of natives, thus placing the new subjects of Rome on the same footing in the army as the conquerors of the world. It is therefore possible that he thought of Britain as a new field of action to be thrown open under Roman control to the military aspirations of the great Gallic clans, whose chiefs he intended to lead to Britain in the following year.

For the moment however, towards the end of the year 55, after having invented a new type of ship and given orders for the construction of a certain number of vessels during the winter, he crossed the Alps to Italy and thence to Illyria, returning again to Cisalpine Gaul to summon the local assemblies, receive the innumerable petitioners who awaited him from Rome, and practise once more on a grander scale his familiar policy of corruption. Being now in possession of enormous resources, he was able to hand over large sums to Balbus and Oppius, his two agents at Rome, to make advances to needy Senators, to build costly villas and to buy up estates, antiques, and works of art of every kind all over Italy, and finally to imitate Pompey in undertaking huge public works at Rome, thus putting money into the pockets of contractors and workmen and satisfying the now almost universal taste for magnificence. His designs were indeed grandiose. He had given orders to Oppius and Cicero to enlarge the narrow confines of the Forum, and he spent the enormous sum of 60 million sesterces to buy up the blocks of old houses which filled a corner of the Comitium at the foot of the Capitol. As the people still assembled in the Campus Martius for the Assembly of the tribes, where they were packed into provisional enclosures, surrounded by palisades and divided by ropes into as many sections as there were tribes, Cæsar was anxious to present the electors with a huge marble palace worthy of the sovereign people, to be called the *Sæpta Julia*. The building was to be in the form of a huge rectangle, with a front corresponding to the present line of palaces on the right-hand side of the Corso, looking from the Piazza del Popolo and the Palazzo Sciarra to the Piazza Venezia. It was to be surrounded by a magnificent colonnade over 300 yards long to which a large public garden was to be attached. This work also was to be superintended by Balbus and Oppius, who were to choose the architects, and contract for and supervise the construction.

Cæsar had now also begun to devote special care to the collection of able and serviceable slaves, whom he either purchased in the open market or chose from among the prisoners of his campaigns. He needed an enormous following of accountants, secretaries, couriers, agents, archivists, and ordinary servants, to administer the huge finances of the State and of his private patrimony, to superintend the government of his province, to provide for the armies and public works, and to assist him in the direction of political intrigues. This huge crowd of personal dependants he distributed throughout Rome, Italy, and Cisalpine and Transalpine Gaul, in the cities, amongst the legions, and along the great roads, wherever, in fact, he thought their presence might be useful to his interests. He had trained it to an unrivalled pitch of efficiency, superintending the whole body down to the humblest slaves and the smallest detail, maintaining the strictest discipline by cruel corporal punishments, and arranging a regular hierarchy of promotion by varying his payments from mere food and clothing up to a salary in money, or liberty, or a gift of land, houses and capital. One of the dependants placed in this way amongst the lowest of his household servants was a youth captured in a raid across the German frontier; hearing one day by chance that the boy lent out the leavings of his food to his companions at interest and kept a rough account of his debtors, he instantly promoted him to be an official in the financial administration, thinking no doubt that so decided a gift for figures, if it did not bring him to the cross, would certainly carry him far; and he was not mistaken.

In the spring of 54 Cæsar returned to Gaul taking with him a number of new officers, amongst them Quintus, brother of Cicero, who joined him in the hope of making his fortune in Britain. Just about the same time Crassus, after passing the Bosphorus, entered Syria from the north, relieving Gabinius of his command and making every preparation to invade Mesopotamia early in the year, without a formal declaration of war.

Pompey, on the other hand, had sent his subordinates to Spain, but himself remained in the neighbourhood of Rome. His pretext for doing so was the necessity of providing for the food-supply of the capital; but his real reason for staying was that the Triumvirs did not think it safe for all three at once to be at a distance from Rome. The depleted Opposition was now trying to show its hostility to the military policy of the Democrats by posing as the defender of oppressed nationalities. In Conservative drawing-rooms at Rome laments were heard about the unscrupulous rapacity of Cæsar, and the sudden and suspiciously rapid enrichment of his officers, more particularly Mamurra and Labienus. Men asked if the heroes of popular Imperialism had no greater ambition than rapine and robbery, and made stirring appeals to the slumbering moral conscience of the nation. But the nation was not disposed to give ear to them; the enthusiasm of conquest was far too contagious. Most people regarded Britain and Parthia as already subdued and made haste to borrow money on the treasures they concealed. Cæsar, Crassus and Pompey were still the heroes of the hour among a people that had no thought except for riches, victories and festivals. Cæsar, indeed, for the moment, was the most popular of the three: "our only general," as his admirers called him, was the man on whom all eyes were directed, about whom all had an opinion, whether good or ill. It seems to be true of all societies, that where pleasure and money are the gods of the multitude, there is a slow but steady weakening in the fibre of character. Men feel unable to remain long in a minority; they have a nervous anxiety to justify their position, and are quick to alter their opinions and likings. Very few at Rome were strong enough not to be carried away by the enthusiasm for the Triumvirs, whose career of success seemed only just to be beginning.

They had a striking and influential example in Cicero. He had at last become reconciled with Crassus, just before his departure for the East. Pompey too was taking every occasion to testify to his esteem, and Cæsar, always anxious to win over the greatest orator and writer of Rome, treated his brother Quintus with special consideration, adroitly flattered his literary vanity by praising the writings he sent him, and took pains to be polite to all the persons whom Cicero recommended to his notice. Cicero was genuinely touched by these exhibitions of flattery. He felt a lively gratitude and devotion towards his three great statesmen friends, and an honest desire to show them his appreciation of their behaviour by acting in their support. Every now and then, it is true, his feelings were still stirred by some particularly scandalous incident. He had thoughts, for instance, of accusing Gabinius in the Senate for his conduct in Egypt. But his longing for quiet, the indifference of his colleagues, and a feeling of the futility of anything that he might attempt induced him to abandon the idea and reserve his energies for his work in the courts or in the field of literature. A distressing personal duty had lately fallen to his share. He had to set into order the great unfinished poem of Lucretius, who had put an end to his life in the previous year in a fit of melancholia.

Moreover he had schemes of his own on hand. He meditated composing a poem on Cæsar's achievements in Britain, and was thinking, like many a retired statesman since, of writing a great political treatise, to expound the ideas which the study of the Greek philosophers, the experience of his career, and discussions with his contemporaries had suggested to his mind. Pure democracy had ended, it seemed, in bringing Rome to a state of irremediable chaos; aristocracy no longer existed, and the idea of monarchy was so generally detested that no one could seriously put it forward as a remedy for present evils. There remained nothing but the Aristotelean harmony of monarchy, aristocracy and democracy—the creation of a supreme office to be given for limited periods, and by election, to some eminent citizen of the Republic who would be entrusted with large powers, and enabled to exact a respect for the laws from both the people and the Senate.

Unfortunately, during the course of these profound political meditations, Cicero was weakly yielding to the fashion of the day, and continuing to swell the large volume of his debts. Although he had not yet finished his payments for the house which had been demolished by Clodius, and although the indemnity granted him by the Senate was insufficient to rebuild his town residence and his villas, he continued to spend money on his country house at Pompeii, to buy a second at Pozzuoli, to provide additional accommodation at Rome, and to increase the number of his servants. Cæsar skilfully took advantage of a moment of difficulty and induced him to accept a considerable loan.

Catullus, on the other hand, was fast becoming the most violent of aristocrats, hurling his fierce and biting lampoons against the favourites of the popular party. On his return to Rome from the East he had definitely broken with Clodia, and after one last bitter and sorrowful poem of farewell had changed the subjects, metre and style of his verse. He was now a thorough Conservative in politics and a devotee of the erudite and artificial poetry of the Alexandrian school. It was at this time that he composed his famous Epithalamium on Peleus and Thetis and his strange sixty-third song, a description, in the barbaric galliambic metre, of the orgiastic worship of Cybele. He was also writing a series of short and violent political lyrics in which he attacked Cæsar, Pompey and their principal partisans, affecting, young provincial though he was, sentiments of the most ultra-aristocratic character and a pious horror for the vulgar democracy which was levelling all the old distinctions between class and class, even in the highest offices of the State, "down to Vatinius who swears he is sure of the Consulship. What remains for you, Catullus, except to die?" And indeed his days were running out. Conscious of the near approach of death, he hastily collected the best of his poems into a small volume and gave expression in a few beautiful verses to the profound sadness of his spirit.

> Malest, Cornifici, tuo Catullo
> Malest me hercule ei et laboriose.

Summer was now fast approaching. Crassus had invaded Mesopotamia without formally declaring war and occupied several of the cities. Cæsar was still delaying his invasion of Britain. At Rome the electoral struggle was just commencing; there was a large selection of candidates for all the offices and not less than five for the Consulship. These five were Caius Memmius Gemellus, once an enemy and now the official candidate of Cæsar; Marcus Valerius Messala, a noble of ancient lineage who had the support of the Conservatives; Marcus Æmilius Scaurus; Caius Claudius, another brother of Clodius; and finally Cneius Domitius Calvinus. But what gave rise to particular scandal was the wild medley of ambitions which now came to light. Rome had never witnessed anything quite like it. All the magistrates in office demanded money from the candidates as the price of their assistance. The two Consuls concluded a regular treaty with Memmius and Calvinus, promising their support on condition that after their election they should, by an ingenious system of falsification, secure them the provinces they desired, or in case of failure pay them 400,000 sesterces. The corruption exceeded anything that had ever been known. One candidate having accused one of his rivals of bribery, all the others followed his example, and soon every one of them was at once accuser and accused. An astonished public asked what would happen on the day of the elections. As the voting drew nearer accusations, invectives and threats redoubled in violence, and the bribery became more and more outspoken; on the day itself there would inevitably be bloodshed in the Campus, and many looked forward, as a last deliverance, to the nomination of a dictator. But no one thought it his duty to do more than wring his hands. The intrepid Cato, who happened to be Prætor, finally had a million sesterces deposited in his custody by all the candidates for the Tribuneship and threatened to confiscate them if the electors were corrupted. But Pompey was too irritated and disgusted to interfere. The Senators refused to take any dangerous initiative, and though long and laborious sittings were held no agreement was arrived at. Soon the summer heats supervened; everyone declared "it had never been so hot," and that they could not put off going into the country. The Senate deferred the consular elections until September, hoping that the electoral fever would calm down while the various prosecutions were being discussed.

Cicero too left Rome to enjoy the fresh air of Arpino, and to supervise the construction of a fine villa and other important works ordered by his brother Quintus as a way of spending his Gallic treasure. For Cicero, who was much attached to his brother, the expedition to Britain was the cause of far more lively anxiety than the situation at Rome. But would the expedition really take place? At the beginning of July Quintus had written to him that Cæsar was on the point of giving up the idea. Information had been received, so he wrote, that the Britons were preparing a vigorous defence and that the conquest would bring in neither precious metals nor slaves of any value. Perhaps another risk with which Quintus was not acquainted, or which he did not venture to confide to his brother, caused Cæsar to hesitate. It concerned the internal situation in Gaul, where his attempts at conciliation with the Nationalists were by no means succeeding. The old institutions were working very badly under Roman control; instead of assuring peace and order they were giving rise to all sorts of unexpected difficulties; and measures inspired by the best intentions were leading to results entirely contrary to what had been awaited.

Thus, shortly after his return to Gaul, Cæsar had had to make a short expedition into the country of the Treveri, where, as often under the old *régime*, a civil war was imminent over the election of the first magistrate. Cæsar had checked its outbreak by the nomination of Cingetorix, one of the competitors; but his intervention had not been received with gratitude by the people. He had alienated the whole party of the other competitor Indutiomarus, who could not resign himself to giving up the struggle without a contest. Nor was the idea of the British campaign as a bait to the Gallic nobility producing the desired effect. Many of the Gallic nobles were inclined to oppose it, and Dumnorix was persuading them not to set out on the ground that Cæsar was anxious to put an end to their lives during the voyage.

Disquieted by these general manifestations of discontent Cæsar had asked himself for a moment if it would not be more prudent to renounce the whole enterprise. Perhaps he would have made up his mind to do so if the expedition were not being so eagerly awaited in Italy, and if his preparations had not already been too far advanced. He reduced the enterprise however to the most modest proportions, selecting only five legions and 2,000 horse, and taking with him for his personal attendance not more than three slaves; he left the three remaining legions in Gaul under the command of Labienus, and in short made every disposition for a speedy return and for the protection of Gaul during his absence. After all these precautions, Cæsar led his legions and the Gallic chiefs who were with him to a port which it is difficult to identify on modern maps, and at the first favourable wind began the embarkation. But now a serious incident occurred. Dumnorix disappeared with all the Æduan cavalry. Fearing a general mutiny, Cæsar sent all his cavalry in pursuit of the fugitive, who, on being overtaken, killed himself to avoid surrender. The other Gallic chiefs were thus frightened into following Cæsar; and in the last days of August Cicero heard in a letter from his brother that the army had reached the British coast without further mishaps: probably about the end of July, for letters at that time took about twenty-eight days to reach Rome from Britain. Cicero was reassured. If Cæsar had been able to disembark, his victory seemed inevitable.

Just at this time, towards the end of August or the beginning of September, occurred the death of Julia, the wife of Pompey, shortly after the death of her grandmother, the venerable mother of Cæsar.

In this very same year Catullus too passed away at the age of thirty-three. But the death of Julia produced a very lively impression in Rome because the young wife had, for the last four years, been a bond of union between the two most celebrated men of the day. Everyone asked whether her death would not modify the political situation.

But there were soon new scandals to occupy the public mind. The hope that the postponement of the elections would calm the bitterness of parties proved illusory, and all the old intrigues broke out once more, accompanied this time by violence. Memmius, who had broken with Calvinus, one day publicly read out in the Senate the agreement that had been made with the two Consuls in office. The armed bands of the various candidates engaged in regular street battles, and day after day there were several deaths. The public, disgusted and alarmed, was only too anxious that the struggle should be closed by the holding of the elections without further delay. But when the fixed date arrived, the Tribunes postponed them once more. Memmius, fearing that the scandal would result in his defeat, was anxious to wait until Cæsar returned from Gaul in order to secure his support. He therefore followed the precedent set by Pompey and Crassus in the preceding year.

Unfortunately Cæsar had other anxieties to deal with at the moment. Cicero had received letters from his brother and from Cæsar up to the end of September (the last letter from Cæsar was dated September 1st) which gave no special cause for anxiety. After constructing a camp on the sea-coast Cæsar had advanced into the interior, but within a few days he had left Quintus and the main body of the expedition and returned to the coast to look after his fleet, which had suffered severe injury in a gale. From that time onwards Cicero had received no further letters either from his brother or from Cæsar: nor was anyone else in Rome better informed. Having been without news for at least fifty days, Cicero was beginning to grow anxious and to ask himself what might be going on in that fabulous island of Britain. Letters eventually arrived to reassure him, and his reply to them is dated the 24th of October. Cæsar had again gone into the interior, where King Cassivellaunus, making a feint of retreating, had enticed him far from the sea into the forests and marshes. He had then sent orders to the kings of the territory through which Cæsar had passed to attack him in the rear. His communications with the sea being thus broken, the legions had been forced to spend their energies in fighting the small and agile bands of British cavalry set on them like wasps by Cassivellaunus, without ever achieving a decisive victory. To destroy these flying columns a strong force of cavalry would be needed, and Cæsar had only with him a very weak contingent composed entirely of Gauls. He was soon obliged to recognize the dangers of a further advance and the risk of being cut off from his base of supplies. Commius the Atrebatian, who was a friend of Cassivellaunus, acted as mediator, and peace was finally concluded. Cæsar declares that he imposed a tribute upon Britain; but it is quite certain that, if Cassivellaunus made promises, he made no payments when the Roman army had once recrossed the sea. Cæsar returned to Gaul in the first fortnight of October, bringing back no booty beyond a number of slaves. The Conquest of Britain had been a complete fiasco.

On his disembarkation in Gaul Cæsar heard of the death of Julia. It was a great blow to him as a father, for he was much attached to his gracious daughter. She had been a link to bind him to one of the tenderest memories, perhaps the tenderest of his life—his romance with Cornelia, daughter of Cinna, whom also death had untimely torn away. It was also a blow to the leader of the Democratic party, for whom Julia had been a guarantee of the friendship of Pompey. But he had no time to give way to grief; there was too much grave business on hand.

At Rome the situation was becoming dangerously complicated. Memmius continued his obstruction, the electors had not yet been convened; there were constant acts of violence; and a frightened public was calling for energetic measures, it cared not what, provided only that order was re-established and the elections took place without a return to the services of an *interrex*.

Encouraged by these symptoms, the friends and flatterers of Pompey conceived the idea of making him Dictator. But this only provoked a new struggle. The Conservatives offered the project a desperate opposition, preferring anything to a dictatorship exercised by Pompey. They attempted to make skilful use of the odium which had been attached to that office since the time of Sulla by protesting that it was not Pompey's Dictatorship which they opposed but the Dictatorship in itself. Pompey, who was anxious to re-establish order at Rome and was conscious of the need, now that Cæsar and Crassus were on all men's lips, of doing something to enhance his own prestige, had a secret desire to be made Dictator; but he maintained a vacillating attitude, afraid both of the unpopularity of the office and of a possible failure in holding it. So he pursued his usual plan of allowing his friends to work for him without ever revealing his intentions or compromising himself in one direction or the other. "Does he wish it, does he object to it? Who knows?" wrote Cicero to his brother. Thus the shadow of Pompey the Dictator began to loom over Rome, sometimes advancing, sometimes receding and almost vanishing, but always to return once more.

During the course of this struggle, in September, Gabinius had quietly returned to Rome, closely followed by Rabirius, the Egyptian Minister of Finance, who had been compelled by a popular rising to fly from the country soon after the departure of Gabinius. The whole story had been an outrageous scandal, and the small clique of Conservatives attempted to make use of it to attack the unscrupulous and bellicose democracy in the persons of Gabinius and Rabirius, since it was powerless and tongue-tied against Cæsar, Crassus and Pompey. Gabinius was accused of high treason and extortion, Rabirius simply of extortion. But these prosecutions only gave rise to new intrigues. Pompey in vain attempted to induce Cicero to defend Gabinius. Gabinius was, however, acquitted on the first charge by a small majority, and now prepared to meet the second. Pompey made new efforts to win Cicero's support and succeeded this time in persuading him. He finally made a speech himself before the people in defence of Gabinius, reading letters from Cæsar in his favour. Nevertheless Gabinius was condemned. It seems, however, that Cicero some time afterwards succeeded in securing the acquittal of Rabirius by means of the speech which is still extant.

But it was in vain that Memmius awaited Cæsar's return. Cæsar had scarcely landed from Britain when serious trouble broke out in Gaul. Tasgetus, whom Cæsar had made King of the Carnutes, was suddenly assassinated. It looked as if the Nationalists intended to make his assassination the beginning of a movement of reprisals against all the Gallic leaders who had consented to recognize the Roman dominion. Cæsar at any rate was so disquieted by an incident which was rather symptomatic than serious in itself that he sent a legion into the territory of the Carnutes, as an open menace to the whole of Gaul. He then prepared to return to Italy; but just as he was setting out and had gone as far as Amiens he was met by still more serious news. On his return from Britain, fear of a possible famine had induced him to split up his forces and send them into winter quarters in different parts of the country. Profiting by their dispersion, a small Belgian tribe, the Eburones, had risen in revolt under the leadership of two nobles, Ambiorix and Catuvolcus. They had cleverly enticed from their camp and overwhelmed a legion and five cohorts recently recruited in Cispadane Gaul (probably to make up the numbers of a second legion), who were wintering in their country under the orders of Titurius and Arunculeius; and the entire force had been massacred. Then, calling the other tribes to their standard, they had marched against Quintus Cicero, who was wintering in the country of the Nervii, and had besieged him in his camp. This then was Gaul's reply to the murder of Dumnorix, the chief of the Nationalist party. Cæsar was forced to interrupt his voyage and to hasten at once to the help of Quintus. Thus it happened that Cæsar preoccupied by his campaigns, and Pompey by the intrigues necessary to save his friends, the Consuls powerless since the revelations of Memmius, and the Senate in its usual impotence, between them allowed public affairs to drift on as they pleased. The end of the year was reached without a single election having been made. At the beginning of 53 every one of the offices was empty and anarchy reigned supreme.

CHAPTER XXI

THE INVASION OF PARTHIA

THE disorder at Rome was soon matched by dangers in the provinces. In Gaul, the assassination of Tasgetus had been followed by a revolt against Caverinus, the king whom Cæsar had imposed upon the Senones. When a party of his countrymen, headed by Accon, threatened to put him on his trial, the nominee of the Romans found safety in flight. The revolt of the Eburones also had given rise to other small movements in different parts of the country. After these warnings, Cæsar gave up his intention of spending the winter in Cisalpine Gaul and further increased his army, replacing the fifteen cohorts annihilated by Ambiorix with thirty new cohorts, partly recruited by himself in Cisalpine Gaul, partly supplied him by Pompey, who had himself raised them in the same country. He was soon to learn that these were no heedless precautions.

Cæsar was now in the full vigour of his powers. The healthy outdoor life of the province and the stimulus of success and popularity had hardened a naturally delicate constitution and restored the elastic energy of his mind. He could take up every morning without effort the urgent and onerous tale of work required for the superintendence of Italy, Gaul and the whole of the Empire. Yet the ceaseless anxieties of the Gallic situation were slowly telling upon his strength and temper. He had not neglected, amid the labours of these years, to devote close and searching study to the social conditions of that country; and his lucid and penetrating intelligence, his unequalled faculty for weaving comprehensive and consistent theories out of a multitude of scattered observations, seemed to grow in quickness and concentration as the area of his experience enlarged. He had now succeeded in forming a mental picture, complete in all the essential details, of the great country whose destinies he controlled—a country still largely covered with forest and marshland, but teeming with natural wealth.

Gaul was no longer the same as when she had filled Rome with panic in distant centuries or even half a century ago in the time of

Marius. Some relics of those days Cæsar may still have seen among
the Belgæ and Helvetii; but over the rest of the country he could
watch the old agricultural, aristocratic and military traditions making
way, as they had made way in Italy a century before, for a civilization
based on commerce and industry; he could watch the slow and
insidious influence of the foreign trader as he initiated the Gauls into
the mysteries of Græco-Latin life, from the alphabet and the minting
of artistic coins to the temptations of the hot and fiery wines of the
south. Cæsar had indeed been set over the country at a decisive
moment in her history. The increase in the cost of living and the
individual effort necessary to keep pace with it were slowly gathering
to a crisis similar to that which Italy had lived through in the half
century following the Gracchi. The old land-holding aristocracy,
which had formed the political and military backbone of the country,
was gradually succumbing beneath the burden of debt; and the small
proprietors were disappearing with them. The whole power and
wealth of the country was being concentrated into the hands of a
small plutocracy that had grown rich on war, usury, and the farming
of the public taxes; and it was this plutocracy that Cæsar now resolved
to use as the mainstay of his Roman organization. The national
religion, Druidism, was utterly decadent and had lost all hold over
the masses. Of the countless multitude whom debt and war and the
concentration of land in a few large estates had ruined and cast adrift
on the world, many had formed themselves into those bands of
brigands—*perditi homines et latrones*—whom Cæsar mentions so
frequently, while others were engaged in trade with the different
nations of Gaul or with Germans, Britons and Romans, and others
again came to settle in the towns and formed the nucleus of an artisan
class. Scattered about among the rude villages which covered the
whole of the country were a certain number of large towns, such as
Avaricum, Gergovia and Bibracte, which were beginning to attract
population and wealth. A flourishing slave-trade was carried on with
Italy, and several industries, such as pottery, metal-work, goldsmith's
work, weaving and the preparation of ham were making some progress.
As the workers became more numerous in the towns and in the
villages, amid a disturbed and still semi-barbarous country, they felt
the need both of security and of capital; they thus fell naturally into

the clutches of the powerful plutocrats, and gladly accepted their political protection. Gaul was in fact rapidly falling a prey to the disorder and discontent produced in every society by sudden changes in the nature and distribution of wealth and in the timeworn fabric of ideas and customs. Every class in the community was divided and unsettled; and public opinion, capricious and excitable, obeyed neither guide nor rule. If the old governing class of the nobility was in decadence, the new and active plutocracy, despite its money and ambitions, was equally unable either to administer the old political institutions or to establish new ones in their place.

Thus the military and political disorder of Gaul was daily becoming more pronounced. In almost every part of the country the Government had consisted of an assembly of nobles—that is, of rich land-holders— generally distinguished in war, who had also controlled the armies, each of them commanding a small troop formed out of his fellow-citizens and clients. But in proportion as the nobility disappeared and estates fell more and more into the hands of a small plutocracy, the newcomers with their clients forced their way into the army and, by their preponderating influence, disturbed the old equilibrium of Republican liberty. By this time the armies were composed mainly either of the dependants of these plutocrats, men who in return for food and some small remuneration cultivated their lands or acted as their servants in their great riverside mansions in the forests, or of troops of cavalry which they maintained at their own cost to increase their power both in peace and war.

Cæsar had long been aware that the Gallic army was no longer what it had been. Yet the Romans were hardly justified in regarding their military superiority as a serious guarantee of peace. In spite of continual internecine wars the peoples of Gaul were united by community of language, traditions and religion, and cherished a national sentiment which was far deeper than it seemed, and which had been considerably strengthened by the foreign invasion.

This danger in itself was sufficiently serious, but it was still further accentuated by the necessity, in which Cæsar had found himself on several occasions, of offending the interests of different parties or classes. Ruined as it was by continual warfare and threatened by the competition of the classes below it, the aristocracy would perhaps have been ready to accept a Roman protectorate in the hope of re-establishing order and putting an end to a period of distress and agitation. But such a protectorate would never have been accepted with loyalty by the small oligarchy of proprietors and capitalists, whom the possession of riches, the large number of their dependants and the general support which they secured from the people combined to make arrogant in their pretensions and hostile to any settled order. Thus by a policy favourable to the ambitions of the capitalists Cæsar had alienated the sympathies of the Republican aristocracy, without securing the loyal attachment of the plutocratic oligarchy.

The discontent was still further increased by the considerable losses which the foreign dominion entailed. Gaul was compelled to pay a contribution in money, to furnish a large part of the supplies necessary to the Roman army, to provide military contingents for the wars undertaken by Cæsar, which were often unpopular: and she had often to submit to the looting of the soldiery and the expenses necessary to give hospitality to the officers on tours of inspection. In many of the Gallic towns a large number of Italian traders had settled in the wake of the army, and these, as may be imagined, were not satisfied with buying up loot, but fell upon the country like birds of prey, to compete with the few large native capitalists.

At the beginning of spring disquieting news arrived from all parts. The Nervii, the Aduatuci and the Menapii were taking up arms. The Senones refused to furnish their contingents and were making an understanding with the Carnutes. Ambiorix was endeavouring to stir up a fresh outbreak; and it appears also that advances had been made to Ariovistus to secure his help against the common enemy. Disquieted at this widespread disaffection, Cæsar had not the patience to wait till spring. With the object of striking terror into all the rebels at once he made a sudden foray with four legions into the land of the Nervii and took a huge quantity of cattle and many prisoners, distributing them freely amongst his soldiers. Then, in March, he convened an assembly of all the Gallic peoples at Amiens; but he found there representatives neither of the Treveri nor of the Senones nor of the Carnutes. In a fit of anger, and in the hope of terrorizing the country, he adjourned the assembly forthwith, ordering it to meet at a later date at Lutetia amongst the Parisii, which was on the borders of the country of the Senones; and on the very same day he set out on a series of forced marches into the rebel country. Dismayed at the suddenness of the attack, the Senones promptly sued for peace, which was granted on condition that they gave hostages; and the Carnutes at once followed their example.

Intending at last to make an end of Ambiorix, Cæsar then sent on to Labienus, who was in winter quarters in the territory of the Treveri, the whole of his baggage and two legions; he then advanced with five legions into the territory of the Menapii, where he suspected the rebel leader to be in hiding; but the Menapii abandoned their villages on his approach and dispersed in small bands through the marshes and forests. Cæsar divided his army into three columns, entrusting one to Caius Fabius, another to Marcus Crassus, son of the millionaire; while at the head of the third he himself began an organized hunt after men and cattle, destroying the villages as he went. The Menapii were soon frightened into suing for peace; but Ambiorix escaped once more.

During all this time the disorders in the capital had continued and even increased. Month succeeded month and still no elections took place. Pompey was still hoping that the situation would ultimately make his Dictatorship inevitable, but did not venture to make an open profession of his ambition. Thus the situation remained obscure, and the exasperated Conservatives went so far as to accuse Pompey of giving secret encouragement to the rioters in order to force the hands of the Senate. But all these bickerings and uncertainties were soon to be overshadowed by news from the East.

In the spring of 53 Crassus at length took the field for the conquest of Parthia. Destiny had chosen him to be the first victim of the megalomania of his countrymen. When he joined the forces that he had brought from Italy with those which he found in Syria he had an army of 5,000 horse, 4,000 auxiliaries, and nine legions of about 3,500 men each, making about 40,000 in all. He had no sooner reached Syria, at the beginning of 54, than he put into execution what can only be regarded as an excellent plan of campaign. He fortified the bridge over the Euphrates at Zeugma, crossed the river, occupied the Greek cities of Mesopotamia, Apamea, Carrhæ, Icne and Nicephorium, inflicted an easy defeat on a Parthian general who had a small force in that district, and then, leaving 7,000 men (probably two legions) and 1,000 cavalry behind in the cities, he returned into winter quarters in Syria. The ancients have severely criticized this retreat, regarding it as a serious mistake, because the Parthians were thus given time to make preparations; but it is probable that Crassus' aim in taking the Greek cities of Mesopotamia was to draw the enemy out from the interior of Parthia towards the Euphrates and make him give battle at the least possible distance from the Roman province. If he had penetrated deeper into Parthia he would have been committing the same blunder as Napoleon in his advance on Moscow. Crassus was, therefore, well advised in retiring upon Syria in the autumn of 54 to await the spring and the effect of his challenge. He spent the winter in collecting money, laying hands, in the process, on the Treasure of the Temple at Jerusalem. He also made attempts towards an understanding with the King of Armenia and the other independent or semi-independent princes of Mesopotamia, amongst them the Abgar of Edessa, who had been a close friend of Pompey.

His plan at first seemed to promise success. In the spring of 53 the garrisons that he had left behind in Mesopotamia were attacked by the Parthians. The Parthian king had in fact decided to divide his forces: to invade Armenia with the best of his infantry, while he sent almost the whole of his cavalry into Mesopotamia under the command of the Surena, or commander-in-chief, with the object of enticing the Romans as far as possible from their base of operations. The two adversaries had thus proposed to themselves identically the same object and were employing identically the same stratagem to effect it. Unfortunately Crassus was too easily deluded into the belief that he had deluded the other side. As soon as he heard that the Parthians were approaching, his only idea was to throw himself impetuously upon them, and his only fear that he might not come up to them in time. Fugitives who had escaped from the towns besieged by the Parthians brought strange news into camp; the enemy had huge numbers of horsemen, all armed in mail, who were amazingly bold and quick, and amazingly strong and skilful in shooting from their enormous bows. Some of the generals were so impressed by this information that they proposed to revise the whole plan of campaign.

Artabaces, the King of Armenia, had just arrived with 6,000 cavalry and declared himself ready to supply 10,000 more cavalry and 30,000 infantry, if Crassus would only invade the enemy's country through Armenia, where the mountains would prevent the Parthians from making use of their cavalry. But the obstinate old banker, who was growing more impatient daily, refused to abandon the besieged Romans to their fate. He crossed the Euphrates at Zeugma with seven legions, 4,000 cavalry and the auxiliaries, and directed his course across Mesopotamia in the direction of Carrhæ to meet the Parthians. The seven legions, the cavalry, the auxiliaries, and the 500 beasts of burden carrying the supplies and the tents by which each legion was followed must have formed a procession more than twelve miles long.

Scarcely had they set out before scouts began to bring in still more mysterious information. The Parthians had universally abandoned the sieges and retired. The country was clear of them; but everywhere there were traces of numerous horse hoofs which seemed to indicate a retreating army. This news caused a certain agitation amongst the general staff. What could be the enemy's object? Cassius, the son-in-law of Servilia, who was with Crassus in the capacity of Quæstor and was a young man of ability, advised his general to halt in one of the cities already occupied, and gather more precise information about the enemy's movements, or else, since the towns were no longer threatened, to march upon Seleucia, following the course of the Euphrates along the road of Xenophon's 10,000. This would have the advantage of covering the right flank of the army and would also have simplified the provision of supplies. Crassus seemed impressed, and summoned a council of war.

Once more the doubters were in the right. The Surena was trying to draw the Roman army away from its base, and to entice it across the Cabur, a stream which forms the boundary of the desert. Unfortunately, Pompey's friend, the Abgar of Edessa, in whom Crassus had complete confidence, was secretly in agreement with the Parthians, and knew how to play upon the impatience and avarice of the Roman general. He insisted that the Parthians were taking steps to transport their treasures into the mountains, and that the right policy was to pursue the Surena without further delay, and overtake and defeat him before he could join forces with his royal master. In this way he finally persuaded Crassus to commit the mistake which historians reproach him for not having committed in the previous year. His impatience and cupidity, his confidence in his own star, and his repugnance against changing his mind, overwhelmed all the counsels of prudence; and Crassus threw his army upon the track of the Parthians, compelling his soldiers to undertake forced marches during the torrid heats of a Syrian May. But the days passed, the march was continued with increasing hardship, and the enemy was still out of sight. The troops grew weary of pursuing an invisible enemy. Crassus began to grow impatient. He was unwilling to retrace his steps, yet he was also afraid of advancing too far. Rumours of foul play began to circulate. One day ambassadors arrived from the King of Armenia to inform Crassus that no reinforcements could be sent him because the King of Parthia had invaded his kingdom. Crassus was again advised to make Armenia his base of operations. If he rejected that plan it was suggested that he should avoid the desert and the plain, where the cavalry of the Parthians would have easy play.

Cassius at once perceived the wisdom of this counsel; but an elderly general with his nerves unstrung by fatigue and anxiety lost his temper at the suggestion that he was in need of advice. He discourteously dismissed the ambassadors, telling them that when the war was over he would punish the King of Armenia as he deserved. He then continued his march, moving forward without setting eyes on the enemy or hearing news of his whereabouts. At length after long days of weary marching, about the end of May or the beginning of June, just as they had passed the town of Carrhæ and were approaching the banks of the river Belik, scouts came in breathless with the news that they had met a huge Parthian army a few miles off, advancing rapidly on a surprise attack and that most of the scouts had already been cut off. What induced the Parthians to turn back to attack in this way? Perhaps they had received secret information from the Abgar of Edessa that the Roman army was discouraged and perplexed. It is certain, at any rate, that the tired legions were somewhat troubled by the news, and that many of the officers were in favour of encamping on the bank of the river, there to await the enemy and study his method of fighting before giving battle. But after a moment's hesitation Crassus decided at once to try the fortune of battle, lest the enemy should escape him once more.

He began by giving orders that the seventy cohorts should be disposed in a single line ten files deep. This was what the Roman tacticians advised should be done when an army was attacked by great masses of cavalry. But to draw up on a front nearly eight miles long (for this is the space that seventy cohorts would occupy when placed alongside one another) an army which in column of march took up some twelve miles is not a manœuvre which can be executed in a few moments. Crassus lost patience in the middle of the operation and decided to arrange the four first legions in a square with twelve cohorts, each strengthened by cavalry, on each front, eight cohorts on each flank, and the beasts and the baggage in the centre. He gave the command of one wing to his son and of the other to Cassius, placed himself in the centre, gave his soldiers time to take a rapid meal in their lines, and then ordered the square, followed by the three legions, to cross the river and throw itself on the enemy.

It was not long before dark groups of horsemen appeared on the horizon, advancing slowly and with caution, little like the wild hordes that had been awaited. But gradually their numbers increased; the plain began to be filled with noise, the air to be dazzled with the glitter of armour; and finally the heavy cavalry forming the head of the army, which the Surena had concealed behind a hill, darted from its ambush and hurled a heavy mass of armoured horsemen against the Roman square. The cohorts stood firm against the shock, meeting charge after charge with the Roman spear. Gradually the assaults grew less frequent, and at last the cavalry slowly withdrew, as though weary of the fight. Fearing that the battle would be over too soon Crassus sent his archers, slingers and light infantry in pursuit of the fugitives; but they were soon overwhelmed by an irresistible hail of arrows from the light cavalry of the Parthians, which was entirely composed of archers, and appears to have advanced and deployed from the two sides of the heavy horsemen, in the form of a huge semicircle. The troops sent forward by Crassus were soon forced to retreat in disorder towards the legions. Meanwhile the light cavalry of the Parthians were moving up, and their arrows, passing in a huge parabola right over their own lines, fell, hissing and whistling, piercing shields and armour, first among the front ranks and then in the centre of the Roman square. Crassus and the officers tried to rally their men; let them only have patience and the arrows must be exhausted; let them show their mettle in a counter-attack. But as soon as the Romans advanced the Parthians retreated, shooting as they went, facing backwards on their horses; and the cohorts were obliged to take refuge once more in the square, upon which the relentless rain of arrows soon descended anew. The Parthian supply of arrows seemed mysteriously inexhaustible, till at length the officers descried a long troop of camels on the horizon towards which a group of horsemen dashed up from time to time—a moving storehouse from which the Parthian quivers were replenished.

The legions were now fast becoming demoralized under the Parthian archery. Crassus decided to make a supreme effort to break through the moving circle of horsemen which enveloped his army, and ordered his son Publius with 1,300 horse, including his 1,000 Gauls, 500 archers, and eight cohorts to charge the enemy. The Parthians made show of yielding and disappeared beyond the horizon in clouds of dust. The stinging hail of arrows ceased at last. Crassus used the respite to march his army to a hill and, thinking the battle ended, quietly awaited the return of Publius. But before long the scouts were galloping up to the lines. Publius was begging for reinforcements. The flying Parthians had enticed his small force too far from the main body, and then suddenly turned back and surrounded it. A wild hand-to-hand struggle was in progress and the whole detachment would be cut to pieces unless reinforcements were promptly sent. Crassus hurriedly took the march with his whole army; but no sooner had he set out than the familiar dust-clouds beat up once more from the horizon, with a glitter of armour in their midst, heralded by a chorus of barbaric cries. The Parthians were returning at full gallop, and a horseman at their head was carrying a black object on his lance. The Romans stopped and waited. When the Parthians came a little nearer keen eyes detected that the black object on the spear-point was the head of Publius Crassus. His force had been annihilated. The troops were almost paralysed with horror; but Crassus, who had kept his nerve so far against the whole violence of the onset, did not break down now; he went through the ranks telling his men that it was their general alone that suffered through the death of Publius; that Roman soldiers must do their duty and stand firm against the fresh assault. For by now the enemy had drawn a huge semicircle of archers all round the army while heavy masses of cavalry charged up ceaselessly from its centre against the opposing square. But once more the Roman infantry held their ground; and at length the Parthians, wearied by a succession of furious charges, retired with empty quivers and blunted sabres as the sun sank below the horizon.

It is probable that by this time the Parthians thought victory beyond their grasp. They had hoped to take the Roman army by surprise and cut it in pieces; yet despite the heavy losses they had inflicted, the battle had ended in no definite result. The check would have had no influence upon the issue of the campaign if the army of Crassus had been one of those old and experienced forces which Rome used in old days to send into battle. But at this moment there was only one trained army in the Empire, and that was in Gaul. In the ranks of Crassus young recruits far outnumbered older soldiers, the officers were almost all drawn from the frivolous gilded youth of Rome and had no real knowledge of the military art, while their chief, although a man of ability, was too old to be a good general and had been deceived by his successes in the war against Spartacus. None of them had been inured to the hardships of campaigning. They were so demoralized that evening by the heavy losses, the unaccustomed tactics of the enemy, their distance from their base in Syria, and the loss of the detachment of cavalry, that both soldiers and officers took the day's fighting for a defeat. Crassus himself, after commanding during the whole day with remarkable energy, now lost heart. He felt sure that the Parthians would be encouraged by their victory to renew the attack next day on his exhausted forces; and that very night, acting, as it seems, upon the advice of Cassius, he gave orders for a hasty retreat upon Carrhæ. He was obliged to leave behind him on the field of battle some 4,000 wounded, who were killed by the Parthians next morning; and during the night, in the darkness and disorder, four cohorts went astray and suffered a similar fate.

Nevertheless, once at Carrhæ, the Romans were in a position to rest, reorganize their forces and retire without further danger along the track of their outward march, where the Parthians, through lack of water and forage, would have been unable to keep up the pursuit. This was indeed what the Parthian commander-in-chief anticipated that they would do. Unfortunately they were so completely demoralized by the hurried retreat, with its abandonment of the wounded, and the massacre of the stragglers, that both soldiers and officers refused to recognize that the crisis was past. They were in such dismay of the Parthians that they dared not move out of the town into the plain. At a council of war it was decided to ask help from the King of Armenia, to wait at Carrhæ until these reinforcements arrived, and only then to retreat, probably through Armenia.

When the Parthian commander-in-chief, who had advanced up to the walls of Carrhæ, ascertained the condition of the army, he attempted to win by craft what he had failed to achieve in open battle. He let the Roman soldiers know that he would permit them to return in liberty, if they consented to deliver up Crassus and Cassius. The plot was skilfully devised. If the soldiers mutinied and put their two most capable leaders into his hands, it would be easy to cut the whole army to pieces. But the discipline in the Roman ranks was too strong; the attempts of the Surena would have failed outright, if the Roman officers had kept confidence in their men. But this was just what they were not in the mood to do. As soon as they learnt that the loyalty of their troops was being secretly undermined by emissaries from the Surena, they refused to remain a moment longer at Carrhæ for fear the legions should yield to their tempters. Overcome by the urgent demands of his officers, Crassus changed his mind and gave orders for immediate evacuation without the reinforcements from Armenia, which he was, moreover, by no means sure of receiving.

But what road was he to take? Cassius suggested the route by which they had come, but Crassus, perhaps deceived by Andromachus, a noble of Carrhæ, perhaps still afraid to venture with his soldiers into the plain, decided for the mountainous road through Armenia. The Romans set out over the mountains, marching almost always at night and choosing the most difficult paths, very often through marshes, where the Parthian cavalry would be unable to follow them. One last effort and they would be safe. But the hardships of the retreat increased the nervousness of the soldiers and the irritability of the officers. Open dissensions broke out between the chiefs. Crassus lost his temper during the deliberations and sacrificed all his authority over his subordinates. One day he had a violent altercation with Cassius, who criticized all his plans, and ended by telling him that if he was unwilling to follow him he had only to take an escort and retire by whatever road he thought good. Cassius at once accepted the suggestion, and turned back with 500 horsemen to Carrhæ, where he resumed, in the direction of the Euphrates, the road that the army had taken on its previous march.

Thus the force gradually broke up. Yet in spite of all Crassus continued his retreat. As they drew daily nearer to the mountains, the Parthian commander saw his prey on the point of escaping him. At this crisis he devised a masterpiece of perfidy. One morning he sent an ambassador into the Roman camp to say that he desired to enter into negotiations with Crassus for the conclusion of peace. Crassus, who suspected treachery and saw the success of his retreat assured, would not listen to the offer. But when the tired soldiers heard that they might hope to retire unmolested, they would listen to no arguments, and threatened to mutiny if Crassus refused to negotiate. Fate had gripped him at last. Neither his years, nor his renown, nor his almost sacred authority as Imperator, nor the immense treasures he had left behind him in Italy, could avail to save him. For all his faults, Crassus was every inch a man, and when death suddenly stared him in the face amid the mountains of Armenia, far from his family and his home, like a criminal given but a few minutes to prepare for his fate, he revealed no sign of weakness. He summoned the officers and told them that he was going out to the Parthians; he knew that there was treachery, but preferred to die by the Parthians rather than by his own soldiers. He set out with an escort and was killed on the 9th of June.

Crassus was a man of great gifts. He had conducted this campaign with considerable skill; but his haste, his excess of self-confidence, the carelessness of his preparations, the military slackness of the age, and finally a succession of unfortunate accidents caused him to suffer the fate which Cæsar had only escaped by miracle in his war against the Helvetii. His death was in some sort an expiation for his blunders and the vainglory of his countrymen. His head was cut off and sent to the Parthian Court; his body was left unburied. Deprived of its leaders, the army broke up in confusion, many of the soldiers being killed, and many others, the small remnant of the great army which had crossed the Euphrates, finally straggling into Syria.

The news of this disaster reached Rome in July 53 just as the elections for the offices of that year were about to take place after seven months of anarchy. The disorder had been still further increased by disputes as to how best to put an end to it. Some wished to re-establish the *Tribuni militum consulari potestate* of the old days; others proposed to nominate Pompey Dictator. This latter proposal finally appeared the more advisable. But at the last moment Pompey had shrank before the detested memories of Sulla and merely consented to allow his troops to enter the city. This had been sufficient to enable the elections to take place, and Marcus Valerius Messala and Cneius Domitius Calvinus had been thus eventually elected Consuls. It is easy to imagine the sensation produced in Italy by the news of Crassus' death, coming just at a moment when confidence was reviving after the interminable scandal of the elections. The Conservatives, who had always mistrusted the mad enthusiasm for the expedition, had thus been justified after all.

Meanwhile in Gaul the war was being continued with more favourable results, but with methods of increasing barbarism. Labienus had reduced the Treveri; and Cæsar had crossed the Rhine a second time and made a raid into the country of the Suevi, where he successfully deterred Ariovistus from interference with his neighbours. He had then returned to Gaul, where he was again confronted with the Eburones, who were adopting guerilla methods, surprising and massacring small and isolated detachments of Romans. Anxious for once to make an example Cæsar published an edict in all the towns of Gaul, giving free permission for robbery and massacre in the territory of the Eburones, and brought together troops of brigands and adventurers from all parts of the country. But he did not mean to leave the whole of the pillaging to others. Leaving behind him at Aduatuca, under the protection of one legion, the baggage of his whole army, he threw nine legions into the country of the Eburones, divided into three columns, one of which was commanded by himself, the second by Trebonius, and the third by Labienus; for several months they burned the villages, robbed the cattle, and hunted the natives.

But violence, called in as a servant, often exceeds its instructions. A band of Sugcambrian plunderers, who had come to join in the looting at Cæsar's invitation, ascertaining that there was a Roman camp at Aduatuca with all the spoils and baggage of ten legions and the depots of the merchants who followed the army, attempted to take it and very nearly succeeded. Meanwhile Ambiorix, tracked like a wild beast from lair to lair, still eluded the efforts of his pursuers. At the approach of winter Cæsar once more retired. He convoked the assembly of the Gauls, solemnly tried the Senones and Carnutes for rebellion, condemned Acco to death, and many of the nobles compromised in the revolt, who had fled across the Rhine, to exile and confiscation of their goods. Their property was divided among the nobles who had remained faithful and the higher ranks of the soldiers. Cæsar then made preparations to return to Italy.

Thus the pacification of Gaul was rapidly degenerating into a war of extermination; the conciliatory diplomacy of the opening period had been replaced by a *régime* of bloodshed and violence. This is no doubt the history of most conquests; but in this case the temptations to brutality were particularly strong, because these continual revolts unsettled all the labours of the last six years and were gravely affecting Cæsar's credit at Rome. Posterity thinks of the conquest of Gaul as the greatest of Cæsar's achievements; but contemporaries, towards the end of the year 53, looked at the situation in a very different light. The annihilation of the army of Crassus had damped the enthusiasm of the masses for the policy of expansion, and weakened their confidence in its foremost representative. Crassus being safely dead, men could say what they liked about him, and he therefore naturally came off far worse than Cæsar, who was still alive and powerful. He was accused of having directed his campaigns like an amateur, of having committed the most ridiculous mistakes, and of having brought the Roman name into discredit by his miserly persistence. But even against Cæsar disagreeable comparisons were beginning to be made. When Lucullus and Pompey had annexed Pontus and Syria all had been over in quite a short time; in Gaul, on the other hand, he seemed every year to be beginning his work all over again. Surely this must be due, at least in part, to Cæsar's own blunders.

Moreover the public had another cause for irritation. The display which certain generals were making of their Gallic plunder was becoming a public scandal. Cicero was constantly superintending buildings ordered by his brother; Mamurra, who was only an obscure knight from Formia, was building a magnificent palace on the Cælian, with all its walls covered with plaques of marble in the Alexandrine fashion, in a style hitherto unknown in Rome; Labienus, who had bought huge estates in the Marches, was engaged in building a castle at Cingoli which was almost a small fortified town in itself. A wave of sentimentalism was slowly rousing the nation from the narcotics of corruption and vainglory; and it acted with added force when, after a short truce, the elections for the year 52 provoked a renewed outbreak of anarchy. The candidates for the Consulship were Milo, Publius Plautius Hypsæus, and Quintus Cæcilius Metellus Scipio, the adopted son of Metellus Pius. Clodius was a candidate for the Prætorship and Antony, who, after Gabinius' return to Italy, had joined Cæsar in Gaul, for the Quæstorship. Cæsar, who had speedily appreciated his military talents, had allowed him to come home on furlough to stand for this office.

The electoral contest soon became so heated that all the candidates took up arms in the conduct of their campaign. Day after day there was bloodshed between the different bands. Once Cicero was nearly killed on the Sacred Way; another time Antony only just missed putting an end to Clodius. The public anxiously asked what madness was coming over men's minds, and what massacres it would cost to restore the State to order. In vain all eyes were turned upon Pompey. Whether through indecision and weakness, or through the desire of making his dictatorship necessary through the very excess of the disorders, Pompey refused to stir. The Consuls made several ineffectual attempts to hold the elections; and the Senate, too weak to do anything more drastic, passed a law against the Egyptian worships of Serapis and Isis, which were adding their share to the moral difficulties of the day; it also decided to put before the people a proposal that a magistrate should only receive a province five years after the expiration of his office, which was expected somewhat to appease the competition for all the offices. For the third time in four years the end of this year was reached without a consular election; but this time the Senate was not even able to nominate an *interrex*, since one of the Tribunes,

Titus Munatius Plancus, opposed his veto. Some recognized the hand of Pompey in this stratagem and suspected him of wishing to hurry on events and so force the Senate to appoint him Dictator.

In the midst of all these disorders a feat of assassination brought matters suddenly to a climax. On the 18th of January 52, Milo, going out with an armed escort to Lanuvium, happened to fall in on the Appian Way, in the neighbourhood of Bovillæ, with Clodius, who, accompanied by a small suite, was returning from his country house to Rome. The two bands came to blows and Clodius was killed. "At last," said the Conservatives, heaving a sigh of relief. But even after death the mob leader kept his power of setting Rome in a ferment. The people were stirred to excitement by his clients and cut-throats, by the Tribunes of the popular party, and by his wife Fulvia; and they flocked in crowds to see his body when it was laid out for the public view in his house. On all sides there were cries for vengeance, and his funeral was celebrated with a display of almost barbaric pomp. The people accompanied his body to the Curia Hostilia and made display of their hatred of nobles and millionaires by a bonfire of the senatorial seats, tables and desks. The fire spread to the Curia and the Basilica Portia; and the body of the demagogue was dispersed among the ashes of the two oldest and most venerable public buildings in Rome, while the people shouted for Pompey and Cæsar as Dictators. Plancus was frightened into giving up his opposition to the nomination of an *interrex* and the Senate selected Marcus Æmilius Lepidus, son of the Consul who had died during the Revolution of 78. Lepidus was a young man of great wealth who had married a daughter of Servilia, and was a friend of both Cæsar and Pompey; but as he had very little influence, his nomination only increased the prevailing agitation. At the grand funeral banquet in honour of Clodius wild scenes took place. The crowd attempted to set fire to the house of Milo, and also threatened that of Lepidus, who was suspected of being his friend. A popular demonstration went to offer the Consular Insignia to Hypsæus and Scipio; another proclaimed Pompey both Consul and Dictator. In every quarter of Rome there were processions and street fighting, while bandits and burglars seized their opportunity and on the pretext of searching for the accomplices of Milo made their way into many of the private houses.

CHAPTER XXII

THE GREAT CRISIS OF DEMOCRATIC IMPERIALISM—THE REVOLT OF GAUL

WHILST this turmoil was raging in the streets of Rome, Cæsar was crossing the Alps on his way back to Cisalpine Gaul. His natural impetuosity, the serious condition of his party, and the sheer impossibility of the task which he had set himself were driving him on to blunder after blunder. Thus, to gain a short respite for interference in Italy he had ventured upon measures of repression in Gaul which had only consolidated and intensified the hatred of the natives; and he had then left the country without awaiting their effects. Shortly after he had set out, probably while he was still on the road, he heard from Labienus that his old friend and supporter Commius was himself conspiring against him. For once he lost all patience. He gave instructions to Labienus to inveigle the Atrebatian chieftain to his camp and put him to death. Labienus obeyed, but Commius, though wounded, succeeded in making his escape; and the only result of the perfidy was to turn Commius into an implacable enemy of Cæsar and of Rome. Cæsar seemed to be involved in a very labour of Sisyphus; no sooner had he finished in one direction than fresh efforts were required in another, where he had thought that all was secure. These brutal and treacherous expedients bear witness to the strain at which he lived. For the moment, however, Commius, who escaped into the forests of Northern Gaul, caused him less anxiety than Italy, where serious events were once more in progress.

The Democratic party was again, as in 57, losing all credit with the public, through its failure to redeem the extravagant promises that it had proclaimed. The Land Law of 59, like so many of its predecessors, had never been put into execution. The hopes which had so confidently been built upon the expedition into Britain had been completely falsified. In Parthia the Roman army had suffered a shameful defeat, while Gaul, though everyone had regarded it as subdued in two years by "Rome's only general," now appeared to be still in open revolt. Moreover Crassus was dead, and the once powerful Triumvirate was reduced to a discredited government of two, which was not even strong enough to repress the rioting of the metropolitan crowd. Men had for some time since been chafing at a *régime* of violence and corruption, which threatened to obliterate all the old landmarks of the State; but since the death of Clodius the situation had become truly intolerable. At first, quite as much out of fear as out of justice, the public had been inclined to pass severe judgment upon Milo, who had had the wounded Clodius put to death by his slaves. But when the mob began to take to rioting, there was a change in the general feeling. Even in the Conservative camp the party of repression by violence, the party, that is, which approved of the murder of Clodius, gained the upper hand. On the evening of the funeral the Senate decreed a state of siege, and entrusted Pompey and the Tribunes of the people, together with Milo himself, with the execution of the decree. Emboldened by this sudden change in his favour, Milo at once returned to Rome, and, hoping at one blow to take a pusillanimous public by storm, he had the almost incredible insolence to renew his candidature for the Consulship. But this was too much for the proletariat, which threatened to break out in open revolt. This then was the situation. The confusion was at its height; the public was beginning to take alarm; and the enemies of Cæsar were plucking up courage. Since Cæsar was the creator of the whole party he was considered responsible for all the troubles that had ensued—for the ruin of Crassus, who had set out for Parthia on his persuasion; for the universal corruption, which he had nursed by his largesse; for the disorders at Rome, which he had openly encouraged; and for the endless war in Gaul, which his repeated blunders had provoked.

Cæsar was thus faced with the necessity of once more, for the third time, reconstituting the Democratic party. But this was no easy matter now that not only Crassus and Clodius but also Julia had disappeared. The removal of Clodius, the incomparable agitator, meant the gradual break-up of the electoral colleges, on which Cæsar's party so largely relied; while the death of Crassus, following upon that of Julia, made the relations with Pompey, already strained by the events of the last few years, more and more difficult to maintain. Historians are wrong in attributing the discords which from this moment began to break out between Cæsar and Pompey to the effect of rival ambitions latent for many years and now brought to the surface by the disappearance of Crassus. It was not in the ambitions but in the temperaments of the two men that the discord lay; and it was the force of events rather than the reasoned choice of either of their victims that forced it to break out. The struggle which now begins is not a struggle between two ambitious statesmen; it is the supreme issue between Conservatism and Democracy. After years of desultory conflict the two policies were at last personified in the characters of these two old friends. After all, at the bottom of his nature, Pompey was a Conservative. It was only the bitterness and intrigues of the Conservatives and the difficulty which he had felt in fighting at once against them and against Cæsar, Crassus and Clodius, that had forced him into his strange alliance with Cæsar. A few sharp lessons might be expected to frighten him back into the fold. The defeat of Crassus, the perilous instability of the Republic, and the rioting at Rome supplied the necessary stimulus; they awoke all his instinctive reverence for authority and drove him inevitably towards the ideas of the upper classes.

For earnest and educated opinion had now gradually crystallized round a policy of its own; its programme, so plausible that men forgot how chimerical it still was, proclaimed a harmony between aristocracy and democracy, the repression of public and private corruption, and a return to simpler and purer habits of life. As so often happens to the very rich in times when the whole of society has gone mad over money, Pompey was deeply conscious of the vanity of riches and luxury for other people, and was surprised that the competition to secure them should kindle such disorders in the State. It was impossible that things should remain as they were. The Republic had urgent need of peace, order and justice; and if the ordinary magistracies were not sufficient, a new office must be created with paramount and incontestable powers. All these were ideas widely held in the upper classes; Cicero was giving expression to them in his treatise *De Republica*; while Pompey was slowly being stirred from the depths of his Conservative temperament to a new ambition —to become the appointed reorganizer and peacemaker in the unhappy divisions of his country.

Cæsar was alive to the danger and wished before all to have

Pompey on his side. From Ravenna, where he had gone to pass the winter, he helped his son-in-law to make a levy with which the Senate had entrusted him in Cisalpine Gaul and made him a new and double proposal of marriage. Cæsar was to marry the daughter of Pompey, who was at that time pledged to the son of Sulla, while Pompey was to marry the second daughter of one of Cæsar's nieces, Atia, the widow of Caius Octavius, who had died on the eve of his Consulship, and who, besides a son Caius, born in 63 and now eleven years old, had two older daughters. But Pompey refused the offers, to Cæsar's profound mortification.

It now became increasingly necessary for him to take steps beforehand to avert a serious danger with which he was threatened in the future. His Proconsular powers would expire on the 1st of March 49, and according to the law of Sulla, which only allowed a re-election after a lapse of ten years, he could not again become Consul until the year 48. There would thus be an interval of ten months during which he would no longer be shielded by the immunity enjoyed by a magistrate. He knew that he had hosts of private enemies and that, if his party lost influence and he were abandoned by Pompey, there was serious danger of a prosecution; in which case it was as likely as not that the judges might be induced to pronounce a sentence of exile which would abruptly terminate his political career. It was imperative, therefore, that he should keep the government of his province during these ten months. How was this concession to be obtained? Of course it might easily have been managed by securing the postponement of the nomination of his successor until the 1st of January 48, and by remaining in his province as provisional governor until his successor came out. But this would only involve him in a still more serious difficulty, by making it impossible for him to stand as a candidate for the Consulship in 48. Thus if he returned to Rome, he would lose his *imperium* and become a simple citizen, exposed to the attacks of his enemies; if he remained in his province he could not by law pursue his candidature for the Consulship. It was not easy to find a way out of his network of legal and constitutional difficulties; but Cæsar, never at a loss for expedients, soon hit upon a device. Many of his supporters were making the quite unconstitutional demand that he and Pompey should together be elected to the Consulship for that year. Cæsar refused to entertain the suggestion, but asked in return that the ten Tribunes should bring in a law authorizing him to stand for the Consulship while absent from Rome. He could thus at once secure his election as Consul and at the same time, by preventing the nomination of his successor, remain in Gaul till the 1st of January 48. He at once began to make the necessary arrangements at Rome to secure the proposal of this law.

But bad news from Gaul broke in upon these nice calculations. Once more Cæsar had been mistaken in thinking that strong measures would give him the respite he needed. Scarcely had he left Gaul than the leading men of several of the nations, provoked by the pillaging and executions of the preceding year, held a conclave in the forests to discuss the situation of the country, and formed an agreement to rouse to action, not only their own personal following, but the poorer classes throughout the country. The Carnutes had already risen afresh under Gutuatrus and Conconetodumnus and had made a massacre of all the Italian merchants at Orleans, amongst them the knight Caius Fufius Cita, who was acting as a supply officer to the Roman army. Meanwhile in Auvergne his young friend Vercingetorix had kindled a revolution of his own, securing the supreme power for himself in order to raise the standard of revolt. His movement had already been joined by the Senones, the Parisii, the Pictones, the Cadurci, the Turones, the Aulerci, the Lemovices, the Andes and all the tribes living on the Atlantic coast; and Vercingetorix had despatched one force under the Cadurcan Lucterius towards the frontier of the Province, while he himself was invading the territory of the Bituriges, who were tributaries of the Ædui. The surviving forces of both aristocracy and plutocracy were united against the national enemy; Cæsar's opportunist policy of sowing enmity between the rival interests had ended by setting all parties against him; and the revolt had broken out afresh, in a more serious form than ever, unknown and unsuspected by himself or his generals. The Roman army of occupation was dispersed throughout the country in winter quarters, utterly unprepared for rapid action, whilst their general was surprised hundreds of miles away from the scene of action, before he had even set hands to the work of political restoration for which he had so hastily left the country.

Cæsar was indeed in a terrible dilemma. The whole of his work both in Italy and Gaul, the skilful and laborious construction of years, seemed to be crumbling to ruin, threatening to bury him in its fall. But the greatness of the danger found response in the energy and buoyancy of his spirit. Unable simultaneously to face the danger in Gaul and Italy, and obliged to make an instant choice between the two, he unhesitatingly left Italy to its destiny, as he had done in 57, and at once set out, probably about the middle of February, for Narbonese Gaul. As he drew nearer, the news became more and more disquieting. The Ædui, Remi and Lingones, who alone remained faithful in the centre of the country, were surrounded by an immense circle of revolting peoples, broken only in the East, where the Sequani still maintained a wavering allegiance. The strategic problem with which Cæsar had thus to contend seemed almost insoluble. The entire Roman army was stationed on the most northerly point of the circle of revolt. The whole of the rebel country —almost the whole length of Gaul—lay between Cæsar and his legions; he could not take his small force to join them, nor they march South to meet him, without passing straight through the centre of revolt.

In this cruel dilemma, with that rapidity which, as an ancient writer says, was like a lambent flame, Cæsar devised and executed a plan of extraordinary boldness. Within a few days he had arranged for the defence of the Province with part of its garrison, together with the soldiers he had just recruited in Italy. Then, sending a small force of cavalry to Vienne, he set out with what remained of the garrison, forcing a path in mid-winter through the snow-clad Cevennes and threw his men suddenly upon Auvergne. The Arverni had expected no attack while the snow was still on their mountains; at the appearance of the invader they hastily recalled Vercingetorix to defend his country, which was being overrun, they reported, by a countless army. Vercingetorix, none too secure in his new position, had perforce to comply. This was exactly what Cæsar desired. He abandoned the command to Decimus Brutus with orders to ravage the country. Then, recrossing the Cevennes with a small escort, he covered the 100 miles which separated him from Vienne in a few days. There he picked up the small troop of cavalry which had been sent on ahead and, riding day and night, crossed Gaul at a gallop, unrecognized and unmolested. Before anyone had discovered that he was no longer in Auvergne, he had rejoined the two legions who were wintering in the country of the Lingones, and sent orders to the remainder to concentrate in the neighbourhood of Sens. Towards the middle of March he proceeded there in person with his two legions and found himself at the head of his whole army, eleven legions in all, including the Lark. This gave him about 35,000 men, in addition to the Gallic auxiliaries, whose number is difficult to calculate, and the cavalry, which was very much reduced. From Vienne to Sens, partly on horseback and partly at the head of two legions, Cæsar had covered some 300 miles.

Meanwhile, Vercingetorix, discovering that he had been misled, had returned into the territory of the Bituriges and laid siege to Gorgobina; his small army, composed partly of Arverni and partly of contingents contributed by other tribes, amounted probably to some 7,000 or 8,000 horse, and an equal, or perhaps lesser number of infantry, the greater part of whom must have consisted either of his personal retainers or those of other nobles.

What course was Cæsar now to adopt? From the political point of view his best policy was to throw himself at once against Vercingetorix, to rescue the Ædui and assure himself of their fidelity, and thus dismay the rebels, finish off the war as quickly as possible and return without further delay to Italy. From the purely military point of view, on the other hand, it would be far wiser to await the good season when the army would find abundant supplies on its route. But once more military considerations had to be subordinated to politics. Cæsar was more afraid of an Æduan revolt than of any winter campaign, and he desired to revive the reputation of his army by the brilliance and rapidity of his operations. He therefore requested the Ædui to do their utmost to supply him with corn, left two legions and all his baggage at Sens, and within a few days attacked and took Vellaunodunum, burnt Orleans, crossed the Loire, penetrated into the territory of the Bituriges and laid siege to Soissons. The town was about to surrender when Vercingetorix marched up from Gorgobina. It is hardly likely that he wished to engage his small force in open battle with the Roman army, or to make a serious attempt to deliver the town; more probably he was only attempting a feint to give some relief to the besieged and to revive the courage of the Gauls, who were dismayed by Cæsar's quickness, and had already decided upon guerilla warfare as the best method of fighting the national enemy. However this may be, under the walls of Soissons a battle took place, of which Cæsar gives an exaggerated account, resulting in the retirement of Vercingetorix and the surrender of the town. Cæsar then marched upon Bourges, the capital of the Bituriges, one of the richest of the growing and semi-civilized centres in the country.

Vercingetorix now began methodically to put into execution the design which he must long have had in mind, although Cæsar pretends that it was suggested to him by his recent defeat. His plan was to isolate the invader as he gradually advanced into the country, by making a wilderness all round him—burning the villages and towns, not excepting Bourges, cutting his communications, capturing his convoys, breaking up his foraging parties and allowing him no respite day and night, while drawing his own supplies from a secure base at a distance. These tactics were excellent, particularly as he so outnumbered the Romans in cavalry; but they required one condition for their fulfilment—a nation of iron resolution. At first the Bituriges proved equal to the demand. Cæsar pursued his advance through a deserted and devastated country, daily seeing the smoke going up from burning villages on the horizon, and relentlessly harassed by Vercingetorix who followed close on his heels, refusing all open engagements, camping his small army in the safe shelter of the woods and the marshes, and attempting the capture of Cæsar's convoys.

If only Bourges itself had been destroyed the Roman army would have gone astray in an aimless and impossible enterprise. But the Bituriges were proud of their prosperous capital, and had not the heart to sacrifice it for the cause; and Vercingetorix had at length yielded to their demands, and agreed to spare it. Cæsar was thus able to attack the city, which was stoutly defended by the Bituriges. No sooner had he reached it than, with his habitual activity, he set vigorously to work upon the siege, undertaking works of investment on a gigantic scale and keeping his soldiers busy with the spade through the cold and rainy days of early spring, though the attacks of Vercingetorix, which he consistently ignored, sometimes left them without bread for days together. Since the days of Lucullus no Roman army had been in such straits; but Cæsar knew his men far better than Lucullus. In the crisis of the siege, when everything turned upon their labours, he relied rather on comradeship than on discipline to keep them at work, and heaped them with attentions which contrast strangely with the blood-stained records of the campaign. On one occasion he even proposed, if they thought the task above their strength, to withdraw from the siege altogether. He was met, of course, with a unanimous refusal and his men returned to their work in better spirits than ever. Thus despite cold, hunger and the sallies of the enemy, the siege works were at length completed, and the assaulting towers prepared; towards the end of April the attack was made and the city taken. Cæsar decided to make a terrible example, and the town was given over to the soldiers; the entire population was massacred, without Vercingetorix daring to move to the rescue.

In a little more than a month Cæsar had stamped out four separate flames of revolt, strewn his path with ghastly trophies like the burning of Orleans and the sack of Bourges, replenished his coffers with the treasure of towns, temples and natives, and, above all, revived in his troops the confidence so indispensable to a small army fighting in a huge and unfriendly country. His magnificent vigour and impetuosity had triumphed over every obstacle, over distance and climate and hunger, over numbers and fortifications. He now made a small pause at Bourges, as though to take breath. Imagining that the most difficult part of his work was completed, and that the revolt, if not completely suppressed, was at least well under control, Cæsar proposed to rest his army at Bourges, where he had captured large stores, until the approaching spring. With the arrival of better weather he intended to invade the territory of the Arverni and bring the war to a conclusion by the capture of their capital Gergovia. But now occurred one of those dangerous incidents in Gallic policy which had during the last five years caused so much anxiety to Cæsar. The trouble arose out of the election to the chief magistracy of the Ædui, which had fallen vacant just before. Two parties were in competition for the post, one having nominated Cotys and the other Convictoli-tavus, and the conflict had very nearly provoked a civil war. One side was now claiming that the election of Cotys was illegal. Cæsar was obliged to suspend military operations, to repair with his army to Decetia, and to solve the difficulty by recognizing the validity of the election of Convictolitavus, who was in fact the rightful candidate. This occupied his attention for several weeks, during which the rebel forces might have been expected to be slowly breaking up in the prospect of Cæsar's final campaign against Gergovia.

Once more Cæsar's expectations were falsified. The news which reached him clearly indicated that the insurgents were not nearly so much discouraged by his victories as he had allowed himself to hope. In the North the Senones and Parisii were still in arms and confident of victory; Commius was recruiting an army of his own, while Vercingetorix had received help from Aquitainia and was collecting archers, training his men in the Roman methods of encampment, and bringing pressure to bear upon the nations that remained faithful to Rome, such as the Ædui and Sequani, by sending their chiefs huge quantities of gold from the mines in his own territory. Cæsar, however, was still so certain that the war was almost at an end that he felt strong enough to divide his forces. We have no further mention of the native legion, the Lark, and Cæsar always speaks of a total of ten legions; of these he tells us that he gave four to Labienus, sending him northwards towards the middle of May against the Parisii and Sequani, while he himself marched southwards with six legions to invade Auvergne by the valley of the Allier, thus forcing Vercingetorix to accept battle and put an end to the war.

Meanwhile Vercingetorix had reached the banks of the Allier and broken down all the bridges; he now proceeded to march along the left bank of the river following Cæsar's movements on the opposite bank, to prevent him from crossing over into Auvergne. Cæsar was forced to employ a stratagem. He succeeded one morning in concealing twenty cohorts, two from each legion, in a wood near a broken-down bridge; when the rest of the army had disappeared along the river, the cohorts emerged from their hiding-place and rebuilt and occupied the bridge. The legions returned and crossed the Allier; Vercingetorix, unwilling to give battle, allowed them to pass and, adhering to his previous tactics, began once more to retreat before them. Five days later Cæsar arrived in view of Gergovia, which is situated on the top of a steep bluff; and began at once to enter upon the labours of the siege. But six legions were not sufficient to take a city with such strong natural and artificial defences, and the situation of the Roman army soon became critical. Vercingetorix was always encamped a short distance away, keeping himself in the shelter of the forests and the marshes, always in evidence and always unassailable. The Æduan nobles, who resented the recent interference of Cæsar in their State, were beginning to yield to the substantial persuasions of Vercingetorix. Cæsar grew anxious, redoubled his energy, and tried every device to shorten the siege with the insufficient forces at his disposal. But still Gergovia held out. One day Cæsar with difficulty prevented a troop of Æduan auxiliaries from deserting to the enemy. Then he saw that he must make a supreme effort to capture the city and strike terror into the Gauls by a direct attack, and sent six legions to a general assault. But it was a forlorn hope; the Romans were repulsed with heavy losses. Recognizing his mistake and fully conscious of the danger of obstinately continuing the siege, Cæsar decided to withdraw and to march off, probably in the second half of June, to join Labienus in the North.

The decision was no doubt wise; none the less so because, in the general ferment of national feeling throughout the country, it was one that brought with it undeniable risks. To many this first open confession of failure on Cæsar's part seemed the beginning of the end. Vercingetorix now became the hero of a real national uprising, winning supporters to his cause from the most unexpected quarters. Already on his way north Cæsar received news of the revolt of this faithful Ædui, who had captured Soissons, with all his treasure and his hostages, his baggage and his horses, massacred the Roman merchants, cut the bridge over the Loire, burning or throwing into the river all the stores they could not carry off, and were now preparing to bar his passage and drive him back, through sheer starvation, into the Roman Province. This was really the most critical moment in the campaign. The defection of the Ædui, the richest and most powerful nation in Gaul, not only cut him off from Labienus, but deprived him of his best base of supplies, destroyed the entire effect of his preceding victories and lit the flame of rebellion among neutrals and waverers in every corner of Gaul. His attempted organization had definitely broken down; the old Gallic institutions which he had tried to use for his own purposes were being used to weld together the whole country against him. Already from one end of Gaul to the other arrangements were being made for the convocation of a great national Diet at Bibracte.

Once more Cæsar saw himself on the brink of the abyss; but again he displayed neither hesitation nor dismay. He saw that, if he retired alone into the Province, leaving Labienus in the North, the Gauls would make short work of both forces in detail. He therefore decided to rejoin Labienus at all costs at the earliest possible moment. Not wishing to lose time in making a bridge over the Loire, swollen though it was by the melting of the snows, he found a ford by which his soldiers could cross with the water over their armpits, carrying arms and firewood on their heads. He put the cavalry in the van to form a moving dyke against the current and took all his army with him into the river. Then seizing all the corn and cattle he could find, and loading up slaves and mules and the already overburdened legionaries, he advanced northwards by forced marches and finally rejoined Labienus in the territory of the Senones, probably in the neighbourhood of Sens. From Gergovia to Sens Cæsar had covered another 200 miles; if we suppose that this took him some fifteen days, it must have been the beginning of July when once more he found himself with his whole army at his back. Fortunately while he had been unsuccessful at Gergovia, Labienus had won considerable victories over the Senones and Parisii.

Then supervened a slight lull in the operations. The *Commentaries* do not tell us how long it lasted, but it cannot have been less than a month—a time filled with anxious and feverish preparation on both sides. The defeat at Gergovia seemes to have changed all the probabilities of the war. The example of the Ædui had induced almost all the Gallic nations to join the movement; the only exceptions were the Remi, the Lingones, the Treveri, and a few tribes among the Belgæ. Vercingetorix was at Bibracte, the centre of the insurrection, where representatives from all the states of Gaul were coming together in an improvised Diet to discuss the formation of a national army. Gaul was awake and stirring with enthusiasm from one end to the other; the most sceptical and indifferent were drawn into the national cause.

Very different was the outlook and temper of Cæsar. The sudden change in his fortunes, coming as a reaction from the bold self-confidence of a few months before, tended to render him even unduly pessimistic. Isolated with his small army in the depths of a vast and hostile country, with the constant feeling that a new rising might spring up against him from any quarter of the land, he once more restrained his natural tendencies as a strategist and reverted to an almost excessive measure of care and caution. The country itself he gave up for lost; his one thought now was to extricate his army. But this was by no means so easy. New difficulties appeared at every turn to baffle the general who two months before had thought the country reconquered for good. The soldiers were surprised and disheartened by the revolt of the Ædui; supplies, always scanty, were scarcer than ever since the country-people had turned against them; while the experience of Britain and the disaster of Carrhæ brought home to the army a text on which all Italy was preaching—that in every contest between Roman and barbarian the lack of cavalry was a fatal element of weakness. All through this time Cæsar must have been haunted with the memory of Crassus. If he had hitherto ventured to set his legions boldly on the track of the cavalry of Vercingetorix, he was now far too cautious to march his dispirited infantry with their scanty cavalry supports across the country, exposed, like Crassus, to the constant onslaughts of the enemy's horse.

It was doubtless these considerations which caused him to lead his army in the direction of Germany to a spot which some identify with Vitry-sur-Marne, and others with Bar-sur-Aube, where he recruited a considerable force of German cavalry. The general who had entered Gaul seven years before as the destroyer of the German power was now enrolling Germans against Gauls and paying them with the profits of the pillage of Gaul. He spent the whole of July and perhaps part of August in enrolling a large body of German cavalry and making preparations for his retreat. But his soldiers were still very much discouraged by the reports of the enemy and their own position, while confidence and enthusiasm reigned in the councils of the Gauls.

Both sides had strangely miscalculated the situation. Cæsar was mistaken in exaggerating the danger, as he had been mistaken before in thinking that the war was over. Vercingetorix owed all his success to his guerilla methods of warfare; and no doubt had it been possible to organize a war throughout Gaul under party chieftains like himself, Cæsar would ultimately have been forced, through lack of supplies, to evacuate the country. But Cæsar's defeat under the walls of Gergovia was in reality the salvation of the Roman power. Emboldened by their success, a party among the Gauls desired to transform the guerilla tactics into a regular war—a war in which Gaul, disunited as it was, and in the throes of a dangerous social crisis, could not hope to triumph over the armies of so old and tried a military and political system as that of Rome.

The first symptoms of the change were felt at Bibracte, when the question arose of choosing a commander-in-chief and forming a plan of campaign. The Ædui were anxious to elect one of their own countrymen, while another party proposed to confirm Vercingetorix in his command; one party was anxious for war on a large scale, the other voted for the continuance of the present operations. Vercinge-torix and his partisans secured the upper hand; but in order that the Ædui might not unduly resent his authority, and in the hope of harmonizing two opposing notions of strategy, Vercingetorix, who was certainly a man of real ability, proposed the adoption of both tactics simultaneously—one of those unfortunate compromises so frequent in history, because they are fatally imposed even upon the most resolute and intelligent of men by the weakness and folly of their colleagues. The Ædui and Segusiavi were to send 10,000 infantry and 800 cavalry under the command of a noble to invade the territory of the Allobroges in the Roman Province; the Gabali and Arverni were to pillage the territory of the Helvii; the Rutheni and the Cadurci that of the Volcæ Arrecomici, thus breaking into the Province at several points and drawing Cæsar down from the North to its defence. Vercingetorix was to transfer his headquarters to Alesia, a small fortified town of the Mandubii, where all the roads which Cæsar might take in his southward march happened to cross, and which was an excellent post for watching the movements of the enemy. After strengthening the fortifications of Alesia and supplying it abundantly with provisions, Vercingetorix, with a body of 15,000 cavalry and the infantry under his command, was to hamper the

march of the enemy, to cut off his supplies and harass him as he passed
by on his way to the defence of the Province.

It was probably in the first half of August that Cæsar, after
organizing a large body of German cavalry, put himself at the head
of his eleven tired legions to set out on his retreat to the Province,
a disastrous *finale* to the enterprise he had so brilliantly inaugurated.
The country on which he had staked the whole of his political fortune
had played him false after all; the work on which he had laboured
for seven years and which was to make him the equal of Lucullus
and Pompey had been shattered at one blow. These 30,000 men, who
set out, weary and dispirited, dragging behind them on mules in a
long procession the siege-engines, the baggage, the slaves of officers
and legionaries, the remains of the booty, the few Italian merchants
who had escaped massacre—in short, all that still remained Italian
in men or goods in the country which he had for a moment regarded
as conquered—seemed to mark the end of the Roman dominion
beyond the Alps, and the final ruin of that conquering policy in which
Cæsar had thought to imitate, and even excel, his great predecessor
Lucullus.

It is difficult to ascertain exactly by what road he travelled. Some
authorities trace his route from the neighbourhood of the modern
Troyes by Gray and Dijon to Besançon. Others make him set out
from Vitry-sur-Marne to ascend the valley of the Tille, pass aside
to Dijon, cross the Saône near St. Jean de Losne and thus make for
the Province along the right bank of the Saône. Others again make
him start from Bar-sur-Aube in the direction of Pontaillier-sur-
Saône. All that is certain is that on about the fourth day of his march,
at morning, when he had arrived, according to Von Göler, at
Beneuve, between Brevon and the Ource, according to Napoleon III
upon the banks of the Vingeanne, according to the Duke of Aumale
in the neighbourhood of Montigny, or according to the anonymous
writer of the French *Military Spectator* in the neighbourhood of
Allofroy, Cæsar was suddenly attacked by Vercingetorix and forced
to engage in a pitched battle.

What was the reason for this sudden change of tactics? Why had
Vercingetorix abandoned his guerilla system to attempt war on a
grand scale? As the Gallic general comes down to us, even in Cæsar's

account, as a man of intelligence and energy, we must suppose, in the absence of definite evidence, that it must have been the condition of his army which obliged him to seek an encounter which exactly fell in with Cæsar's desires. It is possible to conduct guerilla operations with a small army, with few resources, and without great generals; but it is impossible to conduct them without brave, resolute and patient soldiers. While Vercingetorix had been at the head of small bodies of cavalry and infantry composed almost entirely of Arverni who were his clients, his servants, or his friends, he had had sufficient authority to submit them to the fatigues and hardships of guerilla warfare; but now that he was at the head of a heterogeneous army he found that he had at once more soldiers and less authority. It is probable that discord arose between the numerous chiefs of the separate detachments and that national rivalries were spreading through the ranks. In an army which had been formed within a few months at a moment of exaltation and which had never been submitted to any regular discipline, in which the soldiers were, for the most part, dependants of great barons accustomed to small inter-tribal wars of short duration, or young men hastily recruited from all classes of society and devoid of the necessary military training, Vercingetorix may perhaps have feared that patriotic enthusiasm would die out altogether unless it were rekindled and intensified by some signal success. He probably reckoned on the demoralization of the Romans and hoped to imitate the tactics by which, only a year before, the Parthians had annihilated the legions of Crassus. He therefore threw his cavalry suddenly upon Cæsar's army as it was on the march, keeping his infantry, divided into three corps, out of action in the rear.

Vercingetorix was perhaps unaware that Cæsar had recruited a new cavalry from the other side of the Rhine, and that, instead of the scanty and ineffective Roman squadrons, he was face to face with the vigorous horsemen of Germany. The engagement between the two bodies of horse was violent but short; for Cæsar's Germans, with the help of the legions, soon succeeded in routing the Gauls with considerable loss.

This ended the operations of the actual battle; but its consequences were so momentous that they can only be explained by supposing that the Gallic army was totally lacking in organization and endurance, and that Cæsar had believed it to be far more dangerous than it really was. Immediately after the battle Vercingetorix withdrew his troops to Alesia, and Cæsar, realizing at once that retreat into a fortified town implied the demoralization of the Gallic army, changed his plans once more on the very evening of the battle and, instead of continuing his march towards the Province, resolved to take the offensive, and to strike a final blow. If he succeeded, it would be the end of the war, and the means of recovering his prestige at Rome; if he failed he would perish with his men and meet, in the heart of Gaul itself, the destiny which would certainly await him in the Province if he returned there with a beaten army. On the very next day he set out in pursuit of the Gallic army, arrived in front of Alesia, saw the rock upon which the citadel was perched, and did not hesitate, although in a hostile country and without assured means of supply, to set his 30,000 men to besiege an enemy whose force was greater or at least equal to his own, to await the attacks of the Gallic armies which were now making for the Province, so soon as they returned to the help of the besieged, indeed to give battle under the walls of Alesia, if need be, to the entire forces of insurgent Gaul. The plan was one of almost desperate rashness. But the man who carried within him the destinies of Europe, the great artist in strategy, over-prudent and foolhardy by turns, was resolved for once to stake all upon his luck. The legionaries took shovel and pickaxe from the backs of their beasts, and once more engaged upon the familiar task of digging trenches and raising terraces round a beleaguered city.

Vercingetorix at once attempted to hamper the siege-works of the Romans by constant cavalry skirmishes; but he soon perceived that though he might retard them he could not actually prevent their completion. What then was he to do? To attempt a sally and stake all upon a pitched battle was too dangerous an alternative; yet to allow himself to be shut up was suicidal. At a council of war, after lively discussion, it was decided to send away the cavalry before the investing lines were completed, that they might ask help from the different Celtic peoples and rouse Gaul to make a general levy; the time, place, and numbers of the detachments were settled, and an army of a quarter of a million men was to be collected to be hurled at the Roman trenches. So one evening almost the whole of the Gallic cavalry noiselessly passed the gates, eluded the vigilance of the Roman sentries, crossed the still incomplete siege-works and disappeared in numerous squadrons to the four quarters of the horizon. The first part of the plan had been successful, and great was Cæsar's consternation when he learnt the news. His fate now rested entirely on the reception Gaul gave to the mission. Would the whole country respond to the appeal of the besieged of Alesia, the last surviving defenders of its liberty? Would beacon-fires be lighted on all the roads, to flame across forest and marshland, from village to village, to announce the danger and implore for help? Would the messengers of rebellion penetrate into the most secluded mountain-hamlets to bear news that a common country demanded a supreme and costly sacrifice, and to roll back a great wave of patriots upon the crags of Alesia?

Vain questions, to which Cæsar had no reply! His lot was already cast; retreat was impossible; nor could he, like Lucullus outside Tigranocerta, leave a part of his 30,000 soldiers to continue the siege and march with the rest against the reinforcing army; for his forces were too scanty and a division might entail the annihilation of both parts. He could do nothing but wait, pressing on the siege with all his might till the enemy's reinforcements came up and caught him where he was. Once more his position seemed wellnigh hopeless. It was this harassing suspense that drove the mind which had for the last seven months been like an impetuous spring, seething and boiling as it bursts its way through too narrow an orifice, to conceive and execute with unheard-of and breathless rapidity one of the most amazing and grandiose ideas in all the record of ancient warfare—the enclosure of his own besieging forces in a huge artificial fortification improvised for the occasion. On the side of the plain he constructed a second circumvallation with bastions and towers, leaving a large space between this circle and that which he had already made on the side of the town; between these two circles his army was to remain in a sort of elongated fortress, moving from one line to the other in the narrow space which remained between, to resist the double assault to be delivered by the besieged of Alesia and the quarter of a million recruits who were expected from Gaul. But would his men have the time to finish the enormous works required—works for which it has been calculated that two million cubic metres of earth needed to be displaced? Cæsar ran a grave risk of being besieged in his turn by the reinforcing army, like Mithridates under the walls of Cyzicus, and thus being reduced to death by starvation. It is difficult to exaggerate the horror of the situation. Although the enemy was still at a distance and the Remi and Lingones remained friendly, the provisioning of the troops was already difficult; it would become altogether impossible when a huge horde of armed men occupied the whole country and closed all the roads. Meanwhile from morning to night Cæsar, with the help of Mamurra, Antony, Labienus, Decimus Brutus, Caius Trebonius, Caius Caninius Rebilus, and Caius Antistius Reginus directed the gigantic work and communicated his own enthusiasm to his soldiers. He studied the texts of the manuals of Siege-work; he consulted Mamurra and the eastern slaves most skilled in scientific strategy, and made them sketch him plans which he distributed to the centurions who had become overseers; he sent out on all sides to fetch in fuel and iron; while his 9,000 soldiers remained ceaselessly at work, breaking up the ground, making trenches far out in the plain, putting in hooks of steel and pointed stone which they covered with faggots and grass, to sow the ground with snares and pitfalls.

Thus the weeks went slowly by. Meanwhile in all the villages throughout Gaul young men were being enrolled for the war, contingents were being fitted, arms furbished, beasts of burden taken out of the stable and loaded with grain. At every cross-road young soldiers and convoys met as they moved towards the spots chosen for the concentration, whence all were to proceed to Bibracte, where the nobles of the chief Gallic states had already come together to deliberate upon the command of the army and the plan of campaign. But round the rock of Alesia brooded a lonely and ill-omened silence. Cæsar received but meagre and uncertain news of the reinforcing army; and from the topmost towers of Alesia the watchmen of Vercingetorix swept their eyes in vain over the distant horizon. Famine soon crept into the beleagured city; and the day arrived when Vercingetorix, after putting the town upon rations, found it necessary to get rid of the useless mouths, and to send the whole non-combatant population outside the walls into the space between them and the inner line of the Romans. He hoped that Cæsar would take them in for sale, and that they would thus at least escape with their lives. But Cæsar had not bread enough for his own soldiers. It was in vain that the doomed company of old men, women and children, exposed to all the assaults of the climate and of hunger, huddled round the Roman lines begging for bread. Every day the besieged in Alesia and their Roman besiegers could see the crowd of non-combatants chewing the grass outside their lines, could hear their cries and watch their exhaustion. The space between the trench and the hill was transformed into a field of agony, a ghastly cemetery where the suffering were already skeletons before death released them. Yet their cries fell unmoved upon both Gaul and Roman, who had neither the mood nor the means for mercy. The defenders of Alesia were themselves half-starved, while in the Roman trenches the men worked away on empty stomachs. If, instead of recruiting an enormous army all through the land, the Gallic leaders had sent countless guerillas to devastate the surrounding country and capture the convoys of the Lingones and Remi, the army of Vercingetorix and the whole people of the Mandubii might perhaps have succumbed, but they would certainly have involved their Roman besiegers in their fall.

But this was not to be. Once more regular warfare was to come to Cæsar's rescue. A large Gallic army, even if less than the expected quarter of a million, eventually arrived outside Alesia. It was a rabble of untrained soldiers, hastily recruited from amongst all classes of Gallic society and was commanded by four generals, Commius, Vercassivelaunus, Eporidorix, and Veridomar, who do not seem to have been in agreement. It has been remarked that two of these generals were Æduans, and that the Ædui, who had only at the last moment entered into the revolutionary movement, seem to have behaved in this final campaign with a slackness which soon enabled them to make terms with the victors. However this may be, there can be no doubt that, if this army had been a regular force under capable commanders, it should have succeeded in annihilating Cæsar, even at the cost of sacrificing Vercingetorix. It should have besieged Cæsar, as Lucullus had besieged Mithridates beneath the walls of Cyzicus, by compelling him either to break out by force, or to die of hunger. Instead of this, the lack of agreement between the leaders and of cohesion in the army, together with the general impatience to rescue Vercingetorix, induced the commanders to make repeated assaults against the Roman trenches, while Vercingetorix attacked them from the opposite side. These assaults lasted seven days; but the Gauls did not succeed in breaking through the great rampart of earth and men which the genius of Cæsar had spent but a month in raising. Under the direction of Cæsar, Antony, Labienus, Trebonius, Antistius, and Caninius vigorously repelled the assaults on all the positions attacked. These useless and costly attempts were wearisome and discouraging to the relieving army, which had reckoned securely on victory and was little used to discipline; and it finally disbanded, leaving numerous prisoners with the Romans, without having succeeded in breaking through the circle of forts which enclosed Alesia. In their discouragement the Gallic chieftains in Alesia turned against Vercingetorix. They seized him, sent him out to Cæsar as a prisoner, and then capitulated. The entire army, all that survived of the Mandubii, and a large number of prisoners, were distributed among the soldiers. In this singular fashion, and to the general amazement, the war was suddenly concluded towards the end of September.

A barbarous country just lightly touched by the transforming hand of civilization, Gaul was equally unfitted either for the obstinate and unsystematic fighting of savage tribes, or the skilful and methodical warfare of civilized nations. She attempted to do both by turns. Cæsar's campaigns reveal all the social and moral incoherence which was at that time prevalent in Gallic society, and which alone is adequate to explain how so vast a country could be effectually subdued by a small army of 30,000 men. Vercingetorix was at once the hero and the victim of this transformation in the character and institutions of his countrymen, which could only be completed after immense sacrifice and suffering. Yet the scales, after all, were very evenly balanced. The awful tension of the crisis from which Cæsar and his legions so triumphantly emerged by the capture of Alesia might easily have been relieved in very different fashion. If the general had been cast in a softer mould, or had displayed less signal qualities of daring and resource, if the soldiers had failed either in training or in toughness, or in loyalty to their incomparable leader, they could never have achieved what they did. Certainly, had they been of the quality of the troops of Crassus, they could never have endured the stress of the campaign—alone in the heart of a huge and hostile territory, constantly exposed to attack on all sides, with no base of operations in the country, with their communications with Italy irretrievably cut off. In such a situation as this, even the most inconsequent and unscientific methods of warfare should have brought victory to the native. Cæsar might have fallen on the road to the Province as Crassus fell on the road to Armenia, and the whole history of Europe would have taken another course.

What would have happened had Carrhæ been repeated, within a year, against a Western enemy? The speculation is interesting. It was a critical moment in the development of Italy; and the shock of a second catastrophe, removing Cæsar so soon after his less gifted colleague, would have made a deep, perhaps an indelible, impression. It is tempting to ask whether it would not have converted Italy for good from the gospel of adventure, and prevented her from pressing further into the interior of the continent. The siege of Alesia reads like a hideous nightmare; but it decided the character of the civilization of Europe. Cæsar's enemies were fond of reproaching him with the slowness of his conquests and the smallness of his achievements. But his work was greater than it seemed. In his seven years of campaigning he had created an army, small in numbers but finer in quality than any force Rome had had at her command for generations; and, at the decisive moment in the history of Europe, he and his men had drawn events into a course which their successors would for centuries be unable to deflect.

CHAPTER XXIII

THE DISORDERS AND THE PROGRESS
OF ITALY

WHILST Democratic Imperialism was passing through this supreme ordeal in Gaul, an important change had taken place in the metropolis. Pompey at last made his peace with the Conservatives. Soon after the departure of Cæsar the rioting had become so serious and energetic measures of repression so urgently necessary that the whole of Rome, even his most violent opponents, had been driven in dismay to acquiesce in the Dictatorship of Pompey. Cato had indeed insisted that Pompey's official title should be not Dictator, but sole Consul, in order that he might still be held responsible at the expiration of his term. But this was a mere constitutional subtlety. The fact remained. Pompey had been raised alone to a supreme position in the State, with the duty of re-establishing order at all costs, thereby adding to his long list of extraordinary honours the altogether unprecedented privilege of being at once Consul and Proconsul.

He had bent himself to his task with an energy which Rome had ceased to expect from one who generally exercised authority with such an air of detachment. He had, it is true, made one last concession to the Democrats by securing the approval of the Bill which allowed Cæsar to stand for the Consulship without returning to Rome. But all the rest of his measures were unaffectedly Conservative. He carefully revised the list of citizens from whom the 100 judges of political cases were chosen by lot, reducing them to 950, Senators, knights and plebeians, and admitting only men whom he was in a position to influence. He proposed a *lex Pompeia de ambitu* and a *lex Pompeia de vi* which simplified lawsuits, increased the penalties for all acts of political corruption committed since 70 (that is, during the years when Cæsar's gold had been most lavishly scattered throughout Italy) and introduced a new and more vigorous procedure against crimes of violence. He also brought forward a *lex Pompeia de Provinciis* to legalize a senatorial decree of the previous year, according to which no one could be a Governor of a province less than five years after ceasing to be Prætor or Consul; and finally a *lex Pompeia de jure magistratuum*, which contained, amongst other provisions which have not come down to us, a simple and straightforward confirmation of the old rule against standing for the Consulship without coming to Rome.

These were all measures for which Conservatives had been clamouring for years. Their exultation may therefore easily be imagined. Even the most inveterate of Pompey's critics began to take a more lenient view of his character. Cæsar's supporters, of course, were by no means so delighted; but as Pompey was still regarded as being on friendly terms with Cæsar they did not attempt to oppose any of his measures, confining themselves to the criticism that the *lex de iure magistratuum* seemed on the face of it to annul the very privilege expressly granted so recently to the Proconsul of Gaul. Thus, thanks to his own personal authority and to the support of the upper classes, and an alarmed and disgusted public, Pompey succeeded in passing all his Bills without a struggle and with a minimum of delay. One small concession he made to the friends of Cæsar, by inserting in the *lex de jure magistratuum* a clause the exact terms of which we do not know, but which was so drawn up that Cæsar's enemies were able later on to dispute its legality.

These laws were excellent. But Cæsar's laws had been equally excellent and they had been in force now for several years. Yet they were entirely useless, simply because, in the excitement and intrigues of the party struggle and the universal debasement of Roman public life, no magistrate was able to put them into execution. What was there to prevent the same from taking place now? All depended upon the action of the Dictator. To the astonishment of Rome, Pompey rose to the occasion. From the moment of his election he seemed to become a changed man. The vacillating, indolent and sceptical aristocrat suddenly displayed an almost brutal energy in the administration of his own laws. For a time it was almost as if Sulla had come to life again. Something like a reign of terror prevailed in the law courts. Cases were hurried forward with peremptory haste; the most garrulous of advocates were sternly silenced; and all the authority of the Dictator was used to secure a condemnation. Within a few weeks a large number of the friends of Clodius and Cæsar who had been compromised in the scandals of the preceding years had been summarily tried and sent into exile. Some of the less respectable of the Conservatives, amongst others Milo, went to share their fate.

All this tended to enhance Pompey's popularity and intensify the feeling against the recent disorders. It put all who were desirous of seeing order re-established in the mood to approve severe measures, without inquiring too closely into their literal legality. It was no time for lawyers' scruples. Rome needed something more thorough than rose-water surgery. Such was the talk of the day. Yet, as always will happen when society has grown rich and self-indulgent and is split up into hostile and self-satisfied cliques, these copy-book maxims were somewhat restricted in their application. When it came to a question of his own friends or relations the most relentless of censors showed an unexpected tenderness. Pompey might harden his heart against the low rioters of the streets; he might display something like ferocity against individuals out of the upper classes, as when he told Memmius, who came to ask his help in a lawsuit and found him going from his bath to his dinner, "If you detain me, you will give me a cold dinner: that is all"; yet even he would intervene to save his own friends. He had lately found a new wife in the young and charming Cornelia, a daughter of Scipio and widow of the ill-fated young Publius Crassus.

Pompey's justice was thus not exactly even-handed. But it was effective; and the elections had passed off without disorder. It is true that Cato, who had refused to spend a sesterce upon his candidature, was unsuccessful for the Consulship. But both the elected Consuls were members of his party. One was Marcus Claudius Marcellus, member of an ancient Roman family and an outspoken enemy of Cæsar: the other, Servius Sulpicius Rufus, the lawyer who had stood against Catiline twelve years before, but whom age and experience had taught the wisdom of opportunism. Clearly the tide of feeling against the extravagance and corruption of Cæsar's *régime* was still steadily rising. Cicero, of course, had not escaped its contact. As he neared the end of his great treatise on the Republic, summoning all the eloquence of his pen to expound in sonorous Latin the high wisdom of the political thinkers of Greece, he shook off the palsy of scepticism which had weighed down his spirit during the last ten years. His old enthusiasm for Pompey was reawakened; he began to hope once more; and, with a scrupulousness which is very characteristic of the man, he prepared to repay the debt he had contracted with Cæsar, whose conduct he now judged with increasing severity.

Amidst the suspense and excitements of this anxious year there was one small change which almost escaped the notice of contemporary observers. It was the first year in which oil prepared in Italy was exported for sale in the provinces. Hitherto Greece and Asia had supplied the markets of the Mediterranean, and even of Italy. But the field of cultivation in Italy had been slowly extended and improved; the increase in the supply had steadily diminished the cost of production; and Italy was now at last prepared, not only to satisfy her own increasing demands but to compete with success in oversea markets. This small item of information, accidentally preserved for us by one of the most careful students of ancient times, reminds us how, amidst wars and the rumours of wars, the despised slave immigrants from the East, under the guidance of their Italian masters, persevered in their appointed task. Behind the small knot of warriors and statesmen who crowd with such self-importance before the footlights of history we catch this one fleeting glimpse of the great multitude of workers who, unknown and unregarded, were spending their powers each in his own way, to transform Italy. In every country town in Italy there were freedmen and sons of freedmen and immigrants from the East, small peasant proprietors and well-to-do landlords, retired legionaries and centurions come home from distant parts, or settled with some comrade in a piece of country they had learnt to know during their service, all busily increasing their resources, laying by savings, buying land sold off by noble families in difficulties, buying slaves, improving methods of cultivation, setting up in business, introducing new arts and processes or opening workshops for manufacturers.

The progress in the cultivation of the olive which is revealed to us by this little notice of Pliny, and the progress which was being made simultaneously in the cultivation of the vine, would not have been possible but for one all-important change in the whole structure of society. This was the emergence, between the great landlords and the few surviving members of the old peasant proprietor population, of a new middle class of landowners who were prepared, with the small capital and few skilled slaves at their command, to attempt the scientific and intensive cultivation of the East. The old peasant proprietors would never have acquired the knowledge to do this for themselves; while the large absentee landlords had not at their disposal, or were not inclined to stake, the vast capital required to stock huge tracts of land with olives, vines, fruit-trees and the necessary buildings. Ordinarily, unless their estates happened to be in the immediate neighbourhood of a town or of the capital, they found it more convenient to rely upon pasturage, conducted however with greater care and knowledge than in the old primitive days. In the great forests and prairies of the Po valley, and in South Italy, where the devastations of Hannibal had never been effaced, there were huge herds out at pasture under the slaves of Roman nobles. Most of the strength that still resided in the extreme Conservative party came from a small knot of old aristocrats like Domitius Ahenobarbus, who were cattle-breeders on an immense scale. But such cases were gradually growing to be altogether exceptional. The steady progress which was being made, more especially in North and Central Italy, by the introduction of intensive cultivation and the growing of vine and olive, was due almost entirely to middle-class proprietors who no longer lived, like the old-fashioned middle class, in the open country and made a precarious living by setting their whole family to work on the soil. The new landed middle class spent a good part of each year in the neighbouring town, leaving the whole of the manual work to their slaves and labourers, over whom they maintained the strictest control, often remained bachelors or had very small families, and devoted a large part of their attention to increasing to a maximum the profit drawn from their estates.

These large changes in the whole economy of agriculture could not help causing a corresponding development in the sphere of industry. It is to these days that we are surely justified in assigning the first impetus of that great advance in arts and manufactures which was in the next half-century to penetrate from one end of the peninsula to the other. The agricultural improvements recorded by Pliny were indeed only the natural effects of a general progress in material civilization which necessarily entailed a greater division of labour in every department of society, and not least, therefore, in industry. In primitive Italy the landowner had made everything for himself: his clothes, his furniture, his implements of toil; he was his own workman, and was at pains that his family should wholly satisfy its own needs. But the modern landlord was more intelligent and cultivated, more refined in his taste than his humbler predecessor. He demanded finer clothes, more perfect implements, less precarious profits; and he realized that he could not ask his slaves to be equally accomplished in every department. He saw that it would pay him to reach perfection in one branch, and apply in the open market for many articles which had previously been manufactured at home. In this way commerce and industry advanced hand in hand with agriculture, and Oriental slaves could be bought or hired for industrial uses not only at Rome but in all the smaller towns of Italy. The freedmen, immigrants and vagabonds who were tramping up and down the country for a livelihood, often found employment in a Latin colony or a *municipium*, or in one of these federated towns which from the height of their Cyclopean walls still seemed to threaten death to the stranger who ventured to draw near without making sure of a kindly welcome.

We may therefore confidently fix this period as marking the first appearance of the class of prosperous merchants and artisans which we shall find flourishing fifty years later in all the smaller cities of Italy. It was this generation that, all over North Italy, from Vercelli in the North down to Milan, Modena and Rimini, first began manufacturing the lamps and bowls and pottery that were afterwards so famous; that saw the skilled workmen and merchants of Padua and Verona produce and export the carpets and coverlets which were soon to be known and appreciated in all parts of Italy; that tempted the poor workers of Parma and Modena to make a living by home labour out of the wool of the great flocks at pasture on the big absentee estates outside the town, thus inaugurating the Italian woollen trade; that planted flax in the low land round Faenza and encouraged the city to spin and to weave it; that made Genoa, at the foot of her savage mountains, a great centre for the timber and hides, the cattle and the honey, brought down by the Ligurian natives from the lonely valleys to which they had slowly been driven back; that revived the old Etruscan pottery works at Arezzo, through the cheapness of skilled slave labour, encouraging the proprietors to buy workers who were clever at designing, and would help to make the red ware which afterward became so familiar under the Empire; that worked the iron mines of Elba and developed the resources of Pozzuoli as a great centre for the iron trade, where rich merchants imported the raw material from Elba and turned it into swords and helmets, nails and screws, to find a market in all parts of Italy; that made Naples the city of perfumes and perfumers, and Ancona the seat of a great purple dye industry. All over Italy too there was an increase in the labouring population employed in satisfying local needs: dyers, fullers, cobblers, tailors, military outfitters, porters and waggoners.

The cities of Italy, which had declined so sadly in the last fifty years of social unrest, during the gradual break-up of the territorial aristocracy and the old peasant class, once more recovered their prosperity, widening their borders to welcome the new bourgeoisie of proprietors and merchants, who had no taste for country life and desired to spend on town pleasures the money they had made by wise ventures in business or agriculture, through the labours of well-trained and well-selected slaves. This new bourgeoisie was the heir of the ancient local institutions of Italy; in the colonies and *municipia* it took over the old arrangements made by Rome in her aristocratic period; in the allied cities it had to administer venerable survivals which had served to govern the cities in their days of sovereign independence and had now, after the concession of Roman citizenship and all the transformation and reconstruction of the last fifty years, to sink to a position of purely municipal usefulness. This rising class, or its wealthier and more eligible members, formed a new upper caste in the towns, called the order of *decuriones*, and it was from amongst its ranks, with varying procedure, that the small governing Senate and the magistrates were chosen.

On the whole this new class kept strictly aloof from politics. This was not merely because most of its members lived at a distance from Rome, only going up on chance occasions for an election, and making practically no use of their political rights. It was due principally to the fact that, in the democracy that had been provisionally erected on the ruins of the illustrious aristocracy of ancient Rome, it was not

possible to obtain power or office or to take an active part in public
life without possessing either a great name or immense wealth or
supreme ability. Not unnaturally men turned their energies into other
channels; they made money, and, if families were small, took all the
more pains over the education of their sons, regarding riches and
culture as a fair substitute for personal advancement and political
influence.

Thus from end to end Italy was conscious of a process of social
and intellectual rebirth, which was at once the cause and effect of
the policy of imperialism; it was felt in the rising standard of luxury
and consumption, in the effort of all classes towards increased riches
and influence and improved culture and education. The tide of
emigration from Italy into the provinces, wherever profits were easy
and abundant, showed no sign of slackening. Cæsar welcomed to his
legions young recruits from all parts of Italy who desired to earn
wealth or distinction in business or warfare. Strange indeed were
some of the contrasts to be observed in his camp. Here were descendants of the oldest house of Rome jostling the sons of well-to-do
middle class families from Piacenza or Pozzuoli or Capua, or ex-
dealers in mules like Ventidius Bassus. Ventidius' career may be taken
as typical of the vicissitudes of that adventurous time. A native of the
Marches, he had been taken prisoner, while still a boy, in the Social
War; after his release he had entered business as a contractor for
military transport, but, growing tired of hiring out slaves and mules,
he had gone off to join Cæsar in Gaul. The position of *Præfectus
Fabrum*, or chief engineer officer, in an army provided contractors
who had experience of building with an easy stepping-stone from
business to politics.

Next to war and politics, education was the most powerful factor
in this wholesale process of democratic levelling. Schools were now
almost universal, even in the small country towns. They were maintained by private enterprise, principally by freedmen, to whom the
pupils made a fixed payment. And all schools were common schools.
Distinctions of rank were entirely ignored. The son of a poor freedman sat on the bench next the son of a Senator or a free peasant or
a knight. Rome was becoming the meeting-place of a company of
young men from all parts of Italy, of the most varied rank and breeding,

all ambitious to win fame and fortune. From Etruria there had probably already arrived in the capital a certain Caius Cilnius Mæcenas,
a young man then perhaps twenty years of age, descended from one
of the old royal families of Etruria, which had lately descended to
commerce and contracting; from Cisalpine Gaul came Cornelius
Gallus, a youth of eighteen, born of humble parentage; the Samnium
contributed Asinius Pollio, now aged twenty-three, sprung from a
noble house which is believed to have supplied the insurgents with
a general during the civil war. Then there was Quintilius Varus
from Cremona, Emilius Macer from Verona, and a certain Publius
Vergilius Maro from Mantua. Virgil was at this time eighteen years
old. He was the son—at least so it appears—of a potter in a small
village near Mantua, who had taken up bee-keeping and a timber
business and made sufficient money to send his son to study, first at
Cremona, then at Milan, and finally, in 53, at Rome.

Amongst this group of young Italians, who had been brought
together in the schools of rhetoric and philosophy and were already
united by the deep and lasting friendship which has lent an added
lustre to all their names, the new spirit in literature, which had found
a bold but solitary champion in Catullus a few years earlier, was
preached as the great revolutionary movement of the coming generation, which was to bear down, like a resistless torrent, upon all the
old monuments of Latin thought—the old-fashioned statuesque
epics of Ennius and Pacuvius, the wearisome dramas of the classical
period, the clumsy horseplay of Plautine humour, the uncouth sallies
of Lucilian wit, the ponderous didactic compositions in the slow-footed
monotonous old hexameter verse. Valerius Cato, the literary model
of all the cultured youth of Italy, and a few Greeks, amongst others
Parthenius—an Oriental captured by Lucullus at Nicæa, sold into
Italy and then set free, who settled at Naples to write poetry, teach
Greek literature and make friends with the young literary aspirant
of the day—had been the first to diffuse the taste for a livelier and
more delicate style; Catullus, with the wild burst of his passion, had
brought it suddenly and unexpectedly to the surface; and on his death
his spirit survived among his own friends and the small band of
enthusiasts for the new poetry. Caius Helvius Cinna, probably from
Cisalpine Gaul, and Caius Licinius Calvus, Caius Memmius, and

Quintus Cornificius, all members of noble Roman families, were its most prominent representatives. They were all of them *Young Italians*, as Cicero, who did not like them, somewhere calls them, revolutionaries dissatisfied with the present condition of literature—they all desired to have done with the old national fustian: to fill Italy with a new poetry, written in new metres, bursts of heartfelt lyric or moving elegy, delicate studies in all the moods and experiences of passion, adventures in the strange and elusive by-paths of psychology or in the bewildering labyrinth of Alexandrian mythology. Rare exceptions, like Asinius Pollio, remained faithful, or at least respectful, to the old classical writers; but the majority were carried away by the enthusiasm of the moment and reserved all their admiration for the models of the new literature.

Virgil succumbed like the rest. He had come up from his school at Milan full of old-fashioned ideas, with the naïve intention of composing a great national poem, on the model of Ennius, upon the Kings of Alba, and had begun to study eloquence with the celebrated Elphidius, the favourite master of the young aristocrats of the day. But he soon grew ashamed of his crude ambitions, and gave up the idea. Disheartened at his excessive nervousness and at the difficulty of self-expression, he had abandoned rhetoric for philosophy and passed on to the school of Siro, an Epicurean and a friend of Cicero, to devote himself with enthusiasm to the investigation of the great Mystery of the Universe.

Men of riper years and Conservative inclinations like Cicero were fond of passing strictures on this contempt of the rising generation for the whole venerable past of Rome. They saw in it simply one more manifestation of the revolutionary spirit which was tossing Italy to and fro and allowing her no peace. This clique of young firebrands who professed to think Ennius and Plautus mere vulgar scribblers, were they not animated by just that same spirit of consuming restlessness which drove Cæsar and his party to trample the old constitution under foot? If their example proved infectious, what would remain of the Rome of older days? While the old Republican constitution had been transformed into a giddy alternation of revolutionary dictatorships, the old manners, if they still survived in many departments of life, were contemptuously dismissed by the younger generation. There was many a town whose citizens felt less cramped within the towering walls which remained to remind them of the old era of warfare than by the obdurate rigidity of their ancient local institutions. To imitate the Greeks became the all-absorbing fashion of the day, and the spread of revolutionary ideas threatened to overwhelm Italy and the Empire as the flame of the pyre of Clodius had seized and destroyed the Curia.

It is not surprising that even the more enlightened among the Conservatives, always a sickly and pessimist tribe, began to join the reactionaries in asking if the era of expiation had not already begun. What had Rome to show for the bellicose Democratic demonstrations of the last few years? A serious war in the East, a serious war in Gaul and the irksome burden of debts so confidently assumed during the years when a gullible public had been induced to stake money with both hands on the fancied security of the treasures of Persia and Britain. The great imperial nation that held the world beneath its sway seemed unable to shake itself free from the load of its obligations; the slight relief brought by the influx of capital through Pompey's army was soon exhausted, and Cæsar's assiduous contributions from the spoils of Gaul were not enough to meet new needs. Many of the improvements in agriculture and industry had been brought about by money lent out at high rates of interest; to the mass of old debts still unpaid new and greater obligations were being steadily added; and the whole structure of the new society seemed to rest on the flimsy foundations of credit.

Even the upper classes were in similar difficulties—not least the noble families, many of them conspicuous in the arena of politics, which had inherited huge estates in the country and house property in Rome, with but little capital to keep them up. Not infrequently Senators who had inherited large fortunes and won personal distinction could not raise the small sum required for a daughter's dowry without borrowing at ruinous rates of interest; or an illustrious statesman like Cicero rose to speak in the sovereign assembly of the Empire with the paralysing sense of his immense liabilities, and of the constant and importunate demands for the largesse which was expected from those who had provinces at their disposal. Friendly loans to influential politicians and a cheerful readiness to make allowances for temporary difficulties were obligatory upon rich financiers who desired to have friends at court; and the politicians, of course, were delighted to accept them. Both parties seemed thus enabled to assist one another with impartial generosity; but in reality it was the needy politicians who succumbed to the influence of their wealthier allies. One of the most powerful members of this class was Atticus, to whom many Roman politicians—for instance, Cato, Cicero and his brother Quintus, Hortensius and Aulus Torquatus—had entrusted the administration of their complicated affairs, using him not only as a banker and paymaster in times of embarrassment, but as an intimate adviser in all matters of public or private interest. Yet these widespread difficulties themselves tended to arouse an increasing aversion for money-lenders and capitalists. Even among the upper classes Catiline was making converts, and it was by no means unusual to hear great nobles like Domitius Ahenobarbus raising their voices in the Senate even louder than the men of the popular party against the exactions of tax-farmers and financiers.

CHAPTER XXIV

THE "DE BELLO GALLICO" AND THE
"DE REPUBLICA," 51 B.C.

CÆSAR had emerged from the war against Vercingetorix victorious but discredited. His reputation as the conqueror of Gaul and Rome's one and only general had been seriously imperilled. During the seven long and eventful months of the war against Vercingetorix, in the vicissitudes and excitements of the first revolt and its extinction, of the failure before Gergovia and the last desperate struggle at Alesia, Italy had at length realized that the conquest of Gaul, which Cæsar had so boldly proclaimed in 57 and the Senate ratified in 56, was still far from accomplished; relapsing from a mood of blind confidence to a still blinder pessimism, the public began to think that Cæsar would now take years to carry through the enterprise he had so rashly undertaken. In a capitalist democracy where the general public is composed of nobles and landed proprietors, merchants and professional men, all supremely ignorant of military affairs, success is the sole standard by which a war can be judged. A victorious general is a hero and a genius, while failure becomes the stamp of weakness and incapacity. This is the explanation why armies operating in distant countries are so often distracted by the excited prognostications of the home public. The present juncture was a case in point. Italians had seen Syria and Pontus securely annexed to the Roman dominion after the campaigns of Lucullus and Pompey; they now saw Gaul invaded and annexed, yet still stirring and simmering with constant rebellions. They concluded that the Gallic war was being so indefinitely prolonged because Cæsar had not the skill to bring it to a conclusion. They did not stop to reflect that, unlike Pompey and Lucullus, Cæsar was engaged in combating, not settled kingdoms with regular armies, but the entire strength of a people in whom the sentiment of nationality and the love of independence were still ruling passions. They did not know that ordinary warfare against great armies is mere child's play compared with a struggle against a nation, however insignificant in numbers, which has made up its mind, in whole or in part, to give no quarter to the invader. The conquest of Gaul, which posterity was to reckon as Cæsar's greatest achievement, seemed to observers at the time little better than an inglorious failure, discreditable to its author and proportionately encouraging to his enemies. So the public willingly lent ear to the familiar Conservative comminations. Fiascos such as they had seen in Parthia and Gaul were the inevitable consequence of the corruption and injustice, the aggression and illegality, of the Democratic leaders.

There was another change in the situation at Rome still more menacing to Cæsar. It was becoming obvious that Pompey had now no further need of his services. While the credit of Cæsar was being steadily lowered owing to the difficulties of his campaigns, Pompey, thanks to the success of his drastic measures of repression, had become the dominant figure in Roman politics. He had now all parties on his side. The Democrats still continued to regard him as one of their leaders, while the Conservatives, who flattered him to the top of his bent, only asked him to continue unflinchingly in the new path which he had marked out. He had thus succeeded in obtaining, from the people, without a contest, as the proconsular command attached to his new Consulship, the Governorship of Spain for five additional years, with two extra legions; while the Senate had granted him without discussion the sum of 1,000 talents for the maintenance of his troops during the following year. In short, Pompey's independent position was now so powerful that Cæsar could no longer reckon upon exercising any considerable influence on his policy. Moreover, the Conservatives were already looking forward to the prospect of an open rupture between the two allies, and a complete change of policy on the part of Pompey.

All this must have caused Cæsar much anxious reflection. It was imperative to find means to refute the insinuations of the Conservatives, to repair his reputation and fortify his position as Proconsul. What else indeed had he to set against Pompey? It was with this object that he set hands to what is, second only to money, the greatest instrument of power in a democracy—the pen. In the last months of 52, in spite of innumerable distractions and anxieties, he found time to write his *De Bello Gallico*, a popular work written with consummate art, and intended to demonstrate to the general public of Italy that

Cæsar was a capable and courageous general, and his Gallic policy neither so violent nor so rapacious as his opponents pretended. With a studied modesty he drew a veil over his own personality and achievements, as a reply to those Conservatives who described him as a charlatan, and posed as an emissary of civilization, who had come into Gaul with four legions full of good intentions towards the natives, but was driven by their base ingratitude and provocation, contrary to his own real wishes, to conduct war against them. He concealed his losses and exaggerated his successes, but so skilfully, with such trifling alterations of significant detail, as to avoid incurring any charge of deliberate falsehood, whilst easily misleading the careless reader. Thus he desired to create the impression that he had exterminated in battle huge multitudes of the enemy, yet was careful to disclaim any responsibility for improbable figures. When figures are introduced they are never his own; they come from lists found in the camp of the enemy, or they had been given him by informers, or they are put into the mouth of one of the enemy in a speech. He appears to be impartially recording the exaggerations of others, without letting us see who it is that is imposing them upon the reader. He makes no mention of plunder, except as regards the sale of slaves, which he knew would never be brought up against him. Nor does he waste time over detailed descriptions of strategic movements which the reader, ignorant of the geography of the country, would have been unable to follow. On the other hand he gives minute and coloured descriptions of battles and sieges, to please the peaceful burgher in Italy, who enjoyed, as men in a settled and peaceful society always will enjoy, letting his imagination roam at leisure over scenes of fighting and adventure, as he turned the pages lazily over in the comfortable seclusion of his frescoed veranda. In short, the book was intended to be a military and political essay for the benefit of outsiders, and all the seductions of its style, the lucidity and quickness of the narrative, the simplicity of the diction, were only devised to delude a credulous public.

The book was written with a rapidity which struck Cæsar's friends with amazement, probably in less than two months. It was perhaps intended to prepare the ground for a letter which he meant to address to the Senate at the beginning of the next year to demand the prolongation of his Governorship into 48, at least in the Transalpine portion of his province. But the narrative, which is quiet enough in the earlier books, becomes hurried and excited as it approaches the close. The writer had to finish his story of the war against Vercingetorix in time to be ready for a new campaign. The Gallic nobles who had escaped in the preceding year were once more fanning the flame of revolt, and an outbreak was imminent in the North and West. The war seemed likely to go on indefinitely. Once more Cæsar angrily refused to await the coming of spring, and in full winter despatched his troops into the country of the Bituriges not to fight, but to burn and to pillage and to massacre. From the Bituriges he turned to the Carnutes, who had also arisen again under the command of Gutuatrus, where he repeated the same barbarous operations.

At Rome on the other hand the year had begun under quite unusually peaceable conditions. Pompey's measures had successfully exorcised the violence with which Rome had been so troubled during the preceding year. The partisans of Clodius kept well in the background: party factions and agitators were forgotten for the moment, and the public settled down, after its momentary access of severity, into the habitual mood of complacent indifference. Appeals began to be made for the recall of the exiles, and Cicero made arrangements with the friends of Milo to attempt at least the rescue of his fortune which had been put up to auction. It was agreed that his property should be bought for a nominal sum by Philotimus, a freedman of Cicero's wife, who was to take it over on Milo's behalf. Altogether the times were becoming abnormally quiet. In March the Senate met to arrange about the provinces. Cilicia and Syria called for particular attention, owing to a Parthian incursion into Syria in 52 to avenge the invasion of Crassus. They had easily been repulsed by Cassius, who was only a Quæstor in temporary command as Proconsul; but a new invasion was expected in 51, and it was necessary to send out officers with higher powers. Now according to the law passed in the preceding year only Senators who had been Consuls and Prætors at least five years before were eligible for a Proconsulship or Proprætorship; and it therefore became necessary to collect the names of all ex-magistrates who had not held a province at the expiration of their Consulship or Prætorship and draw lots between them for commands. By a caprice of fortune Syria fell to Bibulus, Cæsar's old colleague in the Consulship, and Cilicia to Cicero.

Cicero was exceedingly vexed. He had just finished his *De Republica*, he had other literary projects on foot, and he had almost entirely given up politics to devote himself to letters. His ambitions were now centred solely upon writing; and now suddenly, by the merest and blindest accident, he who was so obviously a man of the pen rather than of the sword, born rather for the library than for the battlefield, was to be turned out of his beloved Rome and his comfortable villas in the hills and by the seaside, and sent to the other end of the Empire to meet the enemy who had destroyed one of Rome's greatest armies. But after his fierce denunciations in the *De Republica* of the decay of patriotism and the increasing reluctance to undertake civic responsibilities, he could hardly venture in his own person to provide a striking example of the very qualities he condemned, by refusing the first charge that was laid upon him, particularly under circumstances that involved a certain risk. He dared not face the incongruity. There were other less ideal motives to facilitate his acceptance. In spite of bequests which had come to him in this and the preceding year from two friends who had remembered him in their wills, his pecuniary outlook was far from satisfactory. He had been unable to shake himself free from debt. If an unscrupulous man could come home from his province a millionaire, an honest man might perhaps make a modest fortune. Cicero decided to go.

He asked his brother Quintus, who had come home from Gaul, and his friend Caius Promptinus, both of whom knew more about military matters than himself, to keep him company. He then selected out of his slaves and freedmen those whom he thought would be most useful in the government of the province: secretaries, amongst them a freedman who bore his own name, Marcus Tullius, and a young slave, Tiro; couriers, who were to convey his letters to Rome and bring back answers; litter-carriers for the journey; servants for his own attendance and to precede him by stages on the road to prepare lodgings for himself and his suite in the towns where he stopped. He then made arrangements with one of the regular contractors who hired out the animals necessary for the transport of a governor's baggage: loaded up his belongings and those of his suite, including the jars full of gold pieces, containing the sum which the Treasury allowed him for the administration of his province: engaged the slaves required to guard his treasures on the journey, made Cælius promise to send him detailed information of all that went on at home during his absence, and finally set out on the road taking with him Quintus and his young son, and leaving his wife in Italy. Quintus felt no wrench at parting from his wife Pomponia, sister of Atticus, a hysterical and cantankerous woman who was continually making scenes. In Roman high society fashionable ladies were quite used to being left temporarily widowed when their husbands went off on distant governorships or campaigns, and it is probable that they generally suffered their loss with resignation. The Roman family had now become rather a conventional tie than a connection based either on sentiment or duty.

Just before his departure, in April, Cicero witnessed the first skirmishes in the new contest between Cæsar and the Conservatives. Pompey cannot be held responsible for their outbreak. Although his relations with the Conservatives became daily more cordial, he had retired into the background after his Consulship, and was at present in South Italy. No one knew what he thought of the political situation, and Cicero, who was certain to see him on his way out, had actually been requested to sound his views. But the enemies of Cæsar did not now even require Pompey's support. The war in Gaul, which still dragged on, in spite of pillage and devastation, was sufficient to encourage them. Ambiorix, Commius, and Lucturius had again taken up arms; the Bellovaci, the Atrebates, the Cadurci, the Veliocasses, the Aulerci and the Senones were all in open revolt; and Cæsar, compelled to dash in desperation from one end of Gaul to the other, tired of the endless fighting, uneasy as to the panic which these new risings, coming so soon after Vercingetorix, might arouse in Italy, lost the little serenity that he still retained and broke out into unworthy and barbarous reprisals. Having secured Gutuatrus, the chief of the Carnutes in his grasp, he had him flogged to death in the presence of the legions. When he had captured the city of Uxellodunum, where the surviving rebels of the Cadurci had taken refuge, he cut off the hands of all the prisoners.

These final struggles must have been cruelly exhausting to Gaul;

but they were not reassuring to the public at home, and the old confidence in Cæsar was badly shaken. Alarming rumours were continually reaching Rome from the seat of war: and Cæsar's enemies, of course, knew how to make the most of them. On one occasion, for instance, it was reported that Cæsar had lost a legion and all his cavalry; on another, that he was surrounded by the Bellovaci and in a critical situation. Moreover, Cæsar was just now making a serious mistake in lavishly showering upon Italy and the Empire the plunder which he had collected in Gaul that year and during the revolt of Vercingetorix. As he felt himself falling in popular esteem he tried to consolidate his influence by unheard-of prodigality; he lent largely to young Society spendthrifts and to hosts of Senators who were in debt; he doubled the pay of his soldiers, and even went so far as to make presents to the slaves and freedmen of important personages at Rome in order to have friends or spies in their households. He gave an enormous banquet to the people in memory of his daughter Julia, thus putting large sums into the pockets of the butchers and caterers; he made presents to the towns of Greece, sent thousands of Gallic prisoners as gifts to Oriental sovereigns; used and abused the prerogatives of the *lex Vatinia* to make citizens of freedmen from every country and to increase the number of electors who would be favourable to his cause.

Cæsar thoroughly realized that his prestige was on the wane. But the daring with which he applied himself to his policy of corruption only served to increase the discontent against him. Above all, men were indignant at his wholesale conferment of the title of Roman citizen. Thus, when in April there was a discussion in the Senate on his demand to be maintained in the Governorship of Transalpine Gaul till the 1st of January, 48, one of the Consuls, Marcus Claudius Marcellus, did not shrink from meeting it with open opposition, though his colleague, Servius, a politician of more cautious temper, did his best to restrain him. Marcellus was a noble of ancient lineage endowed with all the qualities and all the defects characteristic of an aristocrat who has lived to witness the rising tide of democracy and has the desire, but not the capacity, to control its advance. Carefully educated and very fairly intelligent, he displayed that curious mixture of arrogant self-assertion with weakness of character which takes on different forms by contrast with the encroachments of democracy in politics, manners and ideas. Such a man will at one moment display a lordly and contemptuous indifference to any object too burdensome to attain, any obstacle too difficult to encounter; at another, when his pride happens to be touched to the quick, he will respond with admirable courage and an unexpected tenacity, or sometimes with a sullen and invincible anger. Hitherto Marcellus, though like all the reactionaries he had for some time past railed at the popularity of Cæsar, had not joined vigorously in the struggle against him, nor indeed played any very prominent part in politics, rising by the ordinary stages, slowly and inconspicuously, by the influence of his name, his friends and his connections rather than by any ambitious efforts of his own. But on this particular occasion, being Consul in a year when the fighting spirit of his party had once more been awakened, free from the vulgar ambitions which imposed prudence upon so many of his senatorial colleagues, and feeling the joy of a true aristocrat in stirring the fury of the Democrats and the mob, he could not refrain from making a public display of his hostility to Cæsar when his proposals came to be discussed before the Senate. He therefore proposed, not only to reject Cæsar's request for Transalpine Gaul, but also to annul the privilege of Roman citizenship bestowed by him on the people of Como.

The Tribunes interposed; and the proposal was not approved, but simply registered in the records of the Senate. But the enemies of Cæsar had no reason to be displeased. They had succeeded, without causing a disturbance, in making proposals against Cæsar which a few years before would almost have provoked a revolution. The Conservatives lauded Marcellus up to the skies. But a serious report began to circulate shortly afterwards. It was said that Cæsar intended to take his revenge by granting citizen rights to all the Gauls in the Cisalpine province. But the rumour was not confirmed, and Marcellus was so carried away by his success that he prepared a decisive answer to the tribunician veto. Towards the end of May he had one of the Comacines whom Cæsar had enfranchised flogged with rods, a punishment which it was illegal to inflict upon a Roman citizen. If he could not annul the honour Cæsar had conferred, he could at least show how little he esteemed it. Reasonable men thought the act uncalled for; but reasonable opinion counts for little in times of crisis; and the boldness of one party increased as that of its opponents declined. After the Comacine incident Marcellus was so intoxicated by his achievements that he intended, with the encouragement of his friends, to go further still and at the sitting of the 1st of June to make the startling proposal that Cæsar should at once be recalled, and his successor nominated. The moment was opportune; the public had been thoroughly frightened by Pompey and refused to stir; the Democratic party was discredited and disorganized. Pompey, if not exactly favourable, proved at any rate by his absence that he had no strong feelings against it.

But at this moment the fair prospect became suddenly overclouded. The Conservatives were not mistaken in supposing that Pompey's behaviour in the preceding year indicated a reaction in their favour, and that Sulla's old lieutenant was anxious to re-enter the ranks of the party to which he had served his first apprenticeship. Indeed when Cicero interrupted his journey to see him at Taranto and spent three days discussing politics, Pompey had used language almost as frank and outspoken as Cato himself. Yet for all this he was too prudent a man to adopt Marcellus' crude and precipitate methods of provocation, and at the session of the Senate which was held on the 1st of June or one of the following days he, either directly or indirectly, indicated his dissent from the proposal. Marcellus made a great harangue in which he declared that, since they had Cæsar's own guarantee that Gaul was pacified, they were justified in disbanding the army and recalling the Proconsul. He added that the privilege of standing for the Consulship while absent from Rome, which the people had granted to Cæsar, was valueless, since it had been abolished by the law of Pompey. But Pompey, or some Senator who had been authorized to speak in his name, observed that by the *Lex Licinia Pompeia* of the year 55 it was illegal to discuss the question of Cæsar's successor before the 1st of March 50. From the constitutional point of view this argument was difficult to refute, and Marcellus and his friends were not so blind as light-heartedly to engage in a quarrel with Pompey. Marcellus wisely refrained from pressing his point.

Public opinion was soon diverted to the elections for 50, which took place in June or July. Cæsar sent home a large number of his soldiers to vote, but his candidate for the Consulship, Marcus Calidius, was not elected. The successful candidates were Caius Claudius Marcellus, a cousin of Marcus and a bitter enemy of Cæsar, though related to him through his wife Octavia, whom Cæsar had offered to Pompey: and Lucius Æmilius Paulus, who professed himself a Conservative but was not to be relied upon, because Cæsar had given him some profitable contracts for building at Rome. The other elections had been more favourable to Cæsar, and amongst the Tribunes there was only one, Caius Furnius, who was a supporter of the Conservative party. The Conservatives, however, immediately brought an action for corruption against Servius Pola, one of the elected Tribunes, and succeeded in getting him condemned and finding a successor in Curio, one of Cæsar's most inveterate opponents. The Prætorian elections had been postponed altogether.

The electoral excitement was scarcely at an end before the enemies of Cæsar renewed their attacks. Their tactics were now to force Pompey to make a clear statement of his views, to say what he thought of Cæsar and his policy, and the demands and pretensions in which he indulged. On the 22nd of July, during a discussion in the Senate about the payment of the legions of Pompey, who was anxious to go to Spain, he was asked to account for the legion which he had lent to Cæsar. Pompey declared that he meant to claim it back, but not immediately, in order to avoid putting the enemies of his friend in the right. He was asked again what he thought of Cæsar's recall, and he replied in vague terms that it was the duty of all citizens to be obedient to the Senate. He deferred all further action until his return from a trip to Rimini, where he was expected to superintend the recruiting which was to be made on his behalf in the valley of the Po.

Everyone thought that the matter would be discussed in the sitting of the 13th of August; but the sitting was put off till a later date owing to a discussion on a charge of corruption brought against one of the Consuls designate; and when the Senate next met, on the 1st of September, it was found that there was not a quorum. The Debating Society of business men and dilettantes began to grow uneasy. What was the meaning of all these manœuvres and counter-manœuvres? Despite his drastic behaviour in the preceding year Pompey continued to give himself out as a friend of Cæsar. Those who were leading the movement against Cæsar, despite their illustrious names, were after all men of little mark, who enjoyed the sport of baiting the Proconsul, but whose influence could not be set in the scales against that of his bold, powerful and wealthy ally. However, in spite of an empty house, the enemies of Cæsar succeeded in gaining a step. Pompey gave it to be understood that he did not approve of Cæsar's standing for the Consulship in his absence; and Scipio proposed that on the 1st of March the only question discussed should be that of the Gallic province, a suggestion which caused great concern to Cæsar's agent Cornelius Balbus, as showing that Pompey's conversion to Conservatism was still in progress. Meanwhile at the remaining elections Favonius, one of the Conservative candidates for the Prætorship, had been defeated, but Marcus Cælius Rufus and Marcus Octavius had been elected Curule Ædiles, and Curio Tribune of the people, all three enemies of Cæsar. Finally, at about the same time, the Senate adopted a serious measure to deal with the great increase of indebtedness and the scarcity of money which were the inevitable consequences of the mad gambling of the years 55 and 54. It enacted that the maximum of legal interest should be 12 per cent., and that unpaid interest should be added to the capital, but should not itself bear interest.

It was a strange decision; for it looked as if the Senate, within ten years of the Conspiracy, were inclined to adopt, in however attenuated a form, the old policy of Catiline. Yet this indulgence on the part of the Senate was as symptomatic in its own way as the great success of Cicero's new political study, the *De Republica*, published just at the moment of his impending departure. The book was sought after and read with avidity all through the educated classes; it was copied and re-copied by the slaves and freedmen who worked as copyists and librarians for men like Atticus, who was a bookseller on a considerable scale. With the continuous advance in prosperity and refinement the educated public was more and more disposed to allay political and economic antagonisms by methods of conciliation and compromise rather than to press for a final solution through a decisive conflict.

There was no class or party which retained the energy and courage, or the toughness of fibre, to venture into a death-struggle against its rivals. The days of Marius and Sulla seemed dim and distant. There was a general desire to put an end to all difficulties between creditors and debtors, but without injustice or inconvenience to anyone concerned, by settling the question in a manner agreeable to all parties. So too there was a general desire to reorganize the State, but without a revolution, through a government such as Cicero proposed in his book, which was to be a harmonious blend of democracy, aristocracy and monarchy.

The spirit of conciliation might be in the air, but the enemies of Cæsar were still irreconcilable. On the 30th of September Marcellus, in the presence of Pompey, proposed a decree in the Senate that on the 1st of March in the following year the Consuls should bring up the question of the Gallic command; that the Senate should meet daily until it was decided; and that even those Senators who were acting as judges should be obliged to be present. This proposal was approved; but when Marcellus proposed further that any veto which a Tribune might oppose against these proceedings should be considered null and void, and that all Tribunes who objected to this measure should be considered as public enemies, and when he went on to ask that all requests for furlough made by Cæsar's soldiers should be taken into consideration, as though to invite them to desert their general, several of the Tribunes, amongst them Caius Cælius and Caius Vicius Pansa, made use of their veto.

But all this was of relatively minor importance compared with Pompey's attitude on this same occasion. Not only did he declare that, though it was impossible before next March to enter into discussion of the provinces then in Cæsar's occupation, these matters could and ought to be discussed from the 1st of March onwards; but he added that in his opinion, if Cæsar was instrumental in inducing a Tribune to oppose his veto, he should be considered as a rebel. Under the influence of this declaration, one of the Senators asked him what he would do if Cæsar wished all the same to remain at the head of his army; to which Pompey replied, "What should I do if my son gave me a box on the ear?" This was by far the clearest announcement he had yet made of his separation from Cæsar. Pompey's conversion to Conservatism was proceeding apace, and the great success of the *De Republica*, which was the literary event of the year, was no doubt a contributory factor. Since the book was being read with such universal enthusiasm it seemed clear that Italy was ready for a saviour, who should be at once illustrious, intelligent and aristocratic. Who else but the man who had saved the State from anarchy the year before could be the hero foretold by Cicero, and desired by all his fellow-citizens?

Cæsar was still engaged on his final campaign in Gaul; but Rome was soon disquieted by bad news from the East. Despatches arrived from Cassius and Deiotarus announcing that the Parthians had crossed the Euphrates in considerable force. Malicious wiseacres in the Conservative party at first refused to believe them, declaring that Cassius had invented the invasion in order to attribute to the Parthians ravages he had made himself; but a letter from Deiotarus soon removed all doubt. As usual the public began to grow excited and clamoured at once for energetic measures; some proposed to send Pompey and others Cæsar to the East. Both Consuls were greatly alarmed lest the Senate, to avoid choosing either Cæsar or Pompey, should entrust the campaign to one of themselves, an honour which neither Marcellus nor the old law-dog Servius were at all inclined to accept; for since the death of Crassus the Parthians were a source of considerable dismay to imperialists at home. The Consuls therefore began to postpone the sittings of the Senate and prevent all discussion, at a moment when it was generally believed that the Empire was threatened with a serious war. The friends of Cicero were especially anxious; they asked what would happen to the great writer, who was left with but a small force to support him in the Governorship of a province exposed to so formidable a foe.

And indeed Cicero had found the opening months of this year distinctly disagreeable. In the course of his voyage out, as he was passing by Samos, a deputation of Italian tax-farmers resident in the province had come to bring him their congratulations and beg him to maintain in his edict certain dispositions which had been made by his predecessor. Once disembarked in his province he had stopped some time at Laodicea to arrange for the exchange into the native currency of the sums which he had brought with him from Italy, and to see that it was fairly carried out. But while engaged in these routine duties he was dismayed by the disorder prevalent in his troops. The army which was considered sufficient to defend the province against the Parthians had been broken up by his predecessor into small detachments at the service of the Italian usurers, who infested the country and used the soldiers to extract money by main force from their recalcitrant debtors. In the course of these operations three cohorts had gone astray and no one knew what had become of them. It can be imagined therefore how he felt when news arrived in August that the enemy had crossed the Euphrates in considerable force. He had originally hoped that his Syrian colleague would be able to repulse the Parthians; but when he learnt that Bibulus had not yet arrived in his province he wrote a pressing despatch to the Senate asking for help. The provinces and their revenues were in serious danger; it was urgently necessary to send him soldiers from Italy, for the Asiatic recruits were valueless and it was imprudent to trust the allies, who were sick of Roman maladministration.

In spite of this piteous appeal, it is a tribute to his genuine patriotism as well as to his skill and adaptability that he did his best to collect his small forces and set out with them to defend the road through Cappadocia, in case the Parthians attempted to invade the province of Asia. He calculated that the frontier of Cilicia on the side of Syria was easily defended with a small body of troops. But ascertaining soon afterwards that the Parthians had invaded Syria and were advancing towards Antioch, he hastened back and arrived at Tarsus on the 5th of October, whence he proceeded at once to the mountains of Amanus. But about the 10th of October, hearing that Cassius had routed the Parthians below Antioch and that the enemy were in full retreat, he undertook an expedition against the wild tribes who lived by brigandage in the range of Amanus. Guided by the experience of his brother and Promptinus, he fought a small engagement, laid siege to the town of Pindenissus and received from his soldiers the title of Imperator; he captured a large supply of slaves and horses, selling the slaves on the spot and distributing the proceeds to his soldiers. Then he returned to his province delighted with his short excursion into generalship.

The despatch of Cicero begging for reinforcements and that of

Cassius announcing his victory arrived simultaneously at Rome and were read at the Senate at the same sitting towards the end of October. The one effaced the impression caused by the other; it was believed that the invaders had been successfully routed, and the Roman public once more dismissed the subject from their minds.

CHAPTER XXV

THE CAMPAIGN OF CURIO, AND THE TROUBLES
OF A ROMAN GOVERNOR

MEANWHILE troublous times seemed in store for Cæsar. Since the death of Julia everything seemed to have gone awry. The ruin of Crassus, the disappearance of Clodius, the revolt of Vercingetorix, the doubtful attitude of Pompey, the new war which had broken out in Gaul in 51, had all gravely compromised his reputation. Whereas, but a few years before, every success gained by the Republic had been put down to his credit, most people now inclined to hold him responsible for every conceivable difficulty: for the dangers which seemed to threaten in the East, for the interminable operations in Gaul, for the increasing corruption at home and the imminent break-up of the whole fabric of the State. And now, to crown all, Pompey's open declaration at the sitting of the 30th of September had put in the clearest light the growing likelihood of a rupture between him and his ally. To speak abusively or contemptuously of Cæsar was now the fashion of the day, impartially imposed, with all the tyranny of a social convention, upon landlords and capitalists and all the gilded youth of the Capital. Cato did not mind saying openly he would like to bring him into court and condemn him to exile as soon as his command came to an end. Many who had been his admirers now turned against him, and even Atticus, always on the safe side, demanded the repayment of the fifty talents which he had lent Cæsar before his Consulship. It was little enough that he could set against these manifold influences—the precarious support of the small contractors to whom he had given, and was still giving, so much employment, and the admiring devotion of the poorer classes, the artisans and freedmen, who could not forgive the death of their old patron Clodius.

Cæsar was conscious of this great change in public feeling and of its causes. Cæsar was not the man to yield at fifty—for he had already reached fifty—to the insatiable megalomania which Napoleon found irresistible at thirty-five. Not only had the Roman a more balanced judgment, but he had had to wait far longer for his success. All that he had won so far, riches, reputation, and power, he owed to twenty-five years of hard and uninterrupted labour, and at fifty he was still the best-hated man of his class. He had had to adapt himself to the most various and uncertain moods of public opinion—to the respectable and conciliatory Liberalism of the years 70 to 65, to the subversive and revolutionary Radicalism of 65 to 60, to the bold, grasping and spendthrift Imperialism of 58 to 55. Yet throughout these Protean changes, with all his marvellous adaptability to shifting circumstances, he had remained the same simple and powerful personality—a man with the depth and insight of a scientific truth-seeker, who valued riches not, like Crassus, as an end in themselves, but as a means to his own purpose, who was full-blooded and passionate by nature, yet sober and abstemious in his personal habits; who had built and rebuilt villas and palaces in Italy to make employment, yet continued all the while to live without luxury in the wilds of Gaul; who loved glory, yet despised the servile flattery and the boastful exaggerations of the mob; who had laboured on with the one instinctive and overruling desire to exercise the powers that were in him. Too acute and clear-sighted to be blinded by pride, he was all the more conscious of his own mistakes because it was necessity rather than inclination which had driven him to commit them; he realized the advisability of meeting public opinion at least half-way, and, with not the least startling of his miracles of versatility, turned away from the barbarities of his last campaign to baffle his Italian antagonists by appearing in a new and unexpected character—that of the moderate and exemplary citizen, disposed to every reasonable concession and solely desirous of the public good.

Cæsar was indeed, both by temperament and necessity, far more Conservative than his policy since the Catilinarian conspiracy had enabled him to reveal. He knew only too well that the cosmopolitan city mob, which would be all that was left of his party on Pompey's desertion, could never be made into a really trustworthy instrument of government. At the head of the artisan population of Rome he had been able to seize, almost by a surprise attack, a foremost place in the State—but he would not occupy it for long unless, like Lucullus or Pompey or Cicero, he enjoyed the confidence and respect of the upper and middle classes, the educated and well-to-do bourgeoisie, which, despite its indifference to politics, possessed the two most powerful means of domination in a mercantile democracy—riches and knowledge. The consent of these classes was indispensable to any government; and it was Cæsar's anxiety to secure their favour which is the master-key to his actions since the conspiracy of Catiline; it explains his hasty annexation and hard-won conquest of Gaul; it explains his sudden and striking reversion now to a policy of skilful moderation. He was not at this time hoping—he would have been a madman if he had hoped—for the possession of the supreme power. His sole object was to become Consul in 48 without giving up his command. To come to Rome for his candidature would be to place himself entirely at the mercy of Pompey, who, since the reforms of 52, had all the judges under his control, and of whom Cæsar had now, of course, a profound distrust. How was he to secure his object? To attempt violent methods would have been to court defeat. Weak and weather-beaten as the old Republican constitution appeared, it still stood solid enough against any overt revolution. It was not mere hypocrisy but a real respect for the old machinery of government which induced all would-be usurpers, however they might offend against the spirit of the constitution, to pose as scrupulous observers of it in the letter. There was no way out, then, but by intrigue; and Cæsar set to work, in the midst of his last and not least bloody campaign in Gaul, to extricate himself unhurt, by a series of ingenious and unexpected contortions, from the network of constitutional difficulties in which he had allowed himself gradually to become enmeshed.

There can be no doubt that from the purely constitutional and legal point of view his position was indefensible. He could maintain that the privilege of absence granted him by the people implied approval of the prolongation of his command to the year 48: for otherwise the privilege itself would have been valueless. But the sophistry of this plea was evident; and his adversaries could easily retort that the privilege had only been granted him in case his presence should be necessary in Gaul during the whole of 49. Now he was obliged to reassure the public, whose patience had been exhausted by the length of the war, by declaring that the conquest of Gaul was already concluded—from which the Conservatives of course drew the rigorously logical conclusion that it was no longer necessary to prolong Cæsar's command, and that consequently there was no more reason for the privilege. Cæsar realized that his best policy was to gain time, to secure the postponement of the nomination of his successor, which should have taken place on the 1st of March, 50, but to employ no methods, either violent or scandalous, which might have caused indignation among the general public—even to refrain from the time-honoured expedient of the tribunician veto, which, after Pompey's last declaration, would indeed not have been without danger. Once more therefore it was necessary to surprise his enemies by some bold and unexpected stratagem. He needed a successor to Clodius, whose loss he must often have lamented in these years. He found one, where he was least looked for by the public, in Curio.

Curio was a young man of good education and great abilities, a striking speaker and writer, but ambitious, cynical, and unscrupulous, anxious only to make a name, a true "scoundrel of genius," as one of the ancients defined him, a Clodius, only with more subtlety and a stronger head: in short, a typical representative of the dying brilliance of the old Roman nobility. By proposing to pay his debts and make him a rich man besides, Oppius attracted him to the party of Cæsar. An arrangement was made, in the strictest secrecy, that Curio, pretending all the time to be hostile to Cæsar, should complicate matters in such a way as to make it impossible that a vote should be taken on the 1st of March on the question of the Gallic command. Once more, as in 59, when he formed the Triumvirate, Cæsar concealed his tactics, partly in order to avoid frightening the public, partly, of course, to take his enemies off their guard. At first Curio was to stand up by himself, as Cæsar had stood up for Crassus in 65, to conduct the dangerous intrigues necessary for the attainment of his object. It was not a very difficult secret to keep. The public could hardly suspect that two men whose enmity was of such long standing could be working together towards a common end.

Scarcely had he entered on his office when Curio caused universal surprise by proposing various laws, some of them displeasing to the Conservatives, and others to the Democrats. Numerous pretexts were thus naturally found for postponing their discussion till the two first months of the year; that is, almost till the beginning of March.

Curio made no objection; but as March approached he proposed, in his character of *pontifex*, to interpolate between the 23rd and 24th February the month of Mercedonius, which, according to an old usage, should have been added every second year in order to make the Calendar agree with the course of the sun. There would thus, he said, be time to discuss his proposals before the month of March, which was to be given up to the discussion upon the provinces. Mercedonius of course failed to secure recognition; and Curio, with a show of violent indignation against the Conservatives, forthwith proposed two popular laws, one on the subject of roads, and the other on the price of corn. The necessity of discussing these laws afforded a good pretext for the Consul Lucius Æmilius Paulus, who was that month presiding over the Senate and was a friend of Cæsar, for the postponement of the provincial discussion till later. Cæsar thus attained his object, thanks, it seemed, to the mysterious interposition of one of his enemies. It appeared impossible to reproach him for what had occurred.

Pompey accepted the postponement, in spite of the declaration he had made in the preceding year, without expressing his opinion upon it in public; but he let it be known that, in his view, it was possible to bring Cæsar's pretensions into harmony with the strict observance of the constitution by maintaining him in his command until the 15th of November, by which time the elections would already be over. Pompey was no more anxious than Cæsar to precipitate events. He enjoyed the respect of the popular party, which still remained faithful to him, as well as that of the Conservatives, who had now returned to him. In short, he was the most prominent and powerful man in the Empire. Why should he endanger this privileged position by driving the friends of Cæsar to desperation? Some pessimists were indeed already declaring that a civil war between Cæsar and Pompey was inevitable because both men were too ambitious to remain together at the head of the Republic, and the ominous expression "civil war," words awaking so many sombre memories, were once more whispered abroad. But there were few who believed in its possibility, and still fewer who desired it; it acted rather as a check than as a stimulus upon the parties and their chiefs.

The Senate, after all, consisted mainly of a crowd of politicians, individually of small account, who had managed to secure election to office and win wealth and influence by steering skilfully between the two recognized parties, inclining to Conservatives and Democrats to Cato and Cæsar, Pompey and Cicero, as opportunity offered, without ever openly taking sides with either. These men had no desire to imperil their fortunes in dangerous adventures and were restrained, just as Cæsar was restrained, by the all-powerful, if invisible, authority of public opinion. They realized that if Italy thought ill of the turbulent methods of Cæsar, she would think still worse of a policy of deliberate civil war, provoked by the hotheads in the reactionary camp. The public drew its picture of a future civil war from the memories of the last, which, to a generation that, despite many symptoms of debasement, was distinctly more settled and humanitarian than its predecessors, seemed too horrible to contemplate. It meant the re-emergence at Rome of some monster of violence like Sulla. It meant the burning of workshops, the sacking of houses, the robbing of temples, which the ordinary citizen used for banks; it meant the suspension of credit, now become almost a necessary of life in all classes; above all, it meant the undermining of the foundation on which the whole of that mercantile and bourgeois society reposed—the fidelity of the slaves. Groaning beneath her vast burden of debt, distrustful of all parties and politicians, weary of the unmeasured corruption of public life, exhausted by the great effort of the last ten years, Italy was unanimous against war. No statesman and party dare openly to act counter to this universal sentiment.

But when the times are ripe for great political changes neither parties nor statesmen can alter the stern logic of facts. No sooner had he won his first success, the postponement of the nomination of his successor, than Cæsar moved on to a more daring stroke. It had for some time been evident that the issue of the struggle between the reactionary Conservatives and Cæsar depended in a large measure upon Pompey. With the large army under his control, with his host of relations and dependants and all the influence at his command, Pompey could turn the scale in whichever direction he wished. The Conservatives had long ago grasped this, and they pressed round him with a constant chorus of homage and adulation. It thus naturally became Cæsar's object to loosen the hold which his opponents had gained over his old ally. But how was he to do so? By flattery or by menace? After the refusal of his proposals in March, and the last declaration of Pompey against him, Cæsar could place little reliance upon flattery. Pompey stood too high and was in too little need of patronage and support from others. Yet the alternative method of threatening him, if it were openly adopted, might very possibly so exasperate Pompey as to drive him altogether into the Conservative camp, with the additional disadvantage of making Cæsar appear to be the aggressor. Here again Cæsar conceived the idea of making use of Curio. Calculating on the impressionable character of Pompey, he instructed Curio to continue throwing difficulties and vexations in his path till he was practically worried into withdrawing his underhand opposition to Cæsar's demands. Curio accomplished this difficult task with consummate skill. Turning suddenly upon the man whom everyone in Rome regarded as the model of constitutional propriety, he attacked Pompey in a series of violent speeches, posing, not as a partisan of Cæsar, but as a disinterested supporter of justice and common sense. Why did Pompey affect to be so scrupulously and pedantically correct when it was he himself who, by the laws of 55, had created the present situation? How could he pose as the defender of the constitution after violating nearly all its provisions, after having been simultaneously Consul and Proconsul? This was shrewd and careful hitting: and it left its mark. The public did not know whether to be more surprised that no one should have made these criticisms before or that someone should have been found brave enough to make them now.

Pompey himself was so much concerned that he once more entered the arena to attempt a reply; but soon finding the exertion too great for his strength, he left Rome for Naples, where shortly after his arrival he fell seriously ill. He was thus absent from Rome when, in April, the Consul Marcellus, who was presiding over the Senate, raised the whole issue afresh, by inviting a discussion on the vote of the sums necessary to Pompey's army for the new year and on the unsettled question of the Gallic command. Encouraged by Pompey's absence, Curio declared that Marcellus' proposal to vote money to Pompey was fair enough, but that there was no reason why Cæsar should abandon his command if Pompey kept his. Put in this way the question seemed to resolve itself into a petty personal quarrel between contending commanders. The only means of solving it to the advantage of the Republic was to return to the ground of strict constitutional principle by putting an end to exceptional powers of every kind. Curio therefore proposed to recall both Cæsar and Pompey and put his veto upon all the proposals of Marcellus.

These means were very skilfully chosen. The Conservatives reproached Cæsar for being in an illegal position. Why should they tolerate in Pompey privileges and illegalities of a still more flagrant character, which they now even propose to increase? The impartial public, with the possibility of a civil war before its eyes, thought Curio's proposal excellent. Here at last was a chance of the definite solution of this complicated business. To have done with all exceptional powers, and to return to the constitution which made them illegal, became the rallying-cry of all good citizens. The result was that the Senate rejected the proposal of Marcellus to enforce the decision of the previous year which deprived the tribunician veto of its validity; and Curio became in a moment one of the most popular men in Rome. Only a few clear-sighted politicians suspected the hand of Cæsar behind the whole intrigue.

But Cæsar had counted too securely upon Pompey's timidity. Curio's proposal, however momentarily successful, failed in its principal object, which was to make Pompey more amenable to compromise with Cæsar. The proposals of Curio were too direct an attack upon his prestige and his interests; and so far from drawing him nearer to Cæsar they cemented his alliance with the reactionary Conservatives. The change was not immediately apparent; Pompey even wrote to the Senate from Naples during his convalescence declaring himself ready to renounce his command; but the offer was not made in sincerity. The law had given him the command of the Spanish army for five years, and he had no intention of renouncing his rights to please Curio. As for the notion that the constitution allowed no exceptional powers, it was the merest fiction. If the metropolitan mob had cast flowers upon Curio's path as he left the Senate House, the towns of Campania were now celebrating huge festivals in honour of Pompey's recovery; the man whom Curio was trying to drive back into private life, or to some minor magistracy, was being openly invoked as the mainstay of great fabric of Empire.

After his return to Rome Pompey declared once more that he was ready to accept the compromise proposed by Curio; but his offer was received with such universal scepticism that Curio immediately renewed his attacks, and declared, in a number of speeches, that he could not take Pompey's words at their face value. He added that words were not enough, that he needed actions; and to put the matter to the test he completed his preceding proposal by adding that whichever of the two refused to obey should be declared a public enemy and that troops should be prepared to make war against him. Deeply hurt by this insulting suggestion, Pompey felt more and more inclined to throw in his lot with the extreme Conservatives; and when, in May or June, the Senate decided that Pompey and Cæsar should both detach a legion from their army and send it to Syria against the Parthians, he seized the opportunity to ask back from Cæsar the legions which he had lent him in 53. He was beginning to count up his forces against Cæsar's. He had seven legions in Spain, Cæsar had eleven. After repaying him his legions Cæsar still retained nine. If war were really to break out this would be an appreciable advantage. All discussion was then broken off on the approach of the elections, which were awaited in great excitement by all parties.

During all this time Cæsar in Gaul was slowly repairing the ravages of the last years of war and consolidating the Roman dominion, while Cicero was sincerely but not very successfully endeavouring to effect reforms in the administration of his province. In the course of his voyage he had had reason to see how familiar a figure he had become throughout the whole of the Empire, even in the Hellenic countries. This world-wide admiration, and, above all, the great success of the *De Republica,* of which Cælius kept him informed, revived in him the illusion, which he had lost almost entirely in the ten years since his Consulship—that it was his mission to be a great statesman and ruler of men. He was anxious to act up to the level of his professions and to give his contemporaries the example of a just and wise provincial administration. But the task was more difficult than he had imagined. The provincial governors had become the agents of the political and financial oligarchy of Rome, the representatives of a whole system of powerful and wealthy interests. How could the man who was to be the instrument of the oppressor be at the same time the defender of the oppressed? Yet it was impossible to be blind to the urgent necessity of good government. On his first arrival, in the imminent fear of a Parthian invasion, Cicero had been chiefly struck with the want of discipline and efficiency among his troops. But when the Parthians retired and he was able to consider the condition of the country more at leisure, he realized the full nature of the duties he had undertaken—the government of a vast province which, from one end of his horizon to the other, over leagues and leagues of country, bore witness to the havoc of Italian speculation.

The population of Cilicia consisted partly of native Asiatics, partly of Greek immigrants. The Greeks lived almost entirely in the towns, and were traders, skilled labourers, professional men and proprietors; while the natives were for the most part peasants, shepherds, humble artisans, or brigands in the mountains. The province was divided into a certain number of districts each of which had some important town for its capital and was governed by a senate or council. This council was chosen from amongst the richer section of the population, which was almost exclusively Greek and governed the town according to the existing legal code, under the supreme control of the Roman Governor and Senate. This municipal organization was excellently devised, and the Romans had turned to study it with some interest as a contrast to the complexity and unwieldiness of the old arrangements still in force in Italy. But a period of warfare and anarchy, prolonged through more than a century, had gradually reduced these local councils to monstrous instruments of tyranny and spoliation. Everywhere the councillors banded together to make profits out of the revenues of the municipality, which were generally derived from taxes and town property. They would decree public works, festivals, special missions and every kind of useless expense in order to share in the profits of the contractors; or make ruinous loans with Italian financiers and tax-farmers, or join with them in exploiting the municipal domains, or in pocketing the proceeds of an exorbitant taxation. Soon after his arrival Cicero found the municipalities busily engaged in sending off special missions to Rome to eulogize the virtues of his predecessor before the Senate, and decreeing monuments and temples in his honour throughout the country, according to the degrading custom which survived from the days of the Hellenistic monarchs.

But the extortions and extravagance of these native oligarchies was but the least of the evils which afflicted the unhappy province. Far more terrible was the last expiring effort of the Italian plutocracy to wring blood from an exhausted prey. What financial Imperialism had meant during the last twenty years, as the provinces had gradually less and less to offer to the invader, the accuser of Verres could now judge for himself. The system was only maintained by a systematic application of violence. In every part of the province money was being wrung out of wretched and helpless debtors by the help of the military; and acts of cruelty and violence occurred daily. Finally, to crown all, every year there would arrive in the province a whole shipload of bankrupt Roman politicians—the governor with all his friends and the officers of the legions, who squeezed money out of cities and private individuals, lived in luxury at the expense of the province, and sold every sort of favour at exorbitant prices. Exemptions from giving quarters to the military were especially lucrative—a curious sidelight on the reputation of the Roman army. Meanwhile the poorer classes, the small shop-keepers and artisans, the peasant proprietors and free labourers in the country districts, were being slowly reduced to desperation, and forced to part with all that they held dearest—their land, their houses, the savings of generations, and often their own children.

These depredations shocked Cicero as they had shocked Rutilius Rufus and Lucullus before him; but he was unwilling to follow Rufus and Lucullus in declaring open war against the Italian financiers. Here as elsewhere he preferred, by a characteristic compromise, to typify the curious and contradictory emotions of his age. So far as his own personal integrity permitted it, he was as obliging a governor as most. He treated with the hunters of panthers to satisfy his friend Cælius, who needed wild animals for the games of his Ædileship. He settled a business negotiation for Atticus at Ephesus, and secured him some valuable vases. He welcomed the friends and relatives of friends who came to him with letters of introduction. He asked to dinner the son of Hortensius, who was supposed to be studying but preferred to waste his money in riotous living. He also showed kindness to a young man called Marcus Feridius, a member of a well-to-do Italian family, who had come to Cilicia as the agent of a company which was farming the affairs of a town. He performed all the ordinary duties of a governor —the liquidation of inheritances, the ransome of Italians kidnapped by pirates, the recovery of the interest of sums lent by Italians in Asia.

Yet at the same time he did his best to bring some relief to the unfortunate native population. He refused the celebrations and gifts of cities; he lived, and forced his escort to live, with extreme simplicity, in order to save the province from excessive expense, and showed himself markedly attentive to the principal citizens. He went out into the streets every morning while he was residing at Laodicea, to enable the humblest provincials to approach him if they wished: and he did all he could to expedite the working of the law-courts. On several occasions he refused absolutely to put his soldiers at the disposition of the money-lenders for the recovery of their debts. To beg, to solicit, to write letters he was not unwilling; but he would not stoop to use his army to recover the debts of his friends. This led to some serious difficulties, not the least of which related to the loans made by his friend Brutus to Ariobarzanes, King of Cappadocia. Long since drained dry by Italian usurers, the old king was spending the little money which remained to him in paying the interest he owed to Pompey, which now amounted in all, probably through the accumulation of arrears, to thirty-three talents a month. Almost every month Pompey's agents in Asia sent off to the coast on mules escorted by armed slaves a sum amounting to some £4,800 of our money. Meanwhile the other creditors remained unsatisfied. In vain did Cicero write letter upon letter to the king on their behalf. It was believed throughout Asia that Pompey would shortly be sent into the East with a great army to make war against the Parthians; and Ariobarzanes could think of nothing but the settlement of his accounts with Pompey.

But Cicero went further still. He declared in his edict that, whatever might be the private arrangements of individuals, he would not recognize as governor any annual interest higher than 10 per cent., and would refuse to enforce any claims for arrears of interest, thus reducing interest all round in the same way as the Senate had done at

Rome. At the same time he carefully revised the budgets of all the towns for the last ten years, remorselessly cancelling all superfluous expenses, and ruinous or unjust impositions. He forced numerous financiers to restore to the towns what they had taken, and took care that the reduced interest on loans made to the towns was punctually paid.

But it was not easy for him to be virtuous in such an environment. The suppression of all the decrees voted in honour of Appius Claudius brought Cicero insolent letters from that personage; and the reduction of interest to 10 per cent. was the occasion of a serious disagreement with Brutus. Two business men named Scaptius and Matinius, who figured as creditors of the people of Salamis, had presented themselves before him to demand the payment of the modest interest of 48 per cent. which had been arranged; and on failing to receive it they had acquainted him with the fact that the real creditor was Brutus. This revelation caused great surprise to Cicero, who had always regarded Brutus as a pattern of virtue: but he refused to alter his decision and remained obdurate even after the receipt of insulting letters from Brutus. Encouraged by his clemency, the unfortunate debtors asked permission to deposit in a temple the 10 per cent. interest which Scaptius and Matinius refused to accept and to declare them freed from every obligation. But at this point Cicero lost courage. Not daring to defy Brutus so openly, he left the matter in suspense. This was exactly what Scaptius and Matinius had now been hoping. They knew that Cicero's successor would not be equally obstinate, and would compel the Salaminians to pay according to the original bargain.

But how could a Roman governor administer real justice when everyone round him was a party to transactions of this nature? Cicero did his best to set a good example. He refused to touch a sesterce of the sums that fell to him as booty or of those which were assigned to him by the Senate for the government of his province, leaving the former to the prefects and the latter to the Quæstors. But all his escort were busy making their pile. His Quæstor was the brother of a rich merchant living at Elis whom he had asked to join him as adviser; and one of his staff officers and Lepta his chief engineer were so compromised in an intrigue that he could only extricate them by consenting to an entirely exceptional indulgence. It was the practice of the Roman government never to give out a contract unless the contracting party presented a certain number of guarantors, who engaged to pay a fixed fine in case the contract were not executed. As contracts increased in number and importance, acceptable guarantors were naturally sought after for their wealth or political influence, as eagerly as letters of exchange from endorsers who enjoy a good credit with banks are in demand nowadays. All possible methods were employed to secure them: friendship or political association or the promise of a large profit. It is probable that many politicians at Rome made arrangements to make money with these guarantees. They arranged the guarantee in return for the promise of an indemnity with the contractor; then if it turned out that the contractor did not keep his engagement with the State and the State proceeded against him, they exerted all their influence to avoid payment. Thus it happened that one of Cicero's agents and his chief engineer Lepta had stood security for a certain Valerius, who had undertaken a contract for some public work; but Valerius had not been able to keep his engagements and had passed on his contract (probably for a very small sum) to a usurer named Volusius. Volusius in his turn was probably in agreement with the Quæstor Rufus, and had engaged to execute the contract but not to pay the fine to which Valerius and, in his default, his guarantors were exposed. Valerius and his guarantors were of course in despair and appealed to the Proconsul, who took pity on them. Finding a legal flaw which entitled him to cancel the concession from Valerius to Volusius, Cicero broke off the agreement, paid into the Treasury the sum which still remained to be paid to the contractor, and freed the guarantors from their engagements, to the great annoyance of Volusius, who thus lost both his money and the profits of the agreement. So common were extortion and fraud in a society where financial interest was now the only tie between man and man! Cicero's utmost efforts towards honest administration were doomed to failure; for instance, he was continually receiving letters from his friends asking for loans and suggesting that after the booty of his war he must necessarily be flush with money. Cicero was forced to send polite replies to the effect that this booty belonged not to him but to the Republic and that he could not make advances upon it to anyone.

Cicero's administration of Cilicia is a title to glory of which the unimaginative and pettifogging criticism of modern historians has in vain attempted to deprive him. It is true that succeeding years swept away the results of his labours as the waves sweep over the drawings made by a child in the sand. But Cicero after all was only human. He could not be expected, single-handed, to cure the malady from which a whole generation was suffering. It is not for its results that his work is significant, but for the emotions and intentions with which it was inspired—for his anxious solicitude for the victims of a chronic misrule, and for the spirit of justice and pity and common humanity that endeavoured to transmute philosophic contemplation into active beneficence. At early dawn in the Alps, a few sentinel rocks on the summits catch the first rays of sunshine and proclaim the coming day, while the folds of the mountains, and the sleeping valley beneath, are still wrapped in gloom. Just so did the conscience of this timid man of letters, and a few solitary thinkers like him, tell a world still deep in the night of unrelieved depravity of the sure approach of a happier age.

But Cicero little guessed what he was doing; and the manifold duties of his office, almost all of them disagreeable, vexed him beyond all belief. That the Empire could not last for long, under the conditions in which it was at this time, without involving something like a total collapse of civilization, is proved, not only by the maladministration of the other provinces, but best of all by the utter weariness which overcame one of the few men who attempted to govern uprightly, after a short year at his task. The Proconsulship of Cicero shows that the encyclopædic diversity of functions by which the same man had successively to act as general, orator, judge, administrator, and architect was an obsolete heritage from a simpler epoch, and could not continue indefinitely in an age of increasing specialization. At last there was a governor who was both honest and conscientious and he was impatient to be rid of his harassing responsibilities. He begged all his friends to oppose the prolongation of his command and seemed to have but one desire, to escape as quickly as possible from his pile of *syngraphæ*, securities, contracts and official business and to return to Italy.

There were many public and private reasons to call him home.

His daughter, his dearly loved Tullia, who had already been twice married and twice divorced, was being courted by a number of great personages in the expectation of her father's return from Cilicia and the prospect of a handsome dowry. Her mother, the adroit Terentia, had given the preference to Cneius Cornelius Dolabella, a young man of noble family, but dissolute character. Cicero was not ignorant of his future son-in-law's moral and pecuniary reputation, but his ambition to be allied with a genuinely aristocratic family overbore even considerations of paternal affection. He had always dreamed of intimacy with the great and noble as the supreme recompense for his labours. For in spite of the progress of the democracy and their own impoverishment and degeneration, the surviving aristocratic families still enjoyed great consideration; they maintained the privilege of fairly easy access to office, since the abler men of the middle class, like Atticus, preferred money-making to the hazards of politics; and, through constant intermarriage they had come to form a small and exclusive caste, whose acquaintance was much sought after by social aspirants. His daughter's marriage with Dolabella was almost a charter of nobility for the parvenu from Arpino. The serious aspect of public affairs, too, inclined him to hasten his return to the capital. He had asked Cælius to keep him abreast of the news; and Cælius had paid a certain Crestus, a professional journalist, to send him out a political and social chronicle of all the gossip of Rome. His couriers too, who were generally on the move between Cilicia and Rome, brought him constant news, and he received further information from the couriers of the tax-farming companies, who often came with letters from distinguished friends at home. Yet despite all, the distance was too great to be bridged; news arrived long after it had occurred, and often in the wrong order. Cicero was longing to be home again.

CHAPTER XXVI

INITIUM TUMULTUS, 50 B.C.

THE elections were now at hand and the contest for the Consulship promised to be exceptionally keen. As the question of the Gallic command was at last to be settled in the course of the year, both parties were more than usually anxious to secure the supreme magistracy. Cæsar, who was still in a moderate mood and would have been satisfied to have one of the Consuls on his side, sent soldiers on furlough to Rome to support his old general, Servius Sulpicius Galba. But the Conservatives put up two candidates against him, Lucius Cornelius Lentulus and Caius Claudius Marcellus; the latter was cousin of the Consul then in office and brother of the Consul of the preceding year, and as ill-disposed as his namesakes to the cause of Cæsar. The reaction against the Democrats was bringing the old aristocratic families back into prominence. There was a desperate conflict, and Cæsar was defeated. His friend and supporter Antony was elected to the Tribuneship, but Galba failed to secure the Consulship. The most important of the offices thus fell into the hands of the Conservatives.

The result of the elections left Cæsar's enemies in a state of wild jubilation. They believed they had dealt a final blow to the influence and power of Cæsar. It was indeed a serious check, though not so much in itself as for the impression it made upon the timid and vacillating public, which began to be persuaded that the current rumours about his precarious position in Gaul must be well founded. Cæsar, who was just now preparing to take his troops into winter quarters for the enjoyment of a little well-earned repose, was so much disturbed by his defeat at the elections and the intrigues of his enemies that he decided to cross over in person in September to Cisalpine Gaul to help Antony in his candidature for the Augurship against Lucius Domitius Ahenobarbus.

He was already half-way on his journey when he heard that Antony had been elected; but, instead of turning back, he decided to make use of the opportunity to execute a project which he had long carried in his mind, that of organizing a demonstration in his favour in Cisalpine Gaul. He was already extremely popular in that province. It was well known that he was in favour of granting it full citizen rights; many of his soldiers came from the villages which were springing up amid the forests and fens of that prospering region; and moreover the inhabitants of the Po valley had been quick to understand that the conquest of Transalpine Gaul would tend to increase the wealth of their province by transforming it from a frontier territory into the main thoroughfare to a large and populous *hinterland*. Skilful agents were sent in advance and found no difficulty in persuading the notables of the Cisalpine province to prepare great demonstrations in honour of the conqueror of Gaul. The enthusiasm became infectious, as it generally does, and Cæsar was able to make a regular triumphal progress through his province. Deputations came to meet him outside every village; the municipalities and colonies invited him to festivals; and the country people, who had given him so many soldiers and knew of his exploits from the tales they had brought home, came in crowds to greet him on the road.

These demonstrations were not intended simply to gratify a soldier's vanity. They were to show Italians who were grumbling at the conquest of Gaul what enthusiasm it excited amongst a population which knew and dreaded its northern neighbours. Cæsar was still so inclined to conciliation that, somewhere about this time, he sent back to Italy the legion demanded from him for the war against the Parthians, returned to Pompey the other legion he had borrowed from him, and instructed Curio to abandon his tactics against Pompey and to cancel his veto upon the supplies for the Spanish legions. After causing Pompey all these vexations, Cæsar now judged the moment opportune for agreement, and held out the olive branch. He was so convinced that his enemies would not provoke a civil war upon so futile a pretext that, towards the end of September, he set out on his return journey and once more crossed the Alps to make final arrangements for installing his troops in their winter quarters.

Meanwhile Cicero's year of government, or rather of exile, had at length run out, and he had started post-haste on his homeward journey, without even stopping to draw up the accounts of his administration. He had begged his Quæstor to come at once to Laodicea to settle this with him; but his Quæstor could not be found and he had been too impatient to wait for him. He begged his scribe to collaborate with the Quæstor in drawing up the accounts, and to expose them, in accordance with the *Lex Julia* of 59, in two public places, at Laodicea and Apamea, for the scrutiny of the public. He had then set out on his homeward journey, taking none of the income of the province with him. Part of it he left to his Quæstor, who remained behind as provisional governor, in the hope that it might prevent him from pillaging the country; the rest, amounting to about a million sesterces, he deposited in the provincial Treasury, to the great indignation of his friends and officers, who failed to understand why he should show more consideration for Phrygians and Cilicians than for themselves. His action was indeed without precedent. Yet even with these deductions Cicero could, *salvis legibus*, as he said, bring back to Italy money enough to pay for the triumph which he hoped would be decreed for his victories and to pay in some 2,200,000 sesterces to the tax-farmers at Ephesus, probably his private share in the booty of his little war. Even the honestest of Proconsuls were sufficiently well paid for their year of government. On his way home he received a letter from his Quæstor protesting that his secretary had put into the Treasury some 100,000 sesterces which should have come to him; and he wrote him a consoling answer to say that he was ready to indemnify him personally. He travelled by slow stages, to show his son and his nephew the sights of Asia and Greece, stopping some time at Athens, where he learnt that his friend Pretius had died and left him heir to his property. At Patras Tiro, a young slave, whom he loved as his own child, fell seriously ill, and the journey was again interrupted. As it proved to be a lengthy illness, Cicero was forced, to his great regret, to leave Tiro behind; but he did not set out before making all the arrangements necessary for his comfort, quite regardless of expense. Manius Curius, a rich Italian merchant at Patras with whom he was acquainted, and who was intimate with Atticus, was asked to place at Tiro's disposal any money that he might need from Cicero's account. Finally, on November 24th, he landed at Brindisi.

Meanwhile in Italy the excitement had calmed down somewhat after the elections; but political and educated society had been considerably taken aback by the sudden appearance at Rome of a Censor of quite perverse and old-fashioned severity, a true rival of the older Cato. It was a strange enough circumstance in itself, but what made it still stranger was the personality of the man who had suddenly taken it upon himself to pose as the incarnation of the austerity of a bygone age. It was Appius Claudius, brother of Clodius and the ex-Governor of Cilicia who had caused Cicero so much trouble in repairing the wrongs committed or sanctioned by him during his administration. He had since been accused of extortion by Publius Cornelius Dolabella, the *fiancé* of Tullia, but since one of his daughters was married to Brutus and another to a son of Pompey, Brutus and Pompey had not only had him acquitted but even raised him to the Censorship. Once safely in office, Appius had displayed a severity almost amounting to barbarism. He had expelled numerous Senators from that august body, brought forward several awkward prosecutions, harassed the proprietors of too extensive estates and all who were deeply in debt, and had even interfered with extravagance in pictures and statues. Amongst his victims was Sallust, who lost his seat in the Senate, and Cælius and Curio, who, however, both eventually evaded his clutches. In short, Appius was doing his best to mimic Pompey's behaviour during his sole Consulship. Yet his Censorship was a mere caricature, too ridiculous to excite more than passing amusement and annoyance. The fashions of one year are the absurdities of the next, and the high moral tone so loudly professed by the Conservatives, which two years before Pompey seemed to have re-established as a rule of government, had already become rather a stale and unedifying farce.

However, nobody was seriously concerned about Appius, for Italy was for the moment in absolute quiet. Pompey was once more in Naples, while Cæsar, having concluded his arrangements in Trans-alpine Gaul, was returning into the Cisalpine province to winter there and prepare for his candidature in the following year. So far was he from believing in the possibility of a civil war that he only brought into Italy a single legion to garrison the Cisalpine province, in place of the legion which he had detached for the Parthian war. The remaining eight he left behind him in Gaul, four under Caius Fabius in the country of the Ædui, and four under Trebonius among the

Belgæ, at the furthest possible distance from Italy. Pompey might perhaps no longer be his friend; but he was a man of prudence and discretion; his other enemies were almost all of them, with the exception of Cato, men of good family but devoid of real influence, who could not possibly do violence to the unanimous opinion of Italy in favour of peace. He refused therefore to entertain the slightest doubt about arriving at some sort of an agreement with Pompey and the Senate.

These were wise and careful calculations. That is why they were wrong. In a period of social transition, when the balance of parties and classes is precarious and unstable, the light-headed petulance of a group of amateur politicians, whether on the reactionary or revolutionary side, may be sufficient, against the desire of an overwhelming majority of the nation, to bring latent antagonisms to the surface and precipitate developments of far-reaching significance. It is this that sometimes gives historic importance to the petty tempers and ambitions of men like Marcellus. Marcellus was furious with the unbroken success of Curio, and could not bear to see his year expire without obtaining his revenge. Nor were Cæsar's other enemies inclined to give up their designs; and their determination was strengthened by a new source of encouragement. If it was soon to be demonstrated by the most unimpeachable logic that the fidelity of Cæsar's soldiers was proof against every test, it seems that amongst his officers, particularly amongst those who belonged to noble families, there prevailed a certain amount of dissatisfaction; perhaps they were affected, as it was impossible that the common soldiers should be, by the impression of Cæsar's growing unpopularity among the upper classes. Labienus himself was taking the lead in the movement. Now Rome was just in the mood to mistake the disaffection of a few officers for a feeling of mutiny throughout the whole army, and it was widely believed that Cæsar's troops, worn out with years of continuous warfare, were clamouring to be disbanded. Thus Cæsar's enemies were now confidently reckoning upon the support of his legionaries. Marcellus decided to make a supreme effort in the sitting of the 1st of December —to force a decision that Cæsar's powers should expire on the 1st of March and to defeat an analogous proposal with regard to Pompey. If he succeeded he would attain a double object; he would both humiliate

Curio and, by doing Pompey a service, force him openly to join the Conservatives and become their leader.

On the 1st of December the Senate met; there was almost a full attendance, about 400 members being present. But the greatest indecision was found to prevail; hardly anyone seemed to have come with his mind made up. Whilst they were afraid of displeasing Cæsar, they were equally afraid of offending Pompey. The majority appeared to have but two desires, to avoid compromising themselves, and to avoid provoking a civil war. Marcellus and Curio alone knew what they wanted. At the beginning of the sitting Marcellus rose, and put the definite question whether Cæsar was to return to Rome as a private citizen. It was generally expected that, as on the 1st of March, Curio would make use of his veto, and that the Senate would thus be saved from entering upon so serious and dangerous a discussion. But to the universal amazement Curio remained silent and motionless on his seat. Marcellus' proposal could thus be put to the vote and was approved by a large majority. Without giving Curio a chance to intervene, Marcellus rose again and proposed to submit to the Senate the other question which had been raised, whether Pompey should resign his command. Thus formulated, the proposal seemed to be aimed definitely at Pompey and so to violate a law specifically approved by the people. Marcellus had couched it in this form on purpose to anticipate any proposal by Curio. In its fear of offending Pompey the Senate of course rejected the proposal. Thus the surprise had been completely successful. Curio and Cæsar had again been defeated and nothing remained but to adjourn the assembly. But Marcellus had not reckoned with Curio. With great presence of mind he rose and begged leave to put another proposal before the Senate—that Cæsar and Pompey should both simultaneously abandon their commands. Expressed in these terms and supported by the skilful pleading of the Tribune, the proposal lost its character of personal hostility against Pompey and seemed simply a measure conceived in the interests of equity and concord, which only a bad citizen could oppose. Marcellus put it to the vote in the full belief that the Senate, being already bound by its preceding decision, would reject it decisively and so complete Curio's discomfiture. But deliberative assemblies are not always guided by strictly logical considerations. Curio's proposal corresponded, as the Senators knew, with the general feeling of Italy, and when it was put to the vote there were 370 against 22 in its favour. Curio was thus once more successful, and the defeat was the more disastrous for Cæsar's enemies because it showed that they could place absolute reliance upon only 22 votes in the Senate. Marcellus adjourned the Senate in disgust, with the ejaculation that they had voted in favour of the tyranny of Cæsar.

If it had not given its vote in favour of tyranny the Senate had unconsciously, and in its desire to maintain the peace, given a vote for war. This vote was the direct cause of the outbreak of the civil war. Marcellus and the small group of Cæsar's enemies were furious at the turn affairs had taken. But they realized at once that one vital advantage had been gained. The vote was as great a blow to Pompey as it was to themselves, and it might achieve what they had been vainly trying to do since 58—it might bring Pompey over to the Conservative side. Marcellus decided to suggest to Pompey the adoption of a supreme expedient—he would propose in the Senate to declare Cæsar a public enemy, and, if the Tribunes intervened or the Senate did not approve, he would on his own authority declare a state of siege and entrust Pompey with the charge of public affairs and the command of the two legions of Cæsar which were to go to Parthia and were still at Lucera. The success of such a *coup d'état* could not surely be doubtful. With the two legions to be given him by the Consul the army of Pompey would amount to nine legions, which was as much as the total force at Cæsar's disposal. With Pompey in command of equal forces and in a position to offer him serious resistance, was it likely that Cæsar and his friends would continue their opposition at the risk of provoking a war which would be disastrous to themselves? If so, the majority of the Senate would certainly succumb to the greater fear and vote all that the enemies of Cæsar desired. It is true that an impartial observer might have objected that the military position was hardly so favourable to Pompey as it appeared. For while his nine legions were scattered, two being in Italy and seven in Spain, Cæsar had his nine legions under his own hand in Gaul. But there was general confidence in the prestige and skill of Pompey, and it was also believed that Cæsar would not run the risk of a new outbreak in Gaul by withdrawing his army from the province

Letters and messages soon began to pass to and fro, in all secrecy, between Rome and Naples. Marcellus and his friends had calculated rightly. Pompey, who had never had any serious intention of giving up his Proconsular command, was more decided than ever after the vote in the Senate not to yield to the suggestions of Curio, who was evidently acting on Cæsar's behalf. He did not mean to resign a right which had been legally conferred upon him or to recognize a surprise vote snatched from the Senate by an intriguing Tribune and inconsistent with a decision made a few minutes before. He would perhaps have been ready to cancel his rights of his own accord, if that would have helped to keep the peace so much desired by the whole of Italy. But it was impossible for him to capitulate before the menaces of a low-class Tribune like Curio. He could not forget that he had been elected Consul without the exercise of any previous magistracy; that he had a long record of distinguished service to his credit; that he was the destroyer of the pirates, the conqueror of Mithridates, the invader of Syria; that he had doubled the State revenues and re-established order in the capital. If Cæsar was short of money and unable to fulfil the delusive promises that he had made, and if he therefore desired to throw Italy into confusion by deliberately provoking a civil war, he must expect no mercy from Pompey. He counted securely upon his own prestige and upon Cæsar's mutinous officers; with some of these he was personally related and they seem to have inspired him with dangerous illusions. With Labienus he was already in communication and the officer escorting the two Parthian legions had told him that Cæsar's troops would never take up arms against him. Pompey in short felt himself complete master of the situation. At the first whisper of hostilities Italy would rise and give him all the legions he wanted. Civil war was an impossibility; he had only to threaten and Cæsar would give way.

Pompey therefore accepted the proposals of Marcellus; and the public soon noticed that the situation was becoming threatening without in the least understanding the reason. Cicero, who was travelling to Rome by the Appian Way, stopped at Naples and visited Pompey on the 10th of December. He was disagreeably surprised to find him in an irritable and pessimistic temper and to hear him say that war was inevitable, that it was now impossible to come to an understanding with Cæsar. Cicero, who had no knowledge of the intrigues which were going on between Rome and Naples, failed entirely to understand why this should be. At Rome Cæsar's friends, particularly Cornelius Balbus, were exceedingly anxious. Scenting danger in the air, they kept close watch over the minority of the 1st of December and waited impatiently for Cæsar's arrival. Cæsar was at this time quietly travelling through Cisalpine Gaul without any suspicion of his danger, and was actually under the impression that on his arrival he would find an agreement with the Senate already concluded. On the 8th of December Hirtius, one of Cæsar's officers, arrived at Rome, bringing letters for Pompey, and stayed in the house of Balbus. Balbus dissuaded him from continuing his journey to Naples, begged him to leave his message with Scipio, Pompey's father-in-law, and made Hirtius set out the same evening post-haste to rejoin Cæsar, to inform him more fully than could be done by correspondence of the sudden and ominous change in the situation.

But the suspense did not last long. So soon as Pompey's consent was received, probably on the 9th of December, Marcellus convened the Senate and made a violent speech in which he attacked Cæsar as a brigand and proposed to declare him a public enemy, at the same time ordering Pompey to take command of the legions which were at Lucera waiting to be embarked for Syria. Curio declared that the proposal could not be seriously meant and opposed his veto. Then Marcellus brought up his big battalions. He declared that, since he was hindered by factious interference from defending the Republic, he would have recourse to other than the ordinary constitutional means. He left the Senate and set out from Rome on the same day with a band of enthusiastic aristocrats, travelling in all haste to Naples to join Pompey, whom he reached on the 13th of December.

His sudden departure must have caused consternation among the public, which was ignorant of the intrigues of which it was the outcome. Would Pompey accept the rash offer that was being made him? On the 10th of December Curio became once more a private citizen, and he decided that, whatever happened, it would be wiser for him to be away from Rome. He set out to rejoin Cæsar who was marching his legions along the Æmilian Road on his way from Piacenza to Ravenna, where he intended to spend the winter. Cæsar clearly still believed in the maintenance of peace. But towards the 18th or 19th of December terrible news reached Rome, whence it penetrated three or four days later to Ravenna. In a speech of studied moderation Pompey had accepted the proposal of Marcellus and had started for Lucera, where he would shortly arrive to take over the command of the legions. The panic and indignation this news evoked among the public were indescribable. Impartial men, particularly the rich financiers, shared Cicero's disapproval of Pompey's behaviour in precipitating a war: while the chiefs of the Cæsarian party gave full rein to their anger. Antony summoned a mass meeting and delivered a violent address, recalling, amongst other things, the great number of citizens whom Pompey was already responsible for sending into exile. The extreme Conservative clique were of course openly exultant.

But nobody was more disconcerted than Cæsar when the news reached him at Ravenna, immediately after his arrival on the 24th or 25th of December. He saw all his hopes of a peaceful settlement dashed at one blow. It was impossible to entertain any illusions. Pompey's sudden resolution would at once drive into the Conservative camp a number of Senators who, under the impression that Pompey was inclined to be conciliatory, had voted on the 1st of December for the simultaneous retirement of the two generals. With Pompey openly arrayed against him, the last remnants of his popularity with the upper classes were taken from him, and their personal quarrel would gradually assume the form of a conflict between rich and poor, between the *élite* and the proletariat, in which respectability in a body would take Pompey's side. There would be few found bold enough to brave the anger of Pompey, still less that taint of vulgarity which was attached, as in all struggles between rich and poor, to the chiefs of the popular party. If Pompey persisted in his demand that he should abandon his command on the 1st of next March, there was no alternative but open resistance. To return to Rome and face the prosecution threatened him by the Conservatives was no longer possible: for since the revision of the lists of judges, Pompey was master of the law-courts, and his condemnation would be assured.

Cæsar at once summoned his friends to a council of war. Curio proposed to summon the Gallic army and march at once upon Rome. If war was inevitable, better face it at once. But Cæsar was unwilling.

He knew that, though Pompey might carry the whole world of politics against him, the public opinion of Italy was still on the side of peace; and he still hoped to set a united and peaceful Italy between himself and his enemies. Sulla was a distant memory, and the bitter antagonisms between class and class which had provoked the outbreak of the last civil war now existed no longer. Italy would not lightly forgive if the petty squabbles of politicians provoked another. Yet Cæsar could not remain inactive. He recalled two legions, the 12th and the 8th, to Italy, and ordered Caius Fabius to proceed with three legions from Bibracte to Narbonne, to intercept a possible movement on the part of Pompey's legions in Spain. Meanwhile he would make one more effort at conciliation. It was now the 25th or 26th of December. The Senate would meet on the 1st of January. If a courier could reach Rome before that day there would still be time to parry the blow that his enemies certainly intended to deliver in that sitting. Curio declared his readiness to accomplish this miracle of quickness. Cæsar wrote a letter to the Senate and another to the people, and Curio left Ravenna at early dawn on the 27th. In his letter to the Senate Cæsar declared his readiness to abandon his command if Pompey acted likewise; otherwise he would take steps to defend his rights. In his letter to the people he said that he was ready to re-enter private life and to give an account of all he had done, and invited Pompey to do the same.

The last days of the year were a busy and anxious time for all parties. Pompey's declaration had indeed converted, albeit reluctantly, a good number of the Senators and the wealthy classes to his side, for they had not the courage to take an open line against a man in his position; and Cæsar's declared supporters were treated with coldness and almost boycotted. This movement of opinion was of course a further encouragement to Pompey. In a fit of irritation at the violent speeches of Antony he told Cicero on the 25th, in the neighbourhood of Formia, that he would absolutely oppose Cæsar's ever becoming Consul either in 48 or at any other time; a second Consulship of Cæsar would be fatal to the Republic. If he was foolish enough to go to war, let him do his worst; he, Pompey, was not afraid. Only the proletariat, which had supported and admired Catiline, was now united in its attachment to Cæsar. But everyone in either camp was in a state of feverish anxiety. What would happen at the sitting of the 1st of January? Cicero was especially unhappy, and almost regretted having left his province. He felt more indebted to Pompey than to Cæsar, and now that the rupture was imminent he was sorry that he had not quite paid off his debts to the Proconsul of Gaul. But above all he was anxious for peace and still hoped for some agreement to stave off the fatal and almost ludicrous expedient of civil war. For unlike many of his contemporaries he was under no illusions as to Cæsar's strength. Moreover, if a war broke out, what would become of his triumph?

But it is Cæsar in the little town of Ravenna who must have suffered most during these terrible days of suspense. Certainly he had every reason to give way to a blind indignation against mankind and his destiny. All that had gone so well for Pompey had gone ill for him. Together they had courted the crowd, inflamed the passions of the democracy, corrupted the nation, opposed the Senate, tilted against the old republican institutions, all to win glory, riches and power. But Pompey had not been forced painfully by slow degrees to mount the ladder of office. He had been three times Consul: he had celebrated numerous triumphs: his victories over Mithridates and his conquest of Syria had made him the greatest general of his day: he had amassed an immense fortune and enjoyed it at his leisure at Rome, amid the admiration of the people and the nobles He had become the representative of the great without losing the respect of the humble. All his life he had been moving from success to success. He thought of himself. What had all his labours brought him? With endless intrigue and difficulty and danger he had climbed into office; and when, at the age of forty, he had at length obtained a province which was to bring him in glory and riches, fortune had again played him false. He had received a country poor in comparison with the East and very difficult to conquer, where he had fought for nine years against almost continuous insurrections. And at the end of it all what had he to show? Had it brought him glory? He was the most despised and best-hated man among the upper classes, and every Italian who had read a line of Xenophon was in a position to improve upon the strategy of his campaigns. Had it brought him wealth? He came out of that gigantic struggle almost as poor as he went in, having used nearly all that his Gallic ravaging had brought him to corrupt Roman politicians, without even winning the gratitude to which his generosity had entitled him. Italy was united in reproaching him for a policy of pillage of which she alone had reaped the fruits. When Cæsar turned back to the past to inquire into the reason for the strange divergence of their two careers, he could not help seeing that, if Pompey had been the favourite of fortune, he owed it to the part he had taken in the massacres of Sulla. It was then that he had acquired his great influence with the rich classes, which had enabled him later to join the Democrats without forfeiting the respect of the Conservatives. Safely entrenched behind an unassailable popularity, he had been able to secure all that he desired, offices and provinces, extraordinary commands and grandiose triumphs, all with but the smallest concessions to the popular party, until he had become universally recognized as indispensable to every undertaking. He himself on the other hand had excited the hatred of the Cabal during the *régime* of the reaction, and it was this hatred that had dogged him all through his career. His slow and laborious rise, the enormous debts he had contracted in order to make a name at all, his early conflicts with the Conservatives, the revolutionary action which was practically forced upon him during his Consulship, the ultra-Imperialist policy by which he had endeavoured to sustain it, the fatal alliance with the demagogues from which he had never been able to withdraw and which threatened now to drag him to his ruin, all these were but the necessary outcome of his connection with the conqueror of the Cimbri and of the chivalrous behaviour of his earliest days—of his loyalty in the reign of terror to the daughter and to the memory of Cinna, of his haughty defiance of Sulla, of his horror of massacre and fratricide. If he had only consented then to betray the conquered side, his career would have been swift and easy, and he would have risen like Pompey to fortune and power.

In the misfortunes which had befallen Cæsar there was thus a real element of injustice; men and circumstances alike had played him false. That his sense of this injustice did not embitter his nature, or drive him, at this climax of his career, to acts of cruelty and violence, is at once a proof of the serenity of his intellect and one of his most lasting titles to glory. The history of the civil war up to the battle of

Pharsalia is perhaps the finest episode in Cæsar's life. He displays a clear-sightedness and moderation which go far to make up for the indiscretions and barbarism of his Gallic campaign. Even at this very moment, while Curio was galloping breathless upon the Flaminian Road, Cæsar was still confident of peace. He fully expected that his letter, couched as it was in terms at once vigorous and conciliatory, would awaken the reactionaries to wiser counsels. All seemed to depend upon whether it could reach Rome in time.

Once more Curio justified the confidence reposed in him. When the Senate met on the 1st of January the letter was already in the hands of Antony. The Consuls were so afraid of the effect it might produce that they endeavoured to prevent it from being read. Antony and the friends of Cæsar were naturally all the more anxious to read it, in the hope of producing another of those revulsions of feeling which had been so frequent in the last few months. It was only after a long and violent discussion that it was finally read. The result was disastrous for the partisans of Cæsar. Whether out of genuine indignation, or out of fear of Pompey, who was now known to be entirely opposed to Cæsar, or simply out of an instinctive desire to find a vent for the ill-humour with which they had all of them come together, the Senators punctuated the reading of the letter with a running chorus of protest, and denounced it as insolent, dictatorial, and unworthy. Before his supporters realized what had happened, Cæsar had lost his last chance in the Senate. Antony was too much disconcerted to speak, and the Conservatives, forgetting that they had tried to prevent the letter from being read, broke out into cries of exultation. Lentulus and Scipio made violent speeches, saying that it was time to have done with palaver; the defenders of Cæsar could not make themselves heard amid the general hubbub, and even Marcellus, the Consul of 51, was hissed into silence because he dared to ask whether it would not be better, before inviting a war, to examine the state of their resources. Had not Pompey repeatedly reassured anxious inquirers by the assertion that everything was ready? In the midst of this confusion approval was given to a proposal by which Cæsar was declared an enemy of his country if he did not abandon his command before the 1st of July. Thanks to the intervention of Antony and Quintus Cassius the vote was not to take effect at once; but this was almost a matter of indifference to the Conservatives; they were certain of being able to vote a state of siege, which would annul the Tribunician veto, as soon as they wished it.

Then followed ten days of breathless activity. Out came all the figures familiar on the eve of a great conflict—the peacemakers and the mischiefmakers, the inopportune opportunists, and the inconsolable pessimists—all anxious to add their quota to the opinions of the moment. On the evening of the 1st of January Pompey summoned numerous Senators to his house, addressed them words of praise and encouragement and invited them to be present in the Senate on the following day. At the same time a levy was begun, and the veterans were recalled to Rome. Nevertheless there seems to have been a slight reaction among the Senators during the night. On the next day, the Consuls did not venture to dispute the Tribunician veto; the father-in-law of Cæsar and the Prætor Roscius demanded a suspension of six days to attempt conciliation, while others suggested that ambassadors should be sent to him. It so happened that the Senate held no sitting on the 3rd and 4th and that on the 4th Cicero arrived in the neighbourhood of Rome, heartily welcomed by the more reasonable party among the Senators, which was anxious for peace and hoped that Cicero might be able to intervene. Cicero at once undertook the task. He negotiated with the party leaders and proposed that Cæsar should be authorized to stand for the Consulship in his absence, and that Pompey should go to Spain during Cæsar's Consulship. Meanwhile Curio had received still more moderate proposals from Cæsar. He was prepared to be satisfied with Cisalpine Gaul and Illyria with two legions. For one moment it was believed that these two proposals might settle the difficulty. Pompey, who seems to have awoken for a moment to realities, gave secret instructions to Lucius Cæsar, a young man whose father was a general in Cæsar's army, to treat for peace. Lucius Roscius, to whom Pompey had declared that he was inclined to accept the last conditions proposed by Curio, also left on a mission of his own to Cæsar. But Lentulus, Cato and Scipio came to the rescue, and strengthened Pompey's failing resolution. Cæsar was but plotting as usual. Would he allow himself to fall into the trap? Pompey's vacillation had been reflected in the Senate which had held its hand on the 5th and 6th of January, discussing the question without arriving at a decision. But by the evening of the 6th Pompey had been reconverted by the extreme Conservatives. On the 7th the state of siege was declared, and Antony and Quintus Cassius fled the city. Cæsar's enemies heaved a sigh of relief. After a year and a half of plots and counterplots the foe was at last at their mercy. If he wished to become Consul, he must pay the price of a civil war. Let him do so if he dared. With Pompey on their side Cæsar's enemies were now masters of the State. They disposed of the Treasury, the provinces, the allies, and the armies; the most celebrated of Roman generals, the most illustrious of Roman citizens was devoted to their cause. Cæsar had but nine legions, worn out by a long war, and a small province, only recently subdued and still bitterly hostile. The common opinion was that he would never dare to leave Gaul behind him and break into Italy, but would prefer to remain on the defensive in the valley of the Po. On the following days the Senate held several sittings under the presidency of Pompey, who gave a reassuring account of the military situation; various measures directed against Cæsar were approved without difficulty. The State Treasury and the municipal and private funds were placed at Pompey's disposal; he was authorized to make forced loans, and the important provinces were distributed amongst the favourites of the Conservative party. Scipio received Syria, Domitius Transalpine Gaul, and Considius Nonianus Cisalpine Gaul. Finally it was decided to make a general levy. Italy was divided into divisions in each of which a Senator of influence, who possessed estates in the districts, was selected for the chief command. Cicero received Capua, Domitius the territory of the Marsi, Scribonius Libo Etruria, and Lentulus Spinther Picenum. The Conservative government seemed already re-established.

When the Romans awoke on the morning of the 14th of January they found that a thunderbolt had burst upon the city. Cæsar had crossed the Rubicon and occupied Rimini in considerable strength; the first fugitives of the invader were already in the capital. The chief of the demagogues, the patron of bankrupts and adventurers, was marching upon Rome at the head of his legions and the Gallic cavalry.

CHAPTER XXVII

BELLUM CIVILE

WHAT had really happened was not so alarming as report suggested. Cæsar had not the intention so naïvely attributed to him in many quarters of remaining quietly on the defensive in the valley of the Po; but neither was he inclined to march straight upon the capital. By the 4th of January he had probably heard of the reception given by the Senate to his last proposals and he had now to make up his mind how to face the situation. What course should he pursue? To wait quietly in his province, plying the Senate with futile recriminations till his command expired on the 1st of July was hardly practicable; it would have given his enemies just what they needed—time to collect their forces, and opportunities of sowing discord amongst his soldiers; for he had already for some time past been aware that Labienus was untrustworthy. Somehow or other he must find means to stiffen his verbal protests; the Senate needed the vigorous tonic of an open defiance. But defiance was difficult, for it involved the risk of provoking a civil war. Moreover, it was impossible to predict what impression it might produce upon his own soldiers. It was the attitude of the legionaries in the approaching crisis which really formed the pivot of the situation and swayed the calculations of the two opposing parties. They had already been through a lengthy series of exhausting campaigns. Could he ask them now to follow him through the odium and vicissitudes of a civil war?

During the last ten years Cæsar had always taken the greatest pains to win the devotion of his soldiers. True, when on active service he had demanded the most rigorous discipline and almost unexampled exertions; he had constantly appeared at unexpected moments to make sure that all was in order and had never failed to punish most severely any dereliction of duty. But he had provided them on the other hand with the amplest compensation for their loyalty. He had heaped them with gold and prize-money; he had shown the greatest solicitude for their material well-being; he had multiplied the number of centurions by increasing the quantity and diminishing the fighting force of the legions; he had encouraged them in a taste for luxury and a liking for fine arms and helmets and cuirasses; and he had employed all the arts of cajolery generally so successful with simple and ignorant persons, trying to know all their names and the details of their lives, and speaking with high appreciation of their services in his public reports. The soldiers, who were most of them poor peasants from the valley of the Po, had listened with pride as their patrician general harangued them not as "soldiers" but as "my comrades," and he had certainly succeeded in securing their enthusiastic fidelity. Yet, elaborate fiction though it was, the old Republican government was still capable of inspiring unbounded veneration. The Senate, the magistrates, and the whole immemorial structure of the Roman state were still looked up to with respect by the mass of the Italian people. One moment of hesitation or distrust or fear at the beginning of the war and the attachment of his soldiers might have vanished before an age-long sentiment, and the Gallic army that he had so laboriously welded together would have dispersed in a few weeks.

Perhaps Cæsar never lived through so perplexing a time as the five or six days which followed. But the news that the state of siege had been proclaimed at Rome on the 7th of January, and that the Tribunes had fled the city, put an end to all his doubts. Quite suddenly, probably on the morning of the 10th, he made up his mind. He determined to make a sudden dash upon Rimini, the first Italian city across the Rubicon frontier, making it his base for the seizure of other important towns: thus making it clear to the Senate and to Pompey that he was not afraid of a civil war, and that if it was to be a fight to the death he would defend himself with the courage of despair. He would then once more attempt to treat with his enemies, whom fear if not reason might by this time have brought into a more conciliatory mood. He set to work at once with the quickness which was his second nature. He communicated the plan to several friends and officers who were to go with him, of whom Asinius Pollio was one, and concerted skilful arrangements to prevent any report of his intention from reaching Rimini. Each of them was to leave the city alone at nightfall by a different route; they were to form a junction during the night with the cohorts whom Cæsar had already sent forward under the command of Hortensius; and together before dawn they were to occupy Rimini. Meanwhile Cæsar was to do his best to distract the attention of the public. He showed himself all day in the streets of Ravenna; he went to the baths, appeared at a public spectacle, examined the plans for a gladiatorial school; in the evening he even gave a great dinner at which he displayed the most complete self-control. And yet the plan was in itself exceedingly hazardous. If his intentions had become known and Rimini had closed its gates, he and his 1,500 men could never have taken it; while a violation of the Italian frontier, however little he achieved, was a definite provocation of civil war. In the middle of dinner he apologized for having to leave his guests for a short time upon urgent and unexpected business, mounted a tradesman's cart, and left Ravenna by a road going in the opposite direction from Rimini. After driving a little distance he turned back, joined the cohorts and his friends, aroused the soldiers and ordered them to set out on the march with no other arms than their swords. On the morning of the 11th of January, when the burghers of Rimini awoke, Cæsar with his 1,500 legionaries was already in their town.

At Rimini he found Antony, fresh from the capital. The soldiers were introduced to their ex-general the Tribune in the slave costume in which he had fled the city. Cæsar delivered a vigorous speech promising large rewards and declaring that it was his object to defend the liberties of the people against the tyranny of faction. In the excitement of the moment the soldiers eagerly pledged themselves to remain loyal. Cæsar then sent Antony to fetch the five other cohorts who were on the Æmilian Way, probably in the neighbourhood of the modern Forlimpopoli, ordering him to cross the Apennines and seize Arezzo. With the five cohorts under his own command he spent the following days in occupying the principal towns along the coast, Pesaro, Fano and Ancona. He did not do this with the object of beginning a campaign. How could he, with little more than 3,000 soldiers at his disposal? He was merely trying to secure an asset which would enable him to treat for peace on more favourable conditions, and to prove to his enemies that, under provocation, he could answer violence with violence. Thus when, towards the 19th of January, Roscius and Lucius Cæsar reached him in one of the towns on the Adriatic coast, he was ready with his conditions. Pompey was to return to Spain; all the troops recruited in Italy were to be dismissed;

the electors were to meet at Rome in the absence of the military; if this were done he was prepared to renounce his province and to go to Rome to stand for the Consulship in person.

Cæsar, like the other side, had been engaged in bluffing; and his tactics met with a very common, though always unexpected, result. They failed, not because they did not succeed in frightening his enemies, but because they frightened them too much. When on the 14th, 15th and 16th of January the news of the successive occupations along the Adriatic coast reached Rome: when it was reported that Pesaro and Fano had followed Rimini and that Libo was hurriedly abandoning Etruria and retiring upon Rome, a panic broke out among the politicians at Rome which it was far beyond Pompey's powers to allay. Cæsar had certainly never imagined that it was so easy to disconcert, indeed to paralyse his opponents. Everyone was convinced that he was preparing a surprise attack upon the capital; that he was on his way to Rome with a host of Gallic cavalry and legionaries who were thirsting for plunder; that he was already wellnigh at the gates; that all Italy lay helpless at his feet, since Pompey had nothing to set against him but two untrustworthy legions which had actually been returned him by Cæsar. All day long a train of terror-stricken Senators and officials crowded round Pompey's mansion feverishly asking for news or comfort, and proffering futile prognostications or equally futile advice. So great was the confusion that the freedmen and slaves were unable to keep watch over the door; everyone entered as he wished, and burdened the unfortunate Pompey with the outpourings of their hearts. The majority of the Senators, who had never been wholehearted in their acceptance of the war, now suddenly turned against the small Conservative majority, and especially against Pompey; they accused him of miscalculation and impetuosity, they regretted not having accepted Cæsar's proposals, and several even used language which on other occasions they would have been the first to call insulting.

This general panic was highly disconcerting to the Consul, and the small knot of politicians who were responsible for the rupture The preparations which were being hurried on on the 12th were as suddenly interrupted; the Senate was not convened either on the 14th, the 15th, or the 16th, obviously because the Consuls were afraid lest the Senators should vote for unconditional submission. The chiefs of the Conservative clique spent the days in deep debate; but they were unable to arrive at any satisfactory conclusion. Pompey himself seems to have been in a most pitiable state of mind. He had never possessed the amazing quickness and elasticity which carried Cæsar over all his obstacles, and he had for some time past been in feeble health. The dizzy succession of rumours and recriminations crowding in from all sides now threw him utterly off his balance. Just when he should have been a tower of strength amid the universal confusion he seems for a time to have been almost paralysed. He did not even succeed in ascertaining, amid the various conflicting reports, what number of troops Cæsar had at his command, and whether he was really in a position to make a dash upon Rome. He was genuinely frightened, and as he was afraid to reveal it he preferred to remain inactive and to make no plans. His aristocratic *hauteur* gave him the strength to contain his feelings, but beneath a calm and almost nonchalant exterior there lurked a blind fury against the party which had egged him on to war and how, at the first stroke, was threatening to desert him: while he was laying up a store of lasting resentment against Cæsar as the cause of this open and unexpected humiliation. Three whole days he spent in debate with the Consuls and chief persons in Rome without being able to make up his mind. He felt that it was his duty to leave Rome at once to take over the command of the legions which were awaiting him, to hurry on the recruiting and to organize the defence of the country; for, like everyone else, he believed that Cæsar would take the offensive at once. But how could he leave behind him at Rome the government of the State in the hands of a terror-stricken Senate, whom Cæsar could easily intimidate into submission? A short-lived panic would be sufficient to cause the Senate to disavow him, thus placing him in a painful and almost impossible situation. The other alternative was to persuade the Senate and the magistrates to leave Rome in his company, thus taking with him the whole of the constitutional government, and withdrawing it from the actions or threats of Cæsar. But this was a highly serious and complicated undertaking, and at present Pompey did not venture either to propose or to approve it.

But on the 17th came the news that not only Ancona but Arezzo also had been occupied by the enemy. Cæsar seemed full on his march towards Rome. The panic had been bad enough before: it now became insupportable. Pompey at last awoke out of his lethargy, and came to a definite understanding with Cato, the Consuls and the more important persons at Rome. All of them realized that speedy decision was now essential. After due consultation he decided to convene the Senate. The sitting was stormy and confused, lasting many hours and revealing many contradictions. Several Senators reproached Pompey with miscalculation. Volcatius Tullus and Cicero proposed to send ambassadors to Cæsar to treat for peace. Cato, on the other hand, wished to entrust Pompey with full powers for the conduct of the war. Pompey listened with disdainful indifference to everything that was said against him. He refused to disguise the realities of the situation and quietly declared that he would look to the defence of Italy. But he opposed the proposal of Tullus which was equivalent in his mind to a confession of weakness. This resolute attitude caused the war party to prevail; Cato's proposal was approved and the *tumultus* decreed. Pompey then revealed his plan. The Consuls and the Senate were to abandon Rome and to retire to Capua, taking the State Treasury with them; Pompey was to take vengeance on the towns which opened their gates to Cæsar and consider as enemies all Senators who did not leave Rome in his company. It can be imagined with what stupefaction this decision was received. Rome was to be abandoned to the enemy. Here was a *coup d'état* on which Sulla himself would never have ventured.

It seems that Pompey set out for Capua as soon as he left the Senate House. It was already late in the evening and the numerous Senators who had not brought slaves with torches to escort them home and did not wish to venture alone into the unlighted streets of Rome spent the night in the Curia. It would be interesting to know their feelings during those slow-moving hours. The difficulties and inconvenience of so hurried a departure were of course innumerable. Pompey, the rich aristocrat, with his slaves and his secretaries, his friends and his clients, had not stopped to reflect that the majority of the Senate was not equally well circumstanced. What was to be done with the slaves that everyone had in his household? Could they be left behind at Rome during a civil war, with the price of provisions going up and a spirit of revolt in the air? And where to send the women and children? Besides it meant a total stoppage of business. Many of the Senators had not even the money necessary for the journey and not the least idea where to turn for it. Their own friends were themselves in need, dealing in bills was practically suspended, and borrowing was very difficult in face of an imminent civil war.

Nevertheless, now that Pompey knew his mind, he rapidly regained his ascendancy. As people recovered from their first surprise they began to consider what was truly to their interest. Cæsar's victory must surely involve a political revolution in which the rich would be despoiled of their possessions. There was no disputing the cogency of this argument; and thus, although Pompey's conduct caused a good deal of bad temper, the greater number of the Senators decided to set out in his company. Even Caius Cassius, once Quæstor of Crassus, came over to Pompey's side, together with his brother-in-law Brutus, whom Cæsar had almost treated as his son and whose own father had been treacherously put to death by Pompey in the operations against Lepidus at Modena. Brutus had hitherto refused to have relations with Pompey, but at a moment like this he was unable to resist. Cæsar's supporters formed a contemptible handful—Sallust and Cælius, still smarting under the persecution of Appius Claudius, Dolabella, the young libertine who had become the son-in-law of Cicero, and Asinius Pollio, a personal friend of old standing.

Next morning, amid general confusion, preparations began for departure, though many still hoped that some unexpected incident would make it possible for them to remain. To procure money enough for their journey many of the Senators applied to Atticus, who placed at the disposal of his friends the huge sums he had stored in the cellars of his house or deposited in the temples at Rome. Yet many had great difficulty in setting out, and not a few would have still further prolonged their preparations if, fortunately for Pompey, a false rumour had not been spread on the 18th that Cæsar was already marching on Rome at the head of his Gallic cavalry. This suddenly revived the panic. The Consuls went off at once without even emptying the Treasury; those who found most difficulty in their preparations finished them off without further ado, and before evening on that day the Appian Way was blocked with a long train of litters and slaves, waggons and beasts of burden. Crowds of knights, freed-men, and well-to-do plebeians—in short, the whole of the wealthy and educated classes—were evacuating Rome, and, with a strange but not altogether unparalleled inconsequence at a time of revolution, were leaving behind them their women, children and slaves in a city on which Cæsar was hourly expected to pounce with his barbarian cavalry.

Cicero had left before the panic, on the morning of the 18th, in as bad a temper as many of his friends and thoroughly disgusted with Pompey. He did not think it wise to abandon the capital in this hurried fashion. Nor did he believe that Pompey could succeed so rapidly as he expected in collecting a large army in Italy. He was therefore very uneasy. It seemed to him that Pompey had been at once too violent and too weak in face of the resolute attitude of Cæsar. He had no reason to pin his faith on Cæsar, yet he was on the whole more disposed to believe in his success than in Pompey's. Events were confirming the sinister presentiment which he had felt at the beginning of the struggle. He repented of having accepted the mission at Capua, now that Capua was becoming the advance position of Pompey's army, and was anxious to exchange it for a post of general supervision over the plain and coast of Latium. Amidst all these anxieties he was by no means sorry to see his son-in-law Dolabella taking sides with Cæsar. It was no doubt a disgrace to the family, yet if Cæsar were to win, it might turn out a blessing. A son-in-law might serve as a useful intermediary.

Meanwhile Cæsar of course did not in the least intend to march upon Rome. After occupying Ancona and Arezzo he had already, on the 19th of January, sent Curio to seize Gubbio which had been evacuated by the Prætor Thermus with five cohorts; and he had then paused to await reinforcements. With his 3,000 men he could venture no farther. But soon the events which he had set in motion carried him far beyond his wildest calculations. He was much vexed to hear that Pompey, the Consuls and part of the Senate had evacuated Rome, and concluded that Pompey wished to deprive him of the means of negotiating an equitable peace with the Senate and to force him to a regular civil war in any or every part of the Empire, which was just what he least desired. He had immediately written, and persuaded his friends to write, to a large number of the departed Senators, amongst others to Cicero, to induce them to stay at Rome.

Meanwhile a far more serious danger threatened him from Osimo, where Actius Varus was hastily arming a number of cohorts, and seemed inclined to make a move forward against Cæsar's small force of 3,000 men, now dispersed in a great triangle between Arezzo, Ancona and Rimini. Cæsar, who had only his small Gallic army to fall back upon, realized that he must at all costs prevent the enemy from further recruiting. He therefore reunited his legions on the Adriatic coast, perhaps at Ancona, and gave orders to Curio and Antony to evacuate Gubbio and Arezzo, thus clearly revealing that the occupation of Arezzo had been merely a piece of bluff.

It was at this moment, towards the end of January, that he received the answer to the conditions of peace which he had proposed. On his return from his interview with Cæsar, Pompey's ambassador had met the Consuls and several Senators at Teano on the road to Capua. Most of them were so much put out by their sudden departure from Rome on a dangerous adventure of which it was impossible to predict the outcome that they were disposed in Pompey's absence to accept the proposals of Cæsar. Cæsar desired peace and the Senate desired peace. Why should it be impossible to attain it? But events had passed beyond the control of human wisdom or human management. The Senators who met at Teano had added to Cæsar's proposals the condition that he should retire into his province in order that the Senate might have full independence for deliberation. It was a natural demand on their part; they needed some pledge of Cæsar's sincerity. Unfortunately it was a demand that Cæsar could not possibly accept. He knew how easy it would be for his enemies to find a pretext for war the moment they felt themselves strong enough to declare it. All this while, indeed, Actius Varus was continuing to arm his soldiers, and it was imperative for Cæsar at all costs to prevent his adversaries from obtaining further recruits. Thus as soon as the whole of his army was under his command, probably on the 1st of February, he marched upon Osimo, took the city after a brief skirmish, and attached to his side, by the promise of high pay, a large number of Varus' soldiers. He then seized Cingoli and the whole of Picenum. A few days later, perhaps on the 3rd of February, having now been joined by the 12th Legion, he advanced in the direction of Fermo with the intention of marching upon Ascoli, which was held by Lentulus Spinther with ten cohorts.

These operations, which were forced upon Cæsar to prevent the recruiting of his adversaries, put an end to all attempts at conciliation just at the moment when they seemed about to succeed. Fate was dragging both sides remorselessly into civil war. Day by day the forces of Cæsar seemed to swell and those of his enemies to dwindle. The daring of his first operations, the confusion which he had unexpectedly introduced into the enemy's camp, the flight of Pompey, his occupation of a whole district of Italy, prepared the mind of the army for a civil war, and for the revolution which was its inevitable outcome. A report was current that Cæsar would make knights of all the soldiers who followed him; and the hope of this reward had still further excited the enthusiasm of his Gallic troops for their Imperator.

Pompey, on the other hand, though armed with the fullest authority that the State could offer him, found it impossible to carry on the war with efficiency. He had succeeded in inducing the magistrates and the greater part of the Senate to evacuate Rome; but he was unable to make use of them for his own purposes. How could he make his way through the country, stopping at the little towns and villages on the way, dogged by a long and melancholy procession of Senators, who knew nothing that they could do to help him and spent their time quarrelling with him and one another and with the miserable accommodation the country places provided? It is not surprising that, before many days passed, he left the Senators to themselves and set out for Lucera, where he intended to take command of his two legions and concentrate all the troops that were being recruited on the Adriatic coast. Thus left to themselves, the Senators gradually dispersed all through Campania; the Consuls were in one place, the Tribunes in another, while the majority of the Senate retired alone to their homes in solitary villas on the deserted and wintry countryside. The couriers did not know where or to whom to deliver their letters; Pompey and the Consuls were sometimes left in ignorance of the most important intelligence; orders arrived too late or could not possibly be carried out owing to distance. Altogether the Conservatives were

by now in a condition of utter confusion; everyone was complaining
but few were acting, and those few took no pains to obey the
instructions of Pompey, who was only nominally their chief. Levies
were carried out remissly, and there was little enthusiasm. Pompey
sent the Tribune Caius Cassius from Lucera to Capua to tell the
Consuls to return to Rome for the treasure; but the Consuls refused
on the pretext that the roads were not safe. Not only the capital, but
the treasure was thus abandoned to the enemy. Already thoroughly
discouraged by the opening events of the war and by the losses entailed
by the confusion of their departure, the Senators became still more
depressed in the solitude of their country homes, where news which
arrived days after it had happened seemed but the distant echo of a
far-away world. The hurried departure from the capital, evacuated
for the first time in its history, had filled them with something like
superstitious terror. How were men in this temper to be infused with
the energy or the enthusiasm of battle?

It was a grain of comfort at this juncture to learn that Labienus
had at last actually crossed over to Pompey's side. We do not know
the exact reasons for his treachery. It appears that there had for some
time past been friction between Cæsar and his subordinate, and that
after the war against Vercingetorix, during which the only real
victories had been those gained by Labienus over the Senones and
Parisii, the obscure plebeian whose friendship with Cæsar had made
him a rich and prominent personage imagined he was actually Cæsar's
superior in generalship. In any case his defection did something to
relieve the despondency of Pompey's partisans, though it was far from
removing their dissatisfaction. Cicero was going and coming constantly
between Formia and Capua, impatient for news and a prey to constant
and contradictory emotions. At one moment he would wax furious
at the audacity of Cæsar, at another at the unpardonable inertia of
Pompey, then he would hark back once more to his favourite project
for intervention and peace. On the 10th of February a meeting was
arranged on his estate at Formia between various friends and influential
members of Pompey's party, Caius Cassius, Marcus Lepidus and
Lucius Torquatus. They discussed the situation at length, and arrived
unanimously at the conclusion that if a pitched battle was inevitable
there must be one and no more. All serious and patriotic politicians

would then unite in inducing the defeated party to renounce his pretensions and force him to the conclusion of peace.

While his adversaries were organizing the defence with such slackness and want of spirit, Cæsar was moving rapidly and resolutely forward. On his arrival at Fermo he heard that Ascoli had been evacuated and that Lentulus, dismayed by the speed and strength of his advance, had surrendered his command during the retreat to Vibullius Rufus and had retired to Corfinium, where Domitius Ahenobarbus was concentrating a large and formidable army. Lucilius Hirrus, who had abandoned Camerino, was also retiring upon Corfinium with a considerable force. Corfinium was thus becoming the rallying-point of his opponents; and Cæsar was compelled to continue his advance if for no other reason than that his enemies were flying before him. Realizing that it was now impossible to secure terms without first fighting a pitched battle, which would overcome the obstinacy of some and the hesitation of others, he formed a new plan of campaign at Fermo, which he immediately put into execution. He would fight a short and sharp campaign in Italy, break up the army concentrated at Corfinium, force Pompey and the Consuls to conclude a reasonable peace, and thus, within a few weeks restore peace to Italy. He stopped one day at Fermo, collecting supplies, and sending numerous couriers with a reassuring manifesto to the chief cities of Italy to set forth his peaceable intentions. Then with his habitual rapidity he set out once more, on the 8th of February, by forced marches along the coast in the direction of Corfinium.

At Corfinium, and at Sulmona and Alba in the neighbourhood, was a force of thirty-one cohorts in all, a little more than 10,000 men. Pompey wisely desired to concentrate his troops farther south, at Lucera, and if his plans had been carried out Cæsar would have found the country of the Marsi deserted. But Pompey could not yet shake off the uncertainty and slackness which ruined all his best projects. He had unlimited powers, but he hesitated to use them against an influential aristocrat like Domitius Ahenobarbus. He had advised rather than ordered him to fall back on Lucera and had been gratified to hear, on the 10th of February, that Domitius expected to set out on the 9th. Since then he had heard no more from Domitius. It was only some days later that he ascertained indirectly that he had changed his mind and was now anxious to oppose a bold front to Cæsar's advance. Pompey, who knew the weaknesses of the Italian upper classes, concluded that some of the great landowners in the neighbourhood of Corfinium must have joined Domitius and were insisting that the country should be saved from pillage. Himself a large landowner and indulgent towards the foibles of his class, and not vigorous enough to impose his will upon others, Pompey then took a step unworthy of a general. On the 12th of February he begged Domitius to send him nineteen cohorts and to keep the rest for his defence. But on the 13th or 14th of February, having now lost all hopes of seeing Domitius conform to his advice, and persuaded that he was on the point of being surprised by Cæsar, he fell back upon the scheme of retiring to Greece. If it was no longer possible to defend himself in Italy he must leave the peninsula, move eastwards to collect an army, and renew the war later on with a more serious fighting force. But even after coming to this momentous decision Pompey showed a lack of the necessary energy. On the 13th he despatched Decimus Lælius to the Consuls with a despatch in which he begged them, if the advice appeared "opportune," the one to go to Sicily, with the troops recruited in the neighbourhood of Capua and with twelve of the cohorts of Domitius to protect the corn supply, and the other to proceed with the rest of the troops to Brindisi to embark. He also invited Cicero to meet him at Brindisi. Unfortunately the fears that he had entertained on the subject of Domitius were but too well founded. On the 14th of February Domitius allowed himself to be surprised and besieged in Corfinium with eighteen cohorts. This news was of course received with great consternation throughout the peninsula, but it was believed that Pompey would march at once to the relief of the besieged.

The news of the siege and impending disaster at Corfinium at last woke Pompey out of his lethargy; from this time onwards he seems to recover much of his old energy. At the risk of precipitating the Republic into anarchy and of perishing with his party in a gigantic struggle, he decided to have his revenge upon Cæsar. Calculating that the two legions which he had at Lucera were not sufficient to relieve Domitius and that a check would be disastrous to his prestige, he resisted the unanimous entreaties of his fashionable friends, who were impatient to stake all upon the relief of Domitius, and showed sufficient strength of mind to come to the most difficult of all decisions —to confess himself temporarily beaten. He counted as lost all the recruits that had been made on the coast of the Adriatic, abandoned Domitius to his fate, and took the decisive step of retiring to Greece. In view of the insufficiency of his forces he even renounced his idea of securing a hold over Sicily, and sent the Consuls the laconic order to concentrate at Brindisi with all the recruits that they had collected at Capua and all the arms which they could bring together. His calculations were justified. After a seven days' siege Domitius capitulated, while Pompey retired to Brindisi, where the fleet which was to carry him to Greece was already being collected. The surrender of Corfinium was followed by that of Sulmona. During the course of the operations another legion, the 8th, reached Cæsar from Gaul, together with twenty-two cohorts of new recruits and 300 horse sent by the King of Noricum.

The news of the fall of Corfinium caused stupefaction among the Italian upper classes. The terrible demagogue had captured five hostile Senators and a large number of knights and young nobles! But Cæsar promptly set them at liberty, restored them all the money they had on them and treated them with every indulgence. As events carried him gradually forward into a war which he had never desired, Cæsar showed an increasing desire to bring the struggle to a rapid conclusion; he hoped to force Pompey to an honourable agreement satisfactory to a public which desired and indeed clamoured for peace and was ready to adore the man who was in a position to secure it. A civil war, even on the present limited scale, was injurious to innumerable private interests. Credit had become so difficult that debtors were obliged to sell their possessions to pay their interest, thus bringing about a general reduction of prices. There was a dearth of employment and a great increase in distress, particularly at Rome with so many of the wealthy away. Cæsar was anxious at all costs to arrive at an agreement with Pompey, if possible in Italy and within a few weeks, and to conclude it in such a manner as to receive the credit for peace in the eyes of Italy. With his usual fertility of resource he wrote to Cicero to say he was ready to re-enter private life and to leave Pompey his place in the Republic, provided he was allowed to live in security. He sent the nephew of Balbus to the Consul Lentulus to beg him to return to Rome and use his efforts in favour of peace. He wrote to Oppius in Rome asking him to give out that he was not setting up to be the Sulla of the democracy, but was only anxious for a reconciliation with Pompey and his generous permission to a triumph. Finally on the 21st of February, the very day of his capture of the town, he left Corfinium, taking six legions with him, three of which formed part of the army of Gaul, the remaining three having been formed on the spot out of new recruits and the soldiers of Domitius. On his way south he set at liberty any officers and supporters of Pompey with whom he fell in along the route. On the 9th of March, after a series of forced marches, he arrived beneath the walls of Brindisi.

But Pompey had already decided for war and had made his arrangements. Recollecting at last that he had an army in Spain he had sent Vibullius Rufus to take command of it. He had also sent Domitius to Marseilles to retain that town in its allegiance; and he had despatched a part of the army with the Consuls to Epirus and was only waiting the return of their transports to cross over to join them. In the light of these preparations was peace still possible? Cæsar seems to have entertained a last glimmer of hope on the arrival of Magius with proposals from Pompey. It is possible indeed that, at this supreme moment, if Cicero had happened to be at Brindisi he might still have made efforts towards the conciliation for which he had all along been working. Unhappily the veteran writer had not responded to Pompey's invitation, on the pretext that the roads were unsafe, but in reality because he was unwilling to take part in a civil war which was as odious to him as to all sensible Italians. At the time when he should have been acting and travelling he remained on his estate at Formia in dreamy inaction, brooding over the hopes and fears of the situation. He had been deeply impressed by the clemency Cæsar had displayed at Corfinium; and he had also, most unfortunately, been flattered by the letters of Cæsar and Balbus. Though he pretended to conceal his satisfaction under a veil of distrust, he would discuss Cæsar's proposals frequently with his friends and enjoyed listening to their assurances that Cæsar was quite sincere in reckoning upon his help for the conclusion of peace.

Meanwhile the last opportunity was slipping through his fingers,

if indeed it can be said that peace was still possible. Cæsar waited for
some days for the return of Magius, and sent Titus Caninius Rebilus
into the town with equal ill-success to confer with Scribonius Libo,
an intimate friend of Pompey's. Libo's response was that Pompey
could not possibly discuss the question of peace in the absence of the
Consuls. The despatch of Magius had been a device to gain time.
Pompey was anxious for war and desired it on a great and decisive
scale. After the surrender of Corfinium Italy would be certain to
consider him as having been conquered by Cæsar, if he consented to
make peace without taking his revenge. The horror of a civil war,
and the infinite distress it was certain to involve, all this now counted
as nothing to a man intoxicated by the greatness of his position and
swayed by a blind and brutal access of egoism. The extraordinary
fortune which he had hitherto enjoyed was leading him to his ruin.
Cæsar was unable to prevent Pompey from setting sail with all his
fleet on the 17th of March. The small quarrel that had broken out
between two factions at Rome had swollen to gigantic size. The real
civil war had broken out.

CHAPTER XXVIII

THE WAR IN SPAIN, 49 B.C.

CÆSAR stopped only one day at Brindisi and then left hastily for Rome in a violent temper, telling his friends that since Pompey and his Senators asked for war to the death he would take them at their word and move at once to the attack of their stronghold in Spain. Curio and Cælius, who had been filled with admiration at his moderate behaviour hitherto, were dumbfounded to hear him talk in this fashion. But Cæsar had only too much reason for irritation. The effects of what had taken place during the last two months were so far-reaching that Italians had as yet been unable to collect their impressions; the result was a situation so obscure, so unprecedented and so utterly unforeseen that, despite his astonishing momentary success, Cæsar could not bring himself to face it with any degree of assurance. The Italian upper classes had now long been used to thinking of the Republic as on the eve of dissolution, but the truth had proved far worse than their gloomiest predictions. They had seen the Senate and the magistracies, the whole venerable edifice of the old Republican government, crumble to pieces within two months, under the blows of a few legions of trained soldiers, and its *débris* swept from the soil of Italy. It was indeed just the very suddenness and completeness of his success which filled Cæsar with dismay. He was in the perilous position of a usurper who has won one striking success over the legitimate government, thereby only provoking it to renewed exertions; he realized that after their hasty and humiliating flight Pompey and the Senate would never consent to return to Italy before they had crushed their exulting rival. No human force could now avert a civil war; and in a civil war his enemies, despite their initial failure, had far greater forces at their disposal than himself. Practically the whole of the Empire was at their command. They had supreme control of the sea; they had a large army in Spain: while they could recruit another and still more formidable force in the East. He himself on the other hand had but fourteen legions, little money and no fleet; worst of all, he had to be on his guard against the smouldering disaffection of his province. If he recalled his legions from Gaul for the civil war he would be risking the outbreak of a new Gallic rising, a dilemma upon which his adversaries placed great reliance.

Cæsar had realized from the first that his only chance of safety lay in an extreme rapidity of action, and calmer investigation only confirmed this idea. With Pompey now escaped from his clutches, his policy must be to attack the forces of his opponents, collectively so formidable, while they were still dispersed; and he would naturally begin with the army in Spain, which was threatening Gaul at close quarters. It was upon the Spanish legions that Pompey's friends based most of their hopes, and a report was even current that Pompey would shortly take command there himself to lead his troops to the reconquest of Italy. It seems that with characteristic energy Cæsar thought out a large and elaborate scheme on the road between Brindisi and Rome, which he at once began to put into execution, endeavouring through detailed instructions to make his will felt in a hundred different places at once. He placed garrisons in the principal centres of South Italy; he ordered all the coast towns to send a quota of ships to Brindisi, and to set to work upon the construction of others; all this was to be left to Hortensius and Dolabella. He at once took steps too to secure command over the corn-supplying countries nearest to Italy, ordering Quintus Valerius to proceed with one legion to Sardinia, and Curio to occupy Sicily with two legions, crossing over thence into Africa, while Dolabella was to go to Illyria. He also intended immediately on his arrival at Rome to convoke the few Senators and magistrates who remained there and restore a semblance of legitimate government. This was indeed a matter of urgent necessity both for himself and for Italy. The condition of Italy, in the anarchy in which Pompey had left it, was indeed at this moment one of his greatest embarrassments. If in a short two months he and his soldiers had been able to break down the government of the Republic, he could not build it up again with the troops that he needed for his campaign, nor yet could he leave it without any government at all. Moreover, as the weaker party, it was greatly to his interest to secure some sort of legal justification for all that he had done or intended to do: more particularly, to be authorized to carry the war into Spain, and to take the sums which he needed from the State Treasury.

Like all Cæsar's creations this plan was coherent and well thought out; but almost superhuman efforts were needed if he, with his friends and soldiers, was to carry it into execution. The difficulties it involved, social, military and political, were stupendous. Moreover, the state of public opinion, which still seemed dazed by the rapidity of events, must have appeared very alarming. It is true that circumstances had modified it slightly in his favour. On the course of his journey some of the towns which had given Pompey a brilliant reception in the preceding year now turned out to welcome Cæsar; numerous Senators whom Pompey had persuaded to leave Rome were preparing to return with the conqueror and many observers now seemed disposed to grant that Cæsar, and not Pompey, was in the right, that Cæsar had in no way provoked the conflict, and had in fact displayed a conciliatory temper all through. People were even sometimes heard exaggerating his merits and the power which he controlled, saying, for instance, that he could, if he wished, collect innumerable recruits from Gaul and had immense treasures at his command. Yet, at bottom, for Cæsar as for Pompey and all the other leaders in a struggle that they hated, Italians felt little else than distrust and indignation. The reception which was given him by the towns on his journey, friendly though it seemed, was very different from that which had been given forty years before to his uncle on his return from Africa. After all, Italy was no longer the Italy of Marius. The sons and grandsons of the nobles and landlords and downtrodden peasants who, half a century before, had been unconscious victims for the future of their country, now owned slave-worked estates in the country and houses in the towns; they had turned traders, or brokers, or opportunist politicians, or advocates and solicitors with friends in great houses, or hard-working small proprietors whose smartly dressed children were taken to school by a slave with the sons of the best families. Taken in the mass, they made up a public opinion which was selfish, exacting and incompetent, which had no understanding of the inevitability of the present situation and lived in mortal terror of a civil war. They imagined that peace was an easy matter and depended solely on the will of Cæsar and Pompey. No one understood that Cæsar had really no alternative now but to go forward; and the feeble reaction in his favour was in part determined by the hope that he would put an end to hostilities. In short, whether favourable or unfavourable, public opinion with its naïve and contradictory pretensions could not but cause him serious embarrassment.

Cæsar was able to take stock of this difficulty in an interview which he had with Cicero. Formia was on his road to Rome, and wishing at this critical moment to assure himself of the friendship of the most powerful writer of the time he paid him a visit, probably on the morning of the 28th of March. But a meeting which, had it taken place a month earlier, might have been a turning-point in the world's history was now but a futile and conventional ceremony. Cæsar made himself as agreeable as he could and invited Cicero to come to Rome to negotiate for peace. When Cicero asked if he would be free to employ any means he liked, Cæsar replied that he would never venture to impose conditions on a man of his distinction. Cicero then informed him that he was prepared to stand up in the Senate and oppose the contemplated campaign in Spain and Greece. Cæsar was obliged to tell him that this advice was useless, since he lay under the absolute necessity of conducting these campaigns with the least possible delay. "I knew it," replied Cicero, "but I could not possibly say less." The conversation was then continued in a cold and trivial strain, and after various subjects had been raised Cæsar broke it off by begging Cicero to think over his suggestion. Cicero of course promised to do so, and Cæsar set out for Rome. Still more unfavourable was the impression left on his mind by Cæsar's escort, which was composed, he told Atticus, of a crew of criminals, adventurers and bankrupts. After the interview he finally made up his mind that Cæsar and his supporters were engaged in a deliberate conspiracy for the ruin of Pompey, the confiscation of the goods of the rich and the exploitation of the State. Under these circumstances he could not think of going to the sitting of the Senate: far better make up his mind to rejoin his old friend in Greece.

On the 29th of March 48 Cæsar arrived in Rome. It was nine years since he had left it at the commencement of his Proconsulship. He might have paused to reflect on all that had happened during those eventful years, how the city itself had been changed and beautified. But he had no time now to admire the embellishments of the capital. He found the whole population, from the few Senators who had returned down to the common people, aghast at the idea that the war was to go on, at the armies which were encamping in all parts of Italy and at the revival of the memories of Marius and Sulla. He was in a serious dilemma. He was very unwilling to exasperate the upper classes in Italy and the public in general; yet he needed to set out for Spain at the earliest possible moment and to lay hands on the treasure that Pompey had so foolishly left behind. Antony and Quintus Cassius collected the few remaining Senators outside the city boundary. Cæsar pretended to be in the presence of a legitimate meeting of the Senate and delivered a moderate speech justifying his actions. He denied that he had used violence against anyone and declared that he would allow all who wished to go off to join Pompey. He proposed that ambassadors should be sent to Greece to negotiate for peace. He then delivered a similar speech to the people, gave orders for the distribution of corn and promised 300 sesterces to every citizen. All this was intended to reconcile public opinion to the Spanish campaign; but in the prevailing mood of suspicion and uncertainty it only served to intensify the discontent. It was observed that his proposal to negotiate for peace could not possibly be regarded as serious, if he did not suspend his preparations for war until the arrival of a reply. The attempt to find an ambassador proved fruitless, in face of the threats of Pompey; and the proposal was thus made to look even more insincere than it was in reality.

Nevertheless in the early days of April the Senate and Cæsar worked together with fair success to create some sort of a government out of the magistrates who had remained at Rome. It was found that Marcus Æmilius Lepidus, son of the Consul who had died in the revolution of 78 and son-in-law of Servilia, a friend of Cæsar's boyhood and now holding the Prætorship, had stayed behind at Rome owing to his relationship with Servilia and his old intimacy with Cæsar. Here was a fairly trustworthy agent, and the Senate was induced to decide that he should be acting Consul. By another senatorial decree Antony was placed at the head of the troops stationed in Italy, and further decrees ratified Cæsar's selection of Quintus Valerius for Sardinia, Curio for Sicily and Africa, Marcus Licinius Crassus for Transalpine Gaul and Dolabella for Illyricum. Thus for a time all went well. But when Cæsar went on to ask the Senate to authorize his use of the Treasury funds, the trouble broke out. Though Cæsar refused to make an open statement, everyone understood that the treasure was needed for the Spanish war. Whatever the decision of the Senate the idea that public money was to be used by one of the rivals for the prolongation of a wicked and calamitous war was highly unpopular and Lucullus Cæcilius Metellus, one of the Tribunes, went so far as to oppose his sacrosanct person against the blacksmiths and soldiers whom Cæsar sent to break the cellar doors in the Temple of Saturn, where the money was deposited; for the keys had been taken off by the Consuls in their flight. At this Cæsar lost patience; he appeared in person at the head of his soldiers and threatened to put the Tribune to death unless he instantly gave way.

Fortunately for Cæsar, Metellus had no intention of dying in defence of the law and his sacred rights. Cæsar was able to carry off 15,000 pounds in gold bullion, 35,000 pounds in silver bullion and about forty million sesterces in coin without shedding the blood of an inviolable magistrate. But the general public was profoundly moved by this exercise of violence against the most popular and the most sacred of the Republican officers. Men saw in it the first symptoms of a new Sullan tyranny. How could the old chief of the popular party now declare that he had taken up arms in defence of the rights of the Tribunes? Confiscation and pillage would soon reveal his true temper! Cæsar was so much disturbed by this change of feeling that he decided upon a speedy departure, without even waiting for a legal authorization of his campaign. All the rest that he intended to do he put off till his victorious return from Spain. He even gave up the idea of making a great speech before the people, although he had already prepared it. But one reform he still found time to carry through. In order to show the public that he had no intention of becoming a second Sulla, he made Antony propose before the Assembly the abolition of the monstrous and antiquated provision of Sulla excluding the descendants of the proscribed from the privilege of holding office. Then he left the city, six or seven days after his arrival, probably on the 6th of April, with a small escort of friends.

His short stay at Rome had in fact been rather injurious than useful to his cause. During those few days he lost in public esteem all that he had gained in the four preceding months. Many impartial observers, upon whom his moderation in January and February had made a favourable impression, now felt once more attracted towards the party of Pompey. The sincerity of Cæsar's talk of peace began to be suspected by those who actually witnessed his violence towards a Tribune and set eyes on the wretched band of adventurers by whom he was accompanied. It seemed absurd to entertain any further illusions. Most probably he and his precious confederates would not be heard of after another six months; but if by any chance he came out conqueror the old ally of Catiline would surely justify the hopes placed in him by the worst section of the Roman population. Cæsar was therefore all the more anxious for some signal success in Spain. Pompey had two legions in Lusitania under the command of his legate Marcus Petreius; he had three more in Nearer Spain under Lucius Afranius and two in Farther Spain under Varro, making a total of seven legions. True, they were only accustomed to guerilla warfare in the mountains and against barbarians. Yet they were seasoned troops and commanded by trusty and skilful generals. Pompey had sent them orders to remain upon the defensive, hoping to retain part of Cæsar's army in Gaul by threatening the passes of the Pyrenees or to compel Cæsar to the dangerous exploit of an invasion of Spain; and the three generals had formed a common plan of defence. Varro was to remain in Farther Spain with his two legions to hold down the tribes who were as yet but half subdued, while Afranius and Petreius with their united five legions were to advance as far as Lerida, a fortified town in a strong situation near the Pyrenees frontier, to await the enemy if he ventured upon an invasion. Pompey had also induced the nobles of Marseilles to refrain from assisting Cæsar. Without the aid of Marseilles, as Pompey knew very well from his war against Sertorius, it would be difficult to maintain an army in Spain, where the population would certainly be hostile to Cæsar. The conqueror of Sertorius would be fresh in their memories while the name of Cæsar was almost unknown. If the Spanish legions had not done all the service that the ingenuous strategists at Rome expected they were none the less, in conjunction with Marseilles, a formidable barrier upon Cæsar's road.

Cæsar was indeed soon brought to a halt on his march. When

probably on the 19th of April he arrived under the walls of Marseilles, he found the city gates shut and the Senate steadfastly hostile on the pretext of neutrality. As the occupation of Marseilles was necessary to carry on a vigorous campaign in Spain, Cæsar resolved at once to take it by force, and sent for three legions from Gaul. But before his soldiers came up Domitius arrived by sea, threw himself into the town and began to organize the defence. With Domitius against him the siege of Marseilles became a much longer and more difficult undertaking. Yet it was imperative for Cæsar to come to blows with the Spanish army with the least possible delay. Vexed by this unexpected rebuff and resolved to stake all upon a rapid and signal success, Cæsar suddenly decided upon two exceedingly rash enterprises. He resolved to withdraw all his troops from Gaul and to push on operations simultaneously under the walls of Marseilles and in Spain. No sooner had his three legions arrived than he commenced the siege, giving orders at the same time to the three legions which were already in the Narbonese Province under the orders of Caius Fabius and to the two last legions which remained in Gaul to proceed to Spain. Fabius was to attempt to detach the native inhabitants of the country from Pompey, while Cæsar himself continued the siege of Marseilles. With that city once in his possession, he would advance into a country already partially conquered and complete the destruction of the armies of Pompey.

So far as concerned Gaul the venture was entirely successful. Thanks to the measures that Cæsar had taken and to a fortunate conjunction of circumstances, no rising resulted in that country. With his habitual quickness and adaptability Cæsar had prepared for his action by once more exchanging his policy of violence for conciliation. Not only had he done his best to repair the damage caused by the last wars, but he had endeavoured to make peace with the surviving chiefs of the insurrectionary movement. He seems, for instance, to have succeeded in coming to a complete understanding with Commius. But he had achieved yet more. The Gallic nobles were for the most part men of the sword. A large number of the horsemen and foot soldiers who were in the pay of the rich now found themselves without employment and many of the impoverished nobles were only awaiting an opportunity for winning riches and renown. With the money from the Treasury and sums which he had borrowed from military Tribunes and Centurions, at once a useful contribution and a pledge of their fidelity, Cæsar had enrolled a force of cavalry and infantry in Gaul and taken many of the nobles into his service on the promise of restoring their confiscated possessions. He was thus able to send into Spain, in addition to his five legions, no less than 3,000 volunteers and 6,000 cavalry raised from Gaul itself. In short, he had actually succeeded in securing substantial support from the country which according to his adversaries should have been the greatest of his embarrassments.

On the other hand his efforts to bring the war to a rapid conclusion led at first to disappointing results. While he was actively continuing his siege works in Marseilles and constructing a small flotilla, Fabius had crossed the Pyrenees; but he was so easily driven back by the troops of Afranius and Petreius that one is inclined to ask whether the retreat was not a feint to tempt the enemy onwards. Fabius encamped on the banks of the Sègre a few miles from Lerida and began to scatter large sums of money through the town and the neighbouring country to detach the population from Pompey's cause. Although the two legions had now already joined him, he remained on the defensive awaiting the fall of Marseilles.

But the whole of May passed, and Marseilles still held out. This unexpected delay very nearly led to a catastrophe in Italy. The reaction in favour of Pompey, which had begun after Cæsar's departure, was steadily gathering force. The resistance of Marseilles had at first been regarded by Pompey's party merely as a poor compensation for the loss of Sicily, which had been abandoned by Cato and successfully occupied by Curio. But as the weeks went on it began to be thought that Cæsar's simultaneous operations before Marseilles and in Spain could not possibly succeed. The strangest rumours were in circulation; it was said that Pompey had marched across through Illyria and Germany to encounter Cæsar in Gaul. There were other reasons too why the public should be dissatisfied, not least the extraordinary behaviour of Antony.

Antony was the last descendant of one of the noblest families in Rome; yet in some ways he seems more of a typical plebeian than an aristocrat. A regular barbarian, of great physical vigour and powers of enjoyment, a great eater and drinker, jovial, courageous and bloodthirsty, brought up in a primitive independence, removed from all family and social traditions, first among the lowest haunts in Rome and then in the camp, and thus utterly indifferent to the opinions of others, he was gifted by nature with a fair intelligence, a good measure of astuteness and a considerable insight into the more elementary passions of human nature; he could plot and counterplot like the rest and use the ordinary weapons of flattery and intimidation; but he was utterly innocent of any general ideas and had no notion of using his abilities for any other object than the satisfaction of his personal passions. Left by Cæsar the practical master of Italy, he had scandalized even his hardened contemporaries by the shameless licence of his manner of life, keeping a harem of both sexes at Rome, and travelling through the country with Cithæris, a Greek courtesan, in his litter. It is true that such scandals had been seen before in Italy; but Antony's conduct produced an exceptional effect at this moment, when public opinion was particularly impressionable. Several Senators left Rome in disgust; and a rumour was trumpeted abroad, not without reason, that Cicero was anxious to follow their example. Antony was seriously annoyed and he could think of no better remedy than to bring pressure upon Cicero, at first in a politely worded letter and then in more outspoken terms, to remain in Italy.

Unfortunately towards the end of May the war took a still more unfavourable turn for Cæsar. Marseilles was still holding out and Fabius was unsuccessful in his solicitations. The people of Spain remained obstinately faithful to Pompey, partly owing to his reputation in that country, partly to the five legions of Afranius and Petreius, and partly also to the rumours that were skilfully set in circulation. One story was that Pompey was on the point of landing in Africa with a large army. Fabius was soon in great straits for the supplies and began to be afraid that he would be obliged to retreat. Some striking victory was necessary to win Cæsar the support of the Spanish tribes and to induce them to bring in food to his troops, rather than to those of Pompey.

Cæsar therefore decided to take an extreme step—to leave Decimus Brutus and Trebonius at Marseilles and take command of the Spanish army in person to bring about an engagement. Towards the middle of June he left the besieged city with an escort of 900 cavalry, crossed the Pyrenees, rejoined his army, and at once advanced to Lerida, where Afranius was encamped on a hill, and offered him battle. But Afranius, who was aware of the critical position of his adversary, refused to fight. Cæsar was compelled to force the enemy to an engagement. He discovered a small height situated between Lerida and the hill where Afranius was encamped and commanding Afranius' communications with the town and the stone bridge over the Sègre. One day he suddenly detached three legions to make an assault upon this position. But Afranius and Petreius were on their guard. They sent out their cohorts, and after a sanguinary hand-to-hand struggle Cæsar's legionaries were repulsed at the foot of the rise. The check must have been a serious one, for Cæsar, although previously so anxious for an engagement, no longer attempted to take the offensive. Its consequences were soon apparent. The Spanish country towns which Fabius had won over to Cæsar ceased to send in supplies, and provisioning became a matter of difficulty. Cæsar's embarrassments were increased by a sudden flood of the rivers between which he was encamped, carrying away the bridges. The army was soon reduced to the condition in which it had been under the walls of Alesia, in the clutches of the invisible enemy, famine. Within a few days the situation had become almost desperate.

The news of the great danger in which Cæsar was placed spread very rapidly through the whole Roman world and reached Rome, of course, in considerably exaggerated form. At the same time favourable reports of Pompey arrived from Thessalonica. He was making active preparations for war, and was collecting a numerous fleet, provided by the allied states in the East, which he had put under the command of Bibulus. He had recalled one legion from Cilicia to attach it to the five legions he had brought over from Italy; he was recruiting another from amongst the Roman soldiers who had settled in Greece or Macedonia, and two more were being raised in Asia by Lentulus. He had instructed Scipio to send him two from Syria, and by holding out offers of pay he was enrolling cavalry, slingers and archers from amongst Gauls, Germans, Galatians, Cappadocians, Dardanians and Bessi; he was imposing a tribute or the obligation of furnishing military contingents upon the towns of Asia and Syria, the kings and chiefs of the East, and the great Italian trading companies which did business in the East. He would shortly be master of the sea, commander of a formidable army, and at the head of a coalition of all the Eastern states under the protectorate of Rome. This news did not fail to influence the public, which already inclined to Pompey's side, and many of the Senators left for Greece, without Antony being able to interfere with their departure. Cicero had already set sail from Formia on the 7th of June, his fears and hesitations at length subdued. He was angry at the domineering tone adopted towards him by Antony and felt remorse at having allowed Pompey to go off alone on his adventure. He had little confidence in a victory and he realized the full risks of the enterprise; but, when he felt certain that Cæsar was deliberately provoking a war against his friend and benefactor, the writer of the *De Republica* could not display cowardice and ingratitude. It was in vain that his wife begged him at least to wait for the conclusion of the Spanish War.

Cæsar was thus once more in an extremely perilous situation. But fortune again came to his rescue. Towards the middle of July, Decimus Brutus gained a considerable victory over the fleet of Marseilles, and the news of this success, which seemed to make the fall of the city inevitable, was exaggerated by the emissaries of Cæsar and caused some dismay among the natives of Spain, particularly those who lived between the Ebro and the Pyrenees. They expected that the legions which were besieging Marseilles would shortly be crossing the Pyrenees, and that a victory for Cæsar was now assured. Many of them therefore abandoned the cause of Pompey and began to send into Cæsar's camp the supplies which they had been furnishing to Afranius and Petreius. The famine crossed over from one camp to the other and Cæsar was thus almost miraculously saved. The lack of supplies soon forced Afranius and Petreius to prepare to break up their camp and retire across the mountainous district towards Octogesa, then crossing the Ebro and taking refuge among the friendly tribes of Celtiberia. When he heard of their intention Cæsar at once made arrangements for pursuit. Calculating that it would be a slow business to take his army over the weak wooden bridges which crossed the Sègre, he conceived the idea of reducing the size of the river by constructing basins and canals by its banks, thus forming an artificial ford which his soldiers could cross on foot. The troops took pick and shovel and set cheerfully to work; but their labours were still only half completed when the enemy got wind of them and hastily began their retreat. The river was still flowing deep and strong and Afranius and Petreius were in full flight. Cæsar hesitated a moment; then he had all work suspended, drove his army into the ford and crossed the river without losing a man. Once out of the dangerous island he might have attacked Afranius and Petreius on their march, but fearing that the Spanish legions might fight with the courage of despair, he preferred to work for a bloodless capitulation. Throwing his legions, unimpeded by baggage, across the hills and the valleys by a long irregular route and by forced marches, he forged ahead of the enemy's army as it continued its retreat on the high road to Octogesa. Arriving before them at a gorge in the hills through which the road passed, he forced the enemy to retrace their steps in the direction of Lerida; and as soon as they were on the march he advanced on their heels, harassing the stragglers and cutting off supplies. Afranius and Petreius used all their efforts to save the army; but their soldiers rose against them and they were forced to surrender on the 2nd of August.

Cæsar was magnanimous in his conditions. He allowed them all both their life and their money; the soldiers were free to go where they wished, either to retreat to Pompey or to take service under Cæsar's standard, or to re-enter private life. Some time afterwards Varro, who had remained with two legions in Farther Spain, capitulated without a battle. His two legions joined the standard of Cæsar, and the whole of Spain was thus in the power of the Proconsul of Gaul. Cæsar held a sort of Diet at Cordova, made a great number of Spaniards Roman citizens, and imposed a considerable money tribute; then he passed on to Cadiz, which he gave the rights of a Roman city, and thence by sea to Tarragona, leaving Quintus Cassius with four legions to administer the country. He left Spain by land for Marseilles, where he arrived towards the end of September. Here he learned that about the middle of August Marcus Lepidus had made use of the impression produced by his success in Spain to nominate him Dictator. He had done so by passing a law through the Assembly authorizing him to act with the powers of a Consul—an arrangement which had probably been agreed upon beforehand between Lepidus and Cæsar. Cæsar distrusted the Senators who remained behind at Rome and did not wish that the elections for 48 should be presided over in the absence of the Consuls by an *interrex* nominated by them. As Dictator he would, of course, preside over them himself.

CHAPTER XXIX

PHARSALIA, 48 B.C.

For Lepidus and the remnant of the Senate which remained at Rome Cæsar's Dictatorship perhaps provided a welcome means of withdrawing from the alarming responsibilities which were crowding in upon them. Since Cæsar's departure Italy had passed through a time of frightful distress. The suspension of public payments, which had been decreed by the Senate simultaneously with the *tumultus*, the exhaustion of the Treasury, which Cæsar had emptied and from which Pompey was cutting off the tribute of Asia, the interruption of public works, the sudden departure from Italy of a large number of the wealthier citizens, the requisition of all the ships necessary for the transport of troops and supplies, the enormous forced loans that Pompey had raised from the temples of Italy, the recruiting of a large part of the youth of the country, the interruption of normal electoral and political activity, all these had combined to provoke an economic crisis of the gravest character. Trade, in all its branches, was almost at a standstill; the middle class missed the profits it drew from its trained slaves and freedmen, while at Rome especially a large number of artisans and small traders felt the lack of employment. Corn was scarce; bankers and capitalists refused to give loans, for fear of a revolution which might end in the abolition of debts: and money was therefore almost unobtainable. Debtors who had hitherto paid their debts or their interest at fixed seasons, by contracting new debts to pay them, found it impossible to borrow; fathers were no longer in a position to pay the dowries they had promised to their daughters, nor divorced husbands to pay them back as the law required. At Rome and throughout Italy landlords of houses were unable to collect their rents, debtors and creditors were at one another's throats, and many were obliged to sell all that they had if they were lucky enough to find a buyer. But there were many offers and few to take them. Prices fell to an unprecedented level, whether for gold or silver ware, or jewels or stuffs or furniture or land or houses. The decree of the Senate in 51, reducing the rate of interest, afforded little alleviation;

for most people were in such straits that they continued to pile up debts on any conditions imposed upon them by the capitalists, and took no notice of a decree which seems universally to have been regarded as a dead letter. Thus the great question of debt became more and more urgent. Lepidus, the acting Consul, was a man of forty-one, of no great capacity or influence in the State, who had only been prominent in politics hitherto during the unfortunate interregnum which followed on the death of Clodius, and he gladly threw off the whole responsibility of his position upon Cæsar.

Unfortunately Cæsar, who was now returning in all haste to Italy, was hardly in a position to face new difficulties with equanimity. In spite of his remarkable success in Spain his prospects were still very precarious. It is true that, when all hopes of reinforcements from Spain had disappeared, Marseilles had finally capitulated and consented to pay a large indemnity. But in Africa and Illyria Cæsar's party had suffered two serious reverses. Curio, who had ventured into Africa with only two legions, although Cæsar had sent him two more, had paid dear for his rashness. He had at first easily defeated Actius Varus, Cæsar's victim in Picenum, who had fled into Africa to recruit a small army; but he had then been entrapped into an ambush by Pompey's ally Juba, King of Numidia, where he had been surrounded and killed. Only a few stragglers from his little army had found their way back to Italy. Meanwhile Dolabella, who had proceeded with a part of the fleet to attempt the conquest of Illyria, had been severely defeated at sea by Marcus Octavius and Lucius Scribonius Libo. He had then appealed to Antony for reinforcements. Antony sent him the fleet under Hortensius and the three legions which were garrisoning the coast towns under the command of Sallust, Basilus, and his brother Caius; but these reinforcements had been repulsed and Caius himself made prisoner with fifteen cohorts. Illyria and Africa thus remained in the power of the enemy. The advantage that Cæsar had secured from the two legions of Varro and the recruits who had come over from Afranius and Petreius was cancelled by losses of greater importance; and, what was more serious still, a part of the fleet had been destroyed just at the moment when Cæsar most needed it for carrying the war into the East; for the land route to Macedonia was cut off by the defeat in Illyria.

But the difficulties of transport, whether by land or sea, were perhaps the least of those which the new campaign presented. Pompey had collected a force of some 50,000 men, against which Cæsar had only twelve legions, and those so weary after their hardships that the six which returned from Spain by forced marches dropped invalids at every stage and their total after all losses was hardly above 25,000. It would really have been advisable, from the military point of view, to close up the ranks by reducing the number of the legions; but this would have involved cutting off some of the posts for officers, *tribuni militum* and centurions, which Cæsar had always endeavoured to maintain as an avenue of promotion for the best of the common soldiers. Moreover Albania, Macedonia and Greece were poor countries where an army, however small, could not subsist for long unless supported by supplies from oversea—from Egypt or Sardinia or Sicily or the Chersonese. Pompey's command of the sea would enable him to capture the corn-ships, and might reduce Cæsar to the same straits as Sulla during his Mithridatic campaign. Worst of all, Cæsar was short of money, and the war promised to be enormously costly. Almost the whole of the money from the Treasury and from Gaul had been expended in Spain in gifts to the natives. Under these circumstances he could not help asking himself whether his soldiers, hitherto so faithful, would continue to follow him upon this last and most hazardous adventure. One legion had just mutinied at Piacenza and refused to advance unless it received the rewards promised at Brindisi. Cæsar had been so much disquieted by this revolt that he had threatened the rebellious legion with decimation, though he had afterwards yielded to the appeals of his officers and had only punished twelve soldiers whom he pretended to select by lot; in reality, at least so it was believed at the time, he had arranged things in such a way as to select those whom the centurions pointed out as the ringleaders.

Immediately on Cæsar's arrival at Rome his father-in-law and the most influential members of his party begged him to send ambassadors to Pompey. Cæsar would gladly have consented, if he had entertained the slightest hope of their success. He was aware of the difficulties of an Eastern campaign, and the danger of the indefinite continuance of civil war. But he knew that Pompey would listen to no terms, and that his only chance lay in a speedy and vigorous prosecution of the campaign. Thus it was that, partly out of anxiety to put an end to a time of dangerous suspense, partly out of a confidence in sudden and unexpected action confirmed by recent events, he prepared perhaps the most daring of all the surprises of his career. His scheme was to be nominated Consul for 48, and then, at the opening of the year, when he could enter upon his province as the legitimate representative of the Republic, to embark all his troops, without slaves and with the least possible encumbrance, so as to be able to land them at any creek on the coast, without using a harbour; to leave a small garrison of Gallic and Spanish horse to defend Italy, to venture across the sea in midwinter when he would be least expected, and then to face the enemy blindly trusting to fortune and the valour of his men. Before Pompey had recovered from the surprise of his sudden appearance in Epirus, he would offer him terms of peace as legitimate Consul; there was no knowing if he would not accept them. While still on his way to Rome, without divulging his plan even to his intimates, he sent on to Brindisi his twelve legions and all the ships that he could requisition from Italian harbours; and he began to collect war stores as though he were preparing a campaign at leisure in the spring.

But Cæsar could not go on straight to Brindisi without stopping for a few days in Rome, to assume the Dictatorship and to make the most necessary provisions for the ordinary administration. He entered Rome towards the end of November, and stayed there eleven days, perhaps the most crowded even in his crowded life. He presided over the elections, which of course resulted favourably to his party; he was elected Consul with Publius Servilius Vatia, son of the Isauricus under whom Cæsar had fought as a boy, while the new Prætors were Cælius, Trebonius, Quintus Pedius, son of one of his nieces, and perhaps Caius Vibius Pansa. He presided over the Latin holidays; he caused various magistrates to propose to the people the recall of many of those condemned by Pompey's laws in 52 and earlier, amongst others Gabinius, but not Milo; he passed a law granting citizen rights to the whole of Cisalpine Gaul; and he attempted also to deal in some way with the question of debt.

His action in this last question is one of the most important episodes in Cæsar's life, both in itself and for the consequences to which it led. The desperate competition for wealth in which all

Italy was engaged had ended, as it seems that such competition always will end, in a gigantic accumulation of vested interests, which it needed nothing less than a revolution, a cataclysm, to break down. Enormous loans had been contracted at exorbitant rates of interest for the improvement of agriculture and industry or the promotion of a high standard of comfort and culture. These debts were steadily accumulating, and it was impossible for Italy to shake them off. Not even the spoils of a second Gaul or Asia would have sufficed. Yet the age of expansion seemed definitely closed; before long there would be no more unexpected importations of gold and silver captured in war; debtors could place little hope in legislative assistance, and would soon be forced to meet their claims by their own efforts. When this point was reached the liquidation of this immense mass of debt would automatically follow. Yet the injury such a liquidation would entail to the whole structure of Italian life was appalling to contemplate. There were many upper-class families who might still manage to keep afloat by playing off their creditors against their debtors and reducing their scale of living. Not so the middle class. The houses they had built and the slaves they had bought and trained with so much care during the last twenty years would pass into the hands of a small group of capitalist creditors, and with them would disappear the industrious and intelligent bourgeoisie which had been slowly formed during the last half-century. The progress of this class is really the central feature in the history of Cæsar's time. On its prosperity the future of Italy depended, and its ruin would have meant the stifling of all her nascent energies. The fate of this class depended entirely upon the solution of the problem of debt; and this solution could only be achieved by one of those revolutionary strokes which recur periodically in the history of nations. There was no other way out. This is proved by what happened seven years later, when under far less favourable conditions, entailing much greater hardship and suffering, the abolition of debt was finally adopted, like a surgical operation which is the more dangerous and painful the longer it has been delayed.

It is often said that in a great historical crisis a man of genius can divine the future course of events and drive the reluctant multitude along it, thus saving a whole nation by his own single-handed exer-

tions. If this were true, Cæsar, who was indisputably a man of genius,
would have done so now. He had not shrunk from the most revolutionary action when his own life was endangered. He would not have
shrunk from any measures, however high-handed, that were necessary,
had he only known it, to save, not himself, but the combined labour
of a whole generation, the civilization of his people, the spiritual
future of Europe. But Cæsar could see no farther than the other men
of his day; and he acted, like all politicians, according to the impressions and the needs of the moment. In his ambition to win the place
and authority of Pompey, as the controlling personality at Rome, it
was to his interest to appear rigidly law-abiding, to avoid vexing or
frightening the upper classes, the rich knights and capitalists, the
landholding aristocracy and the wealthy members of the middle class.
Ever since he crossed the Rubicon the moneyed classes had accused
him of meditating *novæ tabulæ*, the Abolition of debt. They remembered the pillaging of forty years ago, in the great Democratic upheaval,
and they lived in dread of a wholesale spoliation. They found allies,
curiously enough, among those in their own station of life who were
themselves most deeply in debt. These timid Epigoni of Catiline
shrank from the far-reaching disturbance that Abolition would entail.
They hated the popular party on whose banner it stood inscribed;
they were many of them at the mercy of capitalists who had lent them
money; they shared the strange respect, almost amounting to adoration, which the rich seem destined to inspire; they feared that the
abolition of debt would be merely a prelude to the confiscation of
lands; and they clung to that abstract sentiment of justice which is
often so lively in educated persons and makes them so ill-disposed to
anything savouring of revolution. All these various apprehensions
had been confirmed by Cæsar's nomination to the Dictatorship, with
its memories of Sulla's spoliation at the close of the last civil war.
Cæsar therefore desired to show the rich that he intended before all
to respect the rights of property. Following the precedent set under
similar conditions in the cities of Greece, and imitated by Cicero in
Cilicia, he adopted an ingenious if unpractical device which many
modern admirers of Cæsar, in their contempt for Cicero, have denounced as ridiculous. Debtors were to hand over their goods not at
the existing prices but at what they would have fetched before the

civil war; if creditors and debtors failed to arrive at an agreement about the price arbitrators were to be called in to settle it; the interest already paid was to be subtracted from the capital. It seems that to avoid unpleasant discussions in the Assembly Cæsar sanctioned this arrangement by his own authority as Dictator. He also attempted to bring capital forcibly into circulation by putting an old and long-forgotten law into operation, forbidding persons to keep more than 60,000 sesterces in gold or silver in their houses; and he made a last concession to public opinion by abdicating his Dictatorship at the end of the eleven days, since it was useless to him after the elections. Then he left Rome amidst the plaudits of the people, who seized the opportunity of his departure to make demonstrations in favour of peace. It was still generally hoped that a settlement was in sight.

Cæsar on the other hand was firm in his resolve to precipitate an issue. The ships he had collected were only enough to carry a little more than half his troops, and to make a second journey was perilous. But he refused to wait. He appeared at Brindisi unexpectedly in December, called together his soldiers, told them his plan, made them new and more tempting promises. He then embarked 15,000 men, without corn or slaves or beasts of burden and with only the light baggage that a legionary can carry at the end of his spear. The rest of the troops he left with Gabinius, Fufius Calenus and Antony, with orders to embark them as soon as the ships returned. On the 4th of January 48, he put out to sea, taking with him the young Asinius Pollio and his subordinates Cneius Domitius Calvinus, Publius Vatinius, Publius Sulla, the unfortunate Consul of 65, Lucius Cassius and Caius Calvisius Sabinus. His calculations proved correct. The enemy had not expected him to embark before spring. Bibulus was caught napping. His ships lay rocking on the grey Adriatic in the cold and threatening winter weather, while his sailors sat chattering round the tavern fires in port. When he learnt that the enemy had put out from Brindisi, Cæsar and his army had already landed in a lonely creek near Oricum.

Once safely on shore Cæsar entered upon a twofold policy of conciliation and aggression. He at once sent an ambassador to propose peace once more to Pompey, who was at this moment taking his troops from Macedonia to Durazzo into winter quarters. At the same time he endeavoured to seize the whole coast up to Durazzo, the most important port in that region. His object was to keep open every possible chance of peace, and at the same time to take possession of a huge tract of country, including several towns, from which he could draw not merely corn, but also beasts of burden, leather, wood, iron and necessary implements. He had no difficulty in seizing Oricum and Apollonia, where the small garrisons of Italians were discouraged by the attitude of the natives, who favoured the invader, not because his name was Cæsar but because he was legitimate Consul; but he failed to take Durazzo. Learning on his way that Cæsar had landed and divining his intentions, Pompey advanced his army by forced marches and threw himself into the city before him. Cæsar then encamped on the banks of the Apsus, a small stream to the south of Durazzo, to await the effect of his sudden appearance and the reply to his advances. Pompey and his army were on the opposite bank of the river.

The two rivals were at last face to face, but, as Cæsar had feared, peace was as far off as ever. As soon as Pompey's camp had recovered from the inconvenience of the hasty march, his intimates Lucceius, Theophilus of Mitylene and Libo submitted to him the proposals brought by Cæsar's ambassador. Pompey cut them short at once with an objection to which there was no reply. "I cannot return to Italy by the grace of Cæsar." On the other hand Cæsar's attempted surprise had turned out a failure. Bibulus, not to be caught a second time, had sent Libo with fifty ships to blockade the port of Brindisi, and was keeping careful watch over the sea, despite the inclemency of the season. The troops Cæsar had left behind him in Italy were thus unable to cross and Cæsar found himself isolated with 15,000 men against an enemy almost three times his number. It was hardly likely that Pompey and the Roman aristocrats in his camp would be ready to conclude peace at a moment when Cæsar, who had rashly ventured out of Italy with but a weak force at his disposal, was practically at their mercy. Cæsar was left with no alternative but to alter his plans once more—to send his soldiers into winter quarters, to wait till the rest of his troops could somehow reach him from Brindisi, to seize the country behind him, sending out skirmishing parties on all sides to fetch in supplies, and to keep a careful watch over the coast in order to prevent the fleet of Bibulus from watering and thus obliging it to undertake long and frequent journeys to Corfu, when it would be easier for his ships to slip across from Brindisi. For the fleets of antiquity the taking in of fresh water was a vital need: it bound down their movements to certain points on the mainland.

But would not Pompey take advantage of his numerical superiority and force the enemy to give battle? That was the advice of the majority of officers in his camp. But Pompey had not the untiring nervous resistance of his adversary; the short-lived energy he had displayed before and after his retreat across the Adriatic had once more deserted him, and he seems to have been utterly worn out by the hardships and anxieties inseparable from a civil war in which a single defeat means the break-up of a whole party and army. During all this campaign he is no longer the powerful, if prudent, strategist of the Mithridatic war, but a changed and feebler man. His characteristic aristocratic defects of slowness and irresolution clung to him all through; he seems almost like a man with a disease of doubt, unable to come to even the smallest decision, pleading continually for patience, for consideration, for delay. With a morose and brooding vanity which he thought a mark of strength, but which was really the weakness of exhaustion, he withdrew from the life of the camp and kept his own counsel. The camp as a whole was left to govern itself. It is easy to imagine to what a chaos it was soon reduced, crowded as it was with a motley assemblage of Roman Senators and financiers of all ages and temperaments, with Oriental monarchs and barbarian chieftains. The great personages from Rome, weary of the privations they had been forced to tolerate and of the difficulties to which they had been reduced after lending Pompey all the money they had been able to collect, were impatient to return to Italy, and they emphasized their complaints with threats of vengeance and confiscation which struck the good Cicero with dismay. They regarded one another with unconcealed distrust; they quarrelled over petty points of personal precedence; and they flung accusations of treachery broadcast from morning till night. After all they had nothing better to do. Afranius and Cicero had been received in the camp with distrust and almost with contempt. Atticus himself, who had remained at Rome, was threatened with reprisals as though he were a deserter. Those who, like Brutus, took no interest in the war and stayed reading in their tents could be treated still more lightly. In this temper they were naturally impatient to precipitate a battle. But Pompey paid no attention to their appeals. He listened only to the advice of a few intimate friends, who endeavoured to check the arrival of reinforcements, continued to keep the army under discipline, hastily recalled Scipio from Asia and, instead of attacking Cæsar on the spot, preferred to wait till famine had decimated his forces, in the hope of inflicting a more crushing defeat.

Thus week succeeded week, and nothing of importance took place. In Cæsar's camp supplies became scantier and scantier, and he received neither news nor reinforcements from Italy. Cæsar began to grow anxious. He had failed in his design of surprising the enemy; on the other hand peace was impossible and his commissariat was insecure. To extricate himself from this imbroglio he needed either the immediate arrival of his 10,000 soldiers from Italy or else a victory. Could Gabinius, Antonius and Calenus succeed in crossing the sea, and if so, when? Fortunately, at this juncture, Bibulus died, and Pompey, with his usual indecision, nominated no one in his place. The fleet broke up into numerous small squadrons each of which operated separately in different parts of the Adriatic. As the spring approached there were several occasions on which the wind was favourable. Nevertheless the three generals were so afraid of crossing the Adriatic in the teeth of the Pompeian fleet that they refused to embark. Cæsar became more and more anxious; he began to fear treachery and wrote severe despatches to Calenus and Antony. It is even said that he one day attempted to cross alone on a small ship to Brindisi.

Under the pressure of these repeated appeals the three generals at last decided to act. They divided their forces. Gabinius with fifteen cohorts resolved to attempt the land journey and to pass through Dalmatia to join Cæsar in Albania, while Calenus and Antony ventured to cross by sea. One day the two armies which were encamped opposite one another on the gulf of Durazzo saw a numerous fleet of vessels approaching with a good south wind behind them. There was a general rush to the shore, and it was soon ascertained that the fleet was Antony's. Coponius, the Pompeian admiral who commanded the fleet which lay at anchor in the port of Durazzo sallied out with his ships; and the two squadrons disappeared towards the north. Skirmishers went out from the two camps to learn the news, and the troops were kept under arms and ready to march. Cæsar must have gone through some hours of terrible anxiety. For his fate depended entirely upon the wind. But before long he learnt that, thanks to a favourable breeze, Antony had been able to disembark his four legions almost in their entirety in a small bay not far from Alessio. Pompey and Cæsar at once made for this place with part of their armies and by different routes. Pompey was anxious to defeat Antony before he could join Cæsar, and Cæsar to join Antony and return in safety with his reinforcements. Cæsar arrived first and successfully united his forces; and Pompey was forced to retire southwards towards Durazzo, encamping his troops at Asparagium.

Antony and Calenus brought Cæsar anything but cheering news from Italy. The debt question, which Cæsar thought he had settled by ingenious manipulation, had become more acute than ever after his departure, and seemed on the point of provoking something like a miniature civil war within the ranks of his own party. Cælius, the clever but unbalanced friend of Cicero, who was the son of a banker at Pozzuoli, a Conservative by party and the rival of Catullus in the affections of Lesbia, had been induced by the pressure of his debts and the spur of ambition to propose two laws, one dispensing tenants with the payment of arrears of rent, and another simply abolishing debts altogether. The Consul and Trebonius had opposed them, and disorders had resulted. Milo, who had returned from Marseilles in agreement with Cælius, had recruited bands of gladiators and slaves in southern Italy, and attempted to provoke an insurrection. Finally both Milo and Cælius had been defeated and killed by the Gallic and Spanish cavalry whom Cæsar had left behind to protect Italy.

Cæsar was all the more anxious to bring operations to a rapid conclusion. The war seemed to bring out, in him as in Pompey, the characteristic defects of their qualities. While Pompey was a prey to something like a mania of doubt, Cæsar, always prone to feats of daring, now allowed himself to be carried away by fantastic conceptions of strategy which almost bordered on madness. Difficulties of commissariat impelled him, too, to try to finish the war whatever the risk. He sent Lucius Cassius to Thessaly with a newly recruited legion, Caius Calvisius Sabinus into Ætolia with five cohorts, and Cneius Domitius Calvinus into Macedonia with two legions. Calvinus' orders were to procure corn and to face Scipio, who was moving up and down Asia raising money everywhere, even to the appropriation of considerable deposits left in the temples. Cæsar then moved close up to Pompey and several times offered him battle, but always in vain. Pompey was, of course, as anxious to temporize as Cæsar was anxious to fight. Cæsar then attempted to entice his enemy out by placing himself, after a quick and skilful march, between Pompey's camp and his base at Durazzo. But Pompey still refused to give battle and merely changed the position of his camp, placing it in a spot called Petra on the hills of the Gulf of Durazzo in such a way as to command the coast and communicate by sea with the town.

Cæsar could now no longer control his impatience. Ever since his success at Alesia he had been as confident of victory with the spade as with the sword, and he now adopted the most singular and unprecedented tactics—nothing less than to imprison the enemy between a huge earthwork and the sea, hoping thus to force him to a sortie. His troops took pick and shovel and set to the familiar task. Pompey's soldiers replied by constructing a rampart strengthened with towers on the model of Cæsar's; and soon a campaign of surprises and skirmishing began around these earthworks. Cæsar harassed the army of Pompey by cutting off its water, by preventing it from sending its horses out to pasture, and by enclosing it in a narrow and unhealthy angle of ground. But instead of marching out and giving battle Pompey embarked his cavalry for Durazzo and endeavoured to diminish Cæsar's strength by a policy of passive resistance. Last year's harvest in Epirus and Macedonia was by now exhausted: the Pompeian fleet, now divided into four squadrons commanded by Caius Cassius, Cneius Pompeius, Marcus Octavius and Decimus Lælius, prevented all provisioning by sea; and Cæsar's soldiers were soon forced to live on roots. The whole of the Empire fixed its anxious gaze upon this corner of Epirus, where, in a campaign without battles, a desperate and obstinate conflict was at last being fought out. Which of the two armies could hold out the longer? Cæsar's troops were soon reduced to so pitiful a condition that he himself gave secret instructions to Scipio to interpose for the conclusion of peace. One day, however, one of the ordinary skirmishes round the entrenchments developed by accident into a regular battle, in which Cæsar's exhausted soldiers were severely defeated. Cæsar left 1,000 dead on the field and lost thirty-two ensigns.

If Pompey had only pressed home his success this battle might have proved Cæsar's death-blow. But he refused to run any risks. Satisfied with what he had already achieved, he led his victorious cohorts back into camp. Nevertheless it was a very serious check for Cæsar. Many people began to say that the skill which he had displayed in his campaigns against barbarians would not suffice against a general like Pompey, who had won campaign after campaign from Sulla's civil wars down to the capture of Jerusalem. To crown his misfortunes, news came at this moment that Gabinius had failed to break through to Albania after losing many soldiers on the way in skirmishes with the native Illyrians. He had succeeded in saving Salona, which was being besieged by Marcus Octavius, but there he had fallen ill, and after his death the remains of his small army had dispersed. It would indeed have been disastrous for Cæsar if the confidence of his soldiers and their hope of future recompense had failed him at this moment. In reality, however, his defeat at Durazzo was of great use to him. It calmed the excitement in which he had of late been living and forced him to abandon his fantastic siegeworks and to lead his army into a less desolate region to join Domitius Calvinus and Lucius Cassius, who had meanwhile been fighting against Scipio in Macedonia. Some days after his defeat, towards the end of June, after reassuring his soldiers with new promises, he set out on his retreat for Thessaly, leaving the wounded behind at Apollonia under the care of four cohorts. If Pompey had started immediately in pursuit he might still have overtaken and crushed him. But Pompey as usual preferred to temporize, and his friends and intimates were divided in counsel. Some wished immediately to follow up the enemy, others to return to Italy, others to continue the tactics hitherto pursued. Pompey finally decided to leave Cato and Cicero at Durazzo with fifteen cohorts to protect the baggage, and himself to follow slowly on the heels of the enemy hoping to wear him down by famine, even after he had joined forces with Calvinus.

Cæsar's fate now depended entirely on the patience of his enemy. The two armies marched into Thessaly and drew up opposite to one another in the plain of Pharsalia. Pompey had now joined forces with Scipio, and the tiresome operations which had been going on for the last six months seemed about to recommence. But the Roman nobles, elated by their victory at Durazzo and impatient to return home, were anxious to finish off the campaign. The leading Pompeians could not conceal their contempt for a war in which the sole object appeared to be to avoid giving battle. They told Pompey plainly that he had grown so old and feeble that he did not dare to attack an already conquered foe whose forces were hardly half his own. They set every artifice at work to force their unhappy general to an engagement. Worn out and disgusted by continual criticism, he allowed himself at last to be persuaded to offer battle on the 9th of August in the plain of Pharsalia. He ranged his cohorts in three lines with his right flank on the Enipeus and placed all his cavalry on the left flank. His plan was to throw his horse upon the less numerous cavalry of Cæsar, and thus to break through his right flank. Cæsar marched out the eighty cohorts which were left to him (two others were protecting the camp) and ranged them in three lines. But when he saw the whole of the enemy's cavalry massed on the left he withdrew six cohorts from the third line, and made a fourth line, which he placed on the left flank behind the cavalry so as to help it to repulse any turning movement from Pompey's side. He put Antony on the left wing, Calvinus in the centre, Publius Sulla on the right, himself remaining on the right wing to face Pompey. Then he moved up his first two lines. But the enemy stood firm. Pompey's cavalry then endeavoured to turn Cæsar's right wing, but Cæsar's cavalry, strengthened by the six cohorts of the fourth line, at first stood its ground, then gradually moved forward to the attack, and ended by putting the enemy's cavalry to flight. The six cohorts of the fourth line, finding the road open, repulsed the left wing of Pompey's army and menaced it in the rear. Cæsar at once made use of his opportunity to withdraw the two first lines, which had borne the brunt of the fighting, and brought up his third line, which was still fresh. Pompey's troops were now forced to give way. At this point a general with ordinary presence of mind would at once have arranged for an orderly retreat, fighting his way back to camp, the great fortress which every Roman army always held in its rear. But it was Pompey, not Cæsar, who had to meet the situation. When he saw his wing attacked in the rear and the enemy also massed on his front, he lost his nerve, abandoned the command and fled almost unaccompanied into camp, crying out to the soldiers who guarded it to defend him. Thus left to themselves, the cohorts could not be expected to retire in good order, and a regular rout ensued. Cæsar then moved to the attack of the camp, which was but feebly defended. Pompey, who had retired into his tent, was roused by cries announcing the approach of the enemy, but leaping on horseback he escaped with a few friends by the back gate and galloped off on the road to Larissa. He was no longer in the age to resist what was the first real battle he had had to face since his campaign against Mithridates. On the loss of the camp Pompey's army dispersed; a certain number of cohorts retired with their officers on the road to Larissa; others fled hither and thither in the mountains. Cæsar's losses were small, while Pompey's, though greater, were probably exaggerated later. Amongst the dead was Lucius Domitius Aheno-barbus. The terrible conflict which was to decide the destiny of the world had proved to be a brief and almost bloodless engagement.

CÆSAR at once prepared to drive home his victory. He recalled his soldiers from the pillage of Pompey's baggage, despatched part of them to guard the camp and sent others to defend his own. Then with four legions he dashed in pursuit of the fugitives on the road to Larissa, and already at nightfall overtook the main body of Pompey's army on a hill dominating the road. He encamped at its foot to await the daylight; but next morning the enemy saved him all further trouble by a prompt capitulation. During the night the soldiers had shown so decided a disposition to come to terms that the irreconcilables among their leaders, such as Afranius and Labienus, had fled with small detachments towards Durazzo, leaving the army free to surrender. Without further loss of time Cæsar continued his journey to Larissa, where several of Pompey's officers, amongst others, Brutus, gave themselves up. Here he learned that Pompey had passed through the Vale of Tempe towards the mouth of the Peneus, despatching slaves from his escort on the way to circulate an edict in Greece ordering all young Greeks and Romans resident in Greece to join his standard at Amphipolis. Cæsar then ordered Calenus to reduce Greece, commanded one legion to follow him by forced marches, and set out on the 11th of August at the head of a squadron of cavalry for Amphipolis, in the hope of finding Pompey. Meanwhile Pompey, after taking leave of his slaves at the mouth of the Peneus, had set sail in a small vessel with Lentulus Spinther, Lentulus Crus, Favonius, King Deiotarus, and a few others. Once out at sea he had fallen in with a corn-ship belonging to a Roman merchant, in which he had embarked, and was at this moment nearing Amphipolis. By dint of forced marches Cæsar with his squadron succeeded in covering the 180 Roman miles between Larissa and Amphipolis within six days, and arrived shortly after his rival, but too late. Hearing that his opponent was already in the neighbourhood, Pompey spent only one night in the town, scraped together a little money from his friends and clients and departed hurriedly for Mitylene, where his wife and younger son Sextus were staying, postponing all plans till he was safely at sea. His sudden departure gave Cæsar the impression that he was on his way to Syria, the province which he had conquered. He therefore gave orders to the legion which was behind him to continue the pursuit, sent another to Rhodes, and himself proceeded to Sestos on the Dardanelles.

About the same time, towards the middle of August, Labienus with his Gauls and Germans reached Durazzo, bringing the news that the great army of Pompey had suffered defeat. A terrible panic broke out; men imagined that Cæsar was already at the gates and refused to stay a day longer in the town. It was decided to retire at once with the fleet to Corfu. The soldiers rushed to the magazines and in their haste spilt the grain over all the roads leading to the port; all ships which refused to put out to sea were simply set on fire. At nightfall, in the glare of the burning vessels, the army left port, with Cicero, Varro and Cato on board. Meanwhile the news of Pharsalia passed gradually up the coast of the Adriatic; and all four of Pompey's admirals brought their fleets to Corfu—Caius Cassius from Sicily, Cneius Pompeius from Oricus, Marcus Octavius from a cruise along the coast of Dalmatia, and Decimus Lælius from Brindisi. To Corfu too came, one after another, all those of Pompey's friends who were unwilling to surrender, amongst them Scipio. It was thus possible to hold a sort of Grand Council of War, under the presidency of Cato. We are not told what ensued in the debate; all we know is that Cneius Pompeius nearly murdered Cicero because he proposed to conclude peace, and that after the meeting the majority of the chief personages dispersed in different directions. Cassius took his ships off to Pontus, with no very obvious intentions; Scipio and Labienus sailed for Africa, hoping there to meet Pompey; Marcus Octavius returned to Dalmatia to complete his conquests; and Cato proceeded with Cicero to Patras to collect the fugitives. There he succeeded in taking on board Petreius and Faustus Sulla, but on the approach of Calenus he was forced to set sail for Africa. Cicero, who had no heart to go on fighting, stayed behind at Patras.

In the meantime Pompey, who had reached Mitylene on the 12th of August, took on board Cornelia and Sextus, who had as yet only received the good news of the victory at Durazzo. Taking leave of Deiotarus, who returned to Galatia, he coasted along Asia Minor and Pamphylia, touching land only to take in water and provisions, and stopping but a few hours at Phaselis and at Attalia, where some of the ships of his fleet and a few Senators were stationed. Great discussions took place on the voyage between Pompey and his friends as to the place where it would be possible to collect another army and renew the war. Some proposed Syria, others Egypt, others Africa; it was imperative to come to a decision. The fugitives stopped on Sinedra to deliberate and it was decided to take refuge in Syria.

Meanwhile Cæsar had arrived at Sestos, where, while he waited for his ships and his legions, he received the submission of one of Pompey's admirals, Lucius Cassius, who had ten ships under his command. It was now too that he probably made definite arrangements with regard to Italy, whither he had been unwilling to send any official announcement of his victory. Antony was to lead back his troops to Italy, secure his nomination as Dictator and act as his Master of the Horse or Vice-Dictator. Thus at the expiration of his consular year he would still possess all the powers necessary for the continuance of the war. When his ships and his legions were ready and he had heard of the successful reduction of Greece by Calenus, he set sail for Syria with the intention of touching at Ephesus and Rhodes on the way. He was still under the impression that Pompey would attempt to take refuge in Syria. But Pompey, who had set out for Cyprus towards the 10th of September, had just at this moment received information at Paphos that the inhabitants of Antioch refused to open their gates to him or any of his supporters. He proceeded to raise money from a big syndicate of Italian financiers established at Cyprus, collected a small fleet in the ports of the island, enrolled about 2,000 soldiers from amongst the slaves whom the Italian merchants kept in depot there for sale into Italy, and decided to make his way to Egypt. That country was now under the rule of Ptolemy Dionysus and Cleopatra, the children of the Ptolemy Philometor whom Pompey had had re-established on his throne by Gabinius; according to the will of their father they were to marry one another and reign conjointly. Cæsar, who was at Rhodes awaiting the legion which he had ordered Calenus to send him, soon divined from Pompey's activity at Cyprus that he had changed his plans and was making for

Egypt. As soon as his soldiers arrived, about the end of September, he set sail in haste for the kingdom of the Ptolemies. The two rivals would at last be brought face to face on a narrow stage.

But when Cæsar reached Alexandria on the 2nd of October he was met by unexpected news which formed a fitting *dénouement* to a story full of strange and unforeseen episodes. Pompey was dead. He had arrived to ask Egyptian hospitality at a critical moment in the affairs of that country. The young king was at war with his sister, who had been driven out by his ministers because she was older and cleverer than himself. His counsellors were unwilling to be embroiled with Cæsar; yet they feared that if they refused to receive Pompey he might be driven to take sides with Cleopatra. There was an easy way out—to plot his death. When the few ships of the fugitive arrived in view of Pelusium, where Ptolemy and his army happened to be at the time, a small boat put out to fetch him. Pompey was not without his suspicions; but he consented to step in, remarking that whoever passed the threshold of a royal dwelling became a slave. When the boat approached the bank and Pompey rose to disembark, Cornelia, who was anxiously following him with her eyes from the admiral's vessel, saw a soldier who was in the boat strike him down from behind.

We have now reached the 29th of September in the year 48. On this very date thirteen years before Pompey had entered Rome in the costume of Alexander the Great to celebrate his great Asiatic triumph. Pompey was not a fool, as several modern historians in their enthusiasm for Cæsar have been pleased to call him, but a typical and in some ways exceedingly capable aristocrat, with all the faults and all the virtues of the old nobility, upon whom the circumstances of his time had imposed a task which was far beyond his powers. If he lacked the consuming activity and the unwearied intellectual energy of his successful rival, yet it must be remembered that he owed his fall not merely to the blunders which he himself committed, but also, and in a far greater degree, to the vices and faults of the upper classes, whose champion circumstances rather than any deliberate policy had forced him to become. Nor must we forget the very considerable part which he played in the history of Rome. He annexed to the Roman Empire the country of Christ, with results of perhaps even supremer importance than the occupation of Gaul. Moreover, by the building of his theatre, by the festivals he gave to the people, and by his indiscriminate liberality, he did more almost than anyone to disseminate Eastern culture throughout Italy, to give Rome a taste for the luxury of the imperial epoch whose remains we still continue to admire and even to imitate.

Of all the lucky chances in Cæsar's life the sudden death of Pompey was certainly the luckiest. The rival who would never have laid down his arms disappeared at one blow, cut down by a miserable conspiracy of Oriental eunuchs; and Cæsar was saved from the guilt of having shed his blood. When the news of his death reached Italy towards the middle of November through Diochares, one of Cæsar's fastest couriers, everyone regarded Cæsar as definitely victorious; and as in politics success is the chief criterion of popularity, the impression produced was far greater than Cæsar himself could have expected. The statues of Sulla and Pompey were removed, and the public relapsed into a condition of ecstatic admiration for the man whom they had despised six months before as a criminal. On the proposition of his friends and without any suggestions of opposition, extraordinary and unprecedented honours were voted to him, honours such as Sulla himself had never known. Not only was he given the Dictatorship for the whole of 47 as he desired, but the right of presiding alone over the elections of the magistrates ordinarily presided over by the Consul—that is, of all the magistrates, with the exception of the Tribunes and the Ædiles of the people—the right of himself distributing the provinces amongst the Prætors, instead of drawing lots, and finally that of ranking as a Tribune of the people for life. In short, Cæsar had now regularly taken Pompey's place in public consideration and had become master of the Republic.

This rapid change in opinion is but another example of the great social and moral crisis through which Italy was passing. It is true that the ardent desire for peace, the vacillation and nervousness of public opinion, the marked inclination for moderate measures that Cæsar had hitherto displayed all helped to produce an outburst of enthusiasm that was in part sincere, in part fictitious. But if we look below the surface there are deeper reasons to be found for this strange revulsion. It was the normal and necessary outcome of the new conditions of

Italian society. There no longer existed in Italy classes and parties sufficiently powerful, either politically or economically, to resist the political cliques which centred round the most powerful figure in the State. So long as there had been two rival cliques, many men had been able to preserve a certain measure of independence by skilfully passing from one to the other; but now that Pompey's clique had been broken up at Pharsalia and Cæsar seemed sole master of the Republic and the administration, interest alone compelled a great majority to submit. A large part of the political world lived upon office, and for them to display obstinacy in opposing the victorious clique would have been simply suicidal.

Cicero's experiences at this juncture are a good commentary upon this text. Next to Pompey and Cæsar he was the best-known figure in the Roman world. Yet he was just now in a position of the very greatest embarrassment because everyone considered his political foothold precarious. No one was prepared to advance him money, and many of his creditors were insisting on payment. His family affairs had thus become highly involved. He had had to suspend the payment of Tullia's dowry and was exceedingly alarmed lest Dolabella should demand a divorce. Terentia had been reduced to the most desperate intrigues; his creditors had even threatened to drive him into bankruptcy to force him to sell his goods; perhaps he would really have gone bankrupt if Atticus had not come to his help, and if a fortunate legacy had not arrived just in time. If even Cicero's finances depended entirely on the political situation, it can be imagined what was the predicament of a great number of the obscurer Senators under similar circumstances. Vigorous opposition to the victorious clique, dictated either by sentiment or principle, was simply out of the question; everyone felt his interests so bound up with the State that the small party which controlled the government had for the moment the whole of society on its side.

Never in his life had Cæsar been so happily placed. Fortune had put the whole game in his hands. He had only to make use of the unanimous enthusiasm of Italy, all the more overwhelming because it was inevitably short-lived, to return to Rome and attack the great problems of the age—to adjust the old republican institutions to a mercantile society, to conciliate liberty with imperialism, Latin traditions with the new demands of Eastern luxury and culture. But Cæsar was a man of genius, and not a demigod; he could not discern all that is so clear to us in the perspective of twenty centuries. At this critical moment in his career he allowed himself to be diverted, like any ordinary man, by passing incidents and the immediate necessities of the situation. He needed money. Egypt was a rich country, and Ptolemy had not paid him the whole sum agreed upon in return for the help given him by Gabinius. He decided therefore to go to Alexandria, to claim as Consul the right of settling the difference between brother and sister and interpreting the will of Ptolemy, and thus secure the payment of the father's debt and of his own services as arbitrator before returning to Rome. It is true that he had only some few thousands of soldiers with him, but after his previous successes he could not doubt that the matter would be finished off quickly and without serious difficulty. He therefore sent orders to Cleopatra and Ptolemy to dismiss their armies and submit themselves to his judgment, installed himself in the royal palace and imposed a tribute upon the inhabitants of Alexandria.

But while the king's ministers were haggling with Cæsar and trying to persuade him to leave the city, and while the restless metropolitan populace, excited by the exactions and the orgies of the Roman soldiers, was beginning to break out into rioting, a woman, single-handed, carried the day against them all. The young queen slipped secretly into the town and the palace and penetrated suddenly one evening into Cæsar's apartments. Cæsar had just emerged from one of the most tempestuous periods of his life. It was easy for Cleopatra to persuade him in a single interview, between night and morning, that her cause was the just one. Her interference put a new complexion upon the whole situation. When on the following morning Ptolemy and his ministers learned that Cleopatra had spent the night in Cæsar's company, they knew that their cause was lost. Pothinus, the Minister of Finance who saw in Cæsar a new Rabirius, incited the people to revolt and urged Ptolemy's general to go to Alexandria, to fight the Romans. The Egyptian army was a kind of Stranger's Legion composed of ex-soldiers of Gabinius, of adventurers, of fugitive slaves and deserters from every Mediterranean country. This small force soon compelled Cæsar to retire with his soldiers within the high walls of the palace and submit to a siege while he awaited the reinforcements hastily summoned from Cneius Domitius Calvinus, who had stayed behind in Asia as governor of the province.

Thus up to the 13th of December Cæsar continued to govern Italy and the Empire; he had still time to nominate Antony Master of the Horse, and to promulgate a law forbidding all Pompey's partisans, with the sole exception of Cicero and Decimus Lælius, from returning to Italy. Then winter and the new war cut him off, in the royal palace at Alexandria, from all contact with the outer world. During the first six months of the year Italy and the Empire received no news of his doings. It is to this long absence that Cicero justly attributes much of the trouble which subsequently occurred. The Senators who had left Pompey after Pharsalia and were in hiding in different cities on the Mediterranean coasts, awaiting Cæsar's return before venturing to Italy, were condemned to a long period of delay which allowed them time to meditate upon the moral and material damages they had sustained through the civil war. To form a picture of the suffering and suspense which many distinguished personages went through during these months, we have only to turn to what is told us by Cicero. Cicero spent the whole winter and spring at Brindisi brooding over the friends he had lost in the war, over his quarrel with his brother Quintus, who complained of having been coerced on to Pompey's side, over the Ephesian money he had lent to Pompey, which had disappeared for good, over the penury to which he and his family were now reduced, over the troubles of Tullia, who was being disgracefully treated by Dolabella, over the insolent contempt of the less educated wing of Cæsar's party, and, last but not least, over his loss of popularity with the public, who regarded him with unconcealed suspicion because he had fought on the wrong, or rather, the beaten, side. Pharsalia had brought divisions into his family and ruin into his affairs, destroyed his political prestige and veiled the glories of the *De Republica*. Who was there now who could possibly look up to him as the great political thinker of the day? The meanest of Cæsar's centurions who had fought at Lerida and Pharsalia had better claims than he.

Cicero had at least definitely made up his mind not to take up arms. But there were others in less submissive mood than himself who were beginning to grow impatient, to lend an ear to the rumours which circulated along the Mediterranean coasts and brought hope to exiles longing for vengeance. Though Illyria, now in the hands of Cæsar's Quæstor Quintus Cornificius and of Vatinius, who had sailed from Brindisi to his help, had been definitely abandoned, the Pompeian ex-Governor Marcus Octavius had been able to take his fleet with him to Africa; here he was said to be re-creating an army out of the surviving members of Pompey's force, and to have plans for the invasion of Italy. Cæsar himself was declared to be in danger of his life at Alexandria, and the war might break out afresh at any moment.

Far greater were the troubles in Italy itself. According to the law passed after Pharsalia Cæsar alone was to preside over all the elections ordinarily presided over by a Consul: this meant that no magistrates except Tribunes and Ædiles of the people could be elected during his absence. The State was thus left almost entirely in the power of the Vice-Dictator Antony, who was young, frivolous and debauched, a capable soldier perhaps, but a quite inexperienced administrator, who regarded his position rather as a privilege than as a responsibility, and gave himself up to amusement and self-indulgence in the congenial company of singers, dancers, and the notorious Cithæris. Before long something like a social revolution had broken out almost under his eyes.

In Cæsar's party, as in all democratic parties which represent the most numerous and the poorest section of the community but draw their leaders from the upper classes, there was a latent contradiction which was bound eventually to cause trouble. One part of it, what may be called the educated or aristocratic wing, included representatives of the upper classes such as Caius Trebonius, Marcus and Decimus Brutus, Sulpicius Rufus, Sulpicius Galba and Asinius Pollio, men of means, of good education and decent morality, according to the standard of the age. Some of them had come over to him after Pharsalia, because they wanted peace, and saw no alternative course. Some had been with him from the first, out of personal sympathy or from an over-hasty ambition, or because they were disgusted at the crying misgovernment, the callousness and arrogance of the last genuine survivors of the Roman aristocracy. These men had been brought up in aristocratic and cultivated surroundings, and shared the sentiments and ideas, the prejudices and interests of the upper classes. If they desired a Democratic government which was generous towards the poor, they desired neither the rule of demagogues nor such a revolution as would disturb the upper classes in the enjoyment of luxury and culture. But there was a second and far more numerous section, composed of adventurers, malcontents, criminals, agitators and bankrupts, men drawn from all classes, the highest and the lowest, often bold and energetic but generally ignorant, almost always devoid of principle and of all political ideas, actuated solely by the desire to satisfy their ambition: such men as Dolabella, Vatinius, Fufius Calenus and Ventidius Bassus, Oppius, Cornelius Balbus, and Faberius, the skilful but unscrupulous secretary of Cæsar. These men cared little for public order or tradition, or the tranquillity of the upper classes, so long as they increased their own power; and to obtain that power they were ready to gratify the malice, the madness or the greed of the poor.

So long as they were fighting their way together into office the divergence between the two sections of the party remained latent, and Cæsar did his best to conceal it by alternately playing to the proletariat and coquetting with the Conservatives. But the moment that they felt power at last within their grasp, at the beginning of 47, trouble was inevitable. By this time the distress had reached appalling dimensions; everywhere tenants and debtors were sinking deeper into the slough, and crying out for a rescuer. Dolabella, who was the nearest to bankruptcy among the Tribunes, an unbalanced young politician of twenty-two, refused to take warning by the fate of Cælius. Encouraged by the utter demoralization of the Conservatives and by the chaos to which the Republic had been reduced for lack of magistrates, he attempted to gratify the desires not only of the left wing of Cæsar's party but of the whole of Italy, and to win lasting popularity for himself, by reintroducing, in January, the old proposals of Cælius for the cancelling of rents and the abolition of debt. This caused a panic amongst all owners of house property, such as Atticus, and amongst the wealthy capitalists. The social revolution which had been looming in the distance since the beginning of the civil war, but which they had just begun to hope they might escape after all, was

now suddenly and unexpectedly at their doors. Cæsar had several
times declared his respect for private property; but he was far away;
the Conservative party was crushed, and there remained no authority
in the State capable of maintaining public order. Thus even to those
who feared it most, the present seemed a most favourable moment
for the outbreak of a social revolution.

But to their great surprise the upper classes soon perceived that
safety was to come from a quarter whence they had least expected it.
Partly under the influence of personal friendships and in obedience
to moral and legal scruples, partly because they felt ashamed to be
associated by their social equals, with the politicians of the gutter,
the educated right wing of Cæsar's party treated Dolabella's proposals
as the Conservatives would have treated them under similar conditions. The Tribunes Trebellius and Asinius Pollio, supported by the
Senate, opposed the law. Dolabella insisted, and Antony, at heart
thoroughly indifferent, but pleased to be courted by the rich, for
some time refused to take sides. Finally the multitude of artisans,
small shopkeepers and freedmen, whose profits and corn-doles had
been diminished during the last two years and who were threatened
with eviction by landlords to whom they paid no rent, broke into an
open agitation, and riots ensued. The Senate suspended the constitution and charged Antony with the duty of maintaining order,
employing soldiers if necessary. But this gave rise to a new danger.
The legions in Campania, which had just returned from Greece
elated after their victories and missed the controlling hand of Cæsar,
threatened to mutiny if they did not receive their discharge and the
money grant so frequently promised them. Antony had immediately
to repair to Campania, where he had great difficulty in restoring
discipline. Unfortunately the excitement of the populace was encouraged by the revolt of the soldiers. On his return to Rome Antony
found the situation far worse than when he left. Dolabella was
continuing his agitation, not only delivering panegyrics in memory
of Clodius but organizing armed bands as at the time of the Revolution. Cicero, who had hoped to ennoble his family by marrying him
to Tullia, had the supreme chagrin of seeing a son-in-law of his
own emulating Catiline. Thereupon Antony, impelled it appears by
personal motives (for he suspected Dolabella of being the lover of his

wife), decided to take sides with the partisans of order and set himself vigorously to repress the revolt. Dolabella was not easily to be intimidated. On the day on which his law was discussed in the Assembly he had the Forum barricaded by his partisans in order not to be driven out. Excited by this manœuvre, Antony, always violent and hot-headed, saw Revolution in the air: he hurled his soldiers upon the Forum and dispersed Dolabella's bands, with a loss of 800 killed. It was years since Rome had seen such a slaughter.

This drastic remedy allayed the agitation among the poor for a time; but it greatly discredited Cæsar and his party among the Italian upper classes. Their restlessness was soon augmented by the arrival of more definite news from Africa and Asia. Two of Pompey's sons, together with Cato, Scipio and Labienus, had collected the remains of Pompey's army in Africa and formed an alliance with Juba King of Numidia. They were recruiting archers, slingers and Gallic cavalry, accumulating arms, raiding Sicily and Sardinia with their fleet, and attempting to win over the Spanish natives who were dissatisfied with the government of Quintus Cassius. Meanwhile at the very moment when a new army was preparing to attack Cæsar in Africa under the supreme command of Scipio, Pharnaces son of Mithridates suddenly emerged with an army in Asia from the small principality of the Chersonese, bent on the reconquest of his father's kingdoms, and inflicted a defeat upon Domitius Calvinus. All the hopes that Italy, weary of political discord and civil war, had so joyfully cherished in the autumn of 48 gave place in the spring of 47 to a great and growing uneasiness. The social revolution seemed on the point of breaking out in Italy, the civil war was being revived in Africa, while in the East the Empire of Rome was being disputed by the son of the indomitable Mithridates. And all this time Cæsar gave no sign of life.

It was only towards the end of April that Rome learnt through private sources that after the arrival of his reinforcements, Cæsar had succeeded on the 27th of March in taking Alexandria. Everyone supposed that he would then return immediately to Italy; and the rioting which had already calmed down, stopped as though by magic. But days and weeks passed without any official news of his victory, without even news of his departure from Alexandria. Soon fresh troubles broke out in Rome. The most various rumours were current as to the cause of the delay. Cæsar's friends grew anxious and wrote him pressing letters urging immediate return; many even set out to look for him and hasten his journey. But Cæsar, after having reconquered Alexandria and given the throne of Egypt to Cleopatra (for Ptolemy had died during the war), had committed the additional blunder of taking a trip up the Nile and prolonging for another enjoyable two months his gallant but disastrous adventure with the queen, who was expecting a child. The situation soon became so dangerous at Rome that Cæsar's friends caused the people to vote a series of laws designed to dash the rising hopes of Pompey's partisans. Cæsar was to have the right of making war and peace with all nations and to treat Pompey's supporters as he pleased. At last, in the first days of June, Cæsar set out for Syria, after having wasted nine precious months at a time when days were worth years, and years centuries.

On his arrival at Antioch he found a batch of letters and a great number of persons who urged him to come at once to Italy; yet he allowed a new delay to intervene. He was unwilling to return to Rome until he had done something to re-establish order in the East. A few days sufficed him to reorganize affairs in Syria. He left Antioch in the first days of July, and encountered the Pompeian squadron at the mouth of the Cydnus under the command of Caius Cassius, who had spent a large part of his time studying eloquence at Rhodes with Brutus. Cassius immediately surrendered. Cæsar sailed on to Ephesus, marched up-country with a small army against Pharnaces, using every expedient to extort money on the way, and on the 2nd of August defeated Pharnaces at Zela. He then held a Diet at Nicæa, made a distribution of kingdoms and lands, receiving rich presents in exchange from the kings of the East, but without making reprisals against those who had opposed him at Pharsalia, gave a free pardon to Deiotarus King of Galatia, whose cause was pleaded by Brutus; then, passing by Greece and Athens, he sailed for Italy, disembarked at Taranto on the 26th of September, giving a cordial welcome to Cicero who had come down to meet him, and made his way to Rome.

At last he was back in the capital. But he had let his great opportunity slip by. His long absence and his connection with Cleopatra had damaged his reputation in many quarters; and the revolt of the legions, the discord in his own party and the appearance of a new Pompeian army in Africa had revived the old uncertainty as to the issue of the war. This was particularly the case in the upper classes, where distrust and hatred for Cæsar had been allayed for a time, but were not extinct. Many persons began to ask if the future had not as great surprises in store as the past. The party of Cæsar, which appeared so homogeneous, was distracted by internal dissensions, and the last few years had shown striking and unexpected vicissitudes of fortune. Thus Cæsar was not received with the enthusiasm he might have had a year before. He soon perceived that an attitude of cold respect, and the prospect of a new campaign in Africa, indirectly supported from Rome, were all he had gained by his moderation towards the upper classes and the care with which he had avoided confiscation and plunder even at the risk of goading his legions to revolt. The impression of his striking victory at Pharsalia was in large part effaced, and the situation had again become dangerous and obscure. His reconciliation with the upper classes was only skin-deep, the fidelity of the legions precarious: his party was in danger of breaking up: and he had lost the sympathy of the masses, who had seen their hopes of relief through Dolabella frustrated by the action of a whole group of the Cæsarian party.

Cæsar immediately discerned that the best way to crush the rising hopes of the Conservatives was to strike a blow at once at the new Pompeian army in Africa. But he saw also that he could not again leave Italy without some atttempt to improve the internal situation which his previous vacillation had rendered so confused and even dangerous. If he continued this uncertain policy he ran great risk of losing his popularity among the lower classes without winning the confidence of the upper. Preoccupied by this danger and exasperated by the new campaign with which the Pompeians had replied to his advances, Cæsar decided before his departure to return to his old Democratic policy, and give some clear indication of his intention to benefit the poorer classes, who after all supplied him with legionaries, electors and the indispensable momentum of popularity. At a moment when everyone was expecting him to reward Antony and crush Dolabella, he gave a public proof of his sympathy with Dolabella and his indignation with the man responsible for the murder of 800 plebeians. He even went so far as to adopt one part of Dolabella's proposals, not the universal abolition of debt but the cancelling for a year of all rents below 2,000 sesterces at Rome and 500 sesterces in the other towns of Italy. He refused to accept the nomination of Consul for five years, but passed laws forbidding the mortgage of more than a certain proportion of an estate, forcing capitalists to invest part of their money in land, imposing obligatory loans upon rich individuals and towns, and confiscating for sale the patrimony of many citizens who had fallen in the civil war, amongst others that of Pompey. This was at once an act of reprisal against the irreconcilables, a hint to those who still wavered, and a financial expedient to procure money. Antony purchased Pompey's palace, intending not to pay for it, and laid hands on his works of art, his luxurious furniture and well-stocked cellars. Finally Cæsar presided in place of the Consul over the elections of magistrates for the years 47 and 46, or rather he secured the election of his own nominees and distributed the Proprætorships among his faithful followers. Vatinius and Calenus were to be Consuls in 47, Cæsar himself and Lepidus in 46, Hirtius was to be one of the Prætors, while Decimus Brutus, for whom he had a marked predilection, was to be left in Transalpine Gaul; Marcus Brutus, to whom he showed favour for Servilia's sake, was despatched to Cisalpine Gaul, Trebonius to Farther Spain, his nephew Quintus Pedius and Quintus Fabius Maximus to Nearer Spain, Servius Sulpicius Rufus, the lawyer who had drawn up the Electoral Bill against Catiline, to Achæa, Publius Sulpicius Rufus to Illyria, Pansa to Bithynia, Publius Servilius Isauricus to Asia. But Cæsar was to have an encounter with the legions before he left. When he gave orders to Sallust to lead back the Campanian troops to Sicily with the promise of large sums of money the soldiers mutinied once more, nearly put Sallust to death, and marched in serried bands on Rome, murdering two Senators and spreading pillage and devastation wherever they went. Cæsar was forced to allow them to enter the city and had great difficulty in calming them down. But he was in no mood to delay his departure for Africa. Towards the middle of December he set out for Sicily, arrived at Marsala on the 19th, embarked with six legions on the 25th, landed at Hadrumetum on the 28th and at once commenced operations.

CHAPTER XXXI

CÆSAR'S TRIUMPHS, 46 B.C.

CÆSAR's sudden reversion to a Democratic policy could not fail to set serious issues in motion. Its first result was abruptly to cut short all hopes of a reconciliation with the Conservative classes. No doubt these classes ought really once more to have been grateful to Cæsar for staying his hand after selling the goods of his fallen enemies. But their feelings were so inflamed at the time that the confiscation of Pompey's goods was indignantly resented as a monstrous act of tyranny and revenge. The right wing of Cæsar's own party was equally dissatisfied; it chafed at the unexpected treatment Cæsar had meted out to Antony on the one hand and Dolabella on the other. So the months during which Cæsar was fighting in Africa were a time of anxious suspense for the upper classes in Italy. Great was the speculation and uncertainty as to Cæsar's intentions. What course would he adopt when he had finally crushed the resistance of the Pompeians? The sale of the goods of Pompey's partisans, the law about rents and the indulgence accorded to Dolabella were ominous of trouble. It is true that since the beginning of 46 Cæsar was no longer Dictator. But would he not force them to give him new honours after his victory, a victory which seemed only too well assured? As in the first fitful days of early spring the sky and the earth are darkened by passing storm-clouds, brightening again after a moment only to be darkened once more, so cloud on cloud of foreboding swept over the mind of Italy during these long-drawn months. We can see their shadow still after the lapse of all these centuries over the books written that same spring by the most delicate interpreter of the thoughts and feelings of the upper classes. Under the encouragement of Brutus, with whom oblivious of their quarrel in Cilicia he was becoming increasingly intimate, Cicero had once more taken up his pen, and, early in 46, had begun to compose a history of Latin eloquence, in the form of a Platonic dialogue, with Brutus, Atticus and himself as the speakers; it is the work known as *Brutus seu de claris oratoribus*. But these literary relaxations could not distract his mind from political anxieties: although at the beginning of the dialogue Atticus declares that there will be no politics discussed, there are covert allusions on almost every page. Cicero's heartfelt distress at the renewal of the civil war makes him envy the lot of Hortensius, who had died shortly before, not living to behold the Forum deserted and dumb. A little later Brutus delivers a fine eulogy on the first Consul of the Republic, the destroyer of the monarchy, from whom Atticus, who was something of an antiquarian, had shown that Marcus Brutus was directly descended. Then the dialogue goes on to praise Marcellus, the Consul of 51 and a personal enemy of Cæsar, who had retired to Mitylene, far removed from "the common and destined miseries of mankind."

But only half the book was written when news arrived from Africa of the sudden conclusion of the war, on the 6th of April, by Cæsar's signal victory at Thapsus. For once he had given no quarter. Faustus Sulla, Lucius Afranius and Lucius Julius Cæsar, who fell into his hands, had been summarily put to death. Lucius Manlius Torquatus, Marcus Petreius and Scipio had died by their own hand; only Labienus and Cneius Pompeius had succeeded in escaping to Spain, and Cato to Utica. The gloomy forecasts of the Dialogue had thus been justified by events. The proscriptions were beginning once more! All that remained of the Conservative party withdrew into silence to mourn for its fallen friends and the death-agony of the Republic. For the more ambitious of Cæsar's supporters made use of the victory, as far-seeing men had predicted, to decree him the most extraordinary honours—the Dictatorship for ten years, the Censorial power under the name of *Præfectura Morum*, and the right of proposing candidates for the Tribuneship and the Ædileship. The impression that these measures caused was most disastrous. Not the most pessimistic of observers had predicted such inroads on the constitution. The decennial Dictatorship above all seemed almost the same as a revival of monarchy to a public which had been brought up in a traditional hatred for undivided, long-continued and irresponsible office. It was clear what was going to happen. Cæsar's Dictatorship would be followed by the arbitrary government of a greedy and exclusive cabal. Yet no resistance seemed possible. The left wing of Cæsar's party gained ground daily, and was increasing the power of its chief in order at the same time to increase its own. It was this small clique which, together with a few fanatical admirers and a crowd of parasites, surrounded the new Sulla, who commanded the loyalty of all the soldiers in the Empire. Through him it had supreme control over the Senate and the electorate, and even over the more moderate section of their own party, which, though secretly disapproving of the turn affairs had taken, was not strong enough to offer any open resistance.

So the tone of the *Brutus* becomes more and more despondent. When Brutus mentions Lucius Manlius Torquatus, Cicero begs him to be silent. "The memory of past sorrows is unhappy, and more unhappy still the expectation of sorrows to come." Once more Cicero dwells on the happy lot of Hortensius; he regrets that his earthly journey is ending in this "night of the Republic," and he is almost led to pity Brutus, who is young and will see an infinite succession of still greater troubles. As the book nears its close the tone becomes darker and darker, and the letters written by Cicero to Varro during these months are full of the same melancholy. Private griefs came to reinforce public disasters. His beloved Tullia could no longer live with the discredited Dolabella; while, for reasons which it is difficult to unravel, there had arisen between himself and his wife Terentia one of those strange difficulties between elderly married couples in which an irritable old age sometimes indulges: so serious a quarrel, indeed, that Rome very nearly witnessed father and daughter simultaneously divorced. Now that the excitement of his conflict in the Forum and the Senate House, his cherished ambitions and the pleasures of notoriety, no longer occupied his thoughts, the comparative penury to which he had been reduced and the hopeless entanglement of his affairs began to weigh heavily on his mind. His only consolation was to immerse himself in his favourite studies, in finding answers, for instance, to the numerous questions on Roman history put to him by Atticus, who spent the leisure hours of his business in collecting material for a history of Rome. He found some satisfaction, too, in the esteem with which he was regarded by the most prominent and cultivated members of Cæsar's party, who invited him almost daily to dinner. Hirtius even asked him to give him lessons in oratory and entertained him royally in return. Here too he met Dolabella who had managed somehow, despite his behaviour to Tullia, to keep in the good graces of his father-in-law. With his unfailing charm of manner he had induced the old orator to overlook his behaviour, as he had extorted a similar indulgence from Cæsar and from all the men and even from all the women of his acquaintance. Worn out by the burden of his years and misfortunes, Cicero accepted these invitations just for the pleasures of society, though from time to time he felt a sting of remorse when something happened to recall the miserable catastrophe which had cost him so many of his friends.

To these the name of Cato had by now to be added. The old aristocrat had ended his life with the same inflexible obstinacy with which he had lived it. Despatched after the battle of Thapsus to the defence of Utica, he soon realized that all resistance was useless; unwilling to accept a pardon from Cæsar, he had quietly set his affairs in order, then one evening, after bidding his son farewell, he retired to his room, spent some hours over the *Phædo* and then fell upon his sword. When his friends found him he was already dying.

Meanwhile Cæsar, after annexing the kingdom of Juba to the Roman Empire and raising considerable contributions, left Utica on the 13th of June, disembarked on the 16th at Cagliari, where he stayed till the 27th, despatching Caius Didius and his soldiers to Spain to hunt down the last remnants of the enemy. The winds were contrary and he did not reach Rome till the 25th of July. Immediately on landing he made a speech to the people and another to the Senate celebrating the vast extent of the lands conquered in Africa, their fertility and the abundance of corn they would furnish to Rome, and giving assurances that his government would not be tyrannical and that he intended simply to act as head of the people. He did not at once accept decennial Dictatorship, contenting himself with the position of Consul and the electoral powers of the *præfectura morum*.

But if his speeches were reassuring the upper classes awaited his actions with ill-concealed anxiety; their ancient hostility was reinforced by the helplessness of their position and a sullen jealousy at the honours that were being heaped upon him. While a few sanguine spirits dared to hope that the end of the civil war meant a restoration of republican institutions, the majority dreaded an open, violent and rapacious tyranny. It was not long before both parties discovered that they were mistaken. True, Cæsar had no intention of retiring into private life.

Though he had originally entered upon the war not out of lust for the supreme power but to win a secure and honourable position in the aristocratic republic, yet his overwhelming successes, his intimacy with Cleopatra, and the revolutionary movement which was affecting the whole of Italy, appearing now in the new literary fashions of the younger generation, now in the prevalent affectation of Oriental customs, had left their mark upon his ambitions. Cæsar was no sceptical voluptuary like Sulla, no easy-going dilettante like Pompey, but a restless and ardent spirit for whom feverish activity, engrossing labour, and intense and continuous excitement had become almost a second nature. At last, after years and years of painful effort to win scope for the exercise of these transcendent abilities, he had it within his power to control an army, to put trusted supporters in the chief offices of State and to dispose of huge sums of money. To return to private life, to renounce the execution of the great designs which he was maturing in his brain, was too much to ask of him. Moreover, he was beginning to find pleasure in some, though not in all, the temptations of omnipotence. Supposing he retired into private life, was it likely that Cleopatra would keep her promise to visit him in Rome?

But even had he wished it, to renounce the supremacy was no longer in his power. His hands were tied by the very completeness of his success. He was the prisoner of his own victory. He had won his triumph by exciting in the multitude, as Sulla had done before him, the most dangerous passion of his age, cupidity, by promising his soldiers lands and privileges and money, heaping promise on promise, each greater than the last, the promises of Spain on those of Rimini, and the promises of Brindisi on those of Spain, and on those of Brindisi the recent and still more extravagant promises made after the defeat at Durazzo. And his soldiers had trusted him. They had worked themselves to death in their trust, relying on his untarnished reputation for generosity. Now had come the time for keeping his word. All his other engagements he could disavow, as idle tales for the dupes who had helped him to victory—but not these pledges given to 30,000 or 40,000 men who had either followed him from Gaul or come over to him from the enemy, and who had now for three years been dreaming of settling down at their ease in the country on Cæsar's money. The recent mutinies of the legions, impatient for their rewards and their discharge, had shown him that they were not to be hoodwinked. The civil war and his promises together had raised them to a pitch of dangerous excitement; they would not shrink from taking the law into their own hands and precipitating a military revolution in which their general would be the first victim. Like Sulla, he was personally responsible for all the promises made, all the wild hopes conceived in his name; like Sulla he could not abandon his post at the helm, which was his sole means of fulfilling his multitudinous pledges.

But if the few who expected Cæsar forthwith to lay down his powers had utterly mistaken his position, those who looked for the recurrence of a Sullan *régime* of violence were perhaps even further from the truth. Cæsar had indeed every reason to be indignant with the survivors of the Pompeian party and with the upper classes at Rome for the insincerity of their attitude since Pharsalia, and he made no attempt to conceal his ill-humour on the occasion of his triumphs. He had four triumphs each lasting a whole day, the first over the Gauls, the second over the Egyptians, the third over Pharnaces, and the fourth over Juba. In the last of these Cæsar exhibited the arms taken from his Roman opponents and circulated caricatures of his chief enemies, including Cato. If Cæsar took no pains to conceal his hostility to the aristocrats at Rome and his intention of relying upon the popular classes, if he returned resolved to govern the Republic without considering the prejudices and pretensions of the Conservatives, he knew very well that it was impossible for him to do a tenth part of the work that Sulla had achieved. One of the greatest mistakes made by all historians of Cæsar is the assertion that after Pharsalia and Thapsus he was practically omnipotent, sole master of the Republic and of the Roman world. In truth he was nothing of the kind. Sulla had saved the whole Empire from imminent destruction and rescued an entire class of citizens from political extinction. Cæsar had not emerged triumphant from a revolution; he had merely happened to win in a civil war brought about in a peaceful and peace-loving country through the rivalry of two political cliques. He had neither the prestige to inspire one-tenth of the terror or admiration of Sulla, nor an army on whose fidelity he could rely, nor a body of supporters united in their aims and ideals. On the contrary discord was making way among all classes of his adherents and the solid block of his party showed new fissures every day. Antony himself had refused to obey him in paying for Pompey's goods, which he had bought by auction, and was spreading threats and invectives against his leader broadcast through Rome. It was even whispered that he had made attempts to hire an assassin.

The weakness of Cæsar's position is thus easily explained. The conquest of Gaul had not provided him with prestige adequate to the extraordinary responsibility which he had assumed, while, as for his successive victories since he left his province, they had been gained in a civil war and had better be forgotten than proclaimed. Cæsar saw very clearly that if he was to be truly master of the Republic he must win some greater and purer title to glory by his services to Italy; that all the pains that he had spent hitherto were only a prelude to great work which he was now to undertake. At last he was in a position, not to enjoy but to win a real supremacy in the Republic through the performance of some immortal achievement. Now that the civil war was over he dreamt of forming a government which should be stable, beneficent and memorable to posterity, a government with three essential features in its programme, a large and generous policy towards the poor, a complete reorganization, such as the nation rightly demanded, of the whole disordered machinery of administration, and lastly, in the domain of foreign policy, some great and striking military achievement. He was returning in fact to the old ideas, or the old dreams, of 56.

No sooner was he back in Rome than he set resolutely to work in his usual spirit with the help of several friends and freedmen. With the six hundred million sesterces and vast quantities of precious metals he had brought back from Africa, he paid each citizen the 300 sesterces promised in 49, the 80,000 promised to each soldier, the 160,000 promised to the centurions and the 320,000 promised to the military Tribunes; he also gave a great public banquet and made a free distribution of corn and oil. By using his authority as a Censor or by proposing Bills to the electors he carried through a series of reforms all thoroughly Conservative in spirit. He reorganized the tribunals, giving them a more aristocratic character; he modified the penal laws by strengthening the penalties against crimes of violence; he dissolved all illegal associations, including the *collegia* of workmen organized by Clodius, which had proved so useful to himself in his struggle with the Conservatives; he reduced the number of the poor who had been admitted by the law of Clodius to take part in the distributions of corn; he published a sumptuary law putting a check on the use of pearls and purple and litters; he attempted to check the emigration of young Italians, which had seriously affected the recruiting for the army; he made arrangements for the better administration of his Land Law, which had languished hitherto, by the formation of colonies in Campania in the neighbourhood of Calatia and Casilinum; he made arrangements for the issue of a new gold coin, the *aureus;* he brought Egyptian astronomers to Rome to rectify the calendar; he attempted to regulate the neglected finances of the Republic by re-establishing customs dues and by taking over for the State and leasing out the emery quarries in Crete, which had been largely worked without authorization by private enterprise; and he devoted himself to the working out of the famous *lex Julia municipalis,* of which there will be frequent mention as our story continues and which was to reorganize the government and administration of all the towns of Italy.

But he was nursing still greater projects than these. He intended to revive the old idea of Caius Gracchus, to re-establish the ancient centres of civilization which had been crushed or undermined by the expansion of the Roman dominion, to rebuild Carthage and Corinth, to send out colonies to Provence, to Lampsacus, to Albania, to Sinope, to Heraclea and the coasts of the Black Sea, still smarting from the brutality of the soldiers and officers of Lucullus; last of all he dreamt of returning to the adventure which had cost Crassus his life, the conquest and annexation of Parthia. Hitherto the unkind chances of politics had banished him, sorely against his will, to the cold grey skies of northern Europe. Now that he was free to go his own way he turned towards the East, the land of his early ambitions, which cast its spell over him as over all his contemporaries, and beckoned him to repeat the fabulous exploits of Alexander. Gaul after all was but a poor and barbarous country; the road to the civilization of the future lay through Asia, through the wealthy and highly civilized lands on which the Macedonian and his successors had left immortal marks of their achievement.

Several of these reforms were highly pleasing to the Conservatives, and consoled them somewhat for their mortification at seeing a caricature of Cato carried in the Fourth Triumph. For there was now something like a hero-worship of Cato growing up among the Italian upper classes. Cicero, who, still at Brutus' suggestion, had written a panegyric on him and had now set himself to compose the *Orator*, was constantly wondering whether Cæsar was not going to restore the republican government; he kept watch over all his actions, and waylaid his intimates with questions, in a continual alternation of confidence and despair. He had been very sanguine up to the end of September, so much so that he had even consented to break through what he had regarded as his mourning for the Republic, and to make a speech in the Senate, full of complimentary references to Cæsar, on behalf of the exiled Marcellus, alluding confidently to the reconstruction of a normal civil government.

But his hopes were soon rudely shattered. Towards the end of September Cæsar consecrated a temple to Venus Genetrix and scandalized Cicero and the public by displaying in it a statue of Cleopatra by Archesilaus, one of the most well-known Roman sculptors. The general disgust was increased by the festivals which were celebrated at the inauguration. These were on a far larger scale than those which had been given at the Triumphs; there were wild-beast hunts and gladiatorial fights, and performances given in every quarter and in all languages for the amusement of the cosmopolitan proletariat; there was even a sea fight on an artificial lake. Cæsar then was bent on corrupting the people, just as he was bent on degrading the Senate by electing members from amongst the obscurer ranks of society, including even the professional *haruspices*. Both these new additions to the Senate and Cæsar's inexplicable delay in convening the electors were highly unpopular; and they were soon followed by a series of disagreeable incidents. Cæsar's activity was degenerating into a wild impatience. It was in this spirit that he forced Archesilaus to exhibit his unfinished statue in the Temple of Venus Genetrix in order that he might proceed with the inauguration; and he frequently hurried on preparations with an arbitrary procedure which caused widespread annoyance. Thus one day Cæsar received the thanks of certain Oriental princes for a decree which he had caused to be approved by the Senate, though he had never even heard of the existence of the potentates in question. His nominations of governors for the year 45 proved equally unpopular; with a few exceptions they were all old friends of his own, some of them were peculiarly odious to the Conservatives, the notorious Vatinius, for instance, and Sallust, who had been made Proprætor of Numidia after Thapsus and was allowed to remain there an extra year to recover the fortune which he had wasted on dissipation at Rome.

Thus the situation was becoming more and more difficult. This constant state of inward excitement, the extraordinary nervous tension of the last years, his natural exaltation after his victories, the feeling of strength springing in his case partly out of the very strain at which he lived, all combined to tempt Cæsar to assume responsibilities such as no man, not even he, could carry with impunity. Here again historians are wrong. They are fond of asserting that, because Cæsar had been able to construct so wonderful an instrument of rule as his army, he was thereby placed in a position where he could govern and reorganize the Empire as he wished. He had indeed used his army as an incomparable weapon of destruction; it had helped him to crush the Conservative party and destroy the legitimate government; but it could not help him, except in a wholly insufficient manner, to form a new government on the ruins of the old. The breach was widening on all sides of him. He stood alone, and wellnigh helpless, in the place of power. The nobility, even those of them who had rallied to his side after Pharsalia, had forgiven him nothing; they held suspiciously aloof, and it was only with the greatest difficulty that they could be prevailed upon to accept office. Even in his own party the whole of the right wing was lukewarm and gradually withdrawing from all active support. Only the small and vigorous *coterie* of his partisans from amongst the lower orders remained actively loyal; and they courted the Dictator merely to monopolize his favours and keep off all dangerous intruders. The faithful Oppius, the skilful Balbus, the intriguing Faberius, the gay Dolabella, Vatinius, Calenus, Decimus Brutus, his favourite amongst them all, who had saved him from disaster in Spain and who had, for the last two years, been

Governor of Transalpine Gaul where he had repressed a new revolt amongst the Bellovaci—these were now his chief collaborators in the gigantic task of reorganizing the Empire, a work that called for all the talent and energy in the Roman State. And there were gaps even in that inner circle. Antony had now fallen quite into disgrace and was living in obscurity with his newly married wife, Fulvia, the widow of Clodius and Curio. Cæsar had now neither the time nor the wish to search the crowd, as he had so successfully done hitherto, for the unknown man whom he could use for his purposes; and within the close gathering of his intimates there were few new admissions, only the sons of his two nephews Quintus Pedius and Caius Octavius, and the family of Servilia; these last, Servilia's son Brutus and her two sons-in-law, Caius Cassius and Lepidus, formed a small aristocratic group in Cæsar's party, and were treated by Cæsar with great consideration, though Lepidus was the only one with whom he was really intimate. Caius Octavius was a young man of seventeen who showed promise of great ability; after the death of his father and his mother's second marriage with Lucius Marcius Philippus he had been brought up in the house of his grandmother, Cæsar's sister. Cæsar himself had for some time past taken him under his protection; he supervised his education, introduced him to the public by several special marks of distinction, and was probably instrumental in finding him two new teachers, Athenodorus of Tarsus and Didymus Areus, in addition to the masters under whom he was learning already. Didymus belonged to that small Neo-pythagorean school which we have already seen attempting to spread a new and ascetic morality in the Roman world. But Octavius was a young man of delicate health and was actually at this moment suffering from a serious illness which caused great anxiety to Cæsar.

Thus the loyal and vigorous co-operation which might have enabled him to carry his great projects into execution was not to be found; and the idea that a single man, however remarkable his energy and ability, together with a few friends and freedmen picked up at random at various times in his career during twelve years of war and adventure, could arrest the growing disorder of a long process of social decomposition and change throughout a vast Empire was the idlest of dreams. It had been easy to use his army to triumph over the

Conservative party and the degenerate upper classes of Italy; but it was impossible for one man by mere legislation to reconcile the terrible antagonisms that were raging in a violent, overbearing and money-loving society. One difficulty after another confronted him, often created by his very impatience to overcome them, and the worry, the weariness, the disappointments of his never-ending labours dulled that keen and exquisite sense of what was real and practicable which had stood him in such stead in past years. Sometimes he himself would say, like a man worn out, that he had lived long enough. His intimates, Balbus and Oppius, had noticed for some time how he was daily becoming more irritable, headstrong and strange in his manner; how every suggestion, however guarded, of the wisdom of laying down at least a part of his power caused him increasing annoyance; they had seen him so out of temper at Cicero's panegyric of Cato that he meditated writing a refutation and had encouraged Hirtius to do the same. Yet he refused to have it said that he was violating the constitution, or breaking with Roman tradition, or acting against the spirit, as opposed to the letter, of the laws which had granted him his powers. He was just now engaged in composing his Memoirs of the Civil War, doing his utmost to prove that he had scrupulously observed the constitution, and that it was his opponents and not he who had laid hands on the property and the rights of the citizens. But as the months slowly went by in this endless year, in which there was room for so much to happen because it was increased to fifteen months and 445 days by the astronomers who were reforming the calendar, the situation corresponded less and less with his words and his intentions.

Towards the end of the year Cæsar committed a grave blunder by opening his house to Cleopatra who had come to Rome with a large suite of slaves and ministers. This caused a huge scandal at Rome and in Italy. It had been an open secret for some time past that Cæsar had been giving rein to his passions, particularly in his relations with royal personages, and that during the African war he had a connection with Eunoe, wife of Bogud, King of Mauretania, and had made her enormous presents. But this new scandal shamelessly flaunted before the eyes of Rome shocked and excited a public that was only too ready to find a mark for its criticism. The old Latin family had exercised many judicial and disciplinary functions now reserved for the State, and its dissolution tended to aggravate social disorder in a way quite out of proportion to the relaxation of family ties under modern conditions. Perhaps no other of the many problems of the day was more lamented by contemporaries or seemed more hopeless of remedy. Cleopatra's open appearance in Rome gave fresh emphasis to these complaints. Everyone felt pity for the unhappy Calpurnia, married in 59 for a political intrigue, then left alone for years by a travel-loving husband, and now compelled to receive a rival into her own household. Yet Calpurnia was but a melancholy instance of the lot reserved for all the women in Roman high society who were not either dissolute or criminal. It was the same fate that befel Tullia, in spite of her father's devotion, or Cornelia, the widow of Publius Crassus and of Pompey, and hundreds of others whose names have not come down to us. They were married, abandoned, and remarried from one year to the next, without regard to the age or the character of their husbands; they moved from one home and household and society to another, according to the accidents and vicissitudes of politics; often they had not even the consolation of motherhood and found stepsons older than themselves at their husband's table; at the worst they had to endure the shame of being openly superseded by freedwomen and slaves. This was one of the evils of the age—one of those numberless symptoms of disorder, lamentable, yet inevitable, that marked the great change that was taking place in Roman civilization, to which women had to contribute their share, and more than their share, of suffering. But for once an envious public reserved for Cæsar their resentment against an evil that was common to his class. It was intolerable that the Dictator should make public ostentation of his private vices.

CHAPTER XXXII

CÆSAR'S LAST AMBITION—THE CONQUEST
OF PARTHIA

AMONG the upper classes discontent was thus gathering to a climax. Hereditary pride and dislike of discipline set them naturally against any ordered system of government; and they were still smarting under the effects of the civil war, mourning the loss of parents and friends and damage to their property or interests. The confiscation of the goods of the vanquished had robbed many of windfalls on which they had reckoned: others had lost sums deposited in the temples of Italy and the East, while more still were hard hit by the scarcity of money and the difficulty of raising credit. It was in vain that Cæsar attempted to show in his *Memoirs on the Civil War* that it was Pompey and not he who had laid hands on the deposits of individuals, while they had him to thank for the safety of the great Temple of Diana at Ephesus and the treasure there stored. Pompey was dead and his rival, who was still alive, had to bear the brunt of the blame.

It needed a man of unwearied skill and patience, of unruffled calm and unfailing discretion to steer his way through these difficulties. Deliberate malice and ill-tempered criticism, petty personal quarrels and far-seeing ambitions all joined to block his path. But Cæsar was no longer equal to the work. The strain was at last beginning to tell on his character. The excitement of power and success, the constant adulation, the very weariness that his position entailed, pricked him into the desire to achieve something great and decisive. His dreams of rivalling the romantic exploits of Alexander bore down the habitual restraints of vigilance and good sense. These tendencies were only encouraged by the inevitable pressure of circumstances. In face of the appeals that poured in upon him from all sides he was practically compelled to throw off all semblance of legality. All around him were problems crying out for courageous handling. He can be excused for believing that it was not personal ambition but the imperious necessities of his age that drove him into absolutism. Throughout Italy the distress had grown to appalling dimensions; a large part of the middle class and the proletariat had been driven almost to desperation by the continuance of the depression. A large number of skilled Eastern slaves had been set free in different parts of the country by masters who had been unable to find them employment and could not afford to keep them idle till the arrival of better times. The distress was increased by the reduction that had been found necessary in the number of the recipients of the corn-dole; there were thousands at Rome living in enforced idleness on the verge of starvation. An awful catastrophe seemed inevitable unless some new source of revenue could be discovered. In what direction were these riches to be sought?

There was only one possible answer to the question, and Cæsar had long ago divined it. In Parthia alone lay his hopes of reconstruction; in the fabulous treasures of the East lay the capital that was to relieve the necessities of Italy. It was a great and daring programme. But how could he carry it to a successful conclusion if he had all the while to be considering the absurd prejudices and the petty personal interests of a knot of grumbling Roman Senators? Besides, he owed them no more consideration than they in turn paid him. They had no eyes for the difficulties of his task or the troubles of their fellow-countrymen. At this moment all they cared about was the latest news of some little victory of young Pompey in Spain and the composition of silly and malicious eulogies of Cato. Even Brutus had followed the prevailing fashion and was writing up the suicide at Utica. In his present mood of impatience to be at work the clanking and creaking of the old constitutional machinery was altogether intolerable. He was growing old. He had never yet known failure. He must act, and act quickly, to secure his popularity and win an undying title to renown. He had no old scores to wipe off like Sulla; he did not wish to despoil the rich in order to relieve the poor. But just because his ends were so moderate he felt justified in assuming wide powers, regardless of constitutional propriety, to enable him to achieve them.

It is not improbable that the visit of Cleopatra contributed to produce this change in his attitude. The Queen of Egypt, herself one of the tragic figures of the time, plays a strange and significant part in the tragedy of the Roman Republic. Placed on the throne of Egypt at a moment when the government of Rome had fallen into the hands of a sole military Dictator, she had conceived a new diplomacy for the preservation of her kingdom. Her object it is not difficult to guess, though we are not told it in any well-authenticated document. She desired to become Cæsar's wife; and that by her example and the fascination of her presence and pleading she hoped to awaken in him the passion for kingship is an equally justifiable assumption. How indeed could she think or act otherwise? She was young, ambitious, greedy of pleasure, and still greedier of power; and she was born an Egyptian princess. The conclusion is irresistible. What is certain at least is this—that Cleopatra came to Rome with her infant son to win Cæsar's permission to call him after his father; and that when she left Rome she had, amongst other gifts and privileges, obtained this precious concession. But whatever Cæsar's ultimate ambitions their realization depended at this moment upon the success of his Parthian campaign. This therefore was henceforward his dominant idea, and towards it all his energies were now directed.

Unfortunately in the second half of 46 serious incidents intervened to interrupt his preparations. In Spain Cneius Pompeius and Labienus made play with the popularity of Pompey's name; and through the widespread disgust at Cæsar's governors, assisted by the discontent of some of the legions, they had succeeded in recruiting an army and in conquering a large part of the Peninsula. Cæsar had at first made light of the danger and entrusted the conduct of the war to subordinates; but when all their efforts proved futile they had finally appealed to their chief to come in person. The news from Spain of course only intensified the prevailing excitement and uncertainty, and Cæsar was forced reluctantly to admit that he could not set out for the East leaving a victorious enemy behind him in the West. Truly the civil war seemed to be becoming almost chronic. That a new campaign should be required just at this moment was the most disconcerting thing that could have happened. It obliged him to break off in the very midst of his work of reform and to postpone the great war against Parthia, while it increased his difficulties with Italian public opinion by showing that he had not yet succeeded in granting his promised boon of peace.

Impatient at the prospect of his Spanish campaign, and in the hope of overwhelming his enemies by one bold and unexpected stroke, Cæsar, towards the end of the year, threw off all pretence of constitutional rule and assumed to himself all the supreme powers of government. He took the Dictatorship, choosing this time as his Master of the Horse not Antony, who was still in disgrace, but the faithful Lepidus, who had been nominated Governor of Nearer Spain and Narbonese Gaul and who, to the general astonishment, was authorized to administer these provinces through legates. He also desired to be nominated Consul without a colleague for the year 45; and he postponed till later the election of the other magistrates. As Dictator, and at the same time Consul without a colleague he was for all practical purposes an autocratic ruler.

These measures produced a most disastrous impression. They widened the breach of distrust—already wide enough—which separated him from the upper classes, and encouraged the current apprehension that absolute power in Cæsar's hands was synonymous with a social revolution. A report was suddenly circulated that Cæsar had undertaken a measurement of lands in different parts of Italy with a view to a wholesale confiscation on the Sullan pattern, for the benefit of his troops. For a moment there was a regular panic. But it was soon ascertained that Cæsar was merely putting in a new commission, in accordance with the Land Law of 59, to find land in Italy and Cisalpine Gaul for distribution among his soldiers. On several occasions large portions of the public domain had passed into private hands; but the arrangements had been carried out in such haste and disorder that a few remnants were still left over, either in the possession of the State or leased out to private persons, especially in Etruria and Campania and in the neighbourhood of Leontini. It was this remnant that Cæsar was anxious to divide among his veterans, supplementing it with estates bought from private owners. The lands were to be given on the condition originally laid down by the Gracchi, that they were to be inalienable for twenty years. It was an attempt, somewhat late in the day, to revive the central idea of the Gracchan policy.

No sooner had this excitement abated when new incidents occurred to alarm the public. Cæsar had set out for Spain without convoking the electors, and everyone at Rome expected that in the course of his journey he would provide for the offices in the usual fashion. But towards the end of the year there was a new surprise. Cæsar nominated eight *præfecti urbi* who were to be entrusted with all the powers of the Prætors and certain powers, such as the administration of the Treasury, that belonged properly to the Quæstors, nominally under the direction of Lepidus, but really also controlled by Cornelius Balbus and Oppius. Thus by a stroke of the pen, to the dismay of the public, he created what was practically a system of Cabinet government, in which the people and the Senate were of no account at all. Meanwhile he occupied his spare hours on the journey in writing a book against Cato to combat the recrudescence of Republican sentiment.

This sudden change in Cæsar's policy caused consternation among the upper classes in Italy and even among the right wing of his own supporters, who regarded it as a prelude to the definite victory of the revolutionary section of the party. A whole flood of recriminations broke out. The grant of his own name to the child of Cleopatra was bitterly criticized; while the creation of the *præfecti urbi* was regarded as one of the most arbitrary measures Rome had ever known. Men began to whisper—and the whisper had proved fatal to many an illustrious Roman in the past—that he was stretching out his hands towards the monarchy. It was at this moment that news came that Marcellus the Consul of 51, to whom Cæsar had lately given a free pardon, had been mysteriously assassinated at Athens on his homeward journey; and evil tongues suggested that Cæsar had secretly plotted his death, to gratify a personal hatred whilst pretending in public to grant him a free pardon. The publication of the book against Cato added fuel to the flames. Written in a sour and venomous spirit, it was universally resented as an unworthy calumny on the memory of a great man. All the more striking were the warm references in it to Cicero, which succeeded, as usual, in hitting that tender mark. The old orator sent a hearty note of congratulation through Balbus and Dolabella to the Dictator. But he was alone in his opinion, and even he had not the courage to submit his letter to Atticus for approval. The labours of the Land Commission too were causing widespread anxiety. The common people were being encouraged to indulge in hopes and illusions which might some day prove dangerous to the State. Moreover the inquiries made to identify the public lands were highly disconcerting in many quarters, for if rigorously pressed home they might lead to some unpleasant revelations. Naturally the commissioners were overwhelmed with special appeals from landlords and their friends and relations. Everyone was anxious to own land in Italy, where the soil was under special privileges by law, paid no tax except the *tributum* levied in war-time, and could be held as absolute freehold; whereas in the provinces the soil belonged to Rome and the occupiers might be turned out of their holdings at any moment.

Thus, while Cæsar was fighting in Spain the situation at Rome was far from reassuring. Balbus and Oppius wrote letter after letter to Cæsar and did their best meanwhile to soothe the ruffled feelings of the leaders of opinion. They were particularly attentive to Cicero, now passing into life's evening with the shadow of many troubles upon him. At the end of 46 he had contracted a second marriage with Publilia, a rich young girl of 14; but at the beginning of 45 a great blow had been struck at his happiness. Tullia died in childbirth, shortly after her divorce. Her father could hardly bear up against his grief. To distract his mind he turned resolutely to the execution of a design he had perhaps been contemplating for some time but from which the vicissitudes of politics had always diverted him—to gather up the leading ideas of Greek philosophy in a series of dialogues after the model of Plato, in which all the great Romans of the last generation from Cato to Lucullus and Varro were to appear as interlocutors. It was a project that gave ample scope to the peculiarly dramatic powers of his style. The working out of this idea might have produced one of the masterpieces of literature, creating and reanimating for all posterity, in the calm and intimate atmosphere of philosophic dialogue, the great figures that history only shows us in the strife of war and politics.

But such a task needed the leisure for quiet and continuous workmanship; and Cicero's life at this moment was crowded with petty worries and distractions. He had continually to requisition Dolabella for the recovery by instalments of the dowry of Tullia; and he was trying to find the money for a sumptuous mausoleum to his daughter's memory. Moreover he was tormented by the question of Cæsar's intentions, which formed the subject of constant letters to Brutus, now one of his closest friends, who had only lately returned from the governorship of Cisalpine Gaul. He was also deep in the study of the great Greek books on political philosophy. He had been specially attracted by the letters written by Aristotle and other Greek thinkers to Alexander urging him to reserve autocratic rule for the Asiatics and to remain first citizen, *primus inter pares*, among the Greeks, the noble race which had always lived and could only live under free institutions. Aristotle's letter suggested the idea of writing one in similar terms to Cæsar; and Cicero actually composed an eloquent little treatise which he submitted to Atticus. But the cautious banker advised his friend to submit it first to Oppius and Balbus, who persuaded him not to send it on to the Dictator. The incident was a great disillusion to Cicero and caused renewed suspicions among the educated classes. One touch of brightness came to light up his troubles. A certain Cluvius, who had been one of his most ardent admirers, left him a large bequest which tided him over his pecuniary difficulties. Yet Cicero, like the rest of Rome, was in a continuous state of nervous suspense.

The news which arrived from Spain at the beginning of 45 only increased the general uneasiness. Cæsar had been so busy thinking out his Parthian plans that he had omitted to prepare the details of this preliminary campaign. From the very first the supplies were insufficient and the soldiers suffered severely from famine. It was the same difficulty that had befallen him in the war against Vercingetorix, in his first campaign in Spain, and during the operations in Albania; but with this difference, that it could now only be set down to the carelessness of the master of the great Mediterranean granaries.

Meanwhile a strange and unexpected event intervened to distract the attention of Roman society from the Spanish War. The virtuous Brutus divorced the daughter of Appius Claudius and married Portia, daughter of Cato and widow of Marcus Bibulus, Cæsar's old colleague in the Consulship, the admiral who had died during the war in Albania. A noble of ancient lineage, an enthusiastic student of art, literature and philosophy, Brutus was one of those spoilt children of fortune who succeed in winning general admiration for achievements they have not yet performed. Endowed with certain virtues rare in high society, with sobriety and continence, an unusual austerity in his private habits and a high disdain for vulgar ambitions, he had gained a great reputation among his contemporaries. They overlooked small peccadilloes like his trouble with the Cilician debtors, and universally regarded him, Cæsar included, as a prodigy of will and energy, who had great and enduring achievements to his credit, and could rightfully expect to be offered privileges which others laboured painfully to earn. He could take what liberties he liked: there was none to gainsay him. He had sided with Pompey out of regard for Servilia; yet Cæsar had loaded him with honours and responsibilities. He had become a leading member of the aristocratic Cæsarian party: yet without sacrificing the friendship of Cicero and other distinguished Pompeians. Now he suddenly announced his marriage with the daughter and widow of two of the Dictator's bitterest enemies. All Rome was agog with excitement. What did this new development portend? Hostility on Brutus' part to Cæsar's recent change of policy, or an open reconciliation between Cæsar and his old enemies? Servilia, who feared that the marriage might cost her son the friendship of the Dictator, did her best to dissuade him, and Cicero maintained a judicious reserve. But all in vain. Brutus had set his heart on the marriage, and it had to take place. We may suspect that politics had really very little to do with it; it was an old intimacy between cousins which had been renewed after long years of separation. In any case it is clear that Brutus had no intention of breaking with Cæsar; indeed, perhaps by way of compensation, he wrote a pamphlet in his defence against the current accusation that he had caused the death of Marcellus.

Meanwhile the Spanish War had come to a victorious conclusion, but only after perils and vicissitudes that no one had expected. Cæsar himself had fallen ill on several occasions, and he had conducted operations with so little vigour that in the final battle at Munda, on the 17th of March 45, he was within an ace of being defeated and taken prisoner. Moreover the victory lacked the finality of its predecessors. He had left some notable enemies still in the field. Cneius Pompeius and Labienus had fallen in battle, but the young Sextus Pompeius had successfully made his escape to the north. But Cæsar was impatient to be in Italy. Leaving his subordinates to deal with Sextus, he hastily set out on the homeward journey.

His arrival was anxiously awaited in Italy. The battle of Munda seemed to close the era of the civil war. There was no longer either pretext or reason, so the upper classes held, for the prolongation of the Dictatorship. The decisive moment, then, was approaching; at last the world would know whether Cæsar cared more for liberty or for the temptations of tyranny and revolution. The omens were far from favourable. His party had made immediate use of the victory to propose new honours, which had of course been approved. Cæsar was to bear the title of Imperator as hereditary *prænomen;* he was to be Consul for ten years, and he was also to have the right of nominating the candidates for the Ædileship and the Tribuneship. At the same time Balbus and Oppius, partly to gratify Cæsar, partly to impress the public, sent invitations to all the chief personages in Rome to come out to meet Cæsar on his return and escort him back in state to the city. It seemed clear therefore, unless his partisans were going farther than he wished, that Cæsar was aiming at supreme and absolute power. Amid a welter of hopes and doubts, and endless discussion of his possible intentions, Rome feverishly awaited the conqueror's return.

Yet still he delayed his appearance. He spent some time making several Spanish cities into Roman colonies, including Hispalis, Carthagena, and Tarragona, confiscating a part of their territory and settling a number of discharged soldiers on their lands. He was further detained in Narbonese Gaul, where he entrusted Caius Claudius Nero, a friend who had done him useful service at Alexandria, with the duty of distributing lands to the veterans of the sixth and tenth legions in the neighbourhood of Arles and Narbonne. Two more legions were thus disbanded. Yet even before he crossed the Alps Cæsar was swept into the whirlpool of Roman controversy. Representatives of all the different sections of opinion, Conservatives as well as moderate and extreme members of his own party, had jumped at the invitation of Oppius and Balbus and arrived daily to swell the numbers of his escort. They must have formed a singular company. Amongst them was Antony, who had grown tired of the pleasures of obscurity and had come determined to make his peace with his old master: and Trebonius, who was so indignant at Cæsar's new policy that he was already dreaming of a dagger to cut the knot; and finally Brutus, who had gone out to Cisalpine Gaul, on Cicero's encouragement, to sound Cæsar's intentions and find out what the Dictator thought of his wedding. He had no reason, as it turned out, to be nervous. To Brutus all things were lawful. He found a hearty welcome, and was warmly congratulated on the zeal he had displayed during his provincial administration. Of course he was delighted with his reception, which put all his old apprehensions to sleep. He wrote a most reassuring letter to Cicero, declaring that Cæsar aimed at the re-establishment of an aristocratic government on the Conservative pattern.

And indeed Cæsar had been genuinely impressed by the unanimity of the public and the dissensions within his own party, and was for a moment inclined to make concessions to the right wing of his supporters and the Conservative school of opinion. He was publicly reconciled with Antony, and to show that he had forgiven him his conduct to the rioters in 47 allowed him to make part of the journey in his own litter. Arrived in Rome he deposed the *præfecti urbi*, refused some suggested distinctions, and resigned his sole Consulship; then he convened the electors, and nominated the ordinary magistrates, selecting for the Consulship Quintus Fabius Maximus, one of his Spanish generals, and Trebonius, who was one of the most prominent and disaffected of the moderate Cæsarians.

In an impressionable society this was sufficient to revive the wildest hopes. Many believed that the end of the exceptional *régime* was actually imminent. But Cicero, always far-sighted, could not bring himself to believe it; and he was right. Cæsar was, in fact, not in the least interested in the constitutional question that was absorbing so the leisured classes at Rome; his sole and all-engrossing thought was still the Eastern War and the annexation of Parthia. Moreover his health was growing steadily worse; body and soul were almost worn out. The striking bust of him in the Louvre, the work of a great unknown master, gives a wonderful representation of the last expiring effort of his prodigious vitality. The brow is furrowed with huge wrinkles, the lean and shapeless face bears marks of intense physical suffering, and the expression is that of a man utterly exhausted. In truth he was tired out.

Yet, as so often with tired men, he could not take the rest he needed. The vision of Parthia lured him on to fresh exertions. His short spell of moderation did not last for long. No sooner had he arrived at Rome than he set to work on the military and political preparations for the expedition. One of his first objects was to influence public opinion in favour of the war. Sumptuous festivals were given to celebrate his Spanish triumph, and in the huge popular banquets that accompanied them Cæsar for the first time substituted in place of the usual Greek wines some of the new Italian vintages which, thanks to the skilful cultivation of the Eastern slaves, were now beginning to be widely known. It was a good way of advertising a new home product, and of encouraging the Italian vine-grower, whose prosperity was rapidly increasing, in spite of the prevailing depression. The law on the oversea colonies was at once proposed and approved and settlers were recruited from amongst soldiers, citizens and freedmen. Then followed surprise on surprise. Every day Rome was stupefied to hear of some new and daring project. The Dictator intended to divert the course of the Tiber in order to drain the Pontine marshes; to cut up the Campus Martius into building sites, using the land at the foot of the Vatican Hill in its place; to raise a huge theatre, afterwards completed by Augustus, and familiar to the modern traveller as the great Theatre of Marcellus; to commission Varro to establish large libraries in all parts of Rome; to pierce the Isthmus of Corinth; to lay out a road over the Apennines; to create a huge port at Ostia; to assign great public works to contractors and labourers; to collect and codify all the existing laws: all schemes to be executed, of course, after the completion of the great Parthian campaign, for which they were to serve as an overwhelming justification.

But Cæsar was for once mistaken in thinking that he could dazzle Italy with this profusion of grandiose ideas. The cosmopolitan proletariat of the metropolis might still be deluded into chimerical hopes at the promise of colonies and employment; but the middle class remained sullenly hostile, vainly waiting for a break in the prevailing depression, while the upper ranks of society, touched in their tenderest prejudices by Cæsar's calm assumption of autocratic authority, and always afraid of a social revolution which would despoil them of their riches at the bidding of a dictator, amused themselves by pretending that Cæsar was becoming insane and by heaping derision even on serious projects, such as the reform of the calendar. They took a childish pleasure in working up indignation against the noisy clique of men and women who surrounded the Dictator. To raise the money necessary for his Parthian campaign Cæsar was obliged to make an indiscriminate sale of the property confiscated from his enemies and the public land which was not suitable for settlements, as well as the treasures in the temples; and these hurried auctions were made full use of by his friends, many of whom bought huge lands at purely nominal prices. Servilia, for instance, secured a large confiscated estate in this way, and many centurions, military tribunes and generals in Cæsar's army as well as a few astute freedmen amassed huge fortunes. Amongst these latter was the young German slave named Licinus whom Cæsar had once caught playing the usurer against his companions in servitude and had raised to an important post in the administration, where he had become one of his most skilful coadjutors.

Cæsar could not risk losing the support of his intimates, and he was obliged to let these abuses go on; but his enemies found in them a most useful leverage. In their indiscriminate condemnation of all his acts and intentions they were particularly emphatic against the Parthian War, now the keystone of Cæsar's whole policy. His premature annexation of Gaul had been sufficiently disastrous to the Republic; yet he was still thirsting for fresh conquests. Surely it was inexcusable for him to assume these unprecedented powers only to leave the Republic in the throes of a great crisis in order to go off buccaneering in the East.

Disaffection then was spreading through all classes of the community; yet Cæsar was daily growing less amenable to criticism. Relaxing the self-mastery that had served him so well hitherto, he would let fall violent and indiscreet remarks, such as that Sulla was a fool to lay down his office; that the Republic now only existed in name; that his wish was as good as law. His municipal proposals had been approved by the people, but they bore signs of haste in every line. We may search vainly in the confused and contradictory fragment that has come down to us for the lucidity and distinction of Latin official writing. His other arrangements reveal the same exacting impatience. He entrusted the coining of money and the whole of his financial arrangements to Oriental slaves, most probably Egyptians; he introduced slaves and freedmen into all the public services; he administered a severe rebuke to Pontius Aquila, one of the Tribunes, for not rising when he passed in front of the Tribunician seats; he allowed himself to break out into unworthy and indecent invective; he was furious when he discovered that any of his laws, even the pettiest provisions against luxury, were not being scrupulously carried out, and attempted to secure their better observance by organizing a number of vexatious persecutions on matters of detail. But he refused to listen to the suggestion that he was aiming at monarchy or tyranny and took elaborate pains on several occasions to show his disapproval at any attempt to proclaim him king. Yet he was so tortured by the secret longing for an heir that in the will made on his return from Spain, in view of his approaching departure from Parthia, he named tutors for the child who might be born to him, and actually adopted Octavius, the nephew of his sister, as his son. When two Tribunes removed a diadem that an unknown hand had placed on one of his statues he broke out in fury against what he declared to be a deliberate insult. It is hard to say if Cæsar really intended to found a dynasty analogous to that of the Hellenistic monarchs of Asia, or if he merely toyed with the idea in passing, at the suggestion of Cleopatra, without making up his mind either boldly to accept it or to cast it from him as an unworthy temptation. In any case his enemies had every excuse for circulating the report that he was aiming at the "Kingship." So the rumour went the round of the capital, unsettling all minds, awaking hopes and fears, suspicion and bitterness, and complicating a situation already sufficiently difficult.

Yet amid all this inward and outward confusion there was but one object really on which Cæsar's mind was set. All his serious thoughts, all his remaining energies were directed upon Parthia. It was the one clear path through the maze of his difficulties. Once back in Italy with his legions from Parthia, loaded with Eastern treasure, with the halo of victory round his standard, he would see Rome and Italy at his feet. Already his preparations were well advanced. He was accumulating supplies of money, making a great depot of arms at Demetrias, working out a plan of campaign and sending on the young Octavius to Apollonia with his tutors and sixteen legions composed partly of new recruits. A number of young Italians had been driven by poverty to enlist, in the hope of returning rich on Parthian gold.

Thus in the second half of 45 the right and the left wing of Cæsar's party, the moderates and the extremists, were fighting hard for predominance in the counsels of the Dictator; but the extremists were steadily gaining ground. They had been quick to realize, what their rivals still failed to see, that the Parthian expedition was the inevitable outcome of the situation. Without it their party must inevitably succumb, sooner or later, to difficulties which it was not in a position to surmount. If so, there must be no haggling about constitutional legalities. The Dictator must be given all the powers that he needed, even all the ordinary magistracies united in one hand, to secure his success in the indispensable campaign. It was a difficult and hazardous enterprise that would tax all the energies of their general; and it was imperative that he should enter on it unfettered by constitutional restrictions. These arguments were irresistible, and the men that wielded them had the ear of the Dictator. Amongst them was Dolabella, the bankrupt adventurer, now constantly at Cæsar's side, and Antony, who after two painful years of expiation for his services in the cause of order, had now finally thrown in his lot with the winning side.

Antony's defection was a serious blow to the moderate group, for his distinguished services in the Gallic and Civil Wars gave him a commanding position in Cæsar's party. Soon afterwards, towards the close of 45, the moderates received a still more serious, almost an irreparable check. Cæsar decided to use the right which had been conferred on him after Munda of nominating magistrates to the electors, allowing the people only the power of confirming his nomination. This was a cruel disillusion for all those, and they were very numerous, who had persisted in hoping to the last that Cæsar would refuse to exercise this unprecedented prerogative. What indeed was left of the Republic if a single man had it in his power to distribute all the offices? And how did Cæsar differ from a purely autocratic ruler, if all aspirants to a magistracy were henceforth dependent upon his will and pleasure? Moreover his first set of nominees did not serve to allay the prevailing dissatisfaction. Cæsar attempted, it is true, to give some compensation to the Conservative wing of his party by nominating two of its four most eminent members, Brutus and Cassius, to the Prætorship; but he effaced this concession by his generosity to their enemy the turncoat. Antony was selected as Cæsar's colleague in the Consulship, and his two brothers Caius and Lucius were made Prætor and Tribune respectively. Rome seemed threatened with a government of the House of Antony. The disgust of the public was intensified by an open scandal. Cæsar was anxious to name a *Consul Suffectus* for the time during which he would be absent in Parthia. His choice fell upon his favourite Dolabella, who had not even held the Prætorship. Thus the leader of the revolutionary party would be one of the chief officers of the Republic during Cæsar's absence. But for once his calculations were curiously falsified. Feeling that he had the whole strength of public opinion at his back, Antony, who had an old grudge to pay off against Dolabella, and was perhaps seeking to regain the favour of his old friends on the right wing, declared in the sitting of the 1st of January 44 that in his capacity as Augur he would forbid the electors to meet for Dolabella's nomination. Cæsar bowed to the clamour and refused to intervene.

Rome was in a state of extraordinary confusion. The upper classes, now utterly disgusted, had withdrawn entirely from politics. Cæsar stood practically alone, with a small knot of greedy adventurers. His parasites used their power to induce the Senate and the people, in the first days of 44, to vote him still more extravagant honours borrowed from the disgusting Eastern practice of deification. A temple was decreed in honour of Jupiter Julius; the name of the month Quintilis was changed into Julius, and Cæsar was given the right of being buried inside the City boundary and of maintaining a bodyguard of Senators and knights. These were all the trappings, if not yet the name, of kingship. It was still more ominous that when the Senate went to communicate to him the conferment of these honours, he received the deputation without rising from his seat: that he nominated all sorts and conditions of new members to the Senate, including a number of Gauls: and lastly that, for the Vice-Dictatorship in 44, when Lepidus had left Rome for his province, he proposed to appoint his nephew Caius Octavius who was not yet eighteen years of age. This was openly to violate some of the oldest and most venerated of Roman traditions: a daring application in the sphere of politics of the radical and revolutionary ideas that were widespread among the rising generation of writers and thinkers.

Meanwhile this steady accumulation of honours was accompanied by a progressive weakening of authority. With every fresh access of power Cæsar seemed less able to wield it. He was constantly finding it necessary to make concessions, particularly to his enemies in the

Conservative camp. His situation was indeed almost ludicrously contradictory, inconsistent at once with the supreme position which he occupied and with the idea which most historians have formed of his Dictatorship. The root of all his trouble lay in the Parthian campaign. This forced him at once to assume the fullest possible powers, yet to set out without leaving too many enemies behind his back. He needed, if he could, to have a favourable public. Unfortunately the prolongation of his exceptional authority exposed him to widespread and irreconcilable hostility. Unable as he was to renounce any of these powers, he endeavoured to allay irritation by yielding on minor points, sometimes even to the detriment of the prestige of the State. Alarmed at the excitement caused by his nomination of all the magistrates he went back upon his decision and tried to find a way out by proposing through Lucius Antonius, apparently at the beginning of 44, a very curious *lex de partitione comitiorum* which doubled the number of the Quæstors, enacting that one-half should be elected by the people and one-half nominated by himself and automatically accepted by the electors. The same law perhaps also provided that half the Tribunes and plebeian Ædiles should be nominated by Cæsar, and half elected by the people, and that both the Consuls should be nominated by Cæsar, but the curule Ædiles by the people. By these ingenious arrangements he showed a proper respect for the rights of the people whilst maintaining in office a due proportion of his own adherents. It was no doubt also to gratify the Conservatives that he proposed the *lex Cassia*, an attempt to fill up the number of the old patrician families many of which had become extinct.

The same spirit is displayed in his concessions to the Pompeians. Not only did he reverse his previous policy and proclaim a complete amnesty, but he welcomed them back to Italy with open arms, restored the widows and children of the dead a part of the confiscated property, and heaped favours upon the returning exiles, somewhat to the neglect of his old associates in the dark days of his career. Hirtius and Pansa warned him repeatedly against being too open-hearted. But Cæsar refused to listen. He dismissed his whole bodyguard, including his Spanish slaves, and desired to be accompanied only by lictors on his walks. When told that nocturnal meetings were being held against him in different parts of Rome, and a conspiracy very possibly being set on foot, he did no more than publish an edict declaring his full knowledge of all that was going on, and make a speech to the people in which he warned all would-be evildoers to be careful of their ways. Better to die than to live as a tyrant, as he said one day to Hirtius and Pansa.

Meanwhile he made promises of all sorts, possible and impossible, to everyone who came near him, and no longer even attempted to stop the wholesale pillage of public money which his friends were conducting under his very eyes. The Dictatorship was degenerating into a senile and purposeless opportunism that recalled the feeblest expedients of the old republican government. Many of his veterans had been settled at Volterra and Arezzo, on lands which, originally confiscated but restored by Sulla to their old proprietors, had once more been reclaimed for the State by Cæsar. Many more had been given holdings in various places up and down Italy and had been made members of the order of Decurions, the municipal aristocracy reorganized by the *lex Julia* in many of the smaller Italian towns as at Ravenna and Larino, at Capua and Suessa, at Calatia, Casilino and Sipontum. But the search for what remained of the old State domain proceeded but very slowly, the Commissioners being overwhelmed with appeals for delay from persons of influence. The majority of the veterans had therefore to rest content for the present with the old promises of their general.

Nor were the oversea colonies more successful. It appears that a certain number of settlers actually started for Lampsacus and the Black Sea, but the preparations for Carthage and Corinth were not pushed forward so rapidly, and the idea of founding a colony in Albania had to be abandoned altogether. This had led indeed to a very curious situation. Making use of his rights over provincial land, Cæsar had confiscated part of the municipal domain of Buthrotum which had refused to pay him a fine fixed during the war, intending to distribute it among Italian settlers. But one of the proprietors thus despoiled of their estates happened to be Atticus, who was responsible, it must be remembered, for the investments of a large number of prominent Romans. Atticus brought so much pressure to bear upon Cæsar through his friends at court that the decree was eventually revoked on condition that Atticus be responsible for the original fine. Thus a financier who had never held even the lowest office in the State had got the better of the almighty Dictator. But the sequel is more curious still. Cæsar continued his preparations for the colony as though nothing had happened, till Atticus and Cicero, who had worked hard for his friend in the matter, again became uneasy and asked for an explanation. Cæsar soon reassured them, but begged them to keep the matter quiet. He was unwilling that the public should discover that he had given up his colony to satisfy a Roman plutocrat. He must carry the matter through. He prepared to embark his settlers, and land them in Albania, and then find them some other destination than Buthrotum, though where that should be he had not yet decided. Such were the shifts to which the master of the world was reduced. He was not even successful in allaying the open hostility between Antony and Dolabella; and Antony had actually carried through his threat of preventing the nomination of Dolabella as *Consul Suffectus*. Thus even the apparently omnipotent Dictator was himself entangled in the network of robbery and corruption which encircled Rome as it encircles all mercantile societies where money has become the supreme object of desire. He could no more break through them than the meanest of his dependants.

Yet all these concessions failed utterly in their object; Cæsar's unpopularity increased from day to day. In the whole situation there was a latent contradiction that no human force or ingenuity could resolve, and which was destined indeed to drive Cæsar to his doom. Cæsar endeavoured to justify the prolongation of his exceptional powers on the plea of his Parthian expedition. But it was precisely his Parthian ambitions which set so many, particularly in the upper classes, against his Dictatorship. Everywhere men were asking what more he would do when he returned victorious. Surely then he would be, in fact as well as in name, the absolute master of the Republic? While Cicero was trying to persuade himself that Cæsar was foredoomed to the fate of Crassus, others looked forward with genuine dismay to the exploits of a general who had never known defeat, and did their best to sow suspicion and distrust of his intentions. The strangest rumours were set in circulation. According to one version Cæsar proposed to marry Cleopatra, to transfer the Metropolis of the

Roman Empire to Ilion or Alexandria, and then after the conquest of Parthia to conduct a great expedition against the Getæ and Scythians and return to Italy by way of Gaul. Cleopatra seems to have returned to Rome towards the end of the year 45, in time to play her part in the composition of these fairy tales. On the top of all this came a serious scandal. On the 26th of January 44, as Cæsar was passing through the streets, some of the common people saluted him as king; the two Tribunes of the people with whom he had already come into conflict about the diadem promptly clapped them into prison. Cæsar was furious. He declared that the Tribunes had excited these poor people to make a demonstration in order to cast suspicion upon him for monarchical ambitions. When the two Tribunes objected to his interference, he passed a law to depose them and had them expelled from the Senate, thereby scandalizing the common people who still regarded the Tribune as the most sacred of magistrates.

Meanwhile Cæsar and the extreme party among his associates were breaking down the last barriers of constitutional legality. In the first fortnight of February the Senate of the people nominated Cæsar perpetual Dictator. This was the last and the most important of the measures taken in view of the Parthian War on which Cæsar was almost immediately to set out. Its object was to provide him with the full and unfettered powers which he needed on his campaign without fear of being distracted by the vicissitudes of politics in the metropolis. A perpetual Dictator was, of course, only good Latin for Monarch. In order to weaken the impression of what was really a *coup d'état* and to reassure a public that felt a traditional and almost superstitious horror of monarchy, Cæsar appears to have arranged with Antony for a public pantomime to take place on the Feast of the Lupercals on the 15th of February. Cæsar presided over the festival in person. Antony advanced, diadem in hand, and pretended to be about to place it on his head. Cæsar declined it, but Antony insisted and Cæsar again declined with added emphasis. He was of course long and loudly applauded, after which he had a note inscribed in the Calendar, stating that on this day the people had offered him the royal crown and he had refused it. But this palpable falsehood only increased the public indignation.

All this while Italy was as distracted as ever with the problem of debt, and the middle class was still feeling the pinch of the prevailing crisis, while among the poor population of Italy and Rome there was a strange recrudescence of vague revolutionary propaganda which was becoming daily more alarming to the property-owning classes. The wildest dreams were bandied about in the streets of Rome and over the Italian countryside. Cæsar, with his colonies and his Parthian War, would bring back the age of gold; the tyranny of the rich and powerful was drawing to its close, and a newer and better government was at hand. The memories of the great popular revolution became so lively in men's minds that a certain Erophilos, a native of Magna Græcia, a veterinary surgeon by profession and no doubt more or less weak in the head, passed himself off as the grandson of Marius and immediately became the hero of the hour. Associations of workmen, colonies of veterans and even municipalities chose him as their patron, and he actually formed a sort of Court around him and dared to treat Cæsar and the aristocracy on terms of equality. Afraid to embroil himself with the people, Cæsar did not dare to remove him; and the utmost he would do was to turn him out of the metropolis.

CHAPTER XXXIII

THE IDES OF MARCH

THEN it was that a man took up the idea foreshadowed by Trebonius a few months before—the idea of assassination. It was Cassius who revived it, the Quæstor of Crassus in his Parthian campaign who had married the daughter of Servilia. He was a young man of ability and ambition, but bitter, violent and overbearing, too clever to delude himself that he had more to gain by Cæsar's removal than he might safely expect from his favour. His first step was to discuss the notion cautiously with a few close friends, whom he knew to be opposed to the Dictator. A small group of conspirators was formed, and the possibility of the attempt seriously examined. It was soon agreed that it was indispensable to secure the co-operation of Brutus, the brother-in-law of Cassius, who had great influence amongst all parties as son of Servilia and an intimate of Cæsar's. If it became known that Brutus was actually one of the conspirators many a possible ally would find courage to join.

Like so many another who has been dragged to the front by the caprices of revolutionary history Brutus was the very opposite of a strong man. His was one of those temperaments so common among the hereditary nobility in a civilized age, reasonably intelligent but devoid either of energy or passion, conceited but entirely wrapped up in himself, with few outside ambitions, without a touch of cruelty or vindictiveness, and given to a rather overt display of self-denial and benevolence. Fond of modelling himself on others, like all men of weak character, he had taken for a time to the fashionable pastime of usury; he had joined Pompey in 49, when, in the great panic after the capture of Rimini, the upper classes went blindly after the leader who represented property and order. Later he had made his peace with Cæsar and enjoyed his friendship. Yet by nature he was neither a piler up of millions nor a political aspirant, but a quiet and simple-minded student who in any ordinary age would have developed into nothing more than an aristocratic dilettante, somewhat strange in his ideas and chilling in his manners, finding as much satisfaction in his books as other men in love or fame or riches. But in these troublous times the fervent admiration conceived by the people for his unusual gifts of character had stirred that in him which was stronger even than his taste for study—the insidious passion of vanity. He loved to pose as a hero of iron will and unshrinking resolution, a model of those difficult virtues which can only be exercised by dint of painful self-mastery. This vanity, which a study of the Stoic philosophy had still further excited, together with the underlying feebleness of character which it only partially concealed, are the real keys to a nature which has puzzled generations of historians and moralists.

Cassius was a clever man. He had seen through his brother-in-law, and knew the right bait to use. He began by causing Brutus to find mysterious notes left during the night on his Prætor's seat, or at the foot of the statue of the first Brutus in the Forum; they contained strange and suggestive admonitions, such as "O Brutus, if thou wert still living," or "Thou art asleep, O Brutus." Sometimes too in the street Brutus heard men cry behind him, "We have need of a Brutus." Not guessing whence these missives proceeded the ingenuous student imagined that a whole people was crying out to him as the inflexible hero who was alone capable of the deed of blood. His vanity was touched: he began to reflect on Cæsar's actions, to ask himself if it was not his painful duty to cut them short. No doubt his gentle soul shrank back at first in dismay when he pictured the dangers and the ingratitude of the murder, when he thought of Cæsar's kindness to himself and his old and unbroken friendship with his mother. But once intrenched in that stiffly logical mind the idea of assassination was not to be exorcised. It cast a spell over his narrow and bookish imagination. He called to mind the glory of the tyrant slayers in Greek literature and Roman tradition; he read and re-read the subtle reasoning by which the old philosophers justified regicide on grounds of the highest morality. Argument against argument, emotion against emotion. Cæsar had been his benefactor. That was no reason for forgiveness. All the more necessary to strike him down without flinching, to sacrifice a personal affection to the public good, as his ancestor, the first Consul of the Republic, had put his own children to death for the sake of Rome. It was at this point in the struggle that Cassius intervened. Marcus Brutus must prove no ordinary

Prætor; Rome looked to him with confidence for guidance and inspiration. None so fitted as he to lead her back to freedom! Cæsar, then deep in his Parthian preparations, saw little of Brutus during these critical weeks. So Cassius conquered; and the conspiracy spread, as it had sprung up, among the small group of aristocratic Cæsarians who centred round Servilia, as a natural reaction against the open victory of the radical and revolutionary faction. Lepidus was the only one of the group who knew nothing and remained loyal to his leader.

Brutus and Cassius found many accomplices among the surviving Pompeians and the right wing of Cæsar's party: even some of his best-known generals, such as Caius Trebonius and Servius Sulpicius Galba, were ready to join. Modern historians almost all express surprise at the ease with which the conspiracy was arranged; in their very justifiable admiration for the man who was seeking to reorganize the Roman world they have been unsparing in their judgments upon the treachery, the obstinacy, the short-sightedness of his murderers. Had they tried to form an estimate of the actual situation, as it must have appeared to men at the time, they might have found reason to modify both their surprise and their condemnation. Great man as Cæsar was, it was impossible that his contemporaries should anticipate the childlike hero-worship of posterity or see in him a demigod whose very blunders and self-deceptions were material for adoration! Many of the conspirators may indeed have been actuated by paltry and personal considerations. But these after all were not the real dynamic forces at work. Neither the conspiracy itself nor Cæsar's work as a whole can be judged good or bad by a simple inquiry into the private motives of the actors concerned. We must realize, in all its dramatic intensity, the unique situation which impelled them to action.

Cæsar was a genius. He was at once student, artist and man of action; and in every sphere of his activity he left the imprint of greatness. His soaring yet intensely practical imagination, his wonderfully clear-cut and well-balanced intelligence, his untiring energy and lightning quickness of decision, his marvellous elasticity of temper and iron power of self-control, his indifference even at moments of the greatest strain to anything of the nature of sentiment or mysticism, would have made him, at any time in the world's history, one of the giants of his age. In the Rome of his day both family tradition and personal inclination forced him into politics. Political life is always perilous to a man of genius. There is no sphere of activity which is so much at the mercy of unforeseen accidents or where the effort put out is so incommensurable with the result obtained. In the field of Roman politics Cæsar succeeded in becoming a great general, a great writer, a great character. He failed to become a great statesman.

There were three great political objects for which he fought during his career: the reconstruction of the Constitutional Democratic party in 59, a bold adoption and extension of the Imperialism of Lucullus in 56, and the regeneration of the Roman world by the conquest of Parthia after the death of Pompey. The first and second of these ideas were taken up too late: the third was inherently impossible. The first ended in the revolutionary Radicalism of his Consulship, the second in the field of Carrhæ and the horrors of the death-struggle with Vercingetorix, the third in the Ides of March. It would be unjust to lay the blame for these failures at Cæsar's door. If he was not a statesman, it was because the times forbade him to become one. In a democracy bitten with the mad passion for power, riches and self-indulgence, a man who stands aloof from these temptations may live very happily in retirement and write books upon philosophy; but he must not stray into the hazardous paths of politics. An inexorable destiny seems to dog Cæsar all his days. It was events which drove him to the revolutionary measures of his Consulship. Again it was the necessity under which he lay to save himself, his party and his work from the results of that revolution which drove him to the boldest step in his life, the annexation of Gaul. Annexation once proclaimed, it was no longer in his power to turn back; he was pushed on to those sanguinary acts of repression which form the darkest page in his history. The civil war arose so inevitably out of the policy which he adopted in Gaul that all his efforts to avert it were doomed to failure. His success in the civil war proved even greater than he had hoped—so great, in fact, as to defeat his own object. Victory left him in an unexpected and painfully difficult position. Ostensibly master of the Roman world, he was in reality suspended between two equally impossible alternatives—either to abandon the position he had just triumphantly captured, or, almost single-handed, with the help of a few personal adherents, to administer a huge and disorganized Empire.

He dreamt of escaping from this dilemma by the conquest of Parthia, an enterprise which was to be the beginning of a new era in Roman history. With the experience of twenty centuries to guide us, it is easy to understand how he entertained such an idea: but easy also to understand that it was a fantastic illusion.

Cæsar was not a great statesman; but he was a great destroyer. In him were personified all the revolutionary forces, the magnificent but devastating forces, of a mercantile age in conflict with the traditions of an old-world society—its religious scepticism, its indifference to morality, its insensibility to family affection, its opportunist and undisciplined politics, its contempt for precedent and tradition, its Eastern luxury, its grasping militarism, its passion for the baser forms of commerce and speculation, its first tentative efforts towards intellectual refinement, its naïve enthusiasm for art and science. There is hardly a stranger irony in history than that the rulers of Germany and Russia should have assumed the title of this prince of revolutionaries. For we fail to grasp the true significance of Cæsar's career till we discern that, like Pompey and Crassus and the other great figures of his day, his mission was primarily destructive—to complete the disorganization and dissolution of the old world, both in Italy and the provinces, and thus make way for a stabler and juster system. But when he imagined that he could apply his unrivalled powers of mind and will to all the intellectual and social influences of the time, and direct them to his own purposes, he displeased all parties and was removed from the scene. It matters little that in the later part of his life he displayed more wisdom and moderation than in the earlier; that he attempted in part, though with many inconsistencies, to repair as a reformer the mistakes he had committed as a demagogue; that he had at last come to see that a discontented society, blind and breathless in the race for riches and self-indulgence, has set its selfish course, beyond all turning, for the Abyss. To avert this collapse was beyond any single man's powers. Too many foes were struggling for mastery in the Roman society of his day—from the truceless conflict between riches and poverty or capital and debt, to the antagonism between the spirit of revolution and the spirit of authority, Asiatic profusion and Latin frugality, the new Hellenistic culture and the traditions of Roman life. No doubt Cæsar had displayed a marvellous vigour and elasticity, far beyond that of any contemporary, in his prolonged resistance against the rolling and tossing of the Roman democracy, adrift as it was, like a derelict in a stormy ocean, amid the blasts of a perverse and excitable public opinion. But how could he compose or control these far-reaching conflicts in the whole of society when he could not even dominate those within the ranks of his own party? Until the struggle had reached its climax in the great crisis which began at Cæsar's death and raged without intermission through the whole of the next decade, it was impossible for a new generation to build a sounder and more sheltered society out of the *débris* left by its predecessors—a busy, fortunate, Titanic breed of builders, but too worn and weary, too arrogant, too much embittered by war and hatred, too prone to licence in morals and politics and in their general philosophy of life, to be dowered with lasting happiness. The times called for a quieter, a more cautious, a more patient race of workers. Cæsar's hour had come and gone. He must pass, as Crassus, Pompey, Cato, had passed before him, as Cicero was to follow after a few more months, together with the flower of the aristocracy that had lived through the greatest and most stirring age of Roman history.

It is in this rôle of Titanic destroyer therefore that we must admire him, a rôle which demanded almost superhuman qualities of conception and achievement. We find him, it is true, at the close of his career, busy with the reorganization of a world whose disorder he had done so much to promote, attempting to build on the field which he and his contemporaries had piled with wreckage. But for the success of this work two conditions were necessary. First, Cæsar must retain sufficient vigour and elasticity to adapt himself to the needs of an altered policy; second, the great solvents that had been at work for the last century, loosening the fabric of Italian society, must have finished their work with the civil war. To the former condition fate forbids us the reply. Perhaps the Archdestroyer had still strength enough left him to turn that Protean genius to the work of reconstruction. As to the second, we have the evidence of the next twenty-five years. The forces of dissolution were indeed very far from exhausted. So far were they from being arrested at the time of Cæsar's death that they went on to provoke what was perhaps one of the most tremendous crises in the whole course of world-history.

Moreover the fact that Cæsar did not succeed in healing or even allaying the dissensions within his own party is in itself significant. It does not suggest that he would have been more successful in controlling the similar but far more violent antagonisms in the wider field of society. We need not be surprised that Cæsar, who could not see into the future, had little sense of the realities of the situation: that he naïvely looked forward to the conquest of Parthia as the prelude to an easy reorganization of the Republic. But the modern observer, viewing the centuries behind him in their right perspective, has a clearer vision of his dilemma. He has no excuse for regarding the plot to which Cæsar fell a victim as an unlucky misadventure, due to the weakness or the wickedness of a few isolated individuals. The very opposite is the truth. The conspiracy was the first outcome of an important movement, inevitable both for practical and senti-mental reasons. It marks a genuine alliance between the surviving Conservatives and the right wing of Cæsar's party. Its object was to hinder the Parthian expedition. The conspirators were in fact less concerned with the actual situation than with that which would face them when Cæsar returned victorious from the East. Not all his most emphatic denials could convince them that he was not intending to establish an open kingship. As the representatives of the old Latin and Conservative Republic, the defenders of property and class interest, they banded themselves together against the Asiatic and revolutionary monarchy which they saw looming in the East, between the folds of Cæsar's conquering banners.

The plot was so well taken up that by the 1st of March it comprised according to one account sixty, according to another, no less than eighty Senators. One of the last to join was Decimus Brutus, Cæsar's favourite friend, who had returned to Rome from Gaul towards the end of February. Cicero on the other hand was not admitted into the secret; they were unwilling to expose the veteran writer and speaker to the dangers of conspiracy. The large number of plotters is astonishing in view of the fact that the risk of indiscretions is always necessarily increased with the number of accomplices. But there was probably good reason for their action. The loyalty of the army to their general was regarded as unassailable; while the proletariat, among whom the excitement was rising daily higher, seemed, rightly or wrongly, to be wholly on Cæsar's side. It was therefore absolutely necessary that Cæsar should be struck down not by a few personal enemies but by a practically unanimous Senate. It was the only way in which the coalition of Pompeians and moderate Cæsarians could hope, after his death, to maintain control over the legions, the populace and the Provinces. This is no doubt also the reason why, after lengthy discussion, it was decided that Antony should not meet the same fate as his leader. It was not Brutus, with his scruples against the shedding of Roman blood, that saved him, but more probably the reflection that the simultaneous disappearance of the two Consuls would have prevented the immediate restoration of the old constitution. No doubt they also hoped that so recent a convert to the party of tyranny would return to his old allies on the death of the Dictator.

The place and the method of the assassination are clear evidence of the real intentions of its authors. These details opened up a very difficult question, and a number of alternative plans were discussed during the visits which the conspirators paid to one another in their houses; for to avoid suspicion no common meeting was held. But the days were passing and immediate action was imperative. Cæsar would shortly be starting for Parthia. His veterans, who were to escort him out of the city, were already streaming in from all parts of Italy, finding quarters as best they could in the temples. Several different proposals were made, but no one seemed satisfactory. The conspirators began to lose heart; several already repented of having joined. There was one moment of awful suspense when the weaker section threatened to break off the whole enterprise. But the force of events and the danger in which they were already involved came to strengthen their sinking resolution. Cæsar was moving on from illegality to illegality. He had now gone so far as to pass through the Senate a law providing that before his departure magistrates should be chosen to cover the whole of the next three years, the probable duration of his campaign. Early in March Hirtius and Pansa were nominated Consuls for 43, together with a new batch of Tribunes. According to one report, a Sibylline oracle had declared that only a king could conquer the Parthians, and Lucius Aurelius Cotta, the Consul of 65, against whom Cæsar had conspired in 66, was about to propose his proclamation as king of the whole Roman Empire outside Italy. When at last it was known that Cæsar intended to convoke the Senate on the 15th in the Curia of Pompey to settle the question of Dolabella's Consulship and other outstanding business, and that he was to leave Rome on the 17th, all agreed that this last opportunity must not be allowed to go by. Cut down in the Senate House by a band of eighty influential Senators Cæsar would seem to fall like Romulus at the hands of his country.

There was no more drawing back. On the Ides of March the blow must be struck, cost what it might. The last days before the sitting began slowly to run their course. Every evening in eighty of the richest houses of Rome men who had often and often faced death on the battlefield went trembling to their beds, not knowing whether Cæsar would let them live till morning. At dawn they would recommence the wearisome round of visits to friends' houses, avoiding the curious eyes of passers-by in the streets, baffling the listening ears of the slaves in the houses, with the pretended indifference of a ceremonious visitor. Brutus suffered especially from these torments of doubt and anxiety. If he bore himself in the streets with all the outward marks of serenity, within doors he would plunge into long and melancholy reveries; he would toss and sigh in his sleep, with a trouble that Portia was unable to divine. Fear, gratitude and affection were fighting a hard battle within him against his obstinate ambition to play the hero's part. Meanwhile the days were passing; nothing stirred in Rome; the secret was well kept. Neither Cæsar nor his intimates seemed to dream of danger. Only Portia, by constant questioning, had wrung the truth from her husband. Bit by bit at private meetings all the details of the assassination were arranged. The conspirators were to conceal daggers under their togas; Trebonius was to detain Antony in conversation. In the theatre of Pompey, just outside the Curia, Decimus Brutus was to station a troop of gladiators that he had hired for the Games, who would defend the conspirators in case of need. Immediately after the murder Brutus was to deliver a speech to the Senate explaining the reasons of their action and proposing the reconstitution of the Republic. The 14th of March came and passed without a hint of trouble. Cæsar had arranged to spend that evening with Lepidus, and would return home late—a clear sign that he had no suspicions. How many eyes must have been turned that night towards the sky, to watch for the setting of the stars and the rising of the sun that was to see Cæsar dead and the Republic restored! Only Cæsar, home late from his friend, slept innocent of his doom— the broken sleep of a sick and weary man.

On the morning of the 15th the conspirators were early at their rendezvous, at the colonnade of Pompey, near the present Campo dei Fiori. Brutus, who was Prætor, mounted the judgment-seat and began quietly to attend to his day's litigation, controlling his inward excitement. The rest of the conspirators awaited the opening of the sitting walking up and down the colonnade talking to their friends and trying to conceal their agitation. In the neighbouring theatre of Pompey a performance was going on. There was the usual bustle and traffic in the streets. Cæsar might arrive at any moment.

But Cæsar delayed to come, detained, it seems, by a slight indisposition, which had almost induced him for a moment to postpone the sitting. The conspirators, already excited, began to grow anxious, to start up at every passing noise. A friend approached Casca, one of the conspirators, and said to him, laughing, "You know how to keep a secret, but Brutus has told me everything." Casca, dumbfounded, was about to reveal the whole plot, when his friend's next words showed that he was alluding to Casca's intention of standing for the Ædileship. One of the Senators, Popilius Lena, came up to Brutus and Cassius and whispered into their ear, "Success is possible, but whatever you do do quickly." Still Cæsar did not come. It was perhaps about ten in the morning and the sun was already high in the heavens. The conspirators were exhausted by their long wait. They spoke of treachery and their nerve began to fail. At last Cassius resolved to send Decimus Brutus to Cæsar's house, to see what was detaining him and to bring him to the Curia. Decimus hurriedly threaded the back streets by the Campus Martius, descended into the Forum, and found his way into the *domus publica*, where Cæsar had his official dwelling as Pontifex Maximus. He found him just on the point of postponing the sitting. It was the crucial moment. But Decimus had the nerve, or the ferocity, to drag to the slaughter-house the friend who trusted blindly to his guidance. He engaged him in pleasant conversation, amiably overruled his objections, and persuaded him to come.

At last Cæsar's litter hove in sight. Just outside the Curia the Dictator descended, and the conspirators, who were already collected in the hall, observed Popilius Lena go up to him and address him in low tones. It was a cruel instant of suspense for Brutus and Cassius. Cassius very nearly lost his self-control; but Brutus, calmer than his colleague, had the courage to look Cæsar for an instant in the face. That stern, emaciated, careworn countenance, with the marks of his work lined upon it, was listening unmoved. Brutus beckoned Cassius that all was well. But there was another delay. Cæsar stopped outside the Senate House to make the sacrifices ordained by the State ritual. At last he entered and took his seat, while Trebonius detained Antony in conversation outside. Tullius Cimber approached the Dictator to demand pardon for an exiled brother. The others gathered round him, as though to join their prayers to Cimber's, till Cæsar, feeling that they were pressing him too close, stood up and bade them move farther away. Then Tullius seized him by the toga, which slipped down to his feet, leaving the body covered only with a light tunic. It was the appointed signal. Casca aimed the first blow, but missed in his fright, hitting him in the shoulder. Cæsar turned sharply on him with a cry, seizing his *stilus* in self-defence. Casca called for help to his brother, who plunged his dagger in Cæsar's side. Cassius struck him in the face, Decimus in the groin. In an instant the whole band was upon him, so excited that they hit one another, while Cæsar fought like a wild beast at bay, and the rest of the Senators, after a moment's stupor, fled panic-stricken from the hall, shouting and pushing and stumbling over one another in their haste, Cæsar's own supporters, even Antony, amongst them. Only two rushed forward to rescue Cæsar. Their loyalty was in vain. Still madly beating off his enemies Cæsar had fought his way to the foot of Pompey's statue, where he had fallen at last in a sea of blood.

The murder over, Brutus turned to deliver his speech to the Senate. But the Curia was empty. The conspirators had not reflected that a childish panic might upset their elaborate plan for at once decreeing the restoration of the Republic. What was to be done? In the excitement of the moment they held a brief consultation. Fearing

trouble from the veterans and the people they resolved to summon
the gladiators of Decimus and take them up to a fortified position on
the Capitol, where they could deliberate in greater calm. Then they
emerged from the Curia, with their togas twisted round their left
arms for shields, brandishing their bloody daggers in their right hands,
bearing aloft on a stick the cap, the symbol of liberty, and shouting
to Liberty, to the Republic, and to Cicero, the philosopher of
Republicanism. But outside they found all was noise and confusion.
In the colonnade and the neighbouring streets people had taken fright
at the sudden emergence of the panic-stricken Senators and the
appearance of the armed gladiators. The alarm was raised in an instant
and the public took to their heels. The noise of the shouting reached
the spectators in the theatre of Pompey, who rushed out to join the
fugitives, while pickpockets laid hands on the baskets and carts of the
strolling costers round the theatre. There was a general rush for
refuge into houses and shops, which their owners as promptly closed.
The sudden appearance of a crowd of armed men, reeking with blood,
increased the disorder in the streets they traversed. It was in vain
that, led by Brutus, they shouted and gesticulated to quiet the crowd.
Men were far too frightened to listen. Meanwhile the news was
spreading rapidly to the farthest corners of Rome, and everywhere
people were flying panic-stricken for shelter. Before long Antony was
safely shut up in his house, the conspirators were entrenched in the
Capitol, the frightened public had retired expectant to their homes,
and Rome was wrapped in funereal silence, like a city of the dead.
All parties were afraid of one another.

Parthia was saved. The Archdestroyer had himself been cut down
at the moment when he was setting out to conquer the Empire of
Parthia and set Rome on the road trodden by Alexander. For this was
the dream which had absorbed all his energies during the last months
of his life, while the rumours as to his monarchical ambitions were
probably nothing more than inventions or at least exaggerations on
the part of his enemies. How he would have acted on his return,
supposing he returned victorious, no one can say. Perhaps he did not
know himself. After all, he had been an opportunist all his life
Thrown into politics in an age of unexampled confusion, he had learnt,
by thirty years' experience, to adapt himself to the most widely

divergent conditions. Always entirely engrossed in the question of the hour, he was at this moment only considering how he could use the Dictatorship that he had won in the civil war to become a second Alexander and bring home from Parthia the secret of social reorganization.

But for once the incomparable opportunist had mistaken his reckoning. Cæsar had already, without knowing it, contributed more than all his contemporaries to the future of the world. His greatest work for posterity was the conquest of Gaul, to which he himself attributed so little importance. But to the men of his own day he had no remedy to offer. Before the great regeneration of her society could come about Rome needed, not feats of arms on her distant frontiers, but a great crisis at home in which the forces of dissolution, now at work for a century, could at last run their course. Twenty more long years of storm and tragedy. Then, when all the foremost figures of the age had gone to their deaths by violence and their bones lay scattered through the lands of the Empire they had done so much to extend, an ordered and peaceful world would reap the tardy fruits of their labours. Then at last it would be plain how the conspirators had in part been right; that the hour of military autocracy was still far off; that as yet no citizen could raise an Eastern palace in the capital of the old Latin Republic; that death, the far-seeing liberator, had rescued Cæsar from an entanglement which not even he could have unravelled; that not through absolutism, however inspired, but by the free, patient and often halting development of infinite small social forces, the stormy morning of the Roman Empire would broaden into a clear and tranquil noon.

INDEX

Cæsar, Caius Julius—

Birth of, 100 B.C., 24; marries Cornelia, 46; escape from Sulla, 46; first Eastern journey, 50; at siege of Mitylene, 50; at Court of Nicomedes, 50; his return to Rome, 50, 53; patrimony and vicissitudes of his family, 55; accuses Dolabella and Antonius, 55; his return to the East, 58; his capture by pirates; 58; failure in the prosecutions, 57; he returns from Rhodes and forms the Militia, 77; enters political life, 84–85; Quæstorship of, 120, 124; early political ideas, 121, 123; pecuniary embarrassments, 123, 145, 161; marriage to Pompeia, 129; in pay of Crassus, 145; the conspiracy of 66 B.C., 145–46; as Ædile, 148; struggle with the Conservatives, 65 B.C., 149 et seq.; discredited, 151; and the Tribune Land Law, 157–59; hatred of the Conservatives, 63 B.C., 160; and Pompey's wife, 161; the first Cæsar legend, 63 B.C., 161; made Pontifex Maximus, 163; and the proletariat, 185; the attack upon Catulus, 185–86; and his creditors, 193; governor of Spain, 193, 197; contests Consulship, 201 et seq.; elected Consul, 205; attempt to win over Cicero, 203–4; design of restoring Democratic party of 70 B.C., 203 et seq.; secret coalition with Pompey and Crassus, 204; first actions as Consul, 205; his first Land Bill, 206; sudden change in policy, 59 B.C., 207–8; reduces Asiatic contract, 209; measures taken to consolidate his power, 213–15; alliance with Clodius, 214–15; departs for Gaul, 219; negotiations with the Helvetii, 243, 249–50; his first operations in Gaul, 244 et seq.; battle of Ivry, 252–53; against Ariovistus, 257–61; annexation of Gaul, 270–74; as the Man of Destiny, 273; Cicero and, 289–90; policy in Gaul, 293–95; expeditions into Britain, 297, 306 et seq.; his expenses, 301–2; his slaves, 302; his credit at Rome shaken, 326;

life and character in Gaul, 274; treachery to Commius, 329; discord with Pompey, 330–32; second Consulship contemplated, 332; his strategy, 334; he rejoins his legions, 334–35; his blunder, 338–39; decides to join Labienus, 340; his retreat to the province, 343; causes of his success, 348–50; reaction against, in Italy, 363–65; The Commentaries, 365–66; his cruelty in Gaul, 368; largess in Italy, 368–69; political skirmishes against, 369–74; growing unpopularity, 378–80; his constitutional position, 51 B.C., 380–81; Curio's manœuvres for, 381 et seq.; in Cisalpine Gaul, 394–95; his hopes of peace with Pompey, 397–99; last efforts to avert war, 403–4; his letter to the Senate, 407; and his army, 410–13; his last hesitations, 411; his conditions to the Senate, 412–13; he seizes Picenum, 418; on the road to Corfinium, 421; at Brindisi, 424; after flight of Pompey, 426 et seq.; plan of campaign on leaving Brindisi, 427; on his way to Rome, 427–28; interview with Cicero, 429; his violence against Metellus, 431; at Marseilles, 432–33; critical position outside Lerida, 436; saved by Decimus Brutus, 437; made Dictator, 438; returns to Rome and elected Consul, 49 B.C., 443; and the debt question, 443–46; his first Dictatorship, 445–46; sets sail from Brindisi, 446; Pompey and, on the Apsus, 447; arrival of his reinforcements, 449–50; his defeat at Durazzo, 451–52; battle of Pharsalia, 453–54; pursuit of Pompey, 455–57; honours decreed to, 459; at Alexandria, 461; discord in his party, 463–65; takes Alexandria, 466; his return to Italy, 467; defeats Pharnaces, 467; new honours after Thapsus, 471–72; his triumphs, 475; his reforms, 476–77; contra mundum, 479–81; decline of his intellectual powers, 480–81; his De Bello Civile, 481; his last ambition, 483–84; and the ideas of Caius Gracchus, 486; his negligence

GUGLIELMO FERRERO

Guglielmo Ferrero was born in Portici, near Naples, Italy, on July 31, 1871. A journalist with republican sympathies, he traveled abroad considerably and won a reputation with such books as *Problems of Peace in Europe.* He studied Roman history and in 1902 published his *The Greatness and Decline of Rome,* which established his reputation as a popular historian. He was an outspoken opponent of the Fascist regime in Italy, and his works were proscribed by the Italian government in 1935. In later years, he lived in exile and died in Geneva, Switzerland in 1942.

Among his other works are *Between the Old World and the New, The Ruin of the Ancient Civilization and the Triumph of Christianity,* and *The Reconstruction of Europe.*